INTRODUCTION TO PROGRAMMING CONCEPTS
AND METHODS WITH ADA

McGraw-Hill Series in Computer Science

Senior Consulting Editor

C. L. Liu, *University of Illinois at Urbana-Champaign*

Consulting Editor

Allen B. Tucker, *Bowdoin College*

Fundamentals of Computing and Programming
Computer Organization and Architecture
Systems and Languages
Theoretical Foundations
Software Engineering and Database
Artificial Intelligence
Networks, Parallel and Distributed Computing
Graphics and Visualization
The MIT Electrical Engineering and Computer Science Series

Fundamentals of Computing and Programming

*Abelson and Sussman: *Structure and Interpretation of Computer Programs*
Bergin: *Data Abstraction: The Object Oriented Approach Using C++*
Kernighan and Plauger: *The Elements of Programming Style*
Smith and Frank: *Introduction to Programming Concepts and Methods with Ada*
*Springer and Friedman: *Scheme and the Art of Programming*
Tremblay and Bunt: *Introduction to Computer Science: An Algorithmic Approach*
Tucker, Bradley, Cupper, and Garnick: *Fundamentals of Computing I: Logic, Problem Solving, Programs, and Computers*
Tucker, Bradley, Cupper, and Epstein: *Fundamentals of Computing II: Abstraction, Data Structures, and Large Software Systems*

*Co-published by The MIT Press and McGraw-Hill, Inc.

INTRODUCTION TO PROGRAMMING CONCEPTS AND METHODS WITH

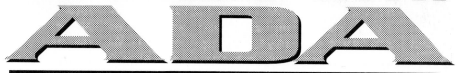

JAMES F. SMITH

THOMAS S. FRANK

Le Moyne College

McGraw-Hill, Inc.

New York   St. Louis   San Francisco   Auckland   Bogotá   Caracas   Lisbon
London   Madrid   Mexico City   Milan   Montreal   New Delhi   San Juan
Singapore   Sydney   Tokyo   Toronto

INRODUCTION TO PROGRAMMING CONCEPTS AND METHODS WITH ADA

 This book is printed on recycled, acid-free paper containing a minimum of 50% recycled de-inked fiber.

1 2 3 4 5 6 7 8 9 0 DOHDOH 9 0 9 8 7 6 5 4 3

P/N 059209-8
PART OF
ISBN 0-07-911725-2

This book was set in Times Roman by the authors and Gail Gottfried.
The editors were Eric M. Munson and Joseph F. Murphy;
the production supervisor was Denise L. Puryear.
The cover was designed by Initial Graphic Systems, Inc.
R. R. Donnelley & Sons Company was printer and binder.

Library of Congress Cataloging-in-Publication Data

Smith, James F., (date).
    Introduction to programming concepts and methods with Ada / James
F. Smith, Thomas S. Frank.
      p.   cm.
    Includes index.
    ISBN 0-07-911725-2 (set)
    1. Ada (Computer program language)   2. Electronic digital
computers—Programming.   I. Frank, Thomas S., (date).   II. Title
QA76.73.A35S65   1994   93-32502
005. 13' 3—dc20

About the Authors

James F. Smith is Professor of Computer Science at Le Moyne College in Syracuse, New York. He received his master's and doctoral degrees in mathematics from the Catholic University of America. Professor Smith is a member of the Association for Computing Machinery and of the IEEE Computer Society. He is a member of ACM's SIGAda and SIGCSE, where he has been active in promoting the use of Ada as the principal language for computer science instruction at the undergraduate level.

Thomas S. Frank is Professor of Computer Science at Le Moyne College in Syracuse, New York. He earned his master's and Ph.D. degrees in mathematics at Syracuse University and has been teaching courses in computer science for the past 24 years. Professor Frank is a member of the Association for Computing Machinery (including SIGCSE and SIGAda) and the IEEE Computer Society, and he is the author of two books on computer architecture and assembly language.

Contents

Preface

This book is intended as a principal textbook for ACM's course CS1 (Introduction to Programming Methodology), a four-credit one-semester course for beginning computer science students. There are no prerequisites for the course.

The language introduced and employed in this book is Ada, and thus the text has been written for use in those universities and colleges that have adopted Ada, or are considering its adoption, as the language of the CS1-CS2 sequence. The limitations of Pascal have prompted widespread reconsideration of the language of instruction in the beginning course. The languages most prominently mentioned as replacements are Modula-2 and Ada (with some interest in C, C++, and Scheme, although these would not appear to meet the language criteria set forth in the CS1 syllabus). Some institutions have adopted Modula-2, but the fact that Modula-2 seems destined to remain an academic language, whereas Ada more firmly resides in the "real world," suggests that Ada is an especially desirable choice.

There are three considerations that have tended to hold back a change to Ada.

(1) The idea that Ada is a "large," complex, and advanced language, along with the unexamined assumption that the whole of a language must be taught in one semester.

   We claim, to the contrary, that the language is at the service of the theoretical content of each course, and that therefore it is entirely appropriate to teach a central core of Ada in CS1, more of the language in CS2 (where it will be used to implement abstract data types), and the rest in more advanced courses in the curriculum. (For example, the concurrency features of Ada might suitably be taken up in the course on operating systems, or in the course on file processing, where two or more parts of a file can be processed concurrently.) Further, our own experience in the classroom with CS1 and CS2 courses has shown that with attention paid to the organization of its topics, Ada can be taught at the introductory level as successfully as Pascal; that in some regards it can be done even more smoothly; and that none of the principal programming concepts needs to be sacrificed. Indeed, some of these concepts are more neatly managed in Ada than in other languages and thus appear to be easier for beginning students to learn.

(2) The former scarcity of acceptable Ada compilers and support software.

   This is a situation of the past, one which no longer exists. More and more good Ada compilers are becoming available, notably inexpensive compilers for use on microcomputers.

(3) The unavailability of textbooks suitable for a CS1-CS2 sequence based on the Ada language.

There are several well-written books on Ada. Originally, however, they did not aim to present the elements of programming methodology, since they were intended for experienced programmers. Thus, until recently none of the books presenting the Ada language was suitable for the introductory college course CS1. The present project is intended to address this situation, joining the small number of CS1/Ada books that have appeared within the past few years. We aim not only at a good organization and clear exposition of the concepts of CS1; we aim also to show how cleanly those concepts can be implemented through the use of Ada's language features.

As its table of contents reveals, this book covers the standard topics of CS1—basic concepts of computer systems, problem solving and algorithm development, program structures, data types, an introduction to searching and sorting—as do other textbooks for this course. In addition, however, it incorporates the following topics:

Topics	Ada language feature
The anticipation of run time events	Exceptions and exception handlers
Data encapsulation	Packages
Information hiding, abstraction by specification	Separation of package specifications and bodies
Generalization of types and procedures	Unconstrained array types, generics

In keeping with top-down programming techniques, other CS1 books demonstrate how program *actions,* along with their associated data, may be localized by means of *subprograms.* This book does the same, but it also demonstrates how program *data,* along with their associated actions, may be localized by means of *packages,* a concept applicable in object-oriented programming.

It is important to understand that the book is not merely an "Ada translation" of a Pascal-based text for CS1. It goes beyond Pascal, and in so doing it goes beyond the original syllabus for CS1 (*CACM* 27, 998-1001). In order to achieve the stated goals without simply adding on new topics to those already specified for CS1, we have cut back somewhat on the considerable overlap of topics that appear in the syllabi for *both* CS1 and CS2 (*CACM* 28, 815-818). In particular, such topics as access types and dynamic storage allocation are *not* covered; we view them as requiring the extensive motivation and implementation that more properly belong to CS2. Similarly, while recursion is discussed briefly (in reference to subprogram calls), the concept is most appropriately motivated by CS2 topics, notably trees and other linked structures.

And some concepts, even those discussed in considerable detail, may not be covered in their complete generality. For example, under the heading of records we omit mention of unconstrained record types and of variant records.

System activities such as text editing, compiling, linking, debugging, and so forth are discussed briefly, but this is done in a general way, without reference to any particular system. Thus, no discussion of how any of these system features are actually *used* is supplied. This doubtless places a burden on the instructor, who will need to give instruction in the local editor and compiler, for example, but this is almost certain to be necessary in any event, when one deals with students who are new, or at least relatively new, to programming.

New topics are frequently introduced by examining a problem or concept and attempting to deal with it via the currently-available programming techniques, prior to disclosing the new feature itself.

There are two main pedagogical devices employed throughout the text. The first of these is the *example program or program segment*. Students who are learning a new programming language—especially those for whom the language is their first—need simple programs with guaranteed, known behavior, to which they make modifications in various experimental ways. In addition to a wide variety of small programs and program segments used to illustrate Ada topics, a few programs extend across several chapters, beginning as simple examples and being expanded or modified as new language features are developed.

The second learning device that is stressed in the text is exercises. Exercises are considered to be of the highest importance in developing the skills that are required of the student who successfully completes the text material. The numerous exercises consist of routine "drill" problems, those which might be called "oral exercises," and problems calling for the writing of program segments or complete programs.

To assist the student's *practice* in understanding programming concepts and methods, we have included with this book a diskette containing two types of materials corresponding to the pedagogical devices we have described above. First of all, we have provided magnetic copies of the source code for all complete programs, subprograms, and packages (as well as a few program fragments) displayed in the text. These should assist the student carrying out the "keyboard experimentation" whose importance we have stressed. Without having to engage in tedious keyboarding, the student may copy these listings; compile, link and run them; modify them; add to them; and in general "play" with them—profitable play, indeed!—in various ways. Secondly, to help the student learn concepts and develop skills from working out the text exercises, we have included on the diskette solutions to about half of these exercises.

While the concepts of problem analysis and algorithm design, as well as those of program documentation and self-documentation, are formally discussed in the text, the skills and attitudes they instill are developed more by example than by precept.

The authors are aware that Ada is not the language of the vast majority of CS1 courses. Indeed, one of their motivations in writing the book was to demonstrate that using Ada at this level is both feasible and advantageous, points not yet widely recognized. We especially wish to encourage those in the computer science education community to consider Ada as the CS1-CS2 language; thus, for purposes of familiarity and comparability we have purposely designed the organization and exposition to be suggestive of the ACM CS1 syllabus. However, this has not constrained us from freely making use of Ada features not found in Pascal, or from extending the traditional CS1 approach to accommodate recent developments in language design and programming methodology, especially those that are directly supported by the Ada language.

The authors wish to express their gratitude to the following reviewers, and to Eric M. Munson and the editorial staff at McGraw-Hill, Inc.: John Beidler, University of Scranton; Patty Brayton, Oklahoma City University; Joel Carissimo, California State University, Long Beach; J.L. Diaz-Herrera, Carnegie-Mellon University; Patricia T. Montague, Metropolitan State College of Denver; and Annette Schoenberger, St. Cloud University. Their dedicated professionalism has been of great assistance to us.

James F. Smith
Thomas S. Frank

INTRODUCTION TO PROGRAMMING CONCEPTS
AND METHODS WITH ADA

Chapter 1

Introduction to Computers and Programming

In this brief chapter we set the scene for the remainder of the book by describing in very general terms what a computing system is, what computer programs are, what a high-level language is, what compilation and linking are, and how the Ada programming language evolved. We close with an example of a simple Ada program and an explanation of how the program is made up and what its individual parts mean.

1.1 Introduction to computing systems

A **computer** is an electronic device that manipulates *data* in various ways. A typical general-purpose **computer system** consists of several components and features, some of which are described below.

1. **Central processing unit**. The central processing unit (CPU) is at the heart of the computing system, for it is here that the manipulations of data referred to above take place. These CPU capabilities include the usual *arithmetic operations* of addition, subtraction, and so forth, as well as a few *logical operations*, that is, operations whose results are of a True-or-False nature, as when the CPU checks the numbers X and Y to see whether X = Y. In fact, the operations that the CPU can carry out are relatively simple, and their number is really quite small. What gives a computer system the *appearance* of great complexity is that it performs these basic operations—**executes** them, as is said—at very *high speeds* (several million such operations per second). Further, these operations may be combined to form a virtually unlimited number of *sequences* of operations; thus, a general-purpose computing system is just that—it may be used for a wide variety of tasks.

2. **Primary storage**. Since the central processing unit performs operations on data, it will need to obtain its data from somewhere, and it will also need to put the results of

its operations somewhere. The "somewhere" is called **primary storage** (or **main memory**), and it is used in part for the temporary storage of data. The amount of primary storage varies widely depending on the computing system—some of the smaller desktop or personal computers contain storage for only a few thousand items, whereas on large computing systems, several millions of such places to store data— **memory locations**—are by no means unusual.

3. **Secondary storage**. For the more permanent storage of information, most computing systems contain some kind of **secondary storage**, commonly in the form of *magnetic disks*, on which typically from a few million to many billions of data items may be stored. Associated items are grouped together into logical units, called **files**, about which we shall have more to say shortly.

4. **Communication devices**. A computing system would be virtually useless if it were not possible for *us* to provide the CPU with the data to be used in its operations and if *we* could not inspect the results of those operations. Thus devices are provided specifically for the purpose of **communication** between the system and the "outside world." Perhaps the devices that are most familiar to you are the display screen and keyboard of your terminal or personal computer. Other output devices include printers and plotters; other input devices include joysticks and mice.

5. **Software**. Even with a full complement of **hardware**—the computer **equipment**, as described in 1 to 4 above—the system would still be of little value to almost all potential users, without some supporting **software (programs)** to assist those users in managing the system. We shall expand on this statement in the remainder of the present chapter.

1.2 The programming of computers

Machines are designed not only to perform certain tasks better than people can perform them but also to be *controllable* by people. Thus, just as an automobile would be worthless (indeed, dangerous) if we could not steer it or if its gears were engaged randomly at random times, so a computer is of no use to us if *we* cannot select which basic operations it is to perform and in what sequence it is to perform them. That is, we need to be able to present the computing system with a *prescribed* set of commands, to do this, then do that, etc., similar to giving an actor a script—a prescribed sequence of words to speak and activities to perform on stage. In the case of a computing system, the script is referred to as a **controlling program**, **computer program**, or, more simply, **program**.

How do we go about "telling" a computer what to do? You are surely aware that we need to use a **programming language**, such as BASIC or FORTRAN or Pascal—or Ada, the language we use in this book. You may or may not be aware, however, that a computer does not "understand" any of these languages. Instead, each type of computer system understands only the commands that are built into its electronic circuitry. Together these commands make up what is called the computer's **native language, machine language,** or **machine code**. Clearly, since different kinds of computers vary in their design—their **architecture**, as it is technically called—there are as many different machine languages as there are computer architectures. Machine languages are collectively known as **low-level languages**; by contrast, programming languages such as those mentioned above are called **high-level languages**.

It is not necessary for the programmer to understand the details of what a computer's machine language is like. However, we mention two aspects of such languages: (1) Each command in a machine language is expressed in terms of a *numeric* code assigned by the designer of the computer; thus, for example, the command for the operation "add" might be the number 6; (2) these numbers are not represented within the computer in their *decimal* (base 10) form, which uses the digits 0 through 9, but rather in their *binary* (base 2) form, which uses only the digits 0 and 1. We go one step further to point out that *all* numbers—data as well as machine code—are somehow represented within a computer in binary form, as strings of the **bits** (*bi*nary dig*its*) 0 and 1. Numbers are often stored as strings of 8, 16, or 32 bits; thus, in 8-bit form, the number "six" would be represented as 00000110. Fortunately, our present investigation will not require us to express numbers in binary form—the computer will do that for us—and therefore we will not take up the matter of how to convert numbers from one representation to another.

What the programmer *does* have to know, however, is that any program written in a high-level language must first be "translated" into machine code before it can be run. This is accomplished by a complex, commercially produced program known as a **compiler**. A compiler is a program that takes as its input a program written in a high-level language and produces as its output the corresponding program written in machine language. (Thus, any particular compiler is specifically tailored to both the high-level language *from* which it is to translate and the machine language *to* which it is to translate. It follows that a given computer system's FORTRAN compiler is not the same as its Pascal compiler; nor is the Pascal compiler of one type of computer the same as the Pascal compiler of a different type of computer.) The "output" of a compiler is not sent to an ordinary output device, such as the display screen; instead, it is stored, in a form not readable *by us*, on a secondary storage medium (that is, in a **file**). Similarly, the "input" to a compiler does not come *directly* from the keyboard; rather, it comes in the form of a program that the programmer has *previously* keyed into the computer and stored in a file. All of this raises several questions. How does the programmer go about keying in a program to be stored in the file? How does the programmer then submit this program to the compiler to be translated into machine language? Finally, what then? Is the resulting machine-code program ready to be run? Or what?

These are all matters that we take up in the following section, in which we describe, step by step, the process of producing a program that can actually be *run*.

1.3 Creating an executable program

We have seen, rather loosely, what is involved in the creation of a program, in that we know that some commands written in a high-level language are somehow translated by a compiler into machine language, which can then be executed by the computer. But what of the specific details—how exactly would one get started with the creation of a program? The individual steps are easy enough to describe, for basically three *files* need to be built. We briefly mentioned files in Section 1.1; now let us describe a file a bit further by saying that it is a collection of related material—data, or in the present instance, the "words" that go to make up a program—that can be stored as a unit in either primary or secondary storage.

Source file. The lines of program commands (instructions), written in the high-level language in question (FORTRAN, Pascal, Ada, or whatever), and saved as a file on some secondary storage device, make up the program's **source file**. The contents of this file are referred to as the **source program**, made up of **source code**. How is such a file created? Normally, for the creation of source files the programmer uses a **text editor**. This is a program which is typically supplied with the computing system and which allows the user to create files of text—consisting of lines of letters, digits, spaces, and other characters—from the keyboard. That is, the programmer, using the editor program, types at the keyboard the characters that make up the program, and those characters are saved in a file.

Object file. Once the source file has been created, it is submitted to the appropriate compiler as its *input*. The task of the compiler, as we now know, is the generation of the corresponding machine-language program. The translated program created by the compiler is in turn saved in a file, called the **object file**. The contents of this file are known as the **object program**, made up of **object code**. The object file is the *output* of the compiler. Recall that, as we mentioned in the preceding section, "input" and "output" do not refer here to data read directly from the keyboard and data sent to the display screen, respectively. In general, the input of an executing program—in this case, the compiler—consists of data supplied to the program, in any fashion, for processing; similarly, the output of a program consists of data generated by the execution of the program.

Executable file. The object file described above is probably not yet "runnable" as is, since it is likely that it makes reference, at least implicitly, to **modules** (collections of data and/or routines) that have already been written, compiled, and saved as object files for repeated use. To cite an example of this, rather complicated code is needed to implement the programmer's instructions to read data from the keyboard or to display data on the screen; however, all this code has been written and compiled in advance by the supplier of the computer software. Thus the object files containing these routines will have to be combined (to use the technical term, **linked**) with the programmer's object file in such a way as to produce an **executable module**, or **executable file**. To accomplish this, the programmer makes use of a program called the **linker**, which takes as its input the programmer's object file, along with whatever other object files it needs, does the needed linking, and produces the executable file as its output. Note that it is *only* the executable file that *runs*: neither source files nor object files are in a suitable state to be executed by the computer hardware.

Now that we have listed the steps necessary to produce an executable program, it still appears that we have not moved very far in the direction of responding to the question: Precisely what commands do I issue to create a program that will *run* on my computer? Regrettably, we cannot give a truly satisfactory answer to that question for two reasons. First, in order to write statements in a high-level language, a programmer must know the *rules* for the formation of valid statements as set down by the language. The rules specify the **syntax** —the grammar of the language, so to say. And of course this book has as one of its purposes an examination of the syntax of one specific high-level language, Ada. Thus, in part the question is quite premature. But even putting that aside, the second reason for our inability to respond to the question involves our lack of knowledge of the computing system on which you will be creating, compiling, and linking program files. For while the Ada syntax is standardized and thus does not vary from one system to another, the commands to be given to the compiler and linker are *not*, and thus these will require information about your local system, which can be supplied only by those on site who know that system. To push matters back one step further, you will have to learn how to use your system's editor, so that you can type in and save in a file the lines of text that make up your Ada program.

1.4 The origins of the Ada programming language*

A principal goal of this book, in addition to the development of numerous programming skills, is the study of a modern computer language. As you know, we have chosen Ada for this purpose. Ada might be said to trace its origins to the early 1970s, when studies revealed the extreme costliness of developing and maintaining the computer systems in use by the U.S. Department of Defense (DoD). As subsequent investigations brought to light, more than 450 computer languages had been employed in producing the systems that controlled radar, aircraft, missiles, and other military equipment and weapons. In this rather chaotic background, the history of ADA began in 1975, when the DoD took an effective step to deal with its problem by establishing the High-Order Language Working Group (HOLWG). With a view to confronting the proliferation of computer languages used in DoD programs, HOLWG was given the task of formulating a set of *requirements* that a language suitable for DoD purposes would need to satisfy; this group was also to investigate several existing languages to see if any of them would meet these requirements. Between 1975 and 1978 HOLWG produced several successive "requirements documents" (to which it gave the curious names Strawman, Woodenman, Tinman, Ironman, Steelman) and, along the way, came to the conclusion that while none of the existing languages proved suitable, it would nonetheless be possible and desirable to develop a single language to do the job.

To launch the development of such a new language, HOLWG invited contractors to submit a preliminary design of a language intended to meet the recently identified requirements. The 17 proposals that were submitted were subsequently narrowed to four, and these were ultimately reduced to two: Green (Honeywell-Bull) and Red (Intermetrics), the color codes being used to preserve the proposers' anonymity. In 1979 DoD announced in favor of the Green proposal, and about that same time the new language was given the name **Ada**. After initial acceptance of the language design, the language underwent a succession of revisions, and in 1980 it was adopted as a Military Standard. In February 1983 the version of Ada that had by then evolved was accepted as the *Ada Standard* by the **American National Standards Institute (ANSI/MIL-STD-1815A-1983)**. At present, considerable effort is being spent to develop a revised version of the language, and with the expectation that this work will be completed "sometime" within the 1990s, this version is usually referred to as Ada 9X.

The language was named after Lady Augusta Ada, Countess of Lovelace (1815-1851), daughter of the English poet George Gordon, Lord Byron. She was a very capable

---

*This section may be omitted; it is not used elsewhere in the text.

mathematician who worked with the eccentric Charles Babbage in his attempts to develop a computing device that he called the "analytical engine." In point of fact, this machine was never completed; had it actually been produced, it would have been the forerunner of the modern computer. What we know about Babbage's plans for the "engine" comes mostly from the writings of Lady Lovelace, who left us better descriptive information about this endeavor than did Babbage himself. In any event, because of her work with Babbage on the development of his machine, Lady Lovelace is often referred to today (perhaps with some shades of the romantic) as "the world's first programmer." It was to do honor to her that DoD chose to adopt her name (with permission of her heirs) for its new programming language.

1.5 Some characteristics of the Ada programming language

As detailed in the preceding section, the Ada programming language was developed in the late 1970s under the sponsorship of the U.S. Department of Defense (DoD). It is possible to cite several characteristics that were incorporated into the language by the DoD working group. For present purposes, however, it will suffice to note some of the language features that stem from the following two aspects of Ada's history.

1. Ada was designed to deal with **embedded computer systems**, that is, computers that form a *part* of (are *embedded in*) larger noncomputer systems such as aircraft, missiles, tanks, and so forth. These computers have as their principal—or only—function the control of the larger system of which they form a part. It is obvious that many such systems are found in the context of weaponry and other military hardware. However, these systems are used in other contexts as well—air-traffic control, industrial robotics, and temperature-regulation systems, to name just a few.

2. Ada was intended for use in very large and complicated programs, whose development would lie beyond the capabilities of a single programmer. Since such programs are produced by teams of programmers, it must be possible to write, compile, run, and test separate "chunks" of the total program, and then somehow to fit the chunks together later in such a way that not only do the interconnections behave as intended but also that no part of the program produced by one team will interfere with another team's efforts.

We shall see some of the consequences of these design characteristics throughout this book. First, because Ada is widely applied in embedded computer systems, its capablilities for input (from the keyboard, say) and output (to the display screen, for example) are *not* automatically called into play when a program runs, contrary to the situation that holds with many other languages; the Ada programmer who wishes to employ even such primitive input and output routines must explicitly call for their inclusion in the program. Second, the language has unusual features aimed at ensuring program *reliability*. (Things are bad enough when a company's payroll program fails to execute properly; things are far, far worse when a rocket-guidance program does not run correctly.) Not only does Ada provide for much data checking within its own syntax, it also gives the programmer several powerful tools for dealing with "exceptional" program behavior—situations in which things go badly, or at least unexpectedly, during program execution.

Thus we see that Ada's design provides for piecemeal development, execution, testing, and revision of separate program sections in such a way that the connections (and thus possible interferences) among them may be kept to a minimum. It is this feature of the language that facilitates team programming, contributes to good program structure, and puts Ada in line with current programming methods.

Before concluding these general remarks about the Ada language, we should make a point of stressing the importance of a document mentioned in the preceding section. This document, which has been given the technical designation **ANSI/MIL-STD-1815A-1983**, goes almost universally by the name *Ada Language Reference Manual* (*LRM*). You will see numerous references to *LRM* throughout this book, and we assume that a copy of the manual is available to you. When a specific reference to a chapter, section, and subsection of *LRM* is given, it will be stated in the form *LRM [Chapter.Section.SubSection]*, for example, *LRM [7.4.3]*. It is a most helpful reference, the more so in view of the fact that it is the *standardized* Ada reference, and you will benefit from it increasingly as your knowledge of Ada develops.

1.6 A sample Ada program

We offer in Figure 1.6.1 our first example of a source program written in the Ada language. Despite being very short, it illustrates many Ada characteristics, and much explanation is required. We cannot explain all the features at the present time, but we can make a beginning. So do not be put off by vague or incomplete discussions; we can assure you that eventually *all* the aspects of this program will be made clear.

```
with Text_IO;

procedure Warranty is

    --  This program calculates the number of miles remaining
    --  on a new-car 25,000 mile warranty.  The program user
    --  enters the car's current mileage (odometer reading).

    package Int_IO is new Text_IO.Integer_IO (INTEGER);

    Warranty_Miles:              constant INTEGER := 25000;

    Current_Miles:               INTEGER;
    Remaining_Miles:             INTEGER;

  begin

    Text_IO.Put ("Enter the current miles (odometer reading): ");
    Int_IO.Get (Current_Miles);

    Remaining_Miles := Warranty_Miles - Current_Miles;

    Text_IO.Put ("The number of miles remaining on the warranty is ");
    Int_IO.Put (Remaining_Miles, 0);
    Text_IO.New_Line (1);

  end Warranty;
```

Figure 1.6.1

Despite the fact that at the present time we cannot expect you to know anything about the Ada programming language, or perhaps even about computer programming at all, you can probably understand enough of Figure 1.6.1 to realize that all it does is obtain a number of miles from the program user, subtract that number from 25,000, and announce the result. As we have already observed, we are dealing with a trivial problem, and were it not for the fact that the program that solves it illustrates some features we wish to examine, it would scarcely be worth considering.

What is shown in the figure is a collection of words, numbers, and special characters —*text*, as we have said—that makes up the program's *source file*. It was created by a text editor, and the resulting file was then submitted to an Ada compiler for translation. The compiler generated a corresponding *object file*, and this was then submitted as input to a linker. Finally, the output of the linker—the *executable file*—can be executed, or **run**. Thus before digging into some of the details, it will be useful to show in Figure 1.6.2 two sample "dialogues" that could occur when the program is run.

```
a     Enter the current miles (odometer reading): 16104
      The number of miles remaining on the warranty is 8896

b     Enter the current miles (odometer reading): 29883
      The number of miles remaining on the warranty is -4883
```

Figure 1.6.2

There should be no real surprises here. In *a* we have entered 16,104 as the current mileage, and the program has subtracted this from 25,000 and responded that 8,896 miles remain on the warranty. In *b*, however, we have entered a number of miles (29,883) which exceeds the warranty miles. The program, however, has slavishly subtracted this from 25,000 and announced that −4,883 miles "remain" on the warranty. Of course such a statement is literally nonsense, although we can *interpret* the result as meaning that the car is now 4,883 miles out of warranty (or beyond its warranty mileage). But the message is clear: Programs, even extremely simple ones, can be accidentally or intentionally abused, and unless they protect themselves against such occurrences, their results can be nonsense. In a case such as this, the result does no real harm, and we easily observe that it is meaningless. But in critical applications (payroll, electronic funds transfer, machine-control systems) nonsense results can be tragic, especially when they are not recognized as such. We shall see throughout the remainder of the book that much effort must be expended to guard against such problems.

To assist us in our discussion of the individual lines of the program text of Figure 1.6.1, we repeat it in Figure 1.6.3, this time with a number in front of each line. These numbers are *not* a part of the source file; we have simply placed them there so that we can easily refer to the text of line 20, lines 5 to 7, and so forth.

```
1     with Text_IO;
2
3  procedure Warranty is
4
5        -- This program calculates the number of miles remaining
6        -- on a new-car 25,000 mile warranty.  The program user
7        -- enters the car's current mileage (odometer reading).
```

```
 8
 9     package Int_IO is new Text_IO.Integer_IO (INTEGER);
10
11     Warranty_Miles:                constant INTEGER := 25000;
12
13     Current_Miles:                 INTEGER;
14     Remaining_Miles:               INTEGER;
15
16  begin
17
18     Text_IO.Put ("Enter the current miles (odometer reading): ");
19     Int_IO.Get (Current_Miles);
20
21     Remaining_Miles := Warranty_Miles - Current_Miles;
22
23     Text_IO.Put ("The number of miles remaining on the warranty is ");
24     Int_IO.Put (Remaining_Miles, 0);
25     Text_IO.New_Line (1);
26
27  end Warranty;
```

Figure 1.6.3

*Line
numbers*   *Comment*

2, 4, ...   The Ada compiler will tolerate blank lines—lines on which *no* text
                   appears. They are useful for separating parts of the program, thereby
                   assisting in its readability.

1   We noted in the preceding section that since Ada is designed to be used in
                   embedded systems, the programmer's keyboard and display screen are no
                   more "natural" devices than any others—and in fact, in many systems
                   which employ Ada, a keyboard and screen would be fairly unnatural
                   devices. Thus we must explicitly call for the software that provides for
                   keyboard input and display output. In Ada, the appropriate routines are
                   "packaged" as a module named Text_IO, for the input and output of text-
                   type data, such as characters and words. This module is supplied by the
                   vendor as a part of the total Ada compiler package.

                   Observe that line 1 ends with a semicolon. In fact, a glance through the rest
                   of the program reveals that most, but not all, lines also end with a
                   semicolon. This concluding of lines with or without semicolons is not
                   arbitrary, of course; there are rules of the Ada language to be obeyed here,
                   and we shall begin to present these in the next chapter.

3   The **procedure <name> is** clause begins every program in Ada, and the
                   name inserted here (in this case, "Warranty") becomes the **name**, or
                   identifier, of the program.

5-7 These three lines each begin with a double hyphen, and this character pair is the signal to Ada that a **comment** is about to begin. Specifically, whenever the Ada compiler detects the "--" pair, it takes these characters and the *remainder of the line* as a comment and ignores it. Thus comments mean nothing to the compiler—they are there only for *our* use, typically to explain what a program or module does, how a particular line of code affects the program, and so forth. Comments may begin anywhere on a line, although in this case they begin at the start of the line, and thus the entire line becomes a comment.

9 This is no doubt an especially mysterious line of the program. Eventually we will offer a full explanation of its purpose and effect. Right now, however, suffice it to say that an Ada program that does input or output of integers must contain "some such" line as this. In fact, we will include this line exactly as it is in our Ada programs for the time being.

11 Here we have created an integer *constant*, to which we have given the name Warranty_Miles. Its value is 25,000, but note that it has been written as 25000, without the comma that is frequently found in a number greater than 999. The reason for this is that Ada will not accept the comma as a valid character in a number representation. We note in the next chapter that the underscore (_) can serve the purpose of the comma here, but in fact we shall rarely use it in this book.

Could we simply have used the *numeric* representation 25000 throughout the program, rather than creating the constant Warranty_Miles having this value? Absolutely, but by *naming* the constant in this suggestive fashion, we help remind ourselves what the number 25000 means in this program.

The underscore character is also legitimate in a *name*, such as Warranty_Miles. We have used it since we want a name that is suggestive of what it represents, and yet we need some kind of "spacing" character for legibility; we claim that the name Warrantymiles or even WarrantyMiles is not as easily read. Neither the space character nor the hyphen is legal here, although you might find the resulting names to have a slightly more attractive form (Warranty Miles or Warranty-Miles).

How has the Ada compiler responded to this so-called **constant declaration**? It has taken three actions: (1) The compiler has provided for some storage in main memory to be designated (**allocated**) for this constant, and it has "named" that storage location Warranty_Miles. (2) The compiler has provided for the number (integer) 25,000 to be placed in that storage location. (3) It has marked the memory location named Warranty_Miles as holding a *constant* and thus being *incapable of being modified in any way*. Compare this situation with that of the next paragraph, in which other memory locations are allocated and named but whose contents *may* be modified at will by the program instuctions.

13-14   On these lines we have created two **variables**, named Current_Miles and Remaining_Miles. As with the constant Warranty_Miles of line 11, the compiler provides for the allocation of storage for these numbers and refers to those storage locations by these names, but in this case no predetermined value (such as 25,000) is placed initially in these locations, and whatever values are eventually placed there by the program instructions *may* be changed or varied (hence the use of the term "variable"). Note also that we have indicated to the compiler that the kinds of things that these variables will be asked to hold are *integers*; the Ada compiler insists upon knowing, for every constant and variable, the sorts of objects that can be placed in them, so that, for one thing, it will be able to determine how *much* memory storage it needs to allocate for each of them.

16   The program's **executable** statements *begin* at this line. Observe that up to now, nothing has been written that could ultimately be executed—we have simply been specifying the *environment* within which the program will execute.

18, 23   Here we "Put" a string of *text* to the display screen, and the routine to do so is in the package Text_IO. Thus we have used that **prefix** to specify the specific routine: Text_IO.Put, as opposed to Int_IO.Put, the routine that displays *integers*.

19   Here we "Get" (from the keyboard) an integer (hence the prefix Int_IO) and have it placed in the variable Current_Miles.

21   Here is the sole computation that takes place; the number of current miles is subtracted from 25,000, and the result is placed in the variable Remaining_Miles. Note that the character pair ":=" is the symbol for assigning a value to a variable. Observe that this symbol was also employed in line 11, when the constant was assigned the value 25,000.

24   Here we put (display on the screen) the result of the computation of line 21. Again, note the prefix Int_IO, the name of the package that contains the appropriate output routine. You may well wonder what role is played by the number 0 that appears in this line. This will be explained in detail in Chapter 3, but for now we may simply note that it will cause the value of Remaining_Miles to be displayed without any blanks inserted in front of it. (Of course there will be *one* blank, the one appearing in line 23 as the last character before the final quotation mark.)

25   In some computer languages, when the output routine has completed putting whatever object was specified, it moves the cursor (or printhead)

down one line and returns it to the left margin. In Ada, put does *not* do this; rather, the cursor (or printhead) is simply left wherever it happens to be after displaying the specified object. Thus a separate command is required to force a "new line," and this is New_Line, contained in the package Text_IO. The number 1, enclosed in parentheses, following the reference here to New_Line indicates that *one* new line is to be generated, rather than two or three, say, which would produce double- or triple-spacing.

27   This signals the **end** of the procedure (program). The program name, Warranty, is repeated here as good programming practice, although it is optional. Note that this line ends in a semicolon. In some other popular languages, the line signifying the end of the program concludes with a *period*.

We are aware that this description contains an enormous amount of detail about a topic that at this point can be understood only at the fuzziest level and that we have necessarily left many of its aspects vague at best. In the next chapter many of the details are put carefully in place, and by the time that chapter ends, this program will be far better understood.

1.7 Exercises

1.6.1   (a)   Use your local editor and Ada system to create, compile, and link the sample Ada program of Figure 1.6.1. Then run the program four times, using the following input as responses to the "current miles" query:

   (i)   16104

   (ii)   29883

   (iii)   0

   (iv)   −73

Verify that the results are as expected. How, if at all, can the outputs resulting from inputs *ii* and *iv* be interpreted?

(b)   Modify the program of part *a* above for a 30,000-mile warranty. Compile and link the result. Test your program using the same sample inputs as in part *a*.

(c)   In the program of part *a* above, change line 24 from

```
Int_IO.Put (Remaining_Miles, 0);
```

to

```
Put (Remaining_Miles, 0);
```

and compile the resulting source program. An error should be generated at this line *upon compilation*. What error message does the compiler display? Insofar as is possible at this stage and in light of the detailed, line-by-line discussion immediately following Figure 1.6.3, explain how the error message can be interpreted. (Notes: Compiler error messages are sometimes referred to as **compiler diagnostics**. Depending upon your Ada compiler, a generated diagnostic can range from a terse, cryptic word or two to a message several dozen lines in length.)

1.6.2 Modify the sample program of Figure 1.6.1 by changing line 24 to each of the forms suggested below. In each case recompile and relink the resulting source file; then execute the resulting program and input the sample "current miles" stated. Pay particular attention to the *appearance* of the resulting output.

(a) line 24:   `Int_IO.Put (Remaining_Miles, 5);`
    sample inputs:
        25
        100
        1000
        10000

(b) line 24:   `Int_IO.Put (Remaining_Miles, 10);`
    sample inputs:
        5
        55
        1000
        22450

(c) line 24:   `Int_IO.Put (Remaining_Miles, 2);`
    sample inputs:
        5
        55
        1000
        20000

(d) line 24:   `Int_IO.Put (Remaining_Miles);`
    sample inputs:
        5
        55
        107
        1000
        24550

Based on your observations, conjecture what the number (0, 5, 10, ...) following the variable Remaining_Miles in the Put statement *means* and how the output *behaves* relative to that number. Give as complete an explanation as possible. How can your conjecture be made consistent with the result in part *d*, in which *no* such number was provided at all?

Chapter 2

Developing a Program

In this chapter we pose a simple problem and produce an Ada program that serves as a solution. The technique that we use is a standard method of program development; we will carefully analyze it here and subsequently use it throughout the book. Following this, we continue the study of the structure of Ada programs begun in Chapter 1 but in far greater detail. In doing so, we investigate some of the most basic and important concepts of programming—concepts which, although in an Ada context, are of widespread application in the study of programming languages and therefore of computer programming itself.

2.1 A time-and-day problem and an Ada program solution

The problem we wish to solve involves converting "so-and-so many minutes since the beginning of the week" into the time and day of the week. For example, 125 minutes represents "Sunday morning at 2:05," while 8,612 minutes corresponds to "Friday night at 11:32." Thus, we set ourselves the task of producing a program that will obtain from the user's keyboard an integer (whole number) standing for the number of minutes that have elapsed since the beginning of the week. Since there are 10,080 minutes in a week, the integer obtained should be between 0 and 10,079, inclusive. To simplify what the program must do, we will agree to display the time of day in terms of hours and minutes after midnight and a numerical indication of the day of the week, with Sunday being designated as day 1, Monday as day 2, and so on up to Saturday (day 7). You may find this a somewhat unsatisfying way of indicating the time and day of the week, and understandably so. But it represents a first attempt on our part; in Chapter 6 we will see how the program can be modified to display the time as it would appear on a 12-hour digital clock, along with the actual name of the day of the week.

Let us start by devising a clear, accurate, complete statement of the problem. We have described what is to be done in a fairly natural way; unfortunately, however, our description is not complete: We have left out the heart of the problem. If the program is to obtain the number of minutes since the beginning of the week and display the result described, then somewhere in between these two steps it must compute the numbers to be displayed. We can

16

more accurately describe the problem statement, and put it in a form better suited for analysis, by revising it as follows:

Problem statement. Write a program that first obtains as input an integer in the range from 0 to 10,079, standing for the number of minutes that have elapsed since the beginning of the week; the program should then compute the number of days, "leftover" hours (short of a complete day), and "leftover" minutes (short of a complete hour) since the beginning of the week; and, finally, it displays the time and day of the week in terms of these numbers.

Having arrived at a complete statement of our problem, we are now able to work toward its solution, while developing a programming method that will be generally applicable. The method is called **top-down programming,** described in the next section.

We begin by writing a broad outline of the main steps to be taken in solving the given programming problem:

1.   Obtain the input: minutes since the beginning of the week.

2.   Compute the numbers representing the day of the week and the time in terms of hours and minutes after midnight.

3.   Display the time and day of the week using these three numbers.

This "broad" outline of the "main" steps to be taken is called a **Level 1** outline of a solution. Notice that aspects are deliberately left quite vague at this point; in particular, no details are worked out as to how any of these steps is to be performed. The next stage in our method consists of detailing each solution step, starting with the easiest. We may be tempted—if not now, then at least when we get into more complex programming problems— to work out the details of the more challenging steps of the outline, so as to get them out of the way; however, the discipline of top-down programming would have us first do the part that appears *easiest.* Bearing this in mind, we can develop a Level 2 outline of a solution to the problem we have before us. It looks as though the computational step will require some thinking out; and, meantime, there are more details to be filled in for the input and output steps. We will leave step 2 as it is and work on the other two. We might come up with the following:

1.   Ask the user for the number of minutes that have elapsed since the beginning of the week, with a reminder that this must be between 0 and 10,079 (inclusive), and get the number that the user types.

2.   Compute the numbers representing the day of the week and the time in terms of hours and minutes after midnight.

3.   Display a message telling the time expressed as hours and minutes after midnight and the day of the week.

At this point, we can delay no longer: We must come to grips with the second step of the problem solution and figure out how the computation is to be done. There are at least two ways of proceeding. One is to divide the total number of minutes since the beginning of the week by 1,440, the number of minutes in a day. This would give the number of complete days since the beginning of the week (the quotient of this division) and the number of leftover minutes (the remainder). We would then divide this remainder by 60, the number of minutes in an hour, to split it up into complete hours (the quotient) and remaining minutes (the remainder).

We prefer, however, to start by dividing the original number of minutes since the beginning of the week into hours and minutes. To do this, we divide the given number by 60, the number of minutes in an hour, to yield the total number of hours since the beginning of the week (the quotient) and the number of leftover minutes (the remainder). We then divide the number of complete hours since the beginning of the week by 24, the number of hours in a day, to split it into the number of days since the beginning of the week (the quotient) and the number of leftover hours (the remainder). We approach the problem in this way because it somehow seems more natural to use the fact that there are 60 minutes in an hour and 24 hours in a day; making use of the number of minutes in a day (1,440) seems a bit more removed from our everyday thinking. Clearly, it is mostly a matter of taste.

With this latter procedure in mind, we can further refine the Level 2 outline by spelling out these computational details in step 2. This brings us to the Level 3 outline below:

1. Ask the user for the number of minutes that have elapsed since the beginning of the week, with a reminder that this must be between 0 and 10,079, and get the number that the user types.

2. Divide the number of minutes since the beginning of the week by 60 to obtain the number of hours since the beginning of the week (the quotient) and the number of remaining minutes (the remainder). Divide the resulting number of hours since the beginning of the week by 24 to obtain the number of days since the beginning of the week (the quotient) and the remaining number of hours (the remainder). Use the resulting numbers to indicate the time of day and day of the week.

3. Display a message telling the time expressed as hours and minutes after midnight and the day of the week.

No matter which of these two approaches we take, however, a slight difficulty appears at this point. Suppose we were to enter 70 as the number of minutes that have passed since the beginning of the week. Then, clearly, the correct time is 1 hour and 10 minutes past midnight on Sunday (day 1). However, the computations we have described in step 2 will yield 0, rather than 1, as the number corresponding to the day of the week. In fact, if we stop and think about it, we see that assuming that a number between 0 and 10,079 has been entered, the quotients designating the day of the week will range from 0 to 6, rather than from 1 to 7. These quotients will actually tell us how many *complete* days have elapsed since the beginning of the week. But when 0 complete days have passed, we are actually *in* day 1; when 1 complete day has passed, we are *in* day 2; and so on. This situation is easily adjusted in the obvious fashion: We add 1 to the quotient we obtain, thereby converting the "number of complete days that have elapsed" to the "number of the current day of the week." We incorporate this computational adjustment into step 2 of our Level 3 outline to obtain the final (Level 4) outline of the problem solution:

1. Ask the user for the number of minutes that have elapsed since the beginning of the week, with a reminder that this must be between 0 and 10,079, and get the number that the user types.

2. Divide the number of minutes since the beginning of the week by 60 to obtain the number of hours since the beginning of the week (the quotient) and the number of remaining minutes (the remainder). Divide the resulting number of hours since the beginning of the week by 24 to obtain the number of days since the beginning of the week (the quotient) and the remaining number of hours (the remainder). Add 1 to the number of days since the beginning of the week, which then yields the designation of the *current* day of the week, and use the resulting numbers to indicate the time of day and day of the week.

3. Display a message telling the time expressed as hours and minutes after midnight and the day of the week.

At this stage, we have outlined our problem solution in such detail that it needs only to be translated into Ada code to yield a correct and well-structured program. Accordingly, we turn our attention now to a program that an experienced Ada programmer might produce on the basis of this Level 4 outline. Of course, we have ahead of us the task of investigating what all the parts of this program mean, so we could hardly expect the program to be fully understandable at this point; nevertheless, our analysis of the program in Section 1.6 should make quite a bit of Figure 2.1.1 at least familiar.

```
with Text_IO;

procedure Time_and_Day is

    -- This program asks the user for an integer from 0 to 10079,
    -- representing the number of minutes that have elapsed since
    -- the beginning of the week.  It then determines and displays
    -- the current day of the week (Sunday = Day 1, ...,
    -- Saturday = Day 7), and the 24-hour time of that day
    -- (hours and minutes after midnight).

    -- Declarations

    package Int_IO is new Text_IO.Integer_IO (INTEGER);


    Minutes_Elapsed:        INTEGER;
    Hours_Elapsed:          INTEGER;
    Day, Hour, Minute:      INTEGER;
    Minutes_in_Hour:        constant INTEGER := 60;
    Hours_in_Day:           constant INTEGER := 24;
```

```
begin

    -- INPUT
    -- Obtain the input (minutes elapsed since the week began)

    Text_IO.New_Line (1);
    Text_IO.Put ("How many minutes since the week began (0 to 10079)?  ");
    Int_IO.Get (Minutes_Elapsed);

    -- COMPUTATIONS
    -- Determine the day of the week and the time, obtaining them
    -- in the order: minute, day, hour

    Hours_Elapsed := Minutes_Elapsed / Minutes_in_Hour;
    Minute        := Minutes_Elapsed rem Minutes_in_Hour;
    Day           := Hours_Elapsed / Hours_in_Day;      -- 0 to 6
    Hour          := Hours_Elapsed rem Hours_in_Day;

    -- Adjust Day to range from 1 to 7, instead of 0 to 6

    Day := Day + 1;

    -- OUTPUT
    -- Display the day and time in terms of these numbers

    Text_IO.Put ("The time is ");
    Int_IO.Put (Hour, 0);
    Text_IO.Put (" hours and ");
    Int_IO.Put (Minute, 0);
    Text_IO.Put (" minutes after midnight, on day ");
    Int_IO.Put (Day, 0);
    Text_IO.Put (".");
    Text_IO.New_Line (2);

end Time_and_Day;
```

Figure 2.1.1

To illustrate the effect of executing this program (after it has been compiled and linked), we indicate in Figure 2.1.2 what appears on the display screen over the course of several runs of the program.

```
How many minutes since the week began (0 to 10079)?  3670
The time is 13 hours and 10 minutes after midnight, on day 3.

How many minutes since the week began (0 to 10079)?  7595
The time is 6 hours and 35 minutes after midnight, on day 6.

How many minutes since the week began (0 to 10079)?  0
The time is 0 hours and 0 minutes after midnight, on day 1.

How many minutes since the week began (0 to 10079)?  10079
The time is 23 hours and 59 minutes after midnight, on day 7.
```

Figure 2.1.2

Now that we have this program before us, we will spend considerable time analyzing it in detail, so that we can learn many of the fundamentals of programming in Ada. But before we set out on this project, we take a moment to summarize the top-down method we used in the development of the program.

2.2 Top-down programming

Probably no one would dispute the claim that any program, if it is to be at all acceptable, must be *correct*: The program has to run properly and do the job it is supposed to do. If anything, we might consider the need of correctness to be so obvious as to merit little discussion beyond its affirmation. To the contrary, we believe that there is much to be said on this topic, and we will take it up at length in Chapter 7.

There is a second quality of a good program that deserves our attention right from the start: A program should be *clear* and therefore *easy to read*. It has become customary to point out that a real-world program—one that is actually put to use by a business or government agency—is *written* only once but *read* many times (for purposes of updating or extending it, for example). Furthermore, the reading and maintaining of the program must usually be done by someone, or by several persons, other than the program's original author. For these reasons, the issue of program clarity, often passed over in the earlier days of computing, has now become a matter of much importance in the profession. One of the aspects that contributes greatly to clarity is good program *structure*, whereby a given program is readily seen to be made up of several "pieces" of code, called **modules**, designed in such a way that each piece is self-contained (or as nearly so as is practical), with as little interaction as possible among the pieces. The process of developing a program that fits this description is often called **structured,** or **modular, programming**.

The method of top-down programming, which we have informally described and used in the preceding section, specifically aims at the development of programs that are well structured and consequently clear and easy to read. As an added benefit, top-down programming contributes to program correctness through its systematic analysis of the successive actions that need to be carried out.

Recall that when we applied the top-down method in the previous section, we began— once the problem had been properly stated—by determining what action (broadly described) was to be carried out first, what action was to be carried out next, and so on. This was the process of producing a Level 1 outline of the problem solution. The next stage consisted of refining the Level 1 outline, filling in the "fine" detail of how some of these actions were to be performed. Remember that we dealt with the easier and simpler actions first, putting off the others until a later stage of refinement. This process led to several successive solution outlines, with higher and higher levels of detail. Finally, the actual writing ("coding") of the program consisted of merely translating from English to Ada the specified steps to be carried out in running the program.

Top-down programming is summarized as follows:

1. State the problem clearly, accurately, and completely.

2. Write a broad (Level 1) outline of the main steps to be taken in solving it.

3.   Successively develop outlines at higher (more detailed) levels by refining (spelling out) the steps of the outline, beginning with the simplest. A complicated step may need to be broken down into smaller steps, and these further broken down into yet smaller and more detailed ones, until eventually it becomes clear exactly what specific sequence of instructions needs to be given to the computer to accomplish the necessary action.

4.   As soon as a step has been described in enough detail to allow it to be translated into the programming language, replace it by one or more lines of program code.

5.   Let the resulting program clearly reflect (for example, by comments and good format) the original Level 1 outline of the problem solution's main steps, and the subordinate steps as well, as may contribute to a clear and well-structured program.

As you may have noticed, there is no specific mention of Ada in any of these five steps. In fact, what we have summed up is a method of *program development* independent of the choice of programming language to be used.

2.3 An overview of the program Time_and_Day

Let us begin our examination of the program in Figure 2.1.1, and thus of the Ada language features that it illustrates, by looking at the general makeup of this program. In doing so, we will discover the **syntactic elements**—the building blocks of the Ada language —from which it is constructed, and in the sections that follow we will return to these to study them in detail.

We start by recalling some of the concepts we saw in Section 1.6. The program begins with the **context clause** (the **with** clause) that makes the input/output (I/O) routines contained in the package Text_IO available to the present program. Next, the program has been given the name Time_and_Day in this instance, a name made up by the programmer, preceded by the word "procedure" and followed by the word "is." All our Ada programs will begin this way.

What follow are several **comment** lines describing what the program does. We saw such comments in the program of Figure 1.6.1. Recall that a comment begins with a double hyphen (two successive hyphens), serving as a signal to the compiler that whatever is included from this point to the end of the line is not part of the Ada code of the program; it is simply ignored by the compiler. Clearly, the reason for including comments is to make the source file more readily understandable to anyone who *reads* it.

The next section of the program, preceding the word "begin," is called the **declarative part** of the program, about which we will say more in a moment. The section between "begin" and "end" is called the program's **statement part, or sequence of statements.** Here are found the executable **statements** of the program, which indicate what actions the computer is to perform. The word "statement" is misleading, as these are *commands*, or *instructions*, telling the computer what to do; they do not really state anything. However, the word "statement" has a long history in computing, and its use in this context is well entrenched in the field. Note that each statement in Ada must be terminated with a semicolon. This is also true of the program as a whole, as we observed in Section 1.6. Note, too, that the sequence of statements in this program has been separated into three main sections, or parts, introduced by comments, to bring out the overall (Level 1) outline of our programming problem solution.

The sequence of statements in the program Time_and_Day has three kinds of statements: (1) an **input** statement, beginning with Int_IO.Get, found in the first of the three sections of the statement sequence, (2) **assignment** statements, containing the symbol :=, found in the second section of the statement sequence, and (3) **output** statements (all other statements in the program, beginning with Text_IO.Put, Int_IO.Put, or Text_IO.New_Line). We look further at each kind of statement in Sections 2.10 and 2.11.

Turning to the declarative part of the program, we find **declarations** of several **data objects**: five variables (Minutes_Elapsed, Hours_Elapsed, Day, Hour, Minute) and two constants (Minutes_in_Hour and Hours_in_Day). Each of them is **declared** to belong to the **type** INTEGER, and the constants are **assigned** the values 60 and 24, respectively. Observe that declarations, like statements, must be terminated with a semicolon. Each of the seven data objects in this program, as well as the program itself, has been given a name (technically called an **identifier**) by the programmer.

All of this is to say that we have many fundamental and important concepts of programming to investigate here—identifiers, declarations, types, variables, constants, the specific type INTEGER—and we look into them all in the sections to come.

2.4 Identifiers in Ada

Apart from words included in comments and those found in text enclosed in quotation marks, all words in Ada programs are considered to be identifiers. There are three kinds of identifiers in Ada:

1. **Reserved words.** The reserved words of Ada have meanings specified by the language rules, and are "reserved" for the specific use determined by these rules. Ada has 63 reserved words, of which the following appear in the program Time_and_Day: **with**, **procedure**, **is**, **package**, **new**, **constant**, **begin**, **rem**, **end**. (See the list of reserved words in Appendix A.)

2. Other predefined words. Predefined words in Ada have a special meaning, although the programmer is free to redefine them with other meanings -- something it would be highly confusing, and therefore very unwise, to do. In Time_and_Day, the following words are in this category: Text_IO, INTEGER, New_Line, Put, Get.

3. Programmer-defined names. These are names made up by the programmer. All the identifiers in Time_and_Day, other than those listed above in 1 and 2, are of this kind (including Int_IO; we have more to say about this in the next chapter).

Since the Ada programmer is called upon to devise identifiers for programs, parts of programs, and objects in programs, we need to see what rules the language has in this matter. First, Ada does not distinguish between capital and lowercase letters in identifiers. Thus, the words

```
HOUR        Hour        hour        hoUR
```

are all regarded as the *same* identifier, as are any other variations of this word obtained by using different combinations of capital and lowercase letters. Our practice in this book is in keeping with widespread (though not universal) Ada programming style, which is to write *reserved words* in lowercase letters and names of types in capitals. For all *other identifiers* we capitalize the first letter—in fact, we capitalize the first letter of each of the main "parts" of longer identifiers, such as Minutes_in_Hour. This differs from the style employed in the *LRM* (referred to in Section 1.5), which, while using only lowercase letters in reserved words as we do, displays all other identifiers entirely in capitals: MINUTES_IN_HOUR, INTEGER, NEW_LINE, and so on.

   An identifier in Ada must begin with a letter of the alphabet, followed optionally by one or more letters and/or digits (the characters 0 to 9). Further, an identifier may contain one or more occurrences of the underscore character provided that, in each case, this character is immediately preceded by *and* followed by a letter or digit. No other character is allowed in an identifier; in particular, an identifier may *not* contain a "blank" or "space" character—indeed, the *underscore* character is typically used to substitute for a space. When the underscore character is used in an identifier, it is a significant part of the identifier: therefore, MyName and My_Name are not the same identifier. Here are some examples of legitimate identifiers:

```
X           Index        Count_1_Item    Warranty_Miles    Two_Digits
X0          Index1       Index_1         Current_Miles     Two_Times_3
```

The following are *not* legitimate identifiers:

```
2X          Index 1      Index 1         Warranty Miles    Gain/Loss
2_X         Index1_      Index_1_        Interest_%        2_Times_3
```

   The rules and examples we have given are meant to indicate how the concept of an identifier is implemented in Ada. There is a principle, too, that applies in general to the use of identifiers, whether in Ada or in other languages. The principle is to *use descriptive identifiers*. Identifiers should be chosen so that a reader of the program can readily grasp what is happening. As we have seen before, it is important that a program be easy to read and understand, and comments may be used throughout the program to help achieve this goal; nevertheless, comments are not a substitute for descriptive identifiers, which, if chosen carefully with a view to clarity, can serve to make the program self-documenting and greatly reduce the need for comments. Understandably, programmers may find it annoying to type long identifiers, especially if these names are used repeatedly; however, the immediate understandability of such identifiers as Warranty_Miles and Minutes_In_Hour makes the effort worthwhile. We do mention, though, that in the context of mathematical abstraction and generality, where no specific real-world application is currently referred to, it is acceptable to use the symbols customarily employed in mathematics, such as X, Y, Z, and also A(J) and A(J,K), the computing equivalents of the mathematical notation a_j and a_{jk}, respectively.

2.5 Declarations: Objects and types

Computers perform many different kinds of operations at the bidding of the programmer, but in general computers need to be told what "material" to operate on. Each piece of data in the current program—Minutes_in_Hour, Minutes_Elapsed, Minute, etc.— belongs to a **data type** (or simply **type**), and membership in a type imposes some rules on these data, as to what values they may assume and what operations are valid for them. It would make no sense to try to assign to Minute, for instance, which represents a whole number, a value such as 5.37. A type, then, consists of a set of *values* and a set of *operations* that can be performed on these values. Eventually we will be studying a variety of different types and using constants and variables of these types; for a while, however, our interest is in the type INTEGER, which the Ada language provides for our use. Objects of this type are "whole numbers," and the operations that the language supplies for them include the familiar ones of addition, subtraction, multiplication, and a form of division. The INTEGER type is much used in computing, and we consider it in some detail in the next section. Meanwhile, let us look at the declarations given in the program of Figure 2.1.1.

```
Minutes_Elapsed:        INTEGER;
Hours_Elapsed:          INTEGER;
Day, Hour, Minute:      INTEGER;
Minutes_in_Hour:        constant INTEGER := 60;
Hours_in_Day:           constant INTEGER := 24;
```

We first note that if a declaration contains the word "constant," then, obviously, what is being declared is a *constant*—an object whose value never changes. Significantly, the *absence* of this word indicates that the object being declared is *not* a constant—it is a variable. Second, the given declaration of Day, Hour, and Minute is equivalent to (and has the same effect as) the three separate declarations:

```
Day:        INTEGER;
Hour:       INTEGER;
Minute:     INTEGER;
```

We see here the fundamental form of a variable declaration: the name (identifier) of the variable, followed by a colon, followed by the name (identifier) of the type to which the variable belongs, followed by the terminating semicolon. In the original form of the declaration, we have taken advantage of the fact that if there are several variables of the *same* type to be declared, their names may be listed together, separated by commas, and the type name (which in Ada terminology is referred to as the **type mark**) need only be given once. As you might expect, we could have declared *all five* of the program's INTEGER variables in this grouped fashion; our decision to group Day, Hour, and Minute, while leaving the others separate, was based on a judgment as to what might best contribute to program clarity.

Recall from Section 1.6 that when we declare a variable such as Day, for example, to be of the type INTEGER, the compiler provides a suitable memory location to be designated (in a technical term, **allocated**) for storing an INTEGER value, and it associates the name Day with this memory location. The variable thus declared may then "take on" (or "be given" or "be assigned") several different INTEGER values during the course of the program's execution. As we will see in Section 2.10, a variable may also be assigned an initial value when it is declared, although that has not been done in this case.

By contrast with a variable, which *may* be given an initial value when declared and which may subsequently take on many different values as the program runs, a constant *must* be assigned a value when it is declared, and it may *not* take on any other value at all during the entire run of the program. For example, in Time_and_Day we have declared:

```
Minutes_in_Hour:      constant INTEGER := 60;
Hours_in_Day:         constant INTEGER := 24;
```

The reserved word **constant** precedes the type mark, and the latter is followed by the assignment of a value of this type to the constant that is being declared. Notice that the two-character symbol :=, called the assignment operator, is used to assign a value to a constant. Taking the first of these two constant declarations as an example, we recall from Section 1.6 that upon encountering this declaration, the Ada compiler does several things: (1) It provides for the allocation of a memory location to hold an INTEGER value and it associates the name Minutes_in_Hour with this memory location, (2) it provides for the storage of the INTEGER value 60 in this memory location, and (3) it "marks," or designates, this memory location as holding a value that cannot be changed at all during the run of the program. Could we have omitted these two declarations and value assignments and simply used the numbers 60 and 24 in our computations? The answer is yes, but as we pointed out in Section 1.6, having names to identify what these numbers stand for makes the program much more understandable. Could we then have let Minutes_in_Hour and Hours_in_Day be *variables*, with the respective values 60 and 24 assigned to them? Again, we could have done so, but since these names are used to designate specific, unchanging values, declaring them to be constants provides more accurate information on their role in the program.

While discussing the giving of names to constant values, we note that this practice can have another advantage in certain contexts. Suppose, for example, that a program contains the declaration

```
Tax_Percent:          constant INTEGER := 5;
```

and that this identifier is employed throughout the program in all computations where it is necessary to make use of the 5 percent tax rate. If the government were to change the tax rate to 7 percent, the program could very easily be updated by simply changing 5 to 7 in the declaration of the constant Tax_Percent; otherwise, it would be necessary to find all occurrences of the number 5, determine in each case whether the 5 represented the tax rate or was being used in some other sense, and then change 5 to 7 where appropriate. You can readily see that in a program consisting of thousands—or tens of thousands—of statements, this task could be formidable.

As a final word on constants, if we need a constant of a *numeric* type such as INTEGER—as opposed to some of the types we will be seeing with values that clearly are not "numbers"—we may omit the type name and simply write, for example:

```
Minutes_in_Hour:    constant := 60;
Hours_in_Day:       constant := 24;
Tax_Percent:        constant :=  5;
```

These names are then used in the program in exactly the same way as before.

2.6 The type INTEGER: Values

As we have noted before, a type is characterized by a set of *values* and a set of *operations* on these values. In this section we begin to study the predefined type INTEGER. We consider this type's set of values and see how to write particular INTEGER values in Ada.

To the mathematician, the set of integers (whole numbers) is an infinite set. Specifically, there is no *greatest* integer: If someone names a (presumably large) integer, you can always name a larger one—by doubling it, say, or even by just adding 1 to it. Similarly, there is no *least* integer: If someone names a negative integer of large magnitude (absolute value), subtracting 1 from it yields a smaller integer.

The finiteness of computers as electronic devices rules out the possibility of their dealing with the integers as an infinite set of numbers. As a consequence—one that you may find peculiar and at times even annoying—the set of integer values that a computer can store and process is finite: It contains a *least* integer, a *greatest* integer, and all the integers between them; no more. This is true, in particular, of the set of values that go to make up the type INTEGER in Ada. The least of these values (negative, and of largest absolute value) is referred to by the Ada language as INTEGER'First (read as "integer tick first"), and the greatest of them is referred to as INTEGER'Last. First and Last are called **attributes** of the type INTEGER.

It is impossible to state, in terms of the Ada language itself, what the specific values of the numbers INTEGER'First and INTEGER'Last are: They depend upon the particular computer system on which the language is being implemented. As we saw in Section 1.2, a computer generally represents a number as a sequence of *bi*nary dig*its* (bits) 0 and 1, which, taken together, yield the binary (base 2) representation of the number. Many computers represent integers internally as 32-bit numbers, using leading zeros, if necessary, to fill out the integer to 32 bits; for these computers, we have the specific values

INTEGER'First: -2^{31}
INTEGER'Last: $2^{31} - 1$

where, for compactness, we have expressed these numbers in terms of the thirty-first power of 2. In the more familiar decimal form, the numbers are

$-2,147,483,648$ and $2,147,483,647$

respectively. However, personal computers (microcomputers) often use a 16-bit representation of integers; for Ada systems implemented on these computers, the values of INTEGER'First and INTEGER'Last will usually be -2^{15} and $2^{15} - 1$, which evaluate to $-32,768$ and $32,767$, respectively.

We have just had occasion to write several specific integer values. Strings of characters that represent particular values of a given type are called the **literals** of the type. Some examples of INTEGER literals are 23, 0, 1776, and 318, as well as 60 and 24, which designate the values we assigned to the constants in the Time_and_Day program of Figure 2.1.1. As noted in Section 1.6, we are not allowed in Ada to use commas within an INTEGER literal and write it in a form such as 32,767 (the way we did above), although we could write it as 32767 or as 32_767, using the underscore character in place of a comma. To describe an INTEGER literal, we say that (provided we remain within our computer's span of numbers for the type INTEGER) any uninterrupted sequence of one or more digits constitutes an INTEGER literal. Moreover, Ada allows us to insert underscore characters into this sequence of digits, as long as each underscore is immediately preceded and followed by a digit. This means that the literal may not begin or end with an underscore, nor may there be two or more *successive* underscores in it. The underscore character, properly used, has no effect on the value of the number: Thus, 1066, 1_066, 10_66, and 1_0_6_6 are all legitimate and represent the same INTEGER value. Recall that this situation is just the *opposite* from what we saw in the case of identifiers: NewCount1, New_Count1, NewCount_1, and New_Count_1 are all *different* identifiers, standing for different items. Clearly, the most practical use of the optional underscore character in an INTEGER literal is in grouping digits in meaningful ways for ease of reading. For example, if we are using a computer whose implemention of the type INTEGER includes numbers (six or more digits), it is more difficult to read the literals

    100000   1000000   2147483647

which might occur in a program, than to read their equivalent forms

    100_000   1_000_000   2_147_483_647

At this point, a question has doubtless occurred to you: What about *negative* integers? The answer is quite simple: a negative number of type INTEGER may be written in the form described above, immediately preceded by a minus sign. We offer some examples, borrowing from the ones we have already given:

    -23 -1776 -1_776 -32767 -32_767

2.7 The type INTEGER: Operations

Ada provides us with a useful and fairly extensive set of arithmetic operations that may be performed on objects of type INTEGER. Each such operation is indicated by its respective symbol (+, −, *, /, **) or by a reserved word (**abs**, **rem**, **mod**). These symbols and reserved words are called **operators**; the numbers they operate on—literals, constants, or variables—are called **operands**. Most of these operators (+, −, *, /, **, **rem**, **mod**) involve two operands: They are called **binary** (or **dyadic**) **operators**. The **abs** (absolute value) operator, however, takes just one operand, and + and − may also be used with a single operand, as is done when we use − to indicate the negative of an integer literal. Operators that take one operand are called **unary** (or **monadic**) **operators**. Thus, the symbols + and − are actually used in two senses: Each represents both a unary and a binary operator. We now consider the effects of these operations.

Nothing need be said about the operators + and −, whether binary or unary, since these symbols are used in the same way, and with the same results, as in ordinary arithmetic. In particular, the unary operator + does not affect the value of the operand that follows it; thus, 1492 and +1492 have the same value. Multiplication is indicated in Ada, as well as in many other computer languages, by the operator *, which also behaves as does the multiplication sign in ordinary arithmetic. We note, however, that in the context of computing, multiplication may *not* be indicated by the mere juxtaposition of its operands, as is the case in mathematics: Thus, the products *xy* and *a(b + c)*, as they might be written in algebraic notation, must be written x*y and a*(b+c)—or, as we would prefer, X*Y and A*(B+C)—in a computer program.

Division of INTEGER numbers, indicated by /, calls for discussion. In arithmetic, we may add, subtract, or multiply two integers and always obtain an integer result; but we are not guaranteed an integer result when we take the quotient of a pair of integers. In computing—and specifically when we program in Ada—the situation is different: Dividing one number of the Ada type INTEGER by another such number *does* yield an INTEGER value, even if this result is not mathematically correct. Specifically, the resulting quotient is "truncated toward 0." This means that the *actual* result of the division, if not already an integer, is "chopped off" to the nearest integer smaller in magnitude. Here are some examples that show the / operator applied to several pairs of operands; in each case, the value that results is given in square brackets:

15 / 5	[3]	14 / 5	[2]	8 / 5	[1]	3 / 5	[0]
15/(−5)	[−3]	14/(−5)	[−2]	8/(−5)	[−1]	3/(−5)	[0]
17 / 5	[3]	17/(−5)	[−3]	(−17)/5	[−3]	(−17)/(−5)	[3]

It may be helpful at this point to recall that the operation of division by 0 is undefined in mathematics. In computing, the same is true; moreover, if division by 0 should be attempted during execution of a program, the computer will object to it in some way or other, often by terminating the run of the program. (This situation will be taken up in considerably more detail in Chapter 7.) What has normally happened in this case is that division by 0 was unintended by the programmer, but somewhere in the program there is a division by a *variable* which, earlier in the course of execution, has taken on the value 0.

The operators **rem** (*rem*ainder) and **mod** (*mod*ulo) are related to the mathematical operation of division, and, as in the case of division, their second operand (on the right of the operator) is not allowed to be 0. We will put off discussion of the **mod** operation until Section 2.13; here we consider only **rem**, as it is perhaps easier to understand and, as we have seen in Figure 2.1.1, is of immediate need for us. Also, it is possible to express the effect of the **rem** operation in a general formula:

A **rem** B   has the value   A − ((A/B) * B)

where A/B denotes the (truncated) INTEGER division described above. A **rem** B is therefore the (INTEGER) **remainder** resulting from the division of A by B, just as A/B is the (INTEGER) **quotient** that results from this division. It is not hard to see that A **rem** B is 0 if and only if B exactly divides A, so that no truncation takes place; this is the same as saying that when A is divided by B, the remainder is 0. Furthermore, one may check that, in every case, A **rem** B is less than B in magnitude (absolute value). Finally, when A **rem** B is not 0, its sign is the same as that of A. Thus

    17 **rem** 5   and   17 **rem** (−5)   have the value   2
    (−17) **rem** 5   and   (−17) **rem** (−5) have the value   −2

There are two remaining INTEGER operations. The first of these, exponentiation, uses the operator ****** with two operands, where the operand on the *right* (exponent) indicates the power to which the operand on the *left* (base) is to be raised. The right operand must be positive or 0 (why?). We have then:

    2**15   2 raised to the 15th power
    15**2   15 squared

Finally, the unary operator **abs** produces the absolute value, or magnitude, of its operand, which is 0 if the operand has the value 0, and positive if the operand has any other value:

    abs 25   and   **abs** (−25)   both have the value   25

2.8 Operator precedence

The INTEGER operations that we have described can, of course, be combined in various ways, just as is done in mathematics. In order to deal properly with such combinations of operations, we will need to know, in each case, the exact order in which the computer will perform the indicated operations. Consider, for instance, the value of

    − 7 + 3 * 5 − 4 / 2

Is it −12? or 6? or 2? or what?

Note that a certain priority or ranking—called **operator precedence**—exists among the operators in Ada for the order of computation. The operators we have considered exist on four *precedence*, or *priority, levels,* as shown in Figure 2.8.1.

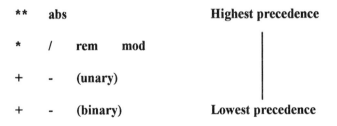

**	abs	Highest precedence
*	/ rem mod	
+	- (unary)	
+	- (binary)	Lowest precedence

Figure 2.8.1

In the process of computing a value, any operations involving ** and **abs** are performed first, followed by those on the next level down, followed by those on the third level, followed by those on the lowest level. Operators on the same level are processed from left to right as they appear in the expression being evaluated (but see Exercise 2.8.4). Thus, in the computation

$$- 7 + 3 * 5 - 4 / 2$$

the operators * and / are applied first, from left to right, to yield

$$- 7 + 15 - 2$$

and then the leading (unary) minus sign is associated with the 7 that follows it, to give the negative integer –7; then the final operations, + and –, both on the same priority level, are carried out, producing

$$8 - 2$$

and, finally,

$$6$$

as the specified value.

The stated order of computation may be overridden by grouping terms in parentheses: The contents of parentheses are evaluated first, starting from the innermost parentheses if there are parentheses "nested" within other parentheses. Thus

$$- (7 + 3) * (5 - 4) / 2$$

becomes

$$- 10 * 1 / 2$$

and then the * and / are carried out (left to right, as they appear), to give

$$- 10 / 2$$

and

$$- 5$$

with the unary minus then operating on the operand 5 to yield the negative integer –5.

For a final example, we offer

$$((- 7 + 3) * 5 - 4) / 2$$

in which the unary minus first is combined with the 7 and the resulting negative integer is added to the 3 to yield the value –4 within the innermost parentheses:

$$(-4 * 5 - 4) / 2$$

Then the multiplication is performed, with a negative result

$$(-20 - 4) / 2$$

followed by the subtraction, which gives the negative value -24 within the outer parentheses

$$(-24) / 2$$

and then the final negative value –12.

There is nothing wrong, by the way, in using redundant parentheses—that is, parentheses that are not really needed—to improve the clarity and readability of what we have written. Thus, our original example could have appeared (in a more readily understandable form) as

$$- 7 + (3 * 5) - (4 / 2)$$

and the result would have been computed in the same way as before, yielding the same value. It is possible to overdo the use of redundant parentheses, however, with the resulting clutter leading to obscurity, rather than to the clarity that is desired.

Applying operator precedence to the unary operators can be a bit tricky; at least, it calls for some care. For instance, –5**2 is –25, not the square of –5. To yield the desired value 25, we write (–5)**2. Finally, since an operation cannot be performed before a value has been provided on each side of the operator (or on the right side, in the case of a unary operator), we cannot write 7 **rem** –4, or **abs** –4, because the computer has not yet carried out the unary minus operation when it attempts to perform the higher-precedence **rem** or **abs** operation. We write 7 **rem** (–4), and **abs** (–4) instead. The same condition pertains to *, /, and **mod**, all of which have higher precedence than the unary minus.

At this point we have finished studying the fundamentals of the type INTEGER, an investigation that we began in Section 2.6. We have seen that this type has a finite number of values consisting of the implementation-dependent numbers INTEGER'First and INTEGER'Last, along with all the integers between them. We have also seen how we may write the individual numbers—literals—of this type. Finally, we have considered the arithmetic operations that Ada provides for values of the type INTEGER and shown for each operation its respective operator symbol or reserved word, as well as the effect the operation has when carried out.

2.9 Other integer types

Up to now we have spoken of the type INTEGER in Ada. In fact, however, the language has many instances of what are called **integer types** (in the plural), with INTEGER being one of them. Our discussion in the remainder of this section and the next pertains to all these integer types, and so we will use the lowercase word "integer" here in such expressions as "integer literals" and "operations on integers." In fact, what we have said already about forming literals of type INTEGER may now be applied, more broadly, to "integer literals."

What are Ada's integer types, other than the type INTEGER, and what use do we make of them? For the moment, we give only a partial answer to the first of these questions by saying that while Ada allows the programmer to *create* integer types (a matter we take up later), the language provides us with two *predefined* integer types, namely, POSITIVE and NATURAL.

Recall from Section 2.5 that a type consists of a set of *values* and a set of *operations* that can be performed on these values. Accordingly, we describe the type POSITIVE as consisting of all values of type INTEGER that are greater than 0 (*positive* in the mathematical sense), along with the same set of operations as those we introduced for the type INTEGER. Similarly, the type NATURAL consists of all the positive values of type INTEGER together with 0 (in mathematical parlance, the set of *natural*, or counting, *numbers*), with the same operations as those pertaining to the type INTEGER. To compare these sets of values with those of the INTEGER type, it may be helpful to consider the attributes First and Last as applied to the types POSITIVE and NATURAL:

```
POSITIVE'First = 1    POSITIVE'Last = INTEGER'Last
NATURAL'First  = 0    NATURAL'Last  = INTEGER'Last
```

POSITIVE and NATURAL each illustrate the Ada concept of a **subtype** of a given type, which consists of a *subset* of the values of the latter type (known as the **base type**), along with the same set of operations as those associated with this type. Clearly, the values of the type POSITIVE constitute a subset of the values of type INTEGER, and the operations pertinent to POSITIVE values are the same as those for INTEGER values; hence, POSITIVE is a subtype of the type INTEGER. Similarly, NATURAL is a subtype of INTEGER. It is easy to verify, from our description of subtypes, that POSITIVE may also be regarded as a subtype of the type NATURAL. In fact, since every set is a subset of itself, it follows that, in the Ada context, every type is a subtype of itself; thus, for example, POSITIVE is a subtype of the type POSITIVE (considered as base type).

The types POSITIVE and NATURAL—just as the type INTEGER—may be used in constant and variable declarations. Consider, for example, the three declarations appearing in the Warranty program of Figure 1.6.1:

```
Warranty_Miles:         constant INTEGER := 25000;
Current_Miles:          INTEGER;
Remaining_Miles:        INTEGER;
```

The constant Warranty_Miles must certainly be a positive integer, inasmuch as it is declared to have the value 25,000; hence, we could have declared, more specifically:

```
Warranty_Miles:         constant POSITIVE := 25000;
```

Also, while the variable Current_Miles, representing a car's odometer reading, may have a value that is either zero or positive, it surely cannot have a negative value; it must be a nonnegative integer, or *natural number*. Thus, the declaration

```
Current_Miles:          NATURAL;
```

gives the program's reader a much more precise—and therefore clearer—idea of the values this variable can assume. In a similar fashion, the constants and variables in the Time_and_Day program (Figure 2.1.1) might be given a better focus if, instead of employing the type INTEGER, we use its subtypes in the declarations:

```
Minutes_Elapsed:        NATURAL;
Hours_Elapsed:          NATURAL;
Day, Hour, Minute:      NATURAL;
Minutes_in_Hour:        constant POSITIVE := 60;
Hours_in_Day:           constant POSITIVE := 24;
```

Admittedly, the assigning of the numbers 60 and 24 makes it immediately evident that the two constants have positive values, and thus little is gained by changing INTEGER to POSITIVE in this case. However, declaring the *variables* to be of type NATURAL (rather than INTEGER) enables the reader to see from the outset that these variables can take on only counting numbers as values—a contribution to ease of understanding.

It may seem that it would be easier to use only the type INTEGER in dealing with integer values, thus sparing ourselves the trouble of singling out which integer variables can meaningfully take on only positive integers, or only natural numbers, as values. However, what we have been trying to point out is the improvement in program clarity and readability that can result from the careful use of subtypes in declarations. Besides helping program clarity, subtypes can also contribute to program correctness, as we now consider by means of some examples.

In the Warranty program (Figure 1.6.1), the user is expected to enter an integer indicating how many miles a car has run (the reading on its odometer), and the program displays how many miles remain on the car's 25,000-mile warranty. Figure 1.6.2 provides two examples of what can occur when the program is run: If the user enters an odometer reading of 16104, the program indicates that 8896 miles remain on the warranty; if the user enters 29883, the program announces that −4883 miles remain. In each case, the program has displayed the value of the variable Remaining_Miles, a value obtained by subtracting the value of Current_Miles (entered by the user) from Warranty_Miles (a constant with a value of 25,000). We have used the declaration

```
Remaining_Miles:        INTEGER;
```

and the program has allowed this variable to take the value −4,883. We pointed out in Section 1.6 that saying −4,883 miles "remain" on the warranty makes no literal sense, although we may interpret this statement as meaning that the mileage has exceeded the warranty by 4,883 miles. Would it have been desirable instead to declare

```
Remaining_Miles:        NATURAL;
```

and, if so, what would have happened if the computer attempted to assign the value −4883 to Remaining_Miles? To answer the latter question first, the computer would surely raise an objection if the attempt were made to assign to a NATURAL variable a value—even an integer value—not of type NATURAL. We have said all along that when we declare a variable to be of a certain type, Ada expects only values of that type to be assigned to this variable. Exactly *how* the computer would object and *what* we might do about it are topics taken up in great detail in Chapter 7; for now let us simply say that any attempt to assign a *negative* value to a NATURAL variable will cause the program to "crash": the Ada system will terminate the run of the program and send a message to the user concerning the offending action. The same will occur if a negative or zero value is assigned to a POSITIVE variable. Is this what we would want? Probably not, in this simple program where it is easy to interpret a negative result as indicating by how many miles the car has exceeded the warranty mileage. Thus, in the Warranty program, we may find it preferable to declare Remaining_Miles to be of type INTEGER and allow the possibility of its assuming *any* integer values, including negative ones.

But consider the case in which the user (by a typographical error, say) enters −3210 as the value of Current_Miles. If Current_Miles has been declared to be of type INTEGER, the resulting dialogue will look like this:

```
Enter the current miles (odometer reading): -3210
The number of miles remaining on the warranty is 28210
```

This wrong answer is not so easily noticed; and, further, the negative *input* here is not as readily interpreted in some meaningful fashion as was the negative *output* −4883 occurring in Figure 1.6.2. As a result, we are better off declaring Current_Miles to be of type NATURAL; an attempt to enter −3210 as the value of this variable would cause the Ada system to terminate program execution and send an error message. While this result may be undesirable, at least it gives a clear indication that something has gone wrong. It is the alternative possibility—receiving wrong output while assuming it to be correct—that constitutes the worst-case scenario in computing. Thus, by appropriate use of subtypes in variable declarations, we may be able to forestall errors resulting from improper data. We dislike finding errors and other problems in our programs, but it is worse *not* to find them.

2.10 Expressions and assignments

The *LRM [4.4]* describes an **expression** as "a formula that defines the computation of a value." If this value is an integer, the expresssion is said to be an **integer expression**. An example of an integer expression is the "formula"

$$-7 + 3 * 5 - 4 / 2$$

discussed in Section 2.8; other examples of integer expressions taken from the Ada program we have been studying are:

```
Minutes_Elapsed / Minutes_in_Hour
Minutes_Elapsed rem Minutes_in_Hour
Hours_Elapsed / Hours_in_Day
Hours_Elapsed rem Hours_in_Day
```

We might expect to see an operator, or several operators, in an expression, as in the examples just cited, for the word "computation" seems to imply that this is the case; however, each of the following is also an integer expression:

An integer literal	such as	60
An integer variable	such as	`Minute`
An integer constant	such as	`Minutes_in_Hour`

The important word in our description of an expression is "value"—an expression is something that has a value. The concept of expression is fundamental in programming. It is especially important to have a clear grasp of the distinction between an *expression* and a *statement*: An expression has a *value* but does not command that anything be done with this value; a statement commands an *action* but does not have a value. An expression is *evaluated*; a statement is *executed*.

One of the simplest yet most important types of statement used in computing is the **assignment statement**, in which a value is assigned, or given, to a variable by means of the **assignment operator :=**. The entire computational section of the Ada program we are studying consists of assignment statements:

```
Hours_Elapsed    := Minutes_Elapsed / Minutes_in_Hour;
Minute           := Minutes_Elapsed rem Minutes_in_Hour;
Day              := Hours_Elapsed / Hours_in_Day;
Hour             := Hours_Elapsed rem Hours_in_Day;
Day              := Day + 1;
```

At the point in the program where these statements occur, each of the constants Minutes_in_Hour and Hours_in_Day has an integer value (60 and 24, respectively), which was assigned to it when it was declared, and the variable Minutes_Elapsed also has a specific integer value, which was given to it when the user's input was obtained from the keyboard with the statement Int_IO.Get (Minutes_Elapsed). The statements above illustrate the general form of an assignment statement: on the left of the assignment operator := is the name of the variable to which a value is to be assigned, and on the right of this operator is an expression. When an assignment statement is executed, the computer evaluates the expression at the right of the assignment operator and then assigns the resulting value to the variable on the left. Thus, in the first statement above, the integer division

Minutes_Elapsed / Minutes_in_Hour

is performed, and its result is assigned to the variable Hours_Elapsed (which, up to this point, had not been assigned any particular value). A similar comment may be made about each of the three following assignment statements. The last assignment statement deserves some special comment, since the variable name Day appears on both the left and the right of the assignment operator. The value of Day, the one it received when the third assignment statement

```
Day := Hours_Elapsed / Hours_in_Day;
```

was executed, is used in the evaluation of the expression Day + 1; the resulting value is then assigned to the variable Day, replacing the value Hours_Elapsed / Hours_in_Day that had formerly been there. At this point, the former value of Day has been lost; but there is no problem, since it is not needed again. A lesson emerges from all this: Whenever a value is assigned to a variable, it replaces the former value of the variable, and this "old" value is no longer available. If necessary to use again, it should be saved by first assigning it to another variable introduced into the program for this purpose.

We cannot leave the topic of assigning values without putting on record one of the very important principles of computer programming: Never make use of a variable without first assigning it a value. As far as the variables dealt with in this book are concerned, we must always assume that any variable we have declared has an *unknown* value until such time as it is explicitly given a value by the program.

How is a variable given its first value—its **initial value**, as is said—in a program the assumption being that, in general, this value may be replaced by one or more subsequent values as the program runs? We distinguish several ways of thus **initializing** a variable. A variable may be given its initial value by means of an **input statement**; this is done in the Time_and_Day program of Figure 2.1.1, in which the variable Minutes_Elapsed is given a starting value when the input statement Int_IO.Get (Minutes_Elapsed) is executed. Notice that all the computations done in the program, as well as its subsequent output, are based on this initial value of Minutes_Elapsed. In this case, the variable receives its initial value from the *user* when the program is run.

In case the *programmer* is in a position to assign an initial value to a program variable (without calling upon the *user* to do so), this may be accomplished in two ways. In order to illustrate them, we introduce a new program, Average_3, which computes and displays the average of three integers entered by the user. To perform the addition, we give an initial value of 0 to a variable Total, and then each number is read as input and added to the current value of Total—Total thus maintains a "running subtotal" of the input numbers. When all the numbers have been read and added to it, Total holds the sum of the three integers, and its value is divided by Count_of_Numbers, a constant with the value 3, to yield the (truncated) average. Note that there is no need to have distinct variables to hold the three numbers that the user enters as input; Number serves as a reusable variable, for once its value has been added to the current value of Total, we may safely overwrite it with the next number entered by the user. But it *is* absolutely essential to give Total the value 0 before we start adding numbers to it, for we have no information on what value this variable holds when the program begins execution. As we noted, this may be accomplished in either of two ways, the first of which is by an assignment statement at the beginning of the program's sequence of statements, as is done in the first version of the program Average_3 shown in Figure 2.10.1.

```ada
with Text_IO;

procedure Average_3 is

    -- This program takes three integers as input.
    -- It computes and displays their (truncated)
    -- average.

    package Int_IO is new Text_IO.Integer_IO (INTEGER);

    Number:           INTEGER;
    Total:            INTEGER;
    Average:          INTEGER;

    Count_of_Numbers:  constant INTEGER := 3;

begin

    Total := 0;    -- assign the value 0 to total
    Text_IO.New_Line (1);
    Text_IO.Put_Line ("Type three integers, one per line:");
    Int_IO.Get (Number);
    Total := Total + Number;
    Int_IO.Get (Number);
    Total := Total + Number;
    Int_IO.Get (Number);
    Total := Total + Number;
    Average := Total / Count_of_Numbers;
    Text_IO.New_Line (1);
    Text_IO.Put ("Average:   " );
    Int_IO.Put (Average, 0);
    Text_IO.New_Line (1);

end Average_3;
```

Figure 2.10.1

We now look at another way of initializing Total. Ada allows the assignment of an initial value to a variable at the time the variable is *declared*. This has been done with the variable Total in the revised version of Average_3 shown in Figure 2.10.2. Here the initialization of Total—the assignment of 0 to this variable—is incorporated into the variable *declaration* and does not need an assignment *statement*.

```ada
with Text_IO;

procedure Average_3 is
```

```
-- This program takes three integers as input.
-- It computes and displays their (truncated)
-- average.

package Int_IO is new Text_IO.Integer_IO (INTEGER);

Number:             INTEGER;
Total:              INTEGER := 0; -- Assign the value 0 to total
Average:            INTEGER;

Count_of_Numbers:   constant INTEGER := 3;

begin

    Text_IO.New_Line (1);
    Text_IO.Put_Line ("Type three integers, one per line:");
    Int_IO.Get (Number);
    Total := Total + Number;
    Int_IO.Get (Number);
    Total := Total + Number;
    Int_IO.Get (Number);
    Total := Total + Number;
    Average := Total / Count_of_Numbers;
    Text_IO.New_Line (1);
    Text_IO.Put ("Average:   " );
    Int_IO.Put (Average, 0);
    Text_IO.New_Line (1);

end Average_3;
```

Figure 2.10.2

Observe that both the *variable* Total and the *constant* Count_of_Numbers have been assigned values in their declarations. There are two differences to be noted: (1) A constant *must* be given a value when it is declared, whereas a variable *may* (but need not) be given a value in its declaration, and (2) the value assigned to a constant in its declaration may *never* be changed, but an initial value assigned to a variable in its declaration *may* be changed, by means of assignment or input statements, when the program runs. To refer once again to the discussion of declarations in Section 1.6, we recall that when the program of Figure 2.10.2 is compiled, the compiler provides for the allocation of four memory locations suitable for holding values of type INTEGER and associates the names Number, Total, Average, and Count_of_Numbers with these locations; it arranges for the values 0 and 3 to be placed in the memory locations associated with the names Total and Count_of_Numbers, respectively. (We may not assume that any particular values are put into the memory locations designated as Number and Average.) Finally, the memory location associated with the name Count_of_Numbers is marked as holding a constant, which means that its value may not be changed during the run of the program.

Values that are assigned in declarations need not be expressed as *literals*, as was the case in the program of Figure 2.10.2. Just as in an assignment statement, the assignment operator in a *declaration* may be followed by *any expression* of the appropriate type, provided that this expression can be evaluated at the point at which it occurs in the program. Thus, for example, the following declarations are legitimate:

```
M:  [constant] INTEGER := 12;
N:  [constant] INTEGER := 2 * M + 1;
```

The square brackets indicate that the word "constant" is optional; that is, for the point we are making it does not matter whether each identifier designates a constant or a variable. Observe that at the point in the program where it is necessary to evaluate the expression

$$2 * M + 1$$

M has already been given the value 12; thus, this expression has the well-determined value 25. On the other hand, we cannot legitimately declare

```
M:  INTEGER;
N:  [constant] INTEGER := 2 * M + 1;
```

because the expression

$$2 * M + 1$$

cannot be evaluated here; M has not been assigned any determinate value. For a similar reason, we must rule out

```
N:  [constant] INTEGER := 2 * M + 1;
M:  [constant] INTEGER := 12;
```

because, although M is given a determined value in the *second* declaration, this value has not *yet* been assigned at the point where the expression

$$2 * M + 1$$

is to be evaluated.

By now we have covered all the parts of the Ada program Time_and_Day in Figure 2.1.1, with the exception of some of the finer points of input and output. We discuss some of these in the next section.

2.11 Input/output of strings and integers

In discussing the program Time_and_Day, we have already mentioned that the inclusion of the context clause **with Text_IO** makes available to this program the routines for I/O contained in the package Text_IO. Of these, we have made direct use of the following:

Text_IO.New_Line (1). This inserts a **line terminator**, which causes subsequent output to start at the beginning of the next line. Text_IO.New_Line (2) brings the output down 2 lines instead of 1, and, in general, Text_IO.New_Line (*n*), where *n* is a positive integer expression, brings it down *n* lines.

Text_IO.Put (string). Here "string" stands for one or more characters enclosed in quotation marks. This causes the given string (or "character string") to be displayed on the screen at the current cursor position. No line terminator is inserted after this string of output.

Text_IO.Put_Line (string). This is the same as Text_IO.Put (string) followed immediately by Text_IO.New_Line (1).

The package Int_IO, which results from the declaration

```
package Int_IO is new Text_IO.Integer_IO (INTEGER);
```

provides us with an input routine Get and an output routine Put, both applicable to integers. Note that in contrast to what we have available for output of strings, there is no routine Int_IO.Put_Line applicable to *integers*. The effects of Get and Put are as follows:

Int_IO.Get (integer-variable). This obtains an integer from the keyboard and assigns this value to the specified integer variable.

Int_IO.Put (integer-expression, 0). This causes the value of the given integer expression to be displayed on the screen at the current cursor position.

Before concluding this section, we should point out that much more can be said about the ways in which the packages Text_IO and Int_IO are similar and dissimilar and, more broadly, about the relationship between them. We leave this discussion for the following chapter, where we can treat it in its proper context.

2.12 Format of an Ada program

We have attempted to lay out the Ada programs presented thus far in a clear and easily understandable format. In particular, we have included spacing by way of indentations and blank lines so as to contribute to the readability of the program. Although it is probably true that too much white space in a program text may make a program harder to read, the real danger to clarity lies in the opposite direction, namely, crowding the text or failing to separate it into coherent sections of program code. Accordingly, since we favor the use of spacing to enhance program clarity, we now discuss what Ada does and does not allow in this matter.

It is convenient to use the word "spaces" in a special way throughout the remainder of this section. By "spaces" we will mean a blank, tab, line terminator (RETURN or ENTER), or any number and combination of these in succession. Using this convention, then, we can lay down two rules on the use of spaces in Ada programs:

1. Spaces *must* be used where their omission would cause words or numbers to run together.

2. Spaces *may* be used anywhere in a program except where their insertion would break up a word or number.

In the Time_and_Day program of Figure 2.1.1, we have written

```
Text_IO.New_Line (2);
Int_IO.Get (Minutes_Elapsed);
Int_IO.Put (Hour);
```

where we might instead have written

```
Text_IO.New_Line(2);
Int_IO.Get(Minutes_Elapsed);
Int_IO.Put(Hour);
```

with no space preceding the left parenthesis, which is an acceptable and often-used style. Also, we have the statements

```
Hours_Elapsed := Minutes_Elapsed / Minutes_in_Hour;
Minute        := Minutes_Elapsed rem Minutes_in_Hour;
Day           := Hours_Elapsed / Hours_in_Day;
Hour          := Hours_Elapsed rem Hours_in_Day;
```

where the extra spaces preceding the assignment operators are included to align the names and bring out the parallelism of the statements. We could have gone even further toward displaying statement parallelism through name alignment if we had inserted further spaces around the / operators, as follows:

```
Hours_Elapsed := Minutes_Elapsed  /  Minutes_in_Hour;
Minute        := Minutes_Elapsed rem Minutes_in_Hour;
Day           := Hours_Elapsed   /  Hours_in_Day;
Hour          := Hours_Elapsed  rem Hours_in_Day;
```

At the opposite extreme, we might have eliminated all spaces from the first of these statements without any violation of syntax (the rules of the language). It would then appear as

```
Hours_Elapsed:=Minutes_Elapsed/Minutes_in_Hour;
```

but the expression on the right of the assignment operator in the second statement could *not* have been written as

```
Minutes_ElapsedremMinutes_in_Hour
```

which, after all, is the same as

```
MINUTES_ELAPSEDREMMINUTES_IN_HOUR
```
or

```
minutes_elapsedremminutes_in_hour
```

a single, very long word, which the compiler is unable to identify as an expression made up of the operator **rem** and its two operands.

Finally, we note the advisability of writing separate statements on separate lines (although the language does not require this), to help bring out the order in which they are performed. We sometimes depart from this practice, however, in the case of clauses or statements that are closely coupled, such as

```
Ans_1 := 0;  Ans_2 := 0;  Ans_3 := 0;    -- Initialize answers
```

2.13 The *mod* operator*

Before we begin our investigation of Ada's **mod** operator, let us first recall a few points about the **rem** operator. We saw in Section 2.7 that A **rem** B is the (integer) *rem*ainder that results from dividing A by B, and its value is A − ((A/B) * B), where A/B is the (integer) quotient resulting from the division of A by B. A **rem** B is 0 if and only if B exactly divides A; otherwise, the sign of A **rem** B is the same as that of A. We repeat the example we offered in Section 2.7, giving the value of each **rem** operation in square brackets:

17	rem	5	[2]	17	rem	(−5)	[2]
(−17)	rem	5	[−2]	(−17)	rem	(−5)	[−2]

The effect of the **mod** operator is somewhat more difficult to describe, and this, along with the fact that we will not be using it again in this book, accounts for our putting off discussing it until now. There are a few aspects that A **rem** B and A **mod** B have in common: (1) Both require that B have a nonzero value; (2) if A and B are both positive, then A **rem** B and A **mod** B have the same value; and (3) both A **rem** B and A **mod** B have the value zero if and only if B evenly divides A, leaving a remainder of 0. If B does *not* exactly divide A, then the value of A **mod** B may be described—in a wordy but accurate fashion—as the (unique) integer strictly *between* 0 and B, which, when subtracted from A, yields an integer multiple of B. (The existence and uniqueness of such an integer are established in mathematics.) Apart from the case where A **mod** B has value zero, it is clear that A **mod** B has the same sign as B, since A **mod** B lies strictly between 0 and B. Some examples of the **mod** operation, with the results in square brackets, follow:

17	mod	5	[2]	17	mod	(−5)	[−3]
(−17)	mod	5	[3]	(−17)	mod	(−5)	[−2]

As you can see, the evaluation of A **mod** B can be rather tricky, especially in the cases where one or both operands are negative. To gain some insight into the situation, consider 17 **mod** (−5). Since the value of this expression lies strictly between 0 and −5 (as we noted above), it must be −1, −2, −3, or −4. We may subtract each of these in turn from 17, to see which

---

*This section may be omitted; it is not used elsewhere in the text.

choice yields a multiple of −5: We obtain, respectively, 18, 19, 20, and 21. Of these, 20—or, 17 − (−3)—is a multiple of −5; hence −3 is the right choice, which is to say that 17 **mod** (−5) = −3.

2.14 Syntax diagrams

Throughout this chapter we have touched on several "parts," or "elements," of the Ada language (identifiers, constant and variable declarations, integer literals, assignment statements, etc.), and in each case we have described how to write and employ the respective language element in constructing an Ada program.

As far as the **syntax** of language elements is concerned—the rules for writing them properly, as opposed to their meaning (semantics) and proper use—there is an excellent way of describing these language elements so that the learner can grasp them very readily. This is by means of **syntax diagrams**, which illustrate how language elements are made up. In this section we consider syntax diagrams for several of the language elements we have been discussing.

In Section 2.4 we described a digit as one of the characters from 0 to 9. This was probably enough to indicate what Ada does and does not take to be a digit. However, to begin our acquaintance with syntax diagrams, we offer the diagram for a *digit* (Figure 2.14.1), which carefully indicates exactly what is meant by this term.

digit

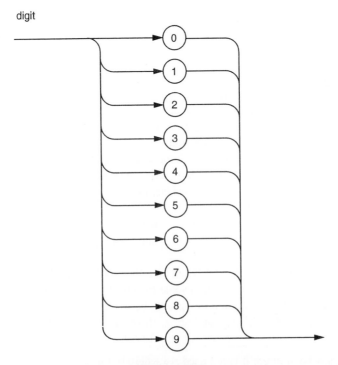

Figure 2.14.1

The interpretation of this syntax diagram, or any syntax diagram, is as follows. Any smooth path through the diagram, starting at its entry point (tail of the arrow at the upper left) and proceeding to its exit point (head of the arrow at the lower right) produces a legitimate instance of the language element being defined; moreover, *all* such instances may be obtained in this way. A path fails to be smooth if it makes a sharp turn or reverses its direction at any point. Thus, in Figure 2.14.1, not only must any smooth path pass through one of the indicated characters, but it cannot subsequently pass through this character again, or through any other character; it must simply continue to the exit point of the diagram. In this way, the syntax diagram indicates clearly and precisely what is meant by a digit. (The circles that enclose the 10 digit characters are not merely stylistic; they serve a purpose that will be explained in the discussion of Figure 2.14.3 below.)

As is obvious, Figure 2.14.1 simply provides an exhaustive list of all possible digits. We could construct a similar (but larger) syntax diagram for the language element *letter*, listing all 52 upper- and lowercase letters of the alphabet, as indicated in Figure 2.14.2.

letter

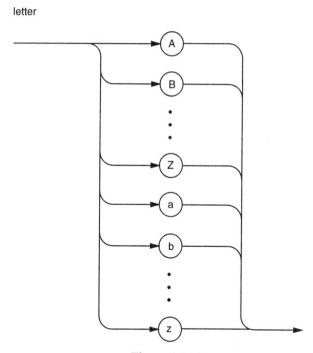

Figure 2.14.2

You might object—and quite rightly—that syntax diagrams are hardly very helpful if they must always list every single legitimate instance of the language element they define, as was done in Figures 2.14.1 and 2.14.2. But these two diagrams are quite special, in that they deal with very simple elements that consist of single characters. Our third syntax diagram, which specifies what is an acceptable Ada *identifier*, brings out how succinctly these diagrams can summarize the rules governing the formation of language elements. The syntax diagram appears in Figure 2.14.3; compare it with the verbal description of an identifier found in Section 2.4.

identifier

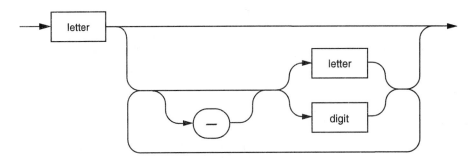

Figure 2.14.3

Observe that we have introduced a second enclosing figure, the rectangle, in addition to the circle that is found in Figures 2.14.1 and 2.14.2, and we use these symbols consistently throughout the book. When a string of characters appears inside a circle (or oval), those characters are to be taken *literally* as they appear. These are either literals from some type or Ada reserved words; they are sometimes referred to as **terminal** symbols. Strings of characters that appear in rectangles are defined in other syntax diagrams; they are called **nonterminals**. In Figure 2.14.3, *letter* and *digit* are nonterminal symbols (defined in the syntax diagrams of Figures 2.14.2 and 2.14.1, respectively); the underscore character, _, is a terminal symbol. In general, here and in future cases, what is required to produce a valid Ada construct—in this case an **identifier**—from its syntax diagram is to use other syntax diagrams to replace *nonterminals* (objects in rectangles) until you eventually arrive at a construction consisting exclusively of *terminals* (objects in ovals or circles).

A similar, though slightly simpler, syntax diagram describes the way in which an integer literal is constructed (Figure 2.14.4).

integer literal

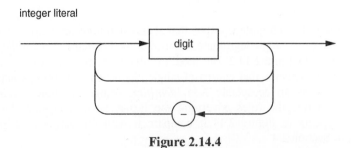

Figure 2.14.4

The syntax diagrams we have seen pertain to language elements that are quite simple in nature, in that they are either individual characters or words or numbers. But syntax diagrams are used for larger and more complex language constructs as well, including some fairly complicated kinds of declarations and statements; in fact, the overall structure of a program may be described in a syntax diagram. Although the declarations we have seen up to now (for constants and variables) have certainly not been very complicated, we sum up what we have said on this topic by presenting syntax diagrams for a *constant declaration* (Figure 2.14.5) and *variable declaration* (Figure 2.14.6). Observe that they are presented in a rather general form, in that they specify *any* type mark, even though INTEGER, POSITIVE, and NATURAL are the only ones that we have discussed so far.

constant declaration

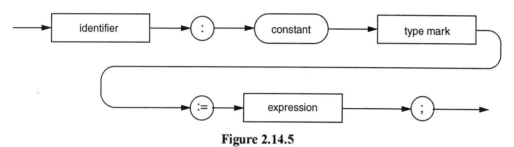

Figure 2.14.5

variable declaration

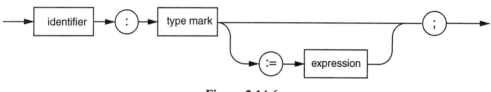

Figure 2.14.6

Note that these last two diagrams make use of the term **expression**. While it is possible to construct a syntax diagram for an *expression* (or, even more specifically, for an *integer expression*), it is quite complicated, and thus we prefer not to do so at present. Instead, we will simply rely on the informal description of integer expressions that we offered in Section 2.10. With the understanding that an expression may be carefully defined in a syntax diagram, we make use of this language element once more in Figure 2.14.7, which sums up the (very simple) syntax of an *assignment statement*.

assignment statement

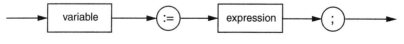

Figure 2.14.7

Throughout the remainder of the book we use diagrams of this sort to describe the syntax of various constructions, particularly when their use will help clarify the structure under consideration. Also, in Appendix C we present a selection of syntax diagrams that may be especially helpful.

2.15 Exercises

2.1.1 Anticipate the output, and give as reasonable an interpretation as you can of its meaning, when each of the following numbers is used as input to the Time_and_Day program of Figure 2.1.1.

(a) 10080
(b) 10123
(c) 12960
(d) −23
(e) −1439
(f) −1440
(g) −1441

2.2.1 Develop successive levels of an outline for a program that accepts as keyboard input an integer from 0 to 100 representing an amount of money in cents and that tells how many quarters, dimes, nickels, and pennies should be used to make up that amount, so that the number of coins is as small as possible.

2.2.2 (a) Develop successive levels of an outline for a program that accepts as keyboard input an integer from 1 to 99 representing the amount of a sale in cents and that tells how many quarters, dimes, nickels, and pennies should be given as change from 1 dollar, so that the number of coins is as small as possible.

(b) What modifications need to be made in the program outline of part *a* if half-dollars are also available for use as change, along with the other coins mentioned?

(c) What modifications need to be made in the program outline of part *a* if no quarters are available, only dimes, nickels, and pennies?

2.4.1 In the program of Figure 1.6.1, determine which of the identifiers are reserved words, which are predefined in Ada, and which are defined by the programmer.

2.4.2 Tell whether or not each of the following is a legitimate identifier in Ada. If not, indicate why not.

(a) `Sales_Total`
(b) `Sales Total`
(c) `SalesTotal`

(d) SALESTOTAL
(e) SalestOtal
(f) Sales_Totle
(g) $_Sales
(h) Sales_in_$
(i) Sales__in__Dollars
(j) I
(k) From
(l) TooPercent
(m) Two_Percent_
(n) 2_Percent
(o) Percent Increase
(p) percentageofincrease
(q) END_OF_PROCEDURE
(r) Taxable
(s) Non-Taxable
(t) Portland,ME
(u) Portland_OR
(v) St._Louis
(w) New_York_New_York
(x) Number1
(y) Number_Two
(z) No._3

2.5.1 Tell what is wrong with each of the following declarations:

(a) constant Percent_Interest: INTEGER := 6;
(b) Inches, Feet, Yards, Miles: INTEGERS;
(c) Fixed_Length: constant INTEGER;
(d) Seconds, Minutes, Days, Weeks, Months, Years;
(e) Magna_Charta_Year: INTEGER constant := 1215;
(f) Amount_of_Change: INTERGER;

2.6.1 Tell whether or not each of the following is a legitimate integer literal in Ada. If not, tell why not.

(a) 513   (e) 513.
(b) 5130   (f) _513
(c) 05130   (g) 0_513
(d) 513.0   (h) 5_13O

2.7.1 Evaluate each of the following:

(a) 17 / 4   (l) 4 rem 12
(b) 17 / (−4)   (m) 4 / 4
(c) −17 / 4   (n) 4 rem 4

(d) −17 / (−4)   (o) 0 / 4
(e) 12 / 4   (p) 0 rem 4
(f) 12 rem 4   (q) 4 ** 3
(g) 12 rem 5   (r) 3 ** 4
(h) 12 rem (−5)   (s) (−4) ** 3
(i) −12 rem 5   (t) (−3) ** 4
(j) −12 rem (−5)   (u) 2 ** 0
(k) 4 / 12   (v) 0 ** 2

2.7.2   Why is it that the right operand of the integer exponentiation operator ** may not be negative?

2.7.3   The binary operators **rem** and **mod** and the unary operator **abs** are unique among the INTEGER operators in the following sense:

X*Y and **X * Y** are both meaningful expressions, and they will always have the same value; that is, whether spaces surround the binary operator symbol * (or +, −, etc.) is immaterial. But explain why **XremY**, **XmodY**, and **absX** are *not* legitimate uses of the **rem**, **mod**, and **abs** operators. How, if at all, will the Ada compiler interpret these "expressions"?

2.8.1   For each of the following, compute the resulting value (if any); or tell why no value can be computed.

(a) 7 + 2 * 5 − 9 / 2
(b) abs 4 − 12 * 3
(c) 2 − 3 rem 4 − 4 rem 3
(d) (9 + (2 * (3 + (−4))))
(e) 4 + abs 5 rem 2 * 21 / 6
(f) 12 rem (abs −5)
(g) 12 rem abs (−5)
(h) (2 ** 2) ** 3
(i) 2 ** (2 ** 3)
(j) −2 ** (2 ** 3)
(k) −12 rem 5 * 2 + 2
(l) 12 rem (−5) * 2 + 2
(m) (−6 * 3) / (5 / 12)
(n) −13 / 5 − 13 rem 5 / 5
(o) (−13 / 5 − 13 rem 5) / 5
(p) −13 / (5 − 13 rem 5) / 5
(q) (8 * (−2 + 4) / ((−3) * (−4) − 2)) ** 3
(r) 3 * 4 ** 2 + 4 * 3
(s) 3 * −4 ** 2 + 4 * 3
(t) 3 / 2 ** 4 + 2 / 3

2.8.2 Let X and Y be INTEGER values, and suppose that we wish to divide X by Y. Show that if, instead of the *truncated* quotient X / Y (provided by the Ada operator /) we want to compute the *rounded* quotient (that is, the quotient rounded to the nearest integer), we may do so by evaluating (2 * X + Y) / (2 * Y).

2.8.3 Show that the INTEGER variable X contains an *even* number if, and only if, X and 2 * (X / 2) have the same value. (But show that there are easier ways to determine whether the value in X is even or odd.)

2.8.4 It was stated in Section 2.8 that operators at the same precedence level are processed left to right. But the exponentiation operator, **, is something of a special case. For example, should 3**2**3 be interpreted as (3**2)**3 = 9**3 = 729 or as 3**(2**3) = 3**8 = 6561? Answer the question by submitting to your Ada compiler a simple program whose only executable statement is

```
Int_IO.Put (3**2**3);
```

2.9.1 In the Warranty program of Figure 1.6.1 declare Current_Miles and Remaining_Miles to be of subtype NATURAL, rather than of type INTEGER. Compile and link the resulting program. Then run the program and observe how your Ada system deals with the inputs 29883 and −3210. Does the program run properly when you enter the input 16104? 25000? 0?

2.10.1 State which of the following declaration sections are valid. For those which are not, explain why they are invalid.

```
(a)     X_High:     constant INTEGER := 17;
        X_Low:      INTEGER := 8;

(b)     X_High:     constant INTEGER := 17;
        X_Low       INTEGER := X_High / 2;

(c)     X_Low:      INTEGER := X_High / 2;
        X_High:     constant INTEGER := 17;

(d)     X_High:     constant INTEGER := 17;
        X_Low:      INTEGER := 2 / x_high;

(e)     X_High:     constant integer := 0;
        X_Low:      INTEGER := 2 / X_High;

(f)     X_High:     constant INTEGER := 17;
        X_Low:      INTEGER := 2 / (X_High - 17);
```

2.13.1 Evaluate each of the following expressions:

(a)   24 mod 7
(b)   −24 mod 7
(c)   24 mod (−7)
(d)   −24 mod (−7)
(e)   12 / 5 + 12 rem 5 + 12 mod 5
(f)   (−12) / 5 + (−12) rem 5 + (−12) mod 5
(g)   12 / (−5) + 12 rem (−5) + 12 mod (−5)
(h)   (−12) / (−5) + (−12) rem (−5) + (−12) mod (−12)
(i)   5 / 12 + 5 rem 12 + 5 mod 12
(j)   (−5) / 12 + (−5) rem 12 + (−5) mod 12
(k)   5 / (−12) + 5 rem (−12) + 5 mod (−12)
(l)   (−5) / (−12) + (−5) rem (−12) + (−5) mod (−12)

Chapter 3

A First Look at Packages

There are several concepts that distinguish Ada from most other programming languages, and one of the central of these is the notion of **package**. Loosely speaking, a package is a collection of declarations and/or routines that have been put together ("packaged") under a specific name; these can then be made available to a program by means of a **context clause** (the **with** clause). The declarations and routines in a package are almost always related somehow, and normally they are such that they can be used in a wide variety of applications. We use the word "routine" here and elsewhere quite informally. For our purposes, we mean a segment of programming instructions, but rarely an entire program, that is "complete" in that it accomplishes some small or perhaps incidental job. Text_IO is a good example of a package, for it consists of a collection of routines, each complete in itself, that do input and output of *text*: characters and strings of characters. The routines can be used by any programmer, even though they have been written by someone else. The programmer needs only to include a reference to the package in his or her current program. Thus we see that one of the features of a package is that it provides **reusable software**— programming that is written only once but can then be used repeatedly.

The few Ada programs we have seen so far are very small—tiny, actually, when compared to the programs of the real world. Typical large programs, called **software systems**, consist of hundreds of thousands of lines of instructions. To manage such complex systems, which must necessarily be written by entire teams of programmers, a great deal of organization must be imposed on the way modules are written; otherwise chaos would surely result. One of the chief ways in which modules and routines are organized is via the package concept, with one programming team writing a package, which in turn is used by another programming team to accomplish an intended job. Thus it is not unusual to find software systems consisting in large part of team-written packages, the main parts of the programs then being reduced to little more than "invoking" the routines within those packages. That is, in the spirit of modular programming, a problem is broken down into subproblems, the subproblems are solved in packages, and the appropriate package routines are invoked as a solution to the main problem.

In this chapter we have an introductory look at some of the details involved in the package concept. This Ada feature is extremely powerful, but it is also quite complex for the beginning programmer. Thus most of the aspects of packages are introduced here only at a most general level, and at that we do not expect you to grasp all the ideas in all of their detail and with all their ramifications. But we can make a beginning, and if nothing else, you can become familiar with some of the terminology and notation. The first packages we investigate are Int_IO and Text_IO. We start with these not because packages that perform input and output are the norm, but because these are the two packages we have already had occasion to use and their actions are at least somewhat familiar. Later in this chapter we introduce a package which has several useful mathematical routines but which has nothing to do with input or output.

3.1 Procedures

In the preceding chapters we have used the commands Put and Get in our programming examples: **Int_IO.Get (Current_miles)**, **Int_IO.Put (Day,0)**, and so forth. We know that Put and Get are not Ada *operations*, which is why we have used the less precise word "command" here, but what exactly are they? The answer is, they are **procedures**.

A procedure is a more or less self-contained collection of Ada instructions whose purpose is typically to carry out a single specified job. A procedure is frequently called a **subprogram**, a term used to indicate that it is executed *within* a program without being a complete program itself. (We realize that we have not defined the term **program**. We refer to collections of instructions that, upon execution, produce solutions to complete problems, as "programs," "main programs," or even "complete programs." By this criterion, the few programming efforts you have seen so far qualify as *programs*.)

Let us begin our investigation of subprograms by examining a statement from the Time_and_Day program of Figure 2.1.1:

```
Text_IO.Put ("The time is ");
```

This statement consists of three components, namely, Text_IO, Put, and ("The time is "), and we examine each of these in turn, beginning with the subprogram Put. Evidently Put consists of instructions which, when executed, result in characters—text—appearing on the display screen, and we have been able to call for Put's execution simply by stating its name. We do not concern ourselves here with just *what* instructions are executed in order to generate the display; our concern is that when we call for the execution of Put, it does its job.

A subprogram is a collection of instructions that accomplishes a complete task. But it is rare that a subprogram can perform its job simply by our calling for its execution. To see why, consider a few sample subprograms. We already know that Put sends strings of characters to the display screen; Square_Root might find the square root of a positive number; and Sort_Up might be used to arrange a list of integers into increasing order. But it makes no sense to invoke these routines simply by name: Put, Square_Root, and Sort_Up. These routines would have to "ask": Display *what* string of characters? Find the square root of *which* positive number? And arrange *what* list of integers into increasing order? Thus while a subprogram might contain all the *instructions* to produce some desired effect on data, it also needs to know to *which* data it is to apply those instructions. This additional information about the data that must be supplied to a subprogram is called a parameter. As we see, the parameter needed by Put is a string of characters, and in Ada a string of characters is defined by placing the characters within double quotes. Evidently Put requires a single parameter, the string itself, but subprograms may require two or more parameters, and we will shortly have an example. A few procedures might require no parameters at all (for example, the procedure that displays *today's* date), but they are the exception.

The third component is the name of the package that contains the routine in question, Put. This package is named Text_IO and is supplied by the compiler vendor as part of a complete Ada system. As described earlier, a package is supposed to be a collection of related routines. Are there other routines in Text_IO? Yes, we already know one of these: New_Line. Is this related to Put? Yes, for New_Line actually sends a *string* of characters to the display, namely, the control character that, rather than "appearing" on the screen, causes the display cursor to move to the extreme left, followed by another control character that causes the cursor to move down one line. (This string of two characters is known as the **new line sequence**.) Note that, like Put, New_Line requires a single parameter; but unlike Put, the parameter is not a string; rather it is a positive integer that "tells" New_Line *how many* lines to move down the display. There are other routines in Text_IO, including one that "gets" strings of characters from the keyboard, and we will examine these as they occur; but the point is that they are all somehow related to strings of characters—"text."

3.2 Package instantiations

As a package, Text_IO is far more elaborate than we have suggested, for not only does it contain routines for the input and output of characters and strings of characters, it even contains several *packages*! Thus packages can be defined within other packages. One of these packages within Text_IO is named **Integer_IO**, and as its name suggests, it provides routines for the input ("Get") and output ("Put") of integers. Now we know from Chapter 2 that there are many different integer types (subtypes of the type INTEGER), among them INTEGER, POSITIVE, and NATURAL, so it is legitimate to ask: On what *type* of integer do the routines in Integer_IO operate? The answer is that no particular integer type is specified in Integer_IO. But if this is the case, how can the routines in Integer_IO input and output integer types, without "knowing" precisely what those types are? Remarkably, the answer is that they cannot! Thus the routines in the package Integer_IO are not usable *until* we notify Integer_IO of the integer type on which its routines are to operate. Once we specify the type, an *instance* of Integer_IO, containing routines for input and output of objects of that type, is brought into existence. A package such as Integer_IO—in which a type, or something else, is missing and must be supplied in order to create a package of usable routines—is called a **generic package**. The creation of an instance of a generic package, by supplying the missing elements, is called an **instantiation** of the package. And since instantiations must always be *named*, we are now in a position to enhance our understanding of the mysterious declaration

```
package Int_IO is new Text_IO.Integer_IO (INTEGER);
```

This indicates that we are creating a package named Int_IO, as a result of specifying that the routines in the package Integer_IO, which is within the package Text_IO, are to operate on the type INTEGER. (We decline to explain the use of the term **new** at this time; suffice it to say that it is required here.) In a similar fashion, if we chose to restrict our input and output to integers of type POSITIVE, then we might declare

```
package Pos_IO is new Text_IO.Integer_IO (POSITIVE);
```

The output routine in Pos_IO would then be capable of displaying values such as 23 and 40227; but an attempt to use Pos_IO.Put to display a value such as −2304 or even 0 would result in an error message. Note that both Int_IO and Pos_IO are names made up by the programmer; they are not given as part of the Ada language.

Is it possible to instantiate *both* Int_IO *and* Pos_IO in the same program? Absolutely, and if you were to do so, then either Int_IO.Put or Pos_IO.Put would be able to display a value such as 6502, but only Int_IO.Put could display −707.

There are principally two routines in any instantiation of Text_IO.Integer_IO, namely, Get and Put. Observe that we said the routines belong to the *instantiation*, not to Integer_IO itself. Thus we have seen in Chapters 1 and 2 references to Int_IO.Put, not to Integer_IO.Put. Get requires a single parameter which must be a variable of some INTEGER type appropriate to the particular instantiation. When Get is invoked, it accepts an integer value from the keyboard and places it in the named variable. See, for example, the statement

```
Int_IO.Get (Minutes_Elapsed);
```

in Figure 2.1.1.

Put requires *two* parameters. One of these is obvious: It is the integer to be displayed. The second parameter requires an explanation. When we send something to the printer or terminal display, it normally appears wherever the typehead or cursor happens to be at the time. That might not always suit our purposes. For example, if we displayed the number 127 and then—without an intervening new line sequence via **Text_IO.New_Line (1)**—displayed 408, what we would see is

```
127408
```

and it would be difficult to know how to interpret this display. We would like at least a blank space or two between the two numbers by inserting, say,

```
Text_IO.Put ("  ");
```

But this is tedious, unnecessary, and, as it turns out, inadequate for many purposes. Instead, Put provides *formatting* capabilities, as follows: The second parameter to Put is a nonnegative integer that specifies the **field width** of the display. That is, beginning at the current cursor (printhead) position, the field width parameter determines the number of character positions on the display that are to be used for the display of the given integer. If the specified field—the positions on the display allocated to the integer—contains more positions than the number of characters in the integer to be displayed, then those characters are shown at the *right-hand end* of the field, the unused positions to the left of the number being filled with space characters (the display is **right-justified**, as is said). If the field width contains exactly the needed number of positions or if the stated field is *inadequate* to hold the display, the entire number is displayed beginning at the current cursor (printhead) position. A few examples will make this notion clear; we use the symbol ƀ here and in the sequel to represent a "space" character, whenever it is necessary or useful to know exactly how many spaces appear in a given display; the underscore character is used to show the cursor position *after* the number has been displayed.

Statement	Display
Int_IO.Put (203,6)	ƀƀƀ203_
Int_IO.Put (203,4)	ƀ203_
Int_IO.Put (203,3)	203_
Int_IO.Put (203,2)	203_
Int_IO.Put (203,0)	203_

As you may have noted, up to now we have always used 0 as the second parameter to the Put routines, thereby ensuring that there could not possibly be any leading spaces displayed, no matter what the number was. The reason for this is that we chose to do the "formatting" ourselves by supplying a *single* space, before and after the number, by means of the immediately preceding and succeeding displayed text strings. (Again, see Figure 2.1.1, which contains several instances of this.)

By now you have surmised that when a subprogram requires more than one parameter, those parameters are *positional* in the sense that there is a *first* parameter, a *second* parameter, and so forth. Indeed, if the variable Volume had the value 7, then

```
Int_IO.Put (Volume,3)
```

would result in the display

```
ƀƀ7
```

whereas

```
Int_IO.Put (3,Volume)
```

would cause

```
ƀƀƀƀƀƀ3
```

to be displayed.

Finally, we note that if you *fail* to supply a field width parameter, then Put will supply one for you—a so-called default value. The default value for the field width parameter depends on the computer system you are using: 6 is a typical value for personal computers and 11 is frequently used on larger machines. As another example of a procedure with a default parameter value, Text_IO's New_Line procedure has a default value of 1. Thus after this, when we need just a single new line sequence, we will frequently invoke it with **Text_IO.New_Line**, rather than the more explicit **Text_IO.New_Line (1)**.

We stated above that Get requires a variable name as a parameter. But the type of parameter that can be passed to Put is far less restricted. What Put requires is an integer *value*. Of course that value might indeed be supplied as a variable name, the value in question then being the value held by that variable. The value could also be in the form of *any* integer expression—anything that can be assigned a value upon execution of the procedure—and, as we know, "integer expression" includes not only variable values but also integer literals and the results of performing algebraic operations on these. Thus

```
Int_IO.Put (Remaining_Miles,0);
Int_IO.Put (Remaining_Miles - 1000,3);
Int_IO.Put (2 * Day,0);
Int_IO.Put (664,Width+6);
```

are all valid instances of parameters given to Put. These notions are expanded in the next two sections.

3.3 The package Int_IO

Since we frequently input and output integer values in our subsequent programs, you may find it a nuisance to have to include a line of **Integer_IO** instantiation. However, it is possible to create a package **Int_IO** (or whatever you may choose to call it) *once and for all* and make its routines available to your future programs exactly as the routines in **Text_IO** are. To achieve this, create a file named **create_int_io.ada** (or whatever you wish) with the following contents:

```
with Text_IO;
package Int_IO is new Text_IO.Integer_IO (INTEGER);
```

If you prefer, substitute your own package name for "Int_IO." Compile this file with your Ada compiler. (Yes, this is a very strange looking source file, but it will compile without errors.) The effect is to create a file in the "library" of your Ada programs which contains this instantiation. Henceforth we will be able to access the routines in **Int_IO** simply by including the context clause

```
with Int_IO;
```

in our programs. Since we will probably also continue to need **Text_IO**, we can combine the two of these in a single context clause:

```
with Text_IO, Int_IO;
```

You may have found it curious, at the time we first introduced the package Integer_IO, to learn that it was a package within the package Text_IO, which we had advertised as being devoted to the input and output of *text*—characters and strings of characters, for **Integer_IO** would seem to involve the input and output of *numbers*, and numbers are not characters. But consider for a moment what you are doing when you write the following on a piece of paper:

12

Are you writing the number twelve? No, you are writing two *characters*,"**1**" and "**2**," whose juxtaposition on the paper is a *representation* of the number twelve, an abstraction that we associate with a dozen eggs, the Apostles, three barbershop quartets, and so forth. Thus twelve is an abstract property of a set or collection; 12 is a pair of characters that represent this abstraction, just as do the three characters "XII" when we use Roman numerals to represent numbers. (The point is a bit fussy and belongs to the realms of the mathematician and logician.) But what difference is there between your writing two characters on the paper and your Ada program "writing" two characters to the display? In a similar fashion, when a program gets a number, what is it really obtaining from the user? A collection of characters —keystrokes on the keyboard. It is apparent that instantiations of Integer_IO actually deal with characters—text—and must convert these strings of digit characters to and from their internal numerical form in order to perform input and output. That is, Text_IO is *precisely* the appropriate package for Integer_IO, since despite its name, it is actually dealing at a keyboard and display level with strings of characters.

3.4 The package Text_IO

The package Text_IO has held a focal position in our discussion, for it contains the "specifications" for almost all the input and output normally done in Ada. As noted, it is supplied by the compiler vendor as a prescribed supplement to the compiler. While we can learn much by looking at the actual package, the details are fairly complex at this stage of our understanding. Thus we will only look at a few of the 100 or so declarations in Text_IO; the complete details will be found in *LRM [14.3.10]*. As a start, we show in Figure 3.4.1 just one of the declarations from Text_IO.

```
package Text_IO is
      .
      .
      .
   procedure Put (Item: in STRING);
      .
      .
      .
end Text_IO;
```

Figure 3.4.1

Notice the familiar **package...is** construction, but this differs from an *instantiation* of a generic package in that the "magic" word **new** is missing. The first line we see here *begins* the declaration of the package named Text_IO, and the last line *ends* that declaration. Let us concentrate on the other line, namely

```
procedure Put (Item: in STRING);
```

We have not yet formally defined the Ada type STRING (see Section 13.3), but we have spoken of "strings of characters" as a collection or list of characters enclosed in quotes, and for the time being this is a quite adequate "definition." As we already know, a procedure is a collection of Ada instructions, possibly along with some declarations as well, that is designed to accomplish a specified job; the procedure is *named*, and it is by its name that it is invoked, or caused to be executed; and typically, some values or variables—*parameters*—are passed along to the procedure as objects on which the procedure is to operate. Thus in order that the Ada compiler be able to manage a procedure, it must be given four items of information in advance: (1) the name of the procedure; (2) the parameter or parameters (if any) that the procedure uses; (3) the types of those parameters; and (4) the *ways* in which the procedure will use those parameters. We have as yet had nothing to say regarding requirement 4, but we deal with it in a moment. The **procedure declarations**, such as those shown in Figure 3.4.1, provide the compiler with the needed information. For example, in the declaration of the procedure Put of Figure 3.4.1, we see the reserved word **procedure**, which notifies the compiler that what is being declared is a procedure (as opposed to, say, a constant or variable). The *name* of this procedure is "Put." The procedure requires one *parameter* any time it is invoked, and for the purposes of the procedure declaration, that parameter is simply named "Item." Item, and in fact any parameter appearing in a procedure's *declaration*, is referred to as a **formal parameter**, in the sense that it is a general formalism that will be replaced by a particular parameter—**actual parameter**, as it is called—when the procedure is *invoked*. At this time of declaration, Item is simply acting as a "placeholder." As is evident, the parameter required by this procedure must be of type STRING. Finally, we see that the parameter Item is declared not simply as being of type STRING but apparently of type "**in STRING**." It is the word "in," of course, that requires some explanation, and its purpose, as we will see immediately, is to indicate what in Ada is known as the **mode** of the parameter.

When a variable is passed to a procedure, the procedure might use that variable in one of three ways. First, it could simply accept the *value* of the variable and use it for whatever purposes it required, and if this is the case, the parameter would not necessarily have to be the value of a variable—anything with a value (that is, any *expression*) would do. Such a parameter is said to be of **mode** *in*, since it is used to pass a value "in" to the procedure. As we have already observed, since Put will display anything that has a STRING value, Put's parameter Item falls into this category. Second, the procedure might not even use the current value of the variable; rather, it might generate a value itself and then place that value in the variable prior to completing its execution. The procedure Int_IO.Get is of this kind, for the value of the variable passed to Get, *prior to* invoking Get, is of no consequence and is not used by Get. Rather, Get obtains an integer value from the keyboard and then places it in the variable passed to it. Thus, for example, in Figure 1.6.1, the variable Current_Miles has no particular value prior to the statement

```
Int_IO.Get (Current_Miles);
```

After invoking and executing the instructions in Get, Current_Miles will contain whatever value was typed at the keyboard. Thus such a variable value is *not* passed "in" to the procedure, but the procedure passes a value back "out" via this variable, and for this reason the parameter is said to be of **mode *out***. The third parameter mode, of which we currently have no example, is **mode *in out***, and it is the mode of any parameter whose value is *used* by the procedure (and is thus "passed *in* to" the procedure) and which also gets a new value due to the procedure's execution (which value is thus "passed *out* from" the procedure). A parameter of mode *in out* must be a variable (why?).

We have been invoking procedures since Chapter 1, and you have undoubtedly deduced most of the rules concerning how this is done. For the sake of completeness, we put these on record.

When one or more actual parameters are passed to a procedure at the time the procedure is invoked:

1.   The actual parameters must be *separated by commas.*

2.   The actual parameters must be supplied in the *same order* as the corresponding formal parameters, as specified in the procedure declaration, since the compiler will associate actual parameters with corresponding formal parameters according to the *order* in which they both appear.

3.   Each actual parameter must match the corresponding formal parameter as to *type.*

Now that we have a better idea of what a procedure is and what is required to declare and invoke it, let us look at a most illuminating set of procedure declarations, namely those in the generic package Integer_IO. Again we look at a few lines from Text_IO.

```
package Integer_IO is
         .
         .
         .
    procedure Get (Item: out NUM);

    procedure Put (Item: in NUM; Width: in NATURAL);
         .
         .
         .
```

Figure 3.4.2

We have already noted the interesting phenomenon of a package such as Text_IO containing the declaration of another package. And we know that this does *not* mean that there is already provided in Text_IO a package capable of putting and getting integers, since Integer_IO is *generic*—it requires additional information to produce a package of usable routines. We have made a start at understanding this notion, but the full explanation is quite complicated and cannot be provided here in all its detail, although we eventually get around to it in Chapter 14. We now show you just enough of Text_IO to suggest what sort of "package" Integer_IO actually is.

```
generic

    type NUM is range <>;

    package Integer_IO is
        .
        .
        .
        procedure Get (Item: out NUM);

        procedure Put (Item: in NUM; Width: in NATURAL);
        .
        .
        .
```

Figure 3.4.3

You may have been surprised (or bothered?) by the fact that, in Figure 3.4.2, the value to Get or to Put was *not* of the expected type INTEGER (or perhaps POSITIVE or NATURAL), but was of type **NUM**, a type we have not yet seen. In fact, there *is* no such type as NUM—NUM is only a formalism. What we have here, as the word "generic" suggests, is not an actual package but a **template** or **pattern** for a package. If the unspecified (generic) piece or pieces are replaced by actual entities, the result *is* a package. In this case, the unspecified piece is the type, referred to here as NUM. If we replace NUM with INTEGER (or POSITIVE or NATURAL), however such a replacement might be made, then the result will be a package of routines capable of performing input and output of objects of the respective integer type. As we have already noted, such a resulting package is a *specific instance* of the many different packages that can be produced by replacing NUM in the generic package Integer_IO with a particular integer type.

We are aware that we have given only a partial explanation at this point—the more so in view of the fact that we have no intention of explaining the mysterious **type NUM "is range <>"**—but perhaps an analogy will help. Just as the routine Int_IO.Put can have no effect *until* its formal parameter Item is replaced by an actual integer value (Remaining_Miles, for example), so Integer_IO becomes a usable package only after its formal type NUM is replaced by an actual integer type (POSITIVE, for instance). Each of these constructs—the procedure Put and the generic package Integer_IO—is acting as a template or model, which becomes useful only after actual values have been "plugged into" them. The analogy is scarcely exact, and we do not want to leave you with the impression that procedures and packages are the same; but for the time being, until we can be more precise, it may be a useful way of thinking of a generic package.

3.5 A sample package of integer functions and procedures

As we already know, the Ada language provides a number of operations on integer variables, operations such as addition, multiplication, and so forth. The language also makes provision for generating the *remainder* of the division of two integers, whenever the two integers are specified. This is actually an Ada operation, called **rem**, which we took advantage of in the preceding chapter. But the language does *not* provide a means of generating the *smaller* of two integers or of rearranging two integers so that they are in *increasing order*. In this section and the next we construct a small package of functions and procedures that provide these and a few other services; in fact, the package is too simple to be useful in actual practice, but it serves as a first example of a package written by *us*, and it introduces us to some of the processes that enter into this central Ada concept.

```
--  Package Int_Pack implements several functions and procedures
--  frequently useful in an INTEGER environment.

--  The package contains the following functions:
--
--    Min (First, Second: INTEGER)
--      returns the smaller of the first and second parameters
--
--    Max (First, Second: INTEGER)
--      returns the larger of the first and second parameters
--
--  and the following procedures:
--
--    Exchange (First, Second: in out INTEGER)
--      exchanges the values in first and second parameters
--
--    Increase (First, Second: in out INTEGER)
--      rearranges the parameters into increasing order
--
--    Decrease (First, Second: in out INTEGER)
--      rearranges the parameters into decreasing order

package Int_Pack is

    function Min (First, Second: in INTEGER) return INTEGER;

    function Max (First, Second: in INTEGER) return INTEGER;

    procedure Exchange (First, Second: in out INTEGER);

    procedure Increase (First, Second: in out INTEGER);

    procedure Decrease (First, Second: in out INTEGER);

end Int_Pack;
```

Figure 3.5.1

There are a few new features to be examined here, and the first is the observation that, unlike the package Integer_IO, there are no "missing" objects to be filled in; this package is *not* generic and thus does not require instantiation to produce a useful collection of routines —the routines are usable as they stand. Second, the first two declarations in Figure 3.5.1 appear very much like the declarations of procedures that we have seen earlier, except for two features: They are called **functions**, not procedures, and they each bear the trailing legend "return INTEGER." We have said that a procedure is a related collection of code—a subprogram—that performs a job when it is executed upon being invoked. Put and Get are good examples, for they each result in some activity when invoked, namely, the putting of some characters on the display and the getting of some characters from the keyboard (with the resulting assignment of a value to a variable). In contrast to the activities that these procedures exhibit, consider what the function Max does. It evidently also consists of some related code (is a subprogram in that sense) which is supplied two values—parameters—and its job is to calculate a value, namely, the *larger* of these two parameters. Thus instead of performing an activity, Max *generates a value*. This is typical of functions: They generate values which are then *used* just as are any other values, such as those of variables or of other expressions. But if a function generates a value (more formally, **returns** a value), then that returned value must have a *type*, and the compiler must be informed of what type to expect. The type of a function's returned value is specified in the function's declaration by means of the phrase

```
... return <type mark>
```

Functions are invoked just as procedures are, by simply specifying their names along with any actual parameters. As a simple example, consider

```
Int_IO.Put (Max (24, -17), 0)
```

which will result in the displaying of the value 24. Note that, since Max represents a *value*, not an action, a "statement" such as

```
Max (24, -17);
```

makes no more sense than the "statement"

```
6 * 3 - 2;
```

As a final point we note that the parameters in the two functions Min and Max have mode **in**. The reason for this is that *all* parameters to *all* functions in Ada *must* have mode **in**, never **out** or **in out**. For this reason we will henceforth almost never explicitly state the mode of function parameters, since Ada uses the only possible value, **in**, as the default.

For the record, we show a simple program that employs the package Int_Pack. It obtains two integers from the keyboard; rearranges them (if necessary) into decreasing order; and then displays the two integers.

```
with Text_IO, Int_IO, Int_Pack;

procedure Test_Int is

    Frst, Scnd:     INTEGER;

begin

    Int_IO.Get (Frst);
    Int_IO.Get (Scnd);
    Int_Pack.Decrease (Frst, Scnd);
    Int_IO.Put (Frst);
    Int_IO.Put (Scnd);
    Text_IO.New_Line;

end Test_Int;
```

Figure 3.5.2

If we enter the numbers 12 and 27 as values for the variables Frst and Scnd, respectively, the program will display

```
27         12
```

If we enter 42 and −783 instead, it will produce

```
42        -783
```

3.6 The package specification and package body

We have seen several examples of packages: segments of Text_IO and Integer_IO, and the complete package Int_Pack. You may be surprised that nowhere in any of these packages did we find even a single executable statement! What we saw is a collection of procedure and function declarations. But we know that if, for instance, Text_IO's Put routine is going to display a string, then something has to be executed. In fact, there is no executable code in the packages we have seen, and the reason is that the executable code is in *another*, related file. In order to understand these important notions, we need to be more specific about the total makeup of a package.

The files we have seen and called "packages" are more precisely called **package specifications**; they contain the specifications of the objects in the package. Thus, in the package specification Int_Pack we find

```
function  Max (First, Second: in INTEGER) return INTEGER;
```

This statement specifies that Max is a function, has two INTEGER parameters of mode **in**, and that it returns an INTEGER value. The associated file that *does* contain the executable code for **Max** (and the other routines declared in Int_Pack) is called the **package body**, and we show the complete package body for Int_Pack in Figure 3.6.1.

```
package body Int_Pack is

   function Min (First, Second: in INTEGER) return INTEGER is

     begin
       if First < Second then
          return First;
       else
          return Second;
       end if;
     end Min;


   function Max (First, Second: in INTEGER) return INTEGER is

     begin
       if First > Second then
          return First;
       else
          return Second;
```

```
      end if;
    end Max;


procedure Exchange (First, Second: in out INTEGER) is

    Temp:  INTEGER;

  begin
    Temp := First;
    First := Second;
    Second := Temp;
  end Exchange;


procedure Increase (First, Second: in out INTEGER) is

  begin
    if Max (First, Second) = First then
        Exchange (First, Second);
    end if;
  end Increase;

procedure Decrease (First, Second: in out INTEGER) is

  begin
    Increase (Second, First);
    end Decrease;

end Int_Pack;
```

Figure 3.6.1

Here we see the code we have been looking for, the statements that are actually executed whenever the function Max is invoked, or called for. Although several constructions here are new to you, you can probably make sense of the logic of the function—it almost reads like plain English.

You may be puzzled that the declaration of Max is repeated here, and the obvious question is, Why do we even bother with the package *specification*, when the declaration and executable code are already in the package *body*? The answer is not easily given; it has to do with the overall structure of the Ada language and its ability to efficiently manage the development of large software systems. But we can give you a hint by looking at the following procedure "call":

```
Int_IO.Put (1274,-3);
```

We have passed a negative parameter −3 as the field width, but that parameter is supposed to be of type NATURAL. Will the Ada compiler complain? Absolutely, the compiler is *very* fussy about parameter passing: The *number* of actual parameters passed to subprogram must be the same as the number of formal parameters specified in the subprogram's declaration, and each actual parameter must match the type of the corresponding formal parameter. In this case the compiler would display a diagnostic message something like "parameter type clash." Does the compiler need to know what *executable* code comprises Int_IO.Put to detect this error? No, it only needs to know what Put's *declaration* looks like, and it can find this in Int_IO's package *specification*. That is, from the compiler's standpoint, the package specification is adequate information for it to do its job—the package body need not even exist at this point. (Of course, the package body—the executable code—must ultimately exist before the program that invokes it can be executed.) These matters are brought up again in Chapter 11, when we will be in a far better position to understand the details.

3.7 A closing comment on packages

We recognize that in discussing details of the package concept at this time, and especially so early in the text, we have been treading on some fairly complicated territory. Indeed, much of what we have seen here is a preview to the remainder of the book. As we have noted, packages are one of the focal points of Ada, and especially of almost all large software systems that are written in Ada. Thus we do not feel that it is too early to enhance your awareness of these notions; the details and understanding required for your own implementation of packages can come later, after you have learned more of the basics of the Ada language and have further developed the necessary programming skills. In the meantime we will use these packages, as you should, in the ways described in their specifications; later we will introduce several other packages that contain useful collections of related procedures.

3.8 Exercises

3.2.1   Since the first parameter to Int_IO.Put may be *any* integer expression (and not merely an integer variable or literal), show how the Time_and_Day program (Figure 2.1.1) could be rewritten in terms of just *one* integer variable, namely, Minutes_Elapsed. Thus, the variables Hours_Elapsed, Minute, Day, and Hour are not really "needed." Would this be a good way to write the program? Explain.

3.2.2   Write a small program to determine the difference (if any) of the run-time behavior when:

(a)   An attempt is made to read (and then display) a negative number into a variable that has been declared to be of type NATURAL, using an I/O package that is the INTEGER instantiation of Integer_IO.

(b)   An attempt is made to read (and then display) a negative number into a variable that has been declared to be of type INTEGER, using an I/O package that is the NATURAL instantiation of Integer_IO.

3.2.3   In a program containing the declaration

```
package Int_IO is new Text_IO.Integer_IO(INTEGER);
```

show what output is displayed by the statements

```
Int_IO.Put (N);
Int_IO.Put (N,5);
Int_IO.Put (N,0);
```

if N is an INTEGER variable which in turn has each of the following values. Assume that the given computer system has 2_147_483_647 as the value of INTEGER'Last; use the symbol ƀ to indicate a leading blank in the display.

(a) 51
(b) 1492
(c) −1492
(d) 1234567
(e) 1231231231
(f) −1231231231

3.2.4 Consider the package Int_IO of Exercise 3.2.3, in which Integer_IO has been instantiated for the type INTEGER. What, if anything, is the difference in effect between the commands

```
Int_IO.Put (N,0);        and      Int_IO.Put (N,1);
```

where N is an INTEGER variable?

3.2.5 Write an Ada program that accepts any three integers as input (as long as they are not too large in absolute value) and then displays each of these integers and their squares in the following format:

Number	Square
16	256
121	14641
-52	2704

3.4.1 It appears that the input procedure Get has a parameter of mode **out** and the output procedure Put has a parameter of mode **in**. Is this correct, or should it be the other way around? Comment on what is going on here.

3.4.2 Why must an actual parameter be a *variable* if it corresponds to a formal parameter of mode **in out**?

3.6.1 Compile the package specification (Figure 3.5.1) and the package body (Figure 3.6.1) for the package Int_Pack, *in that order*. Then write a program to "exercise" the routines in Int_Pack; the program of Figure 3.5.2 is a good starting point, but you should expand on that sample program to verify that *all* the routines are operating properly.

Chapter 4

Floating Point Types

So far the only numerical type we have used—indeed, the only one we know of—is the INTEGER type, or one of the related types POSITIVE and NATURAL. These are probably the most frequently used kinds of numbers in computing, but there are circumstances in which these types are simply inadequate. As an elementary illustration that shows this and also leads to some interesting new concepts, we consider the common problem of maintaining a checkbook balance.

4.1 A checkbook problem

We wish to write a program to manage a checkbook; specifically the program is to maintain the account balance and to adjust that balance whenever a deposit is made or a check is written. Unfortunately, the U.S. monetary system is based on dollars *and* cents, not simply on cents alone, and thus monetary amounts are expressed in terms of dollars and a fractional number of dollars, such as 1.29, 707.66, etc. These do *not* represent numbers of type INTEGER, and thus it appears that we cannot deal with the problem at hand. Suppose, however, we change our focus a bit and consider all dollars-and-cents amounts to be in cents only. That is, instead of dealing with 1.29, 707.66, and so forth, we consider the corresponding *integer* numbers 129, 70766, etc. If we can simply adjust our thinking so that we "think in pennies" whenever dealing with our checkbook, we can easily accomplish our goal. In fact, we could even take advantage of the underscore character that is permitted in the representation of integers by always writing the cents amounts as, for instance, 1_29 and 707_66, as a further reminder that we are *assuming* a decimal point two digits from the right end of the number. (But be careful: Even though 16.40 has the same value—as a fractional number—as 16.4, and thus we might enter $16.40 into a calculator keyboard as 16.4, there is a difference between the *integers* 16_40 and 16_4.) The trivial program of Figure 4.1.1 does what is required. A few sample dialogues are shown in Figure 4.1.2, and observe that although *we* can insert the underscore character appropriately into the input for the sake of appearance, we have no way of demanding that Int_IO.Put do the same; thus the form of the output is somewhat less appealing than that of the input.

```
with Text_IO, Int_IO;

procedure Checkbook is

    --   After establishing an initial balance, the procedure
    --   Checkbook requests and accepts an amount (in cents),
    --   interprets it as a deposit (> 0) or withdrawal (< 0),
    --   and calculates and displays the new account balance.

    Current_Balance:        INTEGER;
    Transaction:            INTEGER;
    New_Balance:            INTEGER;

begin

    Text_IO.Put ("Enter current checking account balance (in cents): ");
    Int_IO.Get (Current_Balance);
    Text_IO.New_Line;
    Text_IO.Put ("Enter the amount of this transaction, in cents");
    Text_IO.New_Line;
    Text_IO.Put ("(deposits are positive, withdrawals are negative): ");

    Int_IO.Get (Transaction);

    New_Balance := Current_Balance + Transaction;
    Text_IO.New_Line;
    Text_IO.Put ("The new account balance is ");
    Int_IO.Put (New_Balance,0);
    Text_IO.New_Line;

end Checkbook;
```

Figure 4.1.1

```
Enter current checking account balance (in cents): 301_92
Enter the amount of this transaction, in cents
(deposits are positive, withdrawals are negative): -13_62

The new account balance is 28830


Enter current checking account balance (in cents): 288_30
Enter the amount of this transaction, in cents
(deposits are positive, withdrawals are negative): 104_29

The new account balance is 39259


Enter current checking account balance (in cents):  17_38
Enter the amount of this transaction, in cents
(deposits are positive, withdrawals are negative): -96_44

The new account balance is -7906
```

Figure 4.1.2

As we see, the Checkbook program has no more substance than, and is virtually identical in form to, the Warranty program of Chapter 1, although in the present case, negative input and output are more meaningful.

Before moving on, we need to make note of a potential problem here. If INTEGER'Last is 32,767 on the computer on which we are executing this program, then numbers such as the 39,259 balance generated above will not be acceptable. Indeed, the largest balance that could be accommodated would be $327.67, and this may be unrealistically small. There are ways around this problem, by means of data types normally supported by Ada compilers intended for use on these small machines, but we will not investigate them here.

As useful as the "assumed-decimal-point" numbers are in some environments, they fail in others, and to see an example in which this is so, consider the following enhancement of our checkbook-balancing program. Suppose that the bank with which we deal gives us 4½ percent interest per year on the balance in our checking account. How are we to calculate the interest? More specifically, how should "4½ percent" be represented? If the balance at the time this interest is calculated happens to be $104.00 (which we would represent as 10400 or 104_00), then the interest *should* be 104.00 * .045 = 4.68. However, we cannot represent .045 as an integer with an implied decimal point two digits from the right end. Even supposing that the interest rate is 4 percent, which is representable (as 4 = 0_04), what should 104_00 * 0_04 = 41600 mean? It cannot mean 416_00, for the interest would then be $416.00, which is absurd. Of course, it should be $4.16 (but should this be written as 4_1600?); however, because of the fact that the assumed decimal point is *fixed* at a position two digits from the right end, the correct result cannot be represented. What is required is a number representation that allows the decimal points to "float" across number representations to their correct positions, a concept to which we devote the remainder of the chapter.

4.2 The type FLOAT

Ada provides a standard data type, called **FLOAT** (short for "floating point"), that has exactly the property described above: The decimal point "floats" and thus always has its correct arithmetic position. Variables and constants may be declared to be of type **FLOAT**, and the "usual" arithmetic operations of addition, subtraction, multiplication, and division apply to floating point expressions just as they do to integer expressions. We do need to make a few comments here:

1. Floating point **literals** *must* be written with a decimal point, and they *must* have at least one digit before and after the decimal point. Thus numbers such as .62, 9., and 63 will not do; instead, these must be written as 0.62, 9.0, and 63.0, respectively.

2. Floating point division is "exact" in the sense that, unlike integer division, floating point division is *not* truncated. For example, whereas 17/5 has the INTEGER value 3, 17.0/5.0 has the FLOAT value 3.4.

3. FLOAT has no operations corresponding to the integer **rem** and **mod** operations.

4.   Exponentiation of floating point numbers is supported, but the exponent itself must be
      of some integer type.

5.   Just as with an integer expression, **abs** will generate the absolute value of a floating
      point expression.

      Floating point variables may be input from the keyboard, floating point values may be
output to the display, and you should create the package Flt_IO, to be added to your Ada
library, by compiling the file

```
with Text_IO;
package Flt_IO is new Text_IO.Float_IO (FLOAT);
```

just as you did for Int_IO. We employ this package throughout the remainder of the text, and
there are two points you need to know when using it. First, the rules stated above for floating
point literals concerning the need for a decimal point with at least one digit on either side of
it apply equally to declarations and assignments, as well as to keyboard input via Flt_IO.Get.
Second, output via Flt_IO.Put is more complex than integer output for several reasons. When
we display an integer value, we must decide the width of the field in which it will appear.
But there are really two separate "numbers" in the visible display of a floating point value,
namely, the **whole number**, or **integer**, portion (*before* the decimal point) and the **fractional**
portion (*after* the decimal point). As with the display of integer values, we can specify the
width of the field in which the integer portion of a floating point value will be displayed, in a
Put parameter named **Fore**. The integer portion will be right-adjusted in a field of the
specified width; the only note we need to add is that a floating point number is always
displayed with at least one digit to the left of the decimal point, even if the floating point
value is between 0 and 1 (in which case the digit 0 will appear in the Fore field). The number
of decimal places displayed is determined by a parameter named **Aft**.
      So far floating point displays seem fairly straightforward. In fact, however, Flt_IO.Put
will normally display these values in **scientific notation**, that is, in the form $W.F \cdot 10^E$, where
W is the whole number (integer) part; F is the fractional part; E is an exponent for the base,
10; and $0 \leq W < 10$. Thus, for example, Put's normal output of the number 123.456 would
appear as $1.23456 \cdot 10^2$. Of course most computer displays cannot actually show exponents
"above the line" as we have done with the 2 here, nor do they have the capability of
displaying the "midline" dot ($\cdot$) that we have used to represent multiplication. If you were
actually to use Flt_IO.Put to display this number, you would see 1.23456E+02, with E
representing Exponent (with an assumed base of 10). Indeed, the declaration of Flt_IO.Put is

```
procedure Put (Item: in FLOAT;
               Fore: in NATURAL;
               Aft:  in NATURAL;
               Exp:  in NATURAL);
```

There are some fairly simple rules as to how various values in the Exp parameter affect the
appearance of the displayed number, but we decline to go into these here (they are
investigated in the exercises); for in the present context and most often throughout the book,
we will want to see floating point numbers with *no* exponent at all. We can achieve this by

passing the value 0 as the Exp parameter, which we will *always* do for the time being. Thus **Flt_IO.Put (123.456,5,4,0)** will yield the display ƀƀ123.4560. (Note the final digit 0 in the fractional part, required by our insistence that *four* decimal places be displayed.)

How would a floating point number such as 123.456 be displayed if we specify *fewer* than three decimal places? For example, what is displayed by **Flt_IO.Put (123.456,5,2,0)**? The answer is, ƀƀ123.46, for the last digit displayed is always *rounded*, up or down depending on whether the *remaining* decimal portion is greater than or less than .00···5. Thus the display generated by **Flt_IO.Put (123.454,5,2,0)** will appear as ƀƀ123.45.

A final example and discussion will serve to assist our understanding of these notions. Assuming that the floating point variable X has the value 238826.9940021,

a.	Flt_IO.Put (X,3,7,4)	will display	ƀƀ2.3882699E+005
b.	Flt_IO.Put (X,0,0,1)	will display	2.4E+5
c.	Flt_IO.Put (X,4,2,0)	will display	238826.99
d.	Flt_IO.Put (X,4,1,0)	will display	238827.0
e.	Flt_IO.Put (X)	will display	ƀ2.388270E+05

(As usual, ƀ stands for a space character.) In *b* and *d*, the apparent discrepancy in the last-displayed digit is, as we already know, a result of rounding. Note also in *b* that even though we specified *no* (or 0) digits after the decimal point, Float_IO ignored the request and insisted on showing at least one such digit. The display in *e* depends on the implementation. (In fact, you might find that executing these calls to Float_IO's Put procedure on your computer may yield slightly different results, typically in the last digit or digits, because of the way the numbers are represented *internally* in the computer.)

4.3 Floating point operations and type conversions

We stated earlier that addition, subtraction, multiplication, division, and exponentiation apply to floating point numbers as well as to integers, and in fact these floating point operations even use the familiar symbols +, −, *, /, and **, respectively. But observe that these must actually mean something different when applied to floating point numbers. This is perhaps most obvious in the case of division, since as we have seen, 17/5 = 3 (*integer* division), whereas 17.0/5.0 = 3.4 (*floating point* division). Since the operation *symbols* are the same for both integer and floating point types, can we mix these types in the same operation? For example, if IX is an integer variable or constant, and FX is a floating point object, are expressions such as IX + 2.78, IX * FX − 2, and 7.0/2 legal? The answer is, absolutely not! While these so-called mixed-type expressions are valid in some programming languages, Ada does not allow them.

The fact that mixed-type expressions are illegal frequently causes some awkwardnesses in our approaches to programming. For example, consider an instructor's task of averaging three student examination grades, 87, 78, and 80. The sum is 245, and if the instructor simply divides this by 3—245/3—the result is 81, whereas the actual average is 81.67. We could solve the problem by writing the grades as 87.0, 78.0 and 80.0 and then dividing by 3.0, the "number" of grades, but since all the values involved are "naturally" integer, you recognize this as an artificiality and a fairly awkward one at that. In a similar fashion, we could not deposit five paychecks, each in the amount of $72.24, by adding 5 * 72.24 to our account balance; instead, we would have to deposit "5.0 paychecks" by adding 5.0 * 72.24.

Each of these problems, and many similar to them, can be circumvented by *converting* the numbers in question (245, 3, and 5 in the examples above) from their integer representation to a *corresponding* floating point version. To convert from integer to floating point, we use the type name FLOAT in the following way:

    FLOAT (<integer expression>)

The result of this "operation" is the floating point number that corresponds to the integer expression. Thus our grade-averaging problem above could be written as

    FLOAT (245) / FLOAT (3)

or, more generally,

```
Ave_Grade := FLOAT (Grade_Sum) / FLOAT (Grade_Count)
```

where we assume that Ave_Grade is a variable of type FLOAT, and Grade_Sum and Grade_Count are INTEGER variables. This **type conversion** has the effect of creating numbers which are the floating point equivalents of integers: 3.0 is the floating point equivalent of the integer 3; 5.0 is equivalent to 5; and so forth.

It is also possible to convert floating point objects to integer values (although this is not nearly as often called for as is the reverse conversion):

    INTEGER (<floating point expression>)

The conversion is accomplished by *rounding* the floating point value, either up or down, depending on whether the fractional part is greater than or less than .5. Thus

Floating point value FX	INTEGER (FX)
12.0	12
12.03	12
12.492	12
12.5	??
12.501	13
12.92	13

The reason for our indecision in converting 12.5 is that the direction of rounding in cases where the fractional portion is exactly one-half is dependent on the particular Ada compiler; you will have to experiment with your compiler to determine its behavior.

4.4 The Checkbook program revisited

Now that we know many of the details of the type FLOAT, let us rewrite the checkbook-balancing program using floating point numbers. The new version is shown in Figure 4.4.1*a*, with sample dialogues given in Figure 4.4.1*b*. Note that the references to Int_IO have been changed to references to Flt_IO, the user-implemented package described in the preceding section; also, all variables are now of type FLOAT, and thus all input must contain a decimal point with at least one digit on either side of it.

a
```
with Text_IO, Flt_IO;

procedure Checkbook is

    --  After establishing an initial balance, the procedure
    --  Checkbook requests and accepts an amount, interprets
    --  it as a deposit (> 0.0) or withdrawal (< 0.0), and
    --  calculates and displays the new account balance.

    Current_Balance:   FLOAT;
    Transaction:       FLOAT;
    New_Balance:       FLOAT;

begin

    Text_IO.Put ("Enter current checking account balance: ");
    Flt_IO.Get (Current_Balance);
    Text_IO.New_Line;

    Text_IO.Put ("Enter the amount of this transaction");
    Text_IO.New_Line;
    Text_IO.Put ("(deposits are positive, withdrawals are negative): ");

    Flt_IO.Get (Transaction);
    New_Balance := Current_Balance + Transaction;
    Text_IO.New_Line;
    Text_IO.Put ("The new account balance is ");
    Flt_IO.Put (New_Balance,0,2,0);
    Text_IO.New_Line;

end Checkbook;
```

b
```
Enter current checking account balance: 301.92
Enter the amount of this transaction
(deposits are positive, withdrawals are negative): -13.62

The new account balance is 288.30


Enter current checking account balance: 288.30
Enter the amount of this transaction
(deposits are positive, withdrawals are negative): 104.29

The new account balance is 392.59
```

```
Enter current checking account balance: 17.38
Enter the amount of this transaction
(deposits are positive, withdrawals are negative): -96.44

The new account balance is -79.06
```

Figure 4.4.1

Note the form of the Put statement here:

```
Flt_IO.Put (New_Balance,0,2,0);
```

We have chosen the Fore parameter to be 0, to ensure that there are no leading spaces; just as before, we have dealt with the formatting of the output ourselves. The Aft parameter has the value 2, for we are dealing in dollars and *hundredths* of dollars. The Exp parameter has been passed the value 0 so that the output will have the usual "dollars and cents" appearance, with the decimal point two digits from the right end of the number, rather than being written in exponential form.

4.5 The accuracy of floating point data*

When we look at an outdoor thermometer to determine the temperature, we might say, "It is 73 degrees"; we might even say, "It is about 73½ degrees." But we recognize it as silly to make statements like, "It is exactly 73.49227 degrees." The thermometer simply does not allow this much *accuracy*. Even though a digital thermometer might be able to display the temperature accurately to, say, two decimal places, nevertheless, beyond that any digits are suspect. A similar phenomenon occurs when we deal with floating point data in Ada or other computer languages.

It will probably not surprise you to learn that Ada cannot represent the number 1/3 = 0.33333... with *complete* accuracy. We know that the representation of data on computers is constrained by the machine's finiteness (which explains why the integers have a *first* and *last* entry rather than having an *infinte* range); so in the case of 1/3 we would expect some kind of truncation to take place internally, just as *we* must ultimately truncate this infinitely repeating decimal and say, for example, that "1/3 is *approximately* 0.3333333." You may also be aware that $\sqrt{2}$ has an infinite (but not repeating) decimal expansion, so once again you would not expect a computer to be able to represent this number with total accuracy. What may surprise you is that computers cannot give an accurate representation of even so simple a number as 1/10 = 0.1! For example, executing

```
Flt_IO.Put (0.1, 1, 10, 0)
```

will yield a display something like

```
0.1000000015
```

---

*This section and the next may be omitted on a first reading.

(This is somewhat dependent on the computer and the version of the Ada compiler running on it, but the result is fairly typical.) The reason behind the phenomenon—the inability of a computer to represent this particular *finite* decimal with complete accuracy—lies with the fact that computers are *not* decimal (base 10) machines, they are *binary* (base 2) machines, and 1/10 does not have a finite expansion when written in base 2. Some other fractions can be represented accurately on a computer. No matter; what counts here is that there are floating point numbers whose computer representations are *not* accurate, and this is a phenomenon of which we must be aware to avoid falling into a variety of errors. When a computer displays a floating point number, we must not slavishly take it as correct just because a computer displayed it; we must be aware of these potential **representational errors**, as they are called.

The failure of a computer to represent accurately some floating point numbers can cause other problems, even more severe than the representational ones noted above (which we might be inclined to claim are merely cosmetic in nature). Suppose for example that the FLOAT variable X is given an initial value of 0.0, and we then add 0.1 to X 100 times. The final value of X *should* be 10.0, of course. However, as we know, 0.1 cannot be represented internally with total accuracy, and by the time we add this very slightly incorrect value to X 100 times, a test such as "Is X = 10.0?" will turn out to be false! The value in X has *accumulated* enough of the representational error inherent in 0.1 to be sufficiently different from the representation of 10.0, so that this test for equality will fail. Thus even though X obviously "equals" 10.0, in fact it does not. We have encountered the result of a **computational error**.

None of these errors is anyone's "fault"; as already noted, they result from the finiteness of machines. An analysis of these errors and various ways to cope with them require mathematical techniques that lie well beyond the scope of this book. The best we can do here is to show you that they exist and how they arise; in some cases they are easily avoided, in others extraordinary measures are required to ensure accurate program results.

4.6 Floating point types

If our thermometer has a scale divided finely enough, we may be able to say, with confidence, that "the temperature is at least 73.4 degrees and is less than 73.5 degrees." In this case we have been able to determine the temperature to within a tenth of a degree. In other words, our reading is accurate to 0.1 degrees, or is accurate to one decimal place. We would be unable to claim that the temperature "is 73.47 degrees" or "73.48 degrees" without an even more finely divided thermometer scale. Thus while we might be able to ensure accuracy to one decimal place, we could not claim accuracy to two places.

This brief discussion raises the question, To what degree of accuracy—to how many decimal places—are numbers of type FLOAT represented? In the preceding section we saw a sample value of 0.1, namely, 0.1000000015. Thus we know that in this particular instance we do not have accuracy beyond eight decimal places. But is this representation accurate to two places? three places? eight places? Once again we are unable to give a definitive answer, since the accuracy depends on the particular implementation of Ada. You can determine this for your machine by displaying the (integer) value of FLOAT's attribute called **Digits**; the command

```
Int_IO.Put (FLOAT'Digits);
```

will yield the accuracy of objects of type FLOAT for your version of Ada. Typical values are 6 and 8, but in some cases it may be as large as 15 or more. Now suppose we are dealing with floating point data which we can measure to an accuracy of, say, nine decimal places (the wave lengths of various kinds of radio waves, for example), but our version of FLOAT is accurate only to six places? Must we simply be satisfied with six-place accuracy? No, we need only declare a floating point type with the desired nine-place accuracy. For the fact of the matter is that the predeclared type FLOAT, and the type we will use throughout the book to represent noninteger numbers, is only *one* of a wide variety of floating point types. A **floating point type** is *declared* by means of the new construct

```
type <type mark> is digits <accuracy>;
```

where *<type mark>* is the name of the type being declared and may be any legal identifier and *<accuracy>* is a positive integer that represents the number of places of accuracy to which objects of the type can be represented. For example,

```
type WAVE_LENGTH is digits 9;
```

declares a type whose objects will have nine-place accuracy.

We must caution you that while increasing the number of digits of accuracy of a floating point type may improve its representation, it does not eliminate the possibility of representational errors, and it certainly does not eliminate the computational errors that were seen in the preceding section. Note also that the floating point I/O routine that has served us so well for so long will no longer do—Flt_IO is not compatible with objects of type WAVE_LENGTH, for example. Fortunately, we need only declare another instantiation of Float_IO:

```
package Wave_IO is new Text_IO.Float_IO (WAVE_LENGTH);
```

In the next chapter we will see how to create *subtypes* of floating point types, such as FLOAT and WAVE_LENGTH—subtypes in the same sense that POSITIVE and NATURAL are subtypes of the INTEGER type. Aside from this, we have said about all we are going to say about floating point numbers. To be sure, there is more to be discovered about these and related types, but what we have done so far is adequate for our purposes, and a further detailed investigation would take us well out of the mainstream of the book.

4.7 Exercises

4.2.1 State what is displayed as a result of executing each of the following commands. Use the symbol ƀ to represent a space character. (We assume that the package Flt_IO has been created, as described in Section 4.2.)

(a) `Flt_IO.Put (12.362, 1, 2, 0);`
(b) `Flt_IO.Put (12.362, 3, 2, 0);`

```
(c) Flt_IO.Put (12.362, 1, 3, 0);
(d) Flt_IO.Put (12.362, 1, 2, 0);
(e) Flt_IO.Put (12.362, 1, 1, 0);
(f) Flt_IO.Put (12.362, 5, 2, 0);
(g) Flt_IO.Put (12.362, 5, 5, 0);
```

4.2.2 Given the variable X with the value 72.90467, write an appropriate Flt_IO.Put command to generate each of the outputs shown below. Note that the answer is not necessarily unique in some cases. (The symbol ƀ is used to represent a space character.)

(a)   ƀƀƀ72.9

(b)   72.90

(c)   ƀ73.0

(d)   ƀƀ72.905

(e)   ƀ72.904670

(f)   72.9047

4.2.3 We have had little to say about the "scientific," or "exponential," form of the display of a floating point number, except to note that for most of our purposes, we do not use it. In fact, it is most useful in a scientific environment, as its name suggests; for everyday use and for business purposes the "integer.fraction" form is preferred. But you should be aware of the rules for the exponential form, and these can fairly easily be deduced by writing a small test program or two. For example, write the following program

```
with Text_IO, Flt_IO;

program Test is

    X:      Float;

begin
    X := 123.468;
    Flt_IO.Put (X, 0, 3, 6);
    Text_IO.New_Line;
        .
        .
        .
    Flt_IO.Put (X, 2, 0, 1);
    Text_IO.New_Line;
end Test;
```

where the statement part consists of a number of statement pairs of the form

```
Flt_IO.Put (X, <fore>, <aft>, <exp>);
Text_IO.New_Line;
```

Include a number of these with various values for <fore>, <aft>, and <exp>. Specifically, let <exp> have all values between, say, 6 and 1 inclusive, and try various combinations of <fore> and <aft> values of 0, 1, and 2.

Next, execute the program again, with the sole change being the value of X:

```
X := 0.0123468;
```

From the results of these experiments, deduce as many of the rules for the output of floating point values in exponential form as you can.

4.2.4 We stated that when the number of digits in the fractional part of a floating point number exceeds the number of digits to be displayed as specified by the aft field in the Flt_IO.Put command, the remaining (undisplayed) digits are used to determine whether the last digit displayed is rounded up or down. However, a careful reading of Section 4.2 will show that we made *no* specific claim as to the rounding up or down if there was only a *single* remaining digit and that digit is 5. The reason for this omission is that the direction of rounding in this one case is dependent on the particular implementation of Ada that you are using.

(a) Write a "scratch" program that includes the statement

```
Flt_IO.Put (12.345,2,2,0);
```

to determine how your version of Ada treats this situation.

(b) Show that, regardless of how your Ada system treats the rounding of such numbers, you can always *force* the rounding *up* of a value X displayed to two decimal places with the statement

```
Flt_IO.Put (X + 0.005, <fore>, 2,0);
```

Verify that this technique not only forces the rounding up of the kinds of numbers in question but also leaves undisturbed the proper rounding up or down of all other values. (Note also that this scheme does not affect the value in the variable X.)

(c) How can you force the rounding up of numbers, such as 12.2345, displayed to *three* decimal places (once again, without disturbing the rounding up or down of numbers that do *not* have 5 in the fourth decimal place)? In general, explain how *any* number can be properly rounded, up or down, when displayed to n decimal places, with numbers having a single trailing digit 5 in the $(n + 1)$st place being rounded *up*. Does your technique work when $n = 0$?

(d) Repeat parts *b* and *c* of this exercise with the intent of forcing the rounding *down* of the special values in question.

(e) Examine the results of this exercise when applied to *negative* floating point numbers. Specifically, what do "rounding up" and "rounding down" mean in this case?

4.3.1 State the integer that results from each of the following type conversions.

(a) INTEGER (−12.708)
(b) INTEGER (12.708)
(c) INTEGER (16.0)
(d) INTEGER (5.001)

4.3.2 State the floating point number that results from each of the following type conversions.

(a) FLOAT (27)
(b) FLOAT (−27)
(c) FLOAT (0)

4.3.3 Let IX be an integer value, and FX be a floating point value. What can be said about the value of

(a) INTEGER (FLOAT (IX))?
(b) FLOAT (INTEGER (FX))?

4.3.4 We noted that the conversion of floating point values to integer values results in rounding up or down but that for floating point numbers of precisely the form xxx.5, the rounding up or down is implementation-dependent. Taking a hint from Exercise 4.2.4 *b* above, show that, regardless of the implementation, it is possible to force

(a) rounding up
(b) rounding down

4.3.5 In Sections 3.5 and 3.6 we created a package of integer routines, named Int_Pack. Write an equivalent package of floating point routines, named Float_Pack. (We are aware that you are on very shaky ground here, for you do not know many of the details of the Ada package concept *and* there are constructs involved there—**if...then**, for example—that have not yet been formally defined. But the desired package can be constructed by literally changing all INTEGER type references in the package Int_Pack's specification and body to type FLOAT.)

Compile the package specification and body (in that order), and write a program similar to the program of Exercise 3.6.1 to verify that your floating point routines seem to be working properly.

4.5.1 One of the statements of Section 4.5 claims that if 0.1 is added to 0.0 one hundred times, the result is *not* exactly 10.0. Verify this by writing a program that assigns to a floating point variable X the initial value 0.0, and then adds 0.1 to X 100d times. We don't expect you to write one hundred statements of the form

```
X := X + 0.1;
```

Instead, use the equivalent construction

```
for K in 1..100 loop
   X := X + 0.1;
end loop;
```

(even if you don't understand it). Then display the value in X to, say, 15 decimal places:

```
Flt_IO.Put (X, 2, 15, 0);
```

4.6.1   We saw in Section 4.6 that it is possible to create floating point *types* with the **type** construct; specifically,

```
type <type mark> is digits <accuracy>;
```

creates a floating point type with the specified number of digits of accuracy. Write a program whose only purpose is to create floating point types of this sort, and try a number of values for <accuracy>, specifically, some fairly large values, such as 10, 15, and 20, and also some small values, such as 2, 1, 0, and −1. These last two *should* make no sense. How does your compiler react to these declarations?

Chapter 5

Some Further Types and Subtypes

In Chapter 2 we saw many examples in which two integer values (INTEGER, POSITIVE, NATURAL) were "combined" by way of a binary *integer* operator (+, −, *, /, **rem**, **mod**) to yield a resulting integer value. Similarly, we saw examples in Chapter 4 where two floating point (FLOAT) values were "combined" with a binary *floating point* operator (+, −, *, /) to produce a real value. It would not be unreasonable, therefore, to conclude that a binary operator is one that combines two values of a given type to yield a resulting value of the same type, but this is not always the case. In this chapter we examine several binary operators that combine *integer* or *floating point* values to yield a "value" of True or False. We then introduce some other types and see how such operators are applicable to these types as well. As you will see, we are really stretching the word "combine" in this instance; what the operators actually do is *compare* a pair of values to produce a response of True or False. The binary operators in question are called **relational operators**, for they deal with how the values of their operands are related to one another.

5.1 Relational operators and comparisons

Consider the following extremely simple construct:

3 = 3

It consists of a binary operator = ("equals" or "is equal to"), along with its left and right operands, both of which have the integer value 3. Taken as a whole, it has a "truth value" of True. It is in fact an example of a comparison employing the relational operator =. As an operator, = has the effect of comparing the left and right operands for equality; since equality holds, the comparison is true, or has a truth value True; otherwise, it would have the truth value False, as is the case with the comparison

3 = 7

You might well object that these comparisons, in which the operands are integer *literals*, are so trivial as to be quite unpromising, as far as applications in programming are concerned. But consider the comparison

    J = 4

where J is an integer *variable*. What is the truth value of this comparison? Is it True? False? The answer, of course, is that its truth value depends on the current value in the variable J. In isolation—without knowing something about the value of J—we cannot say anything about the truth or falsity of the expression **J = 4**. But the notion is nonetheless extremely useful. Consider, for example, a program in which there is an action we want to take at a certain point if J *does* hold the value 4 at that point and that we do *not* want to take otherwise, that is, if J holds a value other than 4. If at that point the expression has the truth value True, we can take the desired action; otherwise (a value of False) that action is not carried out.

All three comparisons we have just looked at involve tests (comparisons) for *equality* of the left and right operands. Similarly, we may test directly to see whether the operands are *unequal* by using the relational operator /= ("does not equal" or "is not equal to"). This operator imitates the mathematical symbol for inequality, which is a "crossed out" equals sign ≠; it is because there is no symbol ≠ on most keyboards that Ada instead uses /=. Thus

    3 /= 3   has the value False

    3 /= 7   has the value True

    J /= 4   has the value False if the variable J holds the value 4; otherwise, has the
                  value True

Besides = and /=, there are four further relational operators that may operate on pairs of integer operands and produce a result of True or False. These operators are:

    <   "is less than" or "comes before"

    <=   "is less than or equal to" or
                  "comes before or has the same value as"

    >   "is greater than" or "comes after"

    >=   "is greater than or equal to" or
                  "comes after or has the same value as"

Notice that these relational operators assume that the integers are *ordered*; that is, given any two distinct values of any integer type, it is always possible to claim that one of them "is less than" (or, in a more general terminology, "comes before" or "precedes") the other one. To continue with further examples of the kind we have seen above:

3 < 3	has the value False
3 <= 3	has the value True
3 < 7	has the value True
3 <= 7	has the value True
3 > 7	has the value False
3 >= 7	has the value False
J < 4	has the value True if J holds any value less than 4; otherwise, has the value False
J <= 4	has the value True if J holds the value 4 or any value less than 4; otherwise, has the value False

The last two examples are easily modified to express the truth values of the comparisons **J > 4** and **J >= 4**.

There is no need for either of the operands in a comparison to be a *literal*, as was the case in the examples given above. Consider, for example, integer variables J and K, with values 4 and 10, respectively:

J = K	has the value False
J /= K	has the value True
J < K	has the value True
J <= K	has the value True
J > K	has the value False
J >= K	has the value False

At the beginning of this section, we introduced the six relational operators by pointing out that, unlike binary operators we had seen earlier, each of them operates on a pair of *integer* operands to yield a truth value. However, having been introduced in Chapter 4 to the Ada type FLOAT—whose values are, after all, numbers—you may suspect that relational operators could be applied to pairs of FLOAT operands, as well as to pairs of integer operands. This is indeed the case. We do point out, though, that when we use these operators to compare numbers, *both* operands must be of type FLOAT or *both* operands must be of an integer type; we are not allowed to mix them in a comparison. It is a simple matter to modify the examples we have seen in this section to produce similar comparisons of FLOAT operands; accordingly, we do so for only a few of them:

3.0 = 7.0	has the value False
3.6 <= 7.12	has the value True
X <= 3.1416	where X is a variable of type FLOAT, has the value True if X holds the value 3.1416 or a value less than 3.1416; otherwise, has the value False

We may also make use of type conversions in this context:

FLOAT (3) = 7.0	has the value False
3.0 = FLOAT (7)	has the value False
INTEGER (3.6) <= 7	has the value True

Having seen that relational operators can be applied to FLOAT operands, as well as to operands of an integer type, we might wonder whether these operators are applicable to any further types. That is, can we use these operators to compare values of any *other* type for equality and inequality and, possibly, with respect to some order that exists among the values of that type? The answer is yes; these operators can be used to compare values of many types. There is a problem in illustrating this, however; we have not yet studied any other type! We will do so immediately, however, taking a first look at the type called CHARACTER. In addition to expanding our knowledge of Ada's types and our insight into comparisons, this also provides us with some interesting techniques we can use in writing programs.

5.2   Introduction   to   the   type   CHARACTER;   more   on comparisons

Ada's CHARACTER type includes among its values all the characters on your keyboard—those, at least, that can appear on the screen. In particular, it includes the digits '0' through '9', the capital letters 'A' through 'Z', and the lowercase letters 'a' through 'z'. It also includes the blank or space character ' ' and various mathematical symbols and punctuation marks. Notice that, in referring to particular characters, we have just enclosed them in apostrophes (or "single" quotation marks); this is how these **literals** of type CHARACTER are written. We may declare variables and constants of type CHARACTER, and little need be said on this point, as these declarations have exactly the same form as all the ones we have seen before. We offer three simple examples:

```
Ch:          CHARACTER;
Initial:     CHARACTER := 'A';
Blank:       constant CHARACTER := ' ';
```

In the data types described previously (INTEGER and FLOAT), we have listed *binary operations* on the type that yield another object of the same type. Addition of INTEGER objects and subtraction of FLOAT objects are examples. But there are no such binary operations among objects of type CHARACTER—Ada does not provide for the combining of two CHARACTER objects to yield another CHARACTER.

However, all six of the *relational* operators may be used with CHARACTER operands. It is easy to see that all the following are correct, where Ch is a variable of type CHARACTER:

'A' = 'A'	has the value True
'A' = 'Q'	has the value False
'A' /= 'a'	has the value True
Ch = 'X'	has the value True if the variable Ch holds the CHARACTER value 'X'; otherwise, it has the value False

What is of equal interest, however, is that we can apply the *other* four relational operators to operands of the CHARACTER type. Recall that if these operators are to be employed with values of a particular type, there must be some *order* among the values of this type, so that given any two distinct values of the type, it will make sense to say that one of these values "is less than," "comes before," or "precedes" the other one. Such an order exists among the values of type CHARACTER, and in Chapter 12 we study it in detail. (Meanwhile, see Exercise 5.2.2.) For our present purposes, it suffices to say that, as CHARACTER values, the capital letters 'A' to 'Z' are in their "usual" alphabetic order, the lowercase letters 'a' to 'z' are also in their usual order, and capital letters *precede* lowercase letters. Thus, each of the following comparisons has the value True:

'C' < 'K'	'v' > 'b'	'Z' >= 'X'
'd' <= 't'	'Q' < 'q'	'Z' >= 'Z'
'm' < 'n'	'Z' < 'a'	'a' > 'A'
't' <= 't'	'M' < 'n'	'm' > 'N'

It is important to distinguish between the CHARACTER literals '0', '1', . . . , '9' and the integer literals 0, 1, . . . , 9. These CHARACTER literals should not be thought of as numbers but as "ordinary" keyboard characters, just as are, for example, 'x', '$', '+', and ' '. However, as CHARACTER values, they do exhibit the same order '0', '1', . . . , '9' as is found among the integer values 0, 1, . . . , 9. Thus:

'2' < '7'	has the value True
'6' <= '1'	has the value False
'0' > '4'	has the value False
'3' <= '8'	has the value True
'5' >= '5'	has the value True

To extend our comments on the ordering of CHARACTER values, we mention that the digit literals '0', . . . , '9' *precede* the alphabetic characters (both capital and lowercase); thus, in summary, we have the following:

$$... < '0' < ... < '9' < ... < 'A' < ... < 'Z' < ... < 'a' < ... < 'z' < ...$$

The final point we need to make at this time concerns input and output for type CHARACTER. To deal with CHARACTER I/O there is no need to devise a special package such as Int_IO or Flt_IO. The package Text_IO itself contains Get and Put routines that are ready for use with parameters of type CHARACTER. Thus, if Ch is a CHARACTER variable and Text_IO has been made available by way of the clause **with Text_IO**, the instruction

```
Text_IO.Get (Ch);
```

obtains the next character from input and assigns it to Ch. Also, Text_IO.Put, with any CHARACTER value as its parameter, will insert this character into the next position in output.

5.3 The type BOOLEAN

In dealing with relational operators, we have consistently been saying that a comparison such as I <= 10 has the (truth) value True or the (truth) value False. Now it is time to reveal that there is actually a predefined *type* in Ada that has the values True and False. This is the type called **BOOLEAN**, named after the English mathematical logician George Boole (1815-1864). The type INTEGER, as we have seen, has very many values—typically 4,294,967,296 of them. By contrast, there are exactly *two* BOOLEAN values: True and False. Thus the relational operators, as applied to objects of type INTEGER, FLOAT or CHARACTER, may now be said to result in values of the type BOOLEAN.

Although we rarely have occasion to refer to them, we note that this type has attributes analogous to those we saw for type INTEGER:

```
BOOLEAN'First:  False      BOOLEAN'Last:  True
```

Thus, while it may seem strange, the two "values" of this type have a definite order, with False preceding True.

When we studied the predefined type INTEGER in Chapter 2, we considered its *values, literals, attributes, objects* (variables and constants), and *operations* (along with operators and operator precedence). We also looked at *expressions* whose values were of the type INTEGER or of other integer types. We now follow the same course in investigating type BOOLEAN.

We may of course declare objects of type BOOLEAN. BOOLEAN variables are heavily used in programming, and we will soon see some examples of them in a program. Since a BOOLEAN object has a value that is either True or False, we choose identifiers that reflect this fact and that are descriptive within their context:

```
Searching:      BOOLEAN := True;
Found:          BOOLEAN := False;
OK:             BOOLEAN;
```

Is there such a thing as a BOOLEAN constant? Yes, there is, at least as far as the Ada language rules go. We might declare

```
Computer_On:    constant BOOLEAN := True;
```

which accurately describes the state of the computer (as long as we are able to use it, at least!). However, examples of BOOLEAN constants usually appear a bit contrived: the usefulness of BOOLEAN variables comes from our being able to change their value as the program runs, which cannot be done with a *constant*. In most cases, instead of declaring a BOOLEAN constant, we would probably be inclined simply to use the corresponding BOOLEAN literal—True or False—and often with a clearer result at that.

We have commented that there are no binary operations on CHARACTER objects that produce CHARACTER results. Now we ask, Are there any binary operations on BOOLEAN objects that produce BOOLEAN results? There are in fact four such operations, called **logical operations**. Three of these are designated by the binary operators **and, or** (inclusive

or), **xor** (exclusive **or**); the other operation is indicated by the unary operator **not**. Because there are only two BOOLEAN values True and False, it is both practical and convenient to show the effect of each of these operators by considering all possible values of their operands. Therefore, taking P and Q to be "objects" (literals, variables, constants) that take on BOOLEAN values, we define the logical operations in Figure 5.3.1.

P	Q	P and Q	P or Q	P xor Q	not P
True	True	True	True	False	False
True	False	False	True	True	False
False	True	False	True	True	True
False	False	False	False	False	True

Figure 5.3.1

The name "logical operators" comes from the use of these operators in logic, or what is called more specifically "propositional logic." Suppose, for example, that P and Q are the propositions (or assertions):

P: Today is Wednesday.

Q: It is raining.

Then we have:

P and Q: Today is Wednesday *and* it is raining.

P or Q: Today is Wednesday *or* it is raining.

In propositional logic, as in ordinary English, the proposition **P and Q** ("Today is Wednesday and it is raining") is taken to be True if *both* P and Q are True; but it is False in every other case. This coincides exactly with the situation indicated in Figure 5.3.1. Similarly, we understand the proposition **P or Q** ("Today is Wednesday or it is raining") to be True when *at least one* of the individual propositions is True.

Notice that logic considers **P or Q** to be true when *both* P and Q are True; in our ordinary speech we sometimes use the word "or" in the sense "one or the other but *not* both." To convey this sense of "or," we introduce the "exclusive or," for which we have no corresponding English word but for which Ada has the logical operator **xor**. In contrast, Ada's operator **or** is often called the "inclusive or." Thus, to borrow the Ada operator **xor** for our example of propositional logic, consider the proposition **P xor Q**, which we are forced to express quite verbosely and awkwardly as

P xor Q: Today is Wednesday or it is raining, but it is not both Wednesday and raining.

This proposition is True when *exactly one* of P and Q is True; it is False when both are True or both are False.

Finally, we readily see that

not P: Today is not Wednesday.

is True if P is False, and False if P is True.

To sum up our discussion, we see that Ada's logical operators on BOOLEAN items (literals, constants, variables) produce the same BOOLEAN values as do the corresponding logical operators on propositions in logic. These are, in fact, the same BOOLEAN values that we would "expect" by reason of our use of the words **and**, **or** (with due account taken of the distinction between inclusive and exclusive **or**), and **not** in ordinary English.

Although we have more to say in Section 5.4 on the topic of operator precedence, we mention for now that the unary operator **not** has higher precedence than the other three logical operators (**and**, **or**, **xor**), which are all on the same "level" of operator precedence:

not P and Q   is the same as   (not P) and Q

not P or Q   is the same as   (not P) or Q

not P xor Q   is the same as   (not P) xor Q

Furthermore, all the following are acceptable

P and not Q   not P and not Q

P or not Q   not P or not Q

P xor not Q   not P xor not Q

because the operator **not** is evaluated *first*. When the respective binary operator is subsequently evaluated, both its operands have already been given well-defined values.

On the other hand, notice that the "left-to-right" rule does not hold in the case of "mixed" binary logical operators, as it did in the case of integer operators on the same level of operator precedence. For example

$10 - 3 + 5$

will be evaluated from left to right, giving the same result as

$(10 - 3) + 5$.

However, although Ada permits

P and Q and R   and   P or Q or R

the expressions

P and Q or R   or   P or Q and R.

are *not* valid without parentheses. Thus, if we want left-to-right evaluation, we must write

(P and Q) or R   and   (P or Q) and R.

And these have different meanings from

P and (Q or R)   and   P or (Q and R).

We mentioned at the beginning of this section that from the fact that BOOLEAN'First and BOOLEAN'Last have the values False and True, respectively, we may infer that the two BOOLEAN values have a definite order, with False preceding True. Thus the relational operators may be applied to the type BOOLEAN (though perhaps not in a very interesting way):

False < True   has the value True
False > True   has the value False

5.4 Boolean expressions

Recall the description of an expression as stated in *LRM [4.4]*: "a formula that defines the computation of a value." When we studied expressions in Chapter 2, we were interested in those whose value was of some integer type; at present, our concern is with expressions having BOOLEAN values. Not surprisingly, these are called **Boolean expressions**. Some simple instances of Boolean expressions are BOOLEAN literals, BOOLEAN constants, and BOOLEAN variables; but we must also include *comparisons*, which, as we have seen, likewise have BOOLEAN values True or False. Further, now that we have looked at BOOLEAN values and the logical operations appropriate to them, we can construct many different Boolean expressions in terms of these values and operations, just as we did with integer values and operations in Sections 2.7 and 2.8.

Here is an example of such a Boolean expression having INTEGER variables J and K, integer operators, relational operators, and a logical operator:

$((3 * J) > (K - 2))$ **and** $((2 * J) < (K + 5))$

If, as in the examples we saw in Section 5.1, J has the value 4 and K has the value 10, then evaluation of this expression, starting with its innermost sets of parentheses, yields

$(12 > 8)$ **and** $(8 < 15)$

which gives

True **and** True

and, finally,

True

Could we omit some of the parentheses in the given expression? Perhaps so; perhaps we could even omit all of them, which would make the expression appear as follows:

3 * J > K – 2 **and** 2 * J < K + 5

Does this make sense? The answer is that it makes sense (and is a legitimate Boolean expression) *if,* and *only if,* at the time that each operator is to be applied, its left and right operands have *already* been evaluated. In other words, it is a matter of the *order* in which operations are performed.

This brings us again—although in a broader context than before—to the question of operator precedence. We need to know that the relational operators are evaluated *after* all the integer operators we considered in Section 2.8 (see Figure 2.8.1) but *before* the binary logical operators **and, or, xor**. In fact, noting that the logical operator **not** is on the same level as ****** and **abs**, we are now in a position to put together all the operators we have seen in the single operator precedence table of Figure 5.4.1.

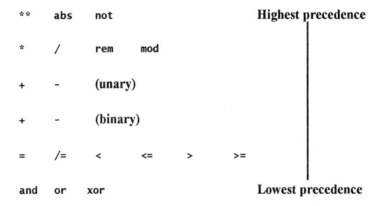

**	abs	not				**Highest precedence**
*	/	rem	mod			
+	-	(unary)				
+	-	(binary)				
=	/=	<	<=	>	>=	
and	or	xor				**Lowest precedence**

Figure 5.4.1

This table reveals that the expression without parentheses is in fact valid; the steps in its evaluation are just the same as in its earlier, parenthesized form. (You should verify this fact.) Despite its syntactic correctness, however, we can see this expression is somewhat more difficult to *read* than the one with parentheses. Thus, parentheses are often an aid to clarity for the reader of a program, even if the programming language does not actually require them.

Here are some examples in which we use the values of J (= 4), K (= 10), Searching (= True), and Found (= False) that we have already considered; additionally, we introduce the

CHARACTER variable Ch, which we will take as having the value 'X'. Note, as a general principle that just as in our earlier examples, parenthesized expressions are evaluated *first*.

Boolean expression	Value
J >= 0 and K <= 100	True
J >= 0 xor K <= 100	False
J < 0 or K <= 100	True
J < 0 or K > 50	False
J > 0 and Searching	True
J > 0 and Found	False
(J > K and K <= 10) or Searching	True
J − K < 0 and J + K > 0	True
J + 2 * K + 1 = 26	False
J + 2 * (K + 1) = 26	True
Ch >= 'A' and Ch <= 'Z'	True
Ch < 'Q' or Ch > 'q'	False
J + 1 >= 5 and Ch <= 'Y'	True
(J < K − 5 xor Ch > 'a') or Found	True

We point out, finally, the use of Boolean expressions in assignment statements, which can seem strange to us until we stop and think about what is going on. The following are valid assignments:

```
Searching := J >= 0;
Found := J = K;
OK :=  Ch <= 'Z' and Searching;
```

What happens here is the same as in the assignment statements for INTEGER variables that we saw in Chapter 2: the expression on the *right* side of the assignment operator is evaluated *first* (in this case, to True or False) and then this BOOLEAN value is assigned to the BOOLEAN variable on the *left* of the assignment operator. Thus, if J, K, and Ch have the respective values 4, 10, and 'X', then the BOOLEAN variables Searching, Found, and OK are assigned the values True, False, and True, respectively. Observe that the assignment of the value True to the BOOLEAN variable OK depends upon the fact that Searching has *already* been given the value True.

5.5 Attributes of types

In Section 2.6 we made very brief mention of the notion of an **attribute** of a type when we introduced First and Last as attributes of the type INTEGER. As you will recall, we were discussing the values of this type, and we stated that the set of INTEGER values in Ada is not infinite, as is the set of mathematical integer values; in fact, it includes only those integers lying between the implementation-dependent values INTEGER'First and INTEGER'Last, inclusive.

Now we point out that the attributes First and Last pertain to all the types we have seen so far and that these types have other attributes as well. We have already mentioned that First and Last pertain to the type BOOLEAN: BOOLEAN'First has the value False, and BOOLEAN'Last has the value True. It is also possible to speak of CHARACTER'First and CHARACTER'Last. But since we have dealt with only *some* of the values of this type (letters and digits) and since neither CHARACTER'First nor CHARACTER'Last is a letter or digit, we put off further consideration of these values until Chapter 12, where we discuss the CHARACTER type in greater detail.

There are also real numbers FLOAT'First and FLOAT'Last. These are analogous to INTEGER'First and INTEGER'Last, in that they represent the least and greatest FLOAT values that a particular Ada implementation can deal with. Thus, like the First and Last values of the type INTEGER, FLOAT'First and FLOAT'Last are implementation-dependent. You may look for their values in the documentation for your particular Ada system, or you may write a short Ada program that outputs their values on your display screen.

Two other very useful type attributes are **Pred** (predecessor) and **Succ** (successor). These are used in conjunction with a particular value of a type to designate the immediate predecessor or successor, respectively, of that value. Thus:

INTEGER'Pred (123)	is 122	INTEGER'Succ (123)	is 124
INTEGER'Pred (−123)	is −124	INTEGER'Succ (−123)	is −122
CHARACTER'Pred ('Q')	is 'P'	CHARACTER'Succ ('Q')	is 'R'
BOOLEAN'Pred (True)	is False	BOOLEAN'Succ (False)	is True

Of course the "first" value of any type has no predecessor, and the "last" value of a type has no successor. For example, we cannot legitimately refer to

INTEGER'Pred (INTEGER'First)   or INTEGER'Succ (INTEGER'Last)

or to

BOOLEAN'Pred (False)   or BOOLEAN'Succ (True)

It is clear that all the type attributes we have mentioned assume that the values of the type are in some kind of *order*, so that it makes sense to speak of the "first" or "last" value of the type. But more than this is required in the case of the attributes Pred and Succ. Recall that these attributes refer to the *immediate* predecessor and successor, respectively, of a type value. For a type to have these attributes, it is required that the values of the type do in fact *have* immediate predecessors and successors. This is indeed the case for integer types and for the types CHARACTER and BOOLEAN. But consider *real* numbers, and their Ada counterparts of type FLOAT. No real number R has an *immediate* predecessor or successor, for if X is *any* number less than R, then $(X + R)/2$—the *average* of X and R—is also less than R, and it is *closer* to R than is X. Likewise, for any Y greater than R, $(R + Y)/2$ is also greater than R, and is closer to R than Y. It is not surprising, then, that the Ada type FLOAT does *not* have the attributes Pred and Succ associated with it. On the other hand, the type FLOAT does have several attributes not pertinent to the integer types or to CHARACTER or BOOLEAN; for example, as we saw in Section 4.6, FLOAT has the attribute Digits.

5.6 Subtypes

In Section 2.9 we remarked that Ada has many instances of "integer types," with three of these—INTEGER, POSITIVE, and NATURAL—being predefined in the language. We mentioned further that POSITIVE and NATURAL are subtypes of the type INTEGER, inasmuch as they consist of a subset of the values of the base type INTEGER, along with the operations that belong to this base type. Ada allows the programmer to create other integer types as well, and each of these is a *subtype* of the INTEGER type. As we will see, it is not only the type INTEGER that can give rise to subtypes; we may define subtypes of the types CHARACTER, FLOAT, and (although it would scarcely be practical) BOOLEAN as well.

We have just recalled from Section 2.9 that a subtype of an Ada data type consists of a subset of the values of the given type, along with this type's set of operations; the given type is known as the **base type** of the subtype. To this information we now add that the values of the subtype must be specified in terms of a **constraint** (restriction) placed upon the values of the base type. One of the most common kinds of constraint used in Ada—and the one with which we are concerned at present—is the **range constraint**, which prescribes that the values of the subtype must lie within some specified *range* of the values of the base type. In general, a **range L..R** of a base type consists of all the values of the base type from L to R, inclusive. If L = R the range consists of one value L (= R); if L > R the range is empty and contains no values. A subtype defined in terms of a range constraint is called a **range subtype** of the given base type.

How do we "define" a range subtype of a base type? The answer is that we *declare* the subtype, in the program's declaration section, using the following format:

```
subtype <identifier> is <type mark> range L..R;
```

In this declaration, the indicated identifier is the one chosen by the programmer to name the subtype, and the type mark referred to is that of the base type. We use **L** and **R** to specify the extent of the range, as in our discussion above. Here are several declarations of range subtypes:

```
subtype MONTHS          is INTEGER range 1..12;
subtype MINUTES_RANGE   is INTEGER range 0..10079;
subtype CENTURY_21      is INTEGER range 2001..2100;
subtype USA_RANGE       is INTEGER range 1776..25000;
subtype HUNDRED         is INTEGER range 1..100;
subtype DIGIT           is CHARACTER range '0'..'9';
subtype CAPITAL         is CHARACTER range 'A'..'Z';
```

```
subtype LIQUID              is FLOAT range 32.0..212.0;
subtype LONG_WAVE           is WAVE_LENGTH range 62.0..64.9;
```

Figure 5.6.1

We should point out expressly that the predefined types POSITIVE and NATURAL are themselves *range subtypes* of the base type INTEGER, although their ranges are not specified by the programmer, but by the Ada environment itself (see the package Standard in Appendix D). In fact, the declarations of these subtypes are already provided with the language:

```
subtype POSITIVE is INTEGER range 1..INTEGER'Last;

subtype NATURAL  is INTEGER range 0..INTEGER'Last;
```

In each of the subtypes declared in Figure 5.6.1, the low and high ends of the range are specified by means of *literals* of the base type (INTEGER, CHARACTER, FLOAT, or WAVE_LENGTH). Although this is frequently done, Ada allows these values to be defined in terms of any *expressions* having values of the base type, provided that these values can be determined at the point in the program where the subtype is declared. If we declare

```
Start:      constant INTEGER := 1;
Finish:     constant INTEGER := 100;
Stretch:    INTEGER := 50;
```

then each of the following ranges could serve in the declaration of an integer subtype:

```
Start .. Finish                    contains 100 numbers
Start-1 .. Finish-2*Stretch        contains 1 number
Start+Stretch .. Finish-Stretch    contains no numbers
```

The syntax of range subtype declarations is shown in Figure 5.6.2, where the indicated type mark is that of the subtype's base type.

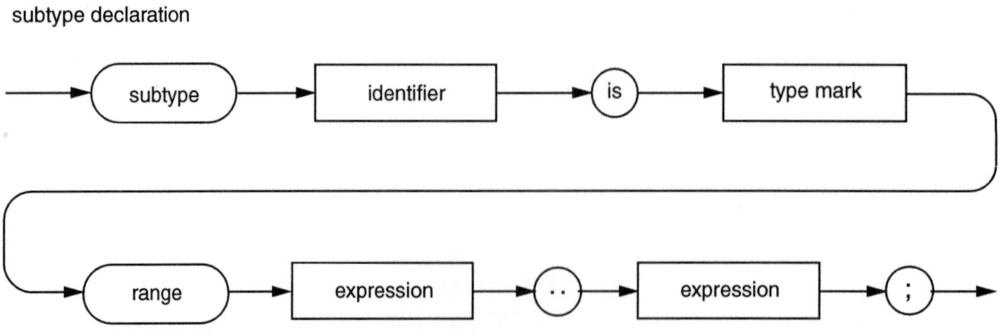

subtype declaration

Figure 5.6.2

Range subtypes, such as those declared above, have the attributes First and Last, just as do their base types. These attributes have the values we expect them to have, namely the low and high values of the subtype's range. We have already observed (Section 2.9) that

```
POSITIVE'First = 1        POSITIVE'Last = INTEGER'Last
NATURAL'First  = 0        NATURAL'Last  = INTEGER'Last
```

With reference to the subtypes declared in Figure 5.6.1, note:

```
MONTHS'First          = 1      MONTHS'Last          = 12
MINUTES_RANGE'First = 0        MINUTES_RANGE'Last = 10079
CENTURY_21'First    = 2001     CENTURY_21'Last    = 2100
USA_RANGE'First     = 1776     USA_RANGE'Last     = 25000
HUNDRED'First       = 1        HUNDRED'Last       = 100
DIGIT'First         = '0'      DIGIT'Last         = '9'
CAPITAL'First       = 'A'      CAPITAL'Last       = 'Z'
LIQUID'First        = 32.0     LIQUID'Last        = 212.0
```

Figure 5.6.3

Now that we have seen several examples of subtypes, we should mention explicitly that the base type of a range subtype may itself be a *subtype*. (We alluded to this briefly in Section 2.9, when we said that POSITIVE may be regarded as a subtype of NATURAL.) Thus, instead of our original subtype declarations, we might have had

```
subtype MONTHS          is POSITIVE range 1..12;
subtype MINUTES_RANGE   is NATURAL range 0..10079;
subtype CENTURY_21      is POSITIVE range 2001..2100;
```

and, further, we might use these subtypes themselves as the base types in new declarations:

```
subtype VACATION_TIME is MONTHS range 6..8;
subtype FIRST_DECADE  is CENTURY_21 range 2001..2010;
```

In an Ada program, we may declare variables and constants to be of any *subtype*, provided that the subtype has been previously declared, either by the Ada language environment or by a prior declaration in the program. We might have

```
Counter:           NATURAL;
Rank:              POSITIVE;
Birth_Month:       MONTHS;
Retirement_Year:   CENTURY_21;
WW2_End:           constant USA_RANGE := 1945;
Initial:           CAPITAL;
```

Operations on values of any of these subtypes are the same as those for the respective base type. However, a variable of any range subtype may *not* be assigned a value that lies outside the range that defines this subtype. Thus, the following assignments are *not* valid:

```
Rank := 0;
Birth_Month := 15;
Retirement_Year := 1995;
Initial := 'q';
```

Of course, these assignment statements would be equally invalid if their right sides were made of *any* expressions (not necessarily literals) whose values were outside the subtype ranges of their respective left-side variables, as for example,

```
Birth_Month := Birth_Month + 24;
```

Note, however, that there is nothing wrong with an *expression* such as Birth_Month + 24; this value could be assigned to an INTEGER variable, say, even though it could not be assigned to Birth_Month, whose values must be between 1 and 12. In Chapter 7 we take up the question of what happens if such an unacceptable assignment is attempted.

5.7 Exercises

5.1.1 Let A and B be INTEGER variables with values 3 and 10, respectively. Find the truth value (True or False) of each of the following comparisons. You may assume that, in each case, the left and right operands of the relational operator are evaluated *first*.

(a) 10 * A = 3 * B
(b) A /= B / A
(c) 5 * A > A + B
(d) A >= A / B + A
(e) B – A < B / 2
(f) B rem A * 12 <= B + B rem 4
(g) A / B < A – B
(h) 2 * A + B >= B / 2 * A

5.1.2 Let X and Y be FLOAT variables with values 2.5 and 1.1, respectively. Find the truth value of each of the following comparisons. As in Exercise 5.1.1, you may expect the left and right operands of each relational operator to be evaluated *first* (with the same arithmetic operator precedence as for integers), before any attempt is made to compare them.

(a) X /= 2.0 * Y
(b) 2.0 * X < 5.0 * Y
(c) X – Y <= (X + Y) / 3.0
(d) X + 2.0 * Y > 2.0 * X
(e) Y / 2.0 >= X – 2.0 * Y

5.2.1   Let Ch be a CHARACTER variable to which 'K' has been assigned. Find the truth value of each of the following comparisons.

(a) Ch /= 'K'   (e) Ch >= 'k'
(b) Ch >= 'C'   (f) Ch < 'T'
(c) Ch >= 'c'   (g) Ch <= 't'
(d) Ch < 'a'   (h) Ch > '6'

5.2.2   It has been stated that the uppercase alphabetic characters are in their "usual" order *among* themselves and that this is true also of the lowercase alphabetic characters and the numeric characters (digits). We know that the digits precede the uppercase letters, which in turn precede the lowercase letters. But what of relations such as

'A' < '?'   'b' = '#'   '<' >= '>'

That is, how are the so-called special characters, which are neither alphabetic nor numeric, related to these "normal" characters and to one another? The details are supplied in Chapter 12, but in the meantime we mention that each character—that is, each literal of type CHARACTER—is assigned an integer *code* called its **ASCII code**, and these are listed in Appendix B. We can tell you now that *any* two characters whatever are related by one of the relational operators (<, >, =, <=, >=, or /=) if, and only if, their corresponding *codes* are in that same relationship as *integers*. Browse through the table of Appendix B, making any observations that you can derive from it (some of the "characters" in that table will be unfamiliar to you; simply ignore those for the time being). Then state the value of each of the following expressions:

(a) 'A' < 'a'
(b) '4' > '['
(c) 's' /= 'S'
(d) ('s' < 'Z') or ('$' > '}')
(e) False < ('~' > '^')
(f) (('q' /= 'Q') and ('p' < '{')) = (('<' > '>') or ('b' > '#'))

5.2.3   So far our knowledge of the CHARACTER type is fairly sketchy. We know from Appendix B what the literals of this type are (although some, such as those labeled DC1 and ESC, for example, cannot be explained at this time); that each literal has a numeric, or ASCII, code; and, from Exercise 5.2.2, that the relational operators are defined for all objects of type CHARACTER and a value of True or False is assigned to a relational expression. But what of operations among the characters themselves? Objects of type INTEGER have binary operations (+, *, **rem**, and so forth). Since each literal of type CHARACTER has a *numeric* code, it may not be outrageous to suggest that expressions such as **'Q' + 1** and **'Z' – '0'** could also have well-defined meanings.

(a) For each of the expressions given below, conjecture as to what the meaning might be, if any; then write, compile, link, and execute a "scratch" program in each case to verify or refute your conjecture. Pay particular attention to any messages generated by the compiler or the run-time system. Note that a "scratch" program is a minimal program that executes and provides information about some situation. It is really an experiment, designed by you, the outcome of which is intended to yield confirmation or refutation of a conjecture. It is minimal in that it does no more than provide this information; it is typically very short, is undocumented, and matters such as readability and proper programming practices are normally pushed to the background. Once it has served its purpose, it is deleted. For example, the complete program

```
with Text_IO;
procedure Op_Test is
begin
   Text_IO.Put ('A' + 'B');
end;
```

will respond to part *iii* below.

(i)   'A' + 1
(ii)   'B' – 1
(iii)   'A' + 'B'
(iv)   'A' * 'B'

(b) There is an operator, **&**, that *does* operate on pairs of objects of type CHARACTER. It has some interesting properties (among them the property of noncommutativity: if X and Y are objects of type CHARACTER, then in general, **X & Y** is *not* the same as **Y & X**). By finding the values of the expressions below (at least those that are valid), conjecture what the **&** operator does and then write scratch programs to establish the validity of your conjecture.

(i)   'A' & 'B'
(ii)   'A' & 1
(iii)   'A' & '1'
(iv)   'A' & 'B' & 'C'
(v)   'a' & "camel"
(vi)   'a' & ' ' & "camel"
(vii)   'a ' & "camel"
(viii)   "a " & "camel"
(ix)   "ca" & 'm' & "el"
(x)   "ca" & "m" & "el"
(xi)   'A' & '' & 'B'
(xii)   'A' & "" & 'B'

(c) Verify that if "R" and 'R' are displayed, the results are identical in *appearance*. Does this mean that "R" and 'R' are the same *object*? If not, what is the difference between these objects? (At the present time you do not have the complete information to give a definitive answer to this question.)

5.3.1 Let P, Q, and R be BOOLEAN variables. Find a combination of True and False for these variables for which

(P and Q) or R and **P and (Q or R)**

do not have the same value. Is this combination unique?

5.3.2 Answer the same questions in Exercise 5.3.1 with respect to

(P or Q) and R and **P or (Q and R)**

5.3.3 Let P, Q, R, ... be BOOLEAN variables. Let E(P,Q,R,...T) represent a BOOLEAN-valued expression involving P, Q, R, ..., T and the operators **and, or, xor,** and **not.** For example, let E(P,Q,R) represent the expression "P and (not Q or R)." We say that two such expressions E_1(P,Q,R,...,T) and E_2(P,Q,R,...,T) are **equivalent,** written E_1(P,Q,R,...T) $\equiv$ E(P,Q,R,...T), if, and only if, both expressions have the same value (True or False) for *each* possible combination of values for the variables P, Q, R, ..., T. For example,

P and Q $\equiv$ Q and P

since both sides of this equivalence have the same values for the various combinations of values for P and Q. (This is trivially verified from Figure 5.3.1.) In a similar fashion, it is easy to check that

P and P $\equiv$ P
P or P $\equiv$ P
not (not P) $\equiv$ P

Establish each of the following equivalences:

(a) not (P and Q) $\equiv$ not P or not Q
(b) not (P or Q) $\equiv$ not P and not Q
(c) P and (Q or R) $\equiv$ (P and Q) or (P and R)
(d) P or (Q and R) $\equiv$ (P or Q) and (P or R)
(e) P xor Q $\equiv$ (P or Q) and not (P and Q)
(f) P xor Q $\equiv$ (not P and Q) or (P and not Q)
(g) not (P xor Q) $\equiv$ (not P or Q) and (P or not Q)
(h) P or not P $\equiv$ True   (the constant-valued expression)
(i) P and not P $\equiv$ False   (the constant-valued expression)

(j)   P and Q and (P or Q) ≡ P and Q
(k)   P and Q and (not P or not Q) ≡ False

5.3.4   For two BOOLEAN items (literals, variables, constants) P and Q, we have:

> P **and** Q is True if and only if P and Q are both True.
> P **or** Q is False if and only if P and Q are both False.

For *three* BOOLEAN items P, Q, and R, are the following assertions correct?

> P **and** Q **and** R is True if and only if P, Q, and R are all True.
> P **or** Q **or** R is False if and only if P, Q, and R are all False.

5.4.1   Let A and B be INTEGER variables to which values have been assigned.

(a)   Is **not (A < B)** the same as **A > B**? Explain.
(b)   Is **not (A >= B)** the same as **A <= B**? Explain.

5.4.2   As in Exercise 5.1.1, let A and B be INTEGER variables with values 3 and 10, respectively. Further, let Ch be a CHARACTER variable to which 'Q' has been assigned. For each of the following, if the expression is valid, find its value; if it is invalid, explain why.

```
(a)  2 * A > B or  2 * B > A
(b)  2 * A > B xor 2 * B > A
(c)  (A > 3) = not (A < 3)
(d)  (not A > 5) and (not B < 5)
(e)  A >= 0 and A < B
(f)  (False or A = B) /= (A = B)
(g)  A < 4 and A > B and B > 4
(h)  A < 4 or  A > B or  B > 4
(i)  A < 4 and A > B or  B > 4
(j)  A < 4 and (A > B or B > 4)
(k)  not (A <= 4 xor A <= B)
(l)  4 * A <= B or 2 * B <= A or 4 * A < 2 * B
(m)  A < 5 and Ch > '5'
(n)  B > 5 and Ch < '5'
(o)  A >= 5 or Ch >= 5
(p)  A >= B or Ch >= B
(q)  Ch > 'Z' or Ch < 'b'
(r)  (A / B < A) and (Ch >= 'K' xor Ch <= 'k')
```

5.4.3   Let Correct be a BOOLEAN variable. For each of the following, tell which value is assigned to Correct.

(a) Correct := 11 / 4 = 3 or 11 rem 4 = 3;
(b) Correct := 8 / 3 = 2 and 8 rem 3 = 2;
(c) Correct := 21 rem (−4) < 0;
(d) Correct := −21 rem 4 = −1;
(e) Correct := 2 ** 4 = 4 ** 2;
(f) Correct := 2 ** 3 > 3 ** 2 or 3 ** 4 > 4 ** 3;

5.4.4 Let R, S, and T be BOOLEAN variables, having the values True, True, and False, respectively. State the value of each of the following.

(a) R < T or S < R
(b) R or T < S or T /= R
(c) R and S /= R and T /= R

5.5.1 Write a small program (which includes Int_IO in a **with** clause) to display the values INTEGER'First and INTEGER'Last for your particular machine.

5.5.2 Write a small program (which includes Flt_IO in a **with** clause) to display the values FLOAT'First and FLOAT'Last for your particular machine. Display the values with an Aft field equal to the number of digits of accuracy for your version of FLOAT. (If you have not already done so, you can determine this number by displaying the *integer* number FLOAT'Digits.)

5.5.3 Explain why it is, or is not, true that for *any* type T having the attributes Pred and Succ and for *any* object X of type T, we always have

$$T'Succ\ (T'Pred\ (X)) = X \qquad and \qquad T'Pred\ (T'Succ\ (X)) = X$$

5.5.4 Determine (by trying it) what happens if you attempt to use the "value" **FLOAT'Succ (12.773)**.

5.6.1 Declare the type SINGLE_DIGIT by

```
subtype SINGLE_DIGIT is INTEGER range -9..9;
```

Then verify (by writing a small program) that SINGLE_DIGIT'First = −9 and SINGLE_DIGIT'Last = 9.

5.6.2 Declare the types SINGLE_DIGIT and POS_DIGIT by

```
subtype SINGLE_DIGIT is INTEGER range -9..9;
subtype POS_DIGIT is SINGLE_DIGIT range 1..9;
```

Let X and Y be declared to be of type POS_DIGIT, assigned values by

```
X := 1;        Y := 9;
```

(a) Is **POS_DIGIT'Pred (X)** meaningful? If so, what is its value?

(b) Is **SINGLE_DIGIT'Pred (X)** meaningful? If so, what is its value?

(c) Is **SINGLE_DIGIT'Succ (Y)** meaningful? if so, what is its value?

(d) Is **POSITIVE'Succ (Y)** meaningful? if so, what is its value?

5.6.3 Write a small program to try each of the following proposed constructions.

(a) We know that a range of, say, INTEGER type can be *empty*—containing no integers at all. For example, if L = 7 and R = 2, then

INTEGER range L..R

is empty. Can a subtype be declared as an empty range of integers? That is, is the following declaration valid for your compiler?

```
subtype EMPTY is INTEGER range 7..2;
```

(b) Assuming that the construction in part *a* is valid, can you then declare a variable of this "empty" type:

```
X:     EMPTY;
```

(c) Assuming that the declaration in part *b* is permitted, what happens if you attempt to assign a value to X in the statement part of a program:

```
X := 3;
```

5.6.4 In Section 4.6 we saw that it is possible to create floating point types with a specified number of digits of accuracy. But we can do even more than was suggested there. At the time the type is declared, a range can also be specified, as in

```
type WAVE_LENGTH is digits 9 range 0.0..65.7500;
```

In Section 5.6 we learned that we can create subtypes of such types; for instance

```
subtype LONG_WAVE is WAVE_LENGTH range 62.0..64.9;
```

In fact, when declaring types such as these we can simultaneously adjust the accuracy, *provided* we do not try to *improve* the accuracy over that of the base type (some reflection should lead you to the conclusion that this would not be possible). Thus

```
subtype SHORT_WAVE is WAVE_LENGTH digits 4 range 1.0..3.0;
```

(a) Write a small program that displays the digits of accuracy for each of the types WAVE_LENGTH, LONG_WAVE, and SHORT_WAVE declared above.

(b) What is the smallest and largest values in each of these types (that is, *<type mark>*'First and *<type mark>*'Last in each case)?

(c) Determine (by trying it!) how your Ada compiler reacts to an attempt to improve the accuracy of a floating point type declared as a subtype; for example

```
subtype SHORT_WAVE is WAVE_LENGTH digits 11 range 1.0..3.0;
```

If your compiler compiles the program (possibly issuing a warning in the process), execute the program and determine the behavior of the Ada run-time system in the presence of this subtype declaration.

Chapter 6

Control Structures: Conditionals and Loops

One common property of the programs we have seen so far is their restriction to "sequential execution" of program statements. That is, the computer begins by executing the first statement of the program, then it executes the next one, the next, and so on until the statement appearing in last place is executed, after which the run of the program is complete. If computers only did this much for us, they would still be useful. But computers can do far more: They can perform an action repeatedly (for example, process one input after another until told to stop), and they can "decide" between alternative courses of action according to the state of affairs at the moment when the decision is made. In fact, it is just such capabilities on a computer's part that make it an extremely versatile tool in the hands of a skilled programmer.

In this chapter we investigate the **control structures** that govern the **flow of control** in the execution of a program, that is, the ways in which a program determines *whether* a given statement is executed (or, instead, skipped over) and, if so, *how often* it is executed. We distinguish three kinds of execution of the statements in a program:

1. sequential execution

2. selective execution

3. repetitive execution

The first of these is the simple program behavior we have already seen. The other two types of execution are associated with **conditional statements** (**if** statements) and **loops**, respectively. In this chapter we take up these latter two types of execution, along with the Ada constructions that implement them.

6.1 Selective execution: *if* statements

As we have remarked above, computer languages allow the programmer to make the computer "decide" whether or not to execute a particular statement or sequence of statements or "decide" which of two possible statement sequences is to be executed. In Ada, the principal way of doing this is to make use of a statement introduced by the reserved word **if**. There are two fundamental forms of an **if** statement; and we will shortly see some other variations on it as well. The first form of an **if** statement is as follows, where the term *condition*, frequently used in this context, is another name for a Boolean expression:

```
if <condition> then
  <statement sequence>
end if;
```

Alternatively, we could describe this kind of **if** statement by a very simple syntax diagram, as is done in Figure 6.1.1. We saw this construction earlier, in Section 3.6, where we simply assumed that you would understand its meaning without a formal definition.

if statement (first form)

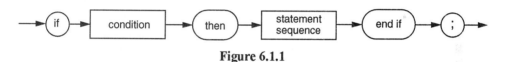

Figure 6.1.1

When this kind of statement is executed, the condition is evaluated first; if it has the value True then the sequence of (one or more) statements between the reserved word **then** and the reserved words **end if** is executed; if the condition has the value False, the statement sequence is *not* executed. In either event, control then passes to the statement following the **end if** (or, if the **end if** is at the end of the program, the program terminates).

As a practical application of this construct, we might use it to decide whether or not to take some action (during the execution of a program), according to the user's preference. For example, we might ask the user if he or she wishes to see the current value of some variable, an INTEGER variable Number, say:

```
Text_IO.Put ("Do you want to see the value of Number (Y/N)?  ");
```

(We assume needed I/O routines have been included by means of a **with** clause.) Having declared a CHARACTER variable Answer in the program, we may obtain the user's affirmative or negative response ('Y' or 'N', respectively) and make use of it in a conditional statement:

```
Text_IO.Get (Answer);
if Answer = 'Y' then
  Text_IO.Put ("Number:  ");
  Int_IO.Put (Number, 0);
  Text_IO.New_Line;
end if;
```

Notice that the program does not bother to check whether the user has entered the negative response 'N' as input. Thus, Number will be displayed if the user types 'Y' but not otherwise. It may happen that the user types a lowercase 'y', and it would be well to allow this as an affirmative response, so that the user is not forced to use a capital letter:

```
Text_IO.Get (Answer);
if Answer = 'Y' or Answer = 'y' then
  Text_IO.Put ("Number:  ");
  Int_IO.Put (Number, 0);
  Text_IO.New_Line;
end if;
```

As another example to illustrate this program construct, consider the following, where A and Maximum are INTEGER variables:

```
if A > Maximum then
  Maximum := A;
end if;
```

When this conditional statement is executed, the condition **A > Maximum** is evaluated first; if it is True, the value of A is assigned to Maximum; otherwise, the value of Maximum is left unaltered (that is, the given assignment is not carried out); in both cases, control then passes to the next statement of the program. The effect of this conditional statement, therefore, is to replace the value of Maximum by that of A if, and only if, A is found to have a greater value than that of Maximum.

Suppose, however, that we want instead to assign to Maximum the value of A or the value of another INTEGER variable B, whichever is greater. To accomplish this, we compare A and B; if A > B, then Maximum is given A as its value; otherwise (that is, if A <= B), Maximum is given the value of B. Notice that, in this case, unlike the preceding one, we definitely want to carry out an assignment: Either the value of A or that of B will be assigned to Maximum. We could write this as follows:

```
if A > B then
  Maximum := A;
end if;
if A <= B then
  Maximum := B;
end if;
```

Observe that if the *first* condition tested (**A > B**) is True, then *necessarily* the other condition (**A <= B**) is False, and it is not necessary to evaluate this condition at all. Similarly, if the first condition is False, the other condition is True, and, again, it is not necessary to test it. To avoid this needless testing of conditions, Ada provides us with another conditional construct that we can apply here, as follows:

```
if A > B then
  Maximum := A;
else
  Maximum := B;
end if;
```

This is an example of Ada's **if...then...else** conditional statement, where **else** is Ada's reserved word for what we might more naturally say in English, "otherwise." This kind of conditional statement can be described in general terms as follows:

```
if <condition> then
  <first statement sequence>
else
  <second statement sequence>
end if;
```

Again, we could use a syntax diagram to describe this form of **if** statement. However, since it is also very simple and since we have other **if** statements to consider, we will wait until we are in a position to present a diagram (Figure 6.1.2) that sums up the syntax of *all* forms of **if** statements. When an **if...then...else..end if** statement is executed, its condition is evaluated first; if this condition has the value True, the *first* statement sequence is executed (but not the second); if it has the value False, the *second* statement sequence is executed (but not the first). Finally, control passes "beyond" the **end if**, as described earlier.

Since the basic forms of conditional statements (**if...then** and **if...then...else**) are so important, we offer another pair of similar examples, this time involving a variable Temperature, of INTEGER type:

1.  ```
    if Temperature > 85 then
       Text_IO.Put_Line ("Too hot!");
       Text_IO.Put_Line ("I prefer it cooler.");
    end if;
    ```

2.  ```
    if Temperature > 85 then
       Text_IO.Put_Line ("Too hot!");
       Text_IO.Put_Line ("I prefer it cooler.");
    else
       Text_IO.Put_Line ("Not bad.");
       Text_IO.Put_Line ("I don't like it too hot.");
    end if;
    ```

These examples illustrate the point that the statement sequences "inside" the **if** statements may consist of several statements, rather than just a single statement.

Ada offers variations or extensions of these basic **if...then** and **if...then...else** statements. For example, suppose that we would like to display a message that will say "Too hot!" if the temperature is above 85 degrees or "Too cold!" if the temperature is below 40 degrees. As a first attempt, we might write:

```
if Temperature > 85 then
  Text_IO.Put_Line ("Too hot!");
end if;
if Temperature < 40 then
  Text_IO.Put_Line ("Too cold!");
end if;
```

Again, if the first condition is True, the second one is necessarily False and there is no need to evaluate it. However, if the first condition is False, we *cannot* conclude that the second one is True, since they may *both* be False. We could ensure that the second condition would be tested when necessary, but not otherwise, by making use of an **if...then...else** construction:

```
if Temperature > 80 then
  Put_Line ("Too hot!");
else
  if Temperature < 40 then
    Put_Line ("Too cold!");
  end if;
end if;
```

In this statement, if the first condition is found to be True, the program displays the message "Too hot!" and control passes immediately beyond the entire **if...then...else** statement. If the first condition is False, the **else** part of the conditional statement is executed, beginning with a test of the condition **Temperature < 40**; if this condition is True, the message "Too cold!" is displayed; if it is False, nothing is displayed, and in each case, control then passes beyond the entire conditional construct. Thus, these lines of Ada code do exactly what we would like to do: Conditions are evaluated if they need to be, but not otherwise, and the "correct" actions are taken in keeping with the BOOLEAN values of the conditions.

There is a certain clumsiness about this latter conditional statement that Ada allows us to avoid. The statement we have constructed could be expressed in general terms as follows:

```
if <first condition> then
  <first statement sequence>
else
  if <second condition> then
    <second statement sequence>
  end if;
end if;
```

An equivalent, and much tidier, form of this conditional statement may be constructed by use of the Ada reserved word **elsif**, in the following manner:

```
if <first condition> then
  <first statement sequence>
elsif <second condition> then
  <second statement sequence>
end if;
```

Just as in the previous conditional statement constructed with **else** followed by **if**, the execution of this statement begins with evaluation of the *first* condition. If it is True, the *first* statement sequence is executed and control immediately passes beyond the **end if**. If it is False, the *second* condition is evaluated, and execution of the *second* statement sequence depends on whether the second condition was found to be True or False. Control then passes beyond the **end if**. In terms of this form of conditional statement, our comments on the temperature would be programmed as follows:

```
if Temperature > 85 then
  Text_IO.Put_Line ("Too hot!");
elsif Temperature < 40 then
  Text_IO.Put_Line ("Too cold!");
end if;
```

There is a final fundamental form of the conditional statement that includes both **elsif** and **else**:

```
if <first condition> then
   <first statement sequence>
elsif <second condition> then
   <second statement sequence>
else
   <third statement sequence>
end if;
```

This type of conditional statement behaves exactly the same as the previous one, except that if the *first* condition is found to be False and the *second* condition is also found to be False, then the *third* statement sequence is executed. Thus, to continue our example on the temperature:

```
if Temperature > 85 then
   Text_IO.Put_Line ("Too hot!");
elsif Temperature < 40 then
   Text_IO.Put_Line ("Too cold!");
else
   Text_IO.Put_Line ("Mild weather.");
end if;
```

These conditional constructs can be generalized to include further occurrences of **elsif**, in the form

```
if <first condition> then
   <first statement sequence>
elsif <second condition> then
   <second statement sequence>
elsif <next condition> then
   <next statement sequence>

        .
        .
        .

elsif <next condition> then
   <next statement sequence>
end if;
```

or in the form

```
if <first condition> then
   <first statement sequence>
elsif <second condition> then
   <second statement sequence>
elsif <next condition> then
   <next statement sequence>

        .
        .
        .

elsif <next condition> then
   <next statement sequence>
else
   <last statement sequence>
end if;
```

In such cases (examples are found in the program of Figure 6.3.1), the conditions are tested in order until the *first* True condition is found; then the statement sequence associated with it is executed and control passes beyond the **end if**. If a True condition is *not* found, the statement sequence associated with the **else** is executed; if there is no **else** (and consequently no such statement sequence), nothing is done; control passes beyond the **end if**.

We close this section with a few comments based on the examples we have seen. First, we have tried to follow the standard Ada format, whereby the words **if...elsif...else...end if** are aligned vertically, with their respective statement sequences being indented. This provides considerable help to the reader, by (1) showing the overall structure of the **if** statement, (2) clearly associating the statements of each statement sequence with one another, and (3) associating each statement sequence with its respective condition.

Second, it is clear that **else**, when used, must introduce the *last* statement sequence before the **end if**. As *LRM [5.3]* points out, **else** has the same effect as if we had put **elsif True then** in its place. Convince yourself that this observation is valid.

To sum up then, Figure 6.1.2 is a syntax diagram that includes all the forms of **if** statements we have described.

if statement

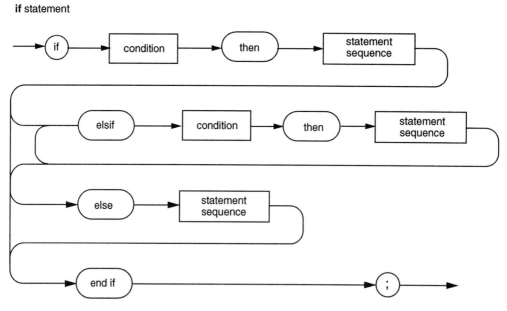

Figure 6.1.2

6.2 Overlapping and redundant conditions

In this section we discuss traps that novice programmers can fall into when using **if** statements involving several conditions. Consider the following:

```
if Temperature > 85 then
  Text_IO.Put_Line ("Too hot!");
end if;
if Temperature >= 60 then
  Text_IO.Put_Line ("Pleasant weather.");
end if;
if Temperature >= 40 then
  Text_IO.Put_Line ("Not bad.");
end if;
if Temperature < 40 then
  Text_IO.Put_Line ("Too cold!");
end if;
```

What will happen on a 90-degree day? The first three messages are displayed, since all four conditions are tested and (because of *overlap* in the temperature ranges) the first three of them are True. Suppose we amend this program fragment as follows:

```
if Temperature > 85 then
  Text_IO.Put_Line ("Too hot!");
end if;
if Temperature >= 60 and Temperature <= 85 then
  Text_IO.Put_Line ("Pleasant weather.");
end if;
if Temperature >= 40 and Temperature < 60 then
  Text_IO.Put_Line ("Not bad.");
end if;
if Temperature < 40 then
  Text_IO.Put_Line ("Too cold!");
end if;
```

We have cleared up the problem of *overlapping* temperature ranges: If the temperature is 90 degrees, the first condition is True and all the others False, and therefore only the *first* message is displayed, as desired. Similarly, if the temperature is 70 degrees, only the second condition is True, and only the *second* message is displayed; and so on. However, there is a lot of *redundant testing* of conditions here: If the first condition turns out to be True, why test all the others? Surely they must be False. If the first condition is False and the second is True, then in this case necessarily the ones that follow will be False. Proceeding in this fashion, we can see that *no more than* one condition can be True. Thus, there are *two* issues at stake here. The first is the inefficiency of the program: Execution time is wasted on the needless evaluation of Boolean expressions. Admittedly, in this case, it is trivial, and the time wasted is negligible. But what if a program construct like this one were to be executed repeatedly, perhaps thousands of times? In such a situation, the resulting waste of computing time could become significant. The second issue is that of *programming logic*. A good programmer would see to it, not only that the program executes correctly, as does the last program fragment shown above, but also that the logic of the program is "clean"— reasonably free of redundancy—and that it makes for easy readability. This is what we mean:

```
if Temperature > 85 then
  Text_IO.Put_Line ("Too hot!");
elsif Temperature >= 60 then
  Text_IO.Put_Line ("Pleasant weather.");
elsif Text_IO.Temperature >= 40 then
  Text_IO.Put_Line ("Not bad.");
```

```
else
  Text_IO.Put_Line ("Too cold!");
end if;
```

Here there is no problem of redundancy: If a condition has been found to be True, no subsequent conditions are evaluated. Nor is there a problem of overlap: If the *second* condition (Temperature >= 60) is tested at all, it is because the *first* condition has turned out False, and thus it has been established that we have Temperature <= 85. Similarly, if the *third* condition is tested, it has already been determined that Temperature < 60.

6.3 Time_and_Day revised: A 12-hour clock version

We now offer a revised version of the program Time_and_Day given in Figure 2.1.1. This new program allows us to show the time in terms of the more familiar 12-hour clock, rather than a 24-hour clock. In fact, we actually display the numbers in the form in which they would appear on a digital clock. Many digital clocks indicate whether the time of day is to be taken as a.m. or p.m. We do this much, and more, by displaying "midnight" or "noon," as well as "a.m." or "p.m.," in giving the time. This requires that we do a few more things in the computational and output sections of the program. We must determine which of these parts of the day to indicate in giving the time. Also, we have to see to it that the "p.m." hours are not given as numbers greater than 12. And (though we might be inclined to forget it) we must make sure that the first hour starting with midnight does not come out to be 0, as it would on a 24-hour clock. We want to make sure that the number of minutes is always displayed as a two-digit integer, even in cases where the tens digit is 0, as on a digital clock. Finally, we give the days of the week their proper names, Sunday through Saturday, rather than day 1 through day 7, as we did in Chapter 2. Making these adjustments requires the application of much that we have had to say about Boolean expressions and **if** statements.

To develop the program described, we again apply the method of top-down programming. First, we need a clear, accurate, and complete statement of the problem:

Problem statement. Write a program that first obtains as input an integer in the range from 0 to 10,079, representing the number of minutes that have elapsed since the beginning of the week; the program then computes and displays the day of the week and the time of day as it would appear on a 12-hour digital clock, indicating whether it is midnight, noon, a.m., or p.m.

To develop a Level 1 outline of this problem, we seek to sum up the task under three headings: (1) input, (2) processing, and (3) output. A moment's reflection should convince us that step 1 of the solution outline, whether in its original form or in any subsequent refinement, is exactly the same as for the Time_and_Day program of Section 2.1; hence we confine our attention to steps 2 and 3. At Level 1, these might appear as follows:

2.   Compute the numbers representing the day of the week and the time (hours and minutes) of that day. Adjust the number of hours as appropriate for indicating time on a 12-hour clock.

3. Using these results, display the time of day with the numbers appearing as on a digital clock, separated by a colon, and with an indication of the appropriate part of the day (midnight, noon, a.m., or p.m.); also, give the day of the week.

As in the first version, it would appear that step 3 is the easier of these two to analyze and refine. Accordingly, it would be well to deal with this one first. The task of refining this step amounts simply to spelling out more details of how the output is to be displayed.

3. Using these results, display the time of day as follows: the number of hours, a colon, the tens digit of the number of minutes, the units digit of this number. Then display an indication of the appropriate part of the day (midnight, noon, a.m., or p.m.), and give the day of the week.

This seems to sum up all the details of step 3. But a question arises: How is the program to "know" at this point which part of the day it is? After all, the hours from 13 to 23 —p.m. hours—have already been reduced by 12 and thus are the same as the morning hours from 1 to 11. The first hour following midnight now has the number 12, as does the first hour following noon. On the other hand, when the number of hours based on *24* is first computed in step 2 and no adjustments have yet been made for 12-hour time, it is easy to determine which part of the day it is. This suggests that it is precisely at this point of the program that we should make the determination and somehow *save* the resulting information for use in the output step.

2. Compute the number of hours and remaining minutes since midnight. Determine what part of the day it is, and, saving this information, adjust the number of hours as appropriate for indicating time on a 12-hour clock.

It is a simple matter to determine what part of the day it is, once the number of minutes since the beginning of the week has been converted to days, hours, and minutes. At midnight and noon, the number of hours is 0 and 12, respectively, with the number of minutes being 0. Any other combination of values with hours at least as big as 12 indicates a time after noon, and all other combinations of values indicate a time before noon. It is easy, then, to *determine* what part of the day it is; but once that is done, how may this information be *saved* for use in the output? One way of doing this is to declare a BOOLEAN variable for each of the parts of the day (Midnight, Noon, PM, AM), with all these variables initialized to False; subsequently, when the actual part of the day is determined, the variable corresponding to it is assigned the value True. When it comes time to do the output, these variables can be checked to find out which one is True and the appropriate indication can be displayed. (In fact, we can get away with using just *three* such BOOLEAN variables, rather than four; if none of the three is ever set to True when the program runs, then the corresponding three parts of the day have been ruled out and the remaining part of the day must be the appropriate one to indicate in the output.)

We can now go back and further refine step 2. Actually, the first computation will undergo the same refinement as it did in the development of Section 2.1. We have already discussed how to determine the part of the day and how to save this information in BOOLEAN variables. To adjust the time for a 12-hour clock, it suffices to recall that if the number of hours since midnight exceeds 12, it is necessary to subtract 12 from it; if, on the other hand, it has the value 0, then this value must be *changed* to 12. We leave you the exercise of summing up all this in a much-refined version of step 2, one that should be considerably closer to the final outline.

Recall that, in our earlier version of Time_and_Day, when we performed the computations to change Minutes_Elapsed into Minute, Day, and Hour, the value of the variable Day ran from 0 to 6, representing the number of complete days that had passed since the beginning of the week. In our original program, we changed these numbers to run from 1 to 7, respectively, indicating the "number" of the current day of the week. In the present program, however, we wish to display the *names* of the days of the week; thus, in each case, we must "convert" a number into a name. To do this, we can make good use of a conditional construction with several occurrences of **elsif**, to display the weekday name corresponding to each possible value of Day. Note that it is not necessary here to add 1 to the value of Day: If Day has the value 0, we can immediately display "Sunday"; if it has the value 1, we can display "Monday"; and so on. This is how we proceed.

In discussing the development of this program, we have used expressions like "determine the part of the day," "adjust the number of hours after midnight," and "check the part of the day for displaying output." It is precisely in carrying out these operations—as well as in displaying the day of the week—that several forms of **if** statements will be put to use. The final outline of steps 2 and 3 should include the details of how these **if** statements are to be constructed; indeed, it is right at this point that the substance of the programming problem and its solution are to be found.

Here is the problem solution in its fully-coded form.

```
with Text_IO, Int_IO;

procedure Time_and_Day is

    -- This program asks the user for an integer from 0 to 10079,
    -- representing the number of minutes that have elapsed since
    -- the beginning of the week.  It then determines and displays
    -- the time of day (as it would appear on a 12-hour digital
    -- clock) and the day of the week.

    -- Variable and constant declarations

    Minutes_Elapsed:      NATURAL;
    Hours_Elapsed:        NATURAL;
    Day, Hour, Minute:    NATURAL;
    Minutes_in_Hour:      constant INTEGER := 60;
    Hours_in_Day:         constant INTEGER := 24;

    Midnight:             BOOLEAN := False;
    Noon:                 BOOLEAN := False;
    PM:                   BOOLEAN := False;

begin

    -- INPUT
    -- Obtain the input (minutes elapsed since the week began)
```

```
Text_IO.New_Line;
Text_IO.Put ("How many minutes since the week began (0 to 10079)?  ");
Int_IO.Get (Minutes_Elapsed);
Text_IO.New_Line;

-- COMPUTATIONS
-- Determine the day of the week and the time (24-hour clock)
-- obtaining them in the order: minute, day, hour

Hours_Elapsed := Minutes_Elapsed  /  Minutes_in_Hour;
Minute       := Minutes_Elapsed rem Minutes_in_Hour;
Day          := Hours_Elapsed   /  Hours_in_Day;      -- 0 to 6
Hour         := Hours_Elapsed   rem Hours_in_Day;

-- Note whether midnight, noon, p.m. (or none of these), and
-- adjust Hours for a 12-hour clock

if Hour = 0 and Minute = 0 then
  Midnight := True;
  Hour := 12;
elsif Hour = 12 and Minute = 0 then
  Noon := True;
elsif Hour >= 12 then
  PM := True;
  if Hour > 12 then
    Hour := Hour - 12;        -- adjust hours from 1 p.m. on
  end if;
elsif Hour = 0 then
  Hour := 12;                 -- adjust hours from midnight to
end if;                       -- 1 a.m.

-- OUTPUT
-- Display the day and time in terms of this information

Text_IO.Put ("The time is ");
Int_IO.Put (Hour, 0);
Text_IO.Put (":");
Int_IO.Put (Minute/10, 0);    -- tens digit for Minute
Int_IO.Put (Minute rem 10, 0); -- units digit for Minute

if Midnight then
  Text_IO.Put (" midnight");
elsif Noon then
  Text_IO.Put (" noon");
elsif PM then
  Text_IO.Put (" p.m.");
else
  Text_IO.Put (" a.m.");
end if;
Text_IO.Put (" on ");
if Day = 0 then
  Text_IO.Put ("Sunday");
elsif Day = 1 then
  Text_IO.Put ("Monday");
elsif Day = 2 then
  Text_IO.Put ("Tuesday");
elsif Day = 3 then
  Text_IO.Put ("Wednesday");
elsif Day = 4 then
```

```
    Text_IO.Put ("Thursday");
  elsif Day = 5 then
    Text_IO.Put ("Friday");
  else
    Text_IO.Put ("Saturday");
  end if;
  Text_IO.Put (".");
  Text_IO.New_Line (2);

end Time_and_Day;
```

Figure 6.3.1

We show below a few sample "dialogues" that might take place when the program is run. We begin by repeating the inputs we gave in Figure 2.1.2, in order to show the corresponding output the revised version of the program produces.

```
How many minutes since the week began (0 to 10079)?   3670

The time is 1:10 p.m. on Tuesday.


How many minutes since the week began (0 to 10079)?   7595

The time is 6:35 a.m. on Friday.


How many minutes since the week began (0 to 10079)?   0

The time is 12:00 midnight on Sunday.


How many minutes since the week began (0 to 10079)?   10079

The time is 11:59 p.m. on Saturday.


How many minutes since the week began (0 to 10079)?   6479

The time is 11:59 a.m. on Thursday.


How many minutes since the week began (0 to 10079)?   6480

The time is 12:00 noon on Thursday.


How many minutes since the week began (0 to 10079)?   6481

The time is 12:01 p.m. on Thursday.
```

Figure 6.3.2

Observe the structure of the **if** statements within this program. In particular, notice that there is an **if** statement that is "nested" within the **elsif Hour >= 12 then** that occurs when the adjustments are made for a 12-hour clock. This is because although there is something we want to do whenever **Hour >= 12** (namely, set the BOOLEAN variable PM to True), we nevertheless do *not* want to subtract 12 from the value of Hours at that point unless this value is at least 13.

There is a final point to be noted about this program. We have made explicit use of the fact that the number of minutes to be displayed does not exceed two digits (it is, of course, less than 60). This allows us to obtain and separately display the tens digit and units digit of this number by finding the quotient and remainder when the number is divided by 10. As we have mentioned, the reason for doing this is to force a leading 0 to be displayed as the tens digit in the case of a number less than 10, as is done on a digital clock. Note that we do not have to compute these numbers and store them in variables in order to display them with the Put procedure; we may simply write expressions like Minutes / 10 and Minutes **rem** 10 inside the parentheses of Put.

6.4 A fundamental loop statement

One aspect that greatly enhances the usefulness of computers is their ability to carry out a sequence of operations repeatedly. It hardly need be pointed out that doing something over and over is very tedious for humans; hence those jobs that require repetition of this kind are especially suited to the computer's capababilities. Ada provides several programming constructs to accomplish **repetitive execution** of a statement sequence. These are all known as **loops**. We will study the various loop structures in Ada, considering some of the ways in which they may be applied.

Suppose we had a program containing several statements—*n* of them, say—to be executed repeatedly, as indicated in the following diagram, where the arrow indicates that, after statement_n is executed, execution is to begin again at statement_1:

```
 ┌──► statement_1;
 │    statement_2;
 │         .
 │         .
 │         .
 │    statement_n;
 └────┘
```

In the Ada language, this can be accomplished by means of a **loop** statement constructed as follows:

```
 ┌──►loop
 │    statement_1;
 │    statement_2;
 │         .
 │         .
 │         .
 │    statement_n;
 └─── end loop
```

Statements 1 through *n* are collectively referred to as the **body of the loop**. This **loop** statement has the structure shown in the syntax diagram of Figure 6.4.1.

loop statement

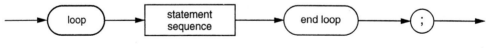

Figure 6.4.1

A simple loop to display successive positive integers might be written as follows (where we assume that K is an INTEGER variable and that Int_IO is available):

```
K := 1;
loop
   Int_IO.Put (K, 0);
   Text_IO.New_Line;
   K := K + 1;
end loop;
```

Here K is given an initial value of 1. When the program containing such a loop is run, the effect of the loop is to cause the value of K to be displayed, after which K is **incremented**; that is, its value is increased by 1. This value of K is then displayed, and K is incremented again, and so on repeatedly. Since nothing in the **loop** statement tells the computer to stop this process, the output and assignment statements are executed over and over until the value of K attempts to go beyond INTEGER'Last. At this point the Ada system signals that something has gone wrong and (in general) terminates not only the loop but the entire program containing it.

What is needed here, obviously, is some way of "taming" this loop and causing it to terminate execution under the control of the programmer. Ada has an **exit** statement that causes execution of the **loop** statement sequence to be abandoned, with control passing "beyond" the loop. Suppose we would like to display only the first 100 positive integers, say, followed by a brief message indicating that the job has been completed. Once again taking K to be an INTEGER variable, and assuming the availability of the necessary I/O routines, we could devise a loop in the form shown in Figure 6.4.2.

```
         .
         .
         .

         .
Text_IO.Put_Line ("First 100 positive integers:");
Text_IO.New_Line;
K := 1;
loop
   Int_IO.Put (K, 3);
   Text_IO.New_Line;
   if K = 100 then
     Text_IO.New_Line;
     Text_IO.Put_Line ("Job completed.");
     exit;
   end if;
   K := K + 1;
```

```
end loop;
Int_IO.Put (K, 0);
Text_IO.Put_Line (" integers displayed.");
    .
    .
    .
```

Figure 6.4.2

We have used an **if** statement containing an **exit** statement within its statement sequence:
When the condition of the **if** statement becomes True (K = 100), then the message, "Job
completed." is displayed and the **exit** is executed, causing control to pass immediately to the
Int_IO.Put (K, 0) statement following the loop (skipping over the assignment statement
K := K + 1 and leaving K unchanged with the value 100). The program displays the
message, "100 integers displayed." Figure 6.4.3 expresses the structure of this loop in general
terms.

```
loop
    <statement sequence>
    if <condition> then
       <statement sequence>
       exit;
    end if;
    <statement sequence>
end loop;
```

Figure 6.4.3

Any of the statement sequences indicated in Figure 6.4.3 may consist of one statement,
several statements, or no statements at all (an "empty" statement sequence). We offer another
example (Figure 6.4.4) of a loop which, when executed, displays the first 100 positive
integers followed by a concluding message; unlike the loop of Figure 6.4.2, this loop contains
no statement following the **end if**. Notice that this loop differs from that of Figure 6.4.2 in
respect to two properties: (1) K is initialized to 0, rather than 1; and (2) K is incremented at
the "top of the loop"—that is, the incrementing of K takes place at the *beginning* of the loop,
rather than at the end, as is done in the loop of Figure 6.4.2. As we will see, it is often
helpful to structure loops so that they have these two properties.

```
    .
    .
    .
Text_IO.Put_Line ("First 100 positive integers:);
Text_IO.New_Line;
K := 0;
loop
   K := K + 1;
   Int_IO.Put (K, 3);
   Text_IO.New_Line;
   if K = 100 then
     Text_IO.New_Line;
     Text_IO.Put_Line ("Job completed.");
     exit;
```

```
   end if;
 end loop;
 Int_IO.Put (K, 0);
 Text_IO.Put_Line (" integers displayed.");
   .
   .
   .
```

Figure 6.4.4

Now let us suppose that since we are quite capable of *observing* whether or not the integers from 1 to 100 have been displayed, we would like to *omit* the concluding message, "Job completed." Of course, this is very easy to do: We have only to take the program segment in Figure 6.4.2, or the one in Figure 6.4.4, and omit the Text_IO.New_Line statement and the Text_IO.Put_Line statement containing the concluding message. Rather than show the resulting adjustment of Figure 6.4.2 or 6.4.4, we show this modification in Figure 6.4.5 in terms of the general loop structure of Figure 6.4.3.

```
loop
  <statement sequence>
  if <condition> then
    exit;
  end if;
  <statement sequence>
end loop;
```

Figure 6.4.5

Notice the form that the conditional statement within the loop now takes:

```
if <condition> then
  exit;
end if;
```

As you might expect, this construct is very useful for controlling the termination of a loop: a condition is tested, and if it is True, control passes beyond the **end loop**; otherwise, control passes just beyond the **end if** and remains in the loop. The construct is so useful, in fact, that Ada provides a shorter way to program it, called a **conditional exit** statement, made up of the reserved words **exit when**, followed by a condition, as in Figure 6.4.6.

```
K := 1;
loop
  Int_IO.Put (K, 3);
  exit when K = 100;
  K := K + 1;
end loop;
```

Figure 6.4.6

When the **exit when** statement is encountered during execution, its condition is evaluated. If this condition is True, control passes beyond the loop; if it is False, control passes to the statement following the **exit when** statement. But suppose that in the body of the loop there is *no* statement following the conditional exit statement, as in Figure 6.4.7.

```
K := 0;
loop
  K := K + 1;
  Int_IO.Put (K, 3);
  exit when K = 100;
end loop;
```

Figure 6.4.7

In this case, as before, if the condition of the **exit when** is True, control passes *beyond* the loop; otherwise, since the body of the loop contains no statement after the conditional **exit** statement, control passes to the **end loop** and from there, as always, to the *beginning* of the **loop** statement.

A conditional **exit** statement may appear anywhere within a loop, as is made clear by Figure 6.4.5 and its "revised version," Figure 6.4.8, in which each of the indicated statement sequences may consist of one or more statements or of no statements at all.

```
loop
  <statement sequence>
  exit when <condition>
  <statement sequence>
end loop;
```

Figure 6.4.8

Figure 6.4.6 shows that we may sometimes use a conditional **exit** statement in the "middle" of a loop, as illustrated in the general structure of Figure 6.4.8. More often, we have occasion to use a loop in which the conditional **exit** statement is placed at the "bottom" of the loop, as was done in Figure 6.4.7. We show the general structure of such a loop in Figure 6.4.9. In a loop with this structure, the indicated statement sequence will be executed at least once (as is often desired) and *then* a test will be performed to see if it should continue.

```
loop
  <statement sequence>
  exit when <condition>
end loop;
```

Figure 6.4.9

The loop structure shown in Figure 6.4.9, in which the conditional exit occurs at the bottom of the loop, is useful if we want to have a program run repeatedly until the user signals a desire to stop. Thus, in the program Checkbook shown in Figure 4.4.1, we might wish to deal with *several* transactions, rather than just one, and have the new balance displayed after each transaction. We may do this by enclosing most of the program statements—all except those used to obtain the user's initial balance—in a loop; this loop is to execute repeatedly until the user indicates that execution should stop. How is the user to do this? In Figure 6.4.10 we illustrate one possible method, in which the computer "converses" with the user after each transaction has been processed.

```
    with Text_IO, Flt_IO;

procedure Checkbook is

    --  After establishing an initial balance, the procedure
    --  Checkbook requests and accepts an amount, interprets
    --  it as a deposit (> 0) or withdrawal (< 0), and
    --  calculates and displays the new account balance.

    --  If, in answer to an inquiry, the user indicates a desire
    --  to enter another transaction, Checkbook processes this
    --  transaction in terms of the balance resulting from the
    --  preceding transaction.  This continues until the user
    --  indicates there are no more transactions to be processed.

    Current_Balance:     FLOAT;
    Transaction:         FLOAT;
    New_Balance:         FLOAT;

    Answer:              CHARACTER;

begin
    Text_IO.Put ("Enter current checking account balance: ");
    Flt_IO.Get (New_Balance);
    Text_IO.New_Line;

    loop
      Current_Balance := New_Balance;

      Text_IO.Put_Line ("Enter the amount of this transaction");
      Text_IO.Put ("(deposits are positive, withdrawals are negative): ");

      Flt_IO.Get (Transaction);

      New_Balance := Current_Balance + Transaction;
      Text_IO.New_Line;
      Text_IO.Put ("The new account balance is ");
      Flt_IO.Put (New_Balance, 0, 2, 0);

      Text_IO.New_Line;
      Text_IO.Put_Line ("Another transaction (Y/N)? ");
      Text_IO.Get (Answer);
      Text_IO.New_Line (2);
      exit when Answer /= 'Y' and answer /= 'y';
    end loop;

    Text_IO.Put_Line ("Processing completed.");
    Text_IO.New_Line;

end Checkbook;
```

Figure 6.4.10

In this version of the Checkbook program, the user who wants to enter another transaction is allowed to type either a capital or a lowercase "Y" in response to the question, "Another transaction (Y/N)?" Furthermore, it is *not* necessary to type "N" (or "n") in order to exit from the loop and terminate the run of the program; any character other than "Y" and "y" will do. The program is written in this way so that, from the novice user's perspective, it is easier to get out of the program than to "get stuck" in it. Observe that the loop begins by assigning to Current_Balance the value of New_Balance, whether this value of New_Balance has come from the user's input (as happens when the program first begins execution) or whether (after the first pass through the loop) the value of New_Balance has been calculated in processing the previous transaction.

As another example, in the Time_and_Day program of Figure 6.3.1, we might have allowed the user to continue giving the program various inputs by declaring a CHARACTER variable Answer and including *all* of the statement part of the program in a loop as follows:

```
begin

   loop
      -- all of the program statements of Figure 6.3.1 go here
      Text_IO.New_Line;
      Text_IO.Put_Line ("Do you want to enter another number (Y/N)?   ");
      Text_IO.Get (Answer);
      Text_IO.New_Line (2);
      exit when Answer /= 'Y' and Answer /= 'y';
      end loop;

end Time_and_Day;
```

Figure 6.4.11

In Figures 6.4.10 and 6.4.11, we could let Answer be an INTEGER variable, rather than a CHARACTER variable, and simply direct the user to enter 1 as an affirmative response and 0 as a negative response to the question about continuing with further inputs. Then the conditional **exit** statement would take the simple form:

```
   exit when Answer /= 1;
```

However, there are at least two reasons for using CHARACTER input instead: (1) It seems more natural to answer a yes-or-no question with "Y" or "N" than with a number and (2) obtaining INTEGER input requires the availability of Int_IO (note that, as it stands, the program of Figure 6.4.10 does not include this package); in contrast, the input of a CHARACTER value requires only Text_IO, which is already available to both programs.

6.5 An iteration scheme: *while* loops

In the preceding section, we saw examples illustrating the Ada construct known as a loop, which brings about repetitive execution of a sequence of statements (the body of the loop). Starting with Figure 6.4.2, our examples showed various ways of using Ada's **exit** and **exit when** statements so as to make the execution of a loop terminate under the programmer's control. There is something that all these examples have in common: At some point in the body of the loop, a condition is tested (evaluated), and depending upon the resulting BOOLEAN value, control either passes immediately beyond the loop or passes to the next statement within the loop (if there *is* a further statement in the loop; if not, control passes to the **end loop** and then to the beginning of the **loop** statement). We saw several examples in which the testing of a condition of this sort took place in the middle of the loop body (Figures 6.4.2 and 6.4.6), and several in which this testing occurred at the bottom of the loop (Figures 6.4.4, 6.4.7, 6.4.10, and 6.4.11). As you might expect, there are important cases in which a condition is tested at the "top" of a loop, to determine whether or not an exit from the loop is to take place at that point. Of course, if the condition is found to be True right away, the first time a test is performed, then the exit occurs immediately, and the remaining statements of the loop body are not executed at all. In terms of a conditional **exit** statement, such a loop construct could be described as in Figure 6.5.1.

```
loop
  exit when <condition>
  <statement sequence>
end loop;
```

Figure 6.5.1

We illustrate the loop structure of Figure 6.5.1 by writing a few lines of Ada code to obtain a POSITIVE integer K from the keyboard, display its square, and display the squares of all succeeding integers as long as these squares do not exceed 5000. We assume that K and Square have been declared to be POSITIVE variables, and we use Int_IO for I/O. Observe that if the user enters 100, say, there is no output, for the square of 100 is 10,000, a number that exceeds 5000; thus the exit from the loop would occur immediately. On the other hand, if there *is* output (for example, if the user enters 10), then it is not evident in advance how many numbers will be displayed or what the largest of them will be. Of course we could figure this out, but the point is that there is no need to do so.

```
Int_IO.Get (K);
Square := K ** 2;
loop
  exit when Square > 5000;
  Int_IO.Put (Square, 4);
  Text_IO.New_Line;
  K := K + 1;
  Square := K ** 2;
end loop;
```

Figure 6.5.2

We now introduce an Ada loop construct that, like the loops shown in Figures 6.5.1 and 6.5.2, tests a condition for exit *before* executing any of the statements in the body of the loop (thus, at the "top" of the loop). However, unlike these examples which contain a condition for an *exit* from the loop, this construct, known as a **while** loop, contains the *opposite*, namely, a condition for remaining in the loop and continuing to execute its statement sequence. In Figure 6.5.3 we show a **while** loop that has the same effect as the loop of Figure 6.5.2.

```
Int_IO.Get (K);
Square := K ** 2;
while Square <= 5000 loop
   Int_IO.Put (Square, 4);
   Text_IO.New_Line;
   K := K + 1;
   Square := K ** 2;
end loop;
```

Figure 6.5.3

Here, the exit condition that appears in Figure 6.5.2 (Square > 5000) has been replaced by the opposite condition (what we might call the "do *not* exit" or "remain in the loop" condition) Square <= 5000, which has the same meaning as **not** (Square > 5000).

The general form of a **while** loop is the following:

```
while <condition> loop
   <statement sequence>
end loop;
```

The syntax diagram for a **while** loop is shown in Figure 6.5.4.

while loop statement

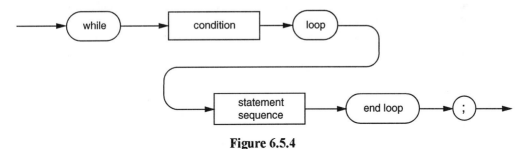

Figure 6.5.4

In a **while** loop, the controlling condition of the loop is built into the loop structure itself. The construct

```
while <condition>
```

is known in Ada as an **iteration scheme**: It is a *scheme* (programming device) that controls the *iteration* (repetition) of the loop. This is how the computer deals with a **while** loop:

1.   The condition is tested (evaluated).

2.   a.   If the condition is False, control passes beyond the loop.
       b.   If the condition is True, the statement sequence in the loop is executed, and then steps 1 and 2 are repeated.

Thus, the first time that the condition is found to be False, the statement sequence is skipped over and control passes beyond the loop.

What we have just said, in effect, is that the statement sequence of the loop will keep executing, *as long as*—that is, *while*—the condition remains True (and if the condition is not False to begin with). Clearly, if the loop is to terminate under the programmer's control, there must be some statement or statements within the loop that will ultimately cause the condition to become False. In the program of Figure 6.5.3, K and Square have been properly initialized before they are used. Furthermore, in each execution of the loop body, the value of Square, which appears in the loop condition (of the iteration scheme), is "updated" in such a way that this condition eventually becomes False, and execution of the loop terminates.

What happens if the condition of a **while** loop is *never* True but is found to be False the very first time the loop is encountered in the run of the program? The answer is simple: The statement sequence of the loop is not executed at all; the computer will simply continue execution beyond the loop. (We considered a similar situation in our discussion of the loop construct of Figures 6.5.1 and 6.5.2.) Often enough, this is just what we want. Check to see that this is consistent with the general description of the behavior of a **while** loop, as given earlier. A typical instance of this kind of behavior might occur if a **while** loop is used to read in data items as input and keep a count of how many items have been read. As a trivial example, Figure 6.5.5 shows a portion of a program that reads and counts nonnegative integers entered as input; it stops counting when the user enters a *negative* integer. This negative integer is not part of the "ordinary" input of the program; its function is to signal that the user has finished entering nonnegative integers and that accordingly the counting is to stop. (Convince yourself that this negative integer will not itself be counted.) A value used to signal the end of input in this way is called an **end-value**, a **terminating value**, or a **terminator**; some would call it a "sentinel," but we prefer to reserve this term for a different use, to be described in Section 10.8. Besides Int_IO, we need the declarations

```
Number:          INTEGER;
Number_Count:    NATURAL;
```

Figure 6.5.5 is a sketch of the program's statement part.

```
begin

  Number_Count := 0;
  Int_IO.Get (Number);
  while Number >= 0 loop
    Number_Count := Number_Count + 1;
      -- Other processing (for example,
      -- adding the inputs) may take place here
    Int_IO.Get (Number);
  end loop;
    -- Possible further processing

end;
```

Figure 6.5.5

Verify that this program performs properly if the user enters *several* nonnegative integers, or just *one* such integer, followed by the terminating negative integer. The program also performs properly if the user enters *no* nonnegative integers for processing but simply inputs a negative integer at the outset to indicate that there are no "further" nonnegative integers to be entered (in fact, there were none at all). Under these circumstances, the body of the **while** loop will not be executed even once—and in particular, Number_Count will be left at its initial value of 0.

At this point we pause to state the cardinal principle of programming with loops: Make sure that execution of the loop will terminate. Since the condition in the iteration scheme of a **while** loop usually involves one or more variables, as does the condition in an **exit when** statement, it is up to the programmer to see to it not only that these variables are properly initialized but also that they are updated in successive executions of the loop. For this reason, it may be helpful to reflect on some loop-handling techniques that occur frequently in programming.

First, you may have noticed that in many of the examples we have seen, the body of the loop contains the assignment statement

```
K := K + 1;
```

whose purpose is to set the value of K to that of the "next" integer to be processed. The assumption here is that we have a loop that processes integers and that we wish to process *successive* integers in *increasing* order, as is very frequently the case. However, there are times when in processing integers we wish to do otherwise. For example, the program segment of Figure 6.4.2 could easily be modified to display only the *even* positive integers up to 100, rather than all the positive integers in this span—we have only to initialize K to 2, rather than 1, and replace the assignment statement in the body of the loop by

```
K := K + 2;
```

Thus, the loop will proceed "by twos," displaying only every *other* integer—that is, only the *even* integers—starting with 2 and ending with 100. Alternatively, we could use these same ideas to write a **while** loop to accomplish our purpose, as shown in Figure 6.5.6.

```
K := 2;
while K <= 100 loop
  Int_IO.Put (K, 3);
  Text_IO.New_Line;
  K := K + 2;
end loop;
```

Figure 6.5.6

On the other hand, we may want to process integers in *decreasing* order, rather than in increasing order, as we have been doing up to now. Suppose we want to be able to display any nonnegative integer up to 9999 in *four-digit* form, even if this means displaying leading zeros (ID numbers and serial numbers are often displayed with a fixed number of digits). Thus, for example, 3 is to appear as 0003, 76 as 0076, 508 as 0508, and 1492 as 1492. To accomplish this, we may first obtain and display the thousands digit of the given number—

1492, say—by dividing the number by 1000 (integer division): This yields the digit 1 (= 1492 / 1000). We then replace the original number by 492 (= 1492 **rem** 1000). Next, we obtain and display the hundreds digit of this number by dividing it by 100: The digit is 4 (= 492 / 100); and we replace 492 by 92 (= 492 **rem** 100). Now we obtain and display the tens digit of 92 by dividing 92 by 10: We obtain the digit 9 (= 92 / 10); and we replace 92 by 2 (= 92 **rem** 10). The resulting number is the units digit of the original number, and we have only to display it to complete the job. If we reflect on this process, we see that we have repeatedly applied the / and **rem** operators with powers of 10 that decrease from 3 to 1. Thus, we could program the entire process in terms of a **while** loop by initializing a variable K to 3 (which is 1 less than the number of digits to be displayed) and then *decrementing* (decreasing) the value of K by 1 on each pass through the loop, as shown in the program segment of Figure 6.5.7, where we assume that Int_IO has been made available to the program.

```
      .
      .
      .
Number, I:        NATURAL;
Num_Digits:       constant POSITIVE := 4;
      .
      .
      .
begin
      .
      .
      .
  Int_IO.Get (Number);
  K := Num_Digits - 1;
  while K > 0 loop
     Int_IO.Put (Number/10**K, 0);
     Number := Number rem 10**K;
     K := K - 1;
  end loop;
  Int_IO.Put (Number, 0);        -- display the units digit
  Text_IO.New_Line;
      .
      .
      .
```

Figure 6.5.7

Of course, the value of the constant Num_Digits could be changed to display numbers of various widths; however, we must be careful that we do not attempt to process any numbers greater than our Ada system's value of INTEGER'Last.

Can a **while** loop contain an **exit** statement? It can; but, in general, it is considered good programming practice (with regard to structure and clarity) to allow only *one* exit point in such a loop. A **while** loop already has a "built-in" exit point at the top of the loop, where the condition is tested and a decision is made whether to exit from the loop or repeat execution of its statement sequence. Thus, if a programmer chooses to use a **while** loop, it is normally best to construct it in such a way that execution of the loop terminates only at this point.

We conclude our discussion of **while** loops by repeating a point that we made in introducing this kind of loop; namely, a **while** loop is equivalent to the loop construct shown in Figure 6.5.1, in which a conditional **exit** statement occurs at the beginning of the loop body. Thus, any **while** loop

```
while <condition> loop
   <statement sequence>
end loop;
```

may be replaced by the following loop structure, in which the same condition is preceded by the logical operator **not**:

```
loop
   exit when not <condition>
   <statement sequence>
end loop;
```

In turn, this can be programmed as shown in Figure 6.5.8.

```
loop
   if not <condition> then
      exit;
   end if;
   <statement sequence>
end loop;
```

Figure 6.5.8

We see then that, given the availability of the **if** statement, the **exit** statement, and the **loop...end loop** construct, there is really no need of having **while** loops at all. However, as commonly happens in programming languages, we are offered a way of replacing a cumbersome programming construction (in this case, Figure 6.5.8) with a far simpler one (the **while** loop), to serve the interests of programming ease and program readability.

6.6 Another iteration scheme: *for* loops with ranges

Let us review briefly what we know about loops so far. In most of the examples of both **loop...end loop** and **while <condition> loop...end loop** constructions that we have seen, there are four fundamental activities that normally take place.

1. A variable (say, K) is *assigned* an initial value.

2. A statement sequence is *executed.*

3. The value of the variable is *adjusted.*

4. The current value of the variable is *tested,* and based on the outcome of that test, the loop is reexecuted or terminated.

Activity 1 must take place first, of course. The remaining activities can take place *in any order*, and we have already seen examples of most of the possible orderings. But for the moment we wish to focus our attention on just the *testing* of the variable that "controls" the loop. There are really two distinguishable cases (with some variations), shown in Figure 6.6.1.

```
a    <beginning-of-loop>          b    <beginning-of-loop>
        <test variable>                  <execute statements>
        <execute statements>             <adjust variable>
        <adjust variable>                <test variable>
     <end-of-loop>                    <end-of-loop>
```

Figure 6.6.1

In Figure 6.6.1 *a*, the variable value is tested at the very beginning of the loop; execution of the loop body takes place or control passes to the statement immediately following the loop, depending on the result of that test. Any loop having the form shown in Figure 6.5.1 is of this kind; and we have already noted that *every* **while** loop conforms to this scheme. A loop with this general structure, in which the test is made at the beginning of the loop, prior to the execution of any loop instructions, is called a **pretest loop**. Any loop having the structure shown in Figure 6.6.1 *b* is called a **posttest loop**; examples are found in Figures 6.4.7, 6.4.9, and 6.4.10.

Because the situation occurs so frequently, we single out for special attention a class of pretest loops in which the loop-controlling variable is assigned some *integer* value and then takes on *all* of the integer values in some *range*. The general structure of such a loop is shown in Figure 6.6.2.

```
K := <initial-value>
while K <= <ending-value> loop
  <statement sequence>
  K := K + 1;
end loop;
```

Figure 6.6.2

As a simple example, consider the loop in Figure 6.6.3 that displays the integers from 1 to 100, followed by the message, "Job completed."

```
K := 1;
while K <= 100 loop
  Int_IO.Put (K,3);
  Text_IO.New_Line;
  K := K + 1;
end loop;
Text_IO.New_Line;
Text_IO.Put ("Job completed.");
```

Figure 6.6.3

When a loop has these characteristics, Ada allows us to program it in terms of a special construct that is very convenient to use, inasmuch as it automatically takes care of the initializing and updating involved in controlling the loop. This is the **for** loop. Figure 6.6.4 is the construction of Figure 6.6.3 written as a **for** loop.

```
for K in INTEGER range 1..100 loop
   Int_IO.Put (K, 3);
   Text_IO.New_Line;
end loop;
Text_IO.New_Line;
Text_IO.Put_Line ("Job completed.");
```

Figure 6.6.4

Recall that, in the case of a **while** loop, the construct

```
while <condition>
```

is called an iteration scheme. A **for** loop also has an iteration scheme; in the loop of Figure 6.6.4 it is

```
for K in INTEGER range 1..100
```

where the identifier K designates the **loop parameter** of the **for** loop. In several regards the loop parameter behaves in a fashion so unlike the variables we have been creating (declaring) and using so far, that you will probably find it somewhat peculiar at first. Some of its properties are discussed in Section 6.8; in the meantime, we note that its special features are:

1. It *comes into existence* at the beginning of the loop and *ceases to exist* when execution of the loop is finished.

2. It can never be referred to in the program except within the loop.

3. No value may be assigned to it (by an assignment or input statement), although, as this example illustrates, it may be used as the parameter of an output procedure— more generally, it may be used in an expression.

Note that, because of properties 1 and 2, we did not insert the statements

```
Int_IO.Put (K, 0);
Text_IO.Put_Line (" integers displayed.");
```

after the loop of Figure 6.6.4, as was done in Figures 6.4.2 and 6.4.4. In Figure 6.6.4, K is a *loop parameter*, not a variable, and it cannot be referred to outside the loop.

The loop parameter K need not—and in fact *may* not—be declared in the declaration section of the program. Ada does allow the program to have a declaration of a variable K in the program's declaration section; however, you may find it strange to learn that this declared variable would be regarded as a *different* entity from the loop parameter K. In this case, any mention of K *outside* the loop would refer to the declared variable K, whereas *inside* the loop, it would refer to the loop parameter K.

In the example above, the **range** of the loop is specified by **INTEGER range 1..100**, which implicitly designates a *range subtype* of INTEGER values from 1 to 100, inclusive. When the loop is encountered, the system sets K to the first (lowest) value of the range; and the statement sequence of the loop is executed; K is then given the next value in the range and the statement sequence is executed again. This process continues until the statement sequence has been executed with K holding the last (highest) value in the range. Execution of the loop is then complete, and control passes beyond it in the program.

It is important to know that **for** loops are *pre*test loops, and in fact they adhere precisely to the scheme of Figure 6.6.1 *a*. As we already know, a **while** loop is also a pretest loop, and because of this there are circumstances in which the body of a **while** loop will not be executed at all, namely, if the test condition is *initially* false. Can a **for** loop fail to execute in the same fashion, that is, because some initial configuration causes the pretesting to terminate the loop immediately? Yes, although the situation is a little more contrived here, since the range of values would have to be *empty*! Although we would probably never write anything such as

```
for K in INTEGER range 27..15 loop
```

we might very well write

```
for K in INTEGER range L..M loop
```

where the integer variables L and M control the range of the loop. It is not inconceivable that in some circumstances, we would find L > M.

Ranges of **for** loops may consist of successive values of type CHARACTER, as well as of integer types (and of other types also, as we will see). This is because corresponding to the notion of the next *integer* in the loop range 1..100 (Figure 6.3.1), there is the next *character* in the range of a loop

```
for Ch in CHARACTER range 'A'..'Z' loop
  Text_IO.Put (Ch);
end loop;
```

which produces the output

```
ABCDEFGHIJKLMNOPQRSTUVWXYZ
```

In Figure 5.6.1 we explicitly declared the CHARACTER subtype CAPITAL as

```
subtype CAPITAL is CHARACTER range 'A'..'Z';
```

This provides us with a range (subtype) to which we have explicitly given the name CAPITAL; and we may use this name to designate the range of a **for** loop:

```
for Ch in CAPITAL loop
   Text_IO.Put (Ch);
end loop;
```

Similarly, having declared (Figure 5.6.1)

```
subtype HUNDRED is INTEGER range 1..100;
```

we may write the **for** loop of Figure 6.6.4 in the form

```
for K in HUNDRED loop
   Int_IO.Put (K, 3);
   Text_IO.New_Line;
end loop;
```

Ranges of **for** loops may be specified in various ways. Frequently, one or both of the values at the "ends" of the ranges are variables or other expressions, rather than literals or constants. We might have

```
for Index in INTEGER range Start..Finish loop
```

where Start and Finish are variables that have been assigned values before the execution of this loop. (See Exercise 6.6.4.) We should note that if Start and Finish have the same value, then the statements in the loop will be executed exactly once. If Start > Finish, then the loop range is said to be **empty**, and the loop's statement sequence will not be executed at all; this might occur if we want the body of a loop to be executed Count times, according to some previously-established value of the variable Count:

```
for K in NATURAL range 1..Count loop
   <statement sequence>
end loop;
```

In case Count has been assigned the value 0, the statements in the body of the loop are executed 0 times (that is, they are not executed at all); thus, as desired, the statements are executed Count times for *any* nonnegative value of Count, even 0.

In Figure 6.5.7 we saw an instance of a **while** loop in which a variable K was initialized to 3 and then the body of the loop was executed with K holding the successive values 3, 2, and 1; termination of the loop occurred when K was given the value 0. In a similar fashion, we may cause a **for** loop to start at the high end of its range and proceed downward through the range values until it has covered all these values. This is done by using the reserved word **reverse**, as follows:

```
for K in reverse INTEGER range 1..100 loop
```

or

```
for K in reverse HUNDRED loop
```

Thus, the program segment of Figure 6.5.7 could be written in terms of a **for** loop, as in Figure 6.6.5:

```
Int_IO.Get (Number);
for K in reverse INTEGER range 1..Num_Digits-1 loop
  Int_IO.Put (Number/10**K, 0);
  Number := Number rem 10**K;
end loop;
Int_.IO.Put (Number, 0); -- display the units digit
```

Figure 6.6.5

In the case of the base type CHARACTER, the loop

```
for Ch in reverse CHARACTER range 'A'..'Z' loop
    Text_IO.Put (Ch);
end loop;
```

will display

```
ZYXWVUTSRQPONMLKJIHGFEDCBA
```

Notice that the range is written in the "usual" way, with the low value at the left and the high value at the right. If we were to write the iteration scheme as

```
for K in INTEGER range 100..1 loop
```
or
```
for K in reverse INTEGER range 100..1 loop
```

we would have, in each case, an empty range, and the body of the loop would not be executed at all.

Is it possible to make a **for** loop proceed over a range of integers "by twos," with the loop parameter taking on every other value in the range, as was done in the **while** loop of Figure 6.5.6? It is *not*, and the reason for this is that in updating the loop parameter K at the bottom of a **for** loop, the Ada system does not formally replace the current value of K by the *sum* K + 1; rather, it makes use of the *attribute* Succ (Section 5.5) and replaces K by INTEGER'Succ (K). Of course, INTEGER'Succ (K) has the same value as K + 1, but consider the loop

```
for Ch in CHARACTER range 'A'..'Z' loop
  Text_IO.Put (Ch);
end loop;
```

It would make no sense to speak of replacing the current value of Ch by Ch + 1 at the bottom of the loop; what is done is to replace the value of Ch by that of CHARACTER'Succ (Ch). And this is true in general: In executing a **for** loop, the Ada system applies the Succ attribute to the loop parameter—or in the case of a **for** loop constructed with the reserved word **reverse**, the Pred attribute is used to "step through" the loop. Thus, we can readily conclude that a loop parameter is never of type FLOAT (why?).

Sometimes **for** loops are called **count-controlled loops**, because unless we use a conditional exit within the loop, the number of times the loop's statement sequence is to be executed must be specified in advance (at least implicitly) by stating the beginning and end of the loop range. We could not, for example, use a "pure" **for** loop (without an **exit** statement) to compute and display the squares of successive positive integers whose squares are less than 5000, as we did using the other kinds of loops. The reason is that we do not know in advance what loop range to use—or, equivalently, how many times to execute the statement sequence of the loop. We could cling to the convenience of the **for** loop by "overestimating" the upper end of the range and using a conditional **exit** statement, as follows (where N and Square are declared to be POSITIVE variables):

```
Int_IO.Get (N);
for K in INTEGER range N..100 loop
  Square := K ** 2;
  exit when Square > 5000;
  Int_IO.Put (Square);
  Text_IO.New_Line;
end loop;
```

Many professional programmers, however, would regard this as clumsy and lacking in the stylistic naturalness and elegance that the other, more versatile kinds of loops afford in such a case. Furthermore, just as we noted in the case of a **while** loop—and for the same reasons—it is generally undesirable to include an **exit** or conditional **exit** statement in the body of a **for** loop.

Figure 6.6.6 shows a syntax diagram for the **for** loop statement in Ada.

for loop statement

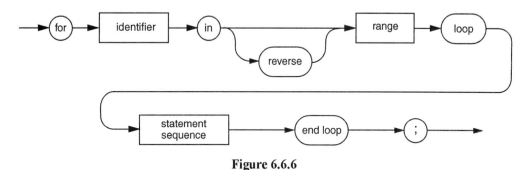

Figure 6.6.6

We sum up this presentation of loop structures by offering four simple loops that compute the sum of the integers from 1 to 10. With each of them we include the declaration

```
Sum:    NATURAL := 0;
```

and with the first two we also include the declaration

```
K:      POSITIVE := 1;
```

Be sure that you understand all the differences between the *variable* K in the first two examples and the *loop parameter* K in the second two shown in Figure 6.6.7.

```
a    loop
        Sum := Sum + K;
        K := K + 1;
        exit when K > 10;
     end loop;


b    while K <= 10 loop
        Sum := Sum + K;
        K := K + 1;
     end loop;


c    for K in INTEGER range 1..10 loop
        Sum := Sum + K;
     end loop;


d    for K in reverse INTEGER range 1..10 loop
        Sum := Sum + K;
     end loop;
```

Figure 6.6.7

6.7 Nested loops and named loops

Consider a situation in which the students in all sections of a college course are given the opportunity to take an optional makeup examination to raise their grades. There are several class sections of this course, and the examination is offered to the students in all of them, with the understanding that no student is obliged to take the examination—presumably some students will be content with the grades they have already achieved. Now we wish to write a program to compute and display the class-section average on this examination for *each* section of the course. To accomplish this, the program will inquire how many class sections there are for the course and then will use this number Num_Sections (in a **for** loop) in computing and displaying the needed information for all the sections. The program segment of Figure 6.7.1, which presupposes the declarations

```
Num_Sections:        NATURAL;
Average:             FLOAT;
```

indicates how this might be done:

```
Text_IO.Put ("How many course sections?  ");
Int_IO.Get (Num_Sections);

for Section_Number in INTEGER range 1..Num_Sections loop

   -- Obtain (from input), count, add the grades for the section with
   -- this section_number, and compute the average for the section.
```

```
      Text_IO.Put ("Average for section ");
      Int_IO.Put (Section_Number, 0);
      Text_IO.Put (":  ");
      Flt_IO.Put (Average, 0, 1, 0);
      Text_IO.New_Line (2);
   end loop;
```

Figure 6.7.1

For any *one* section, the grades are entered from the keyboard, and the computer keeps track of the sum of the grades, along with a count of how many grades have been entered; the average for this section is then computed as the sum divided by the count. Recall that since the examination is optional, it is quite possible that, in a given section, *no* students at all took the examination, and consequently the grade count for that section is 0; to indicate this, the section is assigned a fictitious average of −1.0. To compute the grade sum and grade count (and hence the value of Average) for any individual section, we may initialize the variables Grade_Sum and Grade_Count to 0 and then ask the user to enter the grades for this section, ending the input with a negative integer. As each grade is entered, the Grade_Count is incremented by 1, and Grade is added to Grade_Sum, imitating the method shown in Figure 6.5.5. We include the further declarations

```
   Grade:                     INTEGER;
   Grade_Count, Grade_Sum:    NATURAL;
```

The code to obtain (from input), count, and add the grades for the section with a particular Section_Number and to compute the average for the section is shown in Figure 6.7.2.

```
   Grade_Count := 0;
   Grade_Sum := 0;
   Text_IO.Put ("Enter the grades for section ");
   Int_IO.Put (Section_Number, 0);
   Text_IO.Put_Line ("; then enter a negative integer:");
   Int_IO.Get (Grade);

   while Grade >= 0 loop
     Grade_Count := Grade_Count + 1;
     Grade_Sum := Grade_Sum + Grade;
     Int_IO.Get (Grade);
   end loop;

   if Grade_Count /= 0 then
     Average := FLOAT (Grade_Sum) / FLOAT (Grade_Count);
   else
     Average := -1.0;      -- indicates no grades were averaged
   end if;
```

Figure 6.7.2

We have only to insert this code in place of the comment in Figure 6.7.1, in order to obtain the programming we need to achieve our purpose; we show this in Figure 6.7.3.

```
Text_IO.Put ("How many course sections?  ");
Int_IO.Get (Num_Sections);

for Section_Number in INTEGER range 1..Num_Sections loop
  Grade_Count := 0;
  Grade_Sum := 0;
  Text_IO.Put ("Enter the grades for section ");
  Int_IO.Put (Section_Number);
  Text_IO.Put_Line ("; then enter a negative integer:");
  Int_IO.Get (Grade);

  while Grade >= 0 loop
    Grade_Count := Grade_Count + 1;
    Grade_Sum := Grade_Sum + Grade;
    Int_IO.Get (Grade);
  end loop;

  if Grade_Count /= 0 then
    Average := FLOAT (Grade_Sum) / FLOAT (Grade_Count);
  else
    Average := -1.0;    -- indicates no grades were averaged
  end if;

  Text_IO.Put ("Average for section ");
  Int_IO.Put (Section_Number);
  Text_IO.Put (":  ");
  Flt_IO.Put (Average, 0, 1, 0);
  Text_IO.New_Line (2);
end loop;
```

Figure 6.7.3

Notice that in Figure 6.7.3 the body of the **for** loop contains a **while** loop; the program segment has assumed the form shown in Figure 6.7.4.

```
<statement sequence>
for Section_Number in <range> loop
  <statement sequence>

  while <condition> loop
    <statement sequence>
  end loop;

  <statement sequence>
end loop;
```

Figure 6.7.4

Here, the "outer" **for** loop contains a loop statement (the "inner" **while** loop) among the statements of its body. The inner loop is said to be **nested** within the outer loop. Nested loops are a common occurrence in programming, and we have chosen to introduce them with this example in which a **while** loop is nested inside a **for** loop. Some further comments are necessary:

1. In a nested loops construction, the inner and outer loops may each be *any* of the three kinds of loop structures: **for** loop, **while** loop, or loop without an iteration scheme.

2. The inner loop may occur at any point within the body of the outer loop; in particular, it may be at the beginning or end of this loop body;

3. Loops may be nested to levels greater than two; that is, we may have an outer loop containing an inner loop which itself has a loop nested within it, and so on to "deeper" levels of nesting.

4. Loops may not "overlap"; given any two loops, either we have one loop nested inside the other—totally contained within the body of the outer loop—or else one loop ends before the other begins.

Matters can become somewhat complicated when we are dealing with more than two loops. As we have just noted, a loop that is nested within an enclosing loop may itself have a loop nested within it as part of its own loop body. We show this schematically in Figure 6.7.5, displaying each loop as a loop without an iteration scheme, although each may be *any* kind of loop.

```
loop
   <statement sequence>
   loop
     <statement sequence>
     loop
        <statement sequence>
     end loop;
     <statement sequence>
   end loop;
   <statement sequence>
end loop;
```

Figure 6.7.5

Also, a loop may contain several *successive* loop statements nested within it, as shown in Figure 6.7.6.

```
loop
   <statement sequence>
   loop
     <statement sequence>
   end loop;
   <statement sequence>
   loop
     <statement sequence>
   end loop;
   <statement sequence>
end loop;
```

Figure 6.7.6

Nested loops and consecutive loops can be put together in various ways, and when there are four or more loops involved, it may become a challenge (for the programmer, not the computer) to keep track of them. In particular, it may become difficult to determine just which loop is ending when we encounter an **end loop** in a program. Ada has a way of assisting us in this situation; we are allowed to *name* loops with an identifier. We offer a simple example to illustrate the naming of loops; then we reflect on how loop naming can be helpful. We assume that K and Sum have been declared to be of type NATURAL and have been initialized to 0:

```
Summation:
loop
   K := K + 1;
   Sum := Sum + K;
   exit when K = 10:
end loop Summation;
```

Summation is a programmer-devised identifier. Notice that it is followed by a *colon* (not a semicolon) and placed immediately ahead of the loop statement. If a loop has been named, then the name *must* be included after **end loop**, as above. It *may* also be included in the **exit** or conditional **exit** statement (if the loop has one), in the form

```
if K = 10 then
   <statement sequence>
   exit Summation;
end if;
```

or

```
exit Summation when K = 10;
```

As we have remarked above, it is in situations where loop nesting becomes somewhat complex that the naming of loops is helpful, especially since the repetition of a loop name following the otherwise unrevealing **end loop** enables the reader to see easily just which loop is ending. For an example, consider the statements of Figure 6.7.3 to be part of a program that will run repeatedly (to accommodate several sets of data), as long as the user enters the CHARACTER value 'Y' or 'y' to answer an inquiry about continuing, as in Figures 6.4.10 and 6.4.11. The structure of the resulting program is shown in Figure 6.7.7.

```
begin

   Repeat_Program:
   loop

      Text_IO.Put ("How many course sections?  ");
      Int_IO.Get (Num_Sections);

      Section_Averages:
      for Section_Number in INTEGER range 1..Num_Sections loop
         .
         .
         .
```

```
        while Grade >= 0 loop
            .
            .
            .
        end loop;
        .
        .
        .
    end loop Section_Averages;

    Text_IO.Put_Line ("Another set of course sections (Y/N)?   ");
    Int_IO.Get (Answer);
    Text_IO.New_Line (2);
    exit Repeat_Program when Answer /= 'Y' and Answer /= 'y';
  end loop Repeat_Program;

end;
```

Figure 6.7.7

In Figure 6.7.7 we have named the outer two loops and left the innermost one unnamed because of its brevity, since it is easy to perceive this loop as a whole. In keeping with the idea illustrated in Figures 6.4.10 and 6.4.11, we have placed a conditional **exit** statement at the bottom of the loop Repeat_Program and made use of the option to include the name of the loop in this statement. If, however, we had omitted the name of the loop, the effect of this conditional **exit** statement would have been the same.

What would be the effect of putting an **exit** or conditional **exit** statement in the innermost loop? Consider the case in which the input of a grade greater than 100 causes a conditional **exit** statement to be executed, as in Figure 6.7.8. (Admittedly, the presence of such a statement inside a **while** loop violates the general principle of avoiding multiple exit points in a loop; however, we consider the entry of a grade greater than 100 to be a rare and extreme occurrence, calling for an "emergency" exit!)

```
begin

  Repeat_Program:
  loop
    .
    .
    .

    Section_Averages:
    for Section_Number in INTEGER range 1..Num_Sections loop
      .
      .
      .

      while Grade >= 0 loop
        exit when Grade > 100;
        .
        .
        .

        Int_IO.Get (Grade);
      end loop;
```

```
       .
       .
       .
  end loop Section_Averages;

  Text_IO.Put_Line ("Another set of class sections (Y/N)?  ");
  Text_IO.Get (Answer);
  Text_IO.New_Line (2);
  exit Repeat_Program when Answer /= 'Y' and Answer /= 'y';
end loop Repeat_Program;

end;
```

Figure 6.7.8

It is a general principle in Ada that the execution of an **exit** statement effects an exit from the *innermost* loop containing this statement. Thus, if the condition **Grade > 100** is True and the statement

```
exit when Grade > 100;
```

is encountered, this causes an exit from this innermost loop *only*, with control passing to the statement immediately following the **while** loop. The latter statement, of course, is contained within the body of the loop Section_Averages; hence, no exit from the loop Section_Averages has taken place.

   Is it possible to exit from the loop Section_Averages at the point where the conditional **exit** statement occurs in the inner loop of Figure 6.7.8? It is; and this is the context in which loop names serve a purpose other than that of program clarity. The statement

```
exit Section_Averages when Grade > 100;
```

causes just such an exit, transferring control to the first statement following the loop Section_Averages. Furthermore, as one might therefore expect, it is even possible to exit from the outermost loop of the program (through several levels of nesting) from a point within the **while** loop; the statement

```
exit Repeat_Program when Grade > 100;
```

brings this about if its condition has the value True.

6.8 Loop parameters: Scope and visibility

We stated in Section 6.6 that the loop parameter K of a **for** loop

```
for K in [reverse] <range> loop
  <statement sequence>
end loop;
```

(where the word **reverse** may or may not be present) comes into existence at the beginning of the loop and ceases to exist when execution of the loop is finished. In technical terms, K is *declared* in the loop parameter specification

```
K in [reverse] <range>
```

and it is said to have a **scope** (span of existence) that extends from the loop parameter specification to the end of the loop statement. The programmer may not *reference* (refer to) K outside this scope, since, in effect, it does not exist there.

In general, the loop parameter K may be referenced anywhere *within* the body of the loop. (But recall that, as mentioned in Section 6.6, no value may be assigned to it by either an assignment or an input statement; in this respect it resembles a *constant*.) Thus, the **for** loop

```
for K in INTEGER range 1..3 loop
  Int_IO.Put (K, 0);
  Text_IO.New_Line;
end loop;
```

will cause the numbers 1, 2, and 3 to be displayed—assuming of course, as always, that the needed I/O routines are available. But what if (as Ada allows) the identifier K is used again as the loop parameter of another **for** loop *nested within* the given **for** loop? This would give rise to the structure shown in Figure 6.8.1.

```
for K in INTEGER range 1..3 loop
  .
  .
  .
  for K INTEGER range in 1..5 loop
    Int_IO.Put (K, 0);
  Text_IO.New_Line;
  end loop;
  .
  .
  .
end loop;
```

Figure 6.8.1

What does the K in the Put statement refer to, and what will this statement display when the program runs? The answer is that this K refers to the loop parameter of the *inner* loop, and when the program runs, it displays the sequence of numbers 1, 2, 3, 4, and 5 *three times* (once for each pass through the body of the outer loop). The inner loop contains a *new* declaration of K, with the scope of this loop parameter extending to the end of the inner loop. Throughout this scope, which lies within the scope of the *outer* loop parameter K, the outer K is said to be "hidden" or "invisible"; technically, its **region of visibility**, which normally would consist of the entire body of the outer loop, has been interrupted by the declaration and consequent scope of the *inner* loop parameter bearing the same name. Thus, although the Put statement lies within the *scope* of the outer K, this loop parameter is not *visible* at this point; rather, it is the inner loop parameter that is "seen" by this reference to K. The situation is illustrated in Figure 6.8.2.

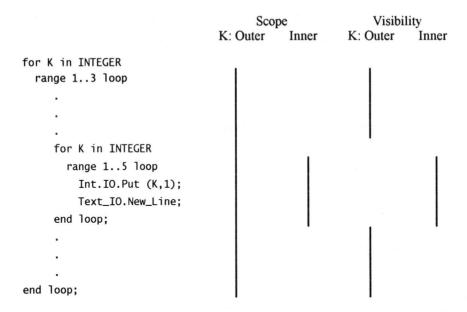

```
for K in INTEGER
  range 1..3 loop
    .

    .

    .
    for K in INTEGER
      range 1..5 loop
        Int.IO.Put (K,1);
        Text_IO.New_Line;
    end loop;
    .

    .

    .
end loop;
```

Figure 6.8.2

Why make a distinction between *scope* and *visibility*? To put it another way, why do we say that the scope of the outer K is not interrupted by the scope of the inner K, whereas the visibility of the outer K is interrupted by the scope of the inner K? The reason is that throughout the scope of the inner K, the outer K still "exists"; even though it is not directly visible. It can be "made visible" here, however—which would not be possible if it had ceased to exist—and consequently can be referenced within the inner loop. This is done by *naming* the outer loop—Outer_Loop, say—and using the **expanded name** Outer_Loop.K to refer to its loop parameter from within the inner loop where this parameter is not otherwise visible. (Just as the names Text_IO.Put and Int_IO.Put can be thought of as meaning "Text_IO's Put" and "Int_IO's Put," respectively, indicating *which* Put is being invoked, so in a similar fashion the expanded name Outer_Loop.K indicates that "Outer_Loop's K" is being referred to.) We could use the program construct shown in Figure 6.8.3.

```
Outer_Loop:
for K in INTEGER range 1..3 loop
  .
  .

  .
  for K in INTEGER range 1..5 loop
    Int_IO.Put (Outer_Loop.K, 0);
    Text_IO.New_Line;
  end loop;
  .
  .

  .
end loop Outer_Loop;
```

Figure 6.8.3

The Put statement of Figure 6.8.3 will now display the loop parameter of the *outer* loop: 1 will be displayed five times, 2 will be displayed five times, and 3 will be displayed five times.

You may wonder if it would not be much simpler to use K for the parameter of the outer loop and then use some other identifier, such as J, for the parameter of the inner loop. The answer is that it certainly would, and it would be better programming practice as well. But there are at least two good reasons for considering the effects of using the same loop parameter more than once:

1. In a lengthy program with much nesting of **for** loops, a programmer might tend to reuse—perhaps inadvertently—such "simple" and conventional loop parameters as I, J, and K; consequently, it is well to have a thorough understanding of the effects this would have.

2. The examples we have looked at, contrived as they may be, serve to illustrate the important Ada concepts of *scope* and *visibility*, which occur in several other contexts in Ada and other languages; we discuss these concepts in detail in Chapter 9 and encounter them several times thereafter.

6.9 Using external files for program input and output*

Figure 6.9.1 shows a sample dialogue that took place during execution of the (improved version of the) Checkbook program, as described in Figure 6.4.10.

```
Enter current checking account balance: 104.72

Enter the amount of this transaction
(deposits are positive, withdrawals are negative): -14.21
The new account balance is 90.51

Another transaction (Y/N)? Y


Enter the amount of this transaction
(deposits are positive, withdrawals are negative): -77.42
The new account balance is 13.09

Another transaction (Y/N)? Y


Enter the amount of this transaction
(deposits are positive, withdrawals are negative): -41.18
The new account balance is -28.09

Another transaction (Y/N)? Y


Enter the amount of this transaction
(deposits are positive, withdrawals are negative): 84.87
The new account balance is 56.78
```

---

*This section may be omitted.

```
Another transaction (Y/N)? Y


Enter the amount of this transaction
(deposits are positive, withdrawals are negative): -12.98
The new account balance is 43.80

Another transaction (Y/N)? N


Processing completed.
```

Figure 6.9.1

The checkbook program is typical of the programs we have written so far, in that the input to the program has always come from the *keyboard* and the output from the program has always been directed to the program user's *display*. In this section we show that there are other possible sources for program input and destinations for program output.

When we write a computer program to solve a problem, there are a number of phases that comprise the process, some quite formal and others somewhat less so. Generally speaking, these involve an analysis of the problem and then a construction of an algorithm— a methodical technique—for its solution. As a next but still intermediate step, the resulting algorithm is cast into the syntax of whatever computer language we choose to use for the problem solution. Finally, the program is submitted to the appropriate compiler and (possibly after some debugging) executed and tested. The question of interest in the present setting is, *In what form* is the source program submitted to the compiler? As indicated in our discussions in Sections 1.2 and 1.3, the answer is almost always: as a *text file*, that is, as a collection of strings of characters (the individual lines of the program), gathered together in a file, and typically a *disk file*. This file of characters acts as *input* to the compiler. And what does the compiler generate as *output*? The answer is: another disk file, the so-called object file. Thus the notion of a program—in this case, a compiler—accepting input from a file (source file) and generating a file as output (object file) is nothing new to us. Indeed, programs whose input comes from the keyboard and whose output goes to the display may be viewed as special cases—in fact, quite special, perhaps more so in the Ada environment than in that of other languages. Could we submit input to the Ada compiler from the keyboard? Curiously, most Ada compilers and operating systems do permit this, although it is almost impossible to contrive circumstances in which this is reasonable to do. Sending the output of a compiler to a display is another matter—it simply is never done, since the object program is not made up of printable characters.

Could we submit transactions to the Checkbook program in the form of a file, rather than from the keyboard? The answer is yes, although we need to expand our understanding of files somewhat. Figure 6.9.2 has a file of text—strings of characters—that you will recognize as consisting of the program user's *keyboard input* exactly as submitted in the dialogue of Figure 6.9.1; that is, all user input has simply been gathered together into a file that we will name TRANSACT.DAT, a name that suggests that this file contains *transact*ions *dat*a.

```
104.72
-14.21
Y
-77.42
Y
-41.18
Y
84.87
Y
-12.98
N
```

Figure 6.9.2

Now as you might expect, in order to use lines of text in the file TRANSACT.DAT as replacements for the keyboard input to Checkbook, two things will have to be done. First, the program has to be notified that input will no longer be coming from the keyboard; rather, it will be coming from a file and, in particular, from the file named TRANSACT.DAT. Second, it is likely that *different* kinds of Get procedures will be required for reading the lines of the file TRANSACT.DAT. You would be correct on both counts, although the differences are perhaps not as great as you might guess.

First, the file TRANSACT.DAT of Figure 6.9.2 is clearly a collection of *text*—strings of characters. Thus it will not surprise you to find that the appropriate routines for managing files of this kind already exist in the package Text_IO. In fact, since one of the objects we will have to "get" from this file is a CHARACTER ('Y' or 'N') to be placed in the variable Answer, let us look at the pair of lines from the package Text_IO that pertain specifically to the getting of characters.

```
package Text_IO is

   procedure Get (Item: out CHARACTER);
   procedure Get (File: in FILE_TYPE; Item: out CHARACTER);
```

The first Get is the familiar one: We supply Text_IO.Get with a CHARACTER variable (such as Answer) and whatever character is typed at the keyboard is placed in that variable. A look at the second version of Get might lead us to conjecture that we are still getting a character (the parameter **Item**), but that the character is now coming from a file and the parameter **File** is being used to tell the Ada system about that file. Both these conjectures are correct. What needs to be investigated is the parameter File, and we will do so momentarily. In the meantime we note that evidently when the Ada system sees the File parameter is *missing*, as in the first version of Text_IO.Get, it *assumes* that characters are coming from the "keyboard file." Thus the *second* version of Get is the more general of the two; the first version is really a special case.

How is our program "told" about the file TRANSACT.DAT via the File parameter? The answer is a little less direct than you might expect. The file actually has *two* names, used for distinct purposes. One of its names is, in fact, TRANSACT.DAT, the name by which *we* know it, and the name known to the operating system. This is the name we use when we edit the file, rename it, delete it, copy it, and so forth; these are operating system activities. The file also has a "name" used internally in our Ada program, and it is *this* name that we supply in place of the File parameter. But then we are going to have to provide the program with some information that associates the *internal* name with the *external* name. Let us look at a few more lines from the package **Text_IO**.

```
type FILE_TYPE is limited private;

type FILE_MODE is (In_File, Out_File);

procedure Open (File: in out FILE_TYPE;
                Mode: in FILE_MODE;
                Name: in STRING);
```

Let us begin with the Open procedure, and in fact let us look at the last parameter: Name. We see that it is a "string of characters," and what is required here is the *familiar* filename, that is, the name both *we* and the operating system use: "TRANSACT.DAT." When a program uses a file, it can do so for one of two purposes: The program can *input* data *from* the file (as is the case here), or it can *output* data *to* the file. It is the purpose of Open's second parameter, Mode, to specify this activity. Since Mode is of type FILE_MODE it can evidently have one of the two values In_File (*in*put data from the file) and Out_File (*out*put data to the file). In the present case of our Checkbook program, the Mode is evidently In_File. The final parameter, File, is simply an identifier by which we refer to the file within the program, an identifier declared to be of type FILE_TYPE. How we name this identifier is no more important than how we name any other identifier, except that it should be suggestive of the file with which it is associated. In the version of the Checkbook program below, we have included the following declaration

```
Trans_File:    Text_IO.FILE_TYPE;
```

which has the name we use as the FILE_TYPE variable associated with the file TRANSACT.DAT. (Note that our use of this type in the declaration has had to specify the package, Text_IO, in which this type is defined.) It is the Open statement in the executable portion of the program that associates the file variable **Trans_File** with the file **TRANSACT.DAT**:

```
Text_IO.Open (Trans_File, Text_IO.In_File, "TRANSACT.DAT");
```

In effect, this statement opens (or establishes) a channel of communication between our program and the actual file TRANSACT.DAT as it exists on a disk and calls that "channel" Trans_File. For the record, we shall informally refer to this variable as a **file variable**.

There is one other procedure from Text_IO relative to files that we need to know about. Having associated the file with our program via the Open procedure, when we no longer need that association, we should "disassociate" the file from the program. This is done with the Close procedure:

```
Close (File: in out FILE_TYPE);
```

We now have everything we need to get CHARACTER objects from the file. But we are going to have to obtain floating point numbers from the file as well—the transactions themselves (deposits and withdrawals). Once again a look at the package Float_IO in Text_IO will show us that the situation is entirely analogous to getting characters. (Recall that Flt_IO is an instantiation of the package Float_IO.)

```
procedure Get (Item: out NUM);
procedure Get (File: in FILE_TYPE; Item: out NUM);
```

(Remember that the "type" NUM will have been replaced by FLOAT when Flt_IO is instantiated.)

With these preliminaries we are now in a position to open the file TRANSACT.DAT, use it to read the various transactions and answers to the "Another transaction" query, and then close the file and exit the program.

```
1    with Text_IO, Flt_IO;
2
3  procedure Checkbook is
4
5     -- After establishing an initial balance, the procedure
6     -- Checkbook requests and accepts an amount, interprets
7     -- it as a deposit (> 0) or withdrawal (< 0), and
8     -- calculates and displays the new account balance.
9
10    -- If, in answer to an inquiry, the user indicates a desire
11    -- to enter another transaction, Checkbook processes this
12    -- transaction in terms of the balance resulting from the
13    -- preceding transaction.  This continues until the user
14    -- indicates there are no more transactions to be processed.
15
16    -- NOTE: In this version of Checkbook, all input comes from
17    --        the transaction file TRANSACT.DAT.
18
19
20    Trans_File:          Text_IO.FILE_TYPE;
21
22    Current_Balance:     FLOAT;
23    Transaction:         FLOAT;
24    New_Balance:         FLOAT;
25
26    Answer:              CHARACTER;
27
28  begin
29
30    Text_IO.Open (Trans_File, Text_IO.In_File, "TRANSACT.DAT");
31
32    Text_IO.Put ("Enter current checking account balance: ");
33    Flt_IO.Get (Trans_File, New_Balance);
34    Text_IO.New_Line;
35
36    loop
37      Current_Balance := New_Balance;
38
39      Text_IO.Put ("Enter the amount of this transaction");
40      Text_IO.New_Line;
41      Text_IO.Put
42        ("(deposits are positive, withdrawals are negative):");
43
```

```
44      Flt_IO.Get (Trans_File, Transaction);
45
46      New_Balance := Current_Balance + Transaction;
47      Text_IO.New_Line;
48      Text_IO.Put ("The new account balance is ");
49      Flt_IO.Put (New_Balance, 0, 2, 0);
50
51      Text_IO.New_Line (2);
52      Text_IO.Put ("Another transaction (Y/N)? ");
53      Text_IO.New_Line;
54      Text_IO.Get (Trans_File, Answer);
55      Text_IO.New_Line (2);
56      exit when Answer /= 'Y' and Answer /= 'y';
57   end loop;
58
59   Text_IO.Close (Trans_File);
60   Text_IO.Put ("Processing completed.");
61   Text_IO.New_Line (2);
62
63 end Checkbook;
```

Figure 6.9.3

There is really very little that remains to be said about this version of the Checkbook program. At line 20 we declare the file variable Trans_File, associated with the file TRANSACT.DAT, and then we use that variable at Line 30 to "open" the file. (The file is closed at line 59.) The only other changes in the earlier version of the program involve the forms of the Get statements at lines 33, 44, and 54, which now specify the file variable, Trans_File. When this program is run, we obtain the (somewhat peculiar) output shown in Figure 6.9.4.

```
Enter current checking account balance:
Enter the amount of this transaction
(deposits are positive, withdrawals are negative):
The new account balance is 90.51

Another transaction (Y/N)?


Enter the amount of this transaction
(deposits are positive, withdrawals are negative):
The new account balance is 13.09

Another transaction (Y/N)?


Enter the amount of this transaction
(deposits are positive, withdrawals are negative):
The new account balance is -28.09

Another transaction (Y/N)?


Enter the amount of this transaction
(deposits are positive, withdrawals are negative):
The new account balance is 56.78

Another transaction (Y/N)?
```

```
Enter the amount of this transaction
(deposits are positive, withdrawals are negative):
The new account balance is 43.80

Another transaction (Y/N)?

Processing completed.
```

Figure 6.9.4

All the lines of text (prompts and other messages), as well as the new account balances, appear on the display, and this is to be expected, since they all result from Put statements—statements that explicitly result in characters being sent to the display. What requires a bit of explanation is why the "current account balance," the transactions themselves (deposit and withdrawal amounts), and "Y/N" responses do *not* show on the display. When a character is sent to the computer system *from* the keyboard, not only is it passed along to the executing program, but it is also sent *back* to the display by the computer system, so that the user can see what he or she has just typed on the keyboard. This phenomenon is called **character echoing**. When a character is sent to the computer system *from a file,* it is *not* echoed to the display. It is for this reason that the initial balance, the transactions, and "Y/N" responses do not appear—even though, of course, they have been sent to the program and, judging from the displayed new balances, have been properly processed.

In Figure 6.9.5*a* we show a modification of Checkbook in which the prompts and other messages have simply been removed. We do not want to eliminate *all* the output, because then we would not even know what the ending balance is. Thus we compromise, and display (1) the initial (beginning) balance; (2) each transaction as it is input from the file; and (3) the closing balance. Figure 6.9.5*b* shows what seems to be the far more pleasing output of this new version.

```
a    with Text_IO, Flt_IO;

     procedure Checkbook is

        Trans_File:          Text_IO.FILE_TYPE;

        Current_Balance:     FLOAT;
        Transaction:         FLOAT;
        New_Balance:         FLOAT;

        Answer:              CHARACTER;

     begin

        Text_IO.Open (Trans_File, Text_IO.In_File, "TRANSACT.DAT");

        Flt_IO.Get (Trans_File, New_Balance);
        Text_IO.Put ("The opening account balance is ");
        Flt_IO.Put (New_Balance, 0, 2, 0);
       Text_IO.New_Line;

        loop
```

```
      Current_Balance := New_Balance;
      Flt_IO.Get (Trans_File, Transaction);

      Text_IO.New_Line;
      Text_IO.Put ("Transaction: ");
      Flt_IO.Put (Transaction, 0, 2, 0);

      New_Balance := Current_Balance + Transaction;
      Text_IO.New_Line;
      Text_IO.Get (Trans_File, Answer);
      exit when Answer /= 'Y' and Answer /= 'y';
   end loop;
   Text_IO.Close (Trans_File);
   Text_IO.New_Line;
   Text_IO.Put ("The closing account balance is ");
   Flt_IO.Put (New_Balance, 0, 2, 0);
   Text_IO.New_Line (2);

end Checkbook;
```

b   The opening account balance is 104.72

          Transaction: -14.21

          Transaction: -77.42

          Transaction: -41.18

          Transaction: 84.87

          Transaction: -12.98

          The closing account balance is 43.80

Figure 6.9.5

What we have accomplished is a very useful little program, for now we can edit the file TRANSACT.DAT at our leisure (perhaps after each transaction actually takes place) and then, when it suits us, we can run Checkbook and record all the transactions in TRANSACT.DAT. If there is room for improvement, it is found in two areas. It is something of an annoyance that each transaction in the file requires the trailing "Y" or "N" to answer the query about "another transaction." In fact we will eliminate the necessity for these responses, simply by removing them from the file. TRANSACT.DAT now has the appearance shown in Figure 6.9.6.

```
104.72
-14.21
-77.42
-41.18
84.87
-12.98
```

Figure 6.9.6

Here the first number in the file (104.72) is the initial balance; the remaining lines represent individual transactions.

Now, with no answers to the "Another transaction?" query, how can the program tell whether to go to the file for the next transaction or to cease accessing the file because it has processed *all* the transactions? The answer lies in a function which is in the package Text_IO and whose name is **End_of_File**. The function is BOOLEAN-valued, and it has the value False as long as the data file (in this case, TRANSACT.DAT) contains data that the program has not yet read as input (via Flt_IO.Get). When the last line of data has been obtained from the file—when we have come to the end of the file—End_of_File takes on the value True. Since several files might be open in the same program, we have to specify, via the **file variable**, *which* file should be tested for the end-of-file condition. That is, End_of_File takes a file variable parameter (in our case, Trans_File). Thus we need only process transactions, one after another, *until* End_of_File (Trans_File) becomes True, that is, *while* End_of_File (Trans_File) has the value False. This modification is shown in Figure 6.9.7; the output is identical to that shown in Figure 6.9.5*b*.

```
with Text_IO, Flt_IO;

procedure Checkbook is

    Trans_File:         Text_IO.FILE_TYPE;

    Current_Balance:    FLOAT;
    Transaction:        FLOAT;
    New_Balance:        FLOAT;

begin

    Text_IO.Open (Trans_File, Text_IO.In_File, "TRANSACT.DAT");

    Flt_IO.Get (Trans_File, New_Balance);
    Text_IO.Put ("The opening account balance is ");
    Flt_IO.Put (New_Balance, 0, 2, 0);
    Text_IO.New_Line;

    while not Text_IO.End_of_File (Trans_File) loop
        Current_Balance := New_Balance;
        Flt_IO.Get (Trans_File, Transaction);

        Text_IO.New_Line;
        Text_IO.Put ("Transaction: ");
        Flt_IO.Put (Transaction, 0, 2, 0);
        Text_IO.New_Line;

        New_Balance := Current_Balance + Transaction;
    end loop;

    Text_IO.Close (Trans_File);
    Text_IO.New_Line;
    Text_IO.Put ("The closing account balance is ");
    Flt_IO.Put (New_Balance, 0, 2, 0);
    Text_IO.New_Line (2);

end Checkbook;
```

Figure 6.9.7

We conclude this section with a final modification to the Checkbook program. Instead of having to maintain the current balance in the transaction file itself, thus making the first line of TRANSACT.DAT a special case, we keep the current balance in a *second* file, which we name BALANCE.CUR. Since the next version of the checkbook program *updates* this file after processing the current transactions found in TRANSACT.DAT, BALANCE.CUR will always have the current balance, and the balance will never have to be kept in the transaction file. The latest version of Checkbook is found in Figure 6.9.8, and we have a few details to explain.

```
with Text_IO, Flt_IO;

procedure Checkbook is

   Trans_File,
   Bal_File:              Text_IO.FILE_TYPE;

   Current_Balance:       FLOAT;
   Transaction:           FLOAT;
   New_Balance:           FLOAT;

begin
   Text_IO.Open (Bal_File, Text_IO.In_File, "BALANCE.CUR");
   Flt_IO.Get (Bal_File, New_Balance);
   Text_IO.Put ("The opening account balance is ");
   Flt_IO.Put (New_Balance, 0, 2, 0);
   Text_IO.New_Line;
   Text_IO.Close (Bal_File);

   Text_IO.Open (Trans_File, Text_IO.In_File, "TRANSACT.DAT");

   while not (Text_IO.End_of_File (Trans_File)) loop
      Current_Balance := New_Balance;
      Flt_IO.Get (Trans_File, Transaction);

      Text_IO.New_Line;
      Text_IO.Put ("Transaction: ");
      Flt_IO.Put (Transaction, 0, 2, 0);
      Text_IO.New_Line;

      New_Balance := Current_Balance + Transaction;
   end loop;

   Text_IO.Close (Trans_File);
   Text_IO.New_Line;
   Text_IO.Put ("The closing account balance is ");
   Flt_IO.Put (New_Balance, 0, 2, 0);
   Text_IO.New_Line (2);

   Text_IO.Create (Bal_File, Text_IO.Out_File, "BALANCE.CUR");
   Flt_IO.Put (Bal_File, New_Balance, 0, 2, 0);
   Text_IO.Close (Bal_File);

end Checkbook;
```

Figure 6.9.8

Note that we begin by opening the BALANCE.CUR file, getting the current balance from it, and *immediately* closing the file again—we have obtained the sole piece of information in the file, and thus there is no longer a need for the program to have a communication channel to it. The program now continues as in its preceding version, by opening the transaction file TRANSACT.DAT, processing transactions until the end of that file is encountered, and then closing TRANSACT.DAT. Now we encounter a new procedure from Text_IO: **Create**, which is applied to the file BALANCE.CUR. The effect of the procedure Create is to *create* a file with the specified name, as an *empty* file (that is, a new file currently containing no data), with the direction of data transmission specified as *from* the program *to* the file, the opposite of the direction permitted when Open is applied to a file. Thus the file BALANCE.CUR is created as a new file, the new balance is put into it (by means of Flt_IO's procedure Put), and BALANCE.CUR is closed. BALANCE.CUR now contains the new balance, and the program is ready to be run again with a new set of transactions.

You will recognize that we have now written a version of the checkbook management program which is clearly superior to its predecessors but which also leaves us with a question that demands attention: When the *new* BALANCE.CUR file is created by means of the Create procedure, what happens to the *original* version of this file—the one containing the original balance, 104.72? We cannot give a definitive answer to this legitimate question, since the answer depends upon the reaction of the computer's operating system to the creation of a new file with the same name as an existing file. There are various possibilities. Many operating systems will simply destroy the original version of the file before creating the new (initially empty) version. Note that we no longer need the original balance, so this would be satisfactory in our case. An operating system might rename the original file, which would then take on the role of a **backup copy** of the original file. Or perhaps an operating system might demand that the original file first be *deleted* before creating a new file with the same name. In any event, the newly created file BALANCE.CUR is the one that will be accessed the *next* time Checkbook is run to update transactions.

You will note that no more than one file is open at any given time in this program: BALANCE.CUR is opened, used, and then closed; TRANSACT.DAT is opened, used, and then closed; and, finally, a new version of BALANCE.CUR is opened (by virtue of its being created), used, and then closed. Does this mean that no more than one file can be open in a program at any given time? Absolutely not; having multiple files open simultaneously is perfectly legal and frequently desirable and even necessary. We need only ensure that they have distinct file variables. That no two files were open simultaneously here is simply a result of the fact that no two files were *needed* simultaneously.

In this section we have afforded you a first glimpse at the file-handling capabilities of Ada, capabilities that go far beyond what we have shown here. As you might expect, judging from our earlier comments that keyboard input and display output play no special role in Ada, the ability to process files in various ways is of paramount importance to the writing of large software systems—and even of small, useful programs, as we have seen in this section. The interested reader will pursue these studies by reading the optional sections in this book that deal with files, doing the accompanying exercises, experimenting with files of various sorts, and investigating those sections of the Ada *LRM* and other sources that pertain to these topics.

6.10 Exercises

6.1.1 Let A, B, and C be INTEGER variables with values 3, 10, and −4, respectively. Tell what, if anything, will be displayed when each of the following program segments is executed.

(a)
```
if A > B then
   Text_IO.Put_Line ("Bigger");
end if;
```

(b)
```
if A > B then
   Text_IO.Put_Line ("Bigger");
else
   Text_IO.Put_Line ("Smaller");
end if;
```

(c)
```
if A < B and A * C > -B then
   Int_IO.Put (A, 0);
else
   Text_IO.Put_Line ("No match");
end if;
```

(d)
```
if A > B or (A < B and A * C > B) then
   Text_IO.Put_Line ("OK");
elsif A < B and -B < -C then
   Text_IO.Put_Line ("No match");
end if;
```

(e)
```
if A > B or (A < B and A * C > B) then
   Text_IO.Put_Line ("OK");
else
   if A < B and -B < -C then
      Text_IO.Put_Line ("No match");
   end if;
end if;
```

(f)
```
if A > B or (A < B and A * C > B) then
   Text_IO.Put_Line ("OK");
elsif A < B and B < -C then
   Text_IO.Put_Line ("No match");
end if;
```

(g)
```
if A > B then
   Text_IO.Put_Line ("OK_1");
elsif A = B and C < A then
   Text_IO.Put_Line ("OK_2");
elsif A < B and C > A then
   Text_IO.Put_Line ("OK_3");
elsif A < B and A * C > B then
   Text_IO.Put_Line ("OK_4");
else
   Text_IO.Put_Line ("No match");
end if;
```

6.1.2 Simplify the following **if** construction. (Assume that A, B, C, D, E, F, G, and H are INTEGER variables.)

```
if A > B then
  if C > D then
    if E > F then
      if G > H then
        Text_IO.Put_Line ("OK");
      end if;
    end if;
  end if;
end if;
```

6.1.3 Given that A, B, C, D, E, and F are INTEGER variables, tell what can be said about each of the following **if** constructions.

(a)
```
if A > B and C > D and E > F then
  if B > C and D > E then
    if A < F then
      Text_IO.Put_Line ("OK");
    end if;
  end if;
end if;
```

(b)
```
if A > B and C > D and E > F then
  if B > C and D > E then
    if A < F then
      Text_IO.Put_Line ("OK");
    else
      Text_IO.Put_Line ("No match");
    end if;
  end if;
end if;
```

(c)
```
if A > B and C > D and E > F then
  if B > C and D > E then
    if A < F then
      Text_IO.Put_Line ("OK");
    end if;
  else
    Text_IO.Put_Line ("No match");
  end if;
end if;
```

(d)
```
if A > B and C > D and E > F then
  if B > C and D > E then
    if A < F then
      Text_IO.Put_Line ("OK");
    end if;
  end if;
else
  Text_IO.Put_Line ("No match");
end if;
```

6.1.4 Let A, B, C, and D be INTEGER variables. Write an **if** construction that will display:

   (a) "OK_1" if A > B; "OK_2" if A < B; and "No match" if neither of these is true.
   (b) "OK_1" if A _ B; "OK_2" if A > B; and "No match" if neither of these is true.
   (c) "OK_1" if A < B; "OK_2" if A > B and C < D; and "No match" if neither of these is true.
   (d) "OK_1" if A > B; "OK_2" if A _ B; "OK_3" if A < B and C > D; and "No match" if none of these is true.
   (e) "OK_1" if A > B and B < D; "OK_2" if A < B and B < D; "OK_3" if A < B and C > D; and "No match" if none of these is true.
   (f) "OK_1" if A > B and B < D; "OK_2" if A < B and B < D; and "OK_3" if A < B and C > D.

6.1.5 Write an Ada program to (a) get three positive integers as input from the keyboard; (b) determine which of these integers is the largest; (c) find out whether these three integers can be the lengths of the three sides of a triangle; and (d) if so, determine whether it is a right triangle, an obtuse triangle, or an acute triangle. Note: the information in step *d* may be obtained by comparing the square of the length of the triangle's longest side with the sum of the squares of the lengths of its other two sides.

6.3.1 It is easy to slip into the misconception that a *condition* is a *comparison* (by means of a relational operator), as is indeed the case with many of the conditions used in computing. In the program of Figure 6.3.1, find some conditions that are *not* comparisons.

6.3.2 Revise the program of Figure 6.3.1 so that, instead of displaying a message, it actually exhibits a display like that of a digital clock, namely (a) a three-letter abbreviation for the day of the week (SUN to SAT); (b) the time (as before); and (c) either AM or PM (but not "midnight" or "noon"); for example:

         TUE   11:05 PM

How should the time be displayed at midnight and noon?

6.3.3 Investigate the use of appropriate integer *subtypes* in the program Time_and_Day of Figure 6.3.1. What would be an especially appropriate subtype for the variable Minutes_Elapsed?

6.4.1 For each of the segments shown below, we assume that K is an INTEGER variable and that Text_IO and Int_IO are available. Tell how the output will appear when each program segment is run.

   (a)
```
K := 0;
loop
  K := K + 1;
  exit when K > 5;
  Text_IO.Put_Line ("Perfect square:  ");
```

```
        Int_IO.Put (K ** 2, 0);
        Text_IO.New_Line (2);
     end loop;
```

(b)   K := 0;
```
       loop
          exit when K > 5;
          K := K + 1;
          PUT_LINE ("Perfect square:   ");
          Int_IO.Put (K ** 2, 0);
          Text_IO.New_Line (2);
       end loop;
```

(c)   K := 0;
```
       loop
          K := K + 1;
          Text_IO.Put_Line ("Perfect square:   ");
          Int_IO.Put (K ** 2, 0);
          Text_IO.New_Line (2);
          exit when K > 5;
       end loop;
```

(d)   K := 1;
```
       loop
          exit when K > 5;
          Int_IO.Put (K ** 2, 0);
          Text_IO.Put ("  Perfect square.");
          Text_IO.New_Line (2);
          K := K + 1;
       end loop;
```

(e)   K := 1;
```
       loop
          Int_IO.Put (K ** 2, 0);
          Text_IO.Put ("  Perfect square.");
          Text_IO.New_Line (2);
          K := K + 1;
          exit when K > 5;
       end loop;
```

(f)   K := 1;
```
       loop
          Int_IO.Put (K ** 2, 0);
          Text_IO.New_Line (2);
          K := K + 1;
          exit when K > 5;
          Text_IO.Put_Line ("Another square:");
       end loop;
```

6.4.2   Write a program that reads integers from the keyboard until the user enters 0 and that then displays the sum of the integers entered.

6.4.3   Write a program that reads from the keyboard nonnegative integers representing examination grades until the user enters some special number that signals the end of the input; the program should then display the (floating point) average of the grades entered.

6.5.1 For each of the program segments in Exercise 6.4.1, write a program segment that produces exactly the same output but that uses a **while** loop in each case instead of a loop without an iteration scheme.

6.5.2 Do Exercise 6.4.2 using a **while** loop.

6.5.3 Do Exercise 6.4.3 using a **while** loop.

6.5.4 Assuming any integer declarations and instantiations that may be required and using any format you wish, write **while** loops to generate the following output:

(a) The integers from 1 to 24.
(b) The even integers between 1 and 24.
(c) The odd integers between 1 and 24.
(d) The integers from 1 to 24, except the multiples of 3.
(e) The odd integers between 1 and 24 which are not also multiples of 5 or 7.

6.5.5 Using **while** loops exclusively and assuming any declarations and instantiations that may be required, write a construction to display the following:

Beginning at n = 1, the nth even integer between 1 and 24 (namely, 2 · n); followed on the next line by all the integers between 1 and *n*, inclusive, displayed on a single line; followed by a blank line; followed by the next even integer, etc.

Thus the first few lines of output should be

```
2
1

4
1   2

6
1   2   3
```

6.6.1 Write a program to add several integers entered from the keyboard and then display their sum. The program should first ask the user how many numbers are to be added and then use a **for** loop to do the reading and adding of the numbers. (Does the program execute properly if the user indicates there are *no* numbers to be added?)

6.6.2 The **for** loop shown below is intended to display the squares of the positive integers, as long as these squares are less than 5000. The needed I/O routines are included in the program, and the variable Square is declared to be of type INTEGER and is assigned the initial value 1. Will this program segment execute as intended? Explain your answer.

```
for K in INTEGER range 2..100 loop
  Int_IO.Put (Square, 4);
  Text_IO.New_Line;
  Square := K ** 2;
  if Square >= 5000 then
    K := 101;
  end if;
end loop;
```

6.6.3   Explain why the loop below will or will not execute forever.

```
for K in INTEGER range 1..10 loop
  Int_IO.Put (K ** 2, 3);
  Text_IO.New_Line;
  K := K - 1;
end loop;
```

6.6.4   In the preceding two exercises the body of the **for** loop contained an assignment statement in which the *loop parameter* was the "target" of the assignment. Now consider the case in which the body of the loop contains an assignment to one or both of the *bounds* of the loop range. In particular, consider the following modified version of the program segment of Exercise 6.6.2, in which Start and Finish have been declared to be INTEGER variables:

```
Square := 1;
Start  := 2;
Finish := 100;
for K in INTEGER range Start..Finish loop
  Int_IO.Put (Square, 4);
  Text_IO.New_Line;
  Square := K ** 2;
  if Square >= 5000 then
    Finish := 1;
  end if;
end loop;
```

Determine what happens when this loop is executed by trying it. Then make a general conjecture about the effect of changing one or both loop bounds within the body of a loop.

6.6.5   Suppose a program contains a **for** loop that begins with

```
for K in INTEGER range -4..18 loop
```

What is the value of K immediately *after* execution of the loop is completed? Explain.

6.6.6   Suppose the loop parameter of a **for** loop does not appear in the loop's statement sequence at all, as in

```
for K in INTEGER range 1..10 loop
  Text_IO.Put_Line ("Go!");
end loop;
```

What happens? Is there anything "wrong" with this loop construction? Compare this situation with that of the "similar" **while** loop:

```
K := 1;
while K <= 10 loop
  Text_IO.Put_Line ("Go!");
end loop;
```

6.6.7   Assuming any integer declarations and instantiations that may be required and using any format you wish, write **for** loops to generate the following output:

(a)   The integers from 1 to 24.
(b)   The even integers between 1 and 24.
(c)   The odd integers between 1 and 24.
(d)   The integers from 1 to 24, except 9.
(e)   The integers from 1 to 24, except the multiples of 3.
(f)   The odd integers between 1 and 24 which are not also multiples of 5 or 7.

6.7.1   Several of the variables used in the program segment of Figure 6.7.3 (namely, Num_Sections, Grade_Count, and Grade_Sum) were declared to be of subtype NATURAL; however, Grade was declared to be of type INTEGER. Would it be possible and advantageous (from the point of view of consistency, if nothing else) to declare Grade to be of subtype NATURAL too? Explain.

6.8.1   The Ada concepts of visibility and expanded names have their counterparts in our ordinary experience. For example, for most residents of northeast Texas, the presence of the city of Paris in that region prevents the French capital with that name from being "directly visible" there, and the latter must be referred to in this part of Texas by its "expanded name," Paris, France (since "Paris" by itself is taken to mean "Paris, Texas"). Think of other instances (not necessarily geographic) where the local meaning of a name blocks out the direct visibility of another, more broadly visible entity with the same name and makes it necessary to refer to this latter by an expanded name.

6.8.2   In a fashion similar to the diagram of Figure 6.8.2, indicate the scope and visibility of each of the variables J, K, and L of the program segment below.

```
        .
        .
        .
    J, K, L:          INTEGER;

begin
    .
    .
    .
    for J in INTEGER range 1..7 loop
```

```
        .
        .
        .
        for K in reverse INTEGER range 12..26 loop
            .
            .
            .
            for L in INTEGER range -6..-2 loop
                .
                .
                .
            end loop;
            .
            .
            .
        end loop;
        .
        .
        .
    end loop;
    .
    .
    .
end;
```

6.8.3 What is the range of the inner (K) loop in the segment shown below? Explain.

```
        .
        .
        .
        J:  INTEGER := 968;
    begin
        .
        .
        .
        for J in INTEGER range 23..1000 loop
            for K in INTEGER range J..1000 loop
                .
                .
                .
            end loop;
            .
            .
            .
        end loop;
        .
        .
        .
    end;
```

6.8.4 Is the **for** construction shown below legal? Explain. If it is, what is the range of the
loop index K? If it is not legal, show how it can easily be repaired so that it will
execute as is evidently intended (that is, with range 3..9).

```
        .
        .
        .
   procedure Sample is
        .
        .
        .
    J:  INTEGER := 3;
   begin
        .
        .
        .
    for K in INTEGER range J..9 loop
       .
       .
       .
    end loop;
        .
        .
        .
   end;
```

6.9.1 There is a minor annoyance in the output of the Checkbook program (Figures 6.9.5, 6.9.7, and 6.9.8); namely, the decimal points in the listing of the transactions (see Figure 6.9.5*b*) are not aligned, since *deposits* do not have the leading minus sign. In fact, if withdrawals (checks) were under $10.00 or over $99.99, then the misalignment would be even more pronounced. Explain how the program might be adjusted to correct this, including any assumptions you need to make to ensure that the output will always be aligned.

6.9.2 In Figure 6.9.8, show that the BALANCE.CUR file can be left open during most of the course of the Checkbook program execution, by moving the first occurrence of

```
   Text_IO.Close (Bal_File);
```

from its present position to later in the statement sequence. When *must* this statement be executed?

6.9.3 Experiment with the Open and Create procedures of the package Text_IO by modifying the line

```
   Text_IO.Create (Bal_File, Text_IO.Out_File, "BALANCE.CUR");
```

in Figure 6.9.8 to read

```
   Text_IO.Open (Bal_File, Text_IO.Out_File, "BALANCE.CUR");
```

(Note that the mode parameter in this call to the Open procedure is Out_File.)

(a)   Verify that this version will compile and link properly.

(b) When the resulting program is executed, what are the contents of BALANCE.CUR?

(c) What is the difference between the two versions? (This may be difficult to determine. If your operating system creates a *new version* of the BALANCE.CUR file when Create is executed, you can observe that it does *not* create a *new* version when the Open procedure is used. If your system does not build new file versions but overwrites old versions, you may still be able to detect a difference between the two programs by examining the "date-and-time stamp" on the BALANCE.CUR file after each version is executed.)

Chapter 7

Program Correctness and Run-Time Events

Up to now our study of computer programming has been focused on the issue of program *development*, the task of designing and writing well-structured programs that are "correct," in the sense that they actually behave in the fashion that we intend. In fact we have had little to say about what *might* happen during program execution ("at run-time," as is said), simply assuming that all will be well. But you may already have had firsthand experience with run-time failures, and they can occur in even the most carefully written programs. At some risk of oversimplification, we can put such failures into two categories: (1) program logic errors and (2) external (input) data errors. We examine these phenomena in this chapter and provide some ways to detect and prevent the problems they cause.

7.1 Compile-time versus run-time

Before beginning our investigation of errors, we need to review in more detail some concepts that we have been dealing with since the beginning of the book, namely, *compilation* and *execution*. In particular, it is essential that we understand the distinction between these two ideas. Recall that the Ada compiler is simply a program, admittedly a very large and sophisticated one; it takes input (the file of text lines we refer to as the **source program**), processes it in some fashion, and generates output (which might consist only of messages announcing language errors but will eventually be the file we call the **object program**). What does the compiler *do*? The very broad subdivision of its activities which is of present interest to us is the following:

1.   The compiler creates and maintains a table of declared types and object names.

2.   It generates code which, at run-time, will cause space in memory to be allocated for variables and constants and ensure that that allocated storage will contain whatever initial values have been assigned in the declarations.

3.   It translates Ada statements into sequences of equivalent machine-executable instructions.

What does the Ada compiler *not* do? That is, what does it leave for the run-time system to handle? There are two things in particular:

1.   It does not actually allocate storage for declared objects; this process, which is called the **elaboration** of declarations, occurs at the beginning of the program's actual execution.

2.   It does not *execute* any of the machine instructions is has generated; this also takes place at run-time.

As a simple but illuminating example of this distinction, consider the lines of Ada programming in Figure 7.1.1.

```
X:   INTEGER := 17;
Y:   INTEGER;
begin
  Y := -24;
```

Figure 7.1.1

Just what does the Ada compiler "know" after processing the two declarations of Figure 7.1.1? It knows that X and Y are integer variables to be allocated an appropriate amount of computer memory for their values; also, it has kept track of the value—17—that is to be placed in the space allocated for X. However, note that when the declaration of Y is elaborated, no particular value will initially be placed in the space allocated for Y, since no explicit initial value has been specified in its declaration. How does the compiler deal with the assignment statement **Y := −24**? It examines this statement for proper syntax and produces the corresponding machine code. Does it keep track of the value −24 to be placed in the space allocated for Y? No, for while the compiler does concern itself with *declarations*, it does *not* anticipate effects that will occur at run-time purely as the result of executing the machine-code *statements* it has generated.

As another example to reinforce our understanding of these concepts, consider the two program segments of Figure 7.1.2. In the case of the first segment, that of Figure 7.1.2*a*, the compiler may issue a warning concerning the statement **Y := 10/X** since it has kept track of the *unchangeable* zero value assigned to the *constant* X in its declaration; hence it "knows" that if this statement is executed, it will result in a division by zero. In the second segment, the compiler does *not* know—or does not "bother to remember"—that X will be 0 when the indicated division takes place, since the assignment of this value to X occurs in an executable *statement*. Thus in this case the error, which will surely occur, must wait until run-time before revealing itself.

```
a    X:    constant := 0;        b    X:    INTEGER;
     Y:    INTEGER;                   Y:    INTEGER;
  begin                            begin
     Y := 10/X;                       X := 0;
                                      Y := 10/X;
```

Figure 7.1.2

7.2 Testing for program correctness

In the introductory section of this chapter we noted that one of our goals to date has been to produce programs which behave in a predetermined fashion. But how can we be reasonably sure, even if not absolutely certain, that a given program actually meets this standard of correctness? A common process, and one that has been practiced ever since the first computer programs were written, is to *test* the program with a relatively small set of data that has been carefully chosen to "exercise" all (or as many as is reasonable and possible) of the pieces of the program. That is, we put the program through its paces with data which *should* generate known theoretical outputs and then compare these with the actual program results. Such tests are necessary since, as we saw in the preceding section, while the Ada compiler does an excellent job of keeping us in line when it comes to correct *grammatical constructs* (syntax), it does not (and in fact cannot) do so with regard to correct programming *logic*. See, for example, Figure 7.1.2*b*, where the constructions make perfect syntactic sense but little if any logical sense.

Testing is one of the most difficult parts of the entire program production process. Designing and writing a program involves an interesting challenge, and when we have met this challenge (or at least appear to have done so), then we understandably experience a sense of accomplishment and satisfaction. By contrast, the task of devising a well-chosen set of test data can seem tedious and dull. Worse yet, the aim of testing is to uncover errors in the program—hardly an appealing endeavor if it is done by the one who has written it in the first place. Finally, if our tests fail to find any mistakes, that does not mean that there *are* none—there may be errors, perhaps subtle ones, that our tests were simply not clever enough to detect.

Making a good set of test data is by no means a trivial task. As far as possible, the *full range* of the program should be examined. That is, data should be selected so that *all* paths through the program are tested—various branches of conditional statements, as well as combinations of such branches, should be executed; loops should be forced to execute their statement sequences, not only many times but also just once, and even not at all; "extreme values" of acceptable data should be tried, including those on the boundaries of the range of valid input and those at which correct program behavior changes from one manner of processing to another. It scarcely need be said that besides carefully selecting a span of data to exercise the program properly, the one who does the testing must know, in each case, which of the program's responses to these data are correct and which are not.

It is sometimes convenient to separate the valid inputs of a program into various categories or "equivalence classes," in each of which we group together those data that we consider similar as inputs to the program (although not necessarily similar as to the processing done on them or the outputs they will produce). We then make certain that each such equivalence class is represented among the test data. For example, in the Time_and_Day program of Figure 6.3.1, we can distinguish three such equivalence classes of inputs: (1) the number 0, in a class by itself, as the extreme value at the *low* end of the valid input range; (2) the number 10,079, again alone in a class, as the extreme value at the *high* end of this range; and (3) all integers between these extremes, which are not considered to have distinct properties *as inputs* (although of course they lead to different *outputs*).

Similarly, we may identify various equivalence classes of *outputs* and see to it that each class is represented (by an appropriate corresponding input) among the test data. Thus in the Time_and_Day program, and concentrating just on the time of day itself (the feature that requires the most adjustment of the *appearance* of the output), we would want to distinguish the following classes of outputs:

1. Midnight, in a class by itself, for which the word "midnight" must be displayed and the hour must be changed from 0 to 12

2. Noon, again in a class by itself

3. Times between midnight and 1 a.m., for which the hour must be changed to 12 and "a.m." must be displayed

4. Times from 1 a.m. to noon

5. Times between noon and 1 p.m., which need to be handled in a fashion analogous to those of category 3 but with the hour remaining at 12

6. The times from 1 p.m. to the following midnight, during which the hour must be reduced by 12, to yield 12-hour rather than 24-hour time.

We want also to be certain that the program correctly manages the output of the day of the week.

If we combine the observations of the preceding paragraphs and lists, we arrive at the test data (and expected program outputs) shown in Figure 7.2.1 where, for space considerations, we have abbreviated somewhat the expected output. You may be justifiably concerned that even so simple a program as Time_and_Day would require the apparently extensive testing shown and that the determination of exactly *which* data would be appropriate for a test set required a nontrivial analysis of the program logic. It may appear that far more elaborate and sophisticated programs would demand testing that could well exceed our abilities to provide. This may indeed be true: Programs may become so complex that *complete* testing of all classes of inputs and outputs and verification of *all* program paths are simply beyond reach. However, in subsequent chapters we will develop techniques of *program modularization* that go far toward subdividing an impossibly complex testing process into many smaller, more manageable tasks.

Input	Expected output		Feature tested
0	12:00 midnight	Sunday	Extreme low input value and "midnight" output
17	12:17 a.m.	Sunday	Time between midnight and 1 a.m.
60	1:00 a.m.	Sunday	1 a.m.
1440	12:00 midnight	Monday	Midnight of the second day
3588	11:48 a.m.	Tuesday	Time between 1 a.m. and noon
3600	12:00 noon	Tuesday	"Noon" output
3627	12:27 p.m.	Tuesday	Time between noon and 1 p.m.
5100	1:00 p.m.	Wednesday	1 p.m.
5225	3:25 p.m.	Wednesday	Time between 1 p.m. and midnight
7199	11:59 p.m.	Thursday	Last minute of the day
7200	12:00 midnight	Friday	First minute of the next day
10079	11:59 p.m.	Saturday	Extreme high input value

Figure 7.2.1

7.3 The problem of invalid external (input) data

Almost all computer programs operate on data whose source is external to the program itself (although there are rare exceptions). That is, data are *input* to the program "from the outside." Sometimes those data are completely predetermined as to their form, range of values, and so forth—for example, the data input to one program may be the data output by another. More frequently, the *programmer* has little or no control over what data the *user* will input to the program, even if it is known what those data *should* be. Consequently even a program that is known to be correct is vulnerable to external data and may fail if those data are not as expected. Thus in the Time_and_Day program, for instance, while the *programmer* may know that the input must be an integer number in the range 0 to 10,079 and while the programmer even warns the program user of this fact, there is no assurance that the program *user* will input numbers in this range or will even input numbers at all. At this point we could investigate the consequences of submitting to Time_and_Day numbers outside the range 0 to 10,079, but instead we encourage you to try this for yourself. We will return to this program later in the chapter (Section 7.14); in the meantime we examine these phenomena via a far simpler little program, the chief virtue of which is the ease with which we can use it to generate the sorts of errors we wish to investigate. (You will find this example reminiscent of both the Warranty and Checkbook programs).

Among the many features of modern cash registers is their ability to calculate the change for the amount tendered on the total cost of the items purchased. The program Change of Figure 7.3.1 assumes that the item purchased costs between 1 and 99 cents, and that the amount tendered is 1 dollar. Hence the change it calculates will be between 99 cents and 1 cent, inclusive. Thus, for example, if the input is 1, the output is 99; if the input is 99, the output is 1; and if, say, 27 is input, 73 is output. There is little question that the program is "correct." But suppose we (inadvertently or maliciously) enter 121. The program will announce that the change should be −21 cents, a nonsense result—although we might *interpret* the result as indicating 21 cents are still due. If −3 is input (an invalid item cost), 103 is announced as the change. Evidently a correct program is exhibiting "incorrect" behavior.

```
    with Text_IO, Int_IO;

procedure Change is

    Cost:       INTEGER;

begin

    Text_IO.Put ("Enter cost in cents (1 to 99) of item: ");
    Int_IO.Get (Cost);
    Text_IO.Put ("The change for one dollar on a ");
    Int_IO.Put (Cost, 0);
    Text_IO.Put ("-cent item is ");
    Int_IO.Put (100-Cost, 0);
    Text_IO.Put_Line (" cents.");

end Change;
```

Figure 7.3.1

Do we need to take the problem underlying this example seriously, or should we simply chalk it up to the aberrant behavior of a contrived situation? The answer, of course, is that we must take this problem very seriously indeed. If the program itself cannot control the data on which it operates, then it must take measures to ensure that any data are valid before it begins processing them. A payroll clerk may easily make a keystroke error at a keyboard and enter 400 as weekly hours worked instead of the intended 40 hours; the program that processes the payroll must recognize this number as nonsense in this context and alert the clerk to the error. The program of Figure 7.3.2 is a simple modification of the Change program of Figure 7.3.1; by our using a conditional statement, it provides a simple test that responds in a reasonable way to invalid data input to the change-making program.

```
    with Text_IO, Int_IO;

procedure Change is

    Cost:        INTEGER;

begin

    Text_IO.Put ("Enter cost in cents (1 to 99) of item: ");
    Int_IO.Get (Cost);

    if Cost < 1 or Cost > 99 then
      Text_IO.Put_Line ("Amount entered is not a valid cost.");
    else
      Text_IO.Put ("The change for one dollar on a ");
      Int_IO.Put (Cost, 0);
      Text_IO.Put ("-cent item is ");
      Int_IO.Put (100-Cost, 0);
      Text_IO.Put_Line (" cents.");
    end if;

end Change;
```

Figure 7.3.2

Actually, we have a serious objection to the *structure* of this new version; namely, most of the program statements lie within the **else** clause, and this has occurred in a rather artificial way. In a more complex program, in which perhaps numerous such tests of data were needed, the nesting of the **else** clauses could result in unnecessarily complex logical structures, with their attendant lack of readability. Of course, the conditional construction itself could be rewritten as

```
    if Cost >= 1 and Cost <= 99 then
      .
      .
      .
    else
      Text_IO.Put_Line ("Amount entered is not a valid cost.");
    end if;
```

While this might seem the more natural test to make (for *correct*, rather than for *incorrect*, input), this would simply force the bulk of the program into the **then** clause. Once again, in a large program, we might have to wait interminably for "the other shoe to drop"—for the **else** clause to put in its appearance. Even worse, we might have to scan forward several pages of program listing to find out if there even *is* an **else** clause.

7.4 Exceptions

It turns out that the program Change of Figure 7.3.2 does not deal with all possible invalid input data, and to see why, we need to know a bit more about the way in which integers are input to a program via the keyboard, a topic that is developed in further detail in

Chapter 12. When we enter the "number" 27 at the keyboard in response to Change's input request, just what are we doing? In fact, we are entering two *keyboard characters*, namely the character 2 and the character 7. How, then, is the variable Cost assigned the *integer value* 27? As we saw in Section 3.3, the answer is that programming within the package Int_IO will convert the sequence of characters 27 (two, seven) to the integer 27 (twenty-seven) and will then store this value in the space allocated to the variable Cost. Suppose now that the user of the program Change enters the sequence of characters "xyz" in response to the input request. Int_IO will attempt the conversion of the input to an integer value, but the first character it encounters—"x"—is not a digit and therefore cannot be converted to an integer form. That is, Int_IO has been given an impossible task, and it must somehow make us aware of its inability to comply with our request.

Int_IO's failure to deal with the input "xyz" is what we will informally call a **run-time event**. The term is appropriate, for it has occurred at run-time (as opposed to compile-time), and it is an occurrence that has prevented the program from continuing its execution—since "xyz" cannot be converted to an integer value, Cost has not received a valid number, and thus any further processing of Cost will be meaningless. You might be inclined to refer to this "event" as a run-time *error*, and that word would certainly be appropriate here. Later we will see other events that, like the one being studied here, require the interruption of program execution but are in fact *expected* to occur during run-time and thus can scarcely be classified as errors.

In the formal Ada terminology, what we have referred to as a run-time event is known as an **exception**, an occurrence that requires that the normal path of statement execution be abandoned. When the event occurs, we say that the exception has been **raised** (much as one might "raise an objection") and some intervening activity must take place. What is the intervening activity? For the moment we can correctly assume that a message concerning the event will be displayed on our screen by the Ada run-time system and the execution of our program will be abandoned.

Thus we see that the second version of our program Change will process valid data correctly and will exit gracefully when it encounters invalid data, *provided* the invalid data are integer in nature (but simply outside of the 1 to 99 range). If the characters input to the program cannot even be converted to an integer value (as, for example, "xyz"), then an exception will be raised, a system message will be displayed, and execution will be aborted, a far more abrupt termination of the program than we might desire. We deal with this problem in the following section.

7.5 Data checking via range constraint

It may already have occurred to you that inasmuch as the valid values of the variable Cost in the Change programs range between 1 and 99, it would be natural to declare a subtype, say CENTS_RANGE, consisting precisely of those integers. We do this in the next version of the Change program, shown in Figure 7.5.1. Note that in addition to declaring the subtype CENTS_RANGE and declaring the variable Cost to be of that type, rather than simply of type INTEGER as before, we have also *removed* the conditional test of the input data. The reason that we have done so is that the test will no longer be useful under any circumstances, a situation that requires explanation.

```
    with Text_IO, Int_IO;

procedure Change is

    subtype CENTS_RANGE is INTEGER range 1..99;

    Cost:        CENTS_RANGE;

begin

    Text_IO.Put ("Enter cost in cents (1 to 99) of item: ");
    Int_IO.Get (Cost);
    Text_IO.Put ("The change for one dollar on a ");
    Int_IO.Put (Cost, 0);
    Text_IO.Put ("-cent item is ");
    Int_IO.Put (100-Cost, 0);
    Text_IO.Put_Line (" cents.");

end Change;
```

Figure 7.5.1

What happens if a "number" such as "xyz" is entered in response to the prompt? As noted in the preceding section, an exception will be raised by the run-time system, since the characters in this input cannot be converted to an integer. But what of input such as −32 or 243? In either case, all will be well initially. Recall that the Get in question is associated with the package Int_IO, an INTEGER instantiation of the (generic) package Text_IO.Integer_IO (see Section 3.3). Since both −32 and 243 are strings of characters that *can* be converted to valid integers, the Get itself will proceed without error. However, the converted number (−32 or 243) is then to be placed in the variable Cost, and it is here that the failure occurs, for Cost has been constrained in such a way that it can only hold integers in the range 1 to 99. Thus an error will occur, an exception will be raised, and program execution will be interrupted by the run-time system. It is for this reason that the (conditional) test that appears in the version of Figure 7.3.2 is no longer meaningful—if a number *outside* the range 1 to 99 is entered, the entire program is aborted (and thus the test would never be executed at all); but if a number *within* that range is entered, then of course the condition would test as True and execution would continue successfully (and the test performs no real service). In any event, the test is no longer useful.

There is a second way we could constrain the input, namely, at the Get procedure itself. Recall that integers outside the range 1 to 99 managed to proceed past the Get procedure in the example above (Figure 7.5.1). In Figure 7.5.2 we abandon the I/O package Int_IO temporarily, and instead we create a *new* instantiation of Integer_IO, one that deals only with integers of type CENTS_RANGE.

```
    with Text_IO;

procedure Change is

    subtype CENTS_RANGE is INTEGER range 1..99;

    package Cents_IO is new Text_IO.Integer_IO (CENTS_RANGE);

    Cost:        CENTS_RANGE;
```

```
begin

    Text_IO.Put ("Enter cost in cents (1 to 99) of item: ");
    Cents_IO.Get (Cost);
    Text_IO.Put ("The change for one dollar on a ");
    Cents_IO.Put (Cost, 0);
    Text_IO.Put ("-cent item is ");
    Cents_IO.Put (100-Cost, 0);
    Text_IO.Put_Line (" cents.");

end Change;
```

Figure 7.5.2

When keyboard characters are entered in response to the input request (Get) statement, Cents_IO must convert those characters to integer values in the range 1 to 99, that is, to values belonging to the type CENTS_RANGE. As before, if for example the sequence of characters "xyz" is entered, then Cents_IO will be unable to convert the "x," and an exception will be raised. But now what of input such as −32 or 243? It would appear that the conversion *will* be possible, since the characters involved *are* numeric in nature (assuming that the sign − will be taken as valid in this context). However, recall that the input data must be converted not just to integer values, but to values that are constrained to the range 1 to 99. And the inputs −32 and 243 cannot be thus converted, and consequently these are just as invalid as is "xyz." Thus an input datum either consists of keyboard characters which can be converted to an integer value between 1 and 99 (in which case the program processes it), or it does not, and an exception will be raised—there is no middle ground here. Once again, input such as −32 and 243 has caused an exception to be raised, but note the difference between this case and the preceding one—here the exception was raised during the Get of the number (more properly, during the attempted conversion of the input characters); in the earlier version the exception occurred *after* the number had successfully been converted. The difference is subtle, but it is also important, and we will shortly return to examine these two distinct exceptions in further detail.

The technique we have employed here—letting the run-time system do checking for us by constraining the range of variables—is both standard and extremely powerful, a scheme that can relieve the programmer of much of the writing of statements used for checking. We will see many further examples throughout the remainder of the book.

7.6 Exception handling: I

In moving from the program Change of Figure 7.3.2 to the version of Figure 7.5.1 or Figure 7.5.2, we have simultaneously gained and lost some ground. On the positive side, constraining values permitted for the package Cents_IO and/or the variable Cost has allowed us to eliminate the data checking statement and to have *all* invalid input (for example, xyz and 243) handled by the run-time system in a uniform (if not identical) fashion. Observe also that by removing the conditional statement, we have overcome our earlier objection; namely, much of the program's statements as shown in Figure 7.3.2 were enclosed in an **else** clause. Now when input data are invalid for *whatever* reason, execution terminates abruptly with a system-devised message. Thus we have had to abandon our earlier, more gentle exit, used when the input was at least numeric but simply out of range. In this and the following sections we see that Ada allows us to maintain all the desirable aspects of these features while circumventing all the undesirable ones: With some careful programming, we can regain all the best aspects of what we have done so far.

Let us examine in some detail just what happens when an exception is raised. When the latest version of the program Change runs, it executes its input request (Get) statement and the user types characters at the keyboard. If those characters can be converted (by routines within Cents_IO) to an integer value in the range 1 to 99, then all is well and processing continues. If Cents_IO cannot do the conversion, an exception is raised. This exception is seen by the Ada run-time system, and it reacts to it by sending an exception message to the user and terminating program execution. However, we have skipped over one crucial step that the Ada run-time system takes prior to aborting the running program. When it sees the exception raised, it *first* asks: Has the executing program made any provision to *deal* with exceptions (in ways we have yet to explain)? If the answer is no, as is the case in all versions of the program Change, the run-time system behaves as described above. But if the answer is yes, the run-time system returns control to the executing program, specifically, to a section of code within that program known as a **programmer-written exception handler**, another feature of the Ada language that is a powerful programmer tool and one that we employ frequently. Before looking into the format of exception handlers, we need a few more details about the events that can result in the raising of exceptions.

7.7 Kinds of exceptions

So far we have alluded to three distinct exceptions. One was suggested in Figure 7.1.2, where we forced a division by zero. This will surely be treated by the Ada system as an exception; since the operation cannot be performed, the statement that contains it must be abandoned. The other two have been the topic of the preceding two sections, namely, the exceptions that occur when (1) a conversion from keyboard characters to numerical values cannot be accomplished (Figure 7.5.2) and (2) the conversion can be accomplished but the resulting number does not satisfy the range constraint of the type of the variable to be assigned the value (Figure 7.5.1). As we will see, there are numerous other causes for exceptions (although all these exceptions result in the same execution-interruption behavior). Note that several different exceptions can occur during the course of program execution, and if the program contains an exception handler, it is likely that not all possible exceptions will be handled in exactly the same way. Thus it is normally necessary that we know not only that an exception occurred but also *why* it occurred so that an action appropriate to the cause of the exception can be taken. The ability to distinguish among the various exceptions is achieved by giving them unique *names* that can then be referred to within the exception handler. In the case of the exceptions we have discussed so far, the names are assigned by the Ada system; we will see in Section 7.13 that it is also possible for the programmer to create and name exceptions. In the table in Figure 7.7.1 we discuss three exceptions, which are perhaps the most common. Others are described and examined later in their appropriate contexts.

Exception name	Cause
Constraint_Error	Raised when a violation of some range constraint is attempted (This exception is predefined in the Ada language.)
Data_Error	Raised by the Get routine when an input character sequence violates the specified syntax or when the input value fails to conform to the range required by the Get routine (This exception is defined as part of the package Text_IO.)
Numeric_Error	Raised when a numeric operation cannot deliver a correct result (This exception is predefined in the Ada language.)

Figure 7.7.1

Constraint_Error is the exception that is raised in the version of the Change program of Figure 7.5.1, when a number outside the range 1 to 99 is supplied as keyboard input. Recall that the Get routine can satisfactorily get—or convert—the number, but the converted number cannot then be placed in the variable Cost, since it violates the constraint of Cost's type, CENTS_RANGE. The description in Figure 7.7.1 of Data_Error is consistent with our discussions of why certain keyboard inputs cannot be valid, specifically why "xyz" can *never* be valid input to any integer implementation of Get, and why −32 or 243 cannot be valid for a CENTS_RANGE version of Get. Thus Data_Error is the exception raised as a result of invalid input to the package Cents_IO of Figure 7.5.2.

Numeric_Error is the exception raised upon a division by zero. However, there are other events that also cause this exception to be raised, and a brief example will show not only that a variety of events can cause this exception to be raised but also that considerable care needs to be taken to ensure that we can distinguish Numeric_Error from other kinds of exceptions.

```
procedure Error_1 is

   X, Y:        INTEGER;

begin

   X := INTEGER'Last;
   Y := X + 1;

end Error_1;
```

Figure 7.7.2

In the program of Figure 7.7.2, the integer variable X is assigned its largest possible positive value. An attempt is then made to assign that value, *plus 1*, to Y, but at this point Numeric_Error would be raised. Why was not Constraint_Error raised, since it appears that the result is simply outside the *range* of permitted values for Y? Recall that the largest possible integer number that can be held in the storage that the Ada compiler allocates for INTEGER variables is INTEGER'Last. An attempt to add 1 to this number has failed not because the result was beyond the range of permitted values for Y but because the addition itself failed—the result could not be generated in the first place. Thus the error is caused by the operation's inability to "deliver a correct result"—a Numeric_Error. This particular kind of numeric error is called, appropriately enough, an **integer overflow error**.

Consider the program of Figure 7.7.3. In this case Constraint_Error is raised. Be certain that you understand why Numeric_Error was not raised in this case (and why Constraint_Error was).

```
procedure Error_2 is

   subtype CENTS_RANGE is INTEGER range 1..99;

   X, Y:          CENTS_RANGE;

begin

   X := CENTS_RANGE'Last;
   Y := X + 1;

end Error_2;
```

Figure 7.7.3

7.8 Exception handling: II

Writing exception handlers is a relatively easy matter, as we will see. First, however, we need to expand our understanding of the structure of a main program. As Figure 7.8.1 indicates, there are three key sections of a main program: (1) the declaration section, (2) the program statement section, and (3) the exception handler section. Note that the exception handler section begins with the reserved word **exception**, it is the *last* section of the program, and no other program statements may appear after it.

```
       .
       .
       .
   procedure <procedure name> is
       .
       .
       .
   <declarations>
       .
       .
       .
   begin
```

```
            .
            .
            .
      <program statements>
            .
            .
            .
      exception
            .
            .
            .
      <exception handler statements>
            .
            .
            .
   end;
```

Figure 7.8.1

Recall that exceptions are *named*, and that different exceptions will probably be handled in different ways. Thus the exception handler section may consist of multiple handlers, each dealing with one or more of the exceptions that might be raised in a given program. The format of these exception handlers is defined by the syntax diagram of Figure 7.8.2. A new symbolism is introduced here, namely, the **when . . . =>** construct. Note that the exception names themselves may be combined using the symbol | representing the logical connective **or**, so that a single sequence of statements can be used to handle two or more exceptions, if it is appropriate to do so. There is no limit to the number or kind of statements in each handler. Finally, the exception name **others** is a catchall, a reserved word that stands for any exception not already explicitly named. If **others** is used in place of an exception name, it may *not* be **or**-ed with any other exception name, and it may be used only in the *last* exception handler.

exception handler

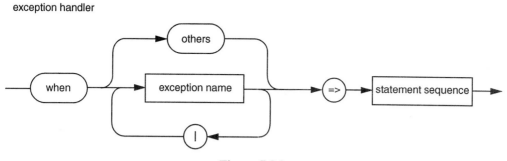

Figure 7.8.2

Figure 7.8.3 gives several examples of exception handler sections. Observe that each handler except the last conforms to the syntax of Figure 7.8.2. Figure 7.8.3*a* is an example of the simplest possible exception handler. It deals with a single kind of exception (Data_Error), and if that exception is raised, it displays an explanatory message. In *b* we deal with two different possible exceptions, each handled separately—again, by displaying a message. These two possible exceptions are combined in Figure 7.8.3*c*, with a more general message being displayed. The exception handler section of Figure 7.8.3*d* takes into account that while perhaps only Data_Error and Constraint_Error exceptions are *anticipated*, other events might occur, and the **others** handler takes care of that possibility. We will explain shortly what would happen if some other exception were raised in the presence of the handlers of *a* to *c*. The section of Figure 7.8.3*e* is invalid, since the **others** handler is not *last*. Finally, the handler of *f* does not even satisfy the definition of an exception handler, since the **others** "exception" may not be combined (via |) with any other type of exception.

```
a    exception
        when Text_IO.Data_Error =>
          Text_IO.Put ("Input data invalid -- ");
          Text_IO.Put_Line ("terminating execution ...");
     end;

b    exception
        when Text_IO.Data_Error =>
          Text_IO.Put ("Input data invalid -- ");
          Text_IO.Put_Line ("terminating execution ...");
        when Constraint_Error =>
          Text_IO.Put ("Input data out-of-range -- ");
          Text_IO.Put_Line ("terminating execution ...");
     end;

c    exception
        when Text_IO.Data_Error | Constraint_Error =>
          Text_IO.Put ("Input data invalid or ");
          Text_IO.Put ("out-of-range -- ");
          Text_IO.Put_Line ("terminating execution ...");
     end;

d    exception
        when Text_IO.Data_Error =>
          Text_IO.Put ("Input data invalid -- ");
          Text_IO.Put_Line ("terminating execution ...");
        when Constraint_Error =>
          Text_IO.Put ("Input data out-of-range -- ");
          Text_IO.Put_Line ("terminating execution ...");
        when others =>
          Text_IO.Put ("Unknown error -- ");
          Text_IO.Put_Line ("terminating execution ...");
     end;

e    exception
        when Text_IO.Data_Error =>
          Text_IO.Put ("Input data invalid -- ");
          Text_IO.Put_Line ("terminating execution ...");
        when others =>
          Text_IO.Put ("Unknown error -- ");
          Text_IO.Put_Line ("terminating execution ...");
        when Constraint_Error =>
          Text_IO.Put ("Input data out-of-range -- ");
          Text_IO.Put_Line ("terminating execution ...");
     end;
```

```
ƒ   exception
      when Text_IO.Data_Error =>
        Text_IO.Put ("Input data invalid -- ");
        Text_IO.Put_Line ("terminating execution ...");
      when Constraint_Error | others =>
        Text_IO.Put ("Input data out-of-range (???) -- ");
        Text_IO.Put_Line ("terminating execution ...");
    end;
```

Figure 7.8.3

Observe that none of these handlers deals with *all possible* exceptions on an individual basis (none will treat Numeric_Error, for example), although the handlers of Figure 7.8.3*d* manage all exceptions via the catchall **others** handler.

What happens if an exception is raised for which no handler is provided? As a concrete example, suppose Numeric_Error is raised in a program which has the section of Figure 7.8.3*b* as exception handlers. When the exception is raised, the run-time system notes that exception handlers are present and passes control to the start of these. It observes that the first handler (**when Text_IO.Data_Error =>**) does not treat the exception in question, so it passes control to the next handler (**when Constraint_Error =>**) which also fails to deal with it. We have come to the end of the exception handler section without having found a handler that deals specifically with Numeric_Error. In this case, the run-time system itself will deal with the exception, in exactly the same way it would have if there had been no exception handlers at all, namely, by displaying an error message and aborting program execution. In Section 7.9 we are a bit more explicit about the ways in which control is passed to and from exception handlers; in the meantime, what we have described here is precisely what will take place in these circumstances.

We can return to our change-making program and employ an exception handler to avoid the graceless termination of execution in the event of invalid input data (Figure 7.8.4). Note that the run-time system would take over if an exception other than Data_Error were raised, but we can state with some confidence that no other exception is possible in this little program.

```
    with Text_IO;

  procedure Change is

    subtype CENTS_RANGE is INTEGER range 1..99;

    package Cents_IO is new Text_IO.Integer_IO (CENTS_RANGE);

    Cost:        CENTS_RANGE;

  begin

    Text_IO.Put ("Enter cost in cents (1 to 99) of item: ");
    Cents_IO.Get (Cost);
    Text_IO.Put ("The change for one dollar on a ");
    Cents_IO.Put (Cost, 0);
    Text_IO.Put ("-cent item is ");
    Cents_IO.Put (100-Cost, 0);
    Text_IO.Put_Line (" cents.");
```

```
exception
   when Text_IO.Data_Error =>
      Text_IO.Put_Line ("Amount entered is not a valid cost.");

end Change;
```

Figure 7.8.4

7.9 The frame concept

You may understandably be unimpressed with the entire concept of exception handling as we have developed it so far. What have we really accomplished? We have said that an exception handler can contain as many of any sorts of statements as we might want, although our examples to date have simply displayed a message. What more might they have done? For whatever is done in the handler, it appears that the program will exit after the handler executes, and in fact this is the case. Thus about all we have managed to do is to replace a system message with a perhaps less rude and more understandable message of our own design, scarcely a giant step forward. At the heart of the matter is the statement that "the program will exit after the handler executes." This happens to be true here, but only because of the simple structure of the program. We now introduce a concept to expand our programming capabilities significantly and especially in the direction of dealing with exceptions.

A **frame** is a programming construct which has the syntax shown in Figure 7.9.1*a* or *b*.


```
a    begin                            b    begin
         <statement sequence>                  <statement sequence>
     end;                                   exception
                                               <exception handlers>
                                        end;
```

Figure 7.9.1

The syntax of Figure 7.9.1*b* is called a **frame with exception handlers**. It is interesting to note that all our programs up to this point consist for the most part of a single frame and that the program Change of Figure 7.8.4 has a single frame with exception handler. The power of the frame concept derives from the following:

1.   A frame may be constructed anywhere within the statement part of a programming module, in particular within other frames (such frames are then called **nested frames**).

2.   If an exception is raised within a frame, then either of the following occurs:

(a) If the frame contains an exception handler which deals with the exception, then the exception is **lowered** (that is, it is no longer raised, or is "turned off"); the statements of that handler are executed; and control passes to the statement that *would* have been executed next had the frame completed execution normally.

(b) If the frame does not contain an exception handler for the exception in question (in particular, if it contains no handler at all), then the exception *remains raised* and control passes to the statement that *would* have been executed next had the frame completed execution normally. Note that since the exception remains raised, control will immediately pass to the exception handler, if it exists, of the outer frame. In this case we say that the exception has been **propagated** from an inner frame to an outer frame.

An example will clarify these ideas. The program segment of Figure 7.9.2 has three nested frames, the outer of which we suppose to be the statement part of a main program. Note that the innermost frame has no corresponding exception handler, and thus the frame construct itself appears not to add anything to the programming here. This may be true in the present instance, but later we will see that frames without exception handlers are by no means unusual. Now suppose that a Numeric_Error exception occurs where indicated. The run-time system looks within Frame 1 for an exception handler, but it finds none. The exception is propagated outward, and control is passed to the statement (Statement_A) immediately following Frame 1—the statement that would have been executed after *normal* completion of Frame 1—while *leaving* the Numeric_Error exception *raised*. (Note that nothing has occurred to *lower* it.) Since there is an exception raised (Numeric_Error), the run-time system again searches for an exception handler in the current frame (Frame 2). This time one is found; however, it does not handle the exception in question. Thus once more control is passed outward, to Frame 3, with the exception *still* raised. As before, Statement_B is not executed because of the propagated exception; instead, control passes to the Frame 3 exception handler, which *does* deal with this error.

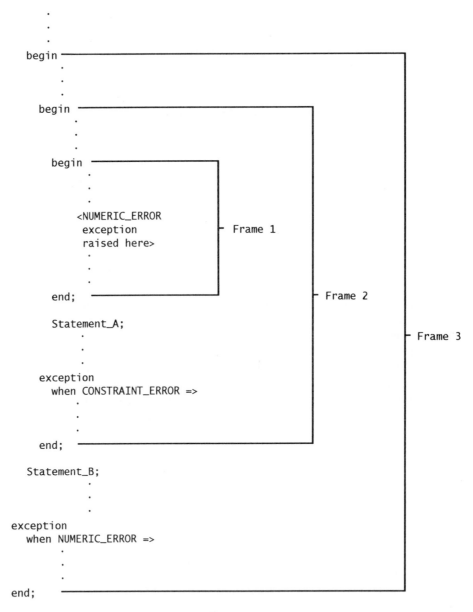

Figure 7.9.2

What would have happened in this example had the outer (and last) frame *not* dealt with the Numeric_Error? To be consistent with what has gone before, the exception would have to be propagated out of the current frame (Frame 3). But if Frame 3 is the entire statement part of the program, is there an "outside"? Yes, as we have mentioned before, we can think of the program itself as being embedded in the run-time system, and thus control would pass to this system with the exception still raised. As we know, the run-time system handles *every* exception, by means of displaying an appropriate message.

Suppose now that instead of a Numeric_Error occurring within Frame 1, Constraint_Error had been raised. (See Figure 7.9.3.) As before, control would pass outward from Frame 1 to Frame 2, with Constraint_Error raised. Thus control would be given over immediately to the Frame 2 exception handler, which *would* deal in some fashion with the exception, and in the course of its execution, it would *lower* the exception. When this exception handler had completed its work, control would be passed outward to Statement_B, which *would* execute since now *no* exception is in a raised state.

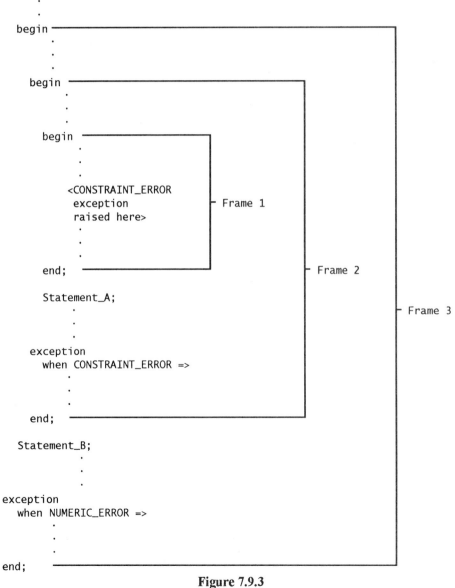

```
              .
              .
              .
  begin ─────────────────────────────────────────────────────┐
              .                                               │
              .                                               │
              .                                               │
      begin ──────────────────────────────────────┐          │
              .                                    │          │
              .                                    │          │
              .                                    │          │
          begin ───────────────────────┐          │          │
                  .                     │          │          │
                  .                     │          │          │
                  .                     │          │          │
              <CONSTRAINT_ERROR         │          │          │
               exception                │─ Frame 1 │          │
               raised here>             │          │          │
                  .                     │          │          │
                  .                     │          │          │
          end; ──────────────────────── ┘          │─ Frame 2 │
          Statement_A;                             │          │─ Frame 3
                  .                                 │          │
                  .                                 │          │
                  .                                 │          │
          exception                                │          │
            when CONSTRAINT_ERROR =>               │          │
                  .                                 │          │
                  .                                 │          │
                  .                                 │          │
          end; ──────────────────────────────────── ┘          │
      Statement_B;                                             │
              .                                                │
              .                                                │
              .                                                │
  exception                                                   │
    when NUMERIC_ERROR =>                                      │
          .                                                    │
          .                                                    │
          .                                                    │
  end; ──────────────────────────────────────────────────────┘
```

Figure 7.9.3

Finally, there is a detail that may not have occurred to you but which needs to be discussed. We have noted that an exception handler consists for the most part of a sequence of ordinary Ada statements. What would happen if in the course of handling an exception, the execution of one of the exception handler statements itself raises an exception (different from or possibly even the same as the exception being handled)? In this case control is passed *directly* to the statement that would normally have been carried out immediately *after* the frame had completed execution; the new exception would be raised (and thus must be handled); the original exception would already have been lowered.

To summarize these concepts, we see that the statement parts of programs consist for the most part of frames, nested in various fashions. When exceptions are raised, control continues to be propagated outward to enclosing frames, until a handler is found that will deal with the exception. The run-time system itself acts as the final "frame" in this sequence —the run-time system contains the "exception handler of last resort." We are now in a position to put this concept to use in our programming.

7.10 Programming with frames and exceptions: I

The program Change of Figure 7.8.4 leaves abundant opportunity for improvement. For example, consider what will happen if we wish to calculate the change for a 52-cent item, but because of a missed keystroke, we enter "r2" instead. The program displays its error message and exits to the operating system. This is no problem, of course, for we merely reexecute the program and supply the correct input. But consider a program which requires perhaps dozens of data items, all from keyboard input. Suppose, after having entered, say, 50 pieces of data, we inadvertently type an invalid number. If the program displays an error message and returns control to the operating system, we are faced with the prospect of running the program again and reentering all the data (including, of course, the 50 inputs that were valid in the first place). We would like to give the user a chance to correct any invalid input *without* having to start the program over again, and this is easily accomplished using frames and appropriately written exception handlers. We illustrate the technique by a new version of the change-making program of Figure 7.10.1, which will process valid data and then exit as before but which now responds to invalid data with an error message and the invitation to reenter the input—the user has as many tries to enter valid data as may be required. (We have included line numbers on the program listing to facilitate our discussion.)

```
1    with Text_IO;
2
3  procedure Change is
4
5    subtype CENTS_RANGE is INTEGER range 1..99;
6
7    package Cents_IO is new Text_IO.Integer_IO (CENTS_RANGE);
8
9    Cost:                CENTS_RANGE;
10
11 begin
12   loop
13     begin
14
```

```
15        Text_IO.Put ("Enter cost in cents (1 to 99) of item: ");
16        Cents_IO.Get (Cost);
17        Text_IO.Put ("The change for one dollar on a ";
18        Cents_IO.Put (Cost, 0);
19        Text_IO.Put ("-cent item is ");
20        Cents_IO.Put (100-Cost, 0);
21        Text_IO.Put_Line (" cents.");
22        exit;
23
24     exception
25        when Text_IO.Data_Error =>
26           Text_IO.Put ("Amount entered ");
27           Text_IO.Put_Line ("is not a valid cost.");
28           Text_IO.New_Line;
30
31     end;
32
33   end loop;
34
35 end Change;
```

Figure 7.10.1

Note that the program contains a frame with exception handler (lines 13 to 31) inside a loop (lines 12 to 33) inside a frame (lines 11 to 35, the statement part of the program itself). When execution begins (at line 11), the loop beginning at line 12 is entered and then comes the frame beginning at line 13. Suppose we enter a *valid* number at the input request (the Get at line 16). The next 5 statements (lines 17 to 22) are executed, and the **exit** statement causes control to pass to the statement following the **end loop** at line 33. (Recall that **exit** always exits the *loop* in which it is located.) Since this is the end of the program, control returns to the operating system. That is, the program behaves exactly as before when it is supplied valid input. But now suppose that the keyboard input entered at line 16 is *invalid*. Then a Data_Error exception is raised, and control passes immediately to the innermost exception handler. This is the handler beginning at line 24, and when it executes, it lowers the Data_Error exception and displays an error message. As is always the case upon completion of execution of an exception handler, control is given over to the point in the enclosing frame to which control would have passed next had the frame completed execution successfully (in this case the point immediately following the current frame), and this is the **end loop** at line 33. Since we are still *in* the loop (not *beyond* it) and in fact at the end of it, the loop reexecutes, so the frame is entered again at line 13, and the input request at line 16 again seeks a valid number. It is clear that the loop (lines 12 to 33) will execute continually until valid data is obtained and the **exit** at line 22 can be executed.

7.11 More about the keyboard input of integers

A potential disaster is lurking in the statements of the Change program of Figure 7.10.1, but to uncover it, we must deepen our understanding of how numbers are input to a program via the keyboard. As you are doubtless aware, when a sequence of keyboard characters is typed, the program requesting the input does not respond to it until the RETURN or ENTER key is pressed. The reason for this is that although the operating system has accepted the keystrokes, it is only after the ENTER key is pressed that the system passes the entire line of input to the executing program. Thus suppose, for example, that the input 52 is supplied to the executing program. After the ENTER key is pressed, Change sees the sequence of characters shown in Figure 7.11.1, stored in an area of memory known as the **keyboard buffer**. (The term *buffer* is in common use in computing for an area of memory in which sequences of data items are stored, usually on a temporary basis.) The arrow in the diagram is called the **keyboard buffer pointer**, and its function will be seen shortly. When the ENTER key is pressed, it is necessary to note in the buffer where that event took place—that is, we need to mark the logical end of the sequence of characters that was entered. The buffer itself, as a set of physical locations, may be quite long; this is the *physical* buffer. The set of characters entered into the buffer through the keyboard is in general much shorter than the physical buffer; we refer to this set of characters as the *logical* buffer. The "mark" in question marks the end of the logical buffer. We show this in the diagrams by the symbol EOL, which we refer to as the **end-of-line marker** or **line terminator**.

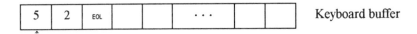

Keyboard buffer

Figure 7.11.1

When Integer_IO (more correctly, some particular instantiation of it) gets an integer number from the keyboard buffer, it does so according to the following rules.

1.   If the keyboard buffer is *empty* (that is, contains no characters—the state of the buffer when the program begins execution, for example), wait for the user to fill the buffer by typing characters, followed by an ENTER. Set the buffer pointer to the first character entered.

2.   If the keyboard buffer pointer is currently pointing at a blank or tab character, move the pointer to the next position in the buffer and repeat Step 2. (That is, the Get routine will skip over *leading* blanks or tabs.)

3.   If the character now pointed at by the buffer pointer (the leftmost nonblank, nontab) is *not* +, −, or a digit character (0 to 9), then raise the Data_Error exception. If the character pointed at by the buffer pointer is + or −, record the sign and move the buffer pointer one position to the right; if the character now being pointed at is not a digit character, raise Data_Error.

4.   If the buffer pointer is pointing at a digit character, convert that character to its corresponding integer value and move the buffer pointer one character to the right. Repeat Step 4 continually until the character pointed at by the buffer pointer is *not* a digit character. *Note:* What happens when the buffer pointer is pointing at a nondigit is somewhat implementation-dependent. Some systems will cause Data_Error to be raised if certain special nondigit characters are encountered, notably the decimal point (.) character; most systems will stop the conversion process under these circumstances. What can be said with assurance is that the character-to-number

conversion process will terminate without error when the buffer pointer encounters either a space character or the end-of-line marker (the two most frequently occurring conditions).

5. If necessary, adjust the sign of the converted integer. If the resulting number does *not* conform to the range associated with the I/O package to which the Get belongs, raise Data_Error. Otherwise the conversion is complete. At this point an attempt is made to assign the converted integer to the item being gotten—the parameter of the Get procedure. If the assignment cannot successfully be made because the converted integer fails to conform to any range constraints of the parameter, Constraint_Error is raised.

Notes: (1) We recognize that the underscore character is also valid when the input is numeric in nature, but in the interest of keeping the algorithm as simple as possible, we have chosen to ignore this special case. You are asked to provide an appropriate modification of the algorithm in the exercises. (2) The algorithm for the input of numbers of type FLOAT is the same as described above, *except* (a) the input must contain a decimal point preceded and followed by a decimal digit (otherwise Data_Error will be raised) and (b) no Constraint_Error is possible. (3) The input of variables of type CHARACTER, beyond what has already been discussed, is taken up in further detail in Chapter 12.

　　Let us examine the sequence of events for the keyboard buffer shown in Figure 7.11.1. We note that the buffer is not empty, and thus the program need not wait for input—Step 1 above. To begin with, the pointer is pointing at the character 5. Thus there are no leading blanks or tabs (Step 2), and so we move on to Step 3. The pointer is not pointing at a + or −, and in fact it is pointing at a digit character. Thus the tests of Step 2 have been passed. Since the pointer is pointing at 5 (a digit character—Step 4), the character 5 is converted to integer form and the pointer is moved to the right and thus points at the character 2. Once again this is a digit (Step 4 repeated), which is converted to an integer. (Because of the digits encountered and their positions in the buffer, the integer that has been "built up" so far is fifty-two.) Once again the pointer is moved, and the test of Step 4 is applied. This time the buffer pointer is pointing at the end-of-line marker, and this is *not* a digit. Thus (Step 5) the conversion stops, and we observe that the buffer pointer is left pointing at the end-of-line marker.
　　As another example of Get's actions on keyboard buffers, consider the buffer of Figure 7.11.2, where we use the symbol Ⱬ to mean a blank, or space, character. In this case the three leading blanks will be skipped over, so the buffer pointer ultimately points at the minus sign. (This is Step 2 above.) Now (Step 3) the sign information is recorded (so that the converted integer can later be negated), and the buffer pointer is moved again, pointing at +. Note that this character does *not* satisfy the conditions of Step 3, and thus the Data_Error exception is raised.

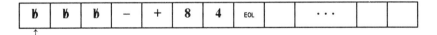

Figure 7.11.2

Next we examine an example that does much to illuminate what might be considered peculiar behavior of Get without a solid understanding of how data is removed from the buffer. (See Figure 7.11.3.) The conversion begins in a fairly straightforward way—the leading blanks are skipped, the sign is noted and skipped, and the digits 1 and 7 are converted (to the integer 17). At this point the buffer pointer is at the character 7, and according to the procedures of Step 4, the pointer is moved so that it now points at the blank character. Since this is not a digit, the conversion stops (Step 5), the converted number being adjusted to −17. Note that the buffer pointer has been left pointing at the blank character (Figure 7.11.4). Thus the program user has evidently entered *two* numbers (−17 and 489) *simultaneously* in response to an input request, but as we have just seen, only the first of these has been gotten—the 489 is unused. What will happen if the program encounters a *second* input request? It checks the keyboard buffer and notes that it is *not* empty (Step 1). Thus this second request can be satisfied from the same buffer—the second request gets the number 489, and we see that the program did not have to wait for the input from the keyboard—it had already been entered.

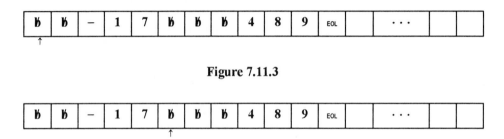

Figure 7.11.3

Figure 7.11.4

This phenomenon of a program user anticipating input requests and *presatisfying* them is sometimes referred to as **type-ahead**. It may be desirable in some circumstances and undesirable in others. We will see that one can ignore characters typed in advance—more accurately, to cause them to be removed from the keyboard buffer. To introduce this notion, we present a final example in which we see that the various actions of the buffer pointer can lead to problems.

Suppose some instantiation of Integer_IO attempts a Get of an integer, and the program user responds with the buffer shown in Figure 7.11.5, probably as a result of a keying error. Since the character being pointed at in the keyboard buffer is not a blank, tab, +, −, or digit character, the Get routine will leave the buffer pointer where it is and raise the Data_Error exception. Now suppose that after the exception has been dealt with, there is a *second* input request for integer data. Since neither the keyboard buffer nor its buffer pointer has changed, Get will see a nonempty buffer and attempt to satisfy this second request from the same buffer. Of course this will simply raise the Data_Error exception again. If this activity is in a *loop*—as it is in the program of Figure 7.10.1—we are destined to execute the loop forever.

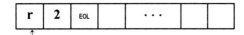

Figure 7.11.5

It is clear that what is needed to solve this last-mentioned dilemma, and also to prevent type-ahead, if desired, is some means—an Ada statement—of *clearing* the keyboard buffer so that any Get will see it as empty and thus wait for the user to refill it. There is such a statement in the package Text_IO; it is **Skip_Line**, and its effect is as stated—it clears the keyboard (input) buffer by *Skipp*ing over anything currently in the buffer, including the end-of-*Line* marker, thereby leaving the buffer with nothing in it. (Please make special note that Skip_Line is an *input* concept, even though its name might suggest that its effect is to skip a *display* line. Do not confuse it with New_Line.) With this new tool we can repair the program of Figure 7.10.1 so that infinite looping within the Get frame cannot occur. Figure 7.11.6 shows a revised version; observe that the only change necessary was the inclusion of the Skip_Line statement in the exception handler.

```ada
with Text_IO;

procedure Change is

    subtype CENTS_RANGE is INTEGER range 1..99;

    package Cents_IO is new Text_IO.Integer_IO (CENTS_RANGE);

    Cost:                 CENTS_RANGE;
begin
    loop
      begin

        Text_IO.Put ("Enter cost in cents (1 to 99) of item: ");
        Cents_IO.Get (Cost);
        Text_IO.Put ("The change for one dollar on a ");
        Cents_IO.Put (Cost, 0);
        Text_IO.Put ("-cent item is ");
        Cents_IO.Put (100-Cost, 0);
        Text_IO.Put_Line (" cents.");
        exit;

      exception
        when Text_IO.Data_Error =>
          Text_IO.Put_Line ("Amount entered is not a valid cost.");
          Text_IO.New_Line;
          Text_IO.Skip_Line;

      end;

    end loop;

end Change;
```

Figure 7.11.6

7.12 Programming with frames and exceptions: II

In this section and the next we make a few final adjustments to the change-making program of this chapter. Our latest version (Figure 7.11.6) allows as many tries at entering a valid number as the user might want. However, in some circumstances this may be unreasonable, for it clearly can trap the user indefinitely in a loop of inputs if, for example, he or she simply does not understand the form that the input is to take. (The description of valid input is completely explicit in the change-making program, but if prompting messages are more vague, abbreviated, or even missing altogether, genuine confusion about what input is expected can arise.) Thus while it may make good sense to allow the user more than one try at input, allowing infinitely many may not. In Figure 7.12.1 we offer a version of the change-making program which allows the user three chances to enter valid input; at the third consecutive invalid input, the program exits with a message.

```
with Text_IO;

procedure Change is

    subtype CENTS_RANGE is INTEGER range 1..99;

    package Cents_IO is new Text_IO.Integer_IO (CENTS_RANGE);

    Cost:       CENTS_RANGE;
    Failures:   NATURAL;
begin
    Failures := 0;

    loop
      begin

        Text_IO.Put ("Enter cost in cents (1 to 99) of item: ");
        Cents_IO.Get (Cost);
        Text_IO.Put ("The change for one dollar on a ");
        Cents_IO.Put (Cost, 0);
        Text_IO.Put ("-cent item is ");
        Cents_IO.Put (100-Cost, 0);
        Text_IO.Put_Line (" cents.");
        exit;
      exception
        when Text_IO.Data_Error =>
          Text_IO.Put_Line ("Amount entered is not a valid cost.");
          Text_IO.New_Line;
          Text_IO.Skip_Line;

          Failures := Failures + 1;
          if Failures = 3 then
          Text_IO.Put ("Terminating execution ");
          Text_IO.Put_Line ("after 3 input failures...");
          exit;
        end if;

      end;

    end loop;

end Change;
```

Figure 7.12.1

There is nothing very esoteric about this version of Change. It keeps track of how many times the exception handler has been executed by means of the variable Failures, which has been given the initial value 0. If Failures reaches the value 3, an **exit** statement forces termination of the loop and, in fact, the program itself. You should verify that if *valid* input is supplied within the first three tries, the program will execute just as each of its earlier versions has.

We have a further objection to the program of Figure 7.12.1, which has more to do with its *structure* than its *behavior*. Notice that the entire executable part of the program lies within the frame inside the loop. Recall that the purpose of constructing this frame was to deal with the problem of invalid input supplied to Get, so certainly we would need to place the **Cents_IO.Get (Cost)** statement within that frame. But by including all the following executable statements within this frame, we are obscuring the frame's true purpose. It would lead to a more readable, logically pleasing program if these statements could be moved out of the frame, to allow the frame and its exception handler to concentrate on the job of managing input and invalid data. The program is easily adjusted to accommodate this structure, as we see from Figure 7.12.2, a simple modification of the version of Figure 7.12.1.

```
    with Text_IO;

procedure Change is

    subtype CENTS_RANGE is INTEGER range 1..99;

    package Cents_IO is new Text_IO.Integer_IO (CENTS_RANGE);

    Cost:               CENTS_RANGE;
begin
    loop
      begin

        Text_IO.Put ("Enter cost in cents (1 to 99) of item: ");
        Cents_IO.Get (Cost);
        exit;

      exception
        when Text_IO.Data_Error =>
          Text_IO.Put_Line ("Amount entered is not a valid cost.");
          Text_IO.New_Line;
          Text_IO.Skip_Line;

      end;

    end loop;

    Text_IO.Put ("The change for one dollar on a ");
    Cents_IO.Put (Cost, 0);
    Text_IO.Put ("-cent item is ");
    Cents_IO.Put (100-Cost, 0);
    Text_IO.Put_Line (" cents.");

end Change;
```

Figure 7.12.2

Can we combine the improvements of our last two attempts (Figures 7.12.1 and
7.12.2)? Yes, but there is a problem here, and solving it leads to a program that is
structurally quite unappealing. We cannot simply move the Put statements of Figure 7.12.1
to a position following the loop as we did in Figure 7.12.2. For in that position they are
programmed to execute under *any* circumstances. Note that if the loop is exited from the
exception handler (because too many failures have occurred), then no further processing is to
be done—the program is to terminate. Thus we must distinguish *how* the loop was exited. If
it was exited after the Get statement, then the input was valid and the Put statements should
be executed. If it exited from the exception handler, then the input was *not* valid and those
Put statements should not be executed. The program of Figure 7.12.3 does execute properly
—note the use of the Boolean variable OK, initialized to True, to determine whether the Put
statements are to be executed. But this program has required the somewhat artificial
introduction of the variable OK, and now we have a significant part of the main program in
an **if** clause, the same kind of objection we had to the program of Figure 7.3.2.

```
with Text_IO;

procedure Change is

   subtype CENTS_RANGE is INTEGER range 1..99;

   package Cents_IO is new Text_IO.Integer_IO (CENTS_RANGE);

   Cost:        CENTS_RANGE;
   Failures:    NATURAL;
   OK:          Boolean;

begin
   Failures := 0;
   OK := True;

   loop
     begin

        Text_IO.Put ("Enter cost in cents (1 to 99) of item: ");
        Cents_IO.Get (Cost);
        exit;

     exception
        when Text_IO.Data_Error =>
          Text_IO.Put_Line ("Amount entered is not a valid cost.");
          Text_IO.New_Line;
          Text_IO.Skip_Line;

          Failures := Failures + 1;
          if Failures = 3 then
            Text_IO.Put ("Terminating execution ");
            Text_IO.Put_Line ("after 3 input failures...");
            OK := False;
            exit;
          end if;

     end;

   end loop;
```

```
  if OK then
    Text_IO.Put ("The change for one dollar on a ");
    Cents_IO.Put (Cost, 0);
    Text_IO.Put ("-cent item is ");
    Cents_IO.Put (100-Cost, 0);
    Text_IO.Put_Line (" cents.");
  end if;

end Change;
```

Figure 7.12.3

7.13 Programmer-declared exceptions

How could the program of Figure 7.12.3 be made to function more smoothly in the event of too many input failures? As it stands, when we leave the exception handler (with the **exit** statement), we leave the inner frame and return to the outer frame. It is at this point that we must make provision for skipping the next set of instructions—that is, for getting to the end of the frame. Now observe that *if* an exception occurred *within the exception handler* in the inner frame, then we would abandon the inner frame and immediately get to the end of the outer frame, since the run-time system would be looking for an exception handler at the end of the outer frame. How can we ensure that an exception will be raised in order to force control to leave the exception handler?

Ada allows the programmer to name and declare new kinds of exceptions, known as **programmer-declared exceptions**. They are "new" in the sense that they are purely creations of the programmer, not predeclared within the Ada system. As we will see, their behavior is almost identical to that of the exceptions we have been studying, the fundamental distinctions being that (1) they must be declared in the declaration section (the reserved word **exception** is used in place of the usual type mark) and (2) a programmer-declared exception is raised *only* via the special Ada instruction **raise <exception name>**; it is lowered as usual by the **when <exception name> =>** exception handler. (Incidentally, immediately upon its declaration, a programmer-declared exception is in its *lowered* state.) The programmer may declare as many exceptions as are appropriate to the programming task, and except for the way in which they reach a "raised" state, they behave and are operated on in the same fashion as any other exception. Using this concept, we present our last and cleanest version of the change-making program (Figure 7.13.1), in which the programmer-declared exception Too_Many_Failures does precisely the job we need.

```
    with Text_IO;

  procedure Change is

    subtype CENTS_RANGE is INTEGER range 1..99;

    package Cents_IO is new Text_IO.Integer_IO (CENTS_RANGE);

    Cost:             CENTS_RANGE;
    Failures:         NATURAL;

    Too_Many_Failures: exception;
```

```
begin
  Failures := 0;

  loop
    begin

      Text_IO.Put ("Enter cost in cents (1 to 99) of item: ");
      Cents_IO.Get (Cost);
      exit;

    exception
      when Text_IO.Data_Error =>
        Text_IO.Put_Line ("Amount entered is not a valid cost.");
        Text_IO.New_Line;
        Text_IO.Skip_Line;

        Failures := Failures + 1;
        if Failures = 3 then
          raise Too_Many_Failures;
        end if;

    end;

  end loop;

  Text_IO.Put ("The change for one dollar on a ");
  Cents_IO.Put (Cost, 0);
  Text_IO.Put ("-cent item is ");
  Cents_IO.Put (100-Cost, 0);
  Text_IO.Put_Line (" cents.");

exception
  when Too_Many_Failures =>
    Text_IO.Put ("Terminating execution ");
    Text_IO.Put_Line ("after 3 input failures...");

end Change;
```

Figure 7.13.1

7.14 The program Time_and_Day revisited

In Figure 7.14.1 we present without great fanfare the latest version of Time_and_Day, the program developed in Chapter 6 (see Figure 6.3.1). Its changes follow closely the development of the change-making program that we have just completed. Specifically, input data checking has taken advantage of Ada's testing of variables that have been constrained to ranges of integers, although observe here that there are *two* instantiations of the Integer_IO package: Int_IO and Minutes_IO. An exception handler is included to deal with any data error exception that might occur as a result of an input integer lying outside its permitted range. Finally, this version of Time_and_Day allows the user a maximum of three faulty inputs, after which it raises a failure exception (here named Time_Up), which is handled in the main program exception handler. Thus the structure of the program is much like that of the Change program of Figure 7.13.1, but since Time_and_Day is a bit more complicated, you should once again verify that the several logical paths through the program, resulting from various inputs (both valid and invalid), do behave as expected.

```
    with Text_IO, Int_IO;

  procedure Time_and_Day is

    subtype MINUTES_RANGE is INTEGER range 0..10079;

    package Minutes_IO is new Text_IO.Integer_IO (MINUTES_RANGE);

    Minutes_Elapsed:        MINUTES_RANGE;
    Hours_Elapsed:          NATURAL;
    Day, Hour, Minute:      NATURAL;
    Minutes_in_Hour:        constant INTEGER := 60;
    Hours_in_Day:           constant INTEGER := 24;

    Midnight:               Boolean := False;
    Noon:                   Boolean := False;
    PM:                     Boolean := False;

    Wrong_Inputs:           NATURAL;

    Time_Up:                exception;


  begin
    Wrong_Inputs := 0;

    Text_IO.New_Line;
    Text_IO.Put ("How many minutes since the week began (0 to 10079)? ");
    Get_Input:
    loop

      begin
        Minutes_IO.Get (Minutes_Elapsed);
        exit Get_Input;
      exception
        when Text_IO.Data_Error =>
          Wrong_Inputs := Wrong_Inputs + 1;
          if Wrong_Inputs = 3 then
            raise Time_Up;
          end if;
          Text_IO.Put_Line ("Minutes must be between 0 and 10079.");
          Text_IO.Put ("Try again: ");
          Text_IO.Skip_Line;
      end;

    end loop Get_Input;

    Text_IO.New_Line;

    Hours_Elapsed := Minutes_Elapsed  /  Minutes_in_Hour;
    Minute        := Minutes_Elapsed rem Minutes_in_Hour;
    Day           := Hours_Elapsed    /  Hours_in_Day;
    Hour          := Hours_Elapsed    rem Hours_in_Day;
```

```
  if Hour = 0 and Minute = 0 then
    Midnight := True;
    Hour := 12;
  elsif Hour = 12 and Minute = 0 then
    Noon := True;
  elsif Hour >= 12 then
    PM := True;
    if Hour > 12 then
      Hour := Hour - 12;
    end if;
  elsif Hour = 0 then
    Hour := 12;
  end if;

  Text_IO.Put ("The time is ");
  Int_IO.Put (Hour, 0);
  Text_IO.Put (":");
  Int_IO.Put (Minute / 10, 0);
  Int_IO.Put (Minute rem 10, 0);
  if Midnight then
    Text_IO.Put (" midnight");
  elsif Noon then
    Text_IO.Put (" noon");
  elsif PM then
    Text_IO.Put (" p.m.");
  else
    Text_IO.Put (" a.m.");
  end if;
  Text_IO.Put (" on ");

  if Day = 0 then
    Text_IO.Put ("Sunday");
  elsif Day = 1 then
    Text_IO.Put ("Monday");
  elsif Day = 2 then
    Text_IO.Put ("Tuesday");
  elsif Day = 3 then
    Text_IO.Put ("Wednesday");
  elsif Day = 4 then
    Text_IO.Put ("Thursday");
  elsif Day = 5 then
    Text_IO.Put ("Friday");
  else
    Text_IO.Put ("Saturday");
  end if;
  Text_IO.Put_Line (."");

exception
  when Time_Up =>
    Text_IO.Put ("Input is still incorrect...");
    Text_IO.Put_Line ("execution is terminated.");

end Time_and_Day;
```

Figure 7.14.1

7.15 On program "debugging"

We began this chapter with a discussion of program correctness and, in particular, the distinction between errors in program logic (an incorrect program) and errors resulting from invalid data (a program operating on incorrect variable values). While we had something to say about the *detection* of logical errors via carefully chosen sets of test data, no attention was paid to the *location* of logical errors—how to find such errors and thus to eliminate them. In fact this error location and elimination process—generally known as **debugging**—can be a terribly time-consuming and frustrating business for which the only help we can offer consists at present mainly of vague guidelines rather than guaranteed techniques.

The first step in program debugging should always be a "desk session" in which the programmer sits down with the program listing and runs through the program statements with data that are known to cause incorrect output. If the program is not too long or complex, this will frequently locate the bug and suggest the appropriate repairs. If this technique fails to find the problem, the insertion of a variety of temporary display (Put) statements in key places in the program may be of assistance. These display statements might (1) display the value of a given variable at the places where it changes its value; (2) display the value of a loop-controlling variable; or (3) display a message announcing that execution had reached a certain point in the program. That is, by inserting these display statements, we are making the program output temporarily far more "verbose" than is actually intended, in order that we might more easily track the progress of execution and the values taken on by key variables (and, in particular, those which led to the incorrect output). Of course, these "tracers"—display statements—will be removed once the program has been debugged.

Sometimes it is useful to have someone else, who is familiar with the problem being solved, examine your program. It is often easy for the programmer to "see" things in a program that are not there or to interpret statements the way they are *supposed* to be, as opposed to the way they *are*. For example, in a **for I in ... loop** construction, the programmer who intended to increment the variable X by 1 can easily look at the statement **X := X + I** and "see" **X := X + 1**. Someone else is less likely to make the same mistake.

Many operating systems feature system programs frequently called **debuggers** or **symbolic debuggers**. These powerful programs give the programmer the capabilities to accomplish the following:

1. Insert **breakpoints** into a program (points at which, during execution, the program temporarily pauses and allows the user to display variable values, jump to other points in the program, or continue with execution).

2. Insert **tracepoints** (which trace the execution of the program without the stopping invoked by a breakpoint).

3. Set **watchpoints** (which cause the displaying of the old and new values of a specified variable each time its value changes).

4. **Step** the program (by causing execution to be suspended, as with a breakpoint, after the execution of each statement).

These are some of the capabilities of debuggers, and many are far more sophisticated than what has been suggested here. However, for the beginning programmer, we feel that debuggers are the "court of last resort" when it comes to the detection of logical program errors, in part because the use of the debugger is "just one more thing to learn" at a time when there are many new concepts to assimilate. A debugger in the hands of a competent programmer is a very powerful tool. Thus we do not mean to discourage its use; rather, we intend that the novice programmer understand that it is one of a sequence of implements that can be brought to bear on a program bug and that it is never the *first* that should be employed.

If the first step in locating a program bug is a desk session, then the best advice we can offer a programmer is to "make sure that your programming is so short and simple that the complexity of its logic can never exceed your ability to grasp it easily." Do not interpret this statement as an expression of our commitment to trivial programs; on the contrary, it is the large, complex tasks that actually need to be computerized. To understand our position, recall that the guiding principle of so-called modular programming is the breaking down of complex problems into simpler and simpler pieces, until the solving of the individual pieces becomes easy. As we will begin to see in the next chapter, Ada supplies facilities aimed precisely at this goal. Indeed, we have already seen numerous instances of Ada constructs that *simplify* the logical structure of programming. As examples we cite the following:

1. The predeclaration of all objects and Ada's strong typing eliminate the possibility of many logical, run-time errors.

2. The **loop ... end loop** construct, including the **for** and **while** variations, is implemented precisely to simplify the logic of programs.

3. We have just seen that frames and exceptions can significantly improve the readability and thus the understandability of some program constructions.

4 Related procedures can be grouped together into *packages* in such a way that they are conveniently available for use at any appropriate time, and yet the programmer who employs them need not be concerned about the actual Ada code that comprises them.

7.16 Exceptions associated with external data files*

In Section 6.9 we presented a program that illustrates how useful external files of alphabetical and numerical data can be. In that final version of the Checkbook program, we not only read from external files the checking account's current balance (BALANCE.CUR) and new transaction data (TRANSACT.DAT), but upon completion of the processing of the transactions, we also created a new current balance file, so that the program would be ready to be executed on the *next* set of transactions.

---

*This section is optional; it is a continuation of, and depends upon, the optional Section 6.9.

There is a pitfall in the overall structure of this "software system," and it is a most mysterious one. The file TRANSACT.DAT used in Section 6.9 has the appearance shown in Figure 7.16.1*a*.

a		*b*	
	−14.21		−14.21
	−77.42		−77.42
	−41.18		−41.18
	84.87		84.87
	−12.98		−12.98
			\<blank line\>

Figure 7.16.1

Suppose instead there was a blank line in the file following the last transaction line, as shown in Figure 7.16.1*b*. (Recall that the transaction file is probably created by means of an editor, so the insertion of a blank line or two at its end could be a fairly common, if inadvertent, occurrence.) If the program is executed using the file of Figure 7.16.1*b*, it will process each transaction correctly:

The opening account balance is 104.72

Transaction: −14.21

Transaction: −77.42

Transaction: −41.18

Transaction: 84.87

Transaction: −12.98

However, before it can exit the **while** loop and write a new BALANCE.CUR file, an End_Error exception is raised. (The exception End_Error is raised whenever an attempt is made to go beyond the end-of-file marker with a Get or Skip_Line.) Since the program makes no provision for handling this or any other exception, the Ada run-time system displays an appropriate error message and terminates execution.

As you must have guessed, the culprit here is the blank line. In effect, what has happened is the following: Normally, immediately after the last number in the file (−12.98) is read via Flt_IO.Get, the end of the transaction file is encountered since there is nothing left in the file, and this causes **Text_IO.End_Of_File (Trans_File)** to return the value True, the value that terminates the **while** loop. In this case, after the last number is read, the end of the file is *not* seen, since there is still more in the file: the blank line. Thus the **while** loop executes once more, and the file is searched for the "next" floating point number. Before such a number can be found (there is none, of course), the end of the file is encountered, and it is this event that raises the End_Error exception. There are a number of important missing details essential to a complete understanding of the phenomenon that has taken place here;

we fill in most of these in Chapter 12. (We can even add to the intrigue by observing that only blank lines at the *end* of the file cause this phenomenon; blank lines between two nonblank lines cause no difficulty whatever!)

Now that we know the cause of the problem, how can we deal with it? The answer is remarkably simple. We read the transaction file in an *uncontrolled* loop rather than a **while** loop and *let* the exception occur. This causes control to pass to an exception handler, in which we acknowledge the End_Error exception. In the present case, the exception handler can contain the entire remainder of the program. The resulting program is shown in Figure 7.16.2.

```
with Text_IO, Flt_IO;

procedure Checkbook is

    Trans_File,
    Bal_File:           Text_IO.FILE_TYPE;

    Current_Balance:    FLOAT;
    Transaction:        FLOAT;
    New_Balance:        FLOAT;

begin
    Text_IO.Open (Bal_File, Text_IO.In_File, "BALANCE.CUR");
    Flt_IO.Get (Bal_File, New_Balance);
    Text_IO.Put ("The opening account balance is ");
    Flt_IO.Put (New_Balance, 0, 2, 0);
    Text_IO.New_Line;
    Text_IO.Close (Bal_File);

    Text_IO.Open (Trans_File, Text_IO.In_File, "TRANSACT.DAT");

    loop
      Current_Balance := New_Balance;
      Flt_IO.Get (Trans_File, Transaction);
      Text_IO.New_Line;
      Text_IO.Put ("Transaction: ");
      Flt_IO.Put (Transaction, 0, 2, 0);
      Text_IO.New_Line;

      New_Balance := Current_Balance + Transaction;
    end loop;

exception

    when Text_IO.End_Error =>

      Text_IO.Close (Trans_File);
      Text_IO.New_Line;
      Text_IO.Put ("The closing account balance is ");
      Flt_IO.Put (New_Balance, 0, 2, 0);
      Text_IO.New_Line (2);
      Text_IO.Create (Bal_File, Text_IO.Out_File, "BALANCE.CUR");
      Flt_IO.Put (Bal_File, New_Balance, 0, 2, 0);
      Text_IO.Close (Bal_File);

end Checkbook;
```

Figure 7.16.2

As you can see, transactions are read from the transaction file until there are no more transactions. At that time, the End_Error exception is raised, and the remaining program details are dealt with in the exception handler. (Note that End_Error is declared in the package Text_IO.)

If there is a deficiency in this program, it has to do with the fact that the entire ending segment of the program—the closing announcements and the updating of the balance file—are in the exception handler. We commented earlier on the undesirability of programs in which the bulk of the code was, for example, in the **then** clause of an **if...then** construction; the same objection could justifiably be raised here. This is easily repaired by appealing to the frame concept, and we show below (Figure 7.16.3) a revised version in which the exception handler treats only the End_Error exception itself, leaving the main part of the program for the concluding activities.

```
with Text_IO, Flt_IO;

procedure Checkbook is

    Trans_File,
    Bal_File:              Text_IO.FILE_TYPE;

    Current_Balance:       FLOAT;
    Transaction:           FLOAT;
    New_Balance:           FLOAT;
begin
    Text_IO.Open (Bal_File, Text_IO.In_File, "BALANCE.CUR");
    Flt_IO.Get (Bal_File, New_Balance);
    Text_IO.Put ("The opening account balance is ");
    Flt_IO.Put (New_Balance, 0, 2, 0);
    Text_IO.New_Line;
    Text_IO.Close (Bal_File);

    Text_IO.Open (Trans_File, Text_IO.In_File, "TRANSACT.DAT");

    begin
      loop
        Current_Balance := New_Balance;
        Flt_IO.Get (Trans_File, Transaction);
        Text_IO.New_Line;
        Text_IO.Put ("Transaction:");
        Flt_IO.Put (Transaction, 0, 2, 0);
        Text_IO.New_Line;

        New_Balance := Current_Balance + Transaction;
      end loop;

    exception

      when Text_IO.End_Error =>
        null;
    end;

    Text_IO.Close (Trans_File);
    Text_IO.New_Line;
    Text_IO.Put ("The closing account balance is ");
    Flt_IO.Put (New_Balance, 0, 2, 0);
```

```
Text_IO.New_Line (2);
Text_IO.Create (Bal_File, Text_IO.Out_File, "BALANCE.CUR");
Flt_IO.Put (Bal_File, New_Balance, 0, 2, 0);
Text_IO.Close (Bal_File);

end Checkbook;
```

Figure 7.16.3

Now there is nothing for the exception handler to do but allow control to pass through to the concluding portion of the main part of the program. In Ada, however, an exception handler cannot be empty; it must contain at least one executable statement. Thus we introduce the new "executable" statement **null**, whose effect is literally to do nothing. This satisfies our intent that nothing be done in the exception handler while also satisfying the Ada syntax rules. We shall have occasion to use **null** in other contexts.

It would appear from these examples that intercepting the End_Error exception is a technique that is superior to examining the End_Of_File function. In fact, it is more *different* than superior. Consider what would happen, for instance, if *two* files were open simultaneously and we were getting data from each of them. Since End_Of_File contains the name of the associated file variable, we can always determine if a specific file has caused End_Of_File to become True. But if the End_Error exception is raised, how can we tell *which* file caused it? We may not be able to determine this without more careful programming. We leave it to you to verify that in the case of Figure 7.16.4*a*, the End_Error exception gives no information about the offending file, whereas in Figure 7.16.4*b*, we take advantage of the frame concept to treat each file separately; in this case we *can* determine what caused the exception to be raised.

```
a    begin
        .
        .
        .
       Flt_IO.Get (File1, X);
       Flt_IO.Get (File2, Y);
        .
        .
        .
     exception
       when Text_IO.End_Error =>
        .
        .
        .
     end;


b    begin
        .
        .
        .
       begin
         Flt_IO.Get (File1, X);
       exception
         when Text_IO.End_Error =>
```

```
        .
        .
        .
   end;

   begin
     Flt_IO.Get (File2, Y);
   exception
     when Text_IO.End_Error =>
        .
        .
        .
   end;
        .
        .
        .
   end;
```

Figure 7.16.4

Another exception sometimes raised when dealing with external files is the **Name_Error**, an exception declared in Text_IO. As the term implies, it is raised when the Ada run-time system detects some kind of error in the name of a file. This may be caused by an *invalid* filename (for example, in almost all operating systems, a name such as AB*C.XYZ is invalid) or, in the case of a file that is being *open*ed, the name of a file that does not exist.

7.17 Exercises

7.2.1 (a) Write the statement part of a program that reads two integers First and Second as input and then displays a brief message giving the value of the larger of these numbers. Then devise test data for this program. How many data sets will you need to try in order to test all the relevant differences that can occur in the input?

(b) Write the statement part of a program that reads three integers First, Second, and Third as input and then displays a brief message giving the value of the largest of the three. Answer the same questions as in part *a*.

7.2.2 (a) Write a program that accepts any integer as input.

(1) If the integer is positive, display this number and all successively smaller integers down to (but not including) 0.

(2) If the integer is not positive, do nothing.

Devise a suitable set of inputs to test this program. (It is clear that if the program is correct, one may enter a very large integer and obtain outrageously lengthy output; but it is also clear that doing this contributes nothing as such to the testing of the program.)

(b) Modify the program of part *a* so that in case *2*, instead of doing nothing, the program displays a message. Again, devise a suitable set of inputs to test the program.

7.3.1 The program of Figure 7.3.1 contains a trivial annoyance, in that its response to an input of 99 (cents) is "1 cents" rather than "1 cent." Insert the small amount of code required to correct this blemish.

7.7.1 Consider the program segment of Figure 7.1.2*b*. What exception does the Ada system raise if a program containing this segment is run?

7.7.2 What kind of exception, if any, is raised when the program Error_3, shown below, is run with each of the following inputs?

(a) −21
(b) 43
(c) 157
(d) xyz

```
with Text_IO;

procedure Error_3 is

   subtype CENTS_RANGE is INTEGER range 1..99;

   package Cents_IO is new Text_IO.Integer_IO (CENTS_RANGE);

   Cost:    CENTS_RANGE;

begin

   Cents_IO.Get (Cost);

end Error_3;
```

7.7.3 Answer Exercise 7.7.2 with respect to the program Error_4, shown below.

```
with Text_IO;

procedure Error_4 is

   subtype CENTS_RANGE is INTEGER range 1..99;

   package Pos_IO is new Text_IO.Integer_IO (POSITIVE);
```

```
   Cost:          CENTS_RANGE;
begin
   Pos_IO.Get (Cost);
end Error_4;
```

7.7.4 Answer Exercise 7.7.2 with respect to the program Error_5, shown below.

```
   with Text_IO, Int_IO;
procedure Error_5 is
   subtype CENTS_RANGE is Integer range 1..99;
   Cost:          CENTS_RANGE;
begin
   Int_IO.Get (Cost);
end Error_5;
```

7.8.1 It is always possible, and sometimes desirable, to use a **when others =>** exception handler by itself, even if it is not preceded by any handlers that name specific exceptions. Tell why it would be disadvantageous to make a general practice of doing this.

7.8.2 Each of the segments shown below is the statement part of a program in which Special_IO, a particular instantiation of Text_IO.Integer_IO, has been declared. Suppose that, in each case, a Data_Error is raised when the system attempts to execute the Get statement. Tell what output is displayed.

(a)
```
   begin

      Special_IO.Get (Number);
      Text_IO.Put_Line ("There is a problem.");

   exception

      when Text_IO.Data_Error =>
        Text_IO.Put_Line ("A data error has occurred.");
      when Constraint_Error =>
        Text_IO.Put_Line ("A constraint error has occurred.");
      when others =>
        Text_IO.Put_Line ("An exception has been raised.");

   end;
```

(b)
```
begin

    Special_IO.Get (Number);
    Text_IO.Put_Line ("There is a problem.");
exception

    when Constraint_Error =>
      Text_IO.Put_Line ("A constraint error has occurred.");
    when Text_IO.Data_Error =>
      Text_IO.Put_Line ("A data error has occurred.");
    when others =>
      Text_IO.Put_Line ("An exception has been raised.");

end;
```

(c)
```
begin

    Special_IO.Get (Number);
    Text_IO.Put_Line ("There is a problem.");

exception

    when Constraint_Error =>
      Text_IO.Put_Line ("A constraint error has occurred.");
    when others =>
      Text_IO.Put_Line ("An exception has been raised.");

end;
```

(d)
```
begin

    Special_IO.Get (Number);
    Text_IO.Put_Line ("There is a problem.");

exception

    when Constraint_Error | Text_IO.Data_Error =>
      Text_IO.Put_Line ("An error has occurred.");
    when others =>
      Text_IO.Put_Line ("An exception has occurred.");

end;
```

(e)
```
begin

    Special_IO.Get (Number);
    Text_IO.Put_Line ("There is a problem.");

exception

    when others =>
      Text_IO.Put_Line ("An exception has been raised.");

end;
```

(f)
```
begin

    Special_IO.Get (Number);
    Text_IO.Put_Line ("There is a problem.");

exception

    when Constraint_Error =>
      Text_IO.Put_Line ("A constraint error has occurred.");

end;
```

(g)
```
begin

    Special_IO.Get (Number);
    Text_IO.Put_Line ("There is a problem.");

end;
```

7.9.1 Each of the segments shown below is the statement part of a program in which Special_IO, a particular instantiation of Text_IO.Integer_IO, has been declared. Suppose that, in each case, a Data_Error is raised when the system attempts to execute the Get statement. Tell what output is displayed.

(a)
```
begin

    Special_IO.Get (Number);
    Text_IO.Put_Line ("There is a problem.");

exception

    when Text_IO.Data_Error =>
      Text_IO.Put_Line ("A data error has occurred.");
    when others =>
      Text_IO.Put_Line ("An exception has been raised.");

end;
```

(b)
```
begin

    Special_IO.Get (Number);

      begin

        Text_IO.Put_Line ("There is a problem.");

      exception

        when Text_IO.Data_Error =>
          Text_IO.Put_Line ("A data error has occurred.");

      end;
```

```
   exception

      when others =>
         Text_IO.Put_Line ("An exception has been raised.");

   end;
```

(c)
```
   begin

      begin

         Special_IO.Get (Number);

      exception
         when others =>
            Text_IO.Put_Line ("An exception has been raised.");

      end;

      Text_IO.Put_Line ("There is a problem.");

   end;
```

(d)
```
   begin

      begin

         Special_IO.Get (Number);

      exception

         when others =>
            Text_IO.Put_Line ("An exception has been raised.");

      end;

      Text_IO.Put_Line ("There is a problem.");

   exception

      when Text_IO.Data_Error =>
         Text_IO.Put_Line ("A data error has occurred.");

   end;
```

(e)
```
   begin

      begin

         Special_IO.Get (Number);

      exception
```

```
    when Constraint_Error =>
        Text_IO.Put_Line ("A constraint error has occurred.");
    end;

    Text_IO.Put_Line ("There is a problem.");
exception

    when Text_IO.Data_Error =>
        Text_IO.Put_Line ("A data error has occurred.");

    end;
```

7.10.1 Allowing the user to try again after entering invalid input (and thereby raising a Data_Error), as is done in Figure 7.10.1, can be considered "user-friendly." Explain, however, why allowing an unlimited number of tries (as in Figure 7.10.1) can be disadvantageous to the user and therefore not as user-friendly as it might seem at first sight.

7.10.2 Consider revising the program Change of Figure 7.10.1 so that its statement part is as shown below.

```
    begin

        begin

            Text_IO.Put ("Enter cost in cents (1 to 99) of item: ");
            Cents_IO.Get (Cost);
            Text_IO.Put ("The change for one dollar on a ");
            Cents_IO.Put (Cost, 0);
            Text_IO.Put ("-cent item is ");
            Cents_IO.Put (100-Cost, 0);
            Text_IO.Put_Line (" cents.");

        exception

            when Text_IO.Data_Error =>
                Text_IO.Put_Line ("This input is incorrect.");
                Text_IO.Put     ("Enter the cost again (1 to 99): ");
                Cents_IO.Get (Cost);
                Text_IO.Put ("The change for one dollar on a ");
                Cents_IO.Put (Cost, 0);
                Text_IO.Put ("-cent item is ");
                Cents_IO.Put (100-Cost, 0);
                Text_IO.Put_Line (" cents.");

        end;

    exception


        when Text_IO.Data_Error =>
            Text_IO.Put_Line ("Sorry, the input is still incorrect.");
    end Change;
```

Tell how the program executes:

(a) If the user initially gives an acceptable input.

(b) If the user gives one or more unacceptable inputs (raising Data_Error).

7.11.1 Consider the program Change of Figure 7.5.1. Tell what the program does when given each of the following lines of input in response to the initial prompt:

(a) 34
(b) +34
(c) 34 56
(d) +34 +56
(e) 34+56
(f) 34, 56
(g) 34,56
(h) 34 cents
(i) 34cents
(j) 34 cents 56 cents
(k) 34 56, each indicating cents

7.11.2 Instead of the program Change of Figure 7.5.1, consider the program shown below, and answer the same questions as in Exercise 7.11.1:

```
with Text_IO;

procedure Change_Twice is

    subtype CENTS_RANGE is INTEGER range 1..99;
    package Cents_IO is new Text_IO.Integer_IO (CENTS_RANGE);
    Cost:      CENTS_RANGE;

begin

    Text_IO.Put_Line ("Enter the two costs (1 to 99 each): ");
    Cents_IO.Get (Cost);
    Text_IO.Put ("Change for the first is ");
    Cents_IO.Put (100-Cost, 0);
    Text_IO.Put (" cents.");
    Text_IO.New_Line;
    Cents_IO.Get (Cost);
    Text_IO.Put ("Change for the second is ");
    Cents_IO.Put (100-Cost, 0);
    Text_IO.Put_Line (" cents.");

end Change_Twice;
```

7.11.3 Change the statement part of the program Change_Twice of Exercise 7.11.2 to that shown below by inserting Text_IO.Skip_Line after each of the Get statements:

```
begin

    Text_IO.Put_Line ("Enter the two costs (1 to 99 each): ");
    Cents_IO.Get (Cost);
    Text_IO.Skip_Line;
    Text_IO.Put ("Change for the first is ");
    Cents_IO.Put (100-Cost, 0);
    Text_IO.Put (" cents.");
    Text_IO.New_Line;
    Cents_IO.Get (Cost);
    Text_IO.Skip_Line;
    Text_IO.Put ("Change for the second is ");
    Cents_IO.Put (100-Cost, 0);
    Text_IO.Put_Line (" cents.");

end Change_Twice;
```

Tell what the program does when given each of the following inputs, in one line or two, as indicated:

(a) 34
    56

(b) 34 56

(c) 34 cents
    56 cents

(d) 34 cents 56 cents

(e) 34.0 cents
    56.0 cents

(f) 34 dollars and
       56 cents.

(g) 34dollars
      +56 cents.

(h) 34 dollars
      + 56 cents.

7.11.4 Draw a syntax diagram that describes the valid contents of the keyboard buffer which can be converted to an integer, according to the conversion algorithm of Section 7.11.

7.11.5 In discussing the algorithm that converts characters in the keyboard buffer to integers, we noted that we had intentionally ignored the fact that the underscore character can also validly be converted in some circumstances. Modify the algorithm to account for this special character. (Recall that the underscore can appear in an integer representation if, and only if, it is both immediately preceded by and followed by a digit character.)

7.11.6 Redo Exercise 7.11.4 for the modified algorithm of Exercise 7.11.5.

7.11.7 Suppose the keyboard buffer is empty at the time the executing program issues an input request (Get), seeking an integer value for some variable. Assume that the user responds to the request by simply pressing ENTER. On the basis of the algorithm of Section 7.11, conjecture how the input routine responds and then write a (very) short program to check your conjecture.

7.12.1 The following questions refer to the program Change of Figure 7.12.3.

(a) Could the Skip_Line statement in the exception handler be placed immediately after the Get statement instead without affecting program execution? Explain.

(b) The program initializes OK to True and sets it to False at an appropriate point (within the exception handler). However, OK may instead be initialized to False and then set to True at an appropriate point in the program without affecting the program's correct execution. If we did this, what would be the "appropriate point" to set OK to True? Explain.

7.14.1 The programs in Figures 7.13.1 and 7.14.1 can serve as models of programming that is both "friendly" and "defensive" as far as user input is concerned. Carefully compare the parts of these programs that deal with input, noting such aspects as the placement of prompts and messages, as well as the contents of the exception handlers.

7.16.1 Verify that blank lines at the *end* of the TRANSACT.DAT file will cause the program of Figure 6.9.8 to fail, as stated in Section 7.16. Also show that blank lines *within* the file will *not* cause any problems. (Do this by inserting blank lines into the transaction file at various places and executing the Checkbook program.)

7.16.2 Suppose that the balance file read by the program of Figure 7.16.3 is named BALANCE.HST and, instead of containing a single checkbook balance, contains an entire *history* of balances, the last of which is the current balance. Such a file might look like:

104.72
43.80
87.29
183.66

Thus the *current* balance that the program should work with is 183.66 found at the *end* of this file. Modify the program of Figure 7.16.3 so that it opens and reads from the file BALANCE.HST, correctly obtains from it the current balance (183.66), and processes a transaction file. Do *not* try to update the balance file (see Exercise 7.16.3 below); remove or "comment out" the last three executable statements of Figure 7.16.3.

7.16.3 Complete the project begun in Exercise 7.16.2 by creating an updated balance "history" file as follows. When BALANCE.HST is opened, create another file, named BALANCE.NEW. Read balances from the BALANCE.HST file, and for each balance read, write that entry to BALANCE.NEW (followed by a new-line sequence). Continue this process until End_Error occurs. Next, process each transaction as before. When the last transaction has been processed, write the remaining balance to BALANCE.NEW and exit the program. At this point you should have two files, BALANCE.HST and BALANCE.NEW, which are identical except that BALANCE.NEW contains the latest balance. Finally, use your operating system's facilities to *delete* BALANCE.HST and to *rename* BALANCE.NEW as BALANCE.HST. (Standard Ada has a procedure that will delete a file, but it has no procedure to rename a file; thus these activities will have to take place *outside* your program.)

7.16.4 There is still a potential pitfall in the program resulting from Exercise 7.16.3; namely, the file BALANCE.HST might not exist, or it might exist but be *empty*. In the first case, the Name_Error exception will be raised; in the second, End_Error will be raised, but before any balance has been read (in which case the variable New_Balance will not contain a meaningful value). Respond to *both* of these problems by exiting the program with the message, "Balance history file not found or is empty."

Chapter 8

Writing and Using Subprograms

Much of the material of the first seven chapters has been devoted to a single goal—the writing of *correct* programs that are also *clear* and *readable*. We have employed the concepts from top-down programming to guide us in the development of program *structure*, and we have consistently used suggestive variable and constant names to enhance your understanding of the program's purpose and methods. In addition, we have seen that the Ada language itself contains many constructs aimed at efficient programming (such as loops and exception handling). In brief, implementation of these powerful techniques and tools not only makes the programmer's life "easier," thereby promoting productivity and efficiency, but it also significantly augments the effectiveness, correctness, reliability, and readability of the code produced by the programmer. In this chapter we study the concept of **subprogram**, a facility of Ada and many other languages as well, that perhaps more than anything else encourages the "modularization" of program code, and along with this modularization come significant improvements in program reliability, readability, and understanding.

The *notion* of subprogram is not new to us, for we have been using the subprograms Get and Put since the beginning of the book. Chapter 3 was devoted for the most part to the topic of *related* subprograms—procedures and functions—grouped together into *packages*. Now that we have had a glimpse at the uses of subprograms, we begin an investigation into the details of writing these subprograms. We will see how they can be used for the effective modularization of programs and how we can decide when a collection of code is a candidate for consolidation into a subprogram. Later, in Chapter 11, we investigate these same questions at the package level.

8.1 Introduction to the *function* concept

In Sections 3.5 and 3.6 we considered a package (Int_Pack) consisting of several simple functions and procedures. But the idea of a function as it is used in computing is quite far-reaching and extends well beyond the examples we have included in Int_Pack. In the present section we show some instances in which the introduction of functions into our computer programs turns out to be of considerable benefit.

Consider the following scenario: We wish to purchase a particular product, of which there are two possible brands, Brand X and Brand Y. Both brands are available at either Store 1 or Store 2. Our task is to determine the "best buy," that is, the lowest price at which the item can be purchased. The problem scarcely requires an extensive analysis, nor would there normally be anything to be gained by writing a computer program to solve it. Nonetheless, we offer a cursory analysis and write a small program for its solution, for some important concepts can be brought to light here.

Evidently we need to obtain from the program user the Brand X and Brand Y costs at Store 1, and then compare these, using a simple **if...then** construction, to find the smaller. We do the same for Store 2, and the desired result is obtained by comparing the results obtained from the two stores. In the interest of simplicity, we assume that all costs are given in terms of cents. Figure 8.1.1 shows a program that does the job.

```ada
with Text_IO;

procedure Best_Buy is

    package Nat_IO is new Text_IO.Integer_IO (NATURAL);

    Brand_X_1,
    Brand_Y_1,
    Brand_X_2,
    Brand_Y_2,

    Store_1,
    Store_2,

    Best:        NATURAL;

begin
    Text_IO.Put ("Enter costs for Brand X and Brand Y, at Store 1: ");
    Nat_IO.Get (Brand_X_1);
    Nat_IO.Get (Brand_Y_1);
```

```ada
if Brand_X_1 < Brand_Y_1 then
   Store_1 := Brand_X_1;
else
  Store_1 := Brand_Y_1;
end if;
```

```ada
    Text_IO.Put ("Enter costs for Brand X and Brand Y, at Store 2: ");
    Nat_IO.Get (Brand_X_2);
    Nat_IO.Get (BRAND_Y_2);
```

```ada
if Brand_X_2 < Brand_Y_2 then
   Store_2 := Brand_X_2;
else
   Store_2 := Brand_Y_2;
end if;
```

```ada
if Store_1 < Store_2 then
   Best:= Store 1;
else
   Best := Store_2;
end if;
```

```
Text_IO.New_Line (2);
Text_IO.Put ("Lowest available cost for the item is ");
Nat_IO.Put (Best, 0);
Text_IO.Put_Line (" cents.");

end Best_Buy;
```

Figure 8.1.1

The three comparisons—those segments of code in which the smaller of two nonnegative integers is determined—have been emphasized by enclosing them in boxes, for it is here that we focus our attention. Note that in each case the instruction sequence consists of a simple **if...then...else...end if** construction; they differ not in *structure* but in the *names* of the variables being compared and the variable ultimately assigned the smaller value.

In Figure 8.1.2 we introduce three new variables A, B, and X, which we refer to as "secondary" variables, to distinguish them from the original ("primary") variables Brand_X_1, Brand_Y_1, Brand_X_2, . . . , Best.

```
with Text_IO;

procedure Best_Buy is

    package Nat_IO is new Text_IO.Integer_IO (NATURAL);

    Brand_X_1,
    Brand_Y_1,
    Brand_X_2,
    Brand_Y_2,

    Store_1,
    Store_2,

    Best:        NATURAL;

    A,
    B,
    X:           NATURAL;

begin

    Text_IO.Put ("Enter costs for Brand X and Brand Y, at Store 1: ");
    Nat_IO.Get (Brand_X_1);
    Nat_IO.Get (Brand_Y_1);
```

```
-- Set up variables

  A := Brand_X_1;    B := Brand_Y_1;

-- Compare

  if A < B then
    X := A;
  else
    X := B;
  end if;

-- Save smaller value

  Store_1 := X;
```

```
Text_IO.Put ("Enter costs for Brand X and Brand Y, at Store 2: ");
Nat_IO.Get (Brand_X_2);
Nat_IO.Get (Brand_Y_2);
```

```
-- Set up variables

  A := Brand_X_2;     B := Brand_Y_2;

-- Compare

  if A < B then
    X := A;
  else
    X := B;
  end if;

-- Save smaller value

  Store_2 := X;
```

```
-- Set up variables

  A := Store_1;    B := Store_2;

-- Compare

  if A < B then
    X := A;
  else
    X := B;
  end if;

-- Save smaller value

  Best := X;
```

```
Text_IO.New_Line (2);
Text_IO.Put ("Lowest available cost for the item is ");
Nat_IO.Put (Best, 0);
Text_IO.Put_Line (" cents.");
```

```
end Best_Buy;
```

Figure 8.1.2

As is easily seen, we have made the code for this program significantly longer, a move that appears to be contrary to the direction of progress. But observe that each segment that performs the comparisons (to find the minimum of two nonnegative integers) has now become a *uniform* process, namely:

1. Copy the values of two (primary) variables into the (secondary) variables A and B.

2. Find the smaller of the values now in A and B, and assign that value to the (secondary) variable X.

3.   Copy the value in X back into some (primary) variable.

The lines that do the actual comparison, shown in Figure 8.1.3, are now *identical* for all three comparisons, and it is this observation, along with the *copying* process noted above, that has major significance.

```
if A < B then
  X := A;
else
  X := B;
end if;
```

Figure 8.1.3

Our immediate goal is somehow to avoid the necessity for having three copies of the code of Figure 8.1.3 in our program, a goal whose desirability would be all the more obvious if dozens of such comparisons were required. This goal can be achieved *provided* there is some mechanism that performs the following services for us.

Each time we wish to find the smaller of two nonnegative integers, we request that the mechanism:

1.   Make the appropriate substitution of actual values (for example, the current values of Store_1 and Store_2) for the "secondary" variables A and B (in effect, perform the assignments **A := Store_1** and **B := Store_2**).

2.   Execute the code of Figure 8.1.3, that is, perform the comparison.

3.   Leave the result in the (secondary) variable X, so that we might use it in any fashion appropriate to X's type (for example, assign it to Best, as in **Best := X**).

Of course, we bear some responsibilities here as well. In particular, we must accomplish the following:

1.   Define the mechanism in advance, in the sense of notifying the Ada compiler which secondary variables the mechanism will use and which sequence of instructions will operate on those variables whenever the mechanism is called for.

2.   Supply actual values for the mechanism to use as replacement values for its secondary variables whenever the mechanism's services are invoked.

3.   Deal in some appropriate fashion with the value calculated by the mechanism.

In fact, the Ada language supports such a mechanism, called the **function** construct, and without further ado we present a version of the program of Figure 8.1.1 that uses it. We have included line numbers in Figure 8.1.4 to aid our discussions.

```
1    with Text_IO;
2
3  procedure Best_Buy is
4
5     package Nat_IO is new Text_IO.Integer_IO (NATURAL);
6
7     Brand_X_1,
8     Brand_Y_1,
9     Brand_X_2,
10    Brand_Y_2,
11
12    Store_1,
13    Store_2,
14
15    Best:        NATURAL;
16
17
18       -- The function "Minimum" returns the smaller of
19       -- the two nonnegative integer values passed to it
20
21    function     Minimum (A, B: NATURAL) return NATURAL is
22
23       X:        NATURAL;
24
25    begin
26
27       if A < B then
28         X := A;
29       else
30         X := B;
31       end if;
32
33       return X;
34
35    end Minimum;
36
37
38 begin
39
40    Text_IO.Put ("Enter costs for Brand X and Brand Y, at Store 1: ");
41    Nat_IO.Get (Brand_X_1);
42    Nat_IO.Get (Brand_Y_1);
43
44    Store_1 := Minimum (Brand_X_1, Brand_Y_1);
45
46    Text_IO.Put ("Enter costs for Brand X and Brand Y, at Store 2: ");
47    Nat_IO.Get (Brand_X_2);
48    Nat_IO.Get (Brand_Y_2);
49
50    Store_2 := Minimum (Brand_X_2, Brand_Y_2);
51
52    Best := Minimum (Store_1, Store_2);
53
54    Text_IO.New_Line (2);
55    Text_IO.Put ("Lowest available cost for the item is ");
56    Nat_IO.Put (Best, 0);
57    Text_IO.Put_Line (" cents.");
58
59 end Best_Buy;
```

Figure 8.1.4

Even a cursory glance at this program reveals numerous constructions that require discussion, and the questions raised here are resolved in the next two sections. In the meantime we can make a couple of observations to suggest in a less detailed way just what will take place upon compilation and execution. We note first a new construction at lines 21 to 35, namely a segment of code headed by the reserved word **function**, followed by a **name** —Minimum. Thus these function mechanisms are *named* constructs. We have encountered a similar phenomenon before, in Chapter 6, where we assigned names to various kinds of *loops*. In fact, this is our notification to the Ada compiler of just what code makes up the named segment Minimum. While there is a good deal of surrounding formalism here to investigate in detail, we observe that lines 27 to 31 are precisely those of Figure 8.1.3, the lines that actually determine which of A and B is the smaller. Observe also that this "telling the compiler about the function—segment of code—named Minimum" appears in the declarative part of the program, a fact that is perhaps not surprising, in view of the fact that it "tells the compiler" something.

Second, we see that the function named Minimum is called into play three times in the executable part of the program, as expected, at lines 44, 50, and 52. What we do *not* see, however, and something that was expected, is the explicit replacement of the secondary variables A and B by the values of the actual variables (Brand_X_1 and Brand_Y_1, for example). To use the terminology we introduced in Chapter 3, the **formal parameters** A and B are replaced by the **actual parameters**, such as Brand_X_1 and Brand_X_2, when the function is **called** or **invoked**. This replacement does take place, for an expression such as

```
Minimum (Brand_X_1, Brand_Y_1)
```

at line 44 means (1) replace the formal parameters A and B by the values of the actual parameters Brand_X_1 and Brand_Y_1, respectively, and then (2) execute the code that makes up the executable part of the function. The value, namely X, calculated as a result of that execution is then "returned by the function," that is, replaces the reference to Minimum. In the specific case under discussion, the smaller of Brand_X_1 and Brand_Y_1 replaces the expression Minimum (Brand_X_1, Brand_Y_1) and thus is assigned as a value to Store_1.

We have observed that the function Minimum has been invoked three times in this program: twice to determine the smaller cost between the two brands and a final time to determine the lower cost between the two stores. In each case the nonnegative integer value calculated by the executable statements that comprise Minimum—the **value returned by Minimum**, as is usually said—has been used on the right side of an assignment statement. Could it have been used in another way? Yes, as we noted in Chapter 3, provided it is used in a way compatible with the ways in which NATURAL numbers are used. We could even have avoided use of the variable Best altogether, if instead of *assigning* the last value that Minimum returned to that variable

```
Best := Minimum (Store_1, Store_2);
```

we had simply *displayed* it at an appropriate place in the program:

```
Nat_IO.Put (Minimum (Store_1, Store_2), 0);
```

In fact,

```
Minimum (Store_1, Store_2)
```

is an *expression* and thus can be used in whatever way is valid for *any* expression.

There are three notable aspects of the development we have followed here, and they are evident from Figure 8.1.4. First, we have made the code—the sequence of instructions—in Minimum *reusable*, inasmuch as it has been used three times without the necessity to replicate it on the second and third occasions. (Recall that this effect was our original goal.) Second, the naming of this collection of Ada statements has had the effect of *compressing* that code segment into one programmer-created superexpression, namely, **Minimum (,)**, with the programmer "filling in the blanks" with the desired nonnegative integer values. This compression of code as described above is frequently referred to as **code encapsulation**. Third, the *readability* and consequent *clarity* of the program (or at least its executable part) has been significantly improved by the encapsulation, since the comparatively lengthier **if...then** constructions have been replaced by the simpler—and even more descriptively named—Minimum construction.

8.2 Further examples of functions

In the next section we study the Ada function concept in a more formal way. In the meantime, we look at two more examples of functions, to get a better idea—on an informal basis, at least—of how they are written, how they are invoked, and how they can improve not only program efficiency but also program appearance. We begin with a function example which differs only trivially from Best_Buy of the preceding section but which is instructive in its own right.

Suppose we wish to purchase any one of three models of a television set. We find that two different dealers have all three models in stock, and they both offer rebates on all three sets. We decide (perhaps naively) that the best buy on a television set is the one having the largest rebate. Thus we go to the first dealer, determine the largest rebate, and note it. Then we find the largest rebate offered by the second dealer. Finally, we calculate the larger of these two amounts. This problem differs from the Best_Buy problem of the preceding section in two ways: First, we need to calculate the *largest* of some numbers, instead of the smallest, and second, we need *two* functions, for in determining the best rebate offered by an individual dealer, we have to find the largest of *three* numbers; then, to compare the dealers themselves, we have to find the larger of *two* numbers. Figure 8.2.1 shows an Ada program solution to the problem which includes two functions, Maximum_2 and Maximum_3. You should have little difficulty following the logic of the functions or of the main part of the program. Maximum_2 is the same as the function Minimum of Section 8.1, in which "less than" has been changed to "greater than," and Maximum_3 is just an easy extension of Maximum_2.

```
with Text_IO;

procedure Rebate is

    package Nat_IO is new Text_IO.Integer_IO (NATURAL);
```

```
      Model_A,
      Model_B,
      Model_C,

      Dealer_1,
      Dealer_2:  NATURAL;


         --  The function "Maximum_2" returns the larger of
         --  the two nonnegative integer values passed to it.

      function Maximum_2 (A, B: NATURAL) return NATURAL is

         X:  NATURAL;

      begin

         if A > B then
           X := A;
         else
           X := B;
         end if;

         return X;

      end Maximum_2;


         --  The function "Maximum_3" returns the largest of
         --  the three nonnegative integer values passed to it.


      function Maximum_3 (A, B, C: NATURAL) return NATURAL is

         X:    NATURAL;
      begin

         if A > B then
           X := A;
         else
           X := B;
         end if;

         if X < C then
           X := C;
         end if;

         return X;

      end Maximum_3;

   begin

      Text_IO.Put ("Enter the Dealer No. 1 rebates for Models A, B, and C: ");
      Nat_IO.Get (Model_A);
      Nat_IO.Get (Model_B);
      Nat_IO.Get (Model_C);

      Dealer_1 := Maximum_3 (Model_A, Model_B, Model_C);
```

```
Text_IO.Put ("Enter the Dealer No. 2 rebates for Models A, B, and C: ");
Nat_IO.Get (Model_A);
Nat_IO.Get (Model_B);
Nat_IO.Get (Model_C);

Dealer_2 := Maximum_3 (Model_A, Model_B, Model_C);

Text_IO.Put ("The largest rebate is $");
Nat_IO.Put (Maximum_2 (Dealer_1, Dealer_2), 0);
Text_IO.New_Line;

end Rebate;
```

Figure 8.2.1

As simple as this program is, it leads to a couple of slightly disturbing thoughts. First, the function Maximum_3, while perfectly straightforward, is a bit more complex than Maximum_2, in that it requires two comparisons instead of one. And it is clear that a Maximum_4 function, following this same pattern, would require three comparisons, with a correspondingly more complex **if...then** structure. Second, it seems that we will need an entire *family* of "Maximum_?" functions to deal with calculating the maximum of so-and-so many integers. As to the first of these observations, we direct your attention to the segment of Figure 8.2.2, where not only is Maximum_3 written *in terms of* Maximum_2 but also the application of a couple of additional programming devices has served to shorten the code required in both Maximum_2 and Maximum_3 even more. (These ideas are further expanded upon in the exercises.)

```
--  The function "Maximum_2" returns the larger of
--  the two nonnegative integer values passed to it.

function Maximum_2 (A, B: NATURAL) return NATURAL is

begin

  if A > B then
    return A;
  else
    return B;
  end if;

end Maximum_2;

--  The function "Maximum_3" returns the largest of
--  the three nonnegative integer values passed to it
--  by invoking Maximum_2 twice.

function Maximum_3 (A, B, C: NATURAL) return NATURAL is

begin

  return Maximum_2 (Maximum_2 (A, B), C);

end Maximum_3;
```

Figure 8.2.2

The question concerning the necessity of an entire family of "Maximum_?" functions is disposed of in Chapter 10. In a sense an entire family of such functions *is* required, but we will see that it is possible to generate *all* of these functions with a single *function declaration*. (The **function...begin...end** sequences of Figures 8.1.4, 8.2.1, and 8.2.2 are referred to as function *declarations*. See Section 8.3 for the details of declaring functions.)

As a second, slightly more complex, and perhaps marginally more interesting example, consider a used car dealer who offers a limited, 10,000-mile repair warranty on cars as follows: The *kinds* of repairs fall into four categories, labeled A, B, C, and D, and the *costs* of these repairs during the first 10,000 miles is split between the vehicle owner and the dealer according to repair category, as described below.

A.   The owner bears the entire cost of the repair.

B.   The dealer bears the entire cost of the repair.

C.   The owner and the dealer each pay 50 percent of the cost of the repair.

D.   For the first 5000 miles, the dealer pays the entire cost of the repair; for the next 2500 miles (up to 7500 miles) the owner and the dealer each pay 50 percent of the cost; and for the final 2500 miles, the owner pays 80 percent of the cost and the dealer pays the remaining 20 percent.

In Figure 8.2.3 we show a program that obtains as input the number of miles on the vehicle since its purchase from the dealer, the cost of the repair, and the category of the repair. The program then displays the shares of the cost to be borne by the owner and the dealer. You should have little difficulty following the logic of the program. Note that we have dealt with the possibility of either lower- or uppercase responses to be used as values for the Category variable and that we have also made provision for an invalid Category value (by raising an exception and then later handling it when necessary).

```
    with Text_IO, Int_IO, Flt_IO;

  procedure Auto_Repair is

      Mileage_Limit:     constant := 10_000;

      Mileage:           NATURAL;
      Repair_Cost:       FLOAT;
      Category:          CHARACTER;
      Percentage:        FLOAT;     -- owner's percent of repair cost
      Owners_Share:      FLOAT;     -- owner's amount of repair cost
      Dealers_Share:     FLOAT;     -- dealer's amount of repair cost

      Invalid_Category: exception;

  begin

      --  Obtain input

      Text_IO.Put ("Enter vehicle miles since purchase: ");
      Int_IO.Get (Mileage);
```

```
      Text_IO.Put ("Enter repair cost: ");
      Flt_IO.Get (Repair_Cost);
      Text_IO.Put ("Enter repair category (A-D): ");
      Text_IO.Get (Category);
      Text_IO.New_Line;

      --  Compute Owner's and Dealer's shares of repair
      --  cost (see text for details of computations for
      --  each of the categories A - D).

      if Category = 'A' or Category = 'a' or
        Mileage >= Mileage_Limit then
          Percentage := 1.00;

      elsif Category = 'B' or Category = 'b' then
        Percentage := 0.00;

      elsif Category = 'C' or Category = 'c' then
        Percentage := 0.50;

      elsif Category = 'D' or Category = 'd' then
        if Mileage <= 5000 then
          Percentage := 0.00;
        elsif Mileage <= 7500 then
          Percentage := 0.50;
        else
          Percentage := 0.80;
        end if;

      else raise Invalid_Category;

      end if;


      Owners_Share := Percentage * Repair_Cost;

      Dealers_Share := Repair_Cost - Owners_Share;


      --  Display Owner's and Dealer's shares of repair cost

      Text_IO.Put ("Owner's share is $");
      Flt_IO.Put (Owners_Share, 0, 2, 0);
      Text_IO.New_Line;

      Text_IO.Put ("Dealer's share is $");
      Flt_IO.Put (Dealers_Share, 0, 2, 0);
      Text_IO.New_Line;
exception
   when Invalid_Category =>
     Text_IO.Put ("The category '");
     Text_IO.Put (Category);
     Text_IO.Put_Line ("' is not valid...aborting execution.");

end Auto_Repair;
```

Figure 8.2.3

The sample dialogues with this program (Figure 8.2.4) suggest that it is working properly—almost—and, in particular, that it deals as expected with lower- and uppercase Category values and with invalid Category values.

```
a   Enter vehicle miles since purchase: 7244
    Enter repair cost: 179.26
    Enter repair category (A-D): B

    Owner's share is $0.00
    Dealer's share is $179.26

b   Enter vehicle miles since purchase: 7244
    Enter repair cost: 179.26
    Enter repair category (A-D): C

    Owner's share is $89.63
    Dealer's share is $89.63

c   Enter vehicle miles since purchase: 7244
    Enter repair cost: 219.75
    Enter repair category (A-D): C

    Owner's share is $109.87
    Dealer's share is $109.87

d   Enter vehicle miles since purchase: 7244
    Enter repair cost: 179.26
    Enter repair category (A-D): d

    Owner's share is $89.63
    Dealer's share is $89.63

e   Enter vehicle miles since purchase: 9421
    Enter repair cost: 305.97
    Enter repair category (A-D): D

    Owner's share is $244.78
    Dealer's share is $61.19

f   Enter vehicle miles since purchase: 9421
    Enter repair cost: 305.97
    Enter repair category (A-D): f

    The category 'f' is not valid...aborting execution.
```

Figure 8.2.4

Note the result in dialogue *c* above: The computation is not quite correct, since the sum of the two shares is a penny short of the cost of the total repair. This is surely strange, for whatever the owner's share is—since the dealer's share is defined to be the total cost less the owner's share—the sum of these two shares *should* be the total repair cost. The problem here lies not with the way the program is written; the difficulties run fairly deep and are not totally within our control. The problem results in part from errors that occur when we use floating point numbers and perform arithmetic with them, as we already noted in Section 4.5. It is a situation that we have to be aware of and deal with whenever we treat floating point numbers.

In the earlier examples of this chapter, we took advantage of the function concept and its ability to gather collections of instructions under a specific name to eliminate the writing of multiple copies of the same code. See, for example, the Minimum and Maximum functions of Figures 8.1.4, 8.2.1, and 8.2.2. A brief investigation of the program statements of Figure 8.2.3 reveals no such repeated code that might be a candidate for bundling into a function. However, it becomes increasingly evident as we develop the concepts of this chapter that the use of functions to avoid the repetitious writing of instructions—the *conservation of code*—is not the only reason for grouping collections of instructions together into a named entity. In fact, it frequently happens that code is written into a function (or a procedure, as we will see later) purely for the purpose of "getting it out of the way," a point that we now illustrate. In the program of Figure 8.2.5 we have written functions, each invoked only *once*, which return as values the owner's share and the dealer's share of a repair cost. You should have no trouble following it, since we have done little beyond regrouping the instructions and rearranging some declarations.

```
    with Text_IO, Int_IO, Flt_IO;

procedure Auto_Repair is

    Mileage:            NATURAL;
    Repair_Cost:        FLOAT;
    Category:           CHARACTER;

    Scratch_Var:        FLOAT;           -- will hold values to be displayed

    Invalid_Category:   exception;

    Function Owners_Share   (Miles: NATURAL;
                             Cost:  FLOAT;
                             Cat:   CHARACTER)

                             return FLOAT is

    Mileage_Limit:          constant INTEGER := 10_000;
    Percentage:             FLOAT;    -- owner's percent of repair cost
    begin

      if Cat = 'A' or Cat = 'a' or Miles >= Mileage_Limit then
        Percentage := 1.00;

      elsif Cat = 'B' or Cat = 'b' then
        Percentage := 0.00;

      elsif Cat = 'C' or Cat = 'c' then
        Percentage := 0.50;

      elsif Cat = 'D' or Cat = 'd' then
        if Miles <= 5000 then
          Percentage := 0.00;
        elsif Miles <= 7500 then
```

```
            Percentage := 0.50;
          else
            Percentage := 0.80;
          end if;

       else raise Invalid_Category;

       end if;

       return Percentage * Cost;

    end Owners_Share;


    function Dealers_Share (Miles: NATURAL;
                           Cost:  FLOAT;
                           Cat:   CHARACTER)

                       return FLOAT is

    begin

       return Cost - Owners_Share (Miles, Cost, Cat);

    end Dealers_Share;

begin

    --  Obtain input

    Text_IO.Put ("Enter vehicle miles since purchase: ");
    Int_IO.Get (Mileage);
    Text_IO.Put ("Enter repair cost: ");
    Flt_IO.Get (Repair_Cost);
    Text_IO.Put ("Enter repair category (A-D): ");
    Text_IO.Get (Category);
    Text_IO.New_Line;

    --  Display Owner's and Dealer's shares of repair cost

    Scratch_Var := Owners_Share (Mileage, Repair_Cost, Category);
    Text_IO.Put ("Owner's share is $");
    Flt_IO.Put (Scratch_Var, 0, 2, 0);
    Text_IO.New_Line;

    Scratch_Var := Dealers_Share (Mileage, Repair_Cost, Category);
    Text_IO.Put ("Dealer's share is $");
    Flt_IO.Put (Scratch_Var, 0, 2, 0);
    Text_IO.New_Line;

exception
    when Invalid_Category =>
       Text_IO.Put ("The category '");
       Text_IO.Put (Category);
       Text_IO.Put_Line ("' is not valid...aborting execution.");

end Auto_Repair;
```

Figure 8.2.5

A comparison of the programs of Figures 8.2.3 and 8.2.5 reveals instantly that the *statement* part of the second version—where the action is, so to speak—is far less cluttered and hence more readable than in the first version. Indeed, the statement part, or "executable code," of Figure 8.2.5 reads almost like an English-language algorithm; there is little question as to what the input is and what results are displayed. In the program of Figure 8.2.3, on the other hand, once the input has been obtained, we are suddenly immersed in the details of the logic of the computations; in Figure 8.2.5, those details have been "gotten out of the way," as was our intent. Of course the details are still there (in the function "bodies"), but we need not be concerned with them *while* we are trying to understand the main flow of the algorithm; when it *suits* us to do so, we can investigate those details at our leisure. The program of Figure 8.2.3 affords us no such option.

The message of this section is that **code encapsulation**—the grouping together of related instructions into a function (or procedure or even a package)—may be done (1) for the purpose of *conservation of code*; (2) to take advantage of the *flexibility* afforded by a function's scheme of substituting actual values for its secondary variables; (3) purely for the momentary "hiding" of complex computations and logic, for later investigation, to improve the appearance and readability of a program; or (4) some combination of these purposes. Of these, item 3 is sometimes the sole motivation, as in the program of Figure 8.2.5, and it is a legitimate one; it is a pleasant fact that the rewards of item 3 are almost always an added benefit of code encapsulation, regardless of the motivations for it. Naturally, all this can be taken to extreme by the overzealous novice, and improved readability can easily give way to the annoyance of dozens of references to trivial pieces of code. The experienced programmer will recognize when a main program would benefit from the compression of a related section of code to a single "name" (function or procedure) and when a set of instructions is best left as is.

8.3 The formal Ada *function* construct

As you know, the construct we are currently studying is called a **function**, and this is a term quite in line with its mathematical namesake, inasmuch as it operates in some well-defined way on *values* of some sort and produces in return a corresponding *function value*. Recall that functions are one of the two classes of *subprograms* that we study in this book, the other being the *procedure*, to be investigated later in this chapter. Again, the term "subprogram" is quite appropriate, since the statements that make up a subprogram generally consist of all the code required to do some complete job or subjob or, in the case of a function, to calculate some value, just as main programs do.

Before investigating the formalisms of Ada functions, we can make a few observations based on our knowledge of Ada and what we already know about functions. We noted earlier on—and verified in Figure 8.1.4—that we must notify the Ada system of our intention that such-and-such code is to comprise a function, that it has a particular name, and that when it is invoked, it will require so-and-so many values to be used as replacements. In view of Ada's insistence on maintaining type compatibility, we saw further that the compiler needs to know in advance the types not only of the expressions used for replacement but also of the value returned by the function. For example, the function Minimum accepts two NATURAL-valued expressions as replacements for A and B, and it returns a NATURAL value, as we have seen. But it could also have returned the same information, in a different form, by answering not the question "Which is the smaller value, A or B?" but rather "Is A smaller than B?" In this case, the return value will be of type BOOLEAN. Assuming that A and B are of type NATURAL but that X is of type BOOLEAN, the code

```
if A < B then
   X := True;
else
   X := False;
end if;
return X;
```

would satisfy this requirement. Moreover, we have seen that each of the functions Owners_Share and Dealers_Share of Figure 8.2.5 requires three replacements of types NATURAL, FLOAT, and CHARACTER—*in that order*—and returns a value of type FLOAT.

The formal definition of an Ada **function body** is given in Figure 8.3.1 in the form of a sequence of syntax diagrams. A discussion of the diagrams, along with several examples, follows.

a

function body

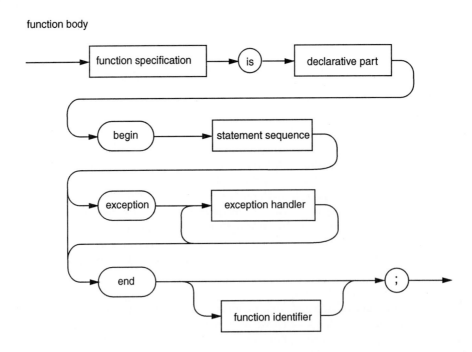

b

function specification

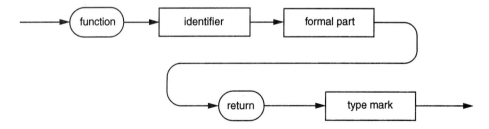

c

formal part

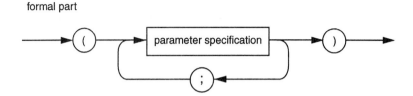

d

parameter specification

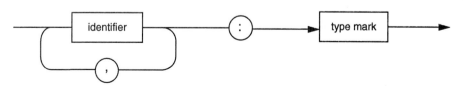

Figure 8.3.1

Rather than discuss these diagrams in this abstract form, we investigate their details for the particular example with which we are already familiar, namely, the function Minimum of Figure 8.1.4, for it is quite representative of many of the functions we will encounter throughout the remainder of the book. The function is shown in Figure 8.3.2.

```
1      -- The function "Minimum" returns the smaller of
2      -- the two nonnegative integer values passed to it
3
4   function  Minimum
5
6              (A:      NATURAL;
7               B:      NATURAL)
8
9              return NATURAL
10
11             is
12
```

```
13    X:        NATURAL;
14
15  begin
16
17    if A < B then
18      X := A;
19    else
20      X := B;
21    end if;
22
23    return X;
24
25  end Minimum;
```

Figure 8.3.2

1.   The combination of Figure 8.3.1*c* and *d* yields the **formal part**, consisting of enclosing parentheses and a sequence of parameter specifications separated by semicolons. In Figure 8.3.2, lines 6 and 7 make up the formal part:

```
(A:        NATURAL;
 B:        NATURAL)
```

It could as well have been written

```
(A: NATURAL; B: NATURAL)
```

or even more simply (but perhaps slightly less clearly) as

```
(A, B: NATURAL)
```

(In fact, we have already used these forms.) Because of its importance we note once more that the identifiers in the formal part (here, A and B) are called **formal parameters**, and it is these that are replaced by actual nonnegative integer values when the function is invoked. It should be noted that although functions *usually* have parameters (that is, usually have a formal part), a formal part is not a *requirement*—there are "parameterless" functions.

2.   The **function specification**, described in Figure 8.3.1*b*, runs from line 4 through line 9, and in Figure 8.3.2 it consists of the reserved word **function**, the *function identifier* (we have used "Minimum" in our example), the *formal part* as described in item 1 above, the reserved word **return**, and the **type** of the value returned by the function, in this case NATURAL.

3.   As described in Figure 8.3.1*a*, the **function body** consists of the following: the *function specification* described above in item 2; the reserved word **is** (line 11 of Figure 8.3.2); a **declarative part** (which may be empty—see the function Dealers_Share of Figure 8.2.5—but here consisting simply of line 13); and a *frame* made up of the reserved word **begin** (at line 15), a *statement sequence* (lines 17

through 23 in Figure 8.3.2), and the reserved word **end.** In this case, **end** is followed by the function identifier, although the inclusion of this identifier is optional. Note that this function contains no exception handlers; however, they frequently are implemented in subprograms, as we will see in the next chapter.

We close this section with a slightly streamlined version of the current program. Figure 8.3.3 exhibits modifications in two places: As noted in Section 8.1, the variable Best is not really needed, and thus it has been removed from the program and replaced by the direct displaying of Minimum's returned value. By a slight rewriting of the function, we have eliminated the need for the variable X (declared *within* the function Minimum), although note that we now have *two* **return** statements, a device we had already employed in the program of Figure 8.2.2 and about which more will be said in Section 8.5.

```
with Text_IO;

procedure Best_Buy is

    package Nat_IO is new Text_IO.Integer_IO (NATURAL);

    Brand_X_1,
    Brand_Y_1,
    Brand_X_2,
    Brand_Y_2,

    Store_1,
    Store_2:    NATURAL;

      -- The function "Minimum" returns the smaller of
      -- the two nonnegative integer values passed to it

    function    Minimum (A, B: NATURAL) return NATURAL is

    begin

      if A < B then
        return A;
      else
        return B;
      end if;

    end Minimum;


  begin

    Text_IO.Put ("Enter costs for Brand X and Brand Y, at Store 1: ");
    Nat_IO.Get (Brand_X_1);
    Nat_IO.Get (Brand_Y_1);

    Store_1 := Minimum (Brand_X_1, Brand_Y_1);

    Text_IO.Put ("Enter costs for Brand X and Brand Y, at Store 2: ");
    Nat_IO.Get (Brand_X_2);
    Nat_IO.Get (Brand_Y_2);
```

```
Store_2 := Minimum (Brand_X_2, Brand_Y_2);

Text_IO.New_Line (2);
Text_IO.Put ("Lowest available cost for the item is ");
Nat_IO.Put (Minimum (Store_1, Store_2), 0);
Text_IO.Put_Line (" cents.");

end Best_Buy;
```

Figure 8.3.3

8.4 Invoking functions

There is really little that needs to be said about invoking functions except for a couple of formalisms that we have already noted. The mechanism by which functions are invoked and return their values is described below:

1. A function is invoked or "called" simply by *using its name in an expression*. Thus the mere occurrence of the name Minimum, as in Figure 8.3.3, is sufficient to invoke it; that is, there is no special Ada reserved word for invoking functions. For example, if Fn is an INTEGER-valued function having three formal parameters of type INTEGER, and if X, Y, and Z are INTEGER variables, then a typical call to Fn might be

    ```
    Z := X + 4 * Fn (X, -3, (Y+4)/5) - 2;
    ```

    Here the replacements for the three formal parameters are expressions of type INTEGER, but we see that they are of somewhat different kinds: the first is the value of a simple INTEGER variable, the second is the negative of an INTEGER literal, and the third involves a slightly more complicated INTEGER-valued arithmetic construction.

2. When a function is invoked, it must be supplied with *substitutes* for its formal parameters. These **actual parameters** may be expressions of any kind, provided only that at the time the function is invoked during program execution, each such expression has a well-defined value of the type specified for its corresponding formal parameter. The substitution of actual parameters for formal parameters is *positional*, in that the first actual parameter replaces the first formal parameter, as described in paragraph 3 below; the second actual parameter replaces the second formal parameter; and so on. (In Section 9.5 we will see another way in which this "parameter association" can take place.)

3. When a function is invoked during program execution, space in main memory (of an appropriate size) is *allocated* for each of the function's formal parameters. Each formal parameter then takes on as its value the value of the corresponding actual parameter. Space is also allocated for any variables or constants declared *within the function*, storage which is said to be **local to the function** (see the variable X of

Figure 8.3.2, for example), although no values are supplied to these "from the outside" as they are to the formal parameters. The statement sequence of the function is then executed.

4. When the value of the function has been calculated, by execution of the function's statements, it is returned to the statement that invoked the function by means of the Ada construct **return**. At this time, the space allocated for the formal parameters and any local items (variables, constants, etc.) is *deallocated.*

5. The statement that invoked the function now continues execution, with the *value* of the function replacing the *call* to the function. For instance (continuing the example of paragraph 1 above), if the value

```
Fn (X, -3, (Y+4)/5)
```

is calculated to be −19, then that value is returned by Fn, it replaces the call to Fn, and the sample statement will execute as

```
Z := X + 4 * (-19) - 2
```

The terms formal parameter and actual parameter, which by now we have used many times, are quite appropriate. A formal parameter—as described in the syntax diagram of Figure 8.3.1 and paragraph 2 above—has no value and does not even exist as a concrete entity until the function is invoked. At that time, an amount of space appropriate to its type is allocated for it, but it takes its value from the *actual* parameter (an expression) that corresponds to it in the function call. The space it occupies is deallocated once execution of the function is complete. Thus *formal* parameters are truly formalisms, without substance; *actual* parameters are expressions having specific values of a certain type.

Before leaving this section we comment on the allocation of space for the formal parameters and so-called local variables of a function. This is not a new idea for us. We know that when we declare a variable in the declarative part of a program, the compiler itself does not allocate space of an appropriate size; rather, it "arranges for" the run-time system to allocate space for that variable once the program begins execution. As we have seen, this run-time space allocation is referred to in Ada as the variable declaration's **elaboration**. In an analogous fashion, the compiler arranges for the run-time elaboration associated with a function's formal parameters and local variables; this is to take place *at the time* the function is invoked. That is, space is not automatically created for these items when the program is executed; this is done if and when the function in question is invoked. Even this much does not involve any new concepts. What is new, however, is that at the close of the function (when the function executes its **return** statement), the space allocated for these items is deallocated. This means that these parameters and variables (and possibly other sorts of declared items) now cease to exist—in technical language, their *lifetime* is said to be *coextensive* with the actual execution of the function. Consequently, they may not be referred to at any point in the program except within the function code itself. To use a formal term that will be discussed in much detail in the next chapter: The **scope** of an item declared within the declarative part of a *program* is (essentially) the entire program; the scope of the formal parameters and other local items of a *function* is the body of the function itself. There are a few imprecisions here that are refined in the next chapter, but what has been said here is essentially correct; in the meantime you should compare the scope ideas brought forth here with those involved in the loop parameters of Section 6.8. (The "visibility" concepts of that section have their counterparts in the subprogram context, and visibility is also discussed in the next chapter.)

8.5 Three rules for writing Ada functions

Rule 1. We have seen that the value a function "takes on" as a result of the execution of its statements is *returned* to the calling statement upon execution of a **return** statement in the function. We have further seen (Figure 8.3.3) that a function may have multiple **return** statements (although only one of these is executed each time the function is invoked). The first of these three rules states that every Ada function *must* contain *at least one* **return** statement.

It is important to understand that a **return** statement has two effects. First, the value specified in the statement is passed back to the statement that invoked the function and is used there as the value of the function. Second, when a **return** statement is executed, control is returned *immediately* to the calling statement and execution of the function's instructions ceases. Consider, for example, the function Minimum of Figure 8.3.3, in which we replace the segment of code found there, namely

```
if A < B then
   return A;
else
   return B;
end if;
```

with the equivalent

```
if A < B then
   return A;
end if;
return B;
```

If the instruction **return A** is executed (because A < B), then the remaining function instruction—**return B**—is *not* executed.

Rule 2. An Ada function can return control to its calling statement *only* as a result of one of the following two conditions:

1.   A **return** statement.

2.   An *exception*. (Here we assume that the function itself makes no provision for handling the exception.) Note that if an exception occurs during execution of a function's statement sequence, then control is passed to the calling statement *with that*

exception raised, and thus control is immediately given to some exception handler (programmer-written or system handler). More will be said about exception handling in the following chapter.

It may seem strange that we have said in discussing rule 1 that every function must have a **return** statement *and* then said here that a function must return via a **return** statement. You might well ask how a function could *fail* to return via its **return** statement, and we offer a simple example in Figure 8.5.1. The function Min described there is innocent-looking enough, and it is the sort of function that the unwary programmer might well write, not anticipating the problems that can occur. The idea is that Min is to return the *smaller* of its two INTEGER parameters, provided there is a smaller. If the two parameters passed to it are equal—presumably an extraordinary event, in the context of this function—a message is to be displayed. As is easily seen, if the two parameters are equal, then the message is displayed but the function does *not* execute a **return** statement. In fact, an Ada-declared exception known as Program_Error is raised, as will always happen whenever a function "runs out of code" before executing **return**.

```
--   CAUTION! This function can cause the Program_Error
--   exception to be raised.

--   The function Min returns as its value the smaller
--   of the two actual parameters passed to it, unless
--   they are equal; in that case, a message is displayed.

function Min (A, B: INTEGER) return INTEGER is

   begin

     if A = B then
       Text_IO.Put_Line ("The parameters are equal!");
     elsif A < B then
       return A;
     else
       return B;
     end if;

   end MIN;
```

Figure 8.5.1

Rule 3. The final rule concerning the writing of Ada functions is that the statement sequence in a function may *not* contain any statement in which the value of any formal parameter is changed, by appearing in an input (Get) statement, or by appearing on the left side of an assignment statement, or any other way. As a simple example, consider the modified version of the function Minimum shown in Figure 8.5.2. Here we simply note that if the parameter A is no larger than B, then A is the minimum and is returned. Otherwise, we assign A the value of B, and once again A's value is returned. We know enough about what happens when the function is invoked, and we have thought far enough ahead to realize that when Minimum is called, memory is allocated *at that time* for A and B, and these locations receive the values of the actual parameters. Since it is these locations—these copies of the actual parameter values—that are manipulated, we are in no danger of changing the values of the *actual* parameters by manipulating the *formal* parameters in this way. All of what we have said here is true, and yet the *language specification* disallows such formal parameter assignments. The restriction appears to be arbitrary (it is, to some small extent), and it is certainly difficult to justify at this point. However, we expand on the concepts involved here in Section 8.7, and at that time we return to the discussion of this restriction. (Incidentally, the Ada compiler will detect and announce the violation of this rule in the function of Figure 8.5.2.)

```
function Minimum (A, B: NATURAL) return NATURAL is

begin

  if A > B then
    A := B;        -- Invalid assignment!!
  end if;
  return A;

end Minimum;
```

Figure 8.5.2

8.6 Using procedures

All the examples we have seen in this chapter up to now reinforce the characteristics of functions as subprograms: (1) A function is (usually) given one or more *values* as parameters when it is invoked; (2) using these values, it carries out a computation that produces a resulting value; (3) this value is returned as the *value of the function*; and (4) because it has a value, a function call is used in a program as an *expression* (for example, on the right side of an assignment statement, either by itself or as an operand of a more complex computational construction).

We turn now to the other kind of subprogram found in Ada and many other programming languages, namely, the *procedure*, which we have already discussed informally in Sections 3.1 and 3.4. Unlike a function, a procedure does not return a value; its purpose is to perform some action. Because it has no value, a procedure call is not used in a program as an expression (something that "has a value"). As noted in Chapter 3, a procedure call, by which the procedure is made to carry out its action, takes the form of a program *statement* (command) that "invokes the name" of the procedure, along with the actual parameter or parameters associated with the procedure call. We have seen many examples of procedure calls, among them:

```
Nat_IO.Get (Brand_X_1);
Nat_IO.Get (Brand_X_2);

Text_IO.New_Line (2);
Text_IO.Put ("Lowest available cost for the item is ");
Nat_IO.Put (Best, 0);
Text_IO.Put_Line ("cents.");
```

A question arises: The form of a procedure call, such as those we have just listed, suggests that, like a function, a procedure can *receive* information from the program that calls it—presumably for use by the procedure in carrying out its action. But if, unlike a function, a procedure does not return a value, how can it *send back* information to the calling program? Or, for that matter, can it do so at all? The answer to this question has been described in Section 3.4, where we briefly discussed *parameter modes*: A procedure takes information in, and sends information out through its *parameters*. Accordingly, each parameter is specified as having a certain "mode," depending on the use that will be made of it in the back-and-forth transmission of information. We take up the matter of parameter modes in the next section; for the moment, let us turn to an example that illustrates why we might want to write and use a procedure.

Suppose we wish to write a program Print_in_Order that will accept three integers as input and then display them in increasing order, with the smallest integer coming first and the the largest one last. The steps are simple:

1. Get the input (three integers).

2. Arrange the integers in increasing order.

3. Display the integers as arranged.

We may regard these three steps as making up a Level 1 outline of the program we are developing. If we declare integer variables Int_1, Int_2, and Int_3, the first and third steps are actually ready for coding (we assume the inclusion of Int_IO):

```
-- (1)
    Text_IO.Put_Line ("Type three integers:");
    Int_IO.Get (Int_1);
    Int_IO.Get (Int_2);
    Int_IO.Get (Int_3);
    Text_IO.New_Line;


-- (2)
    -- Arrange Int_1, Int_2, and Int_3 in increasing order


-- (3)
    Text_IO.Put_Line ("In increasing order, the integers are:");
    Int_IO.Put (Int_1, 0);
    Text_IO.New_Line;
    Int_IO.Put (Int_2, 0);
    Text_IO.New_Line;
    Int_IO.Put (Int_3, 0);
    Text_IO.New_Line;
```

To carry out step 2, we need to compare pairs of numbers and exchange (interchange) the values of the pair if they are "out of order." We may do this as follows:

```
    if Int_1 > Int_2 then
        -- exchange the values of Int_1 and Int_2
```

```
   end if;
      -- Int_1 is now the smaller of Int_1 and Int_2

   if Int_1 > Int_3 then
      -- exchange the values of Int_1 and Int_3
   end if;

         -- Int_1 is now the smallest of the three numbers
         -- Arrange Int_2 and Int_3, if needed

   if Int_2 > Int_3 then
      -- exchange the values of Int_2 and Int_3;
   end if;

         -- The numbers are now in increasing order
```

Suppose we now address the job of exchanging the values of Int_1 and Int_2. Performing an exchange such as this is a frequent operation in programming. Clearly, it is not so simple as

```
   Int_1 := Int_2;
   Int_2 := Int_1;
```

for when the first assignment has been executed, Int_1 has been given the value of Int_2, and the original value of Int_1 has been irretrievably lost. Both variables will end up with the *same* value (the original value of Int_2). Thus, in carrying out an exchange of values, it is always necessary to begin by saving the value of one of the variables in an extra memory location (variable) introduced for this purpose. Accordingly, we will assume the declaration of an integer variable Temp (for *temp*orary location); then the code for the exchange becomes

```
   Temp  := Int_1;
   Int_1 := Int_2;
   Int_2 := Temp;
```

Now we have the job of writing the code for this exchange "action" two more times, each time with different variables. Admittedly, rewriting three assignment statements is no great challenge; nevertheless, it is repetitive. As a matter of fact, we find ourselves in a situation analogous to that of Section 8.1, where "something" is to be done several times—in that case, the computation of a *value* (the minimum of two numbers); in this case, the performing of an *action* (the exchange of two values). Just as before, we are in a position to make good use of a subprogram—this time, a procedure rather than a function—to effect conservation and modularization of program code. Let us suppose that our Print_in_Order program contains all the necessary code (including the declaration of Temp) of a procedure Exchange that will exchange the values of two integer variables passed to it as parameters. Then Print_in_Order assumes the structure shown in Figure 8.6.1, where, for the moment, we omit the code for the procedure Exchange and merely indicate where it is to be placed.

```
   with Text_IO, Int_IO;

procedure Print_in_Order is

   Int_1, Int_2, Int_3: INTEGER;
```

```
    -- the code for procedure Exchange belongs here

begin

    Text_IO.Put_Line ("Type three integers:");
    Int_IO.Get (Int_1);
    Int_IO.Get (Int_2);
    Int_IO.Get (Int_3);
    Text_IO.New_Line;

       -- Arrange the integers in increasing order

    if Int_1 > Int_2 then
       Exchange (Int_1, Int_2);
    end if;

    if Int_1 > Int_3 then
       Exchange (Int_1, Int_3);
    end if;

    if Int_2 > Int_3 then
       Exchange (Int_2, Int_3);
    end if;

       -- The integers are now in increasing order

    Text_IO.Put_Line ("In increasing order, the integers are:");
    Int_IO.Put (Int_1, 0);
    Text_IO.New_Line;
    Int_IO.Put (Int_2, 0);
    Text_IO.New_Line;
    Int_IO.Put (Int_3, 0);

end Print_in_Order;
```

Figure 8.6.1

In this form of the program, our use of Exchange has served both to eliminate repetitive code and to make the conditional statements in the central part of the program quite easy to read. The program would become even easier to read if these conditional statements, which make up the process of ordering, or arranging, the numbers, were themselves removed from the main program and put into a procedure Order, a procedure that takes three integer variables as parameters and does the job of arranging them in increasing order. If we take this step, our program could have the form shown in Figure 8.6.2.

```
    with Text_IO, Int_IO;

procedure Print_in_Order is

    Int_1, Int_2, Int_3: INTEGER;

    -- the code for procedure Exchange belongs here

    -- the code for procedure Order belongs here

begin
```

```
Text_IO.Put_Line ("Type three integers:");
Int_IO.Get (Int_1);
Int_IO.Get (Int_2);
Int_IO.Get (Int_3);
Text_IO.New_Line;

Order (Int_1, Int_2, Int_3);

Text_IO.Put_Line ("In increasing order, the integers are:");
Int_IO.Put (Int_1, 0);
Text_IO.New_Line;
Int_IO.Put (Int_2, 0);
Text_IO.New_Line;
Int_IO.Put (Int_3, 0);
Text_IO.New_Line;

end Print_in_Order;
```

Figure 8.6.2

You will notice that we have left the declaration of procedure Exchange in this program, although it does not appear to be invoked. The reason is that Exchange will be called by the procedure Order when the latter executes, since the statement part of Order will consist essentially of the conditional statements found in Figure 8.6.1, the statements we have now removed from the main program.

What we need to do, of course, is write the code for the procedures Exchange and Order and insert it at the proper places in these programs—the same places, by the way, where it would go if Exchange and Order were functions, rather than procedures. We do this in the following section.

8.7 Parameter modes; writing procedures

From our familiarity with Ada function declarations, we expect that the declarations of the procedures Exchange and Order would begin with the reserved word **procedure**, followed by the respective procedure name, followed by the list (enclosed in parentheses) of formal parameters and their types. And this is indeed correct. But what about the type of the "return value"? As we are aware, procedures, unlike functions, do not return any values; hence in the declaration of a procedure the words "**return <type mark>**," found in function declarations, are simply omitted.

As we have already mentioned, procedures are unlike functions in another way; namely, their parameters are used not only for passing information *in* to the procedure for use when its statements are executed but also for passing information *out* to the calling program when the procedure completes its execution. Thus, as we saw in Chapter 3, provision will be needed for a new *mode* (or kind) of parameter passing, one in which variables whose values were initially given to formal parameters of the procedure are then given (possibly new) values *back* by the procedure just prior to its return. On the other hand, there may be instances in which the assigning of actual parameter values to their formal parameter counterparts is sufficient, that no "handing back" of values to the actual parameter is required, since the values of the parameters are not changed within the procedure. (An example of this is any of the many Put procedures.) Finally, there are cases in which an actual parameter's value upon entry to a procedure is immaterial to the procedure; rather, the procedure's activity *generates* a value that is returned in this parameter. (This is exemplified by any of the Get procedures.)   We describe these three Ada parameter modes (more accurately, perhaps, "modes of parameter passing") below.

Mode	Parameter behavior

---

in   When the procedure is invoked, the formal parameter takes on as its value the value of the corresponding actual parameter. The value of an **in** parameter may be referred to but may *not* be modified (assigned) during execution of the procedure. Mode **in** is the default mode for a parameter if no other mode is specified. (Parameters of functions may *only* be of this mode.)

out   When the procedure is invoked, the formal parameter is allocated space, but that space is *not* given any particular value. Upon return from the procedure, the *actual* parameter is given the value of the *formal* parameter. The value of an **out** parameter may *not* be referred to within the procedure, but the parameter may be (and almost always is) *assigned* a value during execution of the procedure.

in out   When the procedure is invoked, the formal parameter takes on the value of the corresponding actual parameter, and upon return from the procedure, the actual parameter is given the value of the corresponding formal parameter. The value of an **in out** parameter may thus be referred to, and the parameter may also be *assigned* a value during execution of the procedure.

In the declaration of a procedure, the mode of each formal parameter is included before the name of the parameter's type, as we illustrate in the examples below.

We begin by displaying the code for the procedure Exchange discussed in the previous section. Since both parameters are of mode **in out**, the Ada system must copy the values of the actual parameters into the procedure's formal parameters; the values of the formal parameters are then exchanged and copied back by the system (in exchanged form) to the actual parameters. This is precisely the activity that we want to take place in the procedure, and it is for this reason that we have specified the parameter modes as **in out**.

```
procedure Exchange (X: in out INTEGER; Y: in out INTEGER) is

   Temp:     INTEGER;
```

```
begin

  Temp := X;
  X    := Y;
  Y    := Temp;

end Exchange;
```

Figure 8.7.1

Insertion of this code into that of Figure 8.6.1 yields a complete program Print_in_Order. We now turn our attention to developing the procedure Order used in the program of Figure 8.6.2. This procedure will call the procedure Exchange, which we take to be available to it (see the analogous situation for functions in Figure 8.2.2). Actually, there is little to be done, as we have already written the entire statement part of Order (in the main program of Figure 8.6.1). We have only to note once again that at the start of the procedure's execution, the values of the actual parameters must be copied by the Ada system to the formal parameters, and at the conclusion of execution, the (rearranged) values of the formal parameters must be copied back to the respective actual parameters; thus again the formal parameters must be of mode **in out**. Note the more succinct way of listing the formal parameters in their declaration.

```
procedure Order (A, B, C:  in out INTEGER) is

begin

  if A > B then
    Exchange (A, B);
  end if;

  if A > C then
    Exchange (A, C);
  end if;

  if B > C then
    Exchange (B, C);
  end if;

end ORDER;
```

Figure 8.7.2

We may illustrate the use of **in** parameters while further modularizing the program Print_in_Order by incorporating the output statements of Figure 8.6.2 into the body of a procedure Print_Output, which will take care of all the output of Print_in_Order when invoked in the statement part of this program. The procedure Print_Output will have three **in** parameters. Similarly, we may write a procedure Get_Input, with three **out** parameters, that will carry out the input part of Print_in_Order when invoked at the beginning of this program's statement part. Since all the needed code has essentially been written and has only to be put together in a different way, we present the results of this endeavor in Figure 8.7.3 without further comment.

```
     with Text_IO, Int_IO;

procedure Print_in_Order is

     -- This program accepts three integers as input,
     -- arranges the integers in increasing order, and
     -- displays them in this order.

     Int_1, Int_2, Int_3:  INTEGER;


     procedure Get_Input (A, B, C:  out INTEGER) is

     begin

       Text_IO.Put_Line ("Type three integers:");
       Int_IO.Get (A);
       Int_IO.Get (B);
       Int_IO.Get (C);
       Text_IO.New_Line;

     end Get_Input;


     procedure Exchange (X, Y:  in out INTEGER) is

         Temp:    INTEGER;

     begin

       Temp := X;
       X    := Y;
       Y    := Temp;

     end Exchange;


     procedure Order (A, B, C:  in out INTEGER) is

     begin

       if A > B then
         Exchange (A, B);
       end if;

       if A > C then
         Exchange (A, C);
       end if;

       if B > C then
         Exchange (B, C);
       end if;

     end Order;


     procedure Print_Output (A, B, C:  in INTEGER) is

     begin
```

```
          Text_IO.Put_Line ("In increasing order, the integers are:");
          Int_IO.Put (A, 0);
          Text_IO.New_Line;
          Int_IO.Put (B, 0);
          Text_IO.New_Line;
          Int_IO.Put (C, 0);
          Text_IO.New_Line;

      end Print_Output;


   begin   -- Print_in_Order

      Get_Input    (Int_1, Int_2, Int_3);
      Order        (Int_1, Int_2, Int_3);
      Print_Output (Int_1, Int_2, Int_3);

   end Print_in_Order;
```

Figure 8.7.3

A look at this program makes it clear that not only does the inclusion of the procedure Exchange eliminate notable repetition of code (as well as make the body of the procedure Order more readable) but also that the use of the procedures Get_Input, Order, and Print_Output makes it possible to write the statement part of the main program so that it clearly reflects the Level 1 outline of the problem solution. It is an example of the use of subprograms (in this case, procedures) in the process of top-down program development. Each Level 1 step has been coded as a procedure call, and the details of the action have been placed "out of the way" in the declarations of the procedures. In Section 8.10 we present a further example and comment on the use of subprograms to achieve well-structured, modular programs.

Referring once more to Figure 8.7.3, which illustrates all the parameter modes, we offer a few final comments on these modes. First, the formal parameters of a function *must* be of mode **in**; second, whenever the mode is not explicitly stated in a function *or* procedure declaration, it is taken by default to be **in**. We almost never specify it when declaring functions, since there is no other choice. When declaring a *procedure* parameter, however, it is good practice (although not necessary) explicitly to specify **in** parameters, as we did in Figure 8.7.3, since stating the mode tells the reader something about how the parameter will be used.

Could we simply declare *every* procedure parameter to be of mode **in out** and be done with it? Yes, but there are two objections to doing so. First, as noted above, the explicit specification of a parameter's mode tells the reader something significant about the parameter and the way in which it is used in the procedure. Second, suppose we specifically intend that a parameter be *referenced* but not *modified* within a procedure, but we declare it to be of mode **in out** rather than **in**. If, in the procedure's executable part, we inadvertently assign that parameter a value, the assignment will be permitted because of the parameter's mode. If, on the other hand, we had more properly specified that the parameter was of mode **in**, then the Ada compiler would have generated an error message before any damage had been done. Thus the rule that applies here is to declare each procedure parameter to be of the mode that corresponds to the parameter's use in the procedure.

Can *any* object of matching type be used in a subprogram call as the actual parameter corresponding to a formal parameter of the subprogram? If the formal parameter is of mode **in**, the answer is an unqualified yes: Variable values, constants, literals, and function values are all valid formal parameter replacements, as in fact is any expression whose *value* is of the requisite type. But if the parameter is of mode **in out** or **out**, then upon conclusion of the procedure execution, the actual parameter is assigned the value of the formal parameter. Thus only actual parameters that *can be assigned values* are appropriate for formal parameter replacement, and so the only actual parameters appropriate for replacement of **in out** or **out** parameters are *variables*. Verify that the **in out** and **out** parameters of Figure 8.7.3 are used only in this way. Also recall the many forms of integer expressions that we have previously passed as actual parameters to Int_IO.Put, whose formal parameter is of mode **in**, whereas only *variables* have been passed as parameters to Int_IO.Get, whose formal parameter is of mode **out**.

To conclude this section, we give in Figure 8.7.4 the syntax diagrams pertinent to the **procedure** subprogram. We offer them without further comment, except to note that they differ little from those of Figure 8.3.1.

a

procedure body

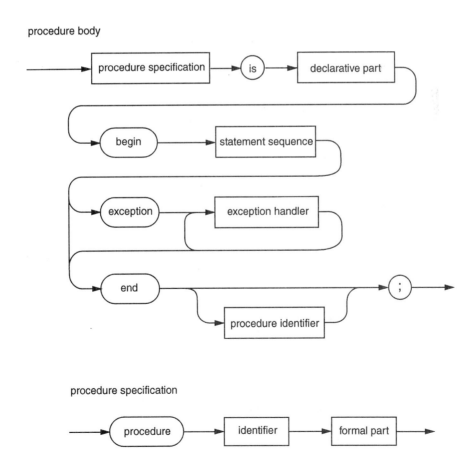

b

procedure specification

c

formal part

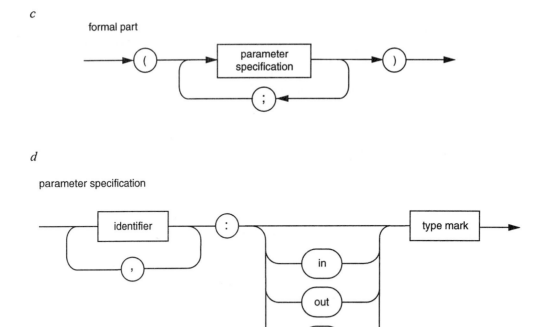

d

parameter specification

Figure 8.7.4

8.8 The *return* statement in procedures*

A glance at the examples of procedures in the previous section reveals that they contain no **return** statement, as you might have expected—being *procedures* (rather than functions), they do not return values, and thus **return** would not even seem to make sense in the context of a procedure. Nonetheless the **return** statement *is* valid in a procedure, but it is used without a value. To discover what effect **return** has in a procedure, recall that in a function, **return** has two effects: It returns control back to the place at which the function was invoked and passes back the calculated value. Since a procedure does not calculate a return value, the effect of **return** in a procedure is simply to return control back to the statement immediately following the statement that invoked the procedure. Since we have already said that a procedure returns back to the module that invoked it (the main program, perhaps) when the code of the procedure "runs out," we can thus think of each procedure as containing an implicit **return** just before the end of the procedure body.

The **return** statement in a procedure affords us a means of abandoning execution of the procedure's statements and returning control back to the calling module. However, abandoning a procedure prior to its normal end is usually the result of some extraordinary event, and in such cases the raising of an exception is frequently the "cleanest" response to

---

*This section may be omitted.

the situation. Can the **return** statement legitimately be used in procedures? The answer is yes, although this is not frequently done. We offer in Figure 8.8.1 an example of a procedure that does use a **return** in this way, to pass a value back to the calling module via an **out** parameter. (The activity here is actually better written as a *function*, and we do so in Section 9.8.) The procedure Find_GCD (for *greatest common divisor*) has three parameters, A, B, and G, all of type POSITIVE; A and B are **in** parameters, while G is an **in out** parameter. It is via G that a value will be passed back to the calling module. The purpose of Find_GCD is to calculate the largest positive integer that exactly divides each of the given integers. We leave it to you to investigate why the code shown will have the greatest common divisor of A and B in G upon returning. Looking at a few examples may be of some help, especially if you are not familiar with the notions involved here.

```
procedure Find_GCD (A, B: in POSITIVE; G: in out POSITIVE)  is

    Num:      POSITIVE := A;
    Temp:     POSITIVE;

begin

    G := B;

    loop
      if Num rem G = 0 then
        return;
      else
        Temp := G;
        G := Num rem G;
        Num := Temp;
      end if;
    end loop;

end Find_GCD;
```

Figure 8.8.1

8.9 The declarative part of a subprogram; nested subprogram declarations

So far we have had little to say concerning the kinds of declarations that can occur within a subprogram's declarative part, beyond the suggestion that simple variables and constants can be declared there. This fact is implicit in Figure 8.1.4, for example, where the NATURAL variable X is declared, and in Figure 8.2.5, where the constant Mileage_Limit is established. In discussing Figure 8.3.2, we did mention, however, that the declarative part of a function might be empty, as is the case with the function Dealers_Share (Figure 8.2.5) and the version of the function Minimum shown in Figure 8.3.3. Similarly, a procedure may have an empty declarative part; this is true of the procedures Get_Input, Order, and Print_Output of Figure 8.7.3.

If a subprogram *does* have a declarative part, as is often the case, what sorts of declarations may this part contain? In fact there are *no* restrictions on what might be declared within a subprogram—almost any kind of entity whose declaration is valid can appear in a subprogram's declarative part. Besides variable and constant declarations, this includes declarations of types and subtypes, packages (instantiations of Text_IO.Integer_IO, for example), and exceptions. Moreover, the declarations themselves may employ the values of the subprogram's formal parameters. We illustrate several of these ideas in Figure 8.9.1.

```
   with Text_IO, Int_IO;

procedure Sample is

   X:        INTEGER;

   function Triple (Lower, Upper, Value: INTEGER) return INTEGER is

      subtype TEMP_RANGE is INTEGER range Lower..Upper;

      Temp:  TEMP_RANGE := Value;

   begin

      Temp := 3 * Temp;
      return Temp;

   end Triple;


begin

   X := 5;

   X := Triple (3, 2*X, X-2);
   Int_IO.Put (X, 0);
   Text_IO.New_Line;

end Sample;
```

Figure 8.9.1

The function Triple declared in Figure 8.9.1 has little merit except as an example, for its purpose is simply to triple the value of one of its parameters (in an unnecessarily complicated way) and to return the resulting number. But there are features here that deserve some discussion. Note first that a *subtype* TEMP_RANGE is declared within Triple and that this subtype depends on the first two of Triple's parameters. Thus we see, as noted above, that (1) types are valid candidates for declaration within a subprogram and (2) the subprogram's formal parameters may validly be used in such type declarations. Next we see that a variable Temp is declared to be of type TEMP_RANGE and assigned as its initial value the third of the subprogram's parameters, Value. In the executable part of the subprogram, Temp is reassigned its triple as a value. Thus, execution of the main program of Figure 8.9.1 amounts to an initialization of X and then a call to Triple; which is, in effect,

```
   X := Triple (3, 10, 3);
```

Within the function Triple, the subtype TEMP_RANGE is declared as the range 3..10. The third actual parameter, 3, is in this range; further, when Temp is tripled (to 9), its value is still within range, so the function returns the value 9, which is assigned to X and then displayed. Other kinds of behavior can occur if X is assigned integer values other than 5 in the first executable statement of the main program; we consider these in the exercises.

What we must bear in mind in this context is the point that we stressed at the end of Section 8.4; namely, although many kinds of entities (including types, variables, constants, packages, and exceptions) may be declared in a subprogram's declarative part, we may refer to these entities *only* within the code that makes up the body of the subprogram itself, not elsewhere in the program. It is instructive to check the function and procedure declarations presented up to this point in the present chapter and verify that this rule has been observed in each case.

We have not yet mentioned a different kind of entity that may be declared within the declarative part of a subprogram, namely, another *subprogram*. Accordingly, we discuss the consequences of declaring one or more subprograms within another (enclosing) subprogram body. Our example, shown in Figure 8.9.2, presents the case in which a *function* is declared within a *function*. Bear in mind that what we have to say here pertains equally to both functions and procedures: A subprogram (whether function or procedure) may be declared and invoked within another subprogram (whether function or procedure).

In Figure 8.9.2 we return to the functions Maximum_2 and Maximum_3 of Figure 8.2.2, which return the largest of two and three NATURAL numbers, respectively. In this sample program we again take advantage of the fact that we already have a function that returns the larger of *two* numbers of type NATURAL in order to calculate the largest of *three* such numbers. What is different here is that, in the case of Figure 8.9.2, the function Maximum_2 is declared *within* the declaration of Maximum_3, whereas in Figure 8.2.2, these functions were declared independently of one another.

```
    with Text_IO;

  procedure Largest is

        package Nat_IO is new Text_IO.Integer_IO (NATURAL);

    Nat_1,
    Nat_2,
    Nat_3:    NATURAL;

    function Maximum_3 (X, Y, Z: NATURAL) return NATURAL is
      function Maximum_2 (A, B: NATURAL) return NATURAL is

      begin     -- function Maximum_2

        if A > B then
          return A;
        else
          return B;
        end if;

      end Maximum_2;

      begin         -- function Maximum_3
```

```
      return Maximum_2 (Maximum_2 (X,Y), Z);

   end Maximum_3;


begin              -- main program

   Text_IO.PUT ("Enter three numbers: ");
   Nat_IO.Get (Nat_1);
   Nat_IO.Get (Nat_2);
   Nat_IO.Get (Nat_3);
   Text_IO.New_Line;

   Text_IO.Put ("The largest of these numbers is ");
   Nat_IO.Put (Maximum_3 (Nat_1, Nat_2, Nat_3), 0);
   Text_IO.New_Line;

end Largest;
```

Figure 8.9.2

The basic structure of the program Largest is depicted in Figure 8.9.3*a*. In Figure 8.9.3*b* we show an acceptable alternative way in which Maximum_2 and Maximum_3 might have been declared—and which is, in fact, the structure of Figure 8.2.2. Finally, we note that the arrangement of Figure 8.9.3*c* is *not* acceptable. (Why not?)

```
a     procedure Largest ...
         .
         .
         .
         function Maximum_3 ...
            .
            .
            .
            function Maximum_2 ...
               .
               .
               .
            end Maximum_2;
            .
            .
            .
         end Maximum_3;
         .
         .
         .
      end Largest;


b     procedure Largest ...
         .
         .
         .
         function Maximum_2 ...
```

```
           .
           .
           .
      end Maximum_2;
        .
        .
        .
      function Maximum_3 ...
           .
           .
           .
      end Maximum_3;
        .
        .
        .
   end Largest;


c    procedure Largest ...
        .
        .
        .
      function Maximum_3 ...
           .
           .
           .
      end Maximum_3;
        .
        .
        .
      function Maximum_2 ...
           .
           .
           .
      end Maximum_2;
        .
        .
        .
   end Largest;
```

Figure 8.9.3

Is there a preference between *a* and *b* of Figure 8.9.3? That depends upon how the function Maximum_2 is to be used. As shown in the sample program of Figure 8.9.2, since Maximum_2 is referenced *only* in the function body of Maximum_3, we prefer version *a*. Note that in this version, since the declaration of Maximum_2 is contained within Maximum_3's body, the function Maximum_2 is known *only* to Maximum_3, and thus the only references to Maximum_2 would have to be from Maximum_3; the main procedure (Largest) itself could not make a reference to Maximum_2. Thus if a reference to Maximum_2 *outside* of Maximum_3 is desired or required, Figure 8.9.3*a* will not do; we have no choice and must use something like version *b*. In cases where there *is* a choice, it is simply a matter of considering what best contributes to good program structure, a point that we discuss further in the next chapter.

8.10 Top-down and modular programming revisited

We stated at the outset of this chapter that subprograms do much to enhance our abilities to write modularized programs having the top-down structure that was investigated briefly in Chapters 2 and 3. We reexamine those ideas once again using the initial example of this chapter, namely, the program Best_Buy. (See Figure 8.3.3 for a good sample version.) Despite its simplicity, the "best buy" problem admits an analysis that discloses a basic activity (procedure) and evaluation (function). In particular, the problem amounts to:

1.   Get the costs of the two brands at the first store.

2.   Find and save the smaller of these two costs.

3.   Get the costs of the two brands at the second store.

4.   Find and save the smaller of these two costs.

5.   Find the smaller of the two numbers saved at steps 2 and 4 above.

6.   Announce (display) the result of the evaluation at step 5 above.

As we see, there are two common activities (steps 1 and 3) and three common evaluations (steps 2, 4, and 5), and thus it is natural to create a procedure in the first case and a function in the second. Our motivations here are twofold. The most obvious is the *conservation* of code, since the procedure and function will need to be written only once, and they can then be reused as often as necessary. Of equal importance is the *compression* of code—we will see that the main (executable) part of the program has a far more pleasing, readable appearance as a result of encapsulating many Ada instructions into a single, programmer-defined "superinstruction." This final version of Best_Buy is shown in Figure 8.10.1, and you should examine it in the context of the notions of this paragraph.

```
    with Text_IO;

  procedure Best_Buy is

    package Nat_IO is new Text_IO.Integer_IO (NATURAL);

    Store_1:  NATURAL;
    Store_2:  NATURAL;


      -- The function "Minimum" returns the smaller of
      -- the two nonnegative integer values passed to it

    function    Minimum (A, B: NATURAL) return NATURAL is

    begin

      if A < B then
        return A;
```

```
    end if;
    return B;

end Minimum;


    --   The procedure Get_Costs gets the cost of both items
    --   (Brand X and Brand Y) at one of the stores.  The
    --   store number is passed to Get_Costs in the parameter
    --   Store_No; the minimum of the costs of the brand X and
    --   Y items is placed in the parameter Min_Cost.

procedure Get_Costs (Store_No:  in  NATURAL;
                     Min_Cost:  out NATURAL) is

    Brand_X,
    Brand_Y:        NATURAL;

begin

    Text_IO.Put ("Enter the costs for Brand X and Brand Y, at Store ");
    Nat_IO.Put (Store_No, 0);
    Text_IO.Put (": ");
    Nat_IO.Get (Brand_X);
    Nat_IO.Get (Brand_Y);

    Min_Cost := Minimum (Brand_X, Brand_Y);

end Get_Costs;


begin

    Get_Costs (1, Store_1);
    Get_Costs (2, Store_2);

    Text_IO.New_Line (2);
    Text_IO.Put ("Lowest available cost for the item is ");
    Nat_IO.Put (Minimum (Store_1, Store_2), 0);
    Text_IO.Put_Line (" cents.");

end Best_Buy;
```

Figure 8.10.1

Our final comment of this section involves the *names* we have given to functions and procedures. In general, as we have said, it is useful to name functions in such a way that they are representative of the *values* that they return, thus Minimum, Minimum_3, and Triple. Since procedures normally involve some *action* (other than a value calculation), we use action or activity names, such as Exchange, Order, and Get_Costs. As is always the case, of course, identifiers should be as suggestive as possible of the entities that they represent; if possible (although we stop short of overstressing it), function names should represent value-type objects and procedure names should represent actions.

In the next chapter we consider a second, and in some respects different, example of the kind of modular, structured programming we have been discussing here. The example consists of yet another version of the Time_and_Day program originally introduced, in somewhat simplistic form, in Chapter 2. As we will see, this new version of Time_and_Day, while illustrating further the use of procedures to modularize programs, leads us into several important concepts associated with subprograms, concepts subsequently considered at length.

8.11 Exercises

8.1.1 Write a function Maximum that takes two NATURAL values and returns as its value the larger of the two. This function may be modeled on the function Minimum found in Figure 8.1.4.

8.1.2 (a) Write a function Minimum that takes two FLOAT values and returns the smaller of them as its value.

(b) Write a function Maximum that takes two FLOAT values and returns the larger of them as its value.

8.2.1 The program in Figure 8.2.1 accommodates a setting in which two dealers offer rebates on each of three models of television sets. Write a program to deal with the situation in which *three* dealers offer rebates on each of *two* models of television sets. What changes, if any, need be made in the functions Maximum_2 and Maximum_3?

8.2.2 Write a function, Maximum_4, that returns the largest of four NATURAL values:

(a) without appealing to any other functions.
(b) using the function Maximum_2 of Figure 8.2.2.
(c) using the functions Maximum_2 and Maximum_3 of Figure 8.2.2.

8.2.3 How will the program of Figure 8.2.3 react if the program user enters:

(a) **25000** for Mileage;
(b) **−1575** for Mileage;
(c) **RATS** for Mileage;
(d) **750** for Repair_Cost;
(e) **−20.46** for Repair_Cost;
(f) **305.62** for Category;
(g) **Elvis** for Repair_Cost.

8.2.4 Based on your answers to Exercise 8.2.3, explain how the Auto_Repair program might be modified to accommodate data entry errors in a better way.

8.3.1 BOOLEAN-valued functions are useful in many computing contexts. Consider the following, which has to do with a citizen's eligibility for voting:

```
function Eligible (Age:  NATURAL) return BOOLEAN is ...
```

Complete the code for this function body so that the function returns the value True if Age >= 18 and returns the value False otherwise. Write the code as follows:

(a) Use a BOOLEAN variable X in the function body and *one* **return** statement.
(b) Do not use a BOOLEAN variable in the function body; use *two* **return** statements.
(c) Do not use a BOOLEAN variable in the function body; use *one* **return** statement. (Recall that a **return** statement may contain *any* expression whose type is that of the value to be returned by the function.)

8.3.2 Consider the following:

```
function Leap_Year (Year: NATURAL) return BOOLEAN is ...
```

Complete the code for this function body so that the function returns the value True if Year is a leap year and returns the value False otherwise. Do this in three ways, as described in parts *a, b,* and *c* of Exercise 8.3.1. (Recall that, in the current Gregorian calendar, "century years"—multiples of 100—are not leap years unless they are multiples of 400.)

8.3.3 (a) Write a function Is_Digit, which, when passed a CHARACTER parameter, returns True or False if the actual parameter is or is not one of the digits '0' to '9'.

(b) Write a function Is_Alpha, which, when passed a CHARACTER parameter, returns True or False if the actual parameter is or is not one of the alphabetic characters 'A' to 'Z' and 'a' to 'z'.

(c) Write a function Is_Upcase, which, when passed a CHARACTER parameter, returns True or False if the actual parameter is or is not one of the uppercase alphabetic characters 'A' to 'Z'.

8.5.1 Consider the function Sample:

```
function Sample (A:    INTEGER;
                 B:    BOOLEAN;
                 C:    CHARACTER) return BOOLEAN is

        X:    INTEGER := 12;
        Y:    CHARACTER;

   begin

        <statement part>

   end Sample;
```

Which of the following statements or statement sequences are syntactically valid within the statement part of the function?

(a) `X := A / 2;`

(b) `Text_IO.Get (C);`

(c) `Text_IO.Get (Y);   C := Y;`

(d) `B := X - A > 4;`

(e) `return A = X;`

(f) `return not B or not Y;`

(g) `B := C > A;`

(h) `B := C > 'A';`

(i) `return not B or not C < Y;`

8.7.1 Tell what is wrong with the procedures Get_2, Increment, Extract_Sign, and Print_2 in the following program:

```
with Text_IO, Int_IO;

procedure Demo is

   A, B:     NATURAL;
   K:        INTEGER;

   procedure Get_2 (X, Y: in NATURAL) is

   begin
     Int_IO.Get (X);
     Int_IO.Get (Y);
   end GET_2;

   procedure Increment (X: in NATURAL) is

   begin
     X := X + 1;
   end Increment;

   procedure Extract_Sign (X: out INTEGER) is

   begin
     if X > 0 then
       X := 1;
     elsif X < 0 then
       X := -1;
     end if;
   end Extract_Sign;

   procedure Print_2 (X, Y: out NATURAL) is

   begin
     Int_IO.Put (X, 0);
     Text_IO.New_Line;
     Int_IO.Put (Y, 0);
     Text_IO.New_Line;
   end PRINT_2;

begin     -- Demo
   .
   .
   .
end Demo;
```

8.7.2 What changes would need to be made in the procedure Order, Figure 8.7.2, to make it arrange three integers in *descending* rather than ascending order?

8.7.3 Write a procedure Order_4 that takes four integers as actual parameters and arranges them into increasing order.

8.7.4 Extend the program Print_in_Order of Figure 8.7.3 by writing a procedure Instruct_User to be called at the beginning of the program's statement part (ahead of the three procedure calls shown in Figure 8.7.3). This parameterless procedure is to display a brief message on the screen telling the user what the program does. (Note that this is not the same as a *comment* at the beginning of the source program telling the *reader* what the program does.)

8.7.5 For purposes of contrast, write a function Sum that returns the sum of three integers passed to it as parameters. Also write a procedure Add that adds three integers passed to it as parameters and returns the result in a fourth parameter. Include these in a main program that invokes and tests both of them.

8.7.6 Consider the procedure Dummy:

```
procedure Dummy is

    X:   INTEGER;

begin
    Int_IO.Put (X, 0);
    Text_IO.New_Line;
    X := 4321;
end DUMMY;
```

Tell what will be displayed the *first* time Dummy is invoked; the *second* time.

8.7.7 Consider previous Ada programs that you have written, and see whether the use of subprograms can help structure them in a better fashion and/or to avoid repetitive code. In particular, determine whether it is reasonable to rewrite them in such a way that each main program consists wholly (or in large part) of a sequence of procedure calls.

8.8.1 Rewrite the program of Figure 8.8.1 without using an **else** part in the conditional statement.

8.9.1 Suppose that the assignment statement

```
    X := 5;
```

in the main program of Figure 8.9.1 is replaced by each of the following assignments:

(a) X := 4;   (c) X := 6;

(b) X := 3;   (d) X := 7;

In each case, describe the behavior of the program when it is run. If a value is displayed, tell what value; if an exception is raised, tell what exception, along with where and why it is raised. Finally, find the set of integers that could be assigned to X in this program without causing an exception to be raised when the program is run.

8.9.2   Rewrite the procedure Exchange (Figure 8.7.1) with the variable Temp initialized in its declaration, rather than in an executable statement.

8.9.3   Answer the question that immediately precedes Figure 8.9.3, namely: Why may we not write the program Largest (Figure 8.9.2) with the functions Maximum_2 and Maximum_3 arranged as in Figure 8.9.3*c*?

8.9.4   Can any of the procedures in Figure 8.7.3 be declared *within* any of the other procedures of this program? If not, tell why not. If so, tell which ones and whether or not this would be desirable.

Chapter 9

More about Subprograms

In the previous chapter we stressed again the importance of writing clear, well-structured programs, and we looked into the use of subprograms, both functions and procedures, as ways of achieving that goal. Our final example of that chapter (Figure 8.10.1) was aimed at illustrating (though not for the first time) how program modularization can be served by employing subprograms to conserve or encapsulate code.

We begin this chapter by considering a new version of the Time_and_Day program, Figure 7.14.1. Careful attention to this program leads to investigation of several ideas associated with subprograms: scope and visibility of declared items, global and local entities, side effects of subprograms, and exception handling as related to subprograms. Then we take up a few final points related to subprograms: For one thing, program modularization and conservation of code can be aided by the ability to compile subprograms *separately*. This capability enables us to write, compile, and store subprograms for use whenever they may be needed, a process often referred to in contemporary terms as the development of "off-the-shelf software."

9.1 Once more, Time_and_Day

In Chapter 2, when we first discussed the problem of converting the number of minutes since midnight Sunday to a clock time and day of the week, we noted that there were essentially three activities to be dealt with: (1) get the number of minutes, (2) convert that number of minutes to days, hours, and minutes, and (3) display the clock time and the day. Now that we have become familiar with subprograms and their uses, we seek to program the three activities as procedures and to code the main program as a sequence of procedure calls. This result is achieved in the program of Figure 9.1.1, where we see that the main program is simplicity itself. It consists of four procedure calls, and all the details of getting the number of minutes, converting it to clock time, and then displaying those results have been compressed into the procedures. They have been "hidden from view" of the main line, or, more properly, temporarily gotten out of the way in the name of simplification and readability—although, of course, the details are still available for investigation. You should have no difficulty seeing how the code of the earlier version has been grouped into these procedures; but take special note of the handling of exceptions, in particular within the procedure Get_Input.

```
    with Text_IO, Int_IO;

procedure Time_and_Day is

    -- This program asks the user for an integer from 0 to 10079,
    -- representing the number of minutes that have elapsed since
    -- the beginning of the week. It then determines and displays
    -- the time of day (as it would appear on a 12-hour digital
    -- clock) and the day of the week.

    subtype MINUTES_RANGE is INTEGER range 0..10079;

    Minutes_Elapsed:            NATURAL;
    Day, Hour, Minute:          NATURAL;

    Midnight:                   BOOLEAN := False;
    Noon:                       BOOLEAN := False;
    PM:                         BOOLEAN := False;

    No_More_Tries:              exception;


    -- Procedure Get_Input requests from the user the number of
    -- minutes since midnight Sunday, and gives the user three
    -- tries to enter a valid number.

    procedure Get_Input (Mins_Elapsed: out MINUTES_RANGE) is

        package Minutes_IO is new Text_IO.Integer_IO (MINUTES_RANGE);
        Wrong_Inputs:   NATURAL := 0;

    begin

        Text_IO.New_Line;
        Text_IO.Put ("How many minutes since the week began (0 to 10079)? ");

        Input_Loop:
        loop

            begin
                Minutes_IO.Get (Mins_Elapsed);
                exit Input_Loop;
            exception
                when Text_IO.Data_Error =>
                    Wrong_Inputs := Wrong_Inputs + 1;
                    if Wrong_Inputs = 3 then
                        raise No_More_Tries;
                    end if;
                    Text_IO.Put_Line ("Minutes must be between 0 and 10079.");
                    Text_IO.Put ("Try again: ");
                    Text_IO.Skip_Line;
            end;

        end loop Input_Loop;
        Text_IO.New_Line;

    end Get_Input;
```

```
-- Procedure Convert generates from the value of Mins_Elapsed
-- the day (0 - 6), left-over hours, and left-over minutes.

procedure Convert (Mins_Elapsed: in MINUTES_RANGE;
                   Dy, Hr, Min:  out NATURAL)            is

   Minutes_in_Hour:    constant INTEGER := 60;
   Hours_in_Day:       constant INTEGER := 24;
   Hours_Elapsed:      NATURAL := Mins_Elapsed / Minutes_in_Hour;

begin

   Min    := Mins_Elapsed  rem Minutes_in_Hour;
   Dy     := Hours_Elapsed  / Hours_in_Day;
   Hr     := Hours_Elapsed rem Hours_in_Day;

end Convert;


-- Procedure SET_HOUR makes any necessary changes in the hour
-- (changing 0 to 12, for example) and also sets the MIDNIGHT,
-- NOON, and PM flags.

procedure Set_Hour (Hr:    in out NATURAL;
                    Min:   in NATURAL) is

begin

  if Hr = 0 and Min = 0 then
    Midnight := True;
    Hr := 12;
  elsif Hr = 12 and Min = 0 then
    Noon := True;
  elsif Hr >= 12 then
    PM := True;
    if Hr > 12 then
      Hr := Hr - 12;
    end if;
  elsif Hr = 0 then
    Hr := 12;
  end if;

end Set_Hour;


-- Procedure Display generates the final output.

procedure Display (Dy, Hr, Min:    in NATURAL)  is

begin

  Text_IO.Put ("The time is ");
  Int_IO.Put (Hr);
  Text_IO.Put (":");
  Int_IO.Put (Min / 10);            -- tens digit for Minute
  Int_IO.Put (Min rem 10);          -- units digit for Minute

  if Midnight then
    Text_IO.Put (" midnight");
```

```
      elsif Noon then
        Text_IO.Put (" noon");
      elsif PM then
        Text_IO.Put (" p.m.");
      else
        Text_IO.Put (" a.m.");
      end if;

      Text_IO.Put (" on ");

      if Dy = 0 then
        Text_IO.Put ("Sunday");
      elsif Dy = 1 then
        Text_IO.Put ("Monday");
      elsif Dy = 2 then
        Text_IO.Put ("Tuesday");
      elsif Dy = 3 then
        Text_IO.Put ("Wednesday");
      elsif Dy = 4 then
        Text_IO.Put ("Thursday");
      elsif Dy = 5 then
        Text_IO.Put ("Friday");
      elsif Dy = 6 then
        Text_IO.Put ("Saturday");
      end if;
      Text_IO.Put (.""");
      Text_IO.New_Line (2);

   end Display;


   -- Main procedure (program) begins here.

begin

   Get_Input (Minutes_Elapsed);
   Convert   (Minutes_Elapsed, Day, Hour, Minute);
   Set_Hour  (Hour, Minute);
   Display   (Day, Hour, Minute);

exception
   when No_More_Tries =>
     Text_IO.Put ("Input is still incorrect...");
     Text_IO.Put_Line ("execution is terminated.");

end Time_and_Day;
```

Figure 9.1.1

At this stage we are thoroughly familiar with the Time_and_Day problem, and it is easy to see exactly what is happening in Figure 9.1.1. There are two special points, however. The first is that we have included a procedure body Get_Input whose statement part contains a frame with an exception handler for Data_Error. This exception handler itself raises (under certain conditions) an exception called No_More_Tries, for which there is no exception handler within the procedure body. Later in this chapter we look into the question of exceptions and exception handlers specifically as they relate to subprograms.

To address the second point, recall that we have stressed several times that entities declared within subprogram bodies may not be referred to anywhere outside these subprogram bodies. But in the procedure Set_Hour we see exactly the *opposite* situation; namely, variables Midnight, Noon, and PM are declared *outside* this procedure (in the main program) and referred to—in fact, assigned values—*within* the body of Set_Hour. Having a subprogram assign values to variables declared outside the subprogram (and not passed to it as actual parameters) is known as a **side effect** of the subprogram's execution. We need to see to what extent side effects are possible and when, if ever, they are desirable. To discuss this issue we must first investigate matters related to the *scope* of names of variables and other entities.

9.2 Scope and visibility considerations for subprograms

In Section 6.8 we first encountered the concepts of **scope** and **visibility** in the context of the loop parameter in a **for** loop; we review some of those concepts here. Consider a program (main procedure) named, say, Sample, in which a variable K is declared. That variable will exist, of course, from its declaration to the program's end, and it may be used in any way that is suitable to and compatible with its declared type. For the sake of concreteness, assume that K is declared to be of type BOOLEAN. Suppose that in the program's statement sequence we have the loop

```
for K in INTEGER range -5..207 loop
```

From our previous discussion we know that a *new* K (a *loop parameter*) is brought into existence for the duration of the **for** loop, and we note that it cannot be the same as the variable declared earlier, since among other things their types do not even match (the newly-created loop parameter K is evidently of type INTEGER). Does the variable K declared earlier now cease to exist? No, for (1) this would deny the statement we just made—namely, the region of existence of this K extends to the end of the program—and (2) it would mean that the value of that variable could not be used—it would have no meaning—after execution of the loop had concluded, and we know from examples that this is not the case. Instead, the earlier-declared K is simply hidden from view within the region of existence of the loop parameter. It becomes visible again once the loop parameter no longer exists, that is, once the loop terminates and we pass beyond the scope of the loop parameter. We know also that the first-declared K (the variable) does not even lose its ability to be referenced within the loop, although now we need to be more explicit in specifying the K to which we are referring —the currently visible one (the loop parameter) may be referred to simply as "K," whereas the version of K that has lost its visibility must now be referred to not only by its name ("K") but also by the name of the module in which it was declared, used as a prefix, as suggested in Section 6.8; that is, this version of K must be referred to by its **expanded name**, "Sample.K".

These questions of scope, visibility, and referencing are as pertinent to subprogram parameters and objects declared "locally" within a subprogram as they are to **for** loop parameters. As we have seen, subprogram parameters, constants, variables, etc., come into existence by virtue of a subprogram call (that is, the Ada system allocates space for these *at that time*), and their existence is terminated upon return from the subprogram. In addition, before a subprogram can be invoked, its body (name, formal parameter list, internal declarations, statement sequence, and, in the case of a function, return value type) must be known to the system. We list here the rules for the placement of subprogram bodies within an Ada program's declarative part, as well as those for the scope and visibility of subprogram names, formal parameters, and other entities declared within a subprogram body.

1. A subprogram *body* (see Figures 8.3.1*a* and 8.7.4*a*) is written within the declarative part of a main program or subprogram. Subprogram bodies must appear *after* the so-called basic declarations: types, subtypes, instantiations, variables, constants, and exceptions. The function body Minimum, Figure 8.1.4, and the procedure bodies in Figure 9.1.1 are examples that illustrate this placement; in each case they are *last* in the declarative part of the main procedure.

2. The scope of the subprogram name (identifier) extends from the subprogram *specification*, where this name is first used (see Figures 8.3.1*b* and 8.7.4*b),* to the end of the program or subprogram in which the given subprogram is declared. As we have seen, it is typically, but not always, within the main *program* that a subprogram is declared.

   The visibility of the subprogram name (identifier) coincides with its scope, except for those regions in which some entity having the same name has been declared. This last situation can occur, and in fact it can even arise somewhat naturally. However, at the present time we can only offer a single, highly contrived example (Figure 9.2.1).

```
with Text_IO, Int_IO;

procedure Sample is

    function Sq (X: INTEGER) return INTEGER is

    begin

        return X * X;

    end Sq;

begin

    Int_IO.Put (Sq (12));
    Text_IO.New_Line (2);

    for sq in 1..5 loop
        Int_IO.Put (Sample.Sq (sq));
        Text_IO.New_Line;
    end loop;

    Text_IO.New_Line;
    Int_IO.Put (Sq (21));
    Text_IO.New_Line;

end Sample;
```

Figure 9.2.1

We see that the function Sq simply returns the square of any actual INTEGER parameter passed to it. Thus as the program Sample begins execution, the reference to Sq (12) will pass the integer 12 to Sq as an actual parameter, and Sq will return 144 as a result. This much is straightforward. Now, however, we execute a **for** loop, and we have made an unfortunate choice of loop parameter, namely, sq. We have written the loop parameter without an initial capital letter, contrary to the standards to which we have adhered throughout this book. Our purpose in doing so is to emphasize the difference between the occurrences of the loop parameter name and function name, although to the compiler there is no such distinction. But within the loop it is not possible to refer to the *function* Sq without further qualifying it with the prefix Sample, for the function has now *lost its visibility*, and without this prefix, Sq would be taken to be a reference to the loop parameter. Finally, once the **for** loop terminates, the function name Sq again becomes visible, so Sq (21) is well defined. For the record, when Sample is executed, the following is displayed:

```
144

  1
  4
  9
 16
 25

441
```

3.   The scope of a formal parameter extends from the end of the subprogram *specification* to the end of the subprogram *body*. Thus in particular a formal parameter exists throughout the *declarative part* of the subprogram body and may be used in declarations.

4.   The scope of an entity declared within a subprogram's declarative part extends from the end of its declaration to the end of the subprogram body. This applies to variables, of course, but also to other entities as well (in Figure 9.1.1, for example, the instantiated package Minutes_IO declared in Get_Input and the constants Minutes_in_Hour and Hours_in_Day declared in Convert).

5.   The visibility of a subprogram identifier, subprogram formal parameter, or an entity declared within a subprogram coincides with that item's scope, except if the visibility is interrupted by an entity of the same name having a "later" declaration within the subprogram body. In these cases the entity can be made visible by using its expanded name.

6.   No identifier can be referenced by any statement which does not lie within the scope of that identifier.

Figure 9.2.2 shows a skeletal program that illustrates some of these scope rules. The rectangle labeled *F* is the scope of the function identifier Fn; the rectangle labeled *P* shows the scope of the formal parameters, Param_1 to Param_J; and the rectangles labeled V_1 to V_K represent the scopes of the variables Var_1 to Var_K.

```
       .
       .
       .
procedure Main is
       .
       .
   Function Fn
       ┌──────────────────────────────────────────────────────────── F ──┐
       │   (Param_1:   P_TYPE_1;                                          │
       │    Param_2:   P_TYPE_2;                                          │
       │       .                                                         │
       │       .                                                         │
       │    Param_J:   P_TYPE_J)                                         │
       │                                                                │
       │   return FN_TYPE is                                            │
       │       ┌──────────────────────────────────────── P ──┐          │
       │       │   .                                         │          │
       │       │   .                                         │          │
       │       │ Var_1:   V_TYPE_1;                          │          │
       │       │   ┌──────────────────────────── V₁ ──┐      │          │
       │       │   │ Var_2:   V_TYPE_2;               │      │          │
       │       │   │   ┌──────────────────── V₂ ──┐   │      │          │
       │       │   │   │   .                      │   │      │          │
       │       │   │   │ Var_K:   V_TYPE_K;       │   │      │          │
       │       │   │   │   ┌────────── Vᴋ ──┐     │   │      │          │
       │       │   │   │   │   .           │     │   │      │          │
       │       │   │   │   │ begin  -- start of Fn execution │          │
       │       │   │   │   │   .           │     │   │      │          │
       │       │   │   │   │ end Fn;       │     │   │      │          │
       │       │   └───┴───┴───────────────┴─────┴───┘      │          │
       │       │   .                                         │          │
       │ begin           -- start of Main execution          │          │
       │       │   .                                         │          │
       └───────┴─────────────────────────────────────────────┘──────────┘
end Main;
```

Figure 9.2.2

We must confess to a certain lack of preciseness in the foregoing discussion of the scope of various kinds of items, and in fact Figure 9.2.2 has inaccuracies. To be pedantically precise about the scope of an entity, we should say that it *begins* at the *start* of its declaration. However, the item does not become visible (and thus able to be referenced) until the *end* of its declaration. In Figure 9.2.2 we have shown the scope of items (for example, the variable Var_1) as beginning at the *end* of their corresponding declarations, whereas this scope extends from the *start* of these declarations. On the other hand, since the items are not visible throughout their declarations, what we have shown is, in effect, the "useful" scope of each entity, namely, the region throughout which the item exists *and* can be referenced. We have no reservations about continuing these slight inaccuracies throughout the remainder of the text and especially when a strict adherence to the formalism would achieve nothing more than to obscure what actually takes place in practice. The formal details will be found in Chapter 8 of *LRM*.

Along with the concept of scope as outlined above, we can introduce two very useful related terms, namely **local** and **global**. We have already used the term "local" several times in an informal but compatible way. First we need to deal with a minor formalism. A declaration is said to be *immediately* within a subprogram body provided it occurs within that subprogram body but is *not* also within another subprogram body enclosed within the first. Thus, for example, in Figure 9.1.1, the declaration of the NATURAL constant Minutes_in_Hour certainly occurs within the scope of the procedure body Time_and_Day, but since it also occurs within the *enclosed* procedure body Convert, we cannot say that this declaration is "immediately within Time_and_Day." However, since the declaration is within the procedure body Convert but not within any further enclosed subprogram body, we can say that it is "immediately within Convert." To put it another way, the procedure body Convert is the innermost one containing the declaration of Minutes_in_Hour. In a similar fashion, the declarations of the parameters Mins_Elapsed, Dy, Hr, and Min are also immediately within Convert. We can now state the following rules:

A declaration occuring immediately within a subprogram body is said to be **local** to that subprogram body.

A declaration occuring in an outer (enclosing) subprogram body is said to be **global** to an inner (enclosed) subprogram body.

A **local entity** is one declared by a local declaration; a **global entity** is one declared by a global declaration.

It would be imprecise to say that "such-and-such variable is *local*" or that "this subtype is *global*," since these concepts are relative to subprogram bodies. For example, referring once more to Figure 9.1.1, to say that the variable Minutes_Elapsed, for example, is global could be unclear; Minutes_Elapsed is global relative to Convert, but it is local relative to Time_and_Day itself. Nonetheless we will occasionally use these terms without further qualification, as long as the context provides the missing relationships. In particular, an entity declared in the main program (procedure) is always global to any subprogram declared within the program and thus will frequently be referred to as "global" without further qualification.

We conclude this section as we began it, by turning briefly to **for** loops. Here we wish to point out that in this familiar context the terms *local* and *global* are pertinent. The *loop parameter* is declared locally within the **for** loop itself and thus is local within that loop. All other entities are global within the **for** loop. However, we will have far less need for these terms in **for** loops than in subprograms.

9.3 Side effects of subprograms

Is it permitted to use a global entity in, say, a subprogram body? That is, can a subprogram make use of items that are not declared within the subprogram iself but in an enclosing subprogram? The answer is a qualified yes, qualified not because there are instances in which such references *cannot* be made but there are cases in which global references within a function *should* not be made. In fact, we appeal to global declarations in subprograms on many occasions. For example, if an INTEGER instantiation of Integer_IO is made in the main procedure (program), it becomes global to all other subprogram bodies of the program. We would feel free to use it wherever necessary, for example, in a procedure body; it would be pointless to redeclare an Integer I/O package within the procedure when an identical one already exists *globally*. In a similar fashion, constants declared in a main program are frequently used in subprogram bodies (that is, in a global fashion).

For a moment let us focus our attention specifically on *function* subprograms. Problems can begin to occur when a function not only *refers* to a global entity (a variable, perhaps) but also *modifies* it. The person who reads a program containing such a function sees a function call and can reasonably expect that (1) the actual parameters—the replacements for the formal parameters—will be unaffected by the function call; (2) the function calculates and returns some useful value, which is then used in some meaningful way by the statement that invoked the function; and (3) there are no effects other than these overt ones. As we know, item 1 is always the case for any function in Ada. Item 2 *should* be true, but consider a BOOLEAN-valued function whose execution simply displays a message and returns the value True; such a function might be invoked simply for its message-displaying role, rather than for any significant use of its return value. Item 3 is *not* true if the function modifies any global entities, and it is this concept that we wish to examine briefly.

If a function modifies a global value of some kind, the result of that modification is called a *side effect* of the function. (Input or output carried out within a function body is also considered a side effect of the function.) Figure 9.3.1 shows a simple example of a function F with a side effect.

```
procedure Side_Effect is

   A: INTEGER;
   B: INTEGER := 5;

   function F (K: INTEGER) return INTEGER is

   begin

      B := B + K;
      return K**2 + 1;

   end F;

begin

   A := F(3) + B;

end Side_Effect;
```

Figure 9.3.1

What value is assigned to A in this program? The Ada language does not specify in which order the two operands of the + operator are evaluated prior to application of the addition operation. Thus, if B is evaluated first, its *original* value, 5, is added to the value 10 returned by F(3), and A is assigned the value 15. On the other hand, if F(3) is evaluated first, and then B, it is the *new* value of B, 8 (resulting from the function execution), that is added to 10 to give 18 as the value assigned to A. Behavior such as this can be confusing at best; worse, side effects may easily be hidden from direct view (if they are unanticipated), and as a result they can generate what appear to be program "bugs" that are frequently difficult to locate. Doubtless it is too strong to say that under *no* circumstances should a function produce side effects—perhaps a function might need to change a BOOLEAN or INTEGER *error flag* (variable) upon its execution, to indicate that some extraordinary event has occurred; the function *must* do so globally, since it cannot manage the flag as a parameter. (Why not?) Nonetheless, we go on record as saying that function side effects should be somewhat rare occurrences, should be well documented, and should be used only for compelling reasons.

Does the same problem apply to procedures? It can, of course, but it *need* not. Any procedure that may modify a global variable can always declare a formal **in out** or **out** parameter, as appropriate, and use that global variable as a corresponding actual parameter in a call to the procedure. This signals the procedure user that there will potentially be a modification to that parameter. Thus procedures provide a mechanism for the avoidance of side effects, and in general we do well to use that mechanism and avoid the dangers inherent in such effects. Nevertheless, while the manipulation of global variables does involve risk, it would be going too far to exclude its use altogether. Indeed, we see in the Time_and_Day program of Figure 9.1.1 that Midnight, Noon, and PM are global variables that are *set* (assigned values) in the procedure Set_Hour and then *used* globally in the procedure Display. This side effect of Set_Hour was tolerated for two reasons: (1) Passing these variables as actual parameters to Set_Hour would require that three corresponding **out** parameters be included in the formal parameter list of this procedure, and this might add more clutter than clarity and (2) it is not unusual programming practice to set **flags** (variables of a yes/no kind, indicating some sort of status) in a global manner. We admit, however, that it would have been well to indicate in the documentation accompanying Set_Hour that these flags are set globally, and we would have done so, had this concept already been discussed at that point.

It is clear that experience and good judgment are required in making decisions about the global use of variables, and these decisions are obviously influenced by the context and environment in which the subprograms reside. Beyond what has been said here, we offer no guidelines in the matter of the use of global variables, local variables, and parameters. But just because *we* offer no such guidelines does not mean that they do not exist. Commercial and research enterprises that deal in the generation of software almost always have not only documentation standards, which frequently run to hundreds of displayed pages, but also *procedural standards* that specify just such matters as we have discussed here—the acceptable use of global variables and parameters, how actual parameters are to be passed to subprograms, the format of packages, and so forth.

9.4 Block statements

Our discussion of the scope of names and of side effects suggests that the Ada language—along with other programming languages—goes to considerable lengths to help the programmer achieve a very important goal, namely, to keep one part of a program from "interfering" with another. Clearly, this goal becomes all the more important when we are dealing with a real-world program consisting of many thousands of lines of code, perhaps produced by a team of several programmers, each of whom is responsible for a section of the overall result. The idea is that by "localizing" names and carefully controlling effects, we may develop and test individual program modules (sections) and then fit these together with assurance that they will not affect one another in unexpected ways.

It often happens that some entity—a variable, say—is needed for use only in a relatively "small" section of a program's statement part. As a simple example, suppose we must interchange the values of two INTEGER variables First and Second during the course of a program's execution. In Chapter 8 we pointed out the advantages of writing a procedure Exchange in a situation where *several* such interchanges, possibly of different pairs of variables, need to be made. Now assume that there is question of only *one* such exchange, specifically affecting First and Second. So little code is needed for an exchange that it hardly seems worthwhile to put it into a procedure that will be called only once; thus we decide that it should be written into the main program. On the other hand, we know that we need an additional INTEGER variable—Temp, say—to carry out this process. Temp will be used only briefly, at *this* point in a (possibly long) program; must we declare it among the (possibly many) global variables of the program? If we do so, Temp will be in existence during the entire run of the program. Moreover, the program's other global variables might all have specific significance within the context of the given programming problem and thus bear correspondingly descriptive names; must we insert the "utility" variable Temp among their declarations? The answer is no, and it is based on a construct found in Ada and several other programming languages, namely, the **code block**. In Ada, code blocks are called **block statements**.

A block statement in Ada may have the form shown in Figure 9.4.1, although, as we will point out, several of the "parts" of this figure are optional.

```
<block name>:

declare

    <local declarations>

begin

    <statement sequence>

exception

    <exception handlers>

end <block name>;
```

Figure 9.4.1

Note that the **begin...end** part of a block statement forms what in Section 7.9 was called a *frame*. As in the case of the frames discussed in that section, the frame of a block statement *need not* have an exception handler section. Further, just as with **for** loops (Section 6.7), a block statement may (but need not) be given a name (identifier) devised by the programmer. If the block statement is to be named, the name appears at the beginning of the statement, followed by a colon; it *must* then be repeated at the conclusion of the block statement, following the reserved word **end**. Finally, we note that the **declare** section of the block is itself optional. This is perhaps surprising since if we omit the declaration section (and the name), the block statement simply reduces to one of the forms of a frame shown in Figure 7.9.1. In fact, when we inserted frames with exception handlers into the statement parts of programs (and subprograms, as in Figure 9.1.1), we were actually employing a particular form of block statement.

Our interest here, however, is in block statements with declaration sections (which begin with the reserved word **declare**), for it is this form of block statement that enables us to introduce variables and other entities that are local to the block—that is, whose scope extends only from their declaration to the end of the block. Such a block is employed in the program skeleton of Figure 9.4.2, where we show how the exchange of the global variables First and Second can be effected by means of a block statement, with the auxiliary variable Temp declared as a local variable of the block. We have indicated the purpose of this block statement by naming it Exchange although, as mentioned above, the name may be omitted.

```
procedure Use_Block is

   .
   .
   .
   First, Second:    INTEGER;
   .
   .
   .
begin   -- Use_Block

   .
   .
   .

   Exchange:

   declare

      Temp:   INTEGER := First;

   begin

      First  := Second;
      Second := Temp;

   end Exchange;

   .
   .
   .

end Use_Block;
```

Figure 9.4.2

Reflecting on this example, we can make some observations concerning block statements. Block statements have certain properties in common with subprograms, principally in that they allow the declaration of local entities and they may have their own exception handler section. Unlike subprograms, block statements are not "declared" in a program's declaration part, nor are they "called"; just as with any other *statement*, they simply execute when their code is encountered in the normal flow of control through the program (or subprogram) in whose statement part they are included. Further, block statements involve no parameter passing. They may use and modify their local variables (although these variables cease to exist upon conclusion of the block statement); more to the point, they may use global entities and modify global variables, and this is their only way of communicating with the remainder of the program "outside" the block.

It may have occurred to you that besides allowing us to localize the variable Temp—thus confining its scope to the small portion of the program where it is needed—our use of the block statement Exchange has allowed us to do something we have never done before (and which many programming languages do not allow). For the first time, we have *declared* an entity (in this case, the variable Temp) within a program's *statement* part. Up to this point, *all* our declarations—including those of subprograms as well as of types, variables, constants, and packages—have had to be placed in the *declaration* part of the program (or subprogram) containing them. The fact that we may now declare an item in a statement means that in making such a declaration, we can employ values that were not available at the time of the program's compilation, values (obtained from input, for example) that are not determined until *after* the program statements have begun to be executed. The significance of this may seem obscure at the moment, and no doubt an example is needed. We defer our response to this need until Chapter 10, where we show what excellent service this feature of the block statement can provide us.

Before leaving this section, we offer a syntax diagram for the block statement; it is shown in Figure 9.4.3.

block statement

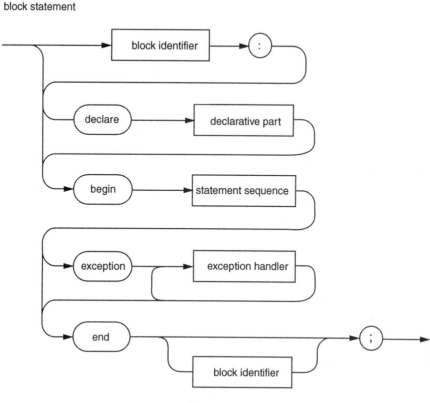

Figure 9.4.3

9.5   Default parameter values and the named association of parameters

In Section 9.1 our reflection on the Time_and_Day program indicated that we should focus on two issues that arose out of the program in Figure 9.1.1: (1) side effects of subprograms and (2) exceptions and exception handling in the context of subprograms. In dealing with the former (Sections 9.2 and 9.3), we paid much attention to questions involving parameters and subprogram names; before turning to the latter issue, namely, exceptions in Section 9.7, we say more about parameter values.

In Section 3.2 we first encountered the notion of **default parameter value** in connection with (1) the display of an integer in which the user supplied *no* field width parameter value when invoking Int_IO.Put and (2) the number of new-line sequences generated when no parameter is passed to Text_IO.New_Line. In this section we show how the programmer can sometimes take advantage of the default parameter value feature of Ada to accommodate those values needed by a subprogram which must be passed as parameters and which frequently have a "standard," "usual," or "default" value. The feature, incidentally, is not exclusive to the Ada programming language.

In Figures 8.3.1 and 8.7.4, we showed the syntax of the parameter specification for a function and procedure to be (in part) as shown in Figure 9.5.1.

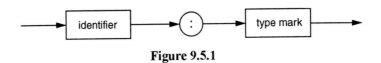

Figure 9.5.1

This part of the syntax diagram is more completely described in Figure 9.5.2.

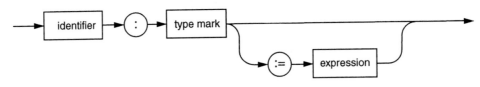

Figure 9.5.2

Here *expression* is the *default value* assigned to the formal parameter *if* no corresponding actual parameter is supplied at the time the function or procedure is invoked. As an important example of this, consider the declaration of Float_IO's Put procedure shown below, in which we disclose more details than were shown to you in Section 4.2.

```
procedure Put (Item: in FLOAT;
               Fore: in NATURAL := 2;
               Aft:  in NATURAL := FLOAT'Digits-1;
               Exp:  in NATURAL := 3);
```

When Put is invoked, it is *not* necessary to provide all four parameters; if any of the last three are missing, the values shown in the declaration will be automatically supplied. Note that the default value given to *Aft* is dependent on the Ada implementation.

Before investigating the details of this concept (there are really very few), we give a simple example of a programmer-written function in which we supply a default value for one of the parameters. Suppose the used car dealer of Section 8.2—see, in particular, Figure 8.2.5—finds that the vast majority of warranty repairs with which he or she must deal fall into category D. The dealer might request that the Owners_Share and Dealers_Share functions use Cat := 'D' as the default value, so that in those cases the category need not even be supplied. Then the function declaration will begin

```
function Owners_Share (Miles: NATURAL;
                       Cost:  FLOAT;
                       Cat:   CHARACTER := 'D') return FLOAT is
```

If this function is invoked as Owners_Share (Some_Miles, Some_Cost), the "missing" parameter will by default have the value 'D'. Of course, if the function is invoked as Owners_Share (Some_Miles, Some_Cost, 'C'), the default will be overridden, and the parameter Cat will have the value 'C'. A similar change should be made to Dealers_Share, since in this case these two functions form a "matched pair."

We can now make some observations about default parameter values. First, it should be obvious that a default value cannot be assigned to a parameter whose mode is either **out** or **in out**, since only *variables* can substitute for such parameters; that is, default values are limited to formal parameters of mode **in**. (Thus *any* parameter of *any* function is a candidate for a default value.) Second, recall that the "substituting" of formal parameters by actual parameters is *positional*; that is, the first actual parameter corresponds to the first formal parameter, the second actual parameter corresponds to the second formal parameter, and so forth. Given this fact, could we rearrange the parameter list to Owners_Share as:

```
function Owners_Share (Miles: NATURAL;
                       Cat:   CHARACTER := 'D';
                       Cost:  FLOAT)          return FLOAT is
```

and then be able to take advantage of the default value for the parameter Cat? The answer is obviously no, for attempting to invoke this function with, say, Owners_Share (6275, 442.76) will generate *two* errors: (1) The second actual parameter does not match its corresponding formal parameter (Cat) in type (CHARACTER) and (2) There is now a missing parameter— Cost has no matching actual parameter, nor does Cat use a default value. An attempt at circumventing the problem with, say, Owners_Share (6275, , 442.76), will fail with a compiler message (although some languages actually permit such constructions). The moral is clear: Place default parameters at the *end* of the parameter list.

As a final example, consider the procedure declaration

```
procedure Do_Something (A: in INTEGER;
                        B: in INTEGER;
                        C: in BOOLEAN := True;
                        D: in CHARACTER := '$') is
```

When invoked as Do_Something (23, −662), the formal parameters C and D take on the values True and '$', respectively. When invoked as

```
Do_Something (23, -662, False);
```

the formal parameters C and D take on the values False and '$', respectively—C by actually having the value False passed to it, D taking its value by default. Is there a way of passing a value to D, to replace its default, without also passing a value explicitly to C? That is, can we allow the default to take over for C while giving D an explicit value? Apparently the answer must be no, for this situation is essentially the same as was just discussed for Owners_Share. The underlying reason for these failures, of course, is that parameters are passed to subprograms *positionally*. But there is a mechanism that permits the assigning of values to parameters in a somewhat more "random" order than what is normally dictated by the subprogram construct.

As we know, each formal parameter in the declaration of a subprogram has an associated identifier, or *name*. In Float_IO's procedure Put, these names are Item, Fore, Aft, and Exp. In the the function Owners_Share, they are Miles, Cost, and Cat. And in the procedure Do_Something above, we have named these simply A, B, C, and D, since we had nothing to guide us to more meaningful names. In Ada, a formal parameter may be assigned a value *by name*, using the following construction:

<formal parameter> => <value>

when this technique is used, the order in which the formal parameters are given is *immaterial*. For example, we could invoke Flt_IO.Put as follows:

```
Flt_IO.Put (Remaining_Balance, 0, 2, 0);
```

or

```
Flt_IO.Put (Item => Remaining_Balance,
            Fore => 0,
            Aft => 2,
            Exp => 0);
```

or

```
Flt_IO.Put (Aft => 2,
            Fore => 0,
            Item => Remaining_Balance,
            Exp => 0);
```

or any of several other orders. We can now respond to the question above concerning the procedure Do_Something. The call

```
Do_Something (A => 23, B => -662, D => '&');
```

gives the parameters A, B, and D the values shown, while C takes on its default value, True.

The technique of assigning actual values to parameters according to the *order* in which the parameters appear in a subprogram's declaration is known as the **positional association** of parameters; assigning parameters by their *names* is called the **named association** of parameters. Can these two methods of parameter assignment be mixed? The answer is yes, with some restrictions. Parameters may be specified positionally until some parameter is specified by name; from that point, all remaining parameters *must* be specified by name (or their default values must be allowed to be used). Thus both

```
Flt_IO.Put (Value, 4, Exp => 0);
```
and

```
Flt_IO.Put (Value, Exp => 0, Aft => 2);
```

are valid, but

```
Flt_IO.Put (Value, 4, Aft =>2, 0);
```

is not. In a similar fashion,

```
Do_Something (23, -662, D => '&');
```

is a simpler way of providing the desired parameters to Do_Something than what was shown above. It will come as no surprise that we take advantage of this construction frequently when invoking Flt_IO.Put, inasmuch as we almost always want the Exp parameter to have the value zero.

There are programmers who insist that all parameters be passed via named association, never positionally. We agree that this practice does improve the readability of subprogram calls, and it even provides some protection against invoking subprograms incorrectly, especially when all parameters have the same type and some parameters have defaults. But this technique requires that we know the *exact names* of *all* formal parameters for *all* subprograms we invoke, and this may be unrealistic. (For example, we know that the function Minimum is passed two INTEGER values; but we might not know or remember the names given to the corrresponding formal parameters when the function was declared.) The position we take is to use positional association whenever possible, except when we want or need to skip over default values by means of named parameter association or when clarity and understanding demand the use of parameter names.

9.6 The overloading of function and procedure names

We have had occasion to make note of the phenomenon in which the same name (identifier) may refer to more than one entity. For example, we have been using the name Put to refer to "the" procedure that displays various kinds of objects—characters, integers, and floating point numbers. The entities in question may be very different from one another, and yet the compiler is able (in most cases) to determine which is intended. These and other examples are instances of the concept known as **name overloading**. We have already commented that while name overloading is not unusual in high-level languages, Ada takes the concept a step farther than most, in allowing the *programmer* to use the same name for distinct objects. Two questions come to mind: (1) *Should* the programmer use duplicate names for different functions (or procedures or whatever), or will this simply make the programmer's products more difficult to read and understand, and (2) if, say, two functions have the same name, how can the compiler determine which is to be used in a particular instance? We answer the first question with a pair of examples, and these in turn suggest an answer to the second.

As written, the procedure Exchange of Figure 8.7.1 exchanges two variables of type INTEGER (or any integer subtype). Its name is about as suggestive as any we might select, for the phrase "Exchange (S, T)" can leave little doubt as to what will happen. Suppose now we wish to be able to exchange the values of two variables of type CHARACTER. The procedure to do so would be identical to that of Figure 8.7.1, except for the types, all of which would now be CHARACTER. What should we name such a procedure? Is there a better name than Exchange when the objects to be exchanged are characters? Probably not, and the remark holds equally for the procedure that exchanges floating point numbers. That is, if we have a name that suggests the activity in question very well, we should not be compelled to abandon it simply because of the type change. In fact, in Ada it is permitted to name all three of these procedures (and perhaps others as well) with the same identifier, Exchange, and then use all three of them in the same program. We leave it to you to create the CHARACTER and FLOAT versions of Exchange and to write a small test program that uses all three of these homonymous procedures.

In an analogous fashion, let us consider rewriting the functions Maximum_2 and Maximum_3 of Figure 8.2.1 with declarations as follows:

```
function Maximum (A, B:  NATURAL) return NATURAL is
```

and

```
function Maximum (A, B, C: NATURAL) return NATURAL is
```

Again, the *name* is so suggestive that we would choose to use it for the maximum of two or of three (or four or more) NATURAL expressions or even for the maximum of however many INTEGER or FLOAT expressions.

How can these duplicate names be acceptable to the Ada compiler? The compiler can distinguish among the three Exchange procedures because, when invoked, the actual parameters that correspond to the formal parameters will be of some *type*, and if that type is CHARACTER, then it must be the CHARACTER version of Exchange that is intended. If the actual parameters are of type INTEGER, then the compiler will use the INTEGER version of Exchange. In a similar fashion, the difference between the two-INTEGER version of Maximum and the two-FLOAT version of Maximum lies, as with Exchange, in the parameter *type*. The difference between the two-INTEGER and three-INTEGER versions of Maximum lies in the parameter *count*, rather than parameter type. Admittedly, the Ada compiler must be fairly "intelligent" to be able to use the surrounding *context* of the function or procedure call in this way, but it can do so, and the result is improved readability and understanding of programs.

9.7 Handling exceptions in functions and procedures

In the program of Figure 8.2.3, we included an exception (Invalid_Category), which was conditionally raised by the programming and dealt with in a short exception handler that did no more than display a message and exit. The raising and handling of that exception was a completely appropriate way to deal with a potential problem, namely, the input of an invalid repair category. In Figure 8.2.5 we improved the appearance (if not the efficiency) of that program by encapsulating the code that made up the computations of the owner's and dealer's shares of the repair cost. In the process we also included, in the Owners_Share function, the *raising* of the Invalid_Category exception but left the *handling* of it to the main part of the program.

In contrast, the procedure Get_Input of Figure 9.1.1 does include an exception handler for dealing with the Data_Error that is raised by an invalid user input. However, if the user fails three times to provide valid input, the exception handler itself raises a new exception No_More_Tries, to be dealt with by the main program.

In offering these examples, we avoided discussing exactly what would happen if these various exceptions were raised, for such issues were out of the mainstream of our discussion at the time. We take up these matters in this section.

The syntax diagrams of Figures 8.3.1 and 8.7.4*a* indicate that it is possible to include an exception handler within a subprogram (function or procedure) body. The ways in which exceptions are managed in programs are as varied as the programs themselves, since run-time event handling is almost always custom-tailored to the programming environment. Thus we cannot cover all possible cases here, nor can we even lay down a set of principles for exception handling. Consequently, we are content in this section to give a few examples to indicate how exception handlers might be used in a subprogram context, what benefits can be accrued, and what problems are encountered. These examples show perhaps the one common thread that runs through most subprogram exception handling: The programming environment (another subprogram, the main program, or whatever) which invoked the subprogram which in turn caused the raising of an exception, must be notified of the event. That is, if a statement calls a subprogram that in turn generates an "error," the calling statement can normally not proceed as if nothing had happened. As you read the examples presented here, keep in mind that they are created for the purpose of illustrating several ways in which exception handlers *might* be used within subprograms and how these handlers and the invoking statements react to exceptions. They are not necessarily intended, in each case, to reflect the best way, or even a logically meaningful way, to handle an exception.

To begin with, we note that the executable part of a subprogram—function or procedure—forms a **frame** in the terminology of Section 7.9, and thus the concepts and results developed there hold here as well. While subprogram behavior is consistent with what was described in Chapter 7, we nonetheless need to proceed a bit carefully, because subprograms *return* out of their frames to the calling statement, rather than *drop* out of them to the statement following the current frame. In one regard, at least, functions behave in a slightly different way from procedures. Thus before getting on with examples, we describe briefly just *how* subprograms return when exceptions are raised as a result of their executions.

If an exception is raised during the course of execution of a subprogram (function or procedure):

1. If the subprogram contains no exception handler for the exception in question (including cases in which the subprogram contains no exception handlers at all), then

    a. If the subprogram is a function, control is returned to the statement that invoked the function.

    b. If the subprogram is a procedure, control is returned to the statement immediately following the statement that invoked the procedure.

    Note that, in either case, the exception in question is still raised, so control passes immediately through to the exception handler section (if any) in the frame that contains the subprogram call. That is, execution of the sequence of statements that contained the offending subprogram call is abandoned.

2. If the subprogram contains an exception handler for the exception that has been raised, then the exception handler is executed and the exception is lowered. Assuming

that the handler itself does not raise a system- or programmer-declared exception, then

a. If the subprogram is a function, control returns to the statement that called the function, *unless* the function's exception handler does *not* contain a **return** statement (functions *must* return via a **return** statement, even out of an exception handler); in this case, Program_Error is raised, the function returns with this exception raised, and the situation reverts to case 1*a*.

b. If the subprogram is a procedure, control returns to the statement immediately following the statement that invoked the procedure.

In the following sample programs (all named Error_Test), we create simple procedures and functions, each of which has the capability of causing a Numeric_Error exception to be raised, by virtue of a division by zero. The subprograms themselves do nothing useful (other than perform an integer division), for it is the exception handling, not the subprogram code, that is the focus of our attention here. We begin with procedures, since they present a slightly simpler situation.

In Figure 9.7.1 we show a procedure in which the first parameter is replaced by the result of dividing it by the second parameter.

```
with Text_IO, Int_IO;

procedure Error_Test is

  A, B:          Integer;

  Error_Flag:    Integer;    -- Global divide-by-zero flag

  procedure Divide (X: in out INTEGER; Y: in INTEGER) is

  begin

    Error_Flag := 0;

    X := X/Y;

  exception

    when Numeric_Error =>    -- If Numeric_Error, then
       Error_Flag := -1;     -- set divide-by-zero flag

  end Divide;

begin

  A := 7;
  B := 2;

  Divide (A, B);
```

```
if Error_Flag /= -1 then
   Int_IO.Put (A, 0);
   Text_IO.New_Line;
else
   Text_IO.Put_Line ("Division-by-zero in procedure Divide");
end if;


A := 7;
B := 0;

Divide (A, B);

if Error_Flag /= -1 then
   Int_IO.Put (A, 0);
   Text_IO.New_Line;
else
   Text_IO.Put_Line ("Division-by-zero in procedure Divide");
end if;

end Error_Test;
```

Figure 9.7.1

Note here that the first parameter, X, is of mode **in out**, while the second is of mode **in**. The global variable Error_Flag is set to 0 in the procedure, the division takes place, and if no division-by-zero error occurs, the value of X is used as the value for the corresponding actual parameter, with the value of Error_Flag remaining at 0. If a division error *does* occur, Error_Flag is set to −1 in the exception handler, and then the "copy-out" of the value of the first formal parameter takes place. (In this case, what value will X's actual parameter replacement have upon return from the procedure Divide?) In either event, control returns at the statement following the call to Divide, namely at the **if...then** construction. The mainline program is designed to examine the global variable Error_Flag prior to continuing with its execution—although normally the calling routine would have to take a more serious action than simply displaying a message and then continuing with its execution. Incidentally, the result of executing this little test program is

```
3
Division-by-zero in procedure Divide
```

You may be somewhat surprised that we have relaxed our campaign *against* side effects here and appear actually to endorse their use. (Note that we have included a few lines of documentation to draw attention to the global nature of Error_Flag.) In fact, we consider this modification of a global variable to be appropriate and even elegant. Such an indicator might be used in a more complex environment to keep track of several different kinds of exceptions, as well as the subprograms in which they were raised, simply by giving the indicator various values. As with all such global uses, there are no substitutes for careful use and complete documentation.

In Figure 9.7.2 we explicitly show the "function counterpart" of Figure 9.7.1, in which we replace the procedure Divide by the function Quotient and make some corresponding adjustments in the code. What is to be noted is that although the subprogram here is a function rather than a procedure, exception handling is carried out in essentially the same manner as before. However, because Quotient is a *function*, its exception handler must return *some* value, which we have arbitrarily chosen to be X. Note that the main program is "expected" to test the error flag before making any use of the function's return value and that if Numeric_Error is raised, the function value is not used by the main program.

```
    with Text_IO, Int_IO;

procedure Error_Test is

    A, B:            Integer;

    Error_Flag:      Integer;      -- Global divide-by-zero flag

    function Quotient (X, Y: INTEGER) return INTEGER is

    begin

      Error_Flag := 0;

      return X/Y;

    exception

        when Numeric_Error =>   -- If Numeric_Error, then
          Error_Flag := -1;     -- set divide-by-zero flag
          return X;             -- and return a "dummy" value

    end Quotient;

begin

    A := 7;
    B := 2;

    A := Quotient (A, B);

    if Error_Flag /= -1 then
      Int_IO.Put (A, 0);
      Text_IO.New_Line;
    else
      Text_IO.Put_Line ("Division-by-zero in function Quotient");
    end if;


    A := 7;
    B := 0;

    A := Quotient (A, B);

    if Error_Flag /= -1 then
      Int_IO.Put (A, 0);
      Text_IO.New_Line;
    else
      Text_IO.Put_Line ("Division-by-zero in function Quotient");
    end if;

end Error_Test;
```

Figure 9.7.2

In Figure 9.7.3 we consider the case in which the procedure includes no handler to deal with the exception that is raised when the procedure executes. In this case, the exception is **propagated** outward to the frame containing the procedure call. When the exception Numeric_Error is raised, control passes to the statement following the procedure call; but because the exception is still raised, control then passes to the exception handler in the main program. The output of this program is the same as that of the previous one.

```
with Text_IO, Int_IO;

procedure Error_Test is

    A, B:             Integer;

    procedure Divide (X: in out INTEGER; Y: in INTEGER) is

    begin

       X := X/Y;

    end Divide;


begin

    A := 7;
    B := 2;

    Divide (A, B);

    Int_IO.Put (A, 0);
    Text_IO.New_Line;

    A := 7;
    B := 0;

    Divide (A, B);

    Int_IO.Put (A, 0);
    Text_IO.New_Line;
exception
    when Numeric_Error =>
       Text_IO.Put_Line ("Division-by-zero in procedure Divide");

end Error_Test;
```

Figure 9.7.3

We may replace the procedure Divide in Figure 9.7.3 by a function Quotient and adjust the program accordingly, just as was done in passing from Figure 9.7.1 to 9.7.2. We then find that the resulting program behaves in a manner very similar to that of Figure 9.7.3; in particular, it produces the same output.

We have considered two cases: (1) one in which the procedure or function includes an error handler that sets an error flag (the flag is tested by the calling program after the subprogram finishes execution) and (2) one in which the procedure or subprogram contains no handler for the pertinent exception but leaves it to the the calling program to handle the exception by sending a message. We look at another case, one in which the subprogram itself contains an exception handler that displays a message. As before, we begin by considering a procedure Divide (Figure 9.7.4); subsequently we deal with its counterpart, the function Quotient (Figure 9.7.5).

```
    with Text_IO, Int_IO;

procedure Error_Test is

    A, B:               Integer;

    procedure Divide (X: in out INTEGER; Y: in INTEGER) is

    begin

      X := X/Y;

    exception

      when Numeric_Error =>
        Text_IO.Put_Line ("Division-by-zero in procedure Divide");

    end Divide;

begin

    A := 7;
    B := 2;

    Divide (A, B);

    Int_IO.Put (A, 0);
    Text_IO.New_Line;


    A := 7;
    B := 0;

    Divide (A, B);

    Int_IO.Put (A, 0);
    Text_IO.New_Line;

end Error_Test;
```

Figure 9.7.4

The output of this program is:

```
3
Division-by-zero in procedure Divide
7
```

It is certainly not as desirable as what we have seen before, for we probably are not interested in knowing that A has been left with the final value 7 (because the quotient that was to be assigned to it could not be computed). But observe that in this structure the main program has not been "notified" that an exception has been raised and, consequently, has no way of "knowing" that something unusual has occurred. If there is any moral here, it is that such information should be communicated to the main program, either by the use of a flag (which the main program can test), by the propagation of the exception to the main program for subsequent handling, or by the return of a "special value," a technique we illustrate in the final example of this section (Figure 9.7.6).

Something even less desirable occurs if we slavishly alter the code of Figure 9.7.4 to replace the procedure Divide by a corresponding function Quotient, as is done in Figure 9.7.5.

```ada
    with Text_IO, Int_IO;

  procedure Error_Test is

    A, B:             Integer;

    function Quotient (X, Y: INTEGER) return INTEGER is

    begin

      return X/Y;

    exception

      when Numeric_Error =>
        Text_IO.Put_Line ("Division-by-zero in function Quotient");

    end Quotient;


  begin

    A := 7;
    B := 2;

    A := Quotient (A, B);

    Int_IO.Put (A, 0);
    Text_IO.New_Line;

    A := 7;
    B := 0;

    A := Quotient (A, B);

    Int_IO.Put (A, 0);
    Text_IO.New_Line;

  end Error_Test;
```

Figure 9.7.5

Here, if a division by zero does take place, the function's exception handler takes over and displays the error message. However, since no provision is made to return via a **return** statement, Program_Error is raised, and control returns to the Ada control system, not the main program that invoked the Divide function. In this case, the output is

```
3
Division-by-zero in function Quotient
<System Program_Error message>
```

Our final example (Figure 9.7.6) handles a division-by-zero error within the function Quotient in an essentially different fashion. In this case the value returned is −1, and we must assume that this is not a normally "valid" return value; that is, the calling module must recognize −1 as an error indication, not a valid return value. (This technique can be a problem when *any* return value is possible.) As we see, the main module does not simply assign the function value to A. Rather, it first *tests* the function value; if it is valid, it assigns it to A; if its value (−1) indicates an error, then a message is displayed and A is not assigned a new value. While this is a useful and common technique for error reporting, in this case a possible objection is that it requires *two* invocations of the function upon its return in order to assign A a valid value. This creates no serious problem here, nor does it elsewhere, as long as the function in question has no side effects. Moreover, this objection can be quite easily removed by a small reprogramming of the statements that invoke Quotient in the main part of the program. We leave this matter to the exercises.

```
  with Text_IO, Int_IO;

procedure Error_Test is

  A, B:            Integer;


  function Quotient (X, Y: INTEGER) return INTEGER is

  begin

    return X/Y;

  exception

    when Numeric_Error =>
      return -1;

  end Quotient;


begin

  A := 7;
  B := 2;

  if Quotient (A, B) = -1 then
    Text_IO.Put_Line ("Division-by-zero in function Quotient");
```

```
  else
    A := Quotient (A, B);
    Int_IO.Put (A, 0);
    Text_IO.New_Line;
  end if;

  A := 7;
  B := 0;

  if Quotient (A, B) = -1 then
    Text_IO.Put_Line ("Division-by-zero in function Quotient");
  else
    A := Quotient (A, B);
    Int_IO.Put (A, 0);
    Text_IO.New_Line;
  end if;

end Error_Test;
```

Figure 9.7.6

9.8 Subprograms as compilation units

The kinds of entities that qualify as candidates for what is known in the Ada language as a **compilation unit** is quite extensive. For this reason we decline to enter into a formal study of this concept at the present time, rather being content to examine a few examples and look at some compilation units with which we are already familiar.

We can informally state, with considerable accuracy, that a compilation unit is simply some collection of Ada source code that will pass the test of "compilability," meaning that it *can*, by itself, be successfully compiled by the Ada compiler. As we already know, main programs (procedures, actually), package specifications, and package bodies fall into this category. But there are other entities that can be compiled, and we look at two simple examples, one a function and the other a procedure that is *not* a main program.

Recall the procedure Find_GCD of Section 8.8. It was introduced in a fairly artificial way to deal with a question that was not really of great significance to begin with (namely, the use of the **return** statement in procedures). We noted at the time that it would probably make more sense to write GCD as a *function*, inasmuch as its primary activity is the calculation of a *value*. Figure 9.8.1 shows the corresponding function.

```
function GCD (A, B:  Positive) return Positive is

  Num_A:        Positive := A;
  Num_B:        Positive := B;
  Temp:         Positive;

begin

  loop
    if Num_A rem Num_B = 0 then
      return Num_B;
```

```
      else
        Temp := Num_B;
        Num_B := Num_A rem Num_B;
        Num_A := Temp;
      end if;
    end loop;

  end GCD;
```

Figure 9.8.1

If the code for this function is compiled, the result will be a compilation unit named GCD, which can then be included in any other programming module by means of the context clause **with GCD**. Figure 9.8.2 shows an example, which does nothing but calculate and display the greatest common divisor of two positive numbers.

```
    with Text_IO, Int_IO;
    with GCD;

procedure GCD_Test is

    X, Y:      Integer;

begin

    Text_IO.Put ("Enter two positive integers: ");
    Int_IO.Get (X);
    Int_IO.Get (Y);

    Text_IO.New_Line;
    Text_IO.Put ("The greatest common divisor of ");
    Int_IO.Put (X, 0);
    Text_IO.Put (" and ");
    Int_IO.Put (Y, 0);
    Text_IO.Put (" is ");
    Int_IO.Put (GCD (X, Y), 0);
    Text_IO.New_Line;

end GCD_Test;
```

Figure 9.8.2

As a second example, consider the procedure Exchange, Figure 8.7.1, whose purpose is simply to interchange two integers. For reference, we repeat this procedure here as Figure 9.8.3.

```
procedure Exchange  (X, Y:  in out INTEGER) is

    Temp:    Integer := X;

begin

    X := Y;
    Y := Temp;

end Exchange;
```

Figure 9.8.3

This procedure has quite wide applicability, for we frequently need to interchange a pair of values, especially when *sorting* data. Thus we could compile it as a separate compilation unit and subsequently include it (by means of a **with** clause) in any other compilation unit that has need of it. We do this in Figure 9.8.4, where we write the code of procedure Order (Figure 8.7.2), this time with a view to separately compiling Order itself for use when needed.

```
with Exchange;

procedure Order (A, B, C: in out INTEGER) is

begin

  if A > B then
    Exchange (A, B);
  end if;

  if A > C then
    Exchange (A, C);
  end if;

  if B > C then
    Exchange (B, C);
  end if;

end Order;
```

Figure 9.8.4

Assuming that we have compiled Order (as it appears in Figure 9.8.4) as a separate compilation unit, we may now rewrite the program Print_in_Order (Figure 8.7.3) in the following compilable form (Figure 9.8.5).

```
with Text_IO, Int_IO, Order;

procedure Print_in_Order is

  -- This program accepts three integers as input,
  -- arranges the integers in increasing order, and
  -- displays them in this order.

  Int_1, Int_2, Int_3: Integer;

  procedure Get_Input (A, B, C:  out Integer) is

  begin

    Text_IO.Put_Line ("Type three integers:");
    Int_IO.Get (A);
    Int_IO.Get (B);
    Int_IO.Get (C);
    Text_IO.New_Line;

  end Get_Input;
```

```
procedure Print_Output (A, B, C:  in Integer) is

begin

   Text_IO.Put ("In increasing order, the integers are:");
   Text_IO.New_Line;
   Int_IO.Put (A, 0);
   Text_IO.New_Line;
   Int_IO.Put (B, 0);
   Text_IO.New_Line;
   Int_IO.Put (C, 0);

end Print_Output;

begin    -- Print_in_Order

  Get_Input    (Int_1, Int_2, Int_3);
  Order        (Int_1, Int_2, Int_3);
  Print_Output (Int_1, Int_2, Int_3);

end Print_in_Order;
```

Figure 9.8.5

We comment only that the separately-compiled procedure Order has been included in this program ("**with** Order"), but it has not been necessary to mention Exchange in a **with** clause, since this has already been included in the compilation unit of Order and is "brought along with it" to the main program for use within Order. However, if it were necessary to invoke Exchange elsewhere in the main program, we would need to include the name of Exchange in the **with** clause. (Why?)

9.9 Introduction to recursive subprograms*

In this chapter we have seen a number of examples of subprograms—functions and procedures—including cases in which a subprogram, when invoked, in turn invokes other subprograms. Indeed, in Figure 9.8.5 (or in its earlier version, Figure 8.7.3) we have an example of a main program that invokes the procedure Order which, in turn, calls Exchange. These nested subprogram calls can in some cases extend fairly deeply, but of course the calling mechanism provides for this. However, consider the following question: Can a subprogram, during the course of its execution, *invoke itself?* Interestingly enough, the answer is yes, and we will shortly see an example of a function that calls itself, a phenomenon known as **recursion**.

The function **factorial** is defined for natural (nonnegative) numbers. One possible definition is the following:

factorial(0) = 1
for $n > 0$,   factorial(n) = n ($n-1$) ($n-2$) . . . 2 · 1

---

*This section may be omitted.

Thus factorial(*n*) is frequently described as "the product of the integers between *n* and 1, inclusive." This mathematical function is easily implemented in Ada, and one such version is shown in Figure 9.9.1, which scarcely requires any discussion.

```
--  Iterative version of the factorial function

function Factorial (Num: NATURAL) return POSITIVE is

   Value:      Positive := 1;

begin

   for K in reverse 1..Num loop
     Value := Value * K;
   end loop;

   return Value;

end Factorial;
```

Figure 9.9.1

Now a mathematician would probably not be much taken with the definition of the factorial function as given above, in part because the ellipsis (the three "dots") is not a very precise construction, in that it leaves to our imagination what is to be filled in. A more acceptable definition, but one that is perhaps a bit more difficult to grasp, is the following:

factorial(0) = 1

for *n* > 0,   **factorial**(*n*) = *n* · **factorial**(*n* − 1)

or, using the more universally accepted notation, **factorial**(*n*) = **n!**

0! = 1;

for *n* > 0,   *n*! = *n* · (*n* − 1)!

Even this version contains deficiencies that require something of the nature of the Principle of Mathematical Induction for their resolution. Observe that in the definition of this function, we actually use the definition itself, and to one not accustomed to this, the definition appears to be circular. This type of definition is referred to as a **recursive definition**.

We offer in Figure 9.9.2 a *recursive* implementation of the factorial function, and unlike its iterative counterpart (Figure 9.9.1) it requires quite a bit of investigation to see exactly how it can return Factorial (Num).

```
--  Recursive version of the factorial function

function Factorial (Num: NATURAL) return POSITIVE is
```

```
begin

    if Num <= 1 then
        return 1;
    end if;
    return Num * Factorial (Num - 1);

end Factorial;
```

Figure 9.9.2

There are perhaps a couple of puzzling constructions here, but surely the principal focus of the discussion is the statement

```
    return Num * Factorial (Num - 1);
```

in which a function (indeed, *the* function in question) is itself invoked on a value of Num one smaller than the current value. Aside from the obvious question about what *values* are being used here, we need also to be convinced that any prior values that have already been created are not now being destroyed. To be more explicit, we know that when Factorial is invoked the first time, the Ada system allocates memory for the formal NATURAL parameter Num and places the actual parameter value in that location. But when Factorial is invoked a second time, with another actual parameter (namely, Num − 1), is the first actual parameter value lost? To answer these questions, we examine a specific invoking of Factorial, and for the sake of definiteness, we assume the call Factorial (3), since the actual parameter 3 yields a situation that is small enough to be manageable while being large enough to be illustrative of the situation in general.

When the function is invoked the first time, an appropriate amount of space is allocated for the formal parameter Num, and the actual parameter 3 is copied into it. We illustrate this situation in Figure 9.9.3, where the space (the small box) is labeled Num_1. The value of the function will also be calculated, and we reserve some temporary space for it as well and label it Val_1. At this point we cannot place a number in the box labeled Val_1, for Num_1 is not equal to 1, and this value depends upon a further computation, in fact another call to Factorial, as we have indicated.

Num_1 [3]

Val_1 [   ]

$$Val_1 = Factorial\ (3)$$
$$= 3 * Factorial\ (3 - 1)$$
$$= 3 * Val_2$$

Figure 9.9.3

What happens when the second call to Factorial, namely Factorial (3 − 1) is executed? The same thing that happened the first time, namely, space is allocated for the actual parameter (3 − 1 = 2) and for the value of the function. The space allocated here is in addition to that allocated earlier, for Num_1 (namely, 3) and Val_1 (namely, ?). As we have indicated in Figure 9.9.4, this second value—Val_2—depends upon a further call to Factorial, and thus the box labeled Val_2 cannot yet be filled in.

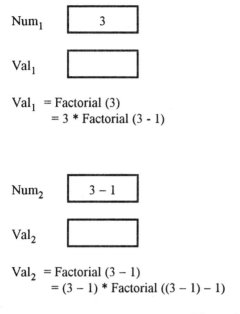

Num_1 | 3

Val_1 |

Val_1 = Factorial (3)
= 3 * Factorial (3 - 1)

Num_2 | 3 − 1

Val_2 |

Val_2 = Factorial (3 − 1)
= (3 − 1) * Factorial ((3 − 1) − 1)

Figure 9.9.4

Note that we have been able to write Val_1 in terms of Val_2 and that a further call to Factorial is necessary, since Num_2 (3 − 1 = 2) is not equal to 1. (Recall that when the parameter value is 1, the recursive step in the function is *not* taken; rather, the function value 1 is returned immediately.)

The next invoking of Factorial is shown in Figure 9.9.5. This time, the actual parameter ((3 − 1) − 1) *does* have the value 1, and the function can immediately return the value 1 (in the box labeled Val_3).

Num_1 | 3

Val_1 |

Val_1 = Factorial (3)
= 3 * Factorial (3 − 1)
= 3 * Val_2

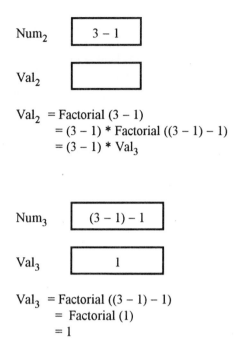

Num_2 $\boxed{3-1}$

Val_2 $\boxed{}$

$\begin{aligned}
\text{Val}_2 \;&= \text{Factorial}\,(3-1) \\
&= (3-1)*\text{Factorial}\,((3-1)-1) \\
&= (3-1)*\text{Val}_3
\end{aligned}$

Num_3 $\boxed{(3-1)-1}$

Val_3 $\boxed{\quad 1 \quad}$

$\begin{aligned}
\text{Val}_3 \;&= \text{Factorial}\,((3-1)-1) \\
&= \;\text{Factorial}\,(1) \\
&= 1
\end{aligned}$

Figure 9.9.5

Finally, as shown in Figure 9.9.6, since Val_3 has been given a value that is *not* dependent upon another function call, the function returns this value to its *last* calling statement, namely, the **return** statement that invoked it with the actual parameter $(3-1)$. As a consequence, Val_2 (2) is now returned to the computation for Val_1, which calculation can now be completed: $\text{Val}_1 = 3 * 2 = 6$, the value of 3!

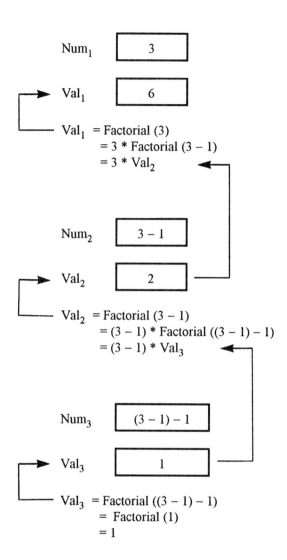

Num_1 3

Val_1 6

Val_1 = Factorial (3)
       = 3 * Factorial (3 − 1)
       = 3 * Val_2

Num_2 3 − 1

Val_2 2

Val_2 = Factorial (3 − 1)
       = (3 − 1) * Factorial ((3 − 1) − 1)
       = (3 − 1) * Val_3

Num_3 (3 − 1) − 1

Val_3 1

Val_3 = Factorial ((3 − 1) − 1)
       = Factorial (1)
       = 1

Figure 9.9.6

    Two facts should be immediately clear about recursive subprogram calls. First, there is a fair amount of computer activity when a function or procedure call is executed, since storage needs to be allocated for formal parameters and local variables, and actual parameters may have to be copied into some of these storage locations. All this is true for *any* function or procedure call. However, when the call is recursive, this activity may have to take place many hundreds or thousands of times, and thus when compared with the corresponding *iterative* version of the same subprogram, the recursive implementation would appear to run more slowly and to be far more "expensive" of computer space. In fact, all of this is true, and we encounter this notion again at the close of this section.

In analyzing the recursive function Factorial, we discover a few principles that, in the more general case, are responsible for the fact that recursion "works" and, in particular, that recursive subprograms eventually *terminate*. First, we note that there is an *alternative* (nonrecursive) statement to the recursive call (in the present instance, **return 1** in the event that Num <= 1). Second, there is actually a *path* to this alternative statement. Third, this alternative path actually will be taken eventually (when Num = 1, which *must* occur, since the number whose factorial is being calculated at each step is initially greater than 1 and is *decreasing*). As a "bad" example, consider the following version of Factorial, evidently a result of a keyboarding error or a lapse of concentration on the part of the programmer (Figure 9.9.7).

```
-- CAUTION! This recursive function contains
-- no provision to terminate the recursion.

-- Recursive version of the factorial function

function Factorial (Num: NATURAL) return POSITIVE is

begin

   if Num <= 1 then
      return 1;
   else
      return Num * Factorial (Num);
   end if;

end Factorial;
```

Figure 9.9.7

It is clear that if, initially, the actual parameter replacement for Num is greater than 1, the function will repeatedly call itself forever, without making any progress toward the "alternate path" case: *<actual parameter>* = 1. In fact, this subprogram will *not* execute "forever," since eventually it will occupy all available space with its repeated demands for space allocation for its formal parameter. The next recursive call will thus fail, with the Ada system exception Storage_Error raised.

We noted above that the recursive implementation of a function or procedure can be expensive, both in terms of time and computer space. While this is true, how should we deal with a process that is "naturally" recursive? What is frequently done is to define or describe the process in its recursive form and perhaps even to write sample descriptive Ada code as a recursive algorithm, all of this for the sake of clarity of presentation. When it comes actually to *implementing* the process, we again fall back to the iterative version, for the sake of efficiency. The factorial function is a case in point—it is best defined and even described algorithmically in a recursive form, but its implementation is best done iteratively. Can an arbitrary *naturally* recursive process always be implemented in an *iterative* fashion? Perhaps, but the way in which this is to be done is by no means always as transparent as in the factorial case. As an example, consider a function that generates the so-called Fibonacci numbers, described as follows.

$$fib(1) = 1$$
$$fib(2) = 1$$
$$fib(n) = fib(n - 1) + fib(n - 2) \quad \text{for } n > 2.$$

The *n*th number in the sequence is the sum of the preceding two numbers (for $n > 2$); thus the sequence of Fibonacci numbers begins

1, 1, 2, 3, 5, 8, 13, 21, 34, 55, . . .

In Figure 9.9.8 we show an Ada implementation of the Fibonacci function. Note that the function Fib described is recursive.

```
--   Function Fib accepts a single POSITIVE parameter N
--   and returns the Nth Fibonacci number

function Fib (N: POSITIVE) return POSITIVE is

begin

  if N <= 2 then
    return 1;
  end if;
  return Fib (N - 1) + Fib (N - 2);

end Fib;
```

Figure 9.9.8

We observe that Fib is an excessively "expensive" subprogram, for not only is it recursive but in fact at each step in the recursion there are *two* (recursive) calls to Fib. Thus for N of any significant size (40 or so), evaluation of Fib (N) can take several *minutes*, even on a relatively fast computer. You will find a version of Fib in the exercises that is not recursive and thus is somewhat more efficient; but at best the function cannot really be made "fast."

We will encounter recursion a few more times in this book, principally in the exercises, but we consider the topic not to be in the mainstream of what we are about here. Thus our brief treatment of the topic is concluded. However, if we have given recursion short shrift, it does not reflect the degree of importance of the subject; there are many areas of computing in which recursion arises naturally and frequently.

9.10 Exercises

9.2.1 (a) Go through the program of Figure 9.1.1 and determine the scope of each identifier. In particular, what about the name Time_and_Day? What would you say about the scope of each of the identifiers INTEGER, NATURAL, BOOLEAN, False, True?

(b) Are there any identifiers in this program whose region of visibility is not the same as their scope? If so, which?

9.2.2 Consider the structure

```
function Fn_Outer (...) return ... is

    function Fn_Inner (...) return ... is
        .
        .
        .
    begin

        <Fn_Inner statement part>

    end Fn_Inner;
    .
    .
    .
begin

    <Fn_Outer statement part>

end Fn_Outer;
```

We know that the function Fn_Inner may be referenced in the statement part of Fn_Outer. (The program of Figure 8.9.2 affords an example of this.)

(a) Can the function Fn_Inner refer to Fn_Outer within Fn_Inner's statement part?

(b) What would be the result of an Fn_Inner reference to Fn_Outer?

(c) As an example of this phenomenon, consider the following program, and tell what is displayed when Main is executed.

```
with Int_IO;

procedure Main is

    function Fn_Outer (X: Integer) return Integer is

        function Fn_Inner (X: Integer) return Integer is

        begin
          if X < 5 then
            return Fn_Outer (X + 1);
          end if;
          return 0;
        end Fn_Inner;

    begin
      if X < 4 then
        return Fn_Inner (X);
      end if;
      return 1;
    end Fn_Outer;
```

```
begin        --  Main procedure

  Int_IO.Put (Fn_Outer (3), 0);

end Main;
```

9.2.3 The discussions and programs of Chapter 8 suggest that it does not matter whether the formal parameter names of a function do or do not coincide with any or all of the actual parameter names—or even, for instance, whether the name of the *first* formal parameter of a function happens to be the same as that of the *second* actual parameter with which it is invoked. (The same is true, of course, of procedures.) In terms of the ideas in Section 9.2, explain why this is so.

9.2.4 Answer the following questions concerning the program of Figure 8.9.2.

(a) What is the scope of the name Maximum_3?
(b) What is the scope of the formal parameters X, Y, and Z of Maximum_3?
(c) Is Maximum_3 a global entity of this program, or is it local to the subprogram body Maximum_3, or both?
(d) What is the scope of the name Maximum_2?
(e) What is the scope of the formal parameters A and B of Maximum_2?
(f) If the formal parameter names A and B were changed to X and Y, respectively, throughout the function body Maximum_2, would the resulting code be acceptable to the Ada compiler? If so, would it execute correctly? Explain.

9.3.1 We have said in Section 9.3 that "a function might need to change a BOOLEAN or INTEGER *error flag* (variable) upon its execution, to indicate that some extraordinary event has occurred; the function *must* do so globally, since it cannot manage the flag as a parameter." Why not?

9.4.1 Use a scheme similiar to that of Figure 6.8.2 to describe the scope and visibility of *all* variables in the program whose outline is given below.

```
procedure Sample is

  A, B:   FLOAT;
    .
    .
    .
begin
    .
    .
    .
  Block_1:
  declare
    A:   INTEGER;
    B:   CHARACTER := 'D';
      .
      .
      .
```

```
        begin

          declare
            B:   FLOAT;
          begin
              .

              .

              .

            for A in CHARACTER range 'A'..Block_1.B loop
                .

                .

                .

            end loop;
                .

                .

                .

          end;
              .

              .

              .

        end Block_1;
            .

            .

            .

      end Sample;
```

9.4.2   Show by a simple programming example that the *block* construction allows *multiple* declarations (one at a time) of the *same* object. That is, it is possible to declare a variable, say Temp, several times in a program, perhaps even of different types each time it is declared.

9.5.1   Make up a *one*-parameter Ada function that has a default value assigned to this parameter. Investigate how you would invoke this function in a main program, making use of its default value.

9.6.1   As suggested in the text, write a test program containing three procedures named Exchange, differing only in their parameter types: INTEGER, CHARACTER, FLOAT. The program should call Exchange with actual parameter pairs of these three types, to verify that the Ada system is able to select the proper procedure in each case, on the basis of the type of the actual parameters with which it is invoked.

9.6.2   Write a test program containing two functions named Minimum, of which one has *two* INTEGER parameters and the other *three*. Each is to return the smallest of the values passed to it as actual parameters. Verify that the Ada system will correctly distinguish between calls to these two functions, on the basis of the number of actual parameters in the function call.

9.6.3   Write a brief Ada program to investigate whether it is permissible to have a procedure and function with the same name in the same program. Find out whether the compiler accepts your program and, if so, whether it executes properly.

9.6.4 In Exercise 9.4.2 we suggested the possibility of multiple declarations of a variable, say Temp, by declaring various versions in *different* block constructions.

    (a) Is this an example of name overloading? Explain.

    (b) Would it be possible to overload a name by declaring, say, *two* variables, of *different* types but with the *same name*, in the same frame? (Try it and see.)

9.7.1 Observe that in each figure of Section 9.7 the main program begins by assigning the values 7 and 2 to A and B, respectively, and then the procedure Divide (or function Quotient) is called; subsequent statements of the program assign the values 7 and 0 to A and B, respectively, and the subprogram is called again. Tell what the output of each program is if these assignment pairs were *reversed*; that is, if A and B were *first* set to 7 and 0, respectively, with the other assignment of values (to 7 and 2) coming after the first call to the subprogram.

9.7.2 The function Quotient of Figure 9.7.2 is a bit awkward, inasmuch as it has a side effect, namely, the setting of the global variable Error. If a statement invokes Quotient, it must examine Error to see if all went well. In fact, the main program that invokes Quotient is quite contrived, in that division by zero causes no real harm.

    (a) Consider the following call to Quotient:

```
Int_IO.Put (Quotient (A,B));
```

    What would be the effect if B has the value 0? What would be displayed by the Put statement? How could the program "recover" from this error? What would be the consequences if Quotient had been invoked in the statement

```
T := Quotient (A,B);
```

    (where T is some INTEGER variable)?

    (b) It might seem more natural for Quotient to leave Numeric_Error raised and let the invoking routine deal with it; for example,

```
function Quotient (X, Y: INTEGER) return INTEGER is

begin

   return X/Y;

exception

   when Numeric_Error =>
      Text_IO.Put ("Division-by-zero in function Quotient");
      raise Numeric_Error;
end Quotient;
```

How would you now write the *two* calls to Quotient that are shown in Figure 9.7.2?

9.7.3 What output would you expect from the program of Figure 9.7.5 if the function Quotient were to be patched up by inserting as the last line of its exception handler (following the call to Put_Line) the statement:

(a) return X;
(b) return Y;

How might you use the latter return value, along with a modified form of the message, so as to produce acceptable output from this program, even in the case of an attempted division by zero?

9.7.4 Modify the program of Figure 9.7.6 so as to preserve the method illustrated in this program while eliminating the need of calling Quotient *twice* when it returns.

9.8.1 Answer the question at the end of Section 9.8: If a procedure Order is separately compiled in a compilation unit containing the context clause **with Exchange** and a main program contains the context clause **with Order**, why is Exchange unavailable to the main program unless the latter also contains the clause **with Exchange**?

9.8.2 What are all the kinds of Ada compilation units we have seen up to this point?

9.9.1 (a) Show that the following function Fib generates the Fibonacci numbers. Pay particular attention to the values Fib(1) and Fib(2). Note that the function is *iterative*, not *recursive*.

```
function Fib (N: NATURAL) return NATURAL is

    A:      NATURAL := 1;
    B:      NATURAL := 1;
    Temp:   NATURAL := 1;

begin

    for K in INTEGER range 1..N-2 loop
      Temp := A + B;
      B := A;
      A := Temp;
    end loop;

    return Temp;

end Fib;
```

(b) Write two programs, each of which obtains a number N from the keyboard and then displays Fib(N), one for the version of Fib given in Section 9.9 and the other for the version shown immediately above. Test both versions for various values of N, with an eye toward the amount of *execution time* required by both versions.

(Note: The recursive version does not slow down noticeably until N reaches values around 30 or so; but if, for your computer, NATURAL'Last = 32767, then you will not be able to use values of N larger than 23. This can be repaired, however, by changing all instances of NATURAL to LONG_INTEGER.)

Chapter 10

Introduction to Arrays

Up to now we have dealt only with integer types (INTEGER, NATURAL, POSITIVE, and other range subtypes), the types FLOAT and BOOLEAN, and, to a lesser extent, the type CHARACTER. These types, along with others that we will be seeing later, are instances of what are called **scalar types** in Ada. There is one characteristic that all scalar types have in common: Objects of these types are *simple* (or *indivisible* or *atomic*); they are not made up of *parts*.

In contrast, almost all high-level computer languages implement **composite types**, which allow the programmer to build complicated data objects out of simpler ones and to deal effectively with these so-called structured objects and their parts. Ada is no exception, and in this chapter we consider a particular kind of structured object called an **array**, whose individual parts are called **components**. We first look into the need for arrays in computing; then we will see how to create arrays and operate with them.

10.1 Why arrays?

Suppose you had to write a program that would read as input 100 integers (examination grades, say) and then display these in reverse order. Using only what we have covered up to now, how could you do it? As indicated in Figure 10.1.1, the program would need 100 variables, as well as 100 input statements and 100 output statements, to carry out its job.

```
with Text_IO, Int_IO;

procedure Reverse_Grades is

   Grade_1,                    -- 100 variable declarations
   Grade_2,
   Grade_3,
      .
      .
      .
   Grade_100:     INTEGER;
```

```
begin

   -- Read 100 grades as input

   Int_IO.Get (Grade_1);              -- 100 input statements
   Int_IO.Get (Grade_2);
   Int_IO.Get (Grade_3);
        .
        .
        .
   Int_IO.Get (Grade_100);

   -- Display 100 grades in reverse order

   Int_IO.Put (Grade_100, 3);         -- 100 output statements
   Text_IO.New_Line;
   Int_IO.Put (Grade_99, 3);
   Text_IO.New_Line;
   Int_IO.Put (Grade_98, 3);
   Text_IO.New_Line;
        .
        .
        .
   Int_IO.Put (Grade_1, 3);
   Text_IO.New_Line;

end Reverse_Grades;
```

Figure 10.1.1

What if, instead of 100 grades, we had to deal with 200 grades in this program? Or 500? We could continue raising the stakes in this fashion, but you might complain—quite rightly, in fact—that such a program would be unrealistic and of almost no consequence. A far more realistic project, and certainly not an insignificant one, would be to write a program to read the 100 grades, rearrange them in decreasing order, and display the resulting list of grades, starting with the highest. How might this be done? Once again, the program would have to have 100 variable declarations for the grades, along with 100 input statements and 100 output statements. Besides all this, there would have to be all kinds of comparisons and exchanges among the data—and you could not be blamed for deciding that the whole process might be carried out far more efficiently with pencil and paper.

The fundamental problem here is having to declare and refer to 100 different names for the 100 grades. Ada's array types allow us to use a single name for the *entire* list of grades, with each grade having its own *position* in the list, the position then distinguishing a particular grade from all the others. Without our getting into all the details of how to deal with lists of integers (these are taken up next), the job carried out by the unwieldly program of Figure 10.1.1 is almost trivially accomplished by the program of Figure 10.1.2, where we need declare only *one* variable (Grades) and subsequently employ it in *two* **for** loops. The fact that the entire list of grades can be referred to as Grades while each grade has its own individual **index** (sometimes referred to as its **array position** or **subscript**) spares us the need of having 100 different identifiers. This construction opens up the possibility of using *loops* to do the needed processing.

```
with Text_IO, Int_IO;

procedure Reverse_Grades is

    subtype RANGE_100 is      INTEGER range 1..100;
    type HUNDRED_INTS is      array (RANGE_100) of INTEGER;
    Grades:                   HUNDRED_INTS;

begin

    -- Read 100 grades

    for Index in RANGE_100 loop
      Int_IO.Get (Grades(Index));
    end loop;

    -- Display 100 grades in reverse order

    for Index in reverse RANGE_100 loop
      Int_IO.Put (Grades(Index), 3);
      Text_IO.New_Line;
    end loop;

end Reverse_Grades;
```

Figure 10.1.2

Array types are a powerful feature of a computer language. In this chapter, we approach arrays in a fairly concrete way, as lists of integers numbered from 1 to *n*, where *n* stands for the number of integers in the list. Later, as we proceed through this chapter and Chapter 13, we learn how this idea and its consequences can be extended to far more general settings.

10.2 Lists of integers

We spoke above of a "list of grades" and of "lists of integers." We should note that the term "list" has a technical meaning in computing; in this book, however, we use it only in the ordinary nontechnical sense. Thus, we might think of a list of five grades as looking like this:

1.   82
2.   78
3.   85
4.   87
5.   90

Such a list could be represented in a computer program by a variable Grades, declared as follows:

```
    subtype RANGE_5        is INTEGER range 1..5;
    type FIVE_INTS         is array (RANGE_5) of INTEGER;
    Grades:                FIVE_INTS;
```

We could picture the array variable Grades as a sequence of numbered "cells" arranged vertically, with each cell containing a grade, as shown in Figure 10.2.1*a*. If we visualize Grades in this way, we have captured the general appearance of the list of five grades as we wrote it above. Alternatively, we might choose to picture the cells arranged horizontally, as in Figure 10.2.1*b*. Clearly, these two ways of imagining an array are equivalent: The cells are identified with their position in the list, and the grade corresponding to each position lies inside the respective cell.

a   Grades

1	82
2	78
3	85
4	87
5	90

b   Grades

82	78	85	87	90
1	2	3	4	5

Figure 10.2.1

An array is made up of parts called the **components** of the array; each component has its own distinctive position in the array indicated by a number called the component's **index**. The indexes make up a range called the **index range** of the array; in our example, this is the integer range 1..5, to which we have given the subtype name RANGE_5. The components of an array must all be of the same type. For the present, we take them to be of type INTEGER; in the next section we consider arrays with components of types other than INTEGER.

Grades is the name of the array variable we have declared and illustrated above. Its individual components are referred to as Grades(1), Grades(2), Grades(3), Grades(4), and Grades(5). Programmers sometimes refer to an array variable as a **subscripted variable**, a term that comes from the use of subscripts in mathematics. You have probably seen examples of the use of subscripts in geometry, where (x_1, y_1) and (x_2, y_2) often denote the coordinates of points in the plane. In computing, however, the "subscripts" (indexes) of the individual array components are not written below the line, since computer keyboards do not generally have the ability to generate subscripts; instead, they are written on the line and enclosed in parentheses (or, in some programming languages, in square brackets). We should point out, too, that the integer literals we have used as indexes in naming these components may be replaced by any expression whose value lies in the appropriate range; this expression is evaluated at run-time (not at compile-time), and its value is used as the respective index. Thus,

```
Grades(Index)
Grades(Index-1)
Grades(2*Index-1)
```

are ways of referring to components of this array, provided that, in each case, the value of the integer Index is such that the given expression has a value in the range 1..5. If the value of the expression lies outside this range, Constraint_Error will be raised. In fact, it is true in general that the Constraint_Error exception will be raised at run-time whenever a reference has been made to a nonexistent component of a given array, that is, a component indexed by a value lying outside the array's index range.

In summary, we observe that in the declarations

```
subtype RANGE_5 is INTEGER range 1..5;
type FIVE_INTS  is array (RANGE_5) of INTEGER;
```

RANGE_5 denotes the **index range** of the array, and INTEGER indicates the type of the array's **component values**. Note that we could omit the declaration of the named subtype RANGE_5 and instead declare the array type immediately, as

```
type FIVE_INTS is array (INTEGER range 1..5) of INTEGER;
```

However, as suggested by the simple examples we have seen so far, **for** loops are frequently used in processing arrays, and as a result it is often convenient to have a *name* for the index range, so that this range can be referenced by name in these **for** loops as well as in the array declaration itself.

The general form of declaration for the array types we are considering at present is given in the syntax diagram of Figure 10.2.2. Note that this is a *type* declaration; hence, it does not bring any object into being. In order to have a variable of this type, we must declare such a variable (in our case, Grades) to be of type FIVE_INTS.

array type

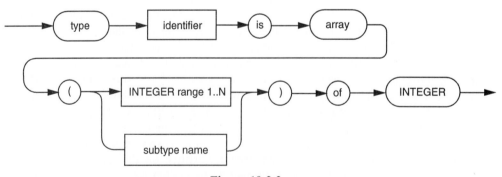

Figure 10.2.2

It should be mentioned that the representations of the array variable Grades in Figure 10.2.1 are based on the assumption that the individual components of Grades have been given values. Figure 10.2.1*a* is meant to show the similarity of this array to the ordinary list with which we began this section. The fact is, however, that when we *declare* the variable

Grades, the contents of the components of this variable remain indeterminate until values have been assigned, just as when we declare an "ordinary" variable.

How are values assigned to an array variable? Often, this must be done by input operations carried out during the execution of the program. Thus we might include the statements

```
Int_IO.Get (Grades(1));
Int_IO.Get (Grades(2));
Int_IO.Get (Grades(3));
Int_IO.Get (Grades(4));
Int_IO.Get (Grades(5));
```

which would require the user to enter input such as

```
82
78
85
87
90
```
or
```
82 78 85 87 90
```

during the program's execution. It is evident that this program segment could be made more efficient by the use of a loop, as was done in Figure 10.1.2:

```
for Index in RANGE_5 loop
   Int_IO.Get (Grades(Index));
end loop;
```

If the problem setting allows assignment of the grades within the program itself, this may be done for each component separately:

```
Grades(1) := 82;
Grades(2) := 78;
Grades(3) := 85;
Grades(4) := 87;
Grades(5) := 90;
```

In this case, there is no way to replace the five assignment statements by a loop structure, since there is no way to represent the five different grade values in terms of a loop.

Sometimes, however, it *is* possible to express the component values by means of a loop parameter. Consider the following:

```
Squares:   FIVE_INTS;
```

If we want this array variable to be assigned the squares of the integers from 1 to 5, we need not write

```
Squares(1) :=  1;
Squares(2) :=  4;
Squares(3) :=  9;
Squares(4) := 16;
Squares(5) := 25;
```

since the relationship between each array index and the value to be assigned to the corresponding component allows us to use the loop

```
for Index in RANGE_5 loop
  Squares(Index) := Index**2;
end loop;
```

In Section 2.6 we described INTEGER *literals*, examples of which are 2001, 0, 57, and 100_000; similarly, in Section 5.2 we spoke of CHARACTER literals, such as 'A', 'z', or '9'. Is there such a thing as an *array* literal? There is, in effect, but in Ada it is called an **array aggregate**. The simplest way of writing an array aggregate is to list the component values of the array, separated by commas and enclosed in parentheses. For the array type FIVE_INTS, we might have the aggregates:

```
(82, 78, 85, 87, 90)
(1, 4, 9, 16, 25)
```

These aggregates can be used with variables of the type FIVE_INTS, just as INTEGER literals are used with INTEGER variables, for example, in an assignment statement

```
Grades := (82, 78, 85, 87, 90);
```

or in an assignment made in a variable declaration

```
Grades:  FIVE_INTS := (82, 78, 85, 87, 90).
```

Similarly, we could have the *declaration*

```
Squares:  FIVE_INTS := (1, 4, 9, 16, 25);
```

or the assignment *statement*

```
Squares := (1, 4, 9, 16, 25);
```

In each case, the given assignment would take effect at run-time, as we saw in Section 7.1: The component values indicated in a *declaration* are assigned to the array variable when the declaration is *elaborated*; those specified in an assignment *statement* are "put into" the array when the statement is *executed*.

There is a good bit more to be said about the various forms in which array aggregates may be written, but most of this is put off until later. For now, because it is frequently quite useful, we introduce one further concept. Often it is necessary to give an array variable an initial assignment in which all components are assigned the same value, such as 0. Of course, this initialization can always be accomplished at run-time, by means of a loop. But, as we have just seen, an array variable—like other variables—can also be given an initial value in its *declaration*. In the case of the array Grades, we could declare

```
Grades:  FIVE_INTS := (0, 0, 0, 0, 0);
```

Suppose we had instead

```
subtype RANGE_100 is   INTEGER range 1.100;
type HUNDRED_INTS is   array (RANGE_100) of INTEGER;
Scores:                HUNDRED_INTS;
```

Would we have to write 100 zeros in order to set all components of Scores to 0 when this variable is declared? Fortunately, it can be done as follows:

```
Scores:  HUNDRED_INTS := (RANGE_100 => 0);
```

or

```
Scores:  HUNDRED_INTS := (1..100 => 0);
```

What should be observed here is the *form* of the array aggregate

```
(RANGE_100 => 0)      or      (1..100 => 0).
```

It makes use of Ada's "arrow" notation, where the arrow => is preceded by the array's index range and followed by the value to be assigned to *all* the components of the array. As this example shows, it is sometimes convenient to write an array aggregate in this form, but there is more to be said about the arrow notation for array aggregates and about the flexibility it allows, and we return to this matter in Chapter 13.

Array aggregates enable us to define an **array constant** which, like any constant, must be assigned a value when it is declared. Letting the aggregate play the role of a literal, we find that the declaration assumes the same form as the constant declarations we have seen before:

```
Five_Primes:  constant FIVE_INTS    := (2, 3, 5, 7, 11);
Multipliers:  constant FIVE_INTS    := (32, 16, 8, 4, 2);
Mean_Scores:  constant HUNDRED_INTS := (RANGE_100 => 500);
```

Array constants are not seen as frequently as, say, INTEGER constants; nevertheless, at times they are useful in programming.

As our examples of array aggregates would seem to suggest, an aggregate must specify a value for *each* component of an array. It is not possible, for example, to use an aggregate to assign values to the first three array components, say, while leaving the values of the remaining components indeterminate. On the other hand, when we are dealing with an array on a component-by-component basis, it is not always necessary or desirable to "fill up and use" *all* the components of an array variable that has been declared. Often the *programmer* does not know exactly how large an array will be needed by the *user* of the program. In this case, one thing that can be done is to declare an array that will be *at least* as large as will ever be necessary, making provision in the program for the array to be only partially used (if not all of it is needed). Of course, the program will have to keep track of how much of the array is actually used for meaningful data, to process only that part of the array. Figure 10.2.3 shows another example of our program Reverse_Grades, in which the programmer allows an array of up to 50 grades, although a shorter list of grades can readily be dealt with; that is, any list containing *no more than* 50 grades can be accommodated. It is assumed that the user of the program enters the grades one by one and then types −1, a number that cannot be a grade, to indicate the end of the list. Notice that the variable Count keeps track of how many grades have been put into the array. (Verify that it works if the number of grades is 0 or 1.) Notice, too, that the range used in the output **for** loop is 1..Count, not 1..50, since the program is to display (in reverse order) only the grades that have been read in as input, ignoring the indeterminate contents of any unused component locations at the end of the array.

```
with Text_IO, Int_IO;

procedure Reverse_Grades is

   -- This program reads a list of up to 50 grades
   -- (nonnegative integers) and displays them in reverse order.
   -- The user enters the list of grades and then enters -1
   -- to signal "no more grades".

   subtype RANGE_50 is      INTEGER range 1..50;
   type FIFTY_INTS is       array (RANGE_50) of INTEGER;
   Grades:                  FIFTY_INTS;
   Input_Value:             INTEGER;
   Count:                   NATURAL := 0;

begin

   -- Read the grades, keeping track of their count

   Int_IO.Get (Input_Value);          -- read the first number
   while Input_Value /= -1 loop       -- while not finished ...
      Count := Count + 1;             -- one more grade read
      Grades(Count) := Input_Value;   -- put it into the array
      Int_IO.Get (Input_Value);       -- read the next number
   end loop;

   -- Display the grades in reverse order.

   for Index in reverse INTEGER range 1..Count loop
      Int_IO.Put (Grades(Index), 3);
      Text_IO.New_Line;
   end loop;

end Reverse_Grades;
```

Figure 10.2.3

10.3 Arrays with noninteger components

As you might have expected, there is no particular reason why the components of arrays should be of the type INTEGER or even of any other integer type. In this section we consider some examples of arrays having components of various types.

Perhaps the most modest extension of the examples we saw in the preceding section results from allowing the components of an array to be *numbers* that are not integers. Thus:

```
subtype MONTH_RANGE is    INTEGER range 1..31;
type MONTHLY_DATA is      array (MONTH_RANGE) of FLOAT;
Rainfall:                 MONTHLY_DATA;
```

These declarations provide an array variable Rainfall whose components, indexed 1..31, allow us to store real numbers representing the rainfall (with inches as the unit of measurement, say) for the respective day of a given month. In fact, there are many other kinds of noninteger numeric data that we might want to maintain on a daily basis over the course of a month: average temperature, perhaps, or daily sales or expenses. Such information could appropriately be stored in array variables of type MONTHLY_DATA.

The data held in the components of an array need not be *numeric* at all. For instance, it is not uncommon in computing to use arrays of BOOLEAN values. Thus, to continue with the idea of saving information for each day of the month, we might have

```
type MONTHLY_INFO is    array (MONTH_RANGE) of BOOLEAN;
Sales_Quota_Reached:    MONTHLY_INFO;
```

In this case, the components of the variable Sales_Quota_Reached might be assigned the value True or False to indicate whether or not, for each day of a given month, the daily sales quota (of some particular business) was reached on that day. Notice that we have reused the range subtype MONTH_RANGE in specifying the index range of the array type MONTHLY_INFO. The array Sales_Quota_Reached is pictured in Figure 10.3.1.

Sales_Quota_Reached

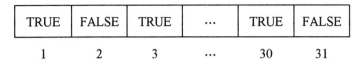

TRUE	FALSE	TRUE	...	TRUE	FALSE
1	2	3	...	30	31

Figure 10.3.1

We can also declare arrays with CHARACTER components, as in the following example:

```
subtype LETTERS is CHARACTER range 'A'..'Z';
type LETTER_ARRAY is array (INTEGER range 1..26) of LETTERS;
Alphabet: LETTER_ARRAY;
```

If we assign values to the components of this array by means of the statements

```
Alphabet(1) := 'A';
for Index in INTEGER range 2..26 loop
  Alphabet(Index) := CHARACTER'Succ (Alphabet(Index-1));
end loop;
```

then the array can be pictured as in Figure 10.3.2. Although probably not very practical, this array does do something that at least is reasonable: For each number from 1 to 26, it gives the corresponding letter of the alphabet. Thus, Alphabet(1) = 'A', Alphabet(2) = 'B', and so on, with Alphabet(26) = 'Z'. Notice that in this example we chose *not* to declare a named subtype to indicate the array range. Even if we had done so, we would not have been able to make convenient use of this name in the **for** loop we have shown, inasmuch as the loop has the range 2..26, which is *not* the same as the array range.

Alphabet

'A'	'B'	'C'	'D'	...	'X'	'Y'	'Z'
1	2	3	4	...	24	25	26

Figure 10.3.2

What types may be used as the component types of arrays in Ada? Actually, there is almost no restriction; the components of an array may be of almost *any* Ada type (although, as our array declarations have implied, all components must be of the *same* type). We could continue to construct examples like those above in which, while using integer index ranges, we vary the component types of the arrays. In terms of the "pictures" of one-dimensional arrays that we introduced in Figure 10.2.1, this would simply mean that the cells representing the array components would contain BOOLEAN values (as in Figure 10.3.1), CHARACTER values (as in Figure 10.3.2), or values of some other type; the cells themselves would continue to be "numbered" by consecutive integers.

10.4 Operations on integer arrays

As the discussion in the preceding section might suggest, much of what is done with arrays (including I/O) is done on a component-by-component basis. Since the indexes of the arrays we are studying are the values of a range of integers, the loop construct (especially the **for** loop) is the programmer's main tool for operating on arrays.

There are some operations, however, that are performed on array objects as a whole. We list four of them for now:

Assignment

An array aggregate, constant, or variable may be assigned to an array variable of the same type. If we declare

```
Five_Integers, Five_Numbers:   FIVE_INTS;
Five_Zeros:                    constant FIVE_INTS := (0, 0, 0, 0, 0);
```

then, as we saw before, we may use an assignment statement with an aggregate such as

```
Five_Integers := (1066, -1492, -1776, 1812, 2001);
```

Other possibilities are

```
Five_Numbers := Five_Integers;
```

where the right side of the assignment statement is a variable; and

```
Five_Nums := Five_Zeros;
```

where the right side is a constant.

Comparison

Two array objects (aggregate, constant, variable) of the same type may be compared by means of the relational operators = and /=. Equality will hold if the arrays have exactly the same component values in the same order; otherwise, the arrays are unequal. Thus, we might have

```
if Five_Integers = (0, 1, 0, 1, 0) then ...

if Five_Numbers = Five_Integers then ...

while Five_Numbers /= Five_Zeros loop ...
```

These comparisons, like the others we saw earlier, are Boolean expressions: They evaluate to True or False. Hence, they find their principal application in conditional and loop constructs, as suggested by the examples.

Parameter passing

An array may be used as a parameter in a procedure or function. We illustrate this by writing a function (Figure 10.4.1) that takes an array as its actual parameter and returns the sum of the components of the array.

```
        .
        .
        .
N:                     constant POSITIVE := <some suitable value>;

subtype RANGE_N is     INTEGER range 1..N;
type SOME_INTS is      array (RANGE_N) of INTEGER;
        .
        .
        .
```

```
-- The following function takes as an actual
-- parameter any array of type SOME_INTS and
-- returns the sum of the components of the array.

function Sum (Int_Data: SOME_INTS) return INTEGER is

  Total: INTEGER := 0;

begin

  for Index in RANGE_N loop
    Total := Total + Int_Data(Index);
  end loop;
  return Total;

end Sum;
```

Figure 10.4.1

Function evaluation

A function may return an array as its value. We will see an example of this later.

This brings us to the end of the fundamentals on arrays. In the next two sections, we turn our attention to the much-used operations of searching and sorting arrays.

10.5 Searching an array

In this section we study two processes in which we search through an integer array—in the first case, to find the largest element of the array and, in the second, to find out where some particular integer is located within the array, if it is there at all. Both these processes are frequently used in computing, and each provides us with an opportunity to see how some of the ideas of the previous sections are applied.

First, we look at a function Max that takes an integer array as a parameter and returns the value of the largest (maximum) integer in the array. As in the case of the function Sum (Figure 10.4.1), we again allow the integer array to be of any positive length specified in advance by the programmer.

Our method is to initialize a local variable Max_Val of the function to the value of the *first* component of the array. Then we compare the value of Max_Val with that of the *second* component of the array, and if the latter is larger, we assign it to Max_Val (otherwise, Max_Val is left as it is); thus, Max_Val will have the value of the largest component inspected so far. Moving on to the *third* array component, we compare Max_Val to this component, and if the latter value is larger, we assign it to Max_Val (otherwise, Max_Val is again left as it is). We continue through the array in this fashion, comparing the current value of Max_Val to that of each array component and replacing the value of Max_Val whenever we find a larger value in the array. At the end of the process, Max_Val holds the largest value in the *entire* array, and we return this value.

```
     .
     .
     .
N:   constant POSITIVE := <some suitable value>;

type SOME_INTS is array (INTEGER range 1..N) of INTEGER;
     .
     .
     .

     -- The following function takes as an actual parameter
     -- any array of type SOME_INTS and returns the value of
     -- the largest integer in the array.

function Max (Int_Data: SOME_INTS) return INTEGER is

   Max_Val:  INTEGER := Int_Data(1);

begin

   for Index in 2..N loop
     if Int_Data(Index) > Max_Val then
       Max_Val := Int_Data(Index);
     end if;
   end loop;

   return Max_Val;

end Max;
```

Figure 10.5.1

This function does all that was asked of it: It reveals *what* the largest integer in the array is, but it does not indicate *where* it occurs. But we can go a step further. If we had a function to tell where the largest integer is in the array, then we could always access this component and find out its value. Thus, a function Index_of_Max that returns the *index* of the largest array component would provide more information than does the function Max, Figure 10.5.1. It is easy to program the function Index_of_Max (Figure 10.5.2); we need only make a few adjustments in the body of Max; the search process is essentially the same.

```
     .
     .
     .
N:   constant POSITIVE := <some suitable value>;

type SOME_INTS is array (INTEGER range 1..N) of INTEGER;
     .
     .
     .

     -- The following function takes as an actual parameter any
     -- array of the type SOME_INTS and returns the index of the
     -- largest integer in the array.  If this integer occurs
     -- more than once in the array, it returns the index of the
     -- location at which it occurs first.
```

```
function Index_of_Max (Int_Data: SOME_INTS) return POSITIVE is

  Max_Loc:  POSITIVE := 1;
  Max_Val:  INTEGER  := Int_Data(Max_Loc);

begin


  for Index in INTEGER range 2..N loop
    if Int_Data(Index) > Max_Val then
      Max_Loc := Index;
      Max_Val := Int_Data(Max_Loc);
    end if;
  end loop;

  return Max_Loc;

end Index_of_Max;
```

Figure 10.5.2

In the next section we examine how the reasoning used in this function body can be applied to the job of rearranging the elements of an array into increasing order. Before leaving these two functions, you might reflect on what slight modifications would need to be made in them to produce the corresponding functions Min and Index_of_Min that return the *least* (minimum) integer in the array and its index, respectively. The latter function (or, specifically, the reasoning used in implementing it) will be applied to sorting the elements of an array into *decreasing* order.

The other problem that we address in this section is that of locating a specified integer in a given array. We will write a function Location that has two parameters, one indicating the array to be searched and the other indicating the integer sought within the array. The function returns the index of the array component at which the given integer is found. The function stops searching when it finds what it is looking for, and therefore, if the number sought occurs several times in the array, the function value will be the position of the *first* occurrence of the number. We discuss several possible versions of this function, beginning with one that will subsequently be revised. Once again, the function deals with an array of the type SOME_INTS, where N is any *fixed* positive integer that has previously been specified by the programmer in a constant declaration.

The fundamental idea of the function Location is quite simple: We search through the given array for the specified number, and when we find it, we stop searching and return its index. This process, which starts at the beginning of the array and inspects each successive element to see if it is the number sought, is often used in computing: It is called a **linear search**. Because we want to stop searching when we find what we are looking for, it is convenient to process the array with a **while** loop, rather than a **for** loop.

```
          .
          .
          .

N:  constant POSITIVE := <some suitable value>;
subtype RANGE_N is INTEGER range 1..N;
type SOME_INTS is array (RANGE_N) of INTEGER;
```

```
          .
          .
          .

    -- The following function takes as actual parameters an
    -- array of type SOME_INTS and an INTEGER value; it
    -- searches the given array for the given integer.  When
    -- it finds the integer in the array, it stops searching
    -- and returns its index as the function value.
    -- Preliminary (deficient) version.

 function Location (Int_Data:   SOME_INTS;
                    Int_Sought: INTEGER)   return POSITIVE is

   Index:  POSITIVE := 1;

 begin

   while Int_Data(Index) /= Int_Sought loop
     Index := Index + 1;
   end loop;

   return Index;

 end Location;
```

Figure 10.5.3

The code for this function is certainly tidy, but there is a problem that is perhaps not immediately obvious. Suppose Int_Sought is *not* in the array—what then? As a matter of fact, we have made no provision at all for this possibility, not even to the extent of stating what the function should do if it fails to find the number it is looking for. The way the function is written, of course, has nothing to stop execution of the loop until Index goes beyond N and an attempt is made to access the nonexistent array location N+1. As we have already noted, when this happens, the system raises the exception Constraint_Error and normal execution of the function is abandoned.

There are two things we ought to do: (1) Determine what value the function is to return if Int_Sought is not in the array (recall that a function must *always* return a value if it is to conclude its execution in a normal manner, without leaving an exception raised) and (2) adjust the statements to provide for the possibility that Int_Sought is not found.

A convenient way to deal with the first of these points is to have the function return a value that cannot possibly be an index of any array of type SOME_INTS, so that the program that calls Location can determine that it has received a value that signals "number not found." Since all arrays of this type are indexed by a positive range, it would seem that 0 might be a good choice. We would then have to declare the type of the function values to be NATURAL rather than POSITIVE, to allow 0 as a value, but this is easily done.

As for the second point, we have to see to it that no attempt is made to access a location "beyond" the end of the array. This is taken care of in the corrected version of the function body shown in Figure 10.5.4.

```
-- The following function takes as actual parameters an
-- array of type SOME_INTS and an INTEGER value; it
-- searches the given array for the given integer.  If
-- it finds this integer in the array, it stops searching
-- and returns its index as the function value.  If it
-- fails to find the given integer, it returns 0.

-- Corrected version.

function Location (Int_Data:    SOME_INTS;
                   Int_Sought: INTEGER)    return NATURAL is
    Index:  POSITIVE := 1;

begin

    while Index < N and Int_Data(Index) /= Int_Sought loop
       Index := Index + 1;
    end loop;

    if Int_Data(Index) = Int_Sought then
       return Index;
    end if;

    return 0;

end Location;
```

Figure 10.5.4

In this version of the function, we have incorporated another test into the iteration scheme of the loop. We check that **Index < N** before incrementing Index in the body of the loop. Thus, we are assured that the *highest* value Index can take is N, and we will never attempt to access an array location beyond this point. On the other hand, when Index has the value N, the looping stops, because the condition **Index < N** is False; however, at this point we cannot say whether the other condition **Int_Data /= Int_Sought** is True or False. For this reason, we must subsequently test the condition **Int_Data(Index) = Int_Sought**, in order to determine whether or not Int_Sought has been found. That is, after termination of the **while** loop, we must determine *which* of the conditions caused that termination. (Could *both* conditions have been False simultaneously?) The examples given in Figure 10.5.5 illustrate the behavior of Location as applied to several arrays with N = 5 and Int_Sought = 1000. In each case, we indicate the BOOLEAN values of the conditions **Index < N** and **Int_Data /= Int_Sought**, respectively, when the loop ceases execution, along with the value returned by the function. You may find it helpful to trace through the execution of Location for each of these arrays, noting especially how the function behaves in the last two cases.

Array searched	Value when loop stops executing		Function value returned
	Index < N	Int_Data(Index) /= Int_Sought	
(a) (32, 1000, −10, −24, 57)	True	False	2
(b) (32, 1000, −10, −24, 57)	True	False	1
(c) (32, −10, −24, 57, 1000)	False	False	5
(d) (32, −10, −24, 57, 15)	False	True	0

N = 5
Int_Sought = 1000

Figure 10.5.5

In general, if we have a loop of the form

```
while P and Q loop
   <statement sequence>;
end loop;
```

where P and Q are conditions (Boolean expressions), it is often necessary to apply a test after the loop to find out whether its execution stopped because P was False, because Q was False, because both were False simultaneously. Thus, we should expect the **while** loop in our function body to be followed by an **if** statement whose purpose is to resolve this question.

Perhaps you would consider it more natural to replace the operator < in the condition **Index < N** by the operator <=; in this case you might arrive at something like the program segment shown in Figure 10.5.6.

```
begin

   while Index <= N and
       Int_Data (Index) /= Int_Sought loop
     Index := Index + 1;
   end loop;

   if Index <= N then
     return Index;
   end if;

   return 0;

end Location;
```

Figure 10.5.6

The reasoning here would be that if Int_Sought is in the array, then when the loop stops executing, Index will have a value <= N; but if Int_Sought is *not* in the array, Index will have been incremented to N+1. This is logically correct, but there are two aspects to consider: (1) The test performed after the loop in this version is quite indirect, for it does not explicitly check to see if Int_Data(Index) = Int_Sought; consequently, it is harder to follow than the one in the previous version of the function. (2) More seriously, there is a possibility that if Int_Sought is not in the array, then Index will reach the value N+1, and the system will raise Constraint_Error as it attempts to evaluate the right operand of the logical operator **and** in the loop condition. Indeed, this possibility frequently arises in linear searches, and Ada has the following way of dealing with it. You may recall that if we employ either of the Boolean expressions

> **P and Q**
> **P or Q**

where P and Q are themselves Boolean expressions, we must expect that the operands P and Q will *first* be evaluated and that the resulting BOOLEAN values will then be combined by means of the respective logical operators **and** and **or**, yielding a final BOOLEAN value. However, Ada also has two **short-circuit control forms,** namely, **and then** and **or else**. In the Boolean expression

> **P and then Q**

which has the same BOOLEAN value as "P and Q," P is *first* evaluated, and if it is found to be False, Q is *not* evaluated at all, since the value of "P and then Q" (same as that of "P and Q") is already determined to be False. Similarly,

> **P or else Q**

has the same BOOLEAN value as "P or Q," but if P is found to be True, then Q is not evaluated at all, since the value of "P or else Q" (same as that of "P or Q") is already determined to be True.

Thus we may take care of the second of the points we raised concerning the version of function Location in Figure 10.5.6. We simply replace the **and** in the condition of the **while** loop by the short-circuit form **and then**. With this slight change, we obtain the version shown in Figure 10.5.7.

```
begin

    while Index <= N and then
        Int_Data (Index) /= Int_Sought loop
      Index := Index + 1;
    end loop;

    if Index <= N then
      return Index;
    end if;

    return 0;

end Location;
```

Figure 10.5.7

We have discussed the process of linear searching at much length, partly because of the importance it has in its own right and partly because it illustrates so many of the issues that must be considered when we deal with arrays. As a consequence, we have added a measure of complexity to the programming of the function Location, in an effort to make this function perform correctly and, in every case, avoid the Constraint_Error that could occur in the very simple function body of Figure 10.5.3. Thus we have arrived at two *correct* versions of the function, those shown in Figures 10.5.4 and 10.5.7. Of these, the programming in Figure 10.5.4 is probably the more direct and perhaps more commendable on that account; however, you should make sure you understand the reasoning employed in Figure 10.5.7, as it has its counterparts in other areas of computing. In Section 10.8 we offer a technique that enables us to do linear searches in a more efficient way.

This brings us to the end of our discussion on searching arrays. As you can easily see, we must step carefully: The main pitfall here is an inadvertent attempt to access a nonexistent array location. It is especially important to be in control of how a loop behaves when an index reaches the end of an array's index range. This is one of the principal lessons to be learned about processing an array—we must be on our guard not to "go beyond" the end of the array.

10.6 Sorting an integer array

In many computing applications it is necessary to rearrange the components of an array so that they occur in the array in *increasing* order, with the smallest component value coming first and the largest one last. Similarly, many contexts call for the components of an array to be arranged in *decreasing* order. The rearranging of an array's component values so that they occur in either ascending or descending order is known as **sorting** the array, a process of the highest importance in computer applications.

In this section, we develop a procedure to sort the numbers in an integer array into ascending order. As we will then see, we can equally well produce a procedure to sort the numbers into descending order instead —changing a single line of program code is all that is required. We call these procedures Sort_Up and Sort_Down, respectively.

Once again, we assume the declarations

```
N:  constant POSITIVE := <some suitable value>;

subtype RANGE_N is INTEGER range 1..N;
type SOME_INTS is array (1..N) of INTEGER;
```

which we use in writing our sort procedures. First, confining our attention to the procedure Sort_Up, we have to consider the method to be used in accomplishing our goal.

There are many ways of sorting an array, some more efficient than others. The method to be used here is called a **selection sort**. It is by no means the fastest of sorting techniques, but for our purposes it has the decided advantage of being quite direct and readily understood. To see how it works, we apply it to the array shown in Figure 10.6.1, which is of type SOME_INTS with N = 8.

−59	129	12	308	−43	9	−88	57
1	2	3	4	5	6	7	8

Figure 10.6.1

We begin by finding the location of the largest element of the array. (In the previous section we saw exactly how this can be done, when we developed the function Index_of_Max.) In the present example, the largest element occurs at position 4 of the array, with value 308. We now *exchange* this component with the last component of the array, which gives us the array shown in Figure 10.6.2.

−59	129	12	57	−43	9	−88	308
1	2	3	4	5	6	7	8

Figure 10.6.2

What we have accomplished, of course, is to place the largest element of the array just where we want it to be: in last place. We therefore need not deal with it any further.

Now we repeat what we have just done but this time only for the part of the array indexed by the range 1..7. Confining our attention to this, we determine the index of its largest component (this index is 2), and we exchange this component with the array component indexed by 7. We then have the array that appears in Figure 10.6.3. The two largest of the given components have been moved into their proper locations in what will eventually be the sorted array.

−59	−88	12	57	−43	9	129	308
1	2	3	4	5	6	7	8

Figure 10.6.3

We continue in this fashion, dealing with the "front end" of the given array and with a shorter portion of it each time, putting the largest component of this portion into its proper place in the sorted list of numbers. The last part of the given array to be dealt with in this way is the one indexed by the range 1..2.

The process involved in an ascending selection sort (for an array of type SOME_INTS) can be summed up as follows:

1. Find, or "select," the index of the largest of the components indexed by the range 1 . . N.
2. Exchange this component and the one with index N.

1. Find the index of the largest of the components indexed by the range 1 . . N − 1.
2. Exchange this component and the one with index N − 1.

1. Find the index of the largest of the components indexed by the range 1 . . N – 2.
2. Exchange this component and the one with index N – 2.

    .

    .

    .

1. Find the index of the largest of the components indexed by the range 1 . . 2.
2. Exchange this component and the one with index 2.

Clearly, we have developed a loop structure, since as we proceed, the last index of the range passes through values from N down to 2. We may summarize our sort procedure as follows:

```
for End_Index in reverse INTEGER range 2..N loop

   -- Find the index of the largest of the components
   -- indexed by the range 1..End_Index;

   -- Exchange this component and the one with index End_Index

end loop;
```

It now becomes a simple matter to complete the writing of the procedure body: The function Index_of_Max (Figure 10.5.2) does the first job that has to be done inside this loop, and it is always easy to program an exchange. However, instead of making use of the function Index_of_Max here, we make our procedure self-contained by incorporating the declarations and statements of this function into the sort procedure itself. You will recall that finding the largest component of an array (or its location in the array) requires a loop; thus, we can expect our procedure to have nested loops. As Figure 10.6.4 shows, this is indeed the case.

```
   -- The following procedure takes as a parameter any array
   -- of type SOME_INTS and sorts it into ascending order.

procedure Sort_Up (Int_Data: in out SOME_INTS) is

   Max_Loc:  POSITIVE; -- location (index) of largest component
   Max_Val:  INTEGER;  -- value of largest component

begin

   for End_Index in reverse INTEGER range 2..N loop

      -- Initialize Max_Loc and Max_Val to beginning of array

      Max_Loc := 1;
      Max_Val := Int_Data(Max_Loc);

      -- Search through array, replacing Max_Loc and Max_Val
      -- whenever a larger component is found

      for Index in INTEGER range 2..End_Index loop
        if Int_Data(Index) > Max_Val then
          Max_Loc := Index;
          Max_Val := Int_Data(Max_Loc);
        end if;
      end loop;
```

```
-- Exchange the largest and the last of the components
-- indexed by the range 1..End_Index; the largest
-- component has already been saved in Max_Val

Int_Data(Max_Loc)   := Int_Data(End_Index);
Int_Data(End_Index) := Max_Val;

    end loop;

end Sort_Up;
```

Figure 10.6.4

What is there about the procedure Sort_Up that makes it sort *up* instead of *down*? To put it another way, how should we change its statements to produce a new procedure to sort the array into descending (decreasing) order? Reflecting on the logic of the selection sort, we see that this can be accomplished if we first find the *smallest* component of the given array and exchange it with the last component of the array, then find the *smallest* component of the remaining part of the array and exchange it with the second-last component, and so on. Further reflection on the process of finding the smallest component of an array should convince us that all that is needed is to change the single occurrence of the operator > in the inner loop of the procedure to a corresponding <. Or, equivalently, we could retain the operator > and reverse its operands:

```
if Max_Val > Int_Data(Index) then ...
```

This would provide us with a procedure Sort_Down. Since we want to maintain descriptive identifiers in our procedure, we have to make some adjustments in the names of variables: changing "Max" to "Min" throughout takes care of this. Finally, we must make the needed updates in the comments.

We now have at our disposal several very useful functions and procedures for dealing with integer arrays. These functions and procedures represent the sort of array processing that is done in real-world information systems. They have their limitations, however; just what these are, and how, to a significant extent, we can get beyond them we take up in the final section of this chapter.

10.7 Dynamically-declared arrays*

In Section 10.2 we brought up a difficulty that can occur when a *programmer* must declare an array for use in a program without knowing exactly how large an array the *user*'s data will require. In fact, it is quite possible in some situations that *several* people will use the program and that each of them will need an array of a particular size, with these sizes varying from user to user. In Figure 10.2.3 we presented an example to illustrate a technique that may be employed in such cases: The programmer declares an array that will be *at least* as large as any user will need, with the understanding that most likely only *part* of the array will be occupied by data and processed when the program runs. In that example the array

---

*This section may be omitted.

was indexed from 1 to 50, and the user was to enter up to 50 nonnegative integer grades and terminate the input by entering the terminal value −1. The program kept track of how many nonnegative integers were entered, using a counter variable called Count, and subsequently it processed only the portion of the array indexed from 1 to Count. Exercise 10.2.4 calls for a variation on this "large-enough-array" technique, in which the user first enters the Count — that is, tells in advance how many nonnegative integers are to be entered—and the program handles the input in a **for** loop, rather than a **while** loop.

Both these examples have shortcomings based on the fact that the programmer must attempt to "overestimate" the size of the array needed by the user's data: (1) At best, there will almost always be wasted space because in declaring the array, the programmer has allocated more computer storage than is actually needed for the user's purposes, and (2) at worst, the programmer may have failed to make the array large enough, and as a result it will be unable to hold all the data in a particular application. But how can the programmer do otherwise? What is desired is that the array range be declared to be 1..Count, where, as before, Count is the number of nonnegative integers to be entered by the user. The problem is that the value of Count has to be used in a *declaration*, whereas this variable is not given any value until *after* the program begins to execute, when its value can be obtained from the user. Is it possible to *declare* an array with range 1..Count after getting the value of Count in an executable statement? In other words, can we place a declaration within the program's statement part? Remarkably, the answer is yes!

As we saw in Section 9.4, Ada provides just such a capability in terms of the **block statement**. The block statement allows us to declare entities **dynamically**, that is, during the actual *execution* of a program. Thus, in making such declarations, we may employ values that are obtained as input after the program has begun to run. We illustrate this approach by revising the program of Figure 10.2.3; by using a block statement, we are able to declare an array of "just the right size" to accommodate the user's needs (Figure 10.7.1). We have left the block statement unnamed; notice that it extends to the end of the program.

```
with Text_IO, Int_IO;

procedure Reverse_Grades is

   -- This program reads a list of grades (nonnegative
   -- integers) and displays them in reverse order.  The
   -- user is first asked to input the number (Count) of
   -- grades to be entered, and then to enter the grades.

   Count:      Natural;

begin

   Text_IO.Put ("How many grades are to be entered?  ");
   Int_IO.Get (Count);
   Text_IO.New_Line;
   Text_IO.Put ("Type the ");
   Int_IO.Put (Count);
   Text_IO.Put_Line (" grades:");

   declare
      type Grade_Array is array (INTEGER range 1..Count) of NATURAL;
      Grades:      Grade_Array;
```

```
begin

    for Index in INTEGER range 1..Count loop
      Int_IO.Get (Grades(Index));
    end loop;

    for Index in reverse INTEGER range 1..Count loop
      Int_IO.Put (Grades(Index));
      Text_IO.New_Line;
    end loop;

  end;

end Reverse_Grades;
```

Figure 10.7.1

10.8 Other index ranges

The integer arrays we have dealt with up to now have all been indexed by the range 1..N, where N stands for a suitable positive integer. In fact we specified that the index range should be of this form, since arrays were introduced as data objects corresponding to the informal idea of a list of integers "numbered" from 1 to N. In this section we look at some other possibilities for the index range of an array.

Suppose a student of economics needs a program that deals with various sets of numeric (integer) data pertinent to the years of President Eisenhower's administration (1953 to 1960). One such data set might consist of the average per capita income of Americans for each of the Eisenhower years; another might contain the median family income for each year of this period. Confining our attention to the first of these data sets—average per capita income (APCI)—we see that it consists of 8 integers, 1 for each of the 8 years of the Eisenhower administration. This is a natural setting for the use of an array, and using the ideas we have developed so far, we might declare

```
subtype RANGE_8 is INTEGER range 1..8;
type EIGHT_INTS is array (RANGE_8) of INTEGER;
APCI:  EIGHT_INTS;
```

The data set in question would fit nicely into this array, with APCI(1) representing the average per capita income for the first year of the Eisenhower administration (1953), and APCI(8) representing the corresponding income figure for the eighth year (1960).

However, there is certainly an inconvenience here. If we refer to APCI(3), it might take us a moment to figure out that this number pertains to the year 1955. Conversely, if we wanted to deal with the annual per capita income for 1958, we would need to determine that this is represented by APCI(6). Admittedly, the simple conversions called for here are more annoying than demanding, mainly because the span of years is so short. But you can easily imagine that they would be more troublesome if we were dealing with a longer period of time.

We can make things more manageable if we use the range 1953..1960, instead of 1..8, to index the array APCI and any other arrays containing data relating to the Eisenhower administration. In fact, using President Eisenhower's initials (DDE), we might set up a type

```
subtype DDE_YEARS is INTEGER range (1953..1960);
type DDE_DATA is array (DDE_YEARS) of INTEGER;
```

and declare whatever array variables we might need to hold the relevant data sets, such as

```
APCI:   DDE_DATA;
```

The point is that there is no need for the index range of an array to begin with 1; indeed, *any* index range is acceptable, and, as this example shows, it is often useful to tailor the range to the problem at hand. In Figure 10.8.1 we show how the choice of the range 1953..1960 is reflected in some simple processing of the array APCI to obtain the average of these annual figures over the period of the Eisenhower years.

```
        .
        .
        .
Sum:        INTEGER;
ACPI_Ave:   FLOAT;
        .
        .
        .
Sum := 0;

for Year in DDE_YEARS loop
  Sum := Sum + APCI(Year);
end loop;

APCI_Ave := FLOAT(Sum)/8.0;
        .
        .
        .
```

Figure 10.8.1

In some situations it is convenient to use an index range of the form 0..N. This might be the case if an economist wished to trace the changes in annual per capita income starting from some year regarded as a "turning point" in economic history. Here the focus would be less on the calendar year number associated with a given income figure than on the year of its occurrence as measured in "years beyond" the significant turning point. For the sake of an example, let us regard 1929 (the year of the great stock market crash) as such a turning point. Providing for a study of 50 years beyond this point, we declare

```
subtype YEARS_SPAN is INTEGER range 0..50;
type DATA_AFTER_1929 is array (YEARS_SPAN) of INTEGER;
APCI:   DATA_AFTER_1929;
```

In this arrangement, APCI(0) can be used to hold the average per capita income for the "base year" 1929; APCI(1) will be the corresponding figure for 1 year later, APCI(2) will be the figure for 2 years later, and so on. It might even be desirable, for comparison purposes, to include data for the 5 years leading up to 1929; in this case, the appropriate type declarations would be

```
subtype YEARS_SPAN is INTEGER range -5..50;
type DATA_AFTER_1929 is array (YEARS_SPAN) of INTEGER;
```

and the array variable APCI would be declared as above. In this case, of course, the negative indexes would be used for the five years *before* the base year 1929.

We leave as an exercise the simple task of modifying the syntax diagram given in Figure 10.2.2 to take account of the more general index ranges introduced in this section.

Before moving on, we would like to point out that it is sometimes advantageous to index an array from 0 to N (whatever the particular value of N may be), rather than from 1 to N, leaving an "unused" array location—the one indexed by 0—for certain special purposes. Foremost among these, perhaps, is the use that can be made of such a location in "streamlining" the linear search process. Recall from our discussion of Figure 10.5.3 that, in some way or other, we must see to it that our search does not run beyond the array, in case the value that is sought fails to be present in the array. We took care of this by replacing the simple but inadequate loop condition of Figure 10.5.3

```
while Int_Data(Index) /= Int_Sought loop ...
```

by the "two-comparison" condition

```
while Index < N and Int_Data(Index) /= Int_Sought loop ...
```

of Figure 10.5.4 or

```
while Index <= N and then Int_Data(Index) /= Int_Sought loop ...
```

of Figure 10.5.7. Clearly, each of these adjustments *doubled* the number of comparisons required for the search as programmed (incorrectly) in Figure 10.5.3. But there is a way in which we can preserve the simplicity and efficiency of the approach taken in Figure 10.5.3 while eliminating its inadequacy. To illustrate it, we redeclare the type SOME_INTS for use in the remainder of this section as follows:

```
N:  constant POSITIVE := <some suitable value>;

subtype RANGE_0_N is INTEGER range 0..N;
type SOME_INTS is array (RANGE_0_N) of INTEGER;
```

While keeping the same names as before, we have now used the range 0..N, rather than 1..N, to index the array type SOME_INTS. Our search method, which we show in the procedure of Figure 10.8.2, is to insert Int_Sought into the "extra" (unused) array component Int_Data(0) and then search *downward* through the array, starting at index N. We will certainly find Int_Sought in the array, at index 0 if not before, and therefore there is no danger of going beyond the array, as there was in Figure 10.5.3. The procedure will communicate to the calling program the value of the index at which it finds Int_Sought, and it will be up to the latter program to check whether this value is 0, meaning that Int_Sought was not in the original array, or whether it is a positive number designating the actual index at which Int_Sought is stored in the array.

```
-- The following procedure takes as actual parameters an
-- array of type SOME_INTS whose first component (with
-- index 0) is unused, along with an INTEGER that is
-- sought in the array, and a NATURAL variable that will
-- hold the index at which the integer sought is found.
-- If the procedure returns the value 0 in this variable,
-- then the integer sought was not in the original array.

procedure Locate (Int_Data:    in out SOME_INTS;
                  Int_Sought:  in INTEGER;
                  Location:    out NATURAL)  is

   Index: Natural := N;

begin

   Int_Data(0) := Int_Sought;

   while Int_Data(Index) /= Int_Sought loop
     Index := Index - 1;
   end loop;

   Location := Index;

end Locate;
```

Figure 10.8.2

It is customary to refer to Int_Data(0), once it is given the value of Int_Sought, as a **sentinel** employed in the search of the array, for it "stands guard" over the low end of the array to make sure that the search does not attempt to go beyond that point. Use of such sentinels is a standard technique in programming.

10.9 Unconstrained array types

By now we have several examples of integer array types with various index ranges. Figure 10.9.1 shows some of them.

```
type FIVE_INTS        is array (INTEGER range 1..5)        of INTEGER;
type HUNDRED_INTS     is array (INTEGER range 1..100)      of INTEGER;
type DDE_DATA         is array (INTEGER range 1953..1960)  of INTEGER;
type DATA_AFTER_1929  is array (INTEGER range -5..50)      of INTEGER;
```

Figure 10.9.1

Besides these, we originally introduced the type SOME_INTS with the declarations

```
N:   constant POSITIVE := <some suitable value>;
subtype RANGE_N is INTEGER range 1..N;
type SOME_INTS is array (1..N) of INTEGER;
```

where the programmer is expected to assign a value to the constant N in advance of the declaration of the type SOME_INTS. This was done so that SOME_INTS could be used in the declaration of functions and procedures capable of dealing with arrays of any positive length. Thus we managed to provide some flexibility to the subprograms Sum, Max, Index_of_Max, Min, Index_of_Min, Location, Sort_Up, and Sort_Down. But it is extremely important to understand that once a value of N has been supplied, each of these procedures and functions can be applied *only* to integer arrays indexed by a range that begins with 1 and ends with *this* value of N. Because of the usefulness of these functions and procedures, it could be advantageous to be able to apply them, within a program, to various integer arrays with *different* index ranges. Can this be done? If so, what modifications would we have to make in the function and procedure bodies, as we have written them?

The array types that we have declared thus far are examples of what in Ada are referred to as **constrained array types**, which means that the type declarations have *constrained*, or *restricted*, the objects of these types to having *specific* index ranges, the ones explicitly declared for the respective types. Ada also has **unconstrained** array types, which constitute a powerful array-handling feature of the language. We illustrate some declarations involving such a type:

```
type INTS is array (INTEGER range <>) of INTEGER;

New_Grades:   INTS(1..5);
New_Scores:   INTS(1..100);
```

The type INTS that we have just declared is an example of an unconstrained array type: Array objects (variables and constants) of this type are indexed by INTEGER ranges, but the type declaration does *not* specify any particular range. Indeed, what is meant by **INTEGER range <>** (where the symbol <> is read "box") is that objects of this type may be indexed by various integer ranges, of different lengths, starting and ending with different pairs of integers. A slight modification of Figure 10.2.2 will yield a syntax diagram for the definition of such a type.

Although Ada has unconstrained array *types*, there is no such thing as an unconstrained array *object* (variable or constant). This is really as we would expect, since the compiler must indicate to the run-time system exactly how much storage space is to be allocated for each array variable or constant when its declaration is elaborated. This in turn requires that the compiler somehow be given such information as part of the array object's declaration. As a consequence, when we declare a variable such as New_Grades, we must supply with it the range constraint that is "missing" from the type declaration. Similarly, we have specified an index range in the declaration of the variable New_Scores. Notice that both of these variables are of type INTS. In fact, an unconstrained array type like INTS may well have objects that exhibit great variety in their index ranges; for example,

```
Six_Numbers:    INTS(-3..2);
Four_Numbers:   INTS(-4..-1);
Pair:           INTS(1..2);
Century_Data:   INTS(1901..2000);
Long_Array:     INTS(0..4999);
```

In Section 10.8 we saw an example in which it was useful to employ negative indexes in arrays. As a matter of fact, although it is possible to find other examples in which negative indexes are meaningful, such applications are relatively rare. For this reason, we do not use negative indexes throughout the remainder of this chapter. The use of 0 as an index, however, is often quite useful and even natural in certain contexts; hence, we continue to allow the possibility of an index range including this number. These remarks may be summed up by saying that our main interest has to do with index ranges that lie within the integer subtype NATURAL. Accordingly, we introduce, and confine our attention to, the unconstrained array type INTEGER_ARRAY:

```
type INTEGER_ARRAY is array (NATURAL range <>) of INTEGER;
```

We have seen above how starting with an unconstrained array type such as INTEGER_ARRAY, we may declare various objects by stating the range constraint that pertains to each object. A second way of dealing with an unconstrained array type and its objects, namely, by way of a constrained *subtype*, follows:

```
type INTEGER_ARRAY is array (NATURAL range <>) of INTEGER;
subtype FIVE_NUMBERED_INTS is INTEGER_ARRAY(1..5);
Grades, Squares:  FIVE_NUMBERED_INTS;
```

We have passed from the *unconstrained* array type INTEGER_ARRAY to the *constrained* array variables Grades and Squares through the intermediate stage of the **constrained subtype** FIVE_NUMBERED_INTS of INTEGER_ARRAY. Perhaps the most interesting point to be noted here is that, for the first time, we have a subtype that is not declared in terms of a range of the values of its base type. In this case, the subtype is related to the base type in a different way: Its "values" are all those of the base type that share a particular index range.

Much of the importance of unconstrained array types stems from the fact that the *formal parameters* of procedures and functions may be of such types. However, the corresponding *actual* parameters with which these subprograms are called must be *constrained* array objects. The use of formal parameters that are of unconstrained array types lends great versatility to the procedures and functions that employ them, as we will see shortly when we revisit the array-processing functions and procedures we have written.

There is one other array concept that we must now put to use. It is the idea of **attributes**, with which we are familiar from our study of integer types and the BOOLEAN type. There are four attributes that are pertinent to arrays: **Range**, **First**, **Last**, and **Length**. Some peculiarities must be noted, however: (1) *Constrained* array types have these attributes, but unconstrained array types do not and (2) array *objects* (not only types) possess these attributes. We illustrate array attributes by looking at the INTEGER_ARRAY variable Long_Array, which we declared above and now redeclare as follows:

```
Long_Array:  INTEGER_ARRAY(0..4999);
```

The attributes of this variable have the following values:

```
Long_Array'Range  = 0..4999    (the index range)
Long_Array'First  = 0          (first element of the index range)
Long_Array'Last   = 4999       (last element of the index range)
Long_Array'Length = 5000       (length of, or number of elements
                                  in, the index range)
```

Similarly, if we had an array variable declared by

```
Special_Data:  INTEGER_ARRAY(12..384);
```
then its attributes would be

```
Special_Data'Range  = 12..384
Special_Data'First  = 12
Special_Data'Last   = 384
Special_Data'Length = 373.
```

Since unconstrained array *types* have no specified range, it is easy to see why these attributes have no meaning for such types, as they do in the case of both *constrained* types and array *objects*, which are always constrained. What is noteworthy—and indeed of great importance—is that while an array used as a *formal parameter* of a procedure or function is allowed to be unconstrained (unlike array variables, constants, or values), it may nevertheless be treated as having the attributes Range, First, Last, and Length. This is because these attributes of the formal parameter will have a meaning derived from the corresponding actual parameter, when the procedure or function is invoked. We see examples of this in Figures 10.9.3 and 10.9.4.

We mention in passing one further point, a most interesting feature of Ada unconstrained array types. A variable or constant of an *unconstrained* array type (which, like every variable and constant of this type, must itself be *constrained*) may be assigned to another variable of this same type, provided that both objects have the same *length*, though not necessarily the same *range*. Thus, recalling again the declaration

```
type INTEGER_ARRAY is array (NATURAL range <>) of INTEGER;
```

we might declare the variables

```
Ten_Integers: INTEGER_ARRAY(1..10);
Ten_Numbers:  INTEGER_ARRAY(17..26);
```

and since both variables are of the same unconstrained type INTEGER_ARRAY and have the same length, we may make the assignment

```
Ten_Integers := Ten_Numbers;
```

even though the two array variables have different ranges.

Finally, we return to the array-processing subprograms Sum, Max, Index_of_Max, Min, Index_of_Min, Location, Sort_Up, and Sort_Down and observe that they can be more applicable if we modify each one to employ a formal parameter of type INTEGER_ARRAY, rather than SOME_INTS. Each of the subprograms can then be called with any array (actual parameter) of type INTEGER_ARRAY, no matter what NATURAL range has been employed to index this array. What modifications will we need to make in order to achieve this end? Besides changing the constrained type SOME_INTS to the unconstrained type INTEGER_ARRAY throughout, we have to change some references to array indexes. Before, we were dealing with an array parameter whose index range was 1..N; now, our formal parameter is of the unconstrained type INTEGER_ARRAY, and it is only in terms of the attributes of this parameter that we can refer to its range, either as Int_Data'Range or as Int_Data'First..Int_Data'Last. Our references to certain specific indexes of the array thus need to be "translated," as is done in Figure 10.9.2.

Former reference	New reference
1	Int_Data'First
2	Int_Data'First+1
N	Int_Data'Last

Figure 10.9.2

Also, whereas our function Location formerly returned 0 to indicate "number sought was not found," our revised function will return −1 in this case, since 0 may now be a legitimate index of the arrays we are dealing with. With these remarks, we offer an updated version of Location (one of several possible versions of it—see Figure 10.9.3) and Sort_Up (Figure 10.9.4), leaving it to you to make the needed modifications in the other array-processing procedure and functions.

```
-- This function takes as actual parameters an array of
-- type INTEGER_ARRAY and an INTEGER value; it searches the
-- given array for the given integer.  If it finds this
-- integer in the array, it stops searching and returns its
-- index as the function value.  If it fails to find the
-- given integer, it returns -1.

function Location (Int_Data:   INTEGER_ARRAY;
                  Int_Sought: INTEGER)        return INTEGER is

   Index:  NATURAL := Int_Data'First;

begin

   while Index < Int_Data'Last and
      Int_Data(Index) /= Int_Sought loop
    Index := Index + 1;
   end loop;
```

```
   if Int_Data(Index) = Int_Sought then
     return Index;
   end if;

   return -1;

end Location;
```

Figure 10.9.3

```
-- The following procedure takes as a parameter any array
-- of type INTEGER_ARRAY and sorts it into ascending order.

procedure Sort_Up (Int_Data: in out INTEGER_ARRAY) is

  Max_Loc:  NATURAL;  -- location (index) of largest component
  Max_Val:  INTEGER;  -- value of largest component

begin

  for End_Index in reverse
    INTEGER range Int_Data'First+1..Int_Data'Last loop

      -- Initialize Max_Loc and Max_Val to beginning of array

    Max_Loc := Int_Data'First;
    Max_Val := Int_Data(Max_Loc);

      -- Search through array, replacing Max_Loc and Max_Val
      -- whenever a larger component is found

    for Index in INTEGER range Int_Data'First+1..End_Index loop
      if Int_Data(Index) > Max_Val then
        Max_Loc := Index;
        Max_Val := Int_Data(Max_Loc);
      end if;
    end loop;

      -- Exchange the largest and the last of the components
      -- indexed by the range Int_Data'First..End_Index

    Int_Data(Max_Loc)   := Int_Data(End_Index);
    Int_Data(End_Index) := Max_Val;

  end loop;

end Sort_Up;
```

Figure 10.9.4

We now have a widely-applicable set of procedures and functions for processing arrays. In the next chapter, we examine how we can package these subprograms and save them for future use in any programming module where they may be needed.

Finally, we recall once more that there is no need to insist that the *component* values of an array be of type INTEGER or even of an integer subtype. They may well be numbers of type FLOAT, BOOLEAN, or CHARACTER or of almost *any* Ada type. What you may find more surprising is that the *indexes* of an array need not be integers; they may be of other types as well. The possibilities and the restrictions in all this are taken up in Chapter 13, when we revisit and extend the array concept.

10.10 Exercises

10.1.1 Without using an array:

(a) Write a program to read three integers Int_1, Int_2, and Int_3, arrange them into decreasing order, and display them in this order.

(b) Do the same for four integers.

(c) Do your programs work properly if two or more of the integers are the same?

10.1.2 (a) Without using an array, write a program to read three integers Int_1, Int_2, and Int_3 and write them in decreasing order. This time, as each integer is read, rearrange this and the ones read earlier (if necessary) so that after each input, the integers already read are maintained in decreasing order before the next integer is read.

(b) Do the same for four integers.

10.2.1 Suppose we have declared an array variable

```
Zeros_and_Ones:  INTS_100;
```

Write a (single) loop to "fill" the array in each of the following ways:

(a) 100 ones.
(b) 50 zeros followed by 50 ones.
(c) 25 zeros, 25 ones, 25 zeros, 25 ones.
(d) (0, 1, 0, 1, 0, 1, ...).
(e) (0, 0, 0, 1, 0, 0, 0, 1, 0, 0, 0, 1, ...).

10.2.2 Given the declarations

```
subtype RANGE_50 is INTEGER range 1..50;
type INTS_50 is array (RANGE_50) of INTEGER;
List, Reversed_List:  INTS_50;
```

write a program to:

(a) Read 50 integers into List and copy them into Reverse_List so that they are in reverse order in the latter array.

(b) Read 50 integers into List, and rearrange them into reverse order within the array List itself. No other array should be used. (An INTEGER variable is needed for exchanges.) Would the program work correctly if List were of type INTS_51 (with an *odd* number of components), rather than of type INTS_50 (assuming, of course, that 50 were replaced by 51 within the program)?

(c) Read *up to* 50 integers (possibly fewer) into List, and keep track of the Count (a variable declaration is needed). Then without using another array, reverse the order of these Count numbers within List.

10.2.3 Consider the program of Figure 10.2.3. For each of the following, tell whether the program would perform correctly if the indicated changes were made. If not, tell why not.

(a) Reverse the order of the statements

```
Count := Count + 1;
Grades(Count) := Input_Value;
```

(b) Initialize Count to 1 instead of 0.

(c) Make the changes indicated in both *a* and *b*.

10.2.4 Revise the program of Figure 10.2.3 so that it first obtains from the user the value of Count (the number of grades to be entered) and then reads the input in a **for** loop, rather than a **while** loop. Is the variable Input_Value needed here? Reconsider the use of Input_Value in the original form of Figure 10.2.3.

10.3.1 Make up some examples of arrays whose components are respectively of types FLOAT, BOOLEAN, and CHARACTER. In each case, try to think of an array that might be of practical use in a program.

10.3.2 We have said that the components of an array may be of almost *any* type. This means that the components of an array may be of an *array* type. What would an array with such components be like? In particular, how might it be pictured? How might it be used in practice, if at all?

10.4.1 Given an array variable List, of type INTS_100, and with values already assigned to each of its components, write statements to accomplish each of the following:

(a) Increment (increase) each component by 1.
(b) Replace each component by 1.
(c) Double each component.
(d) Replace each component by its negative (e.g., 17 is replaced by −17, −23 is replaced by 23, etc.).

Which of these can be done without processing the array on a component-by-component basis?

10.4.2 Write a function Average that accepts an array of type SOME_INTS as a parameter and returns the (integer) average of its component values.

10.4.3 Rewrite the function Sum, Figure 10.4.1, so that it takes a second parameter indicating how many components to sum (starting with the first one). Decide how to deal with a situation in which the function is called upon to add up more components than the array contains.

10.5.1 Does the function Max perform properly if two or more array components are equal? If all are equal?

10.5.2 If two or more array components are equal, what value does Index_of_Max return? If all are equal?

10.5.3 Write the Ada code for the function Index_of_Max *without* using the variable Max_Val.

10.5.4 Write the complete function body of Min.

10.5.5 Write the complete function body of Index_of_Min.

10.5.6 Consider the following:

```
        -- This procedure accepts as an actual parameter
        -- any array of type SOME_INTS and assigns to Max
        -- and Min the values of the greatest and least
        -- components of the array, respectively.

     procedure Find_Extremes (Integer_List: in SOME_INTS;
                     Max, Min:     out INTEGER)    is
```

Write the rest of the procedure body. Use only one loop.

10.5.7 Write a procedure which is similar to the one in Exercise 10.5.6 but which assigns to two **out** parameters the *indexes* (rather than the values) of the greatest and least components of the array.

10.5.8 Comment on the behavior of each of the following, in which a **for** loop is used as an approach to coding the function Location.

```
   (a)    function Location (Int_Data:   SOME_INTS;
                          Int_Sought: INTEGER)    return NATURAL is

          begin

             for Index in RANGE_N loop
               exit when Int_Data(Index) = Int_Sought;
             end loop;
```

```
        if Int_Data(Index) = Int_Sought then
          return Index;
        end if;
        return 0:

    end Location;
```

(b)   function Location (Int_Data: SOME_INTS;
                          Int_Sought: INTEGER)   return NATURAL is

```
    begin

        for Index in RANGE_N loop
          if Int_Data(Index) = Int_Sought then
            return Index;
          end if;
        end loop;
        return 0;

    end Location;
```

(c)   function Location (Int_Data: SOME_INTS;
                          Int_Sought: INTEGER)   return NATURAL is

```
    Loc: NATURAL := 0;

    begin

        for Index in RANGE_N loop
          if Int_Data(Index) = Int_Sought then
            Loc := Index;
          end if;
        end loop;
        return Loc;

    end Location;
```

10.5.9 Write a version of the function Location that uses the construct **loop ... end loop**, along with an **exit when** statement, instead of a **while** loop.

10.5.10 Criticize the following version of the program of Figure 10.2.3, to obtain grades continuously from the keyboard until a signal entry, −1, is entered. (We show here only the fragment that gets the grades; all other code is the same as in Figure 10.2.3.)

```
-- Read the grades, keeping track of their count

loop
  Int_IO.Get (Grades(Count+1));
  exit when Grades(Count+1) < 0;
  Count := Count + 1;
end loop;
```

10.6.1 In the selection sort procedure Sort_Up:

    (a)   Suppose that the largest component of the array is the *last* one (with index N). Is there any problem about exchanging the largest component and the last component when they are the same component? More generally, is there any problem about exchanging Int_Data(Max_Loc) and Int_Data(End_Index) if Max_Loc = End_Index?

    (b)   What if an array element is already in its proper position before the sorting process begins? Is it "moved around" at all? If the entire array as given is already in ascending order, what will the procedure do?

    (c)   What if all the array components are equal?

10.6.2 In a selection sort applied to an array of type SOME_INTS, how many exchanges are carried out?

10.6.3 Trace through the method you used in Exercise 10.1.1, and decide whether or not it was that of a selection sort. If not, analyze the reasoning you employed and generalize it to sort an array of type SOME_INTS.

10.8.1 Sketch a syntax diagram, analogous to the one in Figure 10.2.2, for the definition of an integer array type indexed by an arbitrary integer range (i.e., not restricted to the form 1..N).

10.8.2 Declare an array type whose objects would be suitable and convenient for holding (integer) data relating to each of the years of the twentieth century.

10.8.3 Each of the linear search subprograms of Section 10.5 was written as a *function*, while that of Figure 10.8.2 was written as a *procedure*.

    (a)   The technique of inserting Int_Sought into the array provides a reason for writing a procedure, rather than a function. Explain why this is so, and point out how this change is reflected in the subprogram's formal parameter list.

    (b)   It would be possible to write a function Location using the array component Int_Data(0) as a sentinel, provided it is understood that the calling program must do the "managing" of this array component. How would this be done, and what would be the code for the function body?

10.8.4 Comment on what value the procedure Locate returns by way of its formal parameter Location if the integer sought occurs in the array several times.

10.9.1 Sketch a syntax diagram, analogous to the one in Figure 10.2.2, for the definition of an unconstrained integer array type indexed by an integer range.

10.9.2 (a) Rewrite the function Sum (Figure 10.4.1) to accept a parameter of the unconstrained array type INTEGER_ARRAY.

 (b) Do the same for the function Max (Figure 10.5.1).

 (c) Do the same for the function Index_of_Max (Figure 10.5.2).

 (d) Do the same for the function Min.

 (e) Do the same for the function Index_of_Min.

Chapter 11

More on Packages

We have been using the package concept since our first programming effort in Chapter 1—in that instance, the packages Text_IO and Int_IO. Chapter 3 was devoted to a rather heuristic investigation of packages. However, despite the informal approach we have taken so far, we have actually learned quite a bit about the ideas that surround the concept. Specifically, we know:

1. Packages may consist of functions and procedures (among other things) that can be made available to programs via a **with** context clause.

2. Some packages are generic in nature and require *instantiation* in order to create an "actual," usable package of routines.

3. Packages are not exclusively for input and output (for example, the package Int_Pack of Sections 3.5 and 3.6), although most of our examples thus far are exactly for those purposes.

4. Packages may contain declarations, for example, of types, constants, and exceptions, and all these are made available to the programmer just as the package's subprograms are (see the packages Date_Types and Date_Pack of Section 11.3 below).

Our brief investigations have even revealed that packages consist of two separate but related entities, namely, the package's *specification* and the package's *body*. In this chapter we examine the formalisms involved and the "rules" for writing packages. We also see how packages can be used further to improve the ease of coding and the appearance of our programs.

11.1 Some details of compilation and linking with packages

In Sections 3.5 and 3.6 we introduced the package specification and package body for a small group of functions and procedures that we named Int_Pack (Figures 3.5.1 and 3.6.1); the small program Test_Int of Figure 3.5.2 did a minimal (but scarcely complete) job of testing the package. What underlying activities take place, at the compiler and linker level, when a package such as Int_Pack is "included" in a main program, such as Test_Int, via the **with** context clause? Figure 11.1.1 helps us visualize these activities.

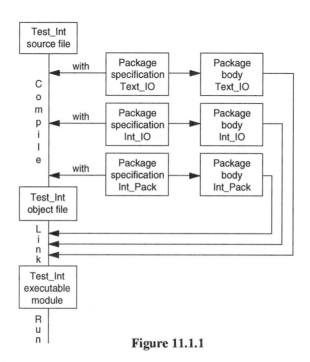

Figure 11.1.1

What will take place when in the course of the translation of the source file Test_Int, the Ada compiler encounters the reference to Decrease? Recall that the context clause **with Int_Pack** makes available the *declared objects* of that package, and thus, the subprogram declaration for Decrease (as well as for Increase and Exchange, etc.) is available to the compiler. The compiler can use Decrease's declaration to verify that the number and type of actual parameters are consistent with the formal parameters of this procedure. In fact, this is the *only* concern of the compiler at this point, namely, verification that the procedure call is *valid*; what will happen when this subprogram executes is of no concern to the compiler. That is, for the successful compilation of a calling statement, all that need be known about the subprogram is its *specification*, as described above. We have indicated this compilation feature in Figure 11.1.1 by the the left-pointing arrow, labeled **"with,"** from each package specification to the vertical line labeled "Compile."

If what is required for a successful compilation as outlined here is important, of equal importance is what is *not* required, and in particular we see that the *compiler* need not know how the procedure Decrease actually implements the rearrangement of the parameters into decreasing order. Once again our Figure 11.1.1 is consistent with this notion, for the *implementations* of the functions and procedures—the *code* for those subprograms—are located in the package bodies, and as we see, there is no direct line in the figure from the package bodies to the "Compile" phase of the process.

Of course the actual Ada code for the procedure Decrease must ultimately be executed, which implies that somewhere along the line it must be translated to its corresponding machine-executable form—it must be compiled. Decrease, along with the other subprograms in the Int_Pack body, has been compiled, but the compilation has been separate from the compilation of Test_Int. We have seen the separate compilation and consequent generation of a compilation unit before; the procedure Decrease was compiled in Section 3.6 when the package body Int_Pack was compiled. This still leaves the following question: Even though the code for the subprograms in the package body of Int_Pack has been compiled (into a separate compilation unit), if that code is not "included" by the compiler in the object file that the compiler creates, how can it ever be executed? The answer lies in the construction of the *executable module* Test_Int, which is created not by the compiler but by the *linker*. It is the linker's responsibility to locate all the references to Decrease in the Test_Int object file and to direct these references to the compiled (and thus executable) code of Decrease in the Int_Pack package body compilation unit. Thus, as indicated in Figure 11.1.1 by the arrows emanating from the package bodies, these units play a role at **link time**.

We return to Figure 11.1.1 later in this chapter, for despite its simple appearance, the concepts embodied in this figure are some of the most far-reaching in the language.

11.2 Two more sample packages

A popular and useful activity frequently found in computing environments has to do with questions about the calendar. For example, we are sometimes interested in the day of the week on which a specified date did or will fall; it is occasionally required to know if a given year is a leap year; and business applications have frequent need for the generation of the date following a given date (or perhaps following a given date by a certain number of days or months). In this section we create two related packages that form a nucleus of declarations, procedures, and functions that you may wish to extend.

In dealing with dates, we need to treat several sorts of integers, namely, the month number (1 to 12), the day number (1 to 31), and a year. Years are restricted to the range 1601 through 10,000; the reasons for these limits are a bit arcane, but the choices ensure that any valid year will be *after* the change in the calendar from the Julian to Gregorian (which took place in 1582) and are still small enough to be valid on a machine whose largest integer is 32,767. We have also included a day-of-the-week number, in which each day is assigned an integer value between 0 and 6. To eliminate some of the errors that can occur, for example, when these numbers are input via the keyboard, it is natural to declare subtypes that constrain the possible values of month, day, and year objects. We do this in the *package* shown in Figure 11.2.1, which can then be included in any program that deals with dates.

```
package Date_Types is

   --  Subtype declarations used to constrain objects of types
   --  MONTH, DAY, and YEAR
```

```
subtype MONTH           is POSITIVE range 1..12;
subtype DAY             is POSITIVE range 1..31;
subtype YEAR            is POSITIVE range 1601..10000;

--  For the days of the week, we take Sunday = 0,
--  Monday = 1, ..., Saturday = 6.

subtype DAY_OF_WEEK     is NATURAL  range 0..6;

end Date_Types;
```

Figure 11.2.1

Figure 11.2.1 is a package specification that can be compiled and then included in any program that needs to declare objects of these types. What is to be in the corresponding package body? The answer is, since the package specification contains the declarations of *no* executable objects (functions or procedures), there simply is *no* package body! When this package is used, it is referenced only for its declarations, never to invoke any executable code that is in it (it has none, of course). We use this package in a second package, Date_Pack, which contains a few subprograms that you will recognize as useful in dealing with dates. Its specification is shown in Figure 11.2.2.

```
with Date_Types;

package Date_Pack is


--  The number of days in the months of a (non-leap) year.

Mon_Length:     constant array (Date_Types.MONTH) of
                     Date_Types.DAY  := (31, 28, 31, 30, 31, 30,
                                         31, 31, 30, 31, 30, 31);

--  Exception raised in package body whenever some date is invalid

Date_Error:     exception;


----------------- Functions and procedures ---------------------

--  Return the length of any month

function Month_Length (Mo: Date_Types.MONTH;
                       Yr: Date_Types.YEAR := 1994)

                         return Date_Types.DAY;


--  Respond to the query: Is the given year a leap year?

function Leap_Year (Yr: Date_Types.YEAR) return BOOLEAN;


--  Convert a date (Month,Day,Year) to the day immediately following
```

```
procedure Next_Day (Mo: in out Date_Types.MONTH;
                    Dy: in out Date_Types.DAY;
                    Yr: in out Date_Types.YEAR);

end Date_Pack;
```

Figure 11.2.2

The array Mon_Length should be obvious; it contains the length of each month, February shown as having 28 days. (You will see in the package body how we accommodate February in leap years.) The purpose of the exception Date_Error is to deal with dates that are invalid. Even though we have constrained the values that objects of types MONTH and DAY can take on, a variable of type DAY could legitimately take on the value 31. But when combined with a MONTH variable having the value 4, we have an invalid date: April 31. Thus simply constraining the ranges of various variables does not take care of all possible invalid dates, and Date_Error is used to warn of these other cases.

The values returned by the functions Month_Length and Leap_Year should be obvious. Note, however, that Month_Length has a default parameter; ordinarily, when we ask for the length of a month, the year is immaterial *unless* the month is February. Thus the function is written so that the user need not supply a year unless the month is February, and even then the year is critical only if it is a leap year. (Why?) The procedure Next_Day accepts a Month/Day/Year date and *changes* some (or all) of the actual parameters to the Month/Day/Year of the day *following*. Its parameters are all of mode **in out**, so that they may be modified to yield the appropriate "return" values.

```
package body Date_Pack is

   --  Internal procedure to verify that a given date is valid.
   --  The procedure returns if the date is valid, raises the
   --  exception Date_Error otherwise.

   procedure Check_Date (Mo: in Date_Types.MONTH;
                         Dy: in Date_Types.DAY;
                         Yr: in Date_Types.YEAR) is

      begin

         if (Mo = 2 and Leap_Year (Yr) and Dy <= 29) or else
            (Dy <= Mon_Length (Mo)) then
               return;
         end if;

         raise Date_Error;

      end Check_Date;

   function Month_Length (Mo: Date_Types.MONTH;
                          Yr: Date_Types.YEAR := 1994)

                          return Date_Types.DAY is
      begin

         if Mo = 2 and then Leap_Year (Yr) then
            return 29;
         end if;
```

```
        return Mon_Length (Mo);

    end Month_Length;



    function Leap_Year (Yr: Date_Types.YEAR) return BOOLEAN is

    begin

        return (Yr rem 400 = 0) or
                ((Yr rem 4 = 0) and (Yr rem 100 /= 0));

    end Leap_Year;


    procedure Next_Day (Mo: in out Date_Types.MONTH;
                        Dy: in out Date_Types.DAY;
                        Yr: in out Date_Types.YEAR) is

    begin

        Check_Date (Mo, Dy, Yr);

        if Dy < Month_Length (Mo, Yr) then
            Dy := Dy + 1;
            return;
        end if;

        Dy := 1;
        if Mo = 12 then
            Mo := 1;
            Yr := Yr + 1;
        else
            Mo := Mo + 1;
        end if;

    exception
        when Constraint_Error =>
            raise Date_Error;

    end Next_Day;

end Date_Pack;
```

Figure 11.2.3

We do not have much to say about the code in this package body (Figure 11.2.3); by now you should be able to follow it without great difficulty. To begin, the function Leap_Year is quite simple, *provided* you know that leap years are those that are multiples of 4 but not multiples of 100 unless they are also multiples of 400. Second, notice that we have written a procedure, Check_Date, that raises the Date_Error exception if the date passed to it is invalid and simply returns otherwise. (Check_Date is *not* declared in the package specification; rather, it is needed only in the package body, which explains the use of the term "internal procedure" in the leading comments of that procedure.) Month_Length is quite straightforward, as is Next_Day; but in the latter we have included an exception handler, which raises Date_Error in response to a Constraint_Error. (Why? How can Constraint_Error be raised in Next_Day?)

We use these packages several times later in the chapter. In the meantime, you may wish to compile, link, and execute the interesting little test program of Figure 11.2.4 which exercises all the subprograms in Date_Pack (although most of them only indirectly). Note that it does nothing to respond to an occurrence of Date_Error.

```
with Text_IO, Int_IO;
with Date_Types, Date_Pack;

procedure Test_Date is

    Mo:     Date_Types.MONTH;
    Dy:     Date_Types.DAY;
    Yr:     Date_Types.YEAR;


    procedure Put_Date is

      begin
        Int_IO.Put (Mo,0);
        Text_IO.Put ('-');
        Int_IO.Put (Dy,0);
        Text_IO.Put ('-');
        Int_IO.Put (Yr,0);
      end Put_Date;

  begin

    Text_IO.Put ("Month Day Year: ");
    Int_IO.Get (Mo);
    Int_IO.Get (Dy);
    Int_IO.Get (Yr);

    Text_IO.Put ("The day following ");
    Put_Date;
    Text_IO.Put (" is ");

    Date_Pack.Next_Day (Mo, Dy, Yr);

    Put_Date;

  end Test_Date;
```

Figure 11.2.4

11.3 Package specifications and package bodies: The formalisms

Figure 11.3.1 shows the syntax of package specifications and package bodies. The diagram for **basic declaration** includes the declarations that we have come to expect in the declarative parts of our programs and subprograms—constants, variables, subprogram *declarations* (but not subprogram *bodies*), types and subtypes, generic instantiations, and exceptions. You will find that the package specifications and bodies we have seen so far fit nicely into these patterns, although there is still room for a couple of surprises.

a   basic declaration

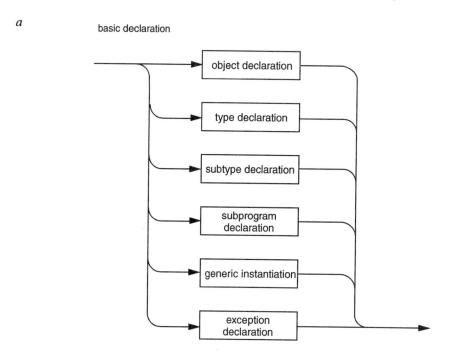

b

package specification

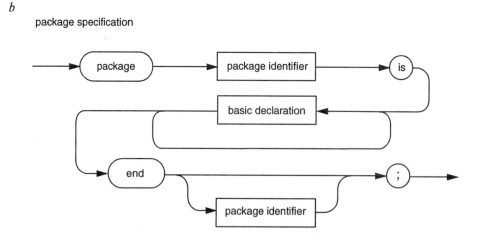

c   package body

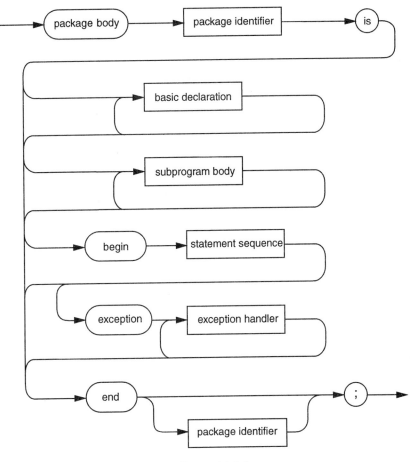

Figure 11.3.1

For example, comparing these diagrams with the package Int_Pack of Figure 3.5.1, we find that in the package specification for Int_Pack there are five *basic declarations*, namely, the declarations of the functions Min and Max and the declarations of the procedures Exchange, Increase, and Decrease. The package body, as shown in Figure 3.6.1, contains no *basic declarations* but five *subprogram bodies* and nothing more. We see from Figure 11.3.1 the possibility of some kind of "frame" structure in the package body, but there is no such frame in Int_Pack, and for the moment we postpone any further discussion of it. As a second example, in Date_Pack (see Figures 11.2.2 and 11.2.3) we find that the package specification contains as basic declarations not just the declarations of three subprograms; it also contains the declaration of the *array* Mon_Length and the *exception* Date_Error. Furthermore, while the package body for Date_Pack, like that for Int_Pack, contains the bodies of the subprograms declared in the package specification, it also contains the declaration and body of a subprogram, Check_Date, which is *not* declared in the package specification. Even granting that this package structure is simple enough, there is nonetheless the interesting fact that the exception Date_Error is *declared* in the package specification but is *raised* in the package body. Evidently both the scope and visibility of Date_Error must extend to the package's body. It is clearly time to make a more formal investigation of the scope and visibility of objects in a package's specification and body, for these are matters of significance to program construction. We take up these considerations in the next section.

We must caution you that the packages we have seen so far are quite simple and perhaps deceptively so. What can go into a package specification is very limited, and our syntax diagram of Figure 11.3.1*b* is, with a couple of minor omissions, about as complex as a package specification can be. But package bodies can include many more sorts of declarations and statements than we have indicated. Package bodies, for example, can themselves include *package specifications* and *package bodies*; and declarations can be placed between the end of a package specification and the beginning of the corresponding package body, which can severely complicate the visibility aspects of objects. Thus the attitude we take at the moment is that we implement as many of the concepts as are needed to support our immediate goals. Some of these concepts are expanded upon in subsequent sections and chapters, but in this book we never discuss the full package implementation. What we do here, therefore, is correct but incomplete; the interested reader who wishes to pursue this concept (and others that we have left intentionally incomplete) can find the details in *LRM*.

11.4 Scope and visibility considerations for packages; the use clause

Before laying down the formal scope and visibility rules for packages, let us see what we can derive based on the known behavior of the Dates packages and test program of Section 11.2 and our understanding of the processes outlined in Figure 11.1.1.

1. We know that any program that includes Date_Pack in a **with** clause has access to the following:

Mon_Length	(array)
Date_Error	(exception)
Month_Length	(function)
Leap_Year	(function)
Next_Day	(procedure)

2. A program that includes Date_Pack in a **with** clause does *not* have direct access to the declarations in Date_Types (even though Date_Pack has), but it can gain access to these by means of an additional **with** clause referencing Date_Types.

3. Since programs can gain access only to declarations in package *specifications*, there is no way that a program can invoke the procedure Check_Date (in the package *body* Date_Pack).

4.   As already suggested, the scope and visibility of the exception Date_Error, as well as the array Mon_Length, must not just extend through the package specification but evidently also extend throughout the package *body*; otherwise, the executable code for Check_Date, Leap_Year, Month_Length, and Next_Day would be unable to refer to them.

5.   Apparently the declaration of Leap_Year, for example, that is made in the package specification must extend to the package body, for we see that in the package body, Check_Date refers to Leap_Year *prior to* its declaration there.

For the purposes of discussing some of the notions that surround the rules for determining scope and visibility of package objects, it is convenient to introduce some informal terminology. The entities—types, subtypes, objects, instantiations, exceptions, and subprograms—that are declared in a package specification are said to be made available for **export** by the package. Any programming module that accesses the package, by way of a **with** clause, and uses one or more of those declarations in some fashion is said to **import** the respective entity. A word of caution: We are using the terms "import" and "export" informally here. You should be aware that there are programming languages and operating systems in which these terms are formal constructs.

The following **scope rules** for package specifications and package bodies do not differ markedly from those for subprograms, as described in Chapter 9:

1.   An entity (type, subtype, object, instantiation, exception, or subprogram) declared within a package *specification* has as its scope *both* of the following:

    a.   The region from the beginning of its declaration to the end of the package body.

    b.   The scope of any **with** clause specifying the package name within any importing module.

2.   An entity declared within a package *body* has as its scope the region from the beginning of its declaration to *either* of the following:

    a.   The end of the package body for entities declared within the declarative part of the package body.

    b.   The end of the subprogram body for entities declared in a subprogram body enclosed within the package body, whether these are formal parameters or other local entities of the subprogram.

The **visibility rules** for identifiers declared within packages are:

1.   An entity declared within a package *specification* has as its visibility:

    a.   The part of its scope contained within the package specification.

b.   The entire package body, except within the (inner) scope of an identically named identifier declared inside the package body (in a subprogram, for example).

2.   An entity declared within a package *body* obeys the visibility rules of Section 9.2 that apply generally to identifiers.

In the preceding section we observed that the exception Date_Error is *declared* in the package specification Date_Pack but *used* (and, equally to the point, not declared) within the corresponding package body, even though the package specification and package body are in different compilation units. We conjectured that the scope and visibility of Date_Error extended through the package body, and we now have confirmation—according to Scope Rule 1*a*, the scope of Date_Error extends to the end of the *body* of Date_Pack, not just to the end of the *specification* of that package. And Visibility Rule 1*b* asserts that Date_Error is visible throughout the entire package body. Finally, from Scope Rule 1*b* we see that the scope of Date_Error (and the array Mon_Length as well) also includes any module that imports Date_Pack via a **with** clause.

In contradistinction to what has just been said about the identifiers Date_Error and Mon_Length in the package specification Date_Pack, consider the procedure Check_Date in the package *body* Date_Pack. The scope of this entity extends only to the end of the package body, by Scope Rule 2*a*, and thus is *not* available to any module that imports Date_Pack via a **with Date_Pack** clause.

The scope and visibility rules for packages also explain a phenomenon that has been with us from the very beginning of the book. Even though a program imports, for example, the packages Text_IO and Flt_IO, each containing a procedure Put, it is not possible for the program to refer simply to "Put"; instead it must explicitly add a prefix to the name "Put" with the name of the package containing it: Text_IO.Put or Flt_IO.Put. The reason is that although Scope Rule 1*b* ensures that both versions of Put exist and thus are accessible throughout the program, there is nothing in the visibility rules to ensure that these procedures can be "seen" by the program. Is there a way to make the objects in an imported package *automatically* visible? The answer is yes, with a new Ada construct, the context clause **use**. The clause

use <package-name>

has the effect of making all the declarations in the named package visible to any program that imports it. This is accomplished by forcing the compiler to search through all packages included in **use** clauses to resolve any reference that is not made explicit by a prefix. Thus if Chr is a CHARACTER variable in a program that imports Text_IO (**with Text_IO**) and includes the statements

```
Text_IO.Put ("The current value of 'Chr' is: ");
Text_IO.Put (Chr);
```

then the inclusion of the context clause **use Text_IO** permits writing these more simply as

```
Put ("The current value of 'Chr' is: ");
Put (Chr);
```

even though these two Puts refer to different procedures (displaying a string of characters is *not* the same as displaying a single character). The **use** clause causes the compiler to search the package Text_IO to find appropriate Put routines (appropriate in the sense of the parameters passed to them).

Inasmuch as many of our programs use the routines from Text_IO, Int_IO, and Flt_IO, would it not make sense—and make the writing of programs less tedious—to routinely include the context clauses

```
with Text_IO, Int_IO, Flt_IO;
use  text_IO, Int_IO, Flt_IO;
```

rather than just the first of these? Yes, this may make the programming a bit easier, but consider a program containing many character, floating point and integer variables. The proposal would allow the sequence of statements

```
Int_IO.Put (X);
Text_IO.Put (C);
Int_IO.Get (Y);
Flt_IO.Put (Z);
```

to be replaced by

```
Put (X);
Put (C);
Get (Y);
Put (Z);
```

While this may be an extreme and contrived example, the point is nonetheless made: The **use** clause, when employed indiscriminately, can significantly reduce the reader's ability to understand the program constructions. For this reason we will continue to use the more lengthy package-name prefix, except in those cases in which a compelling reason exists for the **use** clause. (We see one of these in Section 11.8.)

11.5 The compilation of packages

We have been suggesting throughout the chapter that packages are separate from the modules that use them, in the sense that they undergo *separate* compilation. This is generally true (but not always—the package Integer_IO is declared *within* Text_IO and thus is compiled along with Text_IO, not separately from it). But even given that a package gives rise to a separate compilation unit, we still have two choices, and these are shown in Figure 11.5.1. In Figure 11.5.1*a,* the package specification and the package body are both parts of the *same* **source file**. The rule here is that the package specification must appear first in the source file, and the reason for this should be obvious. (What is it?) In Figure 11.5.1*b* we see that the package specification and body reside in *separate* source files, and thus they undergo separate compilations. As a result of the scope and visibility rules of the preceding section, evidently in these cases the package specification must be compiled first, and upon compilation of the package body, some provision must be made for access to the compiled package specification.

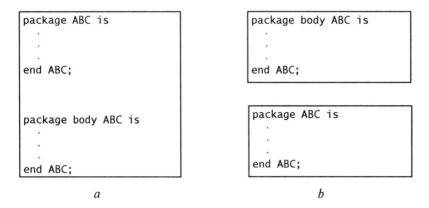

```
package ABC is
  .
  .
  .
end ABC;



package body ABC is
  .
  .
  .
end ABC;
```

```
package body ABC is
  .
  .
  .
end ABC;
```

```
package ABC is
  .
  .
  .
end ABC;
```

a

b

Figure 11.5.1

Most packages can be organized in either way, and neither way is really more difficult for the programmer than the other. Indeed, the technique of Figure 11.5.1*a* would seem to be favored, because all the code for both parts of the package is maintained in the same source file, which appears to improve daily housekeeping chores. In many cases, however, there are significant advantages to keeping the package specification and package body in separate source files. To see why, we return to the package Date_Pack of Figures 11.2.2 and 11.2.3 and the program Test_Date of Figure 11.2.4.

We assume here that the package specification and the package body of Date_Pack have undergone separate compilations, as described in Figure 11.5.1*b*. Later we examine the consequences of a combined compilation of Date_Pack, as in Figure 11.5.1*a*. In the program Test_Date (Figure 11.2.4), we import Date_Pack with the clause **with Date_Pack**. The effect of this clause is to make available to Test_Date the *declarations* found in the package *specification* of Date_Pack. What is notable here is that the package *body* plays no role at this point. Once Test_Date has been compiled, it is linked together with the package body of Date_Pack. All these statements are consistent with Figure 11.1.1.

Suppose that we decide to make a change in the package *body*. For example, we might decide to replace the code in the procedure Next_Day

```
Dy := 1;
if Mo = 12 then
   Mo := 1;
   Yr := Yr + 1;
else
   Mo := Mo + 1;
end if;

exception
   when Constraint_Error =>
      raise Date_Error;
```

by the sequence

```
Dy := 1;
if Mo = 12 then
  Mo := 1;
  if Yr = YEAR'Last then
    raise Date_Error;
  else
    Yr := Yr + 1;
  end if;
else
  Mo := Mo + 1;
end if;
```

in order to eliminate the exception handler. Questions: (1) What effect does this change in the package body have on the package *specification* of Date_Pack? Answer: None. (2) What effect does this change have on the *compilation* of Test_Date? Answer: None, since the package body plays no role in the compilation process of Test_Date. (3) Does the change have an effect on the *linking* of Test_Date? Answer: Yes, since it is precisely the code in the compiled version of the package *body* that is linked with the object file of Test_Date. Finally, we ask the question: (4) After making the change shown above in the package body, what is required to update the executable module for Test_Date? The answer is that the package *body* of Date_Pack must be recompiled (but not the package *specification*) and the Test_Date object file must be relinked (but its source file need not be recompiled).

We now make a second change in the package Date_Pack, in which we *add* a function, Next_PEY (which stands for "next presidential election year") that returns the next year that is a multiple of 4. (All leap years are presidential election years, but the converse is not true.) This change has more far-reaching effects than the previous one. For now, in order to make Next_PEY available to importing routines, we must include its declaration in the package specification of Date_Pack. Since the package specification is what plays a role during *compilations*, evidently modules that include Date_Pack have to be *recompiled*, as well as relinked, whether they invoke Next_PEY or not! The final version of Date_Pack's specification is shown in Figure 11.5.2; we leave it to you to rewrite the package body by including the code for Next_PEY. (Be careful: It is possible that Constraint_Error will be raised in the course of executing this function. How will you handle that occurrence?)

```
    with Date_Types;

  package Date_Pack is


    --  The number of days in the months of a (non-leap) year.

    Mon_Length:     constant array (Date_Types.MONTH) of
                        Date_Types.DAY  := (31, 28, 31, 30, 31, 30,
                                        31, 31, 30, 31, 30, 31);


    --  Exception raised in package body whenever some date is invalid

    Date_Error:     exception;
```

```
------------------ Functions and procedures --------------------

--  Return the length of any month

function Month_Length (Mo: Date_Types.MONTH;
                       Yr: Date_Types.YEAR := 1994)

                       return Date_Types.DAY;


--  Respond to the query: Is the given year a leap year?

function Leap_Year (Yr: Date_Types.YEAR) return BOOLEAN;

--  Convert a date (Month,Day,Year) to the day immediately following

procedure Next_Day (Mo: in out Date_Types.MONTH;
                    Dy: in out Date_Types.DAY;
                    Yr: in out Date_Types.YEAR);


--  Return the Next Presidential Election Year

function Next_PEY (Yr: Date_Types.YEAR) return Date_Types.YEAR;


end Date_Pack;
```

Figure 11.5.2

To sum up this discussion, assume that we have the package ABC (package specification) and the package body ABC, which reside in separate source files, as shown in Figure 11.5.1*b,* and assume that a third source file contains a main program, procedure Main, which begins with the context clause **with ABC**. Then:

1.   To produce an executable version of Main, it is necessary to (a) compile the package specification, (b) compile the package body, (c) compile Main, and (d) link Main. Steps *b* and *c* may be reversed.

2.   If a change is made in the source code of Main, it is necessary to (a) recompile Main and (b) relink Main.

3.   If a change is made in the source code of the package *body,* it is necessary to (a) recompile the package body and (b) relink Main.

4.   If a change is made in the source code of the package *specification,* it is necessary to (a) recompile the package specification, (b) recompile the package body, (c) recompile Main, and (d) relink Main. Steps *b* and *c* may be reversed.

What would have been the consequences of including both the package specification and package body for Date_Pack in the *same* source file, as described in Figure 11.5.1*a*?

Compiling that file would result in the translation of both the package specification and the package body with one compilation, which appears convenient. But note that *any* change in that *file*—whether it affects the package specification or not—will require recompilation of any module that imports the package, for the original package specification has been replaced by a newly compiled one and thus has become obsolete.

11.6 Some package miscellanea

While a package specification normally has a corresponding package body, on occasion it is possible and profitable to write just the specification and delay writing the body. Consider a programming system consisting of a main module Main and many subprograms, which we have grouped together into packages A, B, C, D, and E. We assume that Main requires A, B, C, and D; that B requires D and E; that C requires A; and that D requires C and E. Thus the interrelationships among these modules is somewhat convoluted, and we assume also that the entire system is so large that no one programmer can manage it in a reasonable amount of time. In fact, we assign six programmers, one for each module. It appears that each programmer has to wait for someone else to finish before beginning the assigned module. However, we can take advantage of the package structure in such a way that all programmers can proceed almost immediately: by requiring that the *specification* be created for each package. That is, each programmer decides the types, subtypes, variables, constants, instantiations, and exceptions to be declared in the package which is his or her responsibility. In addition the programmer declares the subprograms in the package specification, complete with user documentation and a formal parameter list. Once this is done, any programmer's module can import needed identifiers from any other programmer's package, and the programmer can successfully *compile* his or her module. As long as a programmer knows how to use another's subprogram, the code making up that subprogram is immaterial—indeed, it is typically "hidden" from the calling programmer anyway. Thus a great deal of progress can be made, even without the existence of *any* package bodies.

Suppose that we have been assigned the task of writing module C, a package whose code relies in part on subprograms in the body of package A. Assume that we have written some of the routines that appear in C's body and we wish to test those subprograms. Thus we write a test program (see, for example, the main program Test_Date of Figure 11.2.4). As long as A's specification module is created and compiled, we can *compile* the test program. But can we link and subsequently execute it? That depends, of course, on just what in A is required by the test program. Suppose the test module requires a procedure P, *declared* within A's specification, but not yet *written* in A's body. Then we will be unable to link the test program *unless* module A's programmer writes a temporary "dummy" version of P— often called a subprogram **stub**—that does nothing except, perhaps, announce that it has been called. Figure 11.6.1 shows a sample procedure stub. When P is invoked by a statement in C, it will not have its ultimate effect; however, we will at least know that we have gotten to P and back, and if necessary, we can write a small segment of code (in module C) to *emulate,* or imitate, what we feel P's action *should* be on the parameters passed to it. This emulator segment will ultimately be removed, once P has been written to achieve its advertised effect.

```
    with Text_IO;          -- To be removed later

procedure P
        (<P's formal parameter list>)
        is

begin

    Text_IO.Put_Line ("Successfully invoked procedure P in package A...");

    end P;
```

Figure 11.6.1

As a final brief comment concerning packages, we expect that you may have been surprised to find *executable statements* ("statement sequence") in the package body, as indicated in Figure 11.3.1c. Recall that a package body owes its existence as a part of an executable module to some external program that accesses it via a **with** clause. Subprogram bodies within the package body are executed by virtue of being called or invoked somewhere in the external program. How then can the executable statements in the package body ever be executed? The answer is quite interesting.

> If a main program contains references to package bodies which in turn contain executable statements, then when the main program is run, any executable statements in any such package bodies are executed *once only* and *prior to the start of execution of the main program.*

If this is the case, to what use might such executable statements be put? The answer is, these executable segments of package bodies are almost always used for *variable initialization.* We give an example in Figure 11.6.2. There are a number of environments in which, in order to handle keyboard input, we need to know where the *tab stops* on the display are; that is, if we encounter a tab character in an input line, we need to know what effect that has had on the display screen's cursor. We assume for the example that the tab stops are in positions 5, 9, 13, 17, ..., 121; that is, each stroke of the tab key moves to a position 4 spaces beyond the last tab stop. You may be aware that positions 9, 17, 25, and so on are the more usual tab stops, but it is frequently useful to reconfigure the display to insert these intermediate positions as well. We wish to create an array of tab stops, in a package specification, so that it is easily imported, and we could do so by declaring, say, Tab_Stops to be a constant array of length 30 and use an array aggregate to assign its value. However, in order to avoid the creation of an obviously long aggregate, we put assignment statements in a **for** loop in the package body. The execution of any module that accesses the package Tabs *first* causes the **for** loop to execute once, which properly loads the array Tab_Stops.

```
    package Tabs is

      subtype Tab_Range is INTEGER range 1..30;

      Tab_Stops:  array (Tab_Range) of INTEGER;

    end Tabs;
```

```
package body Tabs is

begin

  for Tab_Number in Tab_Range loop
    Tab_Stops(Tab_Number) := 4*Tab_Number + 1;
  end loop;

end Tabs;
```

Figure 11.6.2

What of the exception handler section of the executable part of a package body? What exceptions will be sent here for handling? The behavior of exceptions raised in package bodies may be summed up as follows:

1. When an exception is raised *during* execution of the statement part of the package body, then:

    a. If the package body has an exception handler for this exception, the exception is passed to this handler.

    b. If the package body has no exception handler for this exception, then the exception is propagated out to the *Ada run-time system*; that is, the executable segment of a package body executes as a *stand-alone module* embedded in the Ada run-time system, and it is *not* embedded within the main module that has accessed the package.

2. If an exception is raised during execution of the code of a subprogram within the package body that had been called from a module that accessed the package (via a **with** clause) and if the exception is not handled within the subprogram body, then the exception is propagated out to the *calling module* and *not* to the exception handler within the package body's executable segment.

We do not dwell further on these ideas, since these executable segments and their exception handlers are rarely used in day-to-day programming. A few of the exercises will expand a bit on these concepts, and you are encouraged to experiment with the ideas presented here.

11.7 The package Integer_Arrays

The preceding sections have sought to motivate, introduce, and illustrate the important package construct that the Ada language provides. Along the way we have encountered several concepts and language features associated with packages, and we have seen how to use these to our advantage: the distinction between package specifications and package bodies, the scope and visibility rules for packages, and the possibility and utility of separately compiling the specifications and bodies of packages. In this section we develop another Ada package, but this time it is one whose ingredients are already at hand, waiting to be "packaged."

In Section 10.9 we introduced the unconstrained array type INTEGER_ARRAY by the declaration

```
type INTEGER_ARRAY is array (NATURAL range <>) of INTEGER;
```

Objects of this type (for example, the ones we called integer lists, with an index range starting from 1) occur often in information processing. Further, as we have seen, there is a collection of "standard" operations that frequently need to be carried out on such objects—the operations that we have embodied in the array-processing subprograms Sum, Max, Index_of_Max, Min, Index_of_Min, Location, Sort_Up, and Sort_Down. It should be clear at this point that this type declaration and the associated subprograms could be put into a package appropriately named Integer_Arrays. Such a package would be an instance of **reusable software**, a general-purpose programming module (rather than one tailored to a specific need) that could be compiled and saved, then taken "off the shelf" and included (by way of a **with** clause) in any program needing it. Figure 11.7.1 gives the specification for this package.

```
package Integer_Arrays is

    type INTEGER_ARRAY is array (NATURAL range <>) of INTEGER;


        -- Function Sum takes as an actual parameter any array
        -- of type INTEGER_ARRAY and returns the sum of the
        -- components of the array.

    function Sum (Int_Data: INTEGER_ARRAY) return INTEGER;


        -- Function Max takes as an actual parameter any array
        -- of type INTEGER_ARRAY and returns the value of the
        -- greatest integer in the array.

    function MAX (Int_Data: INTEGER_ARRAY) return INTEGER;


        -- Function Index_of_Max takes as an actual parameter any
        -- array of type INTEGER_ARRAY and returns the index of the
        -- greatest integer in the array.  If this integer occurs
        -- more than once in the array, it returns the first
        -- (least) index at which it occurs.

    function Index_of_Max (Int_Data: INTEGER_ARRAY) return NATURAL;


        -- Function Min takes as an actual parameter any array
        -- of type INTEGER_ARRAY and returns the value of the
        -- least integer in the array.

    function Min (Int_Data: INTEGER_ARRAY) return INTEGER;
```

```
            -- Function Index_of_Min takes as an actual parameter any
            -- array of type INTEGER_ARRAY and returns the index of
            -- the least integer in the array.  If this integer occurs
            -- more than once in the array, it returns the first
            -- (least) index at which it occurs.

    function Index_of_Min (Int_Data: INTEGER_ARRAY) return NATURAL;


            -- Function Location takes as actual parameters an array
            -- of type INTEGER_ARRAY and an INTEGER value;  it
            -- searches the given array for the given integer.
            -- If it finds this integer in the array, it returns
            -- as function value the index at which the integer
            -- first occurs.  If it fails to find the given integer,
            -- it returns -1.

    function Location (Int_Data:   INTEGER_ARRAY;
                       Int_Sought: INTEGER)      return INTEGER;


            -- Procedure Sort_Up takes as an actual parameter
            -- any array of type INTEGER_ARRAY and rearranges
            -- its components into ascending order.

    procedure Sort_Up (Int_Data: in out INTEGER_ARRAY);


            -- Procedure Sort_Down takes as an actual parameter
            -- any array of type INTEGER_ARRAY and rearranges
            -- its components into descending order.

    procedure Sort_Down (Int_Data: in out INTEGER_ARRAY);


end Integer_Arrays;
```

Figure 11.7.1

There is little, if anything, to be said about developing the package body Integer_Arrays. All that is needed is to collect the subprogram bodies of the specified functions and procedures, as these were revised in Section 10.9 to accommodate formal parameters of type INTEGER_ARRAY. For the record, however, and to display another instance of the format of a package body, we offer the skeleton package body of Figure 11.7.2.

```
package body Integer_Arrays is

    function Sum (Int_Data: INTEGER_ARRAY) return INTEGER is

        <declarations and statements>


    function Max (Int_Data: INTEGER_ARRAY) return INTEGER is

        <declarations and statements>
```

```
      function Index_of_Max (Int_Data: INTEGER_ARRAY) return NATURAL is

         <declarations and statements>


      function Min (Int_Data: INTEGER_ARRAY) return INTEGER is

         <declarations and statements>


      function Index_of_Min (Int_Data: INTEGER_ARRAY) return NATURAL is

         <declarations and statements>


      function Location (Int_Data:   INTEGER_ARRAY;
                         Int_Sought: INTEGER)        return INTEGER is

         <declarations and statements>


      procedure Sort_Up (Int_Data: in out INTEGER_ARRAY) is

         <declarations and statements>


      procedure Sort_Down (Int_Data: in out INTEGER_ARRAY) is

         <declarations and statements>


   end Integer_Arrays;
```

Figure 11.7.2

What we have accomplished here is far more than the mere packaging of some routines that were created earlier, for the package Integer_Arrays consists of a *type definition*, along with a *set of operations* that can be performed on objects of this type. Packages made up in this way are of frequent occurrence in software development and naturally lend themselves to being reusable, all the more so if the data type declared in them is often needed in programming. Indeed, the concept is of such importance that we devote the next section to it, in which we again create a *type* ("from scratch," this time), along with a collection of permitted *operations* on objects of this newly created type.

11.8 Abstract data types

Throughout the text we have dealt with two numeric data types, namely, INTEGER (and its various subtypes) and FLOAT. Yet it may have occurred to you that there is a quite useful type that has not yet shown itself: the collection of **rational numbers (fractions)** with their familiar arithmetic operations. In fact, this type is *not* defined in Ada. This does not mean that the rationals cannot be defined and used just as any other type. The package Rationals of Figure 11.8.1 (in which we show just the specification) does exactly that—it declares a type, RATIONAL, along with some functions that supply the operations on the rational numbers with which we have come to be familiar, and these can be imported by any program that needs the RATIONAL type. RATIONAL is an example of a what is called an **abstract data type (ADT)**, a term which in general refers to the declaration of a type, along with the specification of the operations that are valid on objects of that type.

```
--  Package Rationals is an implementation of the Abstract
--  Data Type (ADT) consisting of the rational numbers and
--  the arithmetic and comparison operators for that type.

--  Each rational number is a pair of values of type INTEGER,
--  consisting of a Numerator and a Denominator.

--  Rationals which have a negative value always have a negative
--  Numerator.


package Rationals is

    --  The type RATIONAL is declared but its details are private.

    type RATIONAL is private;

    --  The exception Rational_Error is raised whenever a rational
    --  number would be generated having a zero denominator.

    Rational_Error:     exception;


    --  The function Rat returns the rational number whose
    --  numerator and denominator are passed as parameters.

    --  The functions Numerator and Denominator return those
    --  respective parts of the rational number.

    function Rat (Num, Denom: INTEGER) return RATIONAL;

    function Numerator (R: RATIONAL) return INTEGER;

    function Denominator (R: RATIONAL) return INTEGER;

    --  The unary operators "+" and "-" return the rational
    --  itself, and the rational with the sign of its
    --  numerator reversed, respectively. The operator
    --  "abs" returns the absolute value of the rational.

    function "+" (R: RATIONAL) return RATIONAL;

    function "-" (R: RATIONAL) return RATIONAL;

    function "abs" (R: RATIONAL) return RATIONAL;

    --  The binary operators given below return the values
    --  of the results of the corresponding operations on
    --  rational numbers.
```

```
function "+" (Left, Right: RATIONAL) return RATIONAL;

function "-" (Left, Right: RATIONAL) return RATIONAL;

function "*" (Left, Right: RATIONAL) return RATIONAL;

function "/" (Left, Right: RATIONAL) return RATIONAL;


    --  The comparison operators return True or False,
    --  according as the usual comparison between rational
    --  numbers is True or False.

function "<" (Left, Right: RATIONAL) return BOOLEAN;

function ">" (Left, Right: RATIONAL) return BOOLEAN;

function "<=" (Left, Right: RATIONAL) return BOOLEAN;

function ">=" (Left, Right: RATIONAL) return BOOLEAN;


    --  The procedure Get gets two values of type INTEGER
    --  and places in R the rational having those values
    --  as numerator and denominator, respectively.

    --  The procedure Put displays the numerator of the
    --  specified rational value, followed by a slash (/),
    --  followed by the denominator of the rational.  There
    --  are no intervening spaces; there is no provision
    --  for formatting via a field width parameter.

procedure Get (R: in out RATIONAL);

procedure Put (R: in RATIONAL);

private

    type RATIONAL is array (INTEGER range 1..2) of INTEGER;

end Rationals;
```

Figure 11.8.1

You recognize that a few explanations are in order. To begin with, the *type* RATIONAL is declared to be **private**. In effect, this is saying that there is no need to tell the user precisely *how* the type is formed, that is, precisely of *what* Ada objects a rational number consists, as long as the user is assured that an object of type RATIONAL *behaves* like a rational number (fraction)—has a numerator and denominator, has the expected arithmetic, and so forth. It is for this reason that the type is referred to as *abstract;* namely, the details of what the type is and how it is implemented remain "hidden" from the user.

Next, we find a collection of functions, all but one of which operating on rationals (more properly, "objects of type RATIONAL"). That sole exception is an important one, for it allows the user to *form* objects of this type from INTEGERs; specifically, if the user passes to the function Rat two integers, to be used as what we think of as the numerator and denominator of a fraction, then Rat will return a RATIONAL number having those values as numerator and denominator. What is truly curious about most of the remaining functions is their *names*: they are "named" "+", "<=", and so forth. Are these really legal Ada function names? Curiously enough, yes, Ada does allow *some* special names like these, which are familiar symbols. To be specific: The name "Ω"—the quotes are part of the name—may be used for a function name, provided Ω is one of the usual logical, relational, unary, or binary arithmetic operators. (See *LRM [6.7]* for further details.) Note that in most cases we have used the formal parameter names "Left" and "Right." This is not required, of course, but it is quite suggestive, and the names have become traditional.

Consider a program in which we import the package Rationals via the context clause **with Rationals**. If X is of type RATIONAL, how would we represent its absolute value? Surely if we wished to obtain its denominator, we would invoke **Rationals.Denominator (X)**. Would we follow the same pattern and write **Rationals."abs" (X)**? Further, if X and Y are of type RATIONAL, would we represent their product as **Rationals."*" (X, Y)**? Yes, all these function calls are acceptable, but they are unwieldy. However, in the case of operator functions, such as "*" and the like, Ada provides for the more customary "infix" notation (written without the quotes): **X * Y**. But more needs to be said on this point. If the programmer is to employ this simpler way of invoking an operator function, the compiler must be told to look in the package Rationals for the declaration of an operator "*" having two parameters of type RATIONAL. This is done by including in the program, along with the context clause **with Rationals**, a second context clause **use Rationals**. As we learned in Section 11.4, the effect of this is to make it possible to use names and operator symbols declared in the package Rationals (such as **Denominator** and "*") without having to use their respective "expanded names"—in this case, **Rationals.Denominator** and **Rationals."*"**. In fact, operator symbols may then be employed in infix notation (for example, **X*Y**) without the quotation marks.

You may be surprised to observe that *missing* from the list of operators declared in the package Rationals are the *assignment* operator (":=") and the relational operators *equal* ("=") and *unequal* ("/="). The reason for this is that even for private types Ada implicitly defines the assignment of objects of the same (private) type, and can determine when two such objects are the same (=) or not (/=); hence there is no need to redefine these operators for private types. But just as with such operators as "*", the operators "=" and "/=" may not be used in infix form with RATIONAL objects X and Y unless preceded by the clause **use Rationals**; otherwise, instead of **X = Y** we must write **Rationals."=" (X, Y)**.

You may have noticed that in extending the use of operator symbols to objects of type RATIONAL, we have "overloaded" these symbols, much as the procedure name Exchange was overloaded in Section 9.6. In fact, the operators +, -, *, and / have *already* been overloaded by the Ada language itself—they may be applied to operands of integer types and of type FLOAT. Further, the relational operators <, >, <=, and >= apply not only to these same types but with certain other types as well. This phenomenon is known as **operator overloading**; clearly, it is altogether similar to the name overloading we considered in Section 9.6.

Finally, it will seem peculiar that, with all the "secrecy" we seem to be maintaining about just what a RATIONAL is, in the end—at the bottom of the package specification, in a section labeled **private**—we finally come out and tell you: A RATIONAL is an array of two objects of type INTEGER. (We'll be honest with you—the first integer is the numerator of the fraction, the second the denominator.) So now that you know what a RATIONAL is, can you take advantage of that knowledge? No. That is, if you declare a variable, say X, to be of type rational, you may *not* then refer to the numerator of the rational X as X(1), even though that may be what it really is. Why not? Because the type of X (RATIONAL) is *private*. Is this pure perversity on the part of Ada, saying that the type is private and you are not supposed to know anything about it, then telling what it *really* is, and finally not letting you use that information? Not really, and a little reflection will reveal that the *compiler* needs this private information so that it can tell, among other things, how much space in main memory needs to be allocated for any object the programmer declares to be of type RATIONAL. Recall that the compiler must arrange for such allocations and that all the compiler "knows" about the package is what it finds in the package specification. The point here is that except for assignment and tests for equality (= and /=), the programmer who uses this package is not allowed to perform *any* operations on objects of this type except those that are provided in the package specification.

In Figure 11.8.2 we offer a little program that uses rational numbers to calculate the (rational) area of a rectangle having rational dimensions. We have employed the context clause **use Rationals** so that in computing the area, we can write multiplication of rationals as an infix expression. On the other hand, we have continued to use expanded names for the Get and Put procedures of the package Rationals, to make it clear that these names refer to routines declared in this package.

```
      with Text_IO, Rationals;   use Rationals;

   procedure Rectangle is

      Side_1,
      Side_2,

      Area:           RATIONAL;

   begin
      Text_IO.Put_Line ("Enter the sides of the rectangle as rationals:");
      Text_IO.Put ("Side 1: ");
      Rationals.Get (Side_1);
      Text_IO.Put ("Side 2: ");
      Rationals.Get (Side_2);
      Text_IO.New_Line;
      Area := Side_1 * Side_2;

      Text_IO.Put ("The area of the rectangle with dimensions ");
      Rationals.Put (Side_1);
      Text_IO.Put (" by ");
      Rationals.Put (Side_2);
      Text_IO.Put (" is ");
      Rationals.Put (Area);
      Text_IO.Put_Line (".");

   end Rectangle;
```

Figure 11.8.2

If, for example, the numbers (integers)

26 7   and   19 4

are entered in response to the prompts for the sides of the rectangle, the program generates as output the message

```
The area of the rectangle with dimensions 26/7 by 19/4 is 247/14.
```

The package body for Rationals is shown below, and it holds few surprises. It would be completely straightforward (virtually trivial) were it not for the fact that rationals are always maintained in their lowest form; that is, any common factors in the numerator and denominator are always divided out. Thus there are many references to the function (local to the package body) named Reduced, and this fact tends to make the code more untidy than it would otherwise be. Note that the function Reduced makes use of the function GCD of Figure 9.8.1.

```
with Text_IO, Int_IO;

package body Rationals is

   -- Function Reduced returns a rational reduced to lowest terms;
   -- raises Rational_Error if the denominator is zero; and
   -- ensures that the denominator is positive.

   function Reduced (R: RATIONAL) return RATIONAL is

      Sign:       INTEGER := 1;
      CD:         POSITIVE;
      Num:        INTEGER := R(1);
      Denom:      INTEGER := R(2);

      function GCD (A, B: POSITIVE) return POSITIVE is

         Num_A:      Positive := A;
         Num_B:      Positive := B;
         Temp:       Positive;

      begin
        loop
          if Num_A rem Num_B = 0 then
            return Num_B;
          else
            Temp := Num_B;
            Num_B := Num_A rem Num_B;
            Num_A := Temp;
          end if;
        end loop;
      end GCD;

   begin
     if Denom = 0 then
       raise Rational_Error;
     end if;

     if Num = 0 then
       Denom := 1;
       return (Num, Denom);
     end if;
```

```
   if Denom < 0 then
      Denom := -Denom;
      Num := -Num;
   end if;

   if Num < 0 then
      Num := -Num;
      Sign := -1;
   end if;

   CD := GCD (Num, Denom);

   Num := Sign * (Num/CD);
   Denom := Denom/CD;

   return (Num, Denom);

end Reduced;


function Rat (Num, Denom: INTEGER) return RATIONAL is

  begin
    return Reduced ((Num, Denom));
  end rat;


function Numerator (R: RATIONAL) return INTEGER is

  begin
    return R(1);
  end Numerator;


function Denominator (R: RATIONAL) return INTEGER is

  begin
    return R(2);
  end Denominator;

function "+" (R: RATIONAL) return RATIONAL is

  begin
    return R;
  end "+";


function "-" (R: RATIONAL) return RATIONAL is

  begin
    return (-R(1),R(2));
  end "-";


function "abs" (R: RATIONAL) return RATIONAL is

  begin
    return (abs R(1),R(2));
  end "abs";
```

```
function "+" (Left, Right: RATIONAL) return RATIONAL is

  begin
    return Reduced ((Left(1) * Right(2) + Left(2) * Right(1),
                Left(2) * Right(2)));
  end "+";


function "-" (Left, Right: RATIONAL) return RATIONAL is

  begin
    return Reduced ((Left(1) * Right(2) - Left(2) * Right(1),
                Left(2) * Right(2)));
  end "-";


function "*" (Left, Right: RATIONAL) return RATIONAL is

  begin
    return Reduced ((Left(1) * Right(1), Left(2) * Right(2)));
  end "*";


function "/" (Left, Right: RATIONAL) return RATIONAL is

  begin
    return Reduced ((Left(1) * Right(2), Left(2) * Right(1)));
  end "/";

function "<" (Left, Right: RATIONAL) return BOOLEAN is

  begin
    return Left(1) * Right(2) < Left(2) * Right(1);
  end "<";


function ">" (Left, Right: RATIONAL) return BOOLEAN is

  begin
    return Right < Left;
  end ">";


function "<=" (Left, Right: RATIONAL) return BOOLEAN is

  begin
    return not (Left > Right);
  end "<=";


function ">=" (Left, Right: RATIONAL) return BOOLEAN is

  begin
    return not (Left < Right);
  end ">=";


procedure Get (R: in out RATIONAL) is
```

```
begin
  Int_IO.Get (R(1));
  Int_IO.Get (R(2));
  R := Reduced (R);
end Get;

procedure Put (R: in RATIONAL) is

begin
  Int_IO.Put (R(1),0);
  Text_IO.Put ('/');
  Int_IO.Put (R(2),0);
end Put;

end Rationals;
```

Figure 11.8.3

11.9 Packages and subprograms: Modularization and abstraction

In Chapter 8 we noted two advantages to be gained from the use of *subprograms* (procedures and functions) in program development:

Modularization of operations

A subprogram puts together in one "chunk," or **module** (not necessarily one that is separately compiled), whatever programming is necessary for carrying out a specific operation—for example, getting input, performing computations with this input, displaying output. It is said to **encapsulate** the operation by "tying together" the steps (statements) involved in this operation, along with whatever associated data, if any, may be needed, such as locally declared types and objects. In this way, the details of the operation (its steps and auxiliary data—equivalently, its statements and local declarations) are gotten out of the way of the main thrust of the program, with several ensuing advantages, not the least of which is program clarity. The use of subprograms for purposes of modularization is particularly encouraged by the top-down programming method.

Abstraction by parameterization: Reusability

It is possible to write and call a parameterless procedure Exchange to interchange the values of two particular INTEGER variables. Such a procedure may well serve the purpose of modularizing this operation. However, if the procedure is written with two INTEGER formal parameters (of mode **in out**), then the procedure can be applied to *any* pair of integer variables by passing them to it as actual parameters when it is called (see Section 8.7). The procedure has been made *abstract*: It has been freed from the limitation of applicability to only a single specific pair of variables. The parameters have provided the procedure with this quality of abstraction and made it reusable, that is, usable with *various* pairs of INTEGER variables. In general, the use of formal parameters in subprograms makes it possible to call these subprograms with different sets of actual parameters, thus rendering them broadly applicable. They have become abtsract by *parameterization* and, consequently, are reusable in a variety of settings, even if only within a single program module.

If we reflect on the properties and capabilities of packages (in contrast to subprograms) and refer to the examples we have seen in this chapter, we can see that packages offer us similar advantages.

Modularization of data

Packages collect and put together what is needed to specify data types, objects, and associated operations on those objects. This is known as **data encapsulation**. Just as subprograms are concerned with *operations* and their associated data (if any), packages are typically concerned with *data* types and their associated operations (if any). The packages we have developed in this chapter are of this kind: The package specification—"seen" by the program that makes use of the package—contains type or subtype declarations, along with declarations of the operations (subprograms) associated with these types. It is evident that good use of packages serves to keep programming clear and uncluttered: Package specifications and package bodies are usually in different compilation units from (and therefore not in the way of) the program that uses them. Furthermore, implementation details hidden in the package body are completely invisible to this program. Other advantages of the modularization that packages provide were noted in Section 11.6, which discussed the role of packages in the development of very large software projects by programming teams. As a final point under this heading, Ada's package capabilities make it a suitable language for implementing **object-oriented programming**, a method currently much in use, especially for the large software projects to which we have just referred. Top-down programming, as we have seen, proceeds by asking, "What are the successive actions to be carried out, and what are the steps needed to carry out each one?" In contrast, object-oriented programming begins by asking, "What are the (real-world) objects of the program, and how may each one be described in terms of data types and associated operations?" There is much, much more to be said about this programming method, but a great deal of it depends on an acquaintance with data types and structures that lies outside the scope of this book. Our point here is simply that just as subprograms are instrumental in the implementation of top-down programming, packages play a similar role in implementing object-oriented programming, a method that is presently increasing in importance and use.

Abstraction by specification: Modifiability

In our description of the package body Integer_Arrays, whose outline appears in Figure 11.7.2, there is a deliberate ambiguity. We said that to complete the package body, all that was needed was to copy into it the bodies of the various procedures and functions included in Integer_Arrays. But what about the function Location for which *two* correct versions were offered during the course of Section 10.5? Which of these (accommodated to a formal parameter of the unconstrained type INTEGER_ARRAY) should be included in the package body? The answer is that *either* one of them is acceptable, and that is because the package Integer_Arrays (and indeed *any* package) enjoys the property of **abstraction by specification**. This means that the *specification* of the package, which is all that is "known" to and needed by the program using it, is independent of the way in which the package (in particular, any subprogram it contains) is *implemented* in the package body. Thus, the implementation of any subprogram in a package may be selected freely by the programmer of the package body from among all those that correctly do what the specification says the subprogram is to do; furthermore, it may subsequently be modified—for example, to make it faster or more sparing in its use of computer memory. After any such modification, of course, the package body will have to be recompiled. However, as pointed out in Section 11.5, neither the package specification nor the program that uses the package will have to be modified, nor will either have to be recompiled. The main program needs only to be linked again, so that the resulting executable module will incorporate the new object file of the package body. What comes out of all this is the *modifiability* of the package body. The programmer of the package body is free to make changes in it (improvements or other new approaches), provided they are in keeping with the package specification. None of the possibly many source programs that use this package will be affected thereby, nor need any of these source programs be adjusted in any way. This is of enormous importance, for suppose it were *not* so and think of a package used by many programs; then think of all the needed changes in source code that might have to be tracked down and carried out in these programs each time a change was made in the implementation of the package (the package body). As matters stand, package implementations are easy to modify—as long as the package *specification* remains unchanged, there is no danger that such modifications will have "cascading" effects.

11.10 Exercises

11.2.1 In the package Date_Types we declared the day of the week to be a number ranging from 0 to 6, rather than from 1 to 7, which might seem more natural. Justify our choice. (Suggestion: Consider the **rem** operator, its values, and how it might be used in computations involving the day of the week.)

11.2.2 Based on your understanding of Figure 11.1.1, explain why the procedure Check_Date (in the package body of Date_Pack) is *not* accessible to any program that includes Date_Pack in a **with** clause. How could Check_Date be made accessible?

11.2.3 Explain how you would invoke Month_Length for each of the following months.

   (a) January, 1917
   (b) March, 1944
   (c) February, 1907
   (d) February, 1944
   (e) February, 1900

11.2.4 Explain the purpose of the exception handler in the body of the procedure Next_Day in the package Date_Pack.

11.2.5 Include an exception handler in the test program of Figure 11.2.4 to deal, in some reasonable way, with the Date_Error exception. Are there other exceptions that could be raised during the execution of this program?

11.3.1 Verify that the package specifications and package bodies of the packages Int_IO, Flt_IO, Int_Pack (see Figures 3.5.1 and 3.6.1), and Date_Pack are instances of the syntax diagrams of Figure 11.3.1. In each case, relate each object in the actual package to some part of the diagram (for example, basic declaration, exception handler, etc.).

11.4.1 Answer the question of Exercise 11.2.2 again, in the light of what you now know about the scope and visibility of package entities.

11.4.2 Despite the fact that it would seem to be useful in its own right, we might argue that at least in the present form of the package Date_Pack, the function Leap_Year is used *only* in the package body. Could that function be made "local" to the package body, and thus inaccessible by any importing program, simply by removing its declaration from the package specification? (The answer is a qualified yes, but there is more to be done. What is it?)

11.4.3 What would be the consequences of moving the declaration of the exception Date_Error from the package specification to the package body?

11.4.4 What would be the consequences of declaring an exception named Date_Error in the package body of Date_Pack, in addition to the exception Date_Error already declared in the package specification? (First, conjecture the consequences. Then try this to see how the compiler reacts. Can you explain or justify the compiler's rationale for its behavior?)

11.4.5 What changes would you make in the package Date_Pack to make the procedure Check_Date accessible to programs that import this package?

11.4.6 You might find it a bit peculiar that the array Mon_Length is declared in the package *specification* of Date_Pack; it is perhaps unlikely that a program that has imported Date_Pack would actually use Mon_Length, in view of the fact that the function Month_Length can supply (almost) the same values in an apparently more convenient way. State what would be required to move the array into the package body. What effect would this change have on programs using Date_Pack that have already been compiled and linked?

11.4.7 A problem that does not deal directly with the package notion but which *is* related to the scope and visibility concepts of Section 11.4 was brought up in Chapter 8. In Figure 8.9.3c we noted that the configuration was unacceptable, and the reason was that the body of the function Maximum_3 has a reference to Maximum_2, a function yet to be declared and thus one which is not visible during the compilation of

Maximum_3 (in fact, one which does not even exist during that compilation). As a slightly less cluttered example, consider the complete program Sample shown below.

```
with Text_IO, Int_IO;

procedure Sample is

  procedure Pr_1 (X:  INTEGER) is

  begin

    Text_IO.Put ("Executing procedure Pr_1 with a value of ");
    Int_IO.Put (X, 0);
    Text_IO.New_Line;
    Pr_2 (X-1);

  end Pr_1;

  procedure Pr_2 (X:  INTEGER) is

  begin

    Text_IO.Put ("Executing procedure Pr_2 with a value of ");
    Int_IO.Put (X, 0);
    Text_IO.New_Line;
    if X > 0 then
      Pr_1 (X-1);
    end if;

  end Pr_2;

begin          --  Begin Sample execution

  Pr_1 (4);

end Sample;
```

(a) Explain why the compiler should be *unable* to generate the object file for this program. Then create a source file for Sample and submit it to your Ada compiler, to verify that your explanation was correct.

(b) Insert the procedure specification

```
procedure Pr_2 (X:  INTEGER);
```

immediately ahead of the declaration of Pr_1. Verify that your modified source file now compiles without error. Explain why.

(c) What is the output of the program of part (b) when it is linked and executed?

11.6.1 In Section 9.6 we considered several versions of a swapping procedure, and we concluded that the most sensible names for *all* these were identical, say, Exchange. Consider three such swapping procedures, one that exchanges the contents of two

INTEGER variables, another that exchanges the contents of two FLOAT variables, and a third that swaps CHARACTER variables.

(a) Write a package specification (but *not* a package body at this time) that contains the specifications of the three procedures named Exchange noted above. Call this package specification Ex_Pack. Now compile this package specification.

(b) Write a small (mainline) test procedure, Ex_Test, that imports Ex_Pack; declares a pair each of variables of type INTEGER, FLOAT, and CHARACTER; assigns these variables some values and displays them; invokes Exchange on pairs of these variables; and then finally displays the variables again.

(c) Verify that Ex_Test can be *compiled*, even though it invokes a package whose body does not even exist. Can Ex_Test be linked? Explain why or why not, and then verify your assertion by attempting to link Ex_Test.

(d) Write the procedure body for the INTEGER version of Exchange. (In fact, this has already been done; see Figure 8.7.1.) Put this in a source file for the package *body* of Ex_Pack; that is, create a file containing

```
package body Ex_Pack is

  procedure Exchange (A, B: in out INTEGER is

    <body of INTEGER version of Exchange>

  end Exchange;

end Ex_Pack;
```

Our intention here is to compile this package body (at least, as far as it goes), thus yielding a "partial" Ex_Pack package, one that implements the INTEGER version of Exchange. However, show (by trying it) that the compiler insists that bodies for *all* subprograms declared in the package specification be declared in the package body. Thus, in a sense it is not possible to write a partial package; it is all or nothing, as far as the package body is concerned.

(e) To satisfy the compiler's objections to the package body created in part (d) above, expand it to include a procedure body for the other two versions of Exchange. Make the body of each of those two added procedures consist simply of the following code:

```
begin
  null;
end Exchange;
```

Recall that **null** is an Ada construct that really does nothing in this context, but it satisfies the syntax of a subprogram body, which *requires* that there be a statement sequence here. See the syntax diagram of Figure 8.3.1*a* or 8.7.4*b*. The package body should now compile without error.

(f)   In step (a) we created the package specification for Ex_Pack, and in (b) we created a small test program to exercise the package. In step (c) we determined that the test program, Ex_Test, could be compiled but not linked. Now that, in step (e) above, we have successfully created a package body for Ex_Pack which is "complete" as far as the compiler is concerned (despite the fact that two of the procedures in it do precisely nothing), we should be able to link Ex_Test. Does Ex_Test require a recompilation at this point? Explain why it does or does not, and then verify your answer by attempting to link Ex_Pack without recompiling it.

(g)   Complete the writing of *one* of the procedure bodies in the package body Ex_Pack (say, the CHARACTER version of Exchange), and then recompile the package body. Verify once again that Ex_Test does *not* require recompilation and that simply relinking produces an executable module for Ex_Test which now demonstrates the swapping of the two CHARACTER variables. Now complete the writing of the body of the FLOAT version of Exchange in the package body, and test again as above.

(h)   We wish to enhance the total Ex_Pack package by adding an Exchange procedure for variables of type BOOLEAN. Explain carefully and completely what steps have to be taken to accomplish this, and then verify your explanation by carrying out this enhancement of the package.

11.6.2 Some desk calendars tell not only the current date but also the day of the year and the number of days to follow; for example:

March 12, 1994: Day 71, 294 days to follow

To make these computations, we need to know how many days have elapsed from the beginning of the year to the beginning of each month. Suppose we decide to implement some software in Date_Pack to produce such computations. We have use for an array containing the numbers 0, 31, 59, 90, ..., namely, the offsets in days of the beginning of each month. Suppose we call this array Mon_Offset and declare it in the specification for Date_Pack as

```
Mon_Offset:     array (Date_Types.MONTH) of
                   NATURAL := (0, ?, ?, ...);
```

Rather than do "by hand" the calculations required to complete the aggregate to give Mon_Offset its value, we can let the statement part of the package body do the job, much as the tab stops were calculated in Figure 11.6.2. Use the values in Mon_Length, and write a small **for** loop to load this array any time Date_Pack is imported.

11.6.3 Use the results of Exercise 11.6.2, and introduce a function, Day_Of_Year, that gives the number of a specified date within its year. (Thus, for example, the function should return the value 71 when supplied with the parameters **3 12 1994**: March 12, 1994.)

11.8.1 Write a test program that begins with the context clauses **with Rationals** and **use Rationals** and "exercises" as many as possible of the features of the package (ADT) Rationals.

11.8.2 Extend the package Rationals to include an (integer) exponentiation operator, ******. Verify this extension with an appropriate small test program.

11.8.3 Write a small program that after declaring X, Y1, Y2, Z1, and Z2 to be of type RATIONAL, assigns a value to X and attempts the assignments

```
Y1 := "abs" (X);
Y2 := "abs" X;
Z1 := abs (X);
Z2 := abs X;
```

to determine which (if any) of these forms is acceptable. Explain. What context clause(s) did you use, and how do they affect your results?

11.8.4 Write a program that accepts three *positive* rational numbers from the keyboard and announces that they can or cannot be used as the lengths of the sides of a triangle.

11.8.5 A **complex number** can be thought of as a pair of real (FLOAT) numbers, **(R,I)**; **R** and **I** are called the **real part** and **imaginary part**, respectively, of the complex number. Look up in an appropriate reference (if necessary) the rules for the arithmetic of complex numbers—addition, subtraction, multiplication, and division—and create an abstract data type (ADT) for complex numbers, in a fashion similar to the package Rationals. Can the relational operators <, <=, >, and >= be defined for these numbers? What features different from those included in Rationals are appropriate for this type?

Chapter 12

Discrete Types

Thus far in this book we have focused our attention on four different types: INTEGER (and its subtypes), FLOAT, BOOLEAN, and CHARACTER. (We also introduced **array** types in Chapter 10, and more is said about arrays in Chapter 13, but we choose not to include these *structured types* in the present discussion.) Of these four types, we are certainly most familiar with INTEGER. FLOAT has been used occasionally when the need has arisen; the type is not especially complicated, and the details were discussed in Chapter 4. Our interest in BOOLEAN objects has been restricted principally to their uses as *values* in various conditional statements, although we have also found some use for BOOLEAN variables that indicate that some circumstance is in effect or that some event has occurred. CHARACTER entities have been used infrequently, primarily as variables for input (Get) statements, whose values are then used as answers to program queries.

There are a couple of ways in which we might divide these four types into *classes*; one obvious way is to place INTEGER and FLOAT into the class of numeric types, with BOOLEAN and CHARACTER then being in the category of nonnumeric types. Another, perhaps less obvious way, is one discussed in Chapter 5. We know that every object of type INTEGER, BOOLEAN, or CHARACTER has an *immediate successor* and an *immediate predecessor*. Of course, the first value in each of these types has no predecessor, and the last object has no successor. What is important here is that the *concepts* of predecessor and successor are meaningful for such types. In contrast, no object of type FLOAT has either an immediate predecessor or immediate successor. In the type BOOLEAN, False has a successor (True), and True has a predecessor (False), although neither of these enjoys the opposite property. Therefore, even BOOLEAN satisfies the condition, and thus it is legitimate to group it with INTEGER and CHARACTER relative to this criterion. (What are the predecessor and successor of a CHARACTER? At this point a satisfactory answer is the characters that immediately precede and succeed the given character in Appendix B.) These three types belong to the class of **discrete types**, and later in the chapter we are more specific about just what types comprise this category. To begin, we have a more careful look at the nonnumeric types and, in particular, at the important type CHARACTER, which received only a cursory treatment in Section 5.2.

12.1 Nonnumeric types

The management of a type not inherently numeric is not especially difficult. We need to recognize that, generally speaking, the underlying computer operates only on numeric data. As a consequence, we require a segment of code (written in machine language, say, and supplied with the operating system) that converts each nonnumeric item to a numeric datum for storage in the computer's memory and for possible manipulation by the computer's processing unit. When such a converted datum is ready to be presented to the "outside world," another segment of code converts the numeric item back into its original form. These conversions to and from the numeric equivalents are called **encoding** and **decoding**, respectively. The numeric value that replaces a nonnumeric item in the computer's memory is referred to as that item's **code**. (Do not confuse this use of the word "code" with our informal use of the word to mean programming, programming statements, or computer instructions.)

Some of the details of the management of nonnumeric data by the compiler and the run-time system can be illustrated by one of the nonnumeric types with which we have been dealing since Chapter 5, namely, BOOLEAN. A few of the basic facts we know about this type are:

1. Objects of type BOOLEAN can take on one of only two values, True and False.

2. The relational operators <, >, <=, >=, =, /= are applicable to objects of type BOOLEAN, the resulting value being also of type BOOLEAN (and deriving from the fact that False is less than True).

3. BOOLEAN objects also have a special set of operators, namely, the binary operators **and**, **or**, and **xor** and the unary operator **not**.

Just how is, say, a BOOLEAN variable OK managed by the Ada compiler? We can make some educated conjectures about this, and we can assume that when the compiler sees the *declaration* of such a variable, it provides storage to be set aside for it, notes that that storage is associated with the variable which the program has named OK, and that the variable (and hence, in some sense, the associated storage) is of type BOOLEAN. Now what happens, upon compilation, if a statement such as

```
OK := True;
```

is encountered? The compiler verifies that the statement is appropriate, in the sense that the types of the variable and the value match, and it then generates the machine instructions required to place the *code* for the value of True into the storage assigned to the variable OK. Upon execution, this numeric code replaces the contents of that storage location. And what *is* the code assigned by the compiler to the BOOLEAN value True? The answer is really not terribly important to the programmer, whose sole concern here is that the values True and False behave as we have described them. A possible set of values might be: False = −1, True = 0 (although while this particular choice is not unusual, neither is it in any sense *dictated*).

Note that these specific assignments result in numeric codes for True and False that are numerically compatible with the relational operators of item 2 above.

12.2 The type CHARACTER

In order to process *text*—strings of *characters*—we must be able to store the text in the computer's memory, and as we have seen, this requires the encoding of those characters to corresponding numeric values. Unlike the situation encountered with the BOOLEAN type, the choice of encoding scheme for characters has some fairly deep and extensive consequences. There are many more values than just two that require encoding, and while we may have no ideas about how True and False *should* be ordered (False < True? True < False?), we *do* have some preconceived notions about the ordering among the characters, or at least some of them (A < B < ... < Z, a < b < ... < z, for example, taking "<" to mean "precedes in the alphabet"). In particular, there are three easily identified considerations in devising a coding scheme for the characters.

1. The encoding scheme must be unique. That is, no two characters may have the same numeric code. (In mathematics terminology, the function that maps the characters to the integers must be *one to one*.) To see why, suppose that both characters **Q** and *@* were encoded to the number 17. While there would be no problem in *encoding* either character, how would we *decode* the number 17? As **Q**? *@*?

2. The coding scheme should be convenient for the programmer—or better, perhaps, "rational." We cannot be specific about what is meant here, but we can give one simple example. If the numeric codes for A to Z are in increasing order (for example, 10 to 35, or even 21, 23, 53, 64, ...), then determining whether one character precedes another in the alphabet (a task that the computer literally cannot perform) amounts to asking if the first character's code precedes that of the second character, as integers (a task that the computer can perform).

3. The code should be standardized, so that text information generated ("written") by one computer at one site can be decoded ("read") by another computer at a second site.

It is clear that neither item 2 nor 3 is *essential*, but a failure to adhere to them can create vast problems which are mostly unnecessary.

Over the history of electronic computing, literally thousands of encoding schemes have been in use, some special purpose, some experimental. A few general-purpose character encodings have survived, and of these the most pervasive is the scheme known as **ASCII** (American Standard Code for Information Interchange, pronounced "askee"), the code we use in this book. Just what characters are encoded by the ASCII coding scheme, and what properties do the codes have? The answers to these questions will be found by investigating the table of Appendix B, and we can make a few observations here. First, we see that the codes are all nonnegative, begin at 0, run to 127, and contain no gaps. Second, we find that the codes for the alphabetic characters (A to Z and a to z) do indeed increase and, in fact, are *consecutive* increasing integers. The same is true for the *digits* 0 to 9 (which are *characters*, not to be confused with the *numbers* 0 to 9). Third, there are a few mysteries, such as, Why do the alphabetic characters begin at 65 (and 97, for the lowercase characters) rather than, say, 1 or 100? Why don't the codes for the digits—numeric characters—correspond to the digits themselves (that is, why isn't the code for the character *0* the number 0, for the character *1* the number 1, and so forth)? What has prompted the encoding of the so-called special characters—the nonnumeric, nonalphabetic characters, such as [,], =, #, @? And what are the characters called BEL, NUL, HT, VT, ESC, SI, DC3, and so forth? To unveil the meanings of all these symbols, as well as the rationale behind all the choices made in developing the ASCII coding scheme, would require a deeper understanding of the computer as a machine than we wish to pursue, so some of these will simply remain mysteries. In fact, an understanding of them would contribute only marginally, if at all, to our present development.

Let us review briefly what we already know about this type. CHARACTER may be used for the declaration of variables, constants, subprogram parameters, and function values. A CHARACTER literal is signified by enclosing the particular character in single quotes: **'Q'**. Thus, for example, the constructs of Figure 12.2.1 are all valid.

```
Alpha,
Beta,
Gamma:     CHARACTER;                    --  Declare 3 variables

Delta:     CHARACTER := 'D';             --  Declare and initialize
                                         --  one variable

Bracket:   constant CHARACTER := '[';    --  Declare constant

   .
   .
   .

Alpha := Delta;
Gamma := Bracket;

Text_IO.Get (Beta);

if Beta < 'F' then
  Text_IO.Put (Delta);
end if;
```

Figure 12.2.1

We also know that the relational operators (<, <=, /=, and so forth) apply to CHARACTER objects as well as to numerical objects, and we can now tell you that the relationship between two CHARACTER entities is precisely the same as the numerical relationship between their corresponding ASCII codes.

12.3 Input and output of objects of type CHARACTER

As its name implies, the package Text_IO provides for the direct input and output of text, that is, characters and strings of characters, so no instantiation of a package for CHARACTER type is required. Rather, Get, and Put will, respectively, read (from the keyboard) and write (on the display) items of type CHARACTER. Thus the input and output of characters is especially simple, and only a few details need to be examined.

If Ch is an expression (and thus, in particular, a variable or literal) of type CHARACTER, then

```
Text_IO.Put (Ch);
```

causes the CHARACTER value of Ch to be shown at the display's current cursor position (or printhead position, for a printing terminal). Unlike the Put routine derived from the package Integer_IO, the Put procedure for characters has *no* optional field width parameter that can be passed to it. Thus characters are always displayed at the cursor or printhead position. If a character is to be displayed right-justified in a field of width N, then the programmer will have to supply N − 1 leading spaces—for example, by using a loop:

```
for K in INTEGER range 1..N-1 loop
  Text_IO.Put (' ');
end loop;
Text_IO.Put (Ch);
```

Input of characters is as simple as output, but one feature requires discussion. Recall from Section 7.11 that when data are obtained from the user's keyboard, a keyboard buffer is filled with characters, followed by an **end-of-line marker**, and a keyboard **buffer pointer** is set to the first character in the buffer. In Chapter 7 we were in the business of reading *integers* from the keyboard, and so in addition to reading numeric characters—digits—the integer Get routine also converted those characters to INTEGER form. Now, apart from this conversion, the same activity takes place when reading characters, and as an example, suppose we type the string of characters

```
Rats!
```

at the keyboard, followed by RETURN or ENTER. The keyboard buffer and buffer pointer will then have the appearance shown in Figure 12.3.1 where, as before, the symbol EOL represents the end-of-line marker.

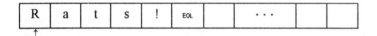

Figure 12.3.1

Now at the first instance of, say, **Text_IO.Get (Ch)**, the character *R* is placed in the variable Ch, and the buffer pointer moves to the character *a*. Another **Text_IO.Get (Ch)** assigns Ch the value *a*, the pointer moves again (to point at the *t*), and after two more occurrences of such a Get statement, the buffer pointer points at the character **!** (Figure 12.3.2).

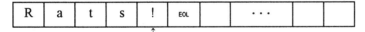

Figure 12.3.2

Now when **Text_IO.Get (Ch)** is executed the next time, three activities take place: (1) The character **!** is assigned to the variable Ch, (2) the buffer pointer moves over and thus points at the end-of-line marker (ᴇᴏʟ), and (3) a BOOLEAN-valued function, End_of_Line, returns the value True (if invoked at this time). Because of this last event, we have a means of determining that we have come to the end of the line of characters which have been entered via the keyboard, and we shortly show how our programming can take advantage of this fact.

What is new here, of course, is the introduction of the function End_of_Line, and there are two questions that come immediately to mind regarding it. First, if encountering the end of an input line causes End_of_Line to return the value True, can we assume that the value returned by this function *prior* to encountering the end-of-line marker, and in particular prior to typing *anything* at the keyboard, will be False? Second, how can we "reset" this function—ensure that it will return False—so that the next Get will not also see End_of_Line returning True? As reasonable as these questions are, it is difficult to give a direct answer to either of them without a bit more insight into this function.

The BOOLEAN-valued function End_of_Line is a function declared within the package Text_IO and, when applied to the *keyboard* buffer, requires no parameter. (But see Section 12.11.) When this function is invoked, as we might do in statements such as

```
if End_of_Line then ...
```

or perhaps

```
while not End_of_Line loop ...
```

the function examines the keyboard buffer and the keyboard buffer pointer. If it finds that characters are in the buffer and that the buffer pointer is not pointing at the end-of-line marker, then the function returns the value False, as we would expect. If it finds that an end-of-line marker is in the buffer and that the buffer pointer is pointing at it, then the function End_of_Line returns the value True, again as anticipated. But what happens if the function sees an *empty* keyboard buffer? In this case it cannot reasonably return *either* value True or False, for if the buffer is empty, there is no end-of-line marker at all. Thus if the buffer is empty, the function End_of_Line *waits for the buffer to fill* with some number of characters (possibly none), *followed by* the end-of-line marker. Then it is able to make a determination as to whether or not the pointer is at end of line.

We can now respond to the two questions posed above. First, the function End_of_Line *will* return False prior to encountering the end-of-line marker in the keyboard, *provided* something is in the buffer; otherwise, the function will wait for the buffer to become nonempty (in particular, the buffer will be nonempty if it contains *only* the end-of-line marker—as a result of pressing ENTER without first pressing some other character key). Thus, when a program first begins its execution, End_of_Line will not return a value; it must wait for something to enter the keyboard buffer. Second, if End_of_Line returns True as a result of the buffer pointer pointing at the end-of-line marker, then executing either another Get or Skip_Line will cause the keyboard buffer to become empty; and, as we have seen, this in turn will cause End_of_Line to *stop* returning the value True. But it will not *start* to return the value False—in fact, it will not return *any* value —until something else is put into the keyboard buffer.

Having examined what appears to be the somewhat aberrant behavior of an otherwise perfectly respectable BOOLEAN (behavior that is actually quite rational once it is understood what End_of_Line really is), we use it to control the execution of a simple but interesting and potentially useful bit of code. The program of Figure 12.3.3 accepts a string of characters from the keyboard, followed as always by ENTER, and displays back the same string of characters, first having reduced consecutive space (or blank) characters to a *single* space.

```
--   Program Trim_Spaces accepts a string of characters
--   from the keyboard and displays on the screen the same
--   string, with consecutive space or blank characters
--   having been reduced to a single space character.

with Text_IO;

procedure Trim_Spaces is

    Ch:         CHARACTER;

    Is_Space:   BOOLEAN := False;

    Space:      constant CHARACTER := ' ';

begin

    while not Text_IO.End_of_Line loop

      Text_IO.Get (Ch);

      if (Ch /= Space) or (not Is_Space) then
        Text_IO.Put (Ch);
        Is_Space := False;
      end if;

      if Ch = Space then
        Is_Space := True;
      end if;

    end loop;

    Text_IO.New_Line;

end Trim_Spaces;
```

Figure 12.3.3

The BOOLEAN variable Is_Space is set to True whenever a space is encountered, so that if *another* space is seen immediately afterward, it can be ignored. Is_Space is set to False each time a nonspace character is encountered. Observe, however, that if a line *begins* with one or more spaces, the program leaves exactly one such "leading blank." Verify that if Is_Space is initialized to True instead of False, all leading blanks are removed, as well as multiple blanks elsewhere. The logic of the use of End_of_Line is quite simple. Initially, End_of_Line can return no value, since the keyboard buffer is empty. Thus it must wait for something to be typed at the keyboard. When that occurs, assuming that what was typed consists of more than just ENTER, End_of_Line returns False and the loop executes, displaying the first character in the buffer. If End_of_Line is still false, the next buffer character (if not a second space) is displayed. And so forth until the end-of-line marker is encountered, End_of_Line returns True, and the loop exits. (What will be output if ENTER is the *only* thing entered at the keyboard?)

As another very simple but highly useful application of character input, consider the frequently arising situation in which the programmer must ask the user a question that is answered yes or no. We have used this technique several times already. (See Figure 6.7.7 for an example of this.) The following segment of code will do the job. Here we are assuming that Ans is a variable declared to be of type CHARACTER.

```
Text_IO.Put ("Do you want to continue processing (Yes/No)? ");
Text_IO.Get (Ans);
Text_IO.Skip_Line;
if Ans = 'Y' or Ans = 'y' then
  <continue processing>;
else
  <discontinue processing>;
end if;
```

Figure 12.3.4

Note that having gotten the *first* character of the user's response, in the variable Ans, we "throw away" any further characters that may have been typed by means of the **Text_IO.Skip_Line** construction. Next we examine this first character to see if it is *Y* or *y*, namely, to see if the user has responded in the affirmative. Recall that, as usual, since we do not know whether the user has typed the answer in uppercase or lowercase, we must examine the response for both possibilities.

Before leaving this section, we note that the behavior of End_of_Line when we get *integers* from the keyboard buffer does not differ substantially from what has just been described for *characters*. That is, End_of_Line has no value until some characters (which we take as making up one or more integers) appear in the buffer, at which time End_of_Line will return False; when all of the characters in the buffer have been read, End_of_Line will return True; and when another Get or Skip_Line is executed, the buffer will again empty, so End_of_Line will no longer return True (or anything else, for that matter). The reason that we did not make a great fuss over the end-of-line marker and its associated BOOLEAN-valued function End_of_Line back in Chapter 7 is that when reading numbers, we typically know *how many* such are to be read; we read that many and stop—and perhaps, to be on the safe side, clear out the buffer with Skip_Line. In reading *text* (characters), it is quite typical that we do not know in advance how many characters there are, and thus we rely on some kind of "signal" that all the available characters have been read—that we have "come to the end of the line."

We do need to note that if an input line of characters, which are to be read as *integers*, contains *trailing* blanks, then upon getting the last integer in the input line, End_of_Line will remain False; and a subsequent integer Get will only empty the buffer of its trailing blanks and again require further filling of the buffer to satisfy the Get. Thus in this special case, End_of_Line will *not* return False when the last integer in the buffer has been read.

12.4 Enumeration types

In several of the examples and exercises so far we have dealt with the days of the week and the months of the year. And on those occasions we have denoted these by the integer ranges 0..6 and 1..12, respectively. Now while our usual method of writing dates has accustomed us to thinking of the months in numerical terms (although most people still prefer "August" to "8"), the assignment of numbers to the days of the week is certainly unnatural. If it was possible to declare days and months by their familiar names rather than by these numerical codes, then for example the declaration

```
JAN_1_1601:          constant DAY_OF_WEEK := 1;
```

or a program statement such as

```
if Mo > 2 and Leap_Year (Yr) then ...
```

could be written in more familiar and pleasing forms as

```
JAN_1_1601:          constant DAY_OF_WEEK := Monday;
```

and

```
if Month > Feb and Leap_Year (Yr) then ...
```

respectively. In a similar fashion, in a program written for the control of street traffic, a statement such as

```
if Light = 2 then ...
```

is less appealing than

```
if Light = Amber then ...
```

What we would like is to be able to use Amber as a *literal* of some *type*, a type to which the variable Light would also have to belong. While it would be quite out of the question for us to expect Ada to supply a *standard* type containing *literals* such as Red, Amber, Green, Defective, Blinking_Yellow, and so forth, Ada does provide the *programmer* the ability to declare types such as this. Such a programmer-declared type is called an enumeration type, since the programmer *lists*—or *enumerates*—the objects that make up the type. More precisely, and in a slightly broader context, an enumeration type is one that is defined by listing its values. The objects making up the type are called the literals of the enumeration type. We offer two simple and, by now, familiar examples.

```
type   DAY_OF_WEEK   is (Sunday, Monday, Tuesday, Wednesday,
                          Thursday, Friday, Saturday);

type   MONTH         is (Jan, Feb, Mar, Apr, May, Jun,
                          Jul, Aug, Sep, Oct, Nov, Dec);
```

For the record we show the syntax diagram for an enumeration type declaration in Figure 12.4.1.

enumeration type definition

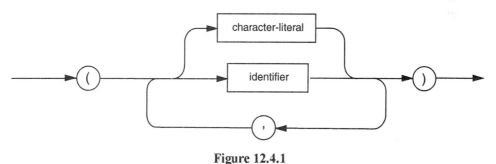

Figure 12.4.1

12.5 Enumeration type input and output

The input of variables and the output of "values" of enumeration types are very similar to their INTEGER counterparts, so there will be little new to learn. The rules for keyboard input of a variable of some enumeration type, via an appropriate Get routine, are the following:

1.   Beginning at the current position of the keyboard buffer pointer, blank (space) and tab characters are discarded. If the only thing remaining in the keyboard buffer after these discards is the end-of-line marker, the buffer is empty and must be refilled. After the buffer is refilled, the buffer pointer is set to the first character position and step 1 is reexecuted.

2.   When the first nonblank, nontab character is encountered, characters are accumulated until a character is encountered that cannot belong to any identifier or character literal (such as blank, or ',' or '$' or, for that matter, the end-of-line marker). This character itself is not "read."

3.   If the string of characters accumulated in step 2 is empty or does not match one of the literals in the enumeration type, Get raises the exception Data_Error. Otherwise, the enumeration literal read is assigned to the variable parameter of the Get.

We offer some examples in Figure 12.5.1, where we assume that X is a variable of type MONTH, as described above. As usual, we use the symbols ƀ, ƚ, and ᴇᴏʟ to represent blanks and tabs, and the end-of-line marker, respectively.

	Keyboard Buffer	Value placed in X by GET(X)	
(a)	ƀ ƀ O C T ƚ 1 9 4 8 ƀ ᴇᴏʟ	OCT	
(b)	ƀ ƀ O c t ƚ 1 9 4 8 ƀ ᴇᴏʟ	OCT	
(c)	ƀ ƀ o c t ƚ 1 9 4 8 ƀ ᴇᴏʟ	OCT	
(d)	ƀ ƀ ƀ ƀ ƀ ƀ ƀ ƀ O C T ᴇᴏʟ	OCT	
(e)	ƀ ƀ O c t 1 9 4 8 ƀ ƀ ᴇᴏʟ	---	(Data_Error raised)
(f)	ƀ ƀ O c t _ 1 9 4 8 ƀ ᴇᴏʟ	---	(Data_Error raised)
(g)	ƀ ƀ O c t @ 1 9 4 8 ƀ ᴇᴏʟ	OCT	
(h)	ƀ ƀ @ O c t 1 9 4 8 ƀ ᴇᴏʟ	---	(Data_Error raised)

Figure 12.5.1

It is clear from examples *a* to *d* that the month name may be entered in either upper- or lowercase or a mixture of these, a reflection of Ada's case insensitivity. In *e* and *f* the exception Data_Error is raised since the identifiers read by Get are Oct1948 and Oct_1948 respectively, and neither of these is defined by the declaration of the type MONTH. That is, the object read is inappropriate to the type of the variable X to which that object is to be assigned. In *g*, character scanning stops with the symbol @, since this symbol cannot belong to an Ada identifier. Note that the situation in *g* is slightly different from those of *a* to *c*. In the first three examples of Figure 12.5.1, if we wished to read both the month and year, the two statements

```
Get (Mo);
Get (Yr);
```

would do the job. Here we assume that Mo is of type MONTH, Yr is of type INTEGER or some subtype thereof that includes 1948, and the two Gets are appropriate input routines, a matter we discuss shortly. But in *g*, we would need something like

```
Get (Mo);
Get (Ch);
Get (Yr);
```

where Ch is of type CHARACTER. (Why?) Finally, the Get in *h* will cause Data_Error to be raised, for the first nonblank, nontab character encountered is @, a character whose use is not valid in an identifier and thus not in an enumeration type literal.

An expression, which may be a variable or literal, of some enumeration type can be output to the user's display via the Put routine in Text_IO. Like the INTEGER version of Put, but unlike the CHARACTER version, the enumeration type version of Put, accepts a *field width* parameter of type NATURAL. But unlike the putting of INTEGERs, enumeration entities are displayed *left*-justified in their specified fields. Thus, if X = Jan and Y = Oct, then (again assuming the appropriate output routine is used in each case) the sequence

```
Put (X,5);
Put (Dec);
Put (Y);
```

results in the output

```
JANØØDECOCT
```

We infer from this example—and in particular from the way in which DEC was displayed— that the default field width for enumeration types is 0; that is, the item is displayed without leading or trailing spaces.

We also note from some of these examples that variables of enumeration types may be entered in either uppercase or lowercase—again, because of Ada's case insensitivity—but apparently the values of expressions of these types are always displayed in uppercase. In fact, Ada displays enumeration type entities in uppercase characters regardless of how they are listed in their type declaration or entered via the keyboard. It is possible to display these values in lower-case characters as well, and how this can be accomplished is found in *LRM [14.3.9]*. However, Ada cannot be instructed to display these as they were entered, or in some mix of upper- and lowercase characters.

It comes as no surprise that in order to get and put entities of programmer-declared enumeration types, an appropriate I/O package must be instantiated. The generic package whose instantiation gives rise to a specific package of input/output routines for a particular enumeration type is named **Enumeration_IO**. It is declared in the package Text_IO, and it is instantiated just as the package Integer_IO is. For example, the instantiations

```
package Mo_IO is new Text_IO.Enumeration_IO (MONTH);
package DoW_IO is new Text_IO.Enumeration_IO (DAY_OF_WEEK);
```

permits the input and output of entities of types MONTH and DAY_OF_WEEK, respectively.

12.6 The packages Standard and ASCII*

In Appendix D is a listing of a package named **Standard**. The first entry in that package is the *declaration* of the type BOOLEAN as an *enumeration type*. That is, BOOLEAN, as a *type*, is no more special than what a programmer might create as any enumeration type. Some operators are also defined there, and we deal with a few of them later in this chapter.

Examining the package Standard a bit further, we encounter another enumeration type declaration, CHARACTER. Thus the CHARACTER type that we introduced in Chapter 5 and expanded upon in the present chapter is another example of an enumeration type. What is peculiar about it, though, is the fact that the literals in the type are enclosed in single quotes. We might have expected, say, R to be a CHARACTER literal, but we find that the literal is 'R' instead. In fact, a glance at the earlier sections of this chapter reveals in our dealings with this type a certain lack of consistency that needs to be addressed.

We make statements such as "*Q* is a CHARACTER" and "the CHARACTER variable X has the value *H*," but we also write statements like

```
Delta:   constant CHARACTER := 'D';
```

and

```
if Beta < 'F' then ...
```

where, in keeping with what we have just recalled, the literals of type CHARACTER are enclosed in single quotes. But what of the CHARACTER versions of the Put and Get routines? When we enter a character from the keyboard in response to a Get request, we enter it as *R*, not 'R'. When a character is put to the user's display, it shows up without the leading and trailing quotes. The explanations of these apparent anomalies are the following:

1.   The literals in the enumeration type **CHARACTER** *are* enclosed in single quotes (except for the first 32 of them, shown in Appendix D in italics).

2.   The routines Get and Put, declared in the package **Text_IO** for input and output of entities of type CHARACTER, are *special cases*. In effect, they do not behave like their Enumeration_IO counterparts since they automatically insert (in the case of Get) or remove (in the case of Put) the leading and trailing quotes that *should* surround each literal of type CHARACTER.

3.   When we speak of the character (or CHARACTER) *R*, we *are* guilty of an imprecision, but it is one that is not serious or apt to lead to misunderstandings and one whose explication would frequently involve untenable circumlocutions.

The first 32 entries in the type CHARACTER, as declared within the package Standard, are a bit peculiar. As the comment that precedes the type declaration indicates,

---

*This section may be omitted.

they are *not* identifiers. However, there is a *package*, named ASCII, that declares (programmer-usable) identifiers for these 32 characters and makes them accessible for programming. As we see, such identifiers as NUL, SOH, ..., RS, US, and DEL are defined, as well as a few others (Exclam, Quotation, Tilde, etc.) that were already accessible. But what do NUL, SOH, and so forth mean? More properly, what is "displayed" or what action is taken by the user's display when such a character is Put? And is it possible to get these characters? For all intents and purposes, the answer to the latter question is no: Most of these characters cannot be directly input through the keyboard. As to what happens when they are Put, we will answer that question for a few of these codes and abandon the others as being essentially useless to us in the present environment. The table in Figure 12.6.1 describes what some of these characters do upon being Put.

Character	Name	Action taken when Put
BEL	Bell	Causes the "bell" to sound
BS	Backspace	Causes the cursor/printhead to back up one space
HT	Horizontal tab	Moves the cursor/printhead to the next tab position
LF	Line feed	Causes the cursor/printhead to move down the display one line (but not change its horizontal position)
CR	Carriage return	Causes the cursor/printhead to move to the first column of the display (but not change its vertical position)

Figure 12.6.1

As a simple application of these "special" codes, consider the program of Figure 12.6.2, in which special symbols are printed by means of **overstriking**, that is, by printing one (standard) character first, *backspacing*, and printing a second character on top of the first. Required here is a hard-copy (or printing) terminal—as opposed to a video terminal—or a printer that has backspacing capabilities. On such a device the output of this program is

$\leq$

$\neq$

θ

On a video output device, the result of executing this program is

```
  _
 /
  _
```

(Why?)

```
    with Text_IO;

  procedure Special_Symbols is

  begin

      Text_IO.Put ('<');    --   'less than or equal'
      Text_IO.Put (ASCII.BS);
      Text_IO.Put ('_');
      Text_IO.New_Line;

      Text_IO.Put ('=');    --   'not equal'
      Text_IO.Put (ASCII.BS);
      Text_IO.Put ('/');
      Text_IO.New_Line;

      Text_IO.Put ('0');    --   Greek letter 'theta'
      Text_IO.Put (ASCII.BS);
      Text_IO.Put ('-');
      Text_IO.New_Line;

  end Special_Symbols;
```

Figure 12.6.2

Observe that we have used the expanded name ASCII.BS for BackSpace, since BS is declared in the package ASCII. But what may seem puzzling is that we have succeeded at all, inasmuch as there is also no **with** clause for this package (more properly, for the package Standard which in turn contains the package ASCII). Our success is accounted for by the fact that the Ada system, in effect, inserts an *implied* **with Standard** clause at the beginning of every compilation unit. Thus the scope of Standard, and with it the scope of ASCII, automatically extends throughout the main procedure.

As a second example of the use of these special ASCII codes, consider the program of Figure 12.6.3, in which a procedure Put_Vertical displays characters in a column, by virtue of preceding each character with a line feed (LF) and backspace (BS). You should verify that the output of this little program is

```
The quick b
          r
          o
          w
          n fox...
```

when the program is executed.

```
   with Text_IO;

procedure ASCII_Sample is

   procedure Put_Vertical (Ch:  in CHARACTER) is

   begin

     Text_IO.Put (ASCII.LF);
     Text_IO.Put (ASCII.BS);
     Text_IO.Put (Ch);

   end Put_Vertical;

begin

   Text_IO.Put ("The quick b");
   Put_Vertical ('r');
   Put_Vertical ('o');
   Put_Vertical ('w');
   Put_Vertical ('n');
   Text_IO.Put (" fox...");
   Text_IO.New_Line;

end ASCII_Sample;
```

Figure 12.6.3

12.7 Discrete types and their attributes

The integer types and the enumeration types (BOOLEAN, CHARACTER, and programmer-declared enumeration types) make up what are known as Ada's **discrete types**.

We use the word "discrete" here more or less in the mathematical sense and in opposition to the term **continuous**, also of mathematical derivation. As we noted at the outset of this chapter, perhaps the most easily described distinction between these concepts is that for the discrete types, with the implied ordering of their literals, each type value (except for the first and last) has an immediate *successor* and *predecessor*. Thus for example, the CHARACTER 'R' has 'A' and 'L' as predecessors, but 'Q' is its sole *immediate* predecessor. Of course, 'S' is its immediate successor. As we know, these are *not* properties shared by the floating point numbers.

In Sections 2.6 and 2.9 we first looked at the type attributes First and Last, and in Section 5.5 we added the notion of Pred and Succ. In this section we add two more important attributes that apply to objects from a discrete type. With each discrete type T is associated an INTEGER-valued function that accepts as its single parameter an expression of type T and returns as its value the **position** of the value of the expression within the type. By *position* we mean the following:

INTEGER   The position of an INTEGER expression X is its value, X.

BOOLEAN   The position of False is 0; the position of True is 1.

CHARACTER   The position of a CHARACTER expression is its ASCII code.

Enumeration   The position of an expression of some programmer-declared enumeration type is the *position* of the expression's value within the enumerated list that defines the type, with the position numbers beginning at 0 and increasing into successive positive integers.

The name of the function that returns the position of the value of an expression of type *T* is **T'Pos** (read "T-tick-Pos").
Consider the enumeration types of Figure 12.7.1.

```
type DAY_OF_WEEK is (Sunday, Monday, Tuesday, Wednesday,
                     Thursday, Friday, Saturday);

type MONTH is      (Jan, Feb, Mar, Apr, May, Jun,
                    Jul, Aug, Sep, Oct, Nov, Dec);

type COLORS is     (Violet, Orange, Red, Green, Blue,
                    Yellow, Brown, Black, White, Grey);

type PRIMARY is    (Red, Blue, Green);
```

Figure 12.7.1

Then we have the following examples of **T'Pos**:

INTEGER'Pos(27 + 2*9 − 6) = 39

INTEGER'Pos(14 − 392/23) = −3

CHARACTER'Pos('B') = 66

CHARACTER'Pos('b') = 98

CHARACTER'Pos(ASCII.LF) = 10

BOOLEAN'Pos(True) = 1

COLORS'Pos(Violet) = 0

COLORS'Pos(White) = 8

COLORS'Pos(Blue) = 4

PRIMARY'Pos(Blue) = 1

DAY_OF_WEEK'Pos(Monday) = 1

MONTH'Pos(Dec) = 11

Each discrete type T has an attribute, denoted T'Val, which is a companion to T'Pos, in that it accepts as a parameter an INTEGER expression and returns as its value the literal of that type having that integer as its *position* (in the sense of Pos). Thus (again using the types of Figure 12.7.1):

INTEGER'Val(28 + 7) = 35

INTEGER'Val(33 − 406/3) = -102

INTEGER'Val(Ex) = value of EX, for any INTEGER expression Ex

COLORS'Val(0) = Violet

PRIMARY'Val(2) = Green

MONTH'Val(2) = Mar

CHARACTER'Val(67) = 'C'

CHARACTER'Val(8) = the BackSpace character, ASCII.BS

Indeed, assume that E_x is an expression of any discrete type T that evaluates to the literal X. Then it should be evident that

$$T\,'\mathrm{Val}(T\,'\mathrm{Pos}(E_x)) = X$$

Similarly, assuming that E_z is an INTEGER expression whose value is Z, we have

$$T\,'\mathrm{Pos}(T\,'\mathrm{Val}(E_z)) = Z$$

Here we must assume something in addition; namely, Z, as an integer, lies within the range of valid positions of literals of type T. If Z is not within this range, Constraint_Error will be raised by the reference to $T\,'\mathrm{Val}(E_z)$.

We can now use the Pos and Val attributes of discrete types to expand to all discrete types attributes that we have already discussed for some of these types. Once again we assume that T is some discrete type and that X is an expression of type T.

$T\,'\mathrm{First}$ The *first* element of T. This is the literal in T having the *smallest* position value. If T is INTEGER, then $T\,'\mathrm{First}$ is implementation-dependent, but some common values are −32,768 and −2,147,483,648.

$T\,'\mathrm{Last}$ The *last* element of T. This is the literal in T having the *largest* position value. Common values for INTEGER'Last are 32,767 and 2,147,483,647.

T'Succ(X)   The *successor* in T of X. This is the literal in T that immediately succeeds (follows) X in the positional ordering of literals in T. T 'Succ(X) can be described as T 'Val(T 'Pos(X) + 1). Observe that T 'Last has no successor.

T'Pred(X)   The *predecessor* in T of X. This is the literal in T that immediately precedes X in the positional ordering of literals in T. T 'Pred(X) can be described as T'Val(T'Pos(X) − 1). T'First has no predecessor.

For the record we offer a few examples of these concepts; for the most part they should give you no great difficulty. (See Figure 12.7.1 for the declarations of the programmer-declared enumeration types.)

MONTH'First = Jan

COLORS'Last = Gray

DAY_OF_WEEK'Succ(Wednesday) = Thursday

MONTH'Succ(Dec) will raise Constraint_Error

CHARACTER'Succ('a') = 'b'

COLORS'Pred(Red) = Orange

PRIMARY'Pred(Red) will raise Constraint_Error

Using the Val attribute, we can now also define several *relations* between expressions of type T (where, as usual, T is one of the discrete types).

EQUALS (=)   An expression X of type T is *equal* to an expression Y of type T, written $X = Y$, provided X and Y both evaluate to the same literal of type T. Another way of putting this is T'Pos(X) = T'Pos(Y), where the equal sign represents the usual equality among the INTEGER literals.

PRECEDES (<)   An expression X of type T *precedes* an expression Y of type T, written $X < Y$, provided T'Pos(X) < T'Pos(Y), where the latter less than sign represents the usual less than among the INTEGERs.

We can now define

$X <= Y$ means $X < Y$ or $X = Y$;

$X > Y$ means $Y < X$;

$X >= Y$ means $Y <= X$;

$X /= Y$ means $X = Y$ is False.

Thus (see again the declarations of Figure 12.7.1):

Monday < Friday

Feb <= Aug

'X' < 'r'

White /= Yellow

Black >= Orange

A final consequence of the extension of the notion of *order* from INTEGER types to enumeration types is that of a *range* of elements of an enumeration type. As a result, we may use the term **discrete range** to designate a range of elements of *any discrete* type. For just as we can refer to the concept of

INTEGER range $A..B$ (*A, B* INTEGER expressions)

as used to declare subtypes, for example, we can also refer to

T range $T_1..T_2$ (T_1, T_2 expressions of type T)

where T is BOOLEAN, CHARACTER, or a programmer-declared enumeration type.
In general, if D is some discrete type and we declare

X: D range $D_1..D_2$

then X is of type D and thus any operation valid for *any* variable of type D is valid for X; the declaration has merely *constrained* the values from D that X may take on to those lying between D_1 and D_2, inclusive. Such constraints are found most frequently in the declarations of subtypes (as with INTEGER types), such as:

```
subtype MONOCHROMATIC is COLORS range Black..Gray;

subtype CAPITALS is CHARACTER range 'A'..'Z';

subtype POSITIVE is INTEGER range 1..INTEGER'Last;
```

What can be said of the *attributes* of a discrete type that results from the constraining of the range of values of some other discrete type? Specifically, let D be a discrete type and declare

subtype S is D range $D_1..D_2$;

Then

S'First $= D_1$ and S'Last $= D_2$

All other attributes are "inherited" from D. In particular, an expression s of type S has as its predecessor and successor *in* S the predecessor and successor it has in D (except, of course, that D_1 has no predecessor *in* S, and D_2 has no successor *in* S), and S'Val and S'Pos are the same as D'Val and D'Pos, respectively.

Another use to which discrete types can be put is as ranges of **for** loops. Indeed, the **for** construct is based on the discrete range and, consequently, is valid for *any* discrete type. Thus loops such as

```
for Day in DAY_OF_WEEK range Monday..Friday loop...
```

and

```
for Color in COLORS range Black..Gray loop...
```

are perfectly valid. In fact, the second of these could as well have been written

```
for Color in MONOCHROMATIC loop...
```

The reserved word **in** used in **for** loops is not restricted to that particular construct; **in** has an existence all its own, and it can be described as follows:

If X is an expression of a discrete type D and if D_1 and D_2 are expressions (frequently literals) of type D, then

$$X \text{ in } D_1..D_2$$

has the same value (True or False) as

$$X >= D_1 \text{ and } X <= D_2$$

Similarly, we define

$$X \text{ not in } D_1..D_2$$

to have the same value (True or False) as

$$X < D_1 \text{ or } X > D_2$$

Note that **not in** is a *new* relation, although its *value* is the same as the construction

$$\text{not } (X \text{ in } D_1..D_2).$$

As concrete examples (and referring again to Figure 12.7.1):

27 in 10..444   is True

27 in 444..10   is False

27 in 30..444	is False
27 not in 30..444	is True
'L' in '2'..'a'	is True
'L' not in CAPITALS	is False
White not in Violet..Blue	is True
White in Black..Gray	is True
White not in MONOCHROMATIC	is False

As a simple application of some of these concepts, consider the little program of Figure 12.7.2. This program accepts an alphabetic character and displays the corresponding uppercase character, which will be the same as the input character if that was already uppercase. Note the use of **not in**, **in**, Val, and Pos. (How does the program terminate?)

```
with Text_IO;

procedure Lower_to_Upper is

   subtype LOWER_CASE is CHARACTER range 'a'..'z';

   subtype UPPER_CASE is CHARACTER range 'A'..'Z';

   Case_Diff:  constant := UPPER_CASE'Pos(UPPER_CASE'First)
                            - LOWER_CASE'Pos(LOWER_CASE'First);

   Ch:    CHARACTER;

begin
   loop
     Text_IO.New_Line;
     Text_IO.Put ("Enter character: ");
     Text_IO.Get (Ch);
     Text_IO.New_Line;

     exit when (Ch not in UPPER_CASE and Ch not in LOWER_CASE);

     if Ch in LOWER_CASE then
       Ch := UPPER_CASE'Val(LOWER_CASE'Pos(CH) + Case_Diff);
     end if;

     Text_IO.Put ("The corresponding uppercase equivalent is ");
     Text_IO.Put (Ch);
     Text_IO.New_Line;
   end loop;

end;
```

Figure 12.7.2

12.8 The *case* statement

In the preceding section we introduced the concept of Ada's *discrete types*, which we saw to be made up of all the integer and enumeration types of the language. Discrete types have certain characteristics in common: For one, they share the attributes Pos, Val, Pred, and Succ; for another, they give rise to discrete ranges and thus are the natural setting of **for** loops.

In this section we take up another construct whose proper setting is that of discrete types, namely, the **case statement**. The **case** statement is a *control structure* that enables us to replace certain rather complicated conditional statements by what is often a shorter and tidier alternative. This appears to be a rather attractive possibility, but we will see that the **case** statement has *limited* use and lacks some of the versatility of the **if** statements that we studied in Chapter 6. A **case** statement may be used *only* in those conditional constructions in which we test the value of a variable (or, more generally, of an expression) that is of a *discrete* type. In contrast, **if** statements are not restricted in this way; the conditions (Boolean expressions) tested in **if** statements may include FLOAT expressions, for example, as well as objects of structured types. Thus, in theory, we could do without the **case** statement (as we have done up to now), relying totally on the forms of conditional statement investigated in Chapter 6. However, **case** statements, where applicable, often provide considerable convenience to the programmer.

We have encountered several instances of the construction

```
if <condition 1> then
  <statement sequence 1>
elsif <condition 2> then
  <statement sequence 2>
elsif <condition 3> then
  <statement sequence 3>
      .
      .
      .
elsif <condition N-1> then
  <statement sequence N-1>
else
  <statement sequence N>
end if;
```

Examples are found in Figures 8.2.5 and 9.1.1, among other places. In Figure 12.8.1 we show the pertinent segment of code from Figure 8.2.5, the Auto_Repair program.

```
if Cat = 'A' or Cat = 'a' or Miles >= Mileage_Limit then
  Percentage := 1.00;

elsif Cat = 'B' or Cat = 'b' then
  Percentage := 0.00;

elsif Cat = 'C' or Cat = 'c' then
  Percentage := 0.50;
elsif Cat = 'D' or Cat = 'd' then
  if Miles <= 5000 then
    Percentage := 0.00;
```

```
   elsif Miles <= 7500 then
      Percentage := 0.50;
   else
      Percentage := 0.80;
   end if;

else raise Invalid_Category;

end if;
```

Figure 12.8.1

The code that selects the category—A, B, C, or D—is essential to the program's execution, so this selection process cannot be eliminated. What *can* be eliminated here, or at least recast in different and more readable form, is the *nesting* of the conditionals and the lack of "cleanness" of code that results from it. For this, Ada supplies the **case** statement, which deals on a case-by-case basis with the possible values of an expresssion, provided the expression is of a *discrete* type, as is the CHARACTER expression (variable) Cat. In the example above, for the *case* Cat = 'A' or 'a', we do one thing; for the *case* Cat = 'B' or 'b', we do something else; and so forth. In Figure 12.8.2 we show the recasting of the code of Figure 12.8.1 in this "case" form, and then we investigate the format and syntax of the **case** statement.

```
if Miles >= Mileage_Limit then
   Percentage := 1.00;
else
   case Cat is

      when 'A' | 'a' =>
         Percentage := 1.00;

      when 'B' | 'b' =>
         Percentage := 0.00;

      when 'C' | 'c' =>
         Percentage := 0.50;

      when 'D' | 'd' =>
         if Miles <= 5000 then
            Percentage := 0.00;
         elsif Miles <= 7500 then
            Percentage := 0.50;
         else
            Percentage := 0.80;
         end if;

      when others =>
         raise Invalid_Category;

   end case;

end if;
```

Figure 12.8.2

Observe that the case in which the Mileage exceeds the Mileage_Limit is now treated separately, instead of being included into the Cat = 'A' option, since it is (and has always been) something of a special situation. The line

```
case Cat is
```

establishes the variable Cat as the **case selector** (the expression to be evaluated). Each line in the form

```
when <...> =>
```

is an **alternative**, and what is between the **when** and the arrow symbol **=>** is a **choice**. The statements following the symbol **=>** are those executed in *case* one of the *choices* matches the *case selector*. For example, if upon entering the segment of code of Figure 12.8.2, Mileage is less than Mileage_Limit and the variable Cat has the value 'b', then the statement

```
Percentage := 0.00;
```

is executed. If Cat has the value 'D', then all the statements between **if** and **end if** in this alternative are executed. Once again we see the use of the symbol | as meaning "or."

The syntax of the **case** statement is shown in Figure 12.8.3*a*, where we note the use of the familiar catch-all **others**.

a

case statement

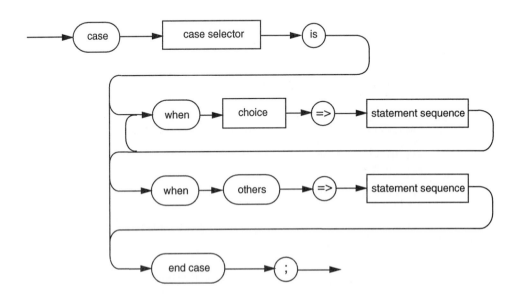

b

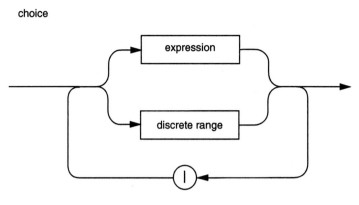

choice

Figure 12.8.3

Since *ranges* of values are permitted as choices in the alternatives in a **case** statement, we can improve on the construct of Figure 12.8.2 by rewriting alternative **'D' | 'd'** with a **nested case statement**, as shown in Figure 12.8.4.

```
when 'D' | 'd' =>
   case Miles is
     when 0..5000 =>
       Percentage := 0.00;
     when 5001..7500 =>
       Percentage := 0.50;
     when 7501..10000 =>
       Percentage := 0.80;
     when others =>
       Percentage := 1.00;
   end case;
```

Figure 12.8.4

We close this section with a brief list of the rules for the formation of **case** statements that either are not obvious from the syntax diagrams or cannot be deduced from them.

Rules for **case** constructions:

1. The case selector expression *must* be of some *discrete* type, and the choices in each alternative must be of that same type. In particular, the case selector may be neither an expression of type FLOAT nor an array.

2. An **others** alternative, if present, must be the *last* alternative.

3.   *Every* possible value of the type of the selector expression *must* be represented somewhere among the choices in the alternative list (including the **others** alternative).

4.   No *two* choices in the alternative list may simultaneously coincide with any one possible value of the selector expression.

To illustrate these rules, especially 2 and 3, we offer the following program segments, in which the simple **if..then..elsif** construction of Figure 12.8.5*a* is translated into the form of a **case** statement in Figure 12.8.5*b*. The variable Temperature is assumed to be of type INTEGER.

```
a       if Temperature >= 85 then
           Text_IO.Put_Line ("Too hot!");
        elsif Temperature <= 40 then
           Text_IO.Put_Line ("Too cold!");
        end if;

b       case Temperature is
           when 85..INTEGER'Last =>
             Text_IO.Put_Line ("Too hot!");
           when INTEGER'First..40 =>
             Text_IO.Put_Line ("Too cold!");
           when others =>
             null;
        end case;
```

Figure 12.8.5

Observe that because the selector expression Temperature is of type INTEGER, all the values of this type must be represented among the choices in the alternative list. Note the role of the **others** alternative in accomplishing this. Also, even though nothing is to be done if the value of Temperature lies strictly between 40 and 85 (which coincides with the **others** alternative in this example), the computer must explicitly be told what "action" to take in this instance. As we saw in the discussion of Figure 7.16.3, this is done by using the reserved word **null** in the form of a statement, which means, "Take no action" or "Do nothing."

12.9 The program Time_and_Day, revisited once again

The program Time_and_Day of Figure 9.1.1 contains a segment of code similar to that found in the Auto_Repair program, namely, a sequence of **if...then...elsif** constructions, used to display the day of the week. That piece of code, along with a case construction that replaces it, are shown in Figure 12.9.1.

```
a        if Dy = 0 then
            Text_IO.Put ("Sunday");
         elsif Dy = 1 then
            Text_IO.Put ("Monday");
         elsif Dy = 2 then
            Text_IO.Put ("Tuesday");
         elsif Dy = 3 then
            Text_IO.Put ("Wednesday");
         elsif Dy = 4 then
            Text_IO.Put ("Thursday");
         elsif Dy = 5 then
            Text_IO.Put ("Friday");
         elsif Dy = 6 then
            Text_IO.Put ("Saturday");
         end if;
         Text_IO.Put (".");
         Text_IO.New_Line (2);

b        case Dy is
            when 0 =>
               Text_IO.Put ("Sunday");
            when 1 =>
               Text_IO.Put ("Monday");
            when 2 =>
               Text_IO.Put ("Tuesday");
            when 3 =>
               Text_IO.Put ("Wednesday");
            when 4 =>
               Text_IO.Put ("Thursday");
            when 5 =>
               Text_IO.Put ("Friday");
            when others =>
               Text_IO.Put ("Saturday");
            end case;

         Text_IO.Put (".");
         Text_IO.New_Line (2);
```

Figure 12.9.1

The version of the Time_and_Day program shown in Figure 12.9.2 eliminates the need for either the nested **if...then...elsif** construction or a **case** statement by creating an enumeration type, DAY_OF_WEEK (as in Figure 12.7.1 above), and then treating the day *number* (0 to 6) as a *position* (Pos) with respect to this type. The modifications should be easy enough to follow, but since the changes are fairly sweeping, we present the entire source program rather than a few segments. We follow the program with a few comments. (The numbers in brackets in the right margin are for annotation purposes.)

```
with Text_IO, Int_IO;

procedure Time_and_Day is

    -- This program asks the user for an integer from 0 to 10079,
    -- representing the number of minutes that have elapsed since
    -- the beginning of the week.  It then determines and displays
    -- the time of day (as it would appear on a 12-hour digital
    -- clock) and the day of the week.
```

```
subtype MINUTES_RANGE is INTEGER range 0..10079;

type DAY_OF_WEEK is (Sunday, Monday, Tuesday, Wednesday,        [1]
                     Thursday, Friday, Saturday);

package Days_IO is new Text_IO.Enumeration_IO (DAY_OF_WEEK);    [2]

Minutes_Elapsed:        NATURAL;
Hour, Minute:           NATURAL;
Day:                    DAY_OF_WEEK;                            [3]

Midnight:               BOOLEAN := False;
Noon:                   BOOLEAN := False;
PM:                     BOOLEAN := False;

Time_Up:                exception;

--   Procedure Get_Input requests from the user the number of
--   minutes since midnight Sunday, and gives the user three
--   tries to enter a valid number.

procedure Get_Input (Mins_Elapsed: out Minutes_Range) is

   package Minutes_IO is new Text_IO.Integer_IO (Minutes_Range);
   Wrong_Inputs:   NATURAL := 0;

begin

   Text_IO.New_Line;
   Text_IO.Put
     ("How many minutes since the week began (0 to 10079)? ");

   Input_Loop:
   loop

      begin
        Minutes_IO.Get (Mins_Elapsed);
        exit Input_Loop;
      exception
        when Text_IO.Data_Error =>
          Wrong_Inputs := Wrong_Inputs + 1;
          if Wrong_Inputs = 3 then
            raise Time_Up;
          end if;
          Text_IO.Put_Line
            ("Minutes must be between 0 and 10079.");
          Text_IO.Put ("Try again: ");
          Text_IO.Skip_Line;
      end;

   end loop Input_Loop;
   Text_IO.New_Line;

end Get_Input;


--   Procedure Convert generates from the value of Mins_Elapsed
--   the day (Sunday - Saturday), left-over hours, and left-over
--   minutes.
```

```
procedure Convert (Mins_Elapsed:   in MINUTES_RANGE;
                   Dy:              out DAY_OF_WEEK;              [4]
                   Hr, Min:         out NATURAL)     is

  Minutes_in_Hour:    constant INTEGER := 60;
  Hours_in_Day:       constant INTEGER := 24;
  Hours_Elapsed:      NATURAL := Mins_Elapsed / Minutes_in_Hour;

begin

  Min    := Mins_Elapsed  rem  Minutes_in_Hour;
  Dy     := DAY_OF_WEEK'Val (Hours_Elapsed / Hours_in_Day);     [5]
  Hr     := Hours_Elapsed rem  Hours_in_Day;

end Convert;


--  Procedure Set_Hour makes any necessary changes in the hour
--  (changing 0 to 12, for example) and globally sets the
--  Midnight, Noon, and PM flags.

procedure Set_Hour (Hr:    in out NATURAL;
                    Min:   in NATURAL) is

begin

  if Hr = 0 and Min = 0 then
    Midnight := True;
    Hr := 12;
  elsif Hr = 12 and Min = 0 then
    Noon := True;
  elsif Hr >= 12 then
    PM := True;
    if Hr > 12 then
      Hr := Hr - 12;
    end if;
  elsif Hr = 0 then
    Hr := 12;
  end if;

end Set_Hour;


--  Procedure Display generates the final output.

procedure Display (Dy:       in DAY_OF_WEEK;                     [6]
                   Hr, Min:  in NATURAL) is

begin

  Text_IO.Put ("The time is ");
  Int_IO.Put (Hr, 0);
  Text_IO.Put (":");
  Int_IO.Put (Min / 10, 0);        -- tens digit for Minute
  Int_IO.Put (Min rem 10, 0);      -- units digit for Minute

  if Midnight then
    Text_IO.Put (" midnight");
```

```
    elsif Noon then
       Text_IO.Put (" noon");
    elsif PM then
       Text_IO.Put (" p.m.");
    else
       Text_IO.Put (" a.m.");
    end if;

    Text_IO.Put (" on ");

    Days_IO.Put (Dy);                                    [7]
    Text_IO.Put (".");
    Text_IO.New_Line (2);

  end Display;



    -- Main procedure (program) begins here.
  begin

    Get_Input (Minutes_Elapsed);
    Convert (Minutes_Elapsed, Day, Hour, Minute);
    Set_Hour (Hour, Minute);
    Display (Day, Hour, Minute);

  exception
    when Time_Up =>
       Text_IO.Put ("Input is still incorrect...");
       Text_IO.Put_Line ("execution is terminated.");

  end Time_and_Day;
```

Figure 12.9.2

The output from this program is the same as before, except for a slight change in appearance. For example, in response to the input 3670, the program generates the line

```
The time is 1:10 p.m. on TUESDAY.
```

This results, of course, from Enumeration_IO's displaying of identifiers in uppercase (or in lowercase), and this is the single, small price we pay for this improvement. As to the code itself, we note the following changes, as indicated by the numbers in the right margin in Figure 12.9.2.

1.   This is the declaration of the enumeration type DAY_OF_WEEK.

2.   The package Days_IO, an instantiation of Enumeration_IO for the enumeration type DAY_OF_WEEK, is used for displaying the day of the week.

3.   The type of the variable Day has been changed from NATURAL to DAY_OF_WEEK.

4.   The formal parameter Dy in the procedure Convert is of type DAY_OF_WEEK.

5.   This is the most significant change in the program. The value of the expression

Hours_Elapsed / Hours_in_Day

will be between 0 and 6. This value is used to generate one of the entries in the type DAY_OF_WEEK, by means of the Val attribute, and in particular, DAY_OF_WEEK'Val. For example, if the expression has the value 2, then instead of setting Dy := 2 as before, we now set Dy := DAY_OF_WEEK'Val(2) = Tuesday.

6.   The formal parameter to Display is now of type DAY_OF_WEEK.

7.   The value of Dy is displayed. Since Dy is of type DAY_OF_WEEK, the Put must be from Days_IO, as indicated in the program.

12.10 Name overloading*

In Section 9.6 we encountered the concept of *name overloading*, and in Section 11.8 we also considered examples of *operator overloading*. In fact, in Section 12.7, there is additional overloading of the relational operators <, >=, and so forth. In the context of enumeration types all this overloading can be a bit less straightforward than what we have already seen. To see why, consider the following examples:

3 < 5

Violet < Green

How would *we* interpret these? We would have no difficulty, since in the first case we would say that inasmuch as 3 and 5 are integers and the < symbol represents *is less than*, the relational expression has the value True. In the second instance, we would conclude also that the value is True, since Violet and Green are bcth literals in the type COLORS, that in enumeration types < means *precedes*, and in COLORS Violet precedes Green. (See Figure 12.7.1.) Observe that we have selected an appropriate interpretation for < based on the *context* of the expressions involved; that is, we have deduced the types in question and then interpreted the meaning of < accordingly.

How would the Ada compiler interpret these relational expressions? The answer is, exactly as we have interpreted them. The compiler would detect that the expressions involved in the < relation are integers, or are COLORS, and it would then proceed to generate code to evaluate these relational expressions based on the appropriate context—INTEGER or COLORS (equivalently, "is less than" among the integers or "precedes" among the COLORS). This evidently requires a certain amount of "intelligence" on the part of the

---

*This section may be omitted.

compiler, but by now we know that it is capable of making basic decisions of this nature since it can determine the types of the expressions entering into the relation to be tested.

What would we—or the Ada compiler—do with the relation

3 < Green

There is no way we can make sense of this. (We are assuming that Green is a literal, not the name of some integer-valued variable.) Although 3 is of integer type, Green is not. Further, there can be no programmer-declared type that contains both 3 and Green. Thus we must conclude, as would the compiler, that this is a relational expression constructed in a syntactically improper fashion.

Suppose that we are operating in an environment in which the declarations of Figure 12.7.1 are in force—in particular, the declarations of *both* enumeration types COLORS and PRIMARY—and consider the relation

Green < Blue

If Green and Blue are literals from COLORS, then the relation is True. But if they are literals from PRIMARY, then the relation has the value False. Can we (or the Ada compiler) determine from this context which is meant? No. Further, the literals Green and Blue belonging to the type PRIMARY have no connection with those same-named literals from the type COLORS. (Why not?) The relational expression above is simply *ambiguous*, and before we or the compiler can assign a True or False value to it, some further disambiguating *qualification* of the expression is required. Thus, if we knew somehow that the Green involved here is from PRIMARY, then we could conclude that the relation is False, because now the only way the relation can be made meaningful is if the Blue is also a literal from PRIMARY. Similarly, if the Blue is known to belong to COLORS, then we could conclude that the Green must also, and we would evaluate the relation as True.

How can we be explicit about the type to which an *ambiguously named* literal belongs? The answer involves what is perhaps the most curious symbolism in Ada. If T is a type and L is a literal in that type, then the **type-qualified name** for L is

$T'(L)$

Thus any of the following (among others) would serve to disambiguate the relation given above:

COLORS'(Green) < COLORS'(Blue)

COLORS'(Green) < BLUE

Green < COLORS'(Blue)

PRIMARY'(Green) < Blue

Green < PRIMARY'(Blue)

Note that we have dealt only with *literals* here, since *expressions* involving enumeration types do not present the problem of context ambiguity. (Why not?)

It is clear that whatever problems are associated with the ambiguities involved here result from the fact that the symbol < (and with it, of course, the other relational symbols) has been endowed with a *multiplicity of meanings*; that is, it has been *overloaded*, having meanings that depend upon the context—integer type, CHARACTER, BOOLEAN, or one of the indefinitely many programmer-declared enumeration types.

Consider now the types declared in Figure 12.10.1.

```
type MONEY is (Peso, Nickel, Dime, Quarter, Dollar,
               Centavo, Ruble, Yen, Kopeck, Mark,
               Pound, Pence, Zloty, Pfennig);

subtype US_MONEY is MONEY range Nickel..Dollar;
```

Figure 12.10.1

Is the relation

Nickel >= Kopeck

ambiguous? No, since these two literals belong only to the type MONEY (and the relation evaluates to False). What of the relation

Nickel >= Quarter

There is *still* no problem, for unlike the example above, we are not faced with multiple *definitions* of Nickel and Quarter; these literals are defined *once* (in the declaration of the type MONEY) and then later *used* to declare a range. While we might wish to think of these two literals as belonging to *both* MONEY and US_MONEY, the precedence relationship between them is defined in MONEY and inherited in US_MONEY. Suppose we add to the declarations of Figure 12.10.1 the further declaration

```
type SMALL_CHANGE is (Pence, Kopeck, Nickel, Dime,
                      Pfennig, Centavo, Quarter,
                      Lepta, Centime);
```

Now the relation

Nickel >= Quarter

is ambiguous and requires further qualification. Note, however, that if Nickel and Quarter were considered relative to either of the types MONEY or SMALL_CHANGE *exclusively*, then the relation would have the value False.

As another simple example of an overloaded name, consider Figure 12.10.2, in which we declare an enumeration type STATES, consisting of the two-character abbreviations for 48 states. (We have intentionally omitted Indiana and Oregon. Why?) In addition, the subtype W_STATES consists of the range of STATES starting with the letter *W*. We then declare and define a function Minimum, having as its two formal parameters objects of type STATES.

```
type STATES is (AL, AK, AR, AZ, CA, CO, CT, DE, FL, GA, HI,
                IA, ID, IL, KS, KY, LA, MA, MD, ME, MI, MN,
                MO, MS, MT, NB, NC, ND, NH, NJ, NM, NV, NY,
                OH, OK, PA, RI, SC, SD, TN, TX, UT, VA, VT,
                WA, WI, WV, WY);

subtype W_STATES is STATES range WA..WY;

-- STATES version of Minimum

function Minimum (S1, S2: STATES) return STATES is

begin

  if S1 <= S2 then
    return S1;
  end if;
  return S2;

end Minimum;
```

Figure 12.10.2

Suppose now that the following references to Min are made in the executable part of a program containing these declarations. We show the value returned by Minimum in each case in square brackets.

1.   Minimum (WI,VT)   [VT]

2.   Minimum (WI,WA)   [WA]

3.   Minimum (VT,NH)   [NH]

Note that in 2, both parameters WI and WA belong to W_STATES as well as to STATES. We have already noted that this is neither a conflict nor an ambiguity.

Suppose we add a new type to this collection, as follows:

```
type NEW_ENGLAND is (CT, MA, ME, NH, RI, VT);
```

Will there be a problem with the call to Minimum shown in item 3 above? No, because even though both NH and VT are now literals in each of STATES and NEW_ENGLAND, Minimum cannot possibly be referring to the NEW_ENGLAND literals, since there is no version of Minimum for parameters of type NEW_ENGLAND.

What if we define a version of Minimum (analogous to the STATES version in Figure 12.10.2) for parameters of type NEW_ENGLAND? Will **Minimum (VT,NH)** be ambiguous to the compiler? Not necessarily, for the compiler may be able to determine the context from other parts of the statement that contains the function call. Consider, for example, the statement

```
for State in AZ .. Minimum (VT,NH) loop...
```

Since AZ is a literal in STATES but *not* in NEW_ENGLAND, the only way the statement can make sense is if **Minimum (VT,NH)** is also in STATES. But it is only the STATES version of Minimum that returns a value of type STATES, and thus the statement is *not* ambiguous. On the other hand,

```
for State in CT .. Minimum (VT,NH) loop...
```

does require further qualification (of CT, or one or both of VT and NH), since it is ambiguous as it stands. These examples give you some idea of the "intelligence"—perhaps "persistence" is a more accurate term—exhibited by the compiler in its attempts at the resolution of what might sometimes appear even to us to be an ambiguous statement.

12.11 Text processing

In Section 6.9 we used Text_IO's file processing procedures to read input from a text file stored on disk, rather than directly from the keyboard. Similarly, we saw that Text_IO also allows us to create a new disk file and write output to it, instead of sending this output to the display screen. Recall that a text file is made up of strings of characters organized into lines. An Ada source file, for example, is a text file—so too is the file TRANSACT.DAT (Figure 6.9.6), in which characters are used to represent FLOAT data. Figure 6.9.7 shows a program that "processes" TRANSACT.DAT to keep track of an opening bank account balance, several transactions (deposits or withdrawals), and a resulting final balance.

In this section we want to consider some of the possibilities for processing ordinary English-language text—Lincoln's "Gettysburg Address," for instance, or a portion of a novel. The processing in question might involve any or all of the following: (1) changing lowercase letters to capitals; (2) counting the number of characters, words, sentences, and lines; (3) counting the number of occurrences of each letter of the alphabet; or (4) encrypting the text in a simple (too simple!) fashion by replacing each letter by its successor, with Z and z being replaced by A and a, respectively. All these things and others can be done by reading the text on a character-by-character basis; that is, by reading one character at a time, inspecting the character that has been read, and taking whatever action (if any) is appropriate.

Reading characters from a text file is not quite the same as reading them from a keyboard input buffer, although the two processes have certain points in common. For instance, the notion of end-of-line marker carries over to text files, and each line of the text may be thought of as a string of characters followed by an end-of-line marker. Also, the buffer pointer that we considered in Section 12.3 finds its counterpart in the **file pointer**, which we visualize as pointing at the next character to be read. But what makes a text file significantly different from the keyboard buffer is the text file's **end-of-file marker**, which, as the name clearly indicates, marks the end of the file. (It is possible to insert an end-of-file marker into the keyboard buffer, although this usually is not done; in many systems, pressing CTRL-Z has this effect.) Every text file concludes with the end-of-file marker, preceded by an end-of-line marker. As a result, there is no such thing as an "empty" text file in the sense in which the keyboard buffer may be empty. Even if the file contains no characters (and is "empty" in that sense), it *does* contain the end-of-file marker and preceding end-of-line marker. Thus, the function End_of_Line (from Text_IO), when applied to a text file, will *always* return either True or False; it will never be without a value, as when it is applied to an empty keyboard buffer. Similarly, Text_IO's function End_of_File will always return a BOOLEAN value: True, if the file pointer is pointing at the end-of-file marker or the end-of-line marker that precedes it; False, otherwise. The presence of the end-of-file marker in a text file leads to a new danger that does not occur in the case of the keyboard buffer, namely, attempting to advance the file pointer beyond the end-of-file marker (by means of a Get or Skip_Line, as described below); this event will cause the raising of Ada's End_Error exception.

We may think of a text file, then, as a "stream" of characters and end-of-line markers, terminated by an end-of-line marker and end-of-file marker. When the file is opened for input (as described in Section 6.9), the file pointer is set to point at the *first* character (or marker) in the file, and it "advances" as the input routines Get and Skip_Line are performed. The effects of applying these routines to a text file are described below, where we use the identifier File_Var as the name of the file variable (of type FILE_TYPE), identified with the physical disk file via the Open statement.

1.   **Get (File_Var, Ch)**, where Ch is a CHARACTER variable:

   a.   If the file pointer is pointing at a character, this character is obtained and assigned to Ch; then the file pointer is advanced to the next position.

   b.   If the file pointer is pointing at an end-of-line marker, it is advanced—repeatedly, if necessary—until it is pointing at a character. It then performs as described in *a*. But if advancing the file pointer causes it to attempt to pass beyond the end-of-file marker, End_Error is raised.

   c.   If the file pointer is pointing at the end-of-file marker, End_Error is raised.

2.   **Skip_Line (File_Var):**

   a.   If the file pointer is pointing at a character, it is advanced to the first position beyond the next end-of-line marker.

   b.   If the file pointer is pointing at an end-of-line marker, it is advanced to the next position in the text.

   c.   If the file pointer is pointing at the end-of-file marker, End_Error is raised.

Because it is necessary to step somewhat carefully in reading a text file, so as not inadvertently to raise the End_Error exception, we offer in Figure 12.11.1 a program structure that can serve as a model for processing a text file, which we have called TEXTFILE.TXT. As you see, we use the BOOLEAN-valued End_of_Line and End_of_File functions to detect the end of a line of text and to ensure that we do not attempt to run beyond the end of the file. These functions take a single parameter, namely, the file variable associated with the file being tested by the function. We shall assume that the file is to be read character by character, that each character is to be inspected as it is read, with appropriate action being taken, and that the result is to be printed on the screen, preserving the line structure of the original file. Note that if *no* action is taken at all between the reading and writing of characters, this program will simply *copy* the text file to the screen.

```
    with Text_IO;

procedure Process_Text is

    Text_Var:          Text_IO.FILE_TYPE;

    Ch:                CHARACTER;

begin

    Text_IO.Open (Text_Var, Text_IO.In_File, "TEXTFILE.TXT");

    while not Text_IO.End_of_File (Text_Var) loop

       while not Text_IO.End_of_Line (Text_Var) loop
          Text_IO.Get (Text_Var, Ch);
          -- Inspect this character and do whatever
          -- is necessary.
          Text_IO.Put (Ch);
       end loop;

       Text_IO.Skip_Line (Text_Var);
       Text_IO.New_Line;

    end loop;

    Text_IO.Close (Text_Var);

end Process_Text;
```

Figure 12.11.1

Notice that the inner loop reads and writes across a line of the text file; at the end of the line —when **End_of_Line(Text_Var)** becomes True—the file pointer is advanced to the beginning of the next input line and the cursor is advanced to the beginning of the next output line. Verify that the nested loop structure, with the loop conditions as given, prevents Text_IO.Get and Text_IO.Skip_Line from causing End_Error to be raised.

To provide a concrete example of text processing, we apply the model of Figure 12.11.1 to the design of a program that changes all the lowercase letters of a text file to the corresponding capital letters, leaving all other characters unaffected. We make direct use of the fact that the ASCII code for each capital letter is 32 *less* than that of the corresponding lowercase letter.

```
     with Text_IO;

  procedure Capitalize is

     Text_Var:         Text_IO.FILE_TYPE;

     Ch:               CHARACTER;

  begin

     Text_IO.Open (Text_Var, Text_IO.In_File, "TEXTFILE.TXT");

     while not Text_IO.End_of_File (Text_Var) loop

        while not Text_IO.End_of_Line (Text_Var) loop
          Text_IO.Get (Text_Var, Ch);
          if Ch in 'a'..'z' then
            Ch := CHARACTER'Val (CHARACTER'Pos (Ch) - 32);
          end if;

          Text_IO.Put (Ch);
        end loop;

        Text_IO.Skip_Line (Text_Var);
        Text_IO.New_Line;

     end loop;

     Text_IO.Close (Text_Var);

  end Capitalize;
```

Figure 12.11.2

12.12 Exercises

12.2.1 In an appropriate reference, look up the character coding known as **EBCDIC** and compare it with the ASCII encodings found in Appendix B. Observe that EBCDIC contains a number of "strange" codes, in particular, codes that do not correspond to the so-called graphic (or printing) characters. Observe also that the organization of EBCDIC seems somewhat less "rational" than that for ASCII. Attempt to find a rationale for this encoding scheme, which has been in widespread use for many decades.

12.3.1 In each of the following, assume that I1 and I2 are variables of type INTEGER and that C1, C2, and C3 are variables of type CHARACTER. Assume also the inclusion of the package Text_IO, as well as some instantiation of Integer_IO for some INTEGER type (Int_IO, for example). Tell what values these five variables have (if any) after the stated sequence of Get procedures has been invoked. The input line is shown just prior to the Gets in each case. The symbol ᴇᴏʟ stands for the end-of-line marker; ƀ is a blank or space character. (If a variable is not assigned a value, state that it is *indeterminate*; if an exception is raised, indicate that fact and assume that any subsequent variables are not read and are thus indeterminate. Finally, assume that each Get is from the package appropriate to its parameter.)

(a) 123ø4,a ᴇᴏʟ   (b) CAT656,x ᴇᴏʟ   (c) aBø1 ᴇᴏʟ

```
     Get (C1);          Get (C1);          Get (C1);
     Get (I1);          Get (C1);          Get (C2);
     Get (C2);          Get (C1);          Get (I1);
     Get (I2);          Get (I2);              Skip_Line;
     Get (C3);          Get (I1);
     Skip_Line;         Get (C3);
                        Skip_Line;
```

(d) 123ø4,a ᴇᴏʟ   (e) 1ø2ø3ø4 ᴇᴏʟ

```
     Get (C1);          Get (I1);
     Get (I1);          Get (I2);
     Get (C2);          Get (C1);
     Get (I2);          Get (I2);
     Get (C3);          Get (C2);
     Get (C2);          Get (C3);
     Skip_Line;         Skip_Line;
```

12.3.2 Write a program that accepts a string of characters from the keyboard and displays the number of characters in the string. Do *not* count the end-of-line marker as a character.

12.3.3 Write a program that accepts a string of characters from the keyboard and displays the number of *nonblank* characters in the string. Do *not* count the end-of-line marker as a character.

12.3.4 Write a program that accepts a string of characters from the keyboard and displays the number of *nonblank, nontab* characters in the string. Do *not* count the end-of-line marker as a character.

12.3.5 Write a program that accepts a string of characters from the keyboard and displays the number of *digit* characters ('0' to '9') in the string.

12.4.1 Declare an enumeration type consisting of the names of the national holidays in the United States.

12.4.2 Declare an enumeration type comprised of the five most popular pet animals. (Declare them in order of popularity, the first being the most popular, the next being the second most popular, etc.)

12.4.3 Declare an enumeration type appropriate for the example in Section 12.4 for use in a traffic control program; (Red, Amber, Green,...) is a beginning.

12.5.1 Given the declarations

```
type VEGGIES is (Corn, Beet, Bean, Pea, Carrot, Green_Bean,
                 Kohlrabi, Lettuce, Snow_Pea, Bean_Sprout,
                 Onion, Broccoli, Asparagus, Bok_Choy);

Veg_Type:       VEGGIES;
Veg_Quantity:   NATURAL;

package Veg_IO      is new Text_IO.Enumeration_IO (VEGGIES);
package Quant_IO    is new Text_IO.Integer_IO (INTEGER);
```

state what values are placed in Veg_Type and Veg_Quantity by the Get statements

```
Veg_IO.Get (Veg_Type);
Quant_IO.Get (Veg_Quantity);
```

for each of the following input lines. If an exception is raised, state explicitly which variable caused the exception to be raised; what value, if any, Veg_Type had when the exception was raised; and specifically what exception was raised and why. (As usual, ƀ stands for a blank or space character, and ᴇᴏʟ is the end-of-line marker.)

   (a)   Beanƀ24 ᴇᴏʟ
   (b)   Beanƀƀ24 ᴇᴏʟ
   (c)   Bean_Sproutƀ19 ᴇᴏʟ
   (d)   Bean-Sproutƀ19 ᴇᴏʟ
   (e)   snow-peaƀ27 ᴇᴏʟ
   (f)   BOK_CHOY,32 ᴇᴏʟ
   (g)   bok_choy-32 ᴇᴏʟ
   (h)   bok_choy32 ᴇᴏʟ

12.5.2 Referring to the declarations of Exercise 12.5.1, state what is displayed by the following sequences of statements.

```
(a)  Veg_IO.Put (Snow_Pea);        (b)  Veg_IO.Put (Snow_Pea,10);
     Veg_IO.Put (Bean);                 Veg_IO.Put (Bean);
     Text_IO.New_Line;                  Text_IO.New_Line;

(c)  Veg_IO.Put (Kohlrabi);        (d)  Veg_IO.Put (Kohlrabi,5);
     Veg_IO.Put (Lettuce,12);           Veg_IO.Put (Lettuce,12);
     Text_IO.New_Line;                  Text_IO.New_Line;

(e)  Text_IO.Put ("Kohlrabi")      (f)  Veg_IO.Put (Kohlrabi);
     Veg_IO.Put (Lettuce,9);            Text_IO.Put ("LETTUCE",9);
     Text_IO.New_Line;                  Text_IO.New_Line;
```

12.5.3 It is stated in the text that an instantiation of Enumeration_IO can be made to display enumeration type values in lowercase. Refer to *LRM [14.3.9]* and the listing of Text_IO in Appendix D, and write a small program to test this feature.

12.5.4 We are aware that, although CHARACTER literals include surrounding quote characters (for example, 'A'), these quote characters are *not* displayed when we use Text_IO's Put routine for objects of type CHARACTER. Similarly, getting a character does not require the user to key in these quote characters. However, since CHARACTER is a particular enumeration type, suppose we instantiate Enumeration_IO for this type and employ it in a program, as follows:

```
with Text_IO;

procedure Char_IO is

    package C_IO is new Text_IO.Enumeration_IO (CHARACTER);

begin

    Text_IO.Put ('A');        -- The "usual" Put for type CHARACTER
    Text_IO.New_Line;
    C_IO.Put ('A');
    Text_IO.New_Line;

end Char_IO;
```

Find the output of this program, and explain what is going on. Is one of these Put routines exhibiting special behavior? If so, which and how?

12.6.1 Tell what is displayed by each of the following programs on a hard-copy terminal and on a video terminal.

(a)
```
    with Text_IO;

procedure ASCII_Test_1 is

begin

    Text_IO.Put ("| | two crosses");
    Text_IO.Put (ASCII.CR);
    Text_IO.Put ("- -");
    Text_IO.Put (ASCII.LF);
    Text_IO.New_Line;

end ASCII_Test_1;
```

(b)
```
    with Text_IO;

procedure ASCII_Test_2 is

begin
```

```
Text_IO.Put (" 1");
Text_IO.Put (ASCII.LF);
Text_IO.Put (ASCII.BS);
Text_IO.Put (ASCII.BS);
Text_IO.Put ("2");
Text_IO.Put (ASCII.LF);
Text_IO.Put (ASCII.BS);
Text_IO.Put (ASCII.BS);
Text_IO.Put ("3");
Text_IO.Put (ASCII.LF);
Text_IO.Put (ASCII.BS);
Text_IO.Put (ASCII.BS);
Text_IO.Put ("4");
Text_IO.New_Line;

end ASCII_Test_2;
```

12.7.1 Referring to the type declaration VEGGIES of Exercise 12.5.1, as well as the I/O packages of that exercise, tell what is displayed by each of the following statements.

    (a)   `Quant_IO.Put (VEGGIES'Pos(Beet));`

    (b)   `Quant_IO.Put (VEGGIES'Pos(Bok_Choy)-3);`

    (c)   `Quant_IO.Put (VEGGIES'Pos(VEGGIES'Pred(Broccoli)));`

    (d)   `Veg_IO.Put (VEGGIES'Succ(Asparagus));`

    (e)   `Veg_IO.Put (VEGGIES'Val(5));`

    (f)   `Veg_IO.Put (VEGGIES'Pred(VEGGIES'Val(VEGGIES'Pos(Corn)+4)));`

    (g)   `Veg_IO.Put (VEGGIES'Last);`

    (h)   `Veg_IO.Put (VEGGIES'Val(VEGGIES'Pos(VEGGIES'Last)+1));`

12.7.2 Referring to the type declaration VEGGIES of Exercise 12.5.1, determine the value (True or False) of each of the following conditionals.

    (a)   Corn < Pea

    (b)   Asparagus >= Green_Bean;

    (c)   VEGGIES'Pos(Bean) < (VEGGIES'Pos(Bok_Choy) - 2) = False

    (d)   Kohlrabi <= VEGGIES'Val(BOOLEAN'Pos(Corn < Pea) + 3)

12.7.3 Referring to the type declaration VEGGIES of Exercise 12.5.1, as well as the package Veg_IO of that exercise, tell what is displayed by each of the following program segments:

    (a)   `Veg_Type := Beet;`

```
        while Veg_Type <= Snow_Pea loop

           Veg_IO.Put (Veg_Type);
           Text_IO.New_Line;
           Veg_Type := VEGGIES'Succ(Veg_Type);

        end loop;
```

```
(b)    for Veg in VEGGIES range Beet..Snow_Pea loop

           if  Veg = Bean or Veg = Pea or Veg = Green_Bean or
               Veg = Lettuce or Veg = Snow_Pea then

                  Veg_IO.Put (Veg);
                  Text_IO.Put_Line (" is a green vegetable.");
           end if;
       end loop;
```

12.8.1 Rewrite the segment of Exercise 12.7.3*b* above by using a **case** construction.

12.8.2 Assuming that Ch is a variable of type CHARACTER, tell what is displayed by each of the following segments of code for various values of Ch. If a segment of code contains compiler-detectable errors, suggest a repair for it.

```
(a)    case Ch is
           when 'A'..'Z' =>
             Text_IO.Put_Line ("Capital letter");
           when others =>
             Text_IO.Put_Line ("Non-capital");
       end case;


(b)    case Ch is
           when CHARACTER'First..'/' | '{'..CHARACTER'Last =>
             Text_IO.Put_Line ("Special character");
       end case;

(c)    case Ch is
           when 'A'..'Z' | 'a'..'z' =>
             Text_IO.Put_Line ("Alphabetic");
           when others =>
             null;
       end case;
```

12.8.3 Rewrite each of the following constructions in the form of a **case** statement, if possible. If it is not possible, explain why. Take Temperature to be of type INTEGER, Cost to be of type FLOAT, and Ch to be of type CHARACTER.

```
(a)    if Temperature >= 85 then
         Text_IO.Put_Line ("Too hot!");
       elsif Temperature <= 40 then
         Text_IO.Put_Line ("Too cold!");
       else
         Text_IO.Put_Line ("Mild weather.");
       end if;

(b)    if Ch >= 'A' and Ch < 'Z' then
         Text_IO.Put (CHARACTER'Succ (Ch));
       elsif Ch = 'Z' then
         Text_IO.Put ('A');
       end if;
```

(c)
```
if Cost >= 10.00 and Cost <= 25.00 then
   Text_IO.Put_Line ("Reasonable price.");
elsif Cost >= 0.0 and Cost <= 9.99 then
   Text_IO.Put_Line ("Cheap merchandise!");
end if;
```

(d)
```
if Temperature = 32 or Temperature = 212 then
   Text_IO.Put_Line ("Critical point of water.");
elsif Temperature > 32 and Temperature < 212 then
   Text_IO.Put_Line ("Liquid range for water.");
end if;
```

(e)
```
if Temperature >= 85 then
   Text_IO.Put_Line ("Too hot!");
elsif Temperature >= 60 then
   Text_IO.Put_Line ("Pleasant weather.");
elsif Temperature >= 40 then
   Text_IO.Put_Line ("Not bad.");
else
   Text_IO.Put_Line ("Too cold!");
end if;
```

(f)
```
if Ch = 'L' and Temperature > 32 then
   Text_IO.Put_Line ("Low temperature above freezing.");
elsif Ch = 'H' and Temperature < 32 then
   Text_IO.Put_Line ("High temperature below freezing.");
else
   Text_IO.Put_Line
      ("Freezing point in range from low to high.");
end if;
```

12.10.1 It was stated in Section 12.10 that while literals having the *same* names in *different* enumeration types require disambiguation, the same is not true for *expressions* involving enumeration types. Explain.

12.10.2 Why were Indiana and Oregon omitted from the list of state name abbreviations in Figure 12.10.2?

12.10.3 It was stated in Section 12.10 that the construction

```
for State in CT..Minimum (VT,NH) loop...
```

is ambiguous.

(a) Verify that with the enumeration types given, the construction actually *is* ambiguous.

(b) State at least two ways in which the ambiguity in part *a* can be resolved.

12.11.1 Create a reasonably short text file by copying some English-language text (preferably several brief paragraphs) from a book by using your system's editor. Then following the program model of Figure 12.11.1, write a program that reads the text file character by character and:

(a) Replace each letter by its predecessor, A and a being replaced by Z and z, respectively, with the resulting characters being written to the screen.

(b) Copy the text to the screen as it is, and then tell (display on the screen) how many characters it contains.

(c) Copy the text to the screen as it is, and then tell how many sentences it contains. Assume that every sentence ends with either a period or a question mark (not a quotation mark) and that these two punctuation marks are not used in the text for any other purpose (as a decimal point, for example).

(d) Copy the text to the screen as it is, and then tell how many lines (including "empty" and blank lines) it contains.

(e) Copy the text to the screen as it is, and then tell how many words it contains. Suggestion: Regard punctuation marks as part of the word with whose letters they are contiguous. (Thus, an opening quotation mark is part of the word that follows it, an apostrophe is part of the word in which it is embedded, and the various punctuation marks at the ends of words are part of the words that precede them.)

(f) Copy the text to the screen as it is, and then present all the information described in parts *b* to *e*.

12.11.2 With reference to the programming projects described in Exercise 12.11.1:

(a) Modify the project described in *d* so that the program counts *only* lines that display visible text, *not* empty lines (those containing no characters) or lines containing only blanks.

(b) For the project described in *e*, if your program does not properly handle the case in which lines may have one or more trailing blanks, modify it so that it does so.

Chapter 13

Composite Types: General Arrays and Records

In Chapter 10 we began our investigation of Ada's *composite types* by studying arrays whose components were of an integer type and whose index ranges were initially taken to be of the form 1..N, with N representing a positive integer. We saw that the components of an array may be of type FLOAT or BOOLEAN or CHARACTER or, in fact, of almost any Ada type. Later we moved on to other integer index ranges and eventually to *unconstrained* array types—but in every case we dealt only with arrays having integer index ranges. Our insistence that the indexes be of integer types was far more restrictive than necessary, as far as Ada's facilities for array-handling are concerned; nevertheless, it did enable us to focus our attention on important concepts and operations associated with arrays, without having to cope with the full span of array types that Ada allows.

In this chapter we extend our investigation of composite types by considering arrays with various index types. After broadening our view somewhat, we again narrow it as we study the special properties of an important predeclared array type, **STRING**. Then we generalize the array concept to take in **multidimensional arrays**, that is, arrays in which each component is specified by two or more indexes, rather than just one. Finally, we turn our attention to **record types**, and we see how arrays and records may be combined to provide useful facilities for the grouping and structuring of information.

13.1 One-dimensional arrays: Generalizations

A **one-dimensional array** is an array in which each component has exactly *one* index associated with it, as is the case with all the arrays we have seen so far. An array of this sort can be pictured as in Figure 10.2.1, namely, as a set of contiguous cells, arranged either vertically or horizontally, with each cell "labeled" by its respective index. Component values may aptly be represented by writing them inside the cells.

Before we take up arrays with different types of indexes, let us revisit the first array type and variable that we looked at in Chapter 10.

```
subtype RANGE_5 is INTEGER range 1..5;
type FIVE_INTS is array (RANGE_5) of INTEGER;
Grades:  FIVE_INTS;
```

Note that we first declared an integer subtype and used it to declare a (constrained) array type FIVE_INTS; we then declared a variable of this type. Ada will allow us, however, to make the following single declaration:

```
Grades:  array (INTEGER range 1..5) of INTEGER;
```

In this case, we have declared the variable Grades and its type, including its index range, in one declaration. The type is

```
array (INTEGER range 1..5) of INTEGER
```

and Grades has been declared to be of this array type. The type itself has *no name* (identifier), and for this reason it is called an **anonymous type**. Declaring an array variable to be of an anonymous array type seems to be an especially quick and easy way of declaring such a variable—after all, it relieves us of the need of separately declaring a *named* array type. Why then did we not introduce this notion in Chapter 10, when we first took up the concept of arrays? The reason is that several restrictions pertain to anonymous types. Anonymous types may not be used for formal or actual parameters of subprograms or for the values returned by functions. Furthermore, if we declare

```
Five_Numbers: array (INTEGER range 1..5) of INTEGER;
Five_Nums:    array (INTEGER range 1..5) of INTEGER;
```

then the array variables Five_Numbers and Five_Nums are of *different* (anonymous) types. This will be true, even with the declaration

```
Five_Numbers, Five_Nums: array (INTEGER range 1..5) of INTEGER;
```

since it only *seems* that both arrays are declared "at once"; the variables are actually declared in succession, just as if the declarations had been written separately. You may think that it is better—and certainly safer—to avoid anonymous types altogether. This is true in general, although there are cases in which the introduction of a named array type for the sake of just one array variable might tend to complicate or clutter the program. In any event, what we have said here about anonymous types applies throughout the rest of this section and in Section 13.4, where we take up multidimensional arrays.

Now we turn our attention to the *index range* of an array type and observe that the indexes of an array need *not* be integers, as they have been in all our examples up to the present. They may be of a character type (the type CHARACTER itself or a range subtype of it), or they may be of any other enumeration type. In general, the index range of an array must be a **discrete range**, which is to say that it must be a range of a discrete (integer or enumeration) type. We look at several examples, starting with one that uses the subtype LETTERS:

```
subtype LETTERS is CHARACTER range 'A'..'Z';
type LETTER_NUMBERS is array (LETTERS) of INTEGER;
Letter_Position:  LETTER_NUMBERS;
```

Values may be assigned to the components of this array with statements similar to those we have used above:

```
Letter_Position('A') := 1;
for Ch in LETTERS range 'B'..'Z' loop
  Letter_Position(Ch) :=
    Letter_Position(LETTERS'Pred(Ch)) + 1;
end loop;
```

Here, the *indexes* are the letters 'A', 'B', ..., 'Z', while the *component values* are the integers 1, 2, ..., 26; thus, the component corresponding to each index (letter) gives the place of that letter in the alphabet, as shown in Figure 13.1.3.

Letter_Position

1	2	3	4	$\cdots$	24	25	26
'A'	'B'	'C'	'D'	$\cdots$	'X'	'Y'	'Z'

Figure 13.1.3

As another example, consider the declarations

```
subtype DIGITS is CHARACTER range '0'..'9';
type DIGIT_NUMBERS is array (DIGITS) of NATURAL;
Digit_Values:  DIGIT_NUMBERS;
```

We fill this array with the integers 0 to 9

```
Digit_Values('0') := 0;
for Ch in DIGITS range '1'..'9' loop
  Digit_Values(Ch) := Digit_Values(DIGITS'Pred(Ch)) + 1;
end loop;
```

and display the result in Figure 13.1.4.

DIGIT_VALUES

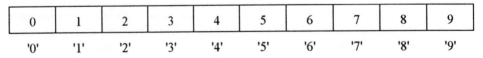

0	1	2	3	4	5	6	7	8	9
'0'	'1'	'2'	'3'	'4'	'5'	'6'	'7'	'8'	'9'

Figure 13.1.4

We saw in Section 7.11 that when the Ada system is instructed to get an integer from the keyboard, it does so by obtaining each successive digit *character* in the input and converting it to the corresponding integer *value*. One way in which such a conversion could be effected (although we do not claim it is the method employed by the Get procedure) is to make use of the array Digit_Values. Besides the declarations of DIGIT_NUMBERS and Digit_Values given above, we would need the additional declarations

```
Num:   INTEGER := 0;
Ch:    CHARACTER;
```

The essentials of the conversion would consist of the code

```
Text_IO.Get(Ch);
while Ch in DIGITS loop
  Num := 10 * Num + Digit_Values(Ch);
  Text_IO.Get(Ch);
end loop;
```

Of course, no provision has been made in this conversion routine for a leading plus or minus sign or for underscores within the number; nor is there any checking for correct integer syntax or allowable size. These are matters that must be dealt with, of course; however, all that is needed is to build on this fundamental loop structure.

In declaring the types LETTER_NUMBERS and DIGIT_NUMBERS, we had at our disposal the previously declared range subtypes LETTERS and DIGITS, which we used to specify the index range of LETTER_NUMBERS and DIGIT_NUMBERS. If this had not been the case, we would have had to declare

```
type LETTER_NUMBERS is array (CHARACTER range 'A'..'Z')
    of INTEGER;
type DIGIT_NUMBERS is array (CHARACTER range '0'..'9')
    of INTEGER;
```

In order to have at hand some further examples of one-dimensional arrays, we repeat a few type and subtype declarations:

```
subtype CAPITALS is CHARACTER range 'A'..'Z';
subtype LOWER_CASE is CHARACTER range 'a'..'z':
type DAYS_OF_WEEK is
    (Sun, Mon, Tue, Wed, Thu, Fri, Sat);
```

As to the last of these, we find it convenient in our present context to use three-letter abbreviations for the days of the week, rather than spell their full names, as was done in the similarly named type DAY_OF_WEEK declared earlier (Figure 12.7.1); hence the introduction of the new type DAYS_OF_WEEK. Now we declare the following:

```
type WEEKLY_INFO is array (DAYS_OF_WEEK) of INTEGER;
type LETTER_NUMBER is array (CAPITALS) of NATURAL;

Hours_Worked:  WEEKLY_INFO;
Letter_Count:  LETTER_NUMBER;
Cap:           array (LOWER_CASE) of CAPITALS;
```

Observe that the array variable Cap is of an anonymous type. In fact, it provides a fairly good example of the use of such a type, since we do not plan to introduce any other variables or constants of this type, nor do we intend to use the type for a parameter or function value. If we fill this array with capital letters in such a way that for each index (lowercase letter) the component "value" is the corresponding capital letter, then we have a convenient way of capitalizing letters in the course of text processing. This initialization may readily be done as for the arrays we have seen before:

```
Cap('a') := 'A';
for Ch in LOWER_CASE range 'b'..'z' loop
  Cap(Ch) := CHARACTER'Succ(Cap(LOWER_CASE'Pred(Ch)));
end loop;
```

Now we have Cap('a') = 'A', Cap('b') = 'B', and so on, as shown in Figure 13.1.5.

Cap

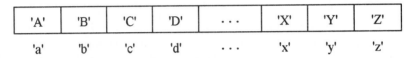

Figure 13.1.5

We could initialize Letter_Count by using a **for** loop:

```
for Ch in CAPITALS loop
  Letter_Count(Ch) := 0;
end loop;
```

Then the arrays Cap and Letter_Count might be employed in reading lines of text, character by character, and counting the number of occurrences of each letter of the alphabet. (Of course, not all characters are *letters*; therefore it is necessary to ensure that only letters are counted.)

```
Text_IO.Get(Ch);
Text_IO.Put(Ch);                 -- if a copy of the input text is desired
if Ch in LOWER_CASE then
  Ch := Cap(Ch);                 -- capitalize the lower case letter
end if;
if Ch in CAPITALS then
  Letter_Count(Ch) := Letter_Count(Ch) + 1;
end if;
```

At the end of this processing, Letter_Count('A') contains a natural number indicating how many times the letter *A* or *a* occurred in the text; and the same holds for each other letter of the alphabet.

When arrays are indexed by enumeration types, rather than integer types, there is apt to be less need for the idea of *unconstrained* array types. They are allowed, however, and although we do not discuss them at any length, we introduce such an array type at this point, since it provides another way of arriving at a declaration of two of the arrays we have used above. We first declare

```
type CHAR_NUMBERS is array (CHARACTER range <>) of NATURAL;
```

then we may subsequently declare:

```
Digit_Values:    CHAR_NUMBERS('0'..'9');
Letter_Count:    CHAR_NUMBERS('A'..'Z');
```

Digit_Values and Letter_Count are now variables of the same array type.

13.2 One-dimensional arrays: Aggregates, attributes, slices, and operations

In view of our experience with integer arrays, you may wonder if we could have used array *aggregates* to initialize the arrays Cap and Letter_Count in the preceding section. We could have done so, either by means of assignment statements or by assignments made in the declarations of these variables. In the case of the array Cap, it would have been somewhat tedious to do this, since we would have had no way of writing down the desired aggregate except in terms of all 26 uppercase letters of the alphabet, each enclosed in apostrophes. On the other hand, since all the components of Letter_Count are to be assigned the same value, we may quite easily initialize this array variable by using an idea introduced in Section 10.2. We need only write

```
Letter_Count := ('A'..'Z' => 0);
```

It is time to point out that what we have actually used in this latter case and what we must now investigate in more detail is **named association** of component values with their respective indexes. Up to now, we have generally used **positional association** in writing array aggregates, the kind of association in which we write out all the component values in the aggregate and understand the first value to be associated with the first index, the second value with the second index, and so on, as in the following:

```
Hours_Worked := (0, 8, 8, 8, 8, 8, 0);
```

The array variable Hours_Worked is indexed by the range Sun..Sat; that is, by the full range of the type DAYS_OF_WEEK. The array may be visualized in Figure 13.2.1.

Hours_Worked

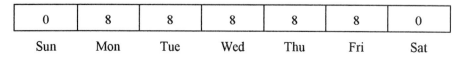

Figure 13.2.1

In using named association to construct an array aggregate, we must in some fashion name each index, whether it is an integer or a value of an enumeration type, and use the symbol => to associate a component value with it. Thus, we could write

```
Hours_Worked := (Sun => 0, Mon => 8, Tue => 8,
                 Wed => 8, Thu => 8, Fri => 8, Sat => 0);
```

In fact, since the association of component values with indexes is based on the explicit *naming* of the latter, rather than on their position in the aggregate, the indexes and their associated values may be listed in any order whatsoever, such as

```
Hours_Worked := (Mon => 8, Wed => 8, Fri => 8,
                 Tue => 8, Thu => 8, Sat => 0, Sun => 0);
```

From this example, it hardly seems that one would choose named association over positional association; after all, rearranging the order of the indexes seems to do nothing for us, and, obviously, there is much more writing to do. But in this context (as in others where the symbol => is used), we are allowed to use the character | to mean "or"; furthermore, we may name *ranges* of indexes with which a common component value is to be associated. Thus, the aggregate we are dealing with can take a much simpler form:

```
Hours_Worked := (Mon..Fri => 8, Sat | Sun => 0);
```

or

```
Hours_Worked := (Sun | Sat => 0, Mon..Fri => 8);
```

Alternatively (as with exception handlers and **case** statements), we might have used the reserved word **others** in last place and by itself:

```
Hours_Worked := (Mon..Fri => 8, others => 0);
```

or

```
Hours_Worked := (Sat | Sun => 0, others => 8);
```

In fact, **others** may be used alone, as in

```
Letter_Count := (others => 0);
```

Two final points about array aggregates are (1) whether an aggregate employs positional association or named association, it must in some way specify values for *all* the components of the array and (2) we may *not* mix positional association and named association in an array aggregate, *except* in the one instance where we begin with positional association and then use a single named association with the word **others**:

```
Five_Nums := (1, -1, others => 0);
```

The idea of array **attributes**, with which we are familiar by now, carries over to index ranges of various types. As we saw in Section 10.9, *unconstrained* array types do not have attributes; however, *constrained* array types and all array constants and variables have them, as do array formal parameters (even of unconstrained array types). For example, the array variable Cap, described above, has the following attributes:

```
Cap'Range  = 'a'..'z' The index range
Cap'First  = 'a'      The first index of the range
Cap'Last   = 'z'      The last index of the range
Cap'Length = 26       Number of indexes in the range
```

Similarly, for the constrained array type WEEKLY_INFO, we have

```
WEEKLY_INFO'Range  = Sun..Sat
WEEKLY_INFO'First  = Sun
WEEKLY_INFO'Last   = Sat
WEEKLY_INFO'Length = 7
```

In Chapter 10 we passed over an Ada feature that was not pertinent to the array operations and processing on which we were concentrating at the time. A **slice** of a given array is itself an array that consists of consecutive components of the given array. To reference a slice, we name the given array and specify the slice's index range in parentheses, as follows:

Reference	Corresponding slice
Hours_Worked(Mon..Fri)	(8, 8, 8, 8, 8)
Hours_Worked(Sun..Mon)	(0, 8)
Hours_Worked(Wed..Wed)	(Wed => 8)
Hours_Worked(Tue..Sun)	a null array
Cap('a'..'c')	('A', 'B', 'C')
Cap('p'..'s')	('P', 'Q', 'R', 'S')

Notice that Hours_Worked(Wed..Wed) is an *array* (slice) with one component, whereas Hours_Worked(Wed) is simply the fourth *component* of the array Hours_Worked (which has the INTEGER value 8). We might expect that an aggregate for an array with a single component could be written in the form (component_value)—as, for example, (8)—but Ada requires us to use a named association in this case, as we have done in (Wed => 8).

Slices may be used in assignments and comparisons, as in the following examples:

```
Five_Nums(3..5) := (2, -2, 3);
Five_Nums(1..4) := Five_Nums(2..5);
if Five_Nums(1..2) = (1, -1) then ...
while Five_Nums(3..5) /= (0, 0, 0) loop ...
```

In the second of these examples, no difficulty arises from the fact that the slices on the two sides of the assignment statement overlap. As always, the (array) expression on the right side is evaluated first, and then the result is assigned to the (array) variable on the left. This example illustrates a convenient way that Ada provides of moving component values "forward" in an array. We could move values toward the back of the array in a similar fashion.

Having used the operations of assignment and comparison in these examples, we should take up in a more careful manner the question of operations on one-dimensional arrays. As we saw in Chapter 10, much of what is done with arrays (including I/O) is done on a component-by-component basis. Further, since the indexes of any array are the values of a discrete range, the **for** loop construct is especially convenient in this setting. Nevertheless, in Section 10.4 we listed four kinds of operations that may involve an array as a whole taken as a single (composite) object: (1) assignment, (2) comparison, (3) parameter passing, and (4) function evaluation. We comment further on the first three of these and extend the list to include logical operations and catenation.

An array aggregate, constant, or variable may be assigned to an array variable of the same *type* and *length*. (Recall that arrays of a given *constrained* type will necessarily have the same index range and, therefore, the same length, but arrays of a given *unconstrained* type may have different index ranges and different lengths.) In this context, the arrays involved in an assignment need *not* have the same index range, and a slice is considered to have the same type as the array of which it is a part. This is why we were able to make the assignment

```
Five_Nums(1..4) := Five_Nums(2..5);
```

above. Recalling the declaration

```
type INTEGER_ARRAY is array (NATURAL range <>)
   of INTEGER;
```

we may declare

```
Six_Ints:   INTEGER_ARRAY(0..5);
Nine_Ints:  INTEGER_ARRAY(1..9);
```

and then the following assignments are valid:

```
Six_Ints          := Nine_Ints(3..8);
Six_Ints(1..3)    := Nine_Ints(5..7);
Nine_Ints(2..5)   := Nine_Ints(4..7);
```

In all these cases, the arrays are of type INTEGER_ARRAY, and the arrays involved in each assignment statement have identical lengths, as required.

With respect to comparison operations, the situation is somewhat different. Two array objects (aggregate, constant, variable) may be compared by means of the relational operators = and /=, provided that they are of the same *type*, as just described for assignments. However, they need not have the same *length* in order to be compared. Equality holds if the arrays do have the same length and also the same component values in the same order; otherwise, they are unequal.

When arrays have components that are of a *discrete* type (integer or enumeration), they may be compared by means of the relational operators <, <=, >, and >= provided, again, that the arrays themselves are of the same *type* (but possibly of different lengths). We describe the meanings of these operations on arrays as follows. Suppose that A and B are arrays of the same type, with components of a discrete type. Initially, we assume for ease of reference that A'Range = $1..M$ and B'Range = $1..N$ for positive integers M and N. (We will subsequently remove this restriction.) Then:

> A < B if A(1) < B(1), or
> > if A(1) = B(1) and A(2) < B(2), or
> > if A(1) = B(1) and A(2) = B(2) and A(3) < B(3), or
> > . . .;
> > or
> > if each component of A equals the corresponding component of B,
> > and also $M < N$ (that is, A is *shorter* than B)

Thus, using aggregates to specify array values, we have

```
(1, 2, 3) < (2, 0)
(1, 2, 3) < (2, 0, 0)
(2, 2, 3) < (2, 3, 0)
(2, 2, 3) < (2, 2, 4)
(2, 3)    < (2, 3, 0)
```

You can see that the order we have described here is like the order used in alphabetizing words, except that in this example we are using "words" (arrays) made up of integers, rather than of letters:

> A < B if A(A'First) < B(B'First).

If A(A'First) = B(B'First), we move on to compare the *second* components of these arrays; if these components are also equal, we then compare the *third* components; and so on. To say that (2, 3) < (2, 3, 0) is analogous to saying that "no" precedes "nod" in the dictionary. In fact, the kind of order used in comparing arrays is often referred to as **lexicographical**, or **dictionary**, **order**. We describe this order somewhat more carefully while removing the restriction we temporarily placed on the ranges of A and B:

Suppose A and B are arrays of the same type with component values of a discrete type, but with A'Range and B'Range not necessarily the same. Then A < B (1) if for some I in A'Range and J in B'Range, A(I) < B(J), with A(I) and B(J) preceded in their respective arrays by the same number of components and with each such component of A (if any) equal to the corresponding component of B, or (2) if A'Length < B'Length and each component of A equals the corresponding component of B.

In particular, the second of these cases holds whenever A'Length = 0 and B'Length > 0, that is, whenever A is a **null array** (one whose index range is *empty*, in the sense described in Section 5.6) and B is *not* a null array. As for the first case described in the definition, we illustrate it by means of the array variables A and B, both of type INTEGER_ARRAY, shown in Figure 13.2.2. Here A < B, because for $I = 1983$ and $J = 2$, we have A(I) < B(J)—that is, A(1983) < B(2)—and each preceding component of A—namely, each of its first two components A(1981) and A(1982)—is equal to the corresponding component of B.

A

6	24	−1	0	−7

  1981   1982   1983   1984   1985

B

6	24	0

  0   1   2

Figure 13.2.2

The array operators <=, >, and >= may be described in a similar fashion.

As a final point on operations applicable to arrays as a whole (as opposed to those array operations that must be programmed on a component-by-component basis), we offer a comment about passing arrays as actual parameters in subprogram calls. Subprogram parameters may indeed be of array types, as is also the case with values returned by functions, but the way in which they are associated with their respective formal parameters when a subprogram is invoked need not be the "copy-in, copy-out" process described in Section 8.7. Recall that when a formal parameter Form_Param and the corresponding actual parameter Act_Param are associated upon the invocation of a subprogram, we are assured by *LRM [6.2]* that the following steps take place, provided that the parameters are of a **scalar** type (that is, any of the types we have seen up to now except array types, which are **composite** types):

1.   Space is allocated for the formal parameter Form_Param.

2.   If Form_Param is of mode **in** or **in out**, the value of Act_Param is copied in to Form_Param.

3.   If Form_Param is of mode **out** or **in out**, then upon conclusion of the subprogram's execution, the current value of Form_Param is copied out to Act_Param.

In the case where Form_Param and Act_Param are of *array* types, the *LRM* does not specify that this particular method of passing parameter information be followed, although it does permit it. Notice that the process would involve creating an entire new array for Form_Param and copying all the values into it, out of it, or both. Instead, an Ada implementation is allowed to pass array parameter information **by reference**. This means that when the subprogram is invoked, the system associates Form_Param and Act_Param in such a way that during the execution of the subprogram, all references to Form_Param are taken as references to Act_Param. Thus, if in the course of the subprogram's execution, a component value of Form_Param is needed, it is obtained from the corresponding component of Act_Param; similarly, a value *assigned* to any component of Form_Param (during the subprogram's execution) is assigned then and there to the respective component of Act_Param. Whatever the mechanism, the *effect* is as if the copying described above had taken place, and this is a convenient and appropriate way for us to view it.

We saw in the preceding section that the components of an array may be of type BOOLEAN. When arrays have BOOLEAN components—and only in this case—we may perform *logical operations* on them. We may apply the unary operator **not** to such an array, and we may apply the binary operators **and**, **or**, and **xor** to pairs of array operands, provided that these operands have the same *type* and *length*. Just as in the case of an assignment statement, the effect of carrying out these operations on whole arrays is the same as if they had been performed on a component-by-component basis. Here is an example:

```
type WEEKLY_PRECIPITATION is array (DAYS_OF_WEEK) of BOOLEAN;
Rain, Snow:  WEEKLY_PRECIPITATION;
```

In the variables Rain and Snow, the component indexed by a particular value of DAYS_OF_WEEK is set to True if the respective kind of precipitation occurred on that day of the week; otherwise, it is set to False. Then we could meaningfully perform the operations

```
Rain and Snow
Rain or Snow
Rain xor Snow
not Rain
not Snow
```

The resulting arrays would hold the appropriate BOOLEAN values for each day of the week. We illustrate the first of these operations in Figure 13.2.3.

Rain

False	True	True	False	False	True	True
Sun	Mon	Tue	Wed	Thu	Fri	Sat

Snow

False	True	True	False	False	True	True
Sun	Mon	Tue	Wed	Thu	Fri	Sat

Rain and Snow

False	True	True	False	False	True	True
Sun	Mon	Tue	Wed	Thu	Fri	Sat

Figure 13.2.3

Finally, we mention the operation of **catenation**, which assumes particular importance in the next section; 2 one-dimensional arrays of the same type may be joined together, or catenated (Latin "catena" for chain), to form a new array of this type. The symbol for this binary operation (which has the same operator precedence as binary + and −) is the ampersand, **&**. When catenation takes place, the right operand of **&** is "appended," or adjoined, to the end of the left operand to form a new array. We may also catenate a one-dimensional array with a single element of its component type, and we may catenate two elements of the component type to form an array. We illustrate these ideas with some aggregates:

```
(1, 0, 3, -4) & (5, -6)  = (1, 0, 3, -4, 5, -6)
(1, 0, 3) & -4           = (1, 0, 3, -4)
1 & (0, 3, -4)           = (1, 0, 3, -4)
1 & 0                    = (1, 0)
```

Catenation is especially practical when we are dealing with arrays of characters, and it is to arrays of this kind—and to an important class of them—that we now turn our attention.

13.3 The type STRING

Ada has an unconstrained array type STRING, which is already predefined by the declaration

```
type STRING is array (POSITIVE range <>) of CHARACTER;
```

The programmer is free to declare (constrained) variables and constants of this type:

```
Word:  STRING(1..16);
Name:  STRING(1..30);
City:  STRING(1..20);
State: STRING(1..2);
Zip:   STRING(1..5);
```

As with other unconstrained types, one may declare constrained subtypes of STRING:

```
subtype Line    is STRING(1..80);
subtype ID      is STRING(1..6);

Title_Line:    LINE;

Student_ID,
Faculty_ID:    ID;
```

Most of what we said in Section 10.9 about one-dimensional unconstrained array types, and their subtypes and objects, pertains to the type STRING—except, of course, that we are now dealing with arrays whose components are specifically of the type CHARACTER and whose index range is a range of POSITIVE numbers. Therefore, in the present section, we confine our attention to a few language features that are peculiar to this type.

First, we may write STRING *literals,* just as for any other one-dimensional array type, thus

```
State := ('N', 'Y');
Zip   := ('1', '3', '2', '1', '4');
```

where State and Zip are as declared above. However, the literals of type STRING and of any other one-dimensional array type whose components are of a character type may be written in a far more manageable way. We simply write the characters of the string next to one another, enclosed in quotation marks (not apostrophes) that serve to **delimit** the string, that is, indicate where it starts and ends. Instead of the assignment statements above, we may write

```
State := "NY";
Zip   := "13214";
```

A single-character string aggregate, such as (1 => 'X') may be written "X"; and a null (empty) string aggregate, which could be expressed in the form (1..0 => 'Q')—where the 'Q' is entirely extraneous and could as well be some other character—may be written "". We mention that the quotation mark itself if used "inside" a string, rather than as a delimiter at its beginning or end, is doubled:

"""No.""" is the same as (' " ', 'N', 'o', '.', ' " ').

Finally, we point out that a string literal delimited by quotation marks can contain only printing characters, including blanks; control characters are not allowed.

Since a string is a one-dimensional array whose component type is discrete (namely, CHARACTER), strings may be compared with one another by means of any of the relational operators. If we recall from the end of the preceding section how the ordering of one-dimensional arrays works and apply it to strings, we see that strings (at least, those consisting of letters only) fall into exactly the same order as the words in a dictionary. Actually, this is not quite true: The component type CHARACTER has the order of the ASCII character listing; therefore, capital letters precede lowercase letters, and we have various curiosities

```
"MOUSE" < "cat"
"Washington" < "government"
```

as well as others that we could make up. Notice that not only does a null string precede any nonnull string (which is true for one-dimensional arrays in general), but a string beginning with a blank precedes a string beginning with any other printable character. (Why?)

We may access the individual components of strings, as well as slices of strings, just as with the other array types we have seen. For example, using the variables declared above, we have

`Name(1)`	is the first character of Name
`Title_Line(80)`	is the last character of Title_Line
`Zip(1..3)`	is the first three characters of Zip
`Student_ID(3..6)`	is the last four characters of Student_ID

Furthermore, we might have an array with components of a string type:

```
subtype NAME_STRING    is STRING(1..30);
type NAME_ARRAY        is array (NATURAL range <>) of NAME_STRING;
Name_List:             NAME_ARRAY(1..100);
```

The variable Name_List is an array with 100 components, each of which is an array with 30 CHARACTER components (that is, a 30-character string). Thus, having noted that the components of an array may be of *any* named type, we find that they may even be of an array type (in this case, a subtype of STRING). It might be worth pointing out that since the components of Name_List can be compared by means of any of the relational operators, the array Name_List can be alphabetized (its components arranged into ascending lexicographical order) by the very same logic coded into the procedure Sort_Up of Figure 10.9.4. Indeed, adapting this procedure to sort arrays of names (that is, parameters of type NAME_ARRAY, rather than INTEGER_ARRAY) requires only a few changes of type marks and some adjusting of identifiers to make them appropriate for the present context. Finally, we should note the following consequences of our declarations:

`Name_List`	is an array of 100 names (30-character strings)
`Name_List(25)`	is the twenty-fifth name (string) in this array
`Name_List(25)(1)`	is the first character in the twenty-fiftth name in this array.

Since strings are one-dimensional arrays—namely, arrays with POSITIVE index ranges and CHARACTER components—we observe that Name_List is a one-dimensional array with components that are themselves one-dimensional arrays. We comment further on this kind of structure in the next section, where we take up the topic of multidimensional arrays.

As suggested at the end of the preceding section, the catenation operation is perhaps more useful in the context of strings than anywhere else. We may catenate two strings, a character and a string, or two characters:

```
"DATA_FILE" & ".DAT" = "DATA_FILE.DAT"
"COUNT" & ';'        = "COUNT;"
'+' & "1999"         = "+1999"
'T' & 'X'            = "TX"
```

This operation can sometimes be of use in output statements when, for example, we want to combine a string literal with the value of a character *variable* (and possibly append a punctuation mark)

```
Text_IO.Put ("The text contains the illegal character " & (Ch & '.'));
```

or when a message is too long for a single line

```
Text_IO.Put_Line ("The input, as given, is not acceptable. "
  & "Please check the data again.");
```

We seem to have moved naturally into the topic of I/O for strings, and we make a few comments about it before we close this section. The first point to mention, although we are aware of it, is that the I/O procedures for strings, contained in the package Text_IO, are not generic; they are ready for use, without any instantiation, as they are for characters (see Section 12.3). We are familiar with the Put operation, which displays the value of its STRING parameter (variable, constant, literal). No operation is performed if the string is null. Put_Line, as we have seen (Section 2.11), is simply Put followed by New_Line. (Recall that Text_IO provides Put_Line for strings *only.*)

The string input procedure Get takes a string variable as its actual parameter. This array variable is constrained, of course, and the Get procedure will determine its length and perform that many successive Get operations for the individual characters of the string. If the input string is too long, only the initial characters of it will be read until the variable (actual parameter) has been "filled." If the string is not long enough, the system will read the input and wait for more characters, until it has read a number of them equal to the length of the variable.

There is an input procedure Get_Line for strings. It takes *two* actual parameters, the first a STRING variable and the second a NATURAL variable. As above, it determines the length of its (actual) string parameter and is ready to perform that many successive Get operations for the individual characters of the string. If the input string is too long, the behavior of the procedure is the same as for the Get procedure above. However, if the input string is shorter than the length of the variable—that is, if End_of_Line becomes true before the specified number of characters has been read—then reading of input stops and Skip_Line is called. In either case, Get_Line returns in its second parameter (an **out** parameter of subtype NATURAL) the index of the last array component into which a character was read from input. If the array indexes start with 1, the value of this second parameter will then coincide with the count of characters read into the array. If only part of the array receives input in this fashion, the remaining components are left with indeterminate character values. We illustrate the input procedure Get_Line with an example. First, we declare

```
Name:       STRING(1..7);
Char_Count: NATURAL;
```

Suppose that we subsequently execute the statement

```
Get_Line(Name,Char_Count);
```

and that the user gives the keyboard input

```
Jefferson<RET>
```

where <RET> denotes the RETURN or ENTER key. Then the string variable Name will have the component values:

'J'	'e'	'f'	'f'	'e'	'r'	's'
1	2	3	4	5	6	7

with Char_Count having the value 7. On the other hand, if the keyboard input is

    Adams<RET>

then Name will have the component values

'A'	'd'	'a'	'm'	's'		
1	2	3	4	5	6	7

where Name(6) and Name(7) are indeterminate; and Char_Count has 5 as its value.

We have finished our investigation of the fundamentals of one-dimensional arrays and of the special type STRING. To complete our present work on arrays, we now turn to the topic of multidimensional arrays.

13.4 Multidimensional arrays

In the introduction to this chapter, we described a **multidimensional array** as one in which each component is specified by two or more indexes, rather than just one. As an equivalent formulation, we could say that a multidimensional array is one that has two or more index ranges associated with it. These index ranges need not be the same, nor need they even be from the same base type. The number of indexes associated with each component (or index ranges associated with the array) is called the **dimension** of the array. In this section we consider examples of arrays with dimension greater than one and see how and to what extent the array properties and operations we have studied are applicable to them. To make matters somewhat specific, we confine our attention for the most part to **two-dimensional** arrays—that is, those in which each component has two indexes—but we also make occasional reference to arrays of higher dimensions. A two-dimensional array is usually called a **matrix** in mathematics; in other contexts (for example, in the social sciences), it is frequently referred to as a **table**.

To begin with, we note that, for a two-dimensional array, it is customary to speak of the first index of each component as its **row index** and to the second index as its **column index**. This terminology stems from the helpful practice of visualizing a two-dimensional array as a collection of cells arranged in horizontal rows and vertical columns, as is done for the array Table in Figure 13.4.1, where the cells have been left empty to indicate that no values have yet been assigned to them. This array has 1..2 as its first index range (the row indexes) and 1..3 as its second index range (the column indexes). In referring to a component of this array, we name its row index first; thus Table(1, 2) is the component in the middle of the top row, and Table(2, 1) is the component in the lower left-hand corner.

Table

Figure 13.4.1

How might we declare an array variable such as Table? As in the case of one-dimensional arrays, there are several ways of doing so, and we mention four possibilities; as you will see, they are just like the ones we saw in our previous investigation of one-dimensional arrays.

```
Table:  array (1..2, 1..3) of INTEGER;
```

declares Table to be of an anonymous array type.

```
subtype ROW_RANGE     is INTEGER range 1..2;
subtype COLUMN_RANGE is INTEGER range 1..3;
type INTS_2X3 is array (ROW_RANGE, COLUMN_RANGE) of INTEGER;
Table: INTS_2X3;
```

declares a constrained array type INTS_2X3 and then declares the variable Table to be of this type.

```
type INTS_TABLE is
  array (INTEGER range <>,INTEGER range <>) of INTEGER;
Table:  INTS_TABLE(1..2, 1..3);
```

declares a two-dimensional unconstrained array type INTS_TABLE and then declares Table to be a variable of this type with index ranges 1..2 and 1..3.

```
type INTS_TABLE is
  array (INTEGER range <>,INTEGER range <>) of INTEGER;
subtype INTS_2X3 is INTS_TABLE(1..2, 1..3);
Table:  INTS_2X3;
```

Here, INTS_2X3 is declared to be a constrained array subtype of the two-dimensional unconstrained array type INTS_TABLE; the variable Table is declared to be of this constrained subtype.

You may wonder if we are allowed to declare a two-dimensional array type with one constrained index range and one unconstrained index range, say

```
type TWO_ROWS is array (1..2, INTEGER range <>) of INTEGER;
```

and then declare

```
Table:  TWO_ROWS(1..3);
```

This approach is disallowed by the Ada language; in any multidimensional array type, *all* the index ranges must be constrained or *all* must be unconstrained—the two may not be mixed.

With these examples and the ones we have seen before as background, you should not find it difficult to trace through the syntax diagram in Figure 13.4.2, which describes the syntax of both one-dimensional and multidimensional arrays.

a

array type

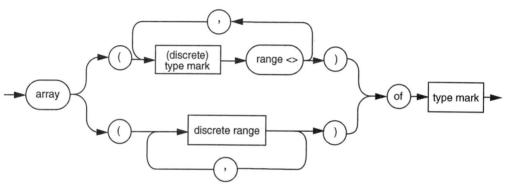

b

discrete range

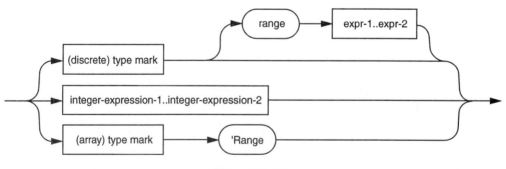

Figure 13.4.2

There are aggregates for multidimensional arrays. For example, we could assign

```
Table := ((4, 5, 6), (7, 8, 9));
```

This aggregate is a one-dimensional array, made up of one-dimensional subaggregates. (In general, an *N*-dimensional aggregate will be a one-dimensional array made up of $N - 1$

dimensional subaggregates.) In this example, we have used positional association of values with indexes; thus, the subaggregate (4, 5, 6) will be assigned to the first row of Table, and the subaggregate (7, 8, 9) will be assigned to the second row of Table. Within each row, the given integers will be assigned to the components in columns 1, 2, and 3, respectively.

We could use named association of values with indexes by writing the aggregate in the form

```
(1 => (4, 5, 6), 2 => (7, 8, 9))
```

or even in the form

```
(1 => (1 => 4, 2 => 5, 3 => 6), 2 => (1 => 7, 2 => 8, 3 => 9)).
```

As is usual with named association, the indexes and their associated values could be named in any order, Also, in employing named association, we may use index ranges, the "or" symbol |, and the reserved word **others**, just as in the case of one-dimensional arrays and with the same restrictions. Finally, positional and named association may be mixed only to the extent allowed for one-dimensional arrays. We make special mention of the usefulness of aggregates in setting all the components of an array to the same value, in this case 0:

```
Table := (1..2 => (1..3 => 0));
```

We should look at how some index ranges with *different* base types might occur in multidimensional arrays. Examples arise in situations where it is necessary to keep a record of some numeric datum—temperature, precipitation, sales, expenditures, or some other—on a daily basis, over a period of several weeks, say. To do this, we can maintain the information in a two-dimensional array, whose first index range stands for the numbering of the weeks that are being tabulated (for example, 1..52, for a period of a year or 1..13, for a period of a quarter) and whose second index range stands for the days of the week. Thus, using again the declaration

```
type DAYS_OF_WEEK is (Sun, Mon, Tue, Wed, Thu, Fri, Sat);
```

that was introduced in Section 13.1, we might include the further declarations

```
Number_of_Weeks:     constant NATURAL := 4;   -- or some other value
subtype WEEK_NUMBERS is INTEGER range 1..Number_of_Weeks;
type WEEKLY_INFO     is array (WEEK_NUMBERS, DAYS_OF_WEEK) of FLOAT;
Avg_Temp:            WEEKLY_INFO;
```

Then the array variable Avg_Temp, as well as others of the type WEEKLY_INFO, could be pictured as in Figure 13.4.3. A typical assignment statement for a component of this array might be

```
Avg_Temp(3, Fri) := 62.5;
```

which assigns 62.5 as the average temperature on Friday of the third week of the 4-week period.

Avg_Temp

	Sun	Mon	Tue	Wed	Thu	Fri	Sat
1							
2							
3						62.5	
4							

Figure 13.4.3

Instead of keeping a *single* number for each day of the four-week period, we might want to record more than one number; for example, we might want to note the high and low temperatures for each day. This can easily be done with a three-dimensional array. We first declare an enumeration type:

```
type EXTREMES is (Low, High);
```

Next we declare a variable, for which we choose to use an anonymous array type, to hold the information we need:

```
Temperature:  array (WEEK_NUMBERS, DAYS_OF_WEEK, EXTREMES) of FLOAT;
```

To picture such an array, we might imagine *two* copies of a table like the one in Figure 13.4.3, with one copy immediately behind the other. The "front" copy would be labeled Low, and the "back" copy would be labeled High, as shown in Figure 13.4.4. A typical reference to a component of this array might be Temperature(2, Mon, High), which, of course, would stand for the high temperature on Monday of the second week.

High

	Sun	Mon	Tue	Wed	Thu	Fri	Sat
1	74.0	75.1	75.6	76.0	75.8	74.3	71.5
2							61.2
3							58.4
4							52.1

Low

	Sun	Mon	Tue	Wed	Thu	Fri	Sat
1	61.5	60.3	58.5	58.0	57.2	58.0	56.1
2	55.6	55.0	54.8	52.7	52.8	51.3	50.1
3	50.4	48.0	48.3	47.8	46.1	45.5	46.2
4	46.0	44.0	45.0	43.7	42.3	41.9	41.5

Figure 13.4.4

Instead of using a three-dimensional array to store this same information, we could take an alternative approach by declaring

```
type EXTREME_VALUES is array (EXTREMES) of FLOAT;

New_Temp:  array (WEEK_NUMBERS, DAYS_OF_WEEK) of EXTREME_VALUES;
```

In this case, New_Temp is a two-dimensional array, and each of its components is a one-dimensional array. Ada regards this as a *different* structure from a three-dimensional array, and we might illustrate this by sketching the array as in Figure 13.4.5. In fact, if we took this approach, we would refer to the high temperature on Monday of the second week as New_Temp(2, Mon)(High).

New_Temp

	Sun	Mon	Tue	Wed	Thu	Fri	Sat	
1	61.5	60.3	58.5	58.0	57.2	58.0	56.1	Low
	74.0	75.1	75.6	76.0	75.8	74.3	71.5	High
2	55.6	55.0	54.8	52.7	52.8	51.3	50.1	Low
	70.1	70.1	69.8	67.9	67.0	64.1	61.2	High
3	50.4	48.0	48.3	47.8	46.1	45.5	46.2	Low
	61.2	60.4	59.3	58.0	57.8	58.0	58.4	High
4	46.0	44.4	45.0	43.7	42.3	41.9	41.5	Low
	57.9	56.6	55.9	54.2	53.8	53.0	52.1	High

Figure 13.4.5

A multidimensional array has the attributes Range, First, Last, and Length associated with *each* of its dimensions. In using these attributes, we indicate which dimension is meant, as follows (where the references are to the three-dimensional array of Figure 13.4.4):

```
Temperature'Range(1)  = 1..4
Temperature'First(1)  = 1
Temperature'Last(1)   = 4
Temperature'Length(1) = 4

Temperature'Range(2)  = Sun..Sat
Temperature'First(2)  = Sun
Temperature'Last(2)   = Sat
Temperature'Length(2) = 7

Temperature'Range(3)  = Low..High
Temperature'First(3)  = Low
Temperature'Last(3)   = High
Temperature'Length(3) = 2
```

The numbers 1, 2, and 3 in parentheses refer to the respective dimension, or index range, of the array. We may omit the number 1 in this context, since Ada defines the attributes Range, First, Last, and Length—without a following integer in parentheses—as referring to the *first* index range of the given array, whether the array has any other index range or not.

The operations on multidimensional arrays—assignment, comparison with the relational operators = and /=, parameter passing, and function evaluation—are the same as for one-dimensional arrays. Note that multidimensional arrays may not be compared by means of the operators <, <=, >, >=, nor may they be catenated. Logical operations may not be performed on multidimensional BOOLEAN arrays as a whole (although they may be applied to the individual components of such arrays). We point out that Ada has no such concept as a *slice* of a multidimensional array.

We conclude this section by illustrating some of the typical processing that is done on multidimensional arrays. We confine our attention to two-dimensional arrays. Using again the array type WEEKLY_INFO, we declare a variable

```
Sales:  WEEKLY_INFO;
```

where Sales is a two-dimensional array that records the dollars' worth of a particular item that is sold on each day of a 4-week period. We assume that the components of this variable have already been assigned values. Now it is easy to see that we might want to add up the numbers across each row, to obtain the total dollars' worth sold in each of the 4 weeks. These sums themselves could be viewed as the components of a one-dimensional array Weekly_Sales having the index range 1..4, the same as Sales'Range(1). Further, we might want to divide each component of Weekly_Sales by 7—which is Sales'Length(2)—to yield another one-dimensional array Avg_Sales, with component values representing the average dollars' worth sold per day in each individual week of the 4-week period.

On the basis of these reflections, we can see that it is desirable to be able to compute the **row sums** and **row averages** of a two-dimensional array. Similarly, we frequently have occasion to find the **column sums** and **column averages** of such an array. (What would be the interpretation of these for the array Sales?) In other contexts, we might need to find the greatest or least element in each row or in each column or to find where these elements are located in the array. Consider, for example, a two-dimensional integer array Grades indexed by 1..Num_Students and 1..Num_Tests, in which the component Grades(S, T) holds the grade attained by student S on test T. Here we might need to know the maximum grade on a given test or the maximum grade achieved by a given student over all the tests. Also, we would probably want to know the test average of each student in the class and perhaps the class average on each test.

These ideas suggest that it would be useful to construct a package Integer_Tables analogous to the package Integer_Arrays of Figures 10.9.1 and 10.9.2. The package would contain a declaration of a two-dimensional array type INTEGER_TABLE, along with a set of operations needed in processing arrays of this type. In the next section we discuss the development of such a package.

13.5 The package Integer_Tables

In Chapter 11 we saw that the use of packages contributes greatly to good program modularization. In Section 11.7 we considered an especially useful kind of package, one that specifies and implements an **abstract data type (ADT)**—in this case, INTEGER_ARRAYS —which consists of a type declaration and a set of operations on objects of this type. As we remarked at that time, a package of this kind provides us with reusable software that can be compiled and saved and then included (by way of a **with** clause) in any program that needs to use the ADT defined in the package.

A feature often desirable in an ADT is that it be as widely applicable as possible. For this reason, we developed a package incorporating the *unconstrained* type INTEGER_ARRAY. In an analogous way, we now introduce a new ADT, which we call INTEGER_TABLES. To do so, we will produce a package in which we first declare a two-dimensional unconstrained array type, INTEGER_TABLE:

```
type INTEGER_TABLE is
    array (NATURAL range <>, NATURAL range <>) of INTEGER;
```

In making this declaration, we have in mind that the ranges used in indexing arrays are "usually" of nonnegative integer types. This is not always the case, however, as we have seen; and the arrays of type WEEKY_INFO that we considered in the previous section have a second index range of the *enumeration* type DAYS_OF_WEEK (as well as components of type FLOAT rather than INTEGER). It must be admitted that our package, though of wide applicability, does not enjoy full generality for all two-dimensional arrays. However, it would be desirable to have a package possessing such generality, and this is a topic we return to in Chapter 14.

Our present situation differs from that of Section 11.7, where we had already written the subprogram bodies needed for the package; all that was necessary was to put the pieces together. Here, our way of proceeding will be to present the entire package specification and then to fill in some parts of the package body, leaving the remaining ones for you to supply. You will notice that all the subprograms in this package are *functions*. In Section 10.4 we mentioned that a function may return an *array* as its "value," and we promised to give an example of this at a later time. The time has come, and we have many examples to show you, for each function included in this package (Figure 13.5.1) returns an array. Indeed, as indicated in the function declarations, each function returns an array belonging to an *unconstrained* type—although as we would expect, the actual array that is returned will itself be constrained.

```
package Integer_Tables is

  type INTEGER_TABLE is array (NATURAL range <>, NATURAL range <>)
      of INTEGER;

  type INTEGER_ARRAY is array (NATURAL range <>) of INTEGER;

    -- for row/column sums, averages, maxima, minima
```

```
-- Function Row_Sums takes as an actual parameter any array
-- of type INTEGER_TABLE and returns a one-dimensional array
-- containing its row sums.

function Row_Sums (Int_Tbl:  INTEGER_TABLE) return INTEGER_ARRAY;


-- Function Row_Avgs takes as an actual parameter any array
-- of type INTEGER_TABLE and returns a one-dimensional array
-- containing its (integer-valued) row averages.

function Row_Avgs (Int_Tbl:  INTEGER_TABLE) return INTEGER_ARRAY;


-- Function Row_Maxs takes as an actual parameter any array
-- of type INTEGER_TABLE and returns a one-dimensional array
-- containing the greatest integer from each of its rows.

function Row_Maxs (Int_Tbl:  INTEGER_TABLE) return INTEGER_ARRAY;


-- Function Indexes_of_Row_Maxs takes as an actual parameter
-- any array of type INTEGER_TABLE and returns a one-dimensional
-- array containing, for each row of this parameter, the column
-- index of the greatest integer in that row.  If, for any
-- row, this integer occurs more than once in that row, the
-- function returns the first column index at which it occurs.

function Indexes_of_Row_Maxs (Int_Tbl:  INTEGER_TABLE)
                                        return INTEGER_ARRAY;


-- Function Row_Mins takes as an actual parameter any array
-- of type INTEGER_TABLE and returns a one-dimensional array
-- containing the least integer from each of its rows.

function Row_Mins (Int_Tbl:  INTEGER_TABLE) return INTEGER_ARRAY;

-- Function Indexes_of_Row_Mins takes as an actual parameter
-- any array of type INTEGER_TABLE and returns a one-dimensional
-- array containing, for each row of this parameter, the column
-- index of the least integer in that row.  If, for any
-- row, this integer occurs more than once in that row, the
-- function returns the first column index at which it occurs.

function Indexes_of_Row_Mins (Int_Tbl:  INTEGER_TABLE)
                                        return INTEGER_ARRAY;


-- Function Col_Sums takes as an actual parameter any array
-- of type INTEGER_TABLE and returns a one-dimensional array
-- containing its column sums.

function Col_Sums (Int_Tbl:  INTEGER_TABLE) return INTEGER_ARRAY;


-- Function Col_Avgs takes as an actual parameter any array
-- of type INTEGER_TABLE and returns a one-dimensional array
-- containing its (integer-valued) column averages.
```

```
        function Col_Avgs (Int_Tbl:  INTEGER_TABLE) return INTEGER_ARRAY;


          -- Function Col_Maxs takes as an actual parameter any array
          -- of type INTEGER_TABLE and returns a one-dimensional array
          -- containing the greatest integer from each of its columns.

        function Col_Maxs (Int_Tbl:  INTEGER_TABLE) return INTEGER_ARRAY;


          -- Function Indexes_of_Col_Maxs takes as an actual parameter
          -- any array of type INTEGER_TABLE and returns a one-dimensional
          -- array containing, for each column of this parameter, the row
          -- index of the greatest integer in that column.  If, for
          -- any column, this integer occurs more than once in that
          -- column, the function returns the first row index at
          -- which it occurs.

        function Indexes_of_Col_Maxs (Int_Tbl:  INTEGER_TABLE)
                                      return INTEGER_ARRAY;


          -- Function Col_Mins takes as an actual parameter any array
          -- of type INTEGER_TABLE and returns a one-dimensional array
          -- containing the least integer from each of its columns.

        function Col_Mins (Int_Tbl:  INTEGER_TABLE) return INTEGER_ARRAY;

          -- Function Indexes_of_Col_Mins takes as an actual parameter
          -- any array of type INTEGER_TABLE and returns a one-dimensional
          -- array containing, for each column of this parameter, the row
          -- index of the least integer in that column.  If, for any
          -- column, this integer occurs more than once in that column,
          -- the function returns the first row index at which it occurs.

        function Indexes_of_Col_Mins (Int_Tbl:  INTEGER_TABLE)
                                      return INTEGER_ARRAY;


    end Integer_Tables;
```

Figure 13.5.1

The principal challenge that we face in writing the code for the functions in this package lies in the management of nested **for** loops and their ranges. We have to remember that moving across a *row* of a two-dimensional array (adding or comparing component values) involves passing through the array's *column* indexes and that moving down a *column* means passing through the array's *row* indexes.

```
    package body Integer_Tables is


        function Row_Sums (Int_Tbl:  INTEGER_TABLE) return INTEGER_ARRAY is

        Sums:   INTEGER_ARRAY(Int_Tbl'Range(1));
        Sum:    INTEGER;
```

```
begin

  for Row in Int_Tbl'Range(1) loop
    Sum := 0;
    for Column in Int_Tbl'Range(2) loop
      Sum := Sum + Int_Tbl(Row, Column);
    end loop;
    Sums(Row) := Sum;
  end loop;
  return Sums;

end Row_Sums;


function Row_Avgs (Int_Tbl:  INTEGER_TABLE) return INTEGER_ARRAY is

  Row_Nums:  INTEGER_ARRAY(Int_Tbl'Range(1))
                                   := Row_Sums(Int_Tbl);
  Row_Size:              INTEGER  := Int_Tbl'Length(2);

begin

  for Row in Int_Tbl'Range(1) loop
    Row_Nums(Row) := Row_Nums(Row) / Row_Size;
  end loop;
  return Row_Nums;

end Row_Avgs;


function Row_Maxs (Int_Tbl:  INTEGER_TABLE) return INTEGER_ARRAY is

    <declarations and statements>


function Indexes_of_Row_Maxs (Int_Tbl:  INTEGER_TABLE)
                                    return INTEGER_ARRAY is

    <declarations and statements>


function Row_Mins (Int_Tbl:  INTEGER_TABLE) return INTEGER_ARRAY is

    <declarations and statements>


function Indexes_of_Row_Mins (Int_Tbl:  INTEGER_TABLE)
                                    return INTEGER_ARRAY is

    <declarations and statements>

function Col_Sums (Int_Tbl:  INTEGER_TABLE) return INTEGER_ARRAY is

    <declarations and statements>


function Col_Avgs (Int_Tbl:  INTEGER_TABLE) return INTEGER_ARRAY is

    <declarations and statements>
```

```
    function Col_Maxs (Int_Tbl:  INTEGER_TABLE) return INTEGER_ARRAY is

      <declarations and statements>


    function Indexes_of_Col_Maxs (Int_Tbl:  INTEGER_TABLE)
                                        return INTEGER_ARRAY is

      <declarations and statements>


    function Col_Mins (Int_Tbl:  INTEGER_TABLE) return INTEGER_ARRAY is

Mins:       INTEGER_ARRAY(Int_Tbl'Range(2));
Min_Val:    INTEGER;

begin
  for Column in Int_Tbl'Range(2) loop
    Min_Val := Int_Tbl(Int_Tbl'First(1), Column)
    for Row in Int_Tbl'First(1)+1..Int_Tbl'Last(1) loop
      if Int_Tbl(Row, Column) < Min_Val then
        Min_Val := Int_Tbl(Row, Column);
      end if;
    end loop;
    Mins(Column) := Min_Val;
  end loop;
  return Mins;

end Col_Mins;


    function Indexes_of_Col_Mins (Int_Tbl:  INTEGER_TABLE)
                                        return INTEGER_ARRAY is

  Min_Indexes:   INTEGER_ARRAY(Int_Tbl'Range(2));
  Min_Loc:       INTEGER;
  Min_Val:       INTEGER;

begin

  for Column in Int_Tbl'Range(2) loop
    Min_Loc := Int_Tbl'First(1));
    Min_Val := Int_Tbl(Min_Loc, Column);
    for Row in Int_Tbl'First(1)+1..Int_Tbl'Last(1) loop
      if Int_Tbl(Row, Column) < Min_Val then
        Min_Loc := Row;
        Min_Val := Int_Table(Min_Loc, Column);
      end if;
    end loop;
    Min_Indexes(Column) := Min_Loc;
  end loop;
  return Min_Indexes;

end Indexes_of_Col_Mins;


end Integer_Tables;
```

Figure 13.5.2

It should be clear that the function bodies that appear in Figure 13.5.2 are similar to those that we developed in Chapter 10 for subsequent incorporation into the package body Integer_Arrays (Figure 11.7.2). As mentioned above, their generalization to two-dimensional arrays requires careful attention to the *two* index ranges now involved. Apart from this logical extension of our previous reasoning, the only point to be mentioned is that, for the first time, we have used a *function call* to initialize a variable in its declaration, namely, when we invoked Row_Sums to give an initial value to the local variable Row_Nums used in the function body Row_Avgs. Recall that a function call is an instance of an *expression*, which is just what is needed in the assignment of a value to a variable.

13.6 Record types

Our initial discussion of arrays in Section 10.1, as well as the applications of arrays that we have seen since, should convince us of the utility—even the need—of having such composite objects at our disposal. Much of the usefulness of arrays stems from the fact that an array as a whole may be referred to and—at least to some extent—used in operations while its individual "parts" (components) may also be referenced and used in operations. The fact that array indexes are ranges of discrete types makes it convenient to process arrays by means of loops (especially **for** loops); however, one of the restrictions placed on arrays is that all the components of a given array must be of the *same type*.

We now turn to **record types**, another class of Ada types whose objects, like those of array types, are **composite**, that is, made up of parts. In this case, however, the parts may be of *different* types; furthermore, they are specified not by indexes but by *identifiers*. We will see that as in the case of arrays, the individual parts of a record may be referenced and used in operations. Similarly, a record as a whole may be referred to and used in various ways.

The need for records arises naturally when we are dealing with data objects made up of different "kinds" of parts. For example, information processing often keeps and manipulates information on dates, and any date is made up of three parts: month, day, and year. Computer games that "play cards" with the user need to refer to playing cards, and a reference to a card usually indicates the card's two characteristics: its face value and its suit. Ada's record types make it possible to declare variables and constants that will "naturally" represent composite real-world objects, such as dates and playing cards. On the other hand, while we may think of a date or a playing card as a *single* object made up of parts, there are cases in which we might want to *create* such an object by bringing together related information into a single unit. A personnel office maintains all sorts of data on an employee: name, street address, city, state, Zip code, telephone number, birth date, social security number, job ID, initial employment date, initial date of current position, hourly wage—and much more. This information is of various types: numeric, character string, and probably some values of other enumeration types as well. What all this has in common, however, is that it pertains to a particular employee. Thus, to organize such information for computer storage and retrieval, the first thing we might want to do is have a single composite data object (corresponding to this employee) with all these various data items making up its parts. Ada allows us to do this by means of a **record** variable.

Perhaps the easiest way to get started on record types is to take up the examples of dates and playing cards we just mentioned and show how they may be implemented in Ada as record types. We note some type and subtype declarations, such as we have seen before, and declare a record type DATES:

```
type MONTHS is (Jan, Feb, Mar, Apr, May, Jun, Jul, Aug,
      Sep, Oct, Nov, Dec);
subtype DAYS is POSITIVE range 1..31;
subtype YEARS is POSITIVE range 1601..5_000_000;

type DATES is
  record
    Month:  MONTHS;
    Day:    DAYS;
    Year:   YEARS;
  end record;
```

Again, with some preliminary type declarations, we declare a record type CARDS:

```
type VALUES is (Two, Three, Four, Five, Six, Seven, Eight,
                Nine, Ten, Jack, Queen, King, Ace);
type SUITS  is (Clubs, Diamonds, Hearts, Spades);

type CARDS is
  record
    Value:  VALUES;
    Suit:   SUITS;
  end record;
```

We now have available two record types, DATES and CARDS.

Let us note that the "parts" making up a record type or object are usually called its **fields**, although they may also be called its **components**. Thus, the type DATES and its objects have three fields, each of which is referred to by an identifier: Month, Day, Year. Similarly, objects of type CARDS are made up of the fields Value and Suit. As we mentioned above, the fields of a record need not be of the same type (although they may be), and the types DATE and CARD provide examples of records having fields of different data types. Observe that in the declaration of a record type, the declarations of the fields are enclosed by **record** and **end record**; the fields themselves are declared just as if they were variables, each with its identifier and type mark.

Of course, with record types, as with other types, the mere declaration of a *type* does not create any *objects* of that type. To do this, we declare some variables:

```
My_Birthday, Today, Tomorrow:  DATES;
Low_Card, High_Card, My_Card:  CARDS;
```

Each of these variables has the fields and corresponding field identifiers named in its respective type declaration.

If we want to refer to an *entire* record object, we do so, just as in the case of arrays, by using its identifier, for example, Today, Low_Card. If we have occasion to refer to a *field* of a record object, we do this by using the record's identifier, followed by a period, followed by the identifier of the field. (Note the similarity of this construct to the "expanded names" we have seen many times, in which the period, or dot, in the expanded name is preceded by the identifier of a package or loop.) Thus, we might make the following assignments:

```
My_Birthday.Year := 1976;
Today.Month      := Oct;
Today.Day        := 16;
Tomorrow.Day     := Today.Day + 1;
```

Each of these fields behaves just like an "ordinary" variable of its respective type and is subject to the operations of this type. As these examples indicate, it may receive an assignment. It may also receive a value from input or send a value to output, where, in each case, an I/O routine appropriate for the field's data type is used. As we have remarked, the manner of referencing a field (for example, Today.Month) is reminiscent of the expanded names we saw in Sections 6.8 and 9.2; what is common to all these contexts is that we use the name of a "larger" entity (such as the record variable Today), followed by a period, followed by the name of a "smaller" entity (such as the field Month) *enclosed* in the larger one. As we will see shortly, this process can be carried even further in dealing with records, in the case where a field of a record is itself of a record type made up of fields of its own.

The fields of a record may be of any named type (anonymous types are not allowed); in particular, they may be of an array or record type. Thus, in order to group into a record various items of information on a particular employee, we might first declare

```
subtype STRING_30 is STRING(1..30);
subtype STRING_20 is STRING(1..20);
subtype STRING_2  is STRING(1..2);
subtype STRING_5  is STRING(1..5);

type ADDRESS is
  record
    Street_Adr:  STRING_30;
    City:        STRING_20;
    State:       STRING_2;
    Zip:         STRING_5;
  end record;
```

and then make the declarations

```
type EMPLOYEE_INFO is
  record
    Name:        STRING_30;
    Adr:         ADDRESS;
    Birth_Date:  DATES;
       .
       .
       .
  end record;

My_Info:  EMPLOYEE_INFO;
```

The variable My_Info is a record with several fields, including Name, Adr, and Birth_Date. Also,

```
My_Info.Birth_Date
```

is a three-field record, of type DATES, but

```
My_Info.Birth_Date.Month
```

is a single field, of type MONTHS. Notice that we must name the "outermost" record My_Info and include intermediate field names, such as Birth_Date, before naming the individual field (Month, Day, or Year) that we want to refer to. This process may be extended to deeper levels of record nesting, when appropriate. To continue with some more examples, consider such references as

`My_Info.Birth_Date.Day`	A number, of type DAYS
`My_Info.Birth_Date.Year`	A number, of type YEARS
`My_Info.Name`	A string of 30 characters
`My_Info.Name(1)`	First character of this string
`My_Info.Adr`	A record with four fields
`My_Info.Adr.State`	A string of 2 characters
`My_Info.Adr.Zip(1..3)`	Three-character slice of string

As you can see, there is a great consistency in all this referencing of record and array components. To extend it further, let us look at an array whose components are of the record type EMPLOYEE_INFO. We declare this array to be of an anonymous array type:

```
Max_Num:     constant := <some suitable POSITIVE value>;
Employees:   array (INTEGER range 1..Max_Num) of EMPLOYEE_INFO;
```

We now consider the employee whose record has index 15 in the array Employees:

`Employees(15):`	This employee's entire employment record
`Employees(15).Birth_Date:`	This employee's birth date, a record with three fields
`Employees(15).Birth_Date.Year:`	The year of this employee's birth
`Employees(15).Name:`	This employee's name, a 30-character string
`Employees(15).Name(1):`	The first character of this employee's name
`Employees(15).Adr:`	This employee's address, a record with 4 fields
`Employees(15).Adr.Zip:`	This employee's zip code, a 5-character string

```
Employees(15).Adr.Zip(4..5):      The last 2 characters of
                                  this employee's Zip code
```

For records, as for arrays, there are **record aggregates** that play the role of literals. A record aggregate is similar to an array aggregate, in that it must specify a value for each field of the record, and it may do this by either positional association or named association. Aggregates may be used in assignments; thus they are useful in declaring record constants. We offer some examples of record aggregates with positional association:

```
Today                := (Oct, 16, 1994);
Low_Card             := (Two, Clubs);
High_Card            := (Ace, Spades);
My_Info.Birth_Date:  := (Aug, 31, 1972);
Independence_Day     := constant DATES := (Jul, 4, 1776);
```

Named association is done in much the same way for record aggregates as for array aggregates. The symbol | may be used, with its usual meaning of "or." Here, however, there is no such thing as a "range" of fields; in general, the association of values and field names has to be done on an individual basis. There is one exception to this: We may use the reserved word **others** as before, alone and in last place, provided that all the fields included under this use of **others** are of the same type (as we might expect, since they are all to be associated with the same value). Here are some examples of named associations:

```
Today := (Month => Oct, Day => 16, Year => 1994);
Today := (Day => 16, Year =: 1994, Month => Oct);
Low_Card := (Suit => Clubs, Value => Two);
```

We may mix positional and named association in the case of record aggregates, but if we do so, we have to begin with positional association, and once we have changed to named association, we must stay with the latter. Thus

```
Today := (Oct, Year => 1994, Day => 16);
Today := (Oct, 16, Year => 1994);
Today := (Oct, 16, others => 1994);
```

One point should be noted before we turn to the topic of operations on record objects. Record types provide the *only* instance in Ada in which the programmer may assign initial values not merely to individual objects but to an *entire type*—which means, more properly, that **default values** may be assigned to one or more fields of the type, and every variable of the type will automatically be given these as initial values at the time of its declaration, unless the programmer specifies otherwise. For example, in declaring the type EMPLOYEE_INFO, we might have initialized all the string fields to strings of blanks. This could be done as follows:

```
type EMPLOYEE_INFO is
   record
     Name:       STRING_30 := (others => ' ');
     Adr:        ADDRESS   := (others => (others => ' '));
     Birth_Date: DATES;
```

```
        .
        .
        .
    end record;
```

Now the declaration

```
    My_Info:  EMPLOYEE_INFO;
```

yields a record variable in which the Name field consists of a string of blanks, as do all the fields (Street_Adr, City, State, Zip) making up the field Adr. The programmer can override these default values; one way of doing this is to use an aggregate to assign other values in declaring My_Info, but recall that if an aggregate is used at all, it must provide values for *all* the fields of the record, even those with default values and even if the value to be provided for a given field is the same as its default value.

We remarked earlier in this section that in the declaration of a record type, the words **record** and **end record** enclose the declarations of the individual fields and these fields themselves are declared just like variables, in terms of their identifiers and types. We now know that these field declarations behave even more like variable declarations, in that the fields may be assigned initial values when they are declared. The Ada language provides other special features of record types that we do not take up in this book; however, for those that we have seen and will continue to use, we sum up in the syntax diagram of Figure 13.6.1 the rules for record type declarations.

a

record type

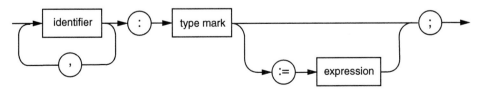

b

component declaration

Figure 13.6.1

When it comes to the matter of **record operations**, the situation is much like that of arrays. Most of the operations involving records (notably I/O) must be done on a field-by-field basis. However, as in the case of arrays, there are four kinds of operations that may be performed on or with *entire* records, without the necessity of dealing separately with their individual fields:

1. **Assignment.** A record aggregate, constant, or variable may be assigned to a record variable of the same type:

    ```
    My_Info.Birth_Date  := (Aug, 31, 1974);     aggregate
    Today               := Independence_Day;    constant
    My_Card             := Low_Card;            variable
    ```

2. **Comparison.** Two record objects (aggregate, constant, variable) of the same type may be compared by means of the relational operators = and /= (but not by the other relational operators). Equality holds if, in both operands, all corresponding pairs of fields have the same values; otherwise, inequality holds.

    ```
    if Today = (Jan, 1, 2000) then ...          aggregate
    if Tomorrow = Independence_Day then         constant
    if My_Card = High_Card then                 variable
    ```

3. **Parameter passing.** A record may be used as a parameter in a procedure or function call. Record types (like array types) are *composite* types; therefore we may apply to parameters that are of a record type the remarks made in Section 13.2 on passing information between actual and formal parameters that are of an array type.

4. **Function evaluation.** A function may return a record as its value.

We illustrate the last two points and conclude this chapter by offering a very simple function associated with the record type CARDS that we have been using in this section. The function compares two cards and returns the value of the "higher" one of them. Its code is shown in Figure 13.6.2.

```
-- Function Higher_Card accepts two actual parameters of type
-- CARDS and returns the value of the higher of them.  Cards
-- are taken to be ordered in terms of their face values (with
-- ace high); for cards with the same face value, the suit
-- determines the rank, by means of the ordering: clubs (low),
-- diamonds, hearts, spades (high).

function Higher_Card (C1, C2: CARDS) return CARDS is

begin

    if C1.Value > C2.Value then
       return C1;
    elsif C2.Value > C1.Value then
       return C2;
    elsif C1.Suit > C2.Suit then     -- cards have the same face value
       return C1;
```

```
      else                              -- C2 has higher suit
         return C2;
      end if;

   end Higher_Card;
```

Figure 13.6.2

13.7 Exercises

13.1.1 Listed below are several possibilities for the *base* type of an array's *index range* and for the type of the array's *components*. For each of these, make up an example (other than those in the text) of an array type with the given characteristics and of an array variable of this type. In each case, try for an array that could actually be put to practical use in a program.

    (a) Index range: INTEGER;   components: an enumeration type other than CHARACTER or BOOLEAN

    (b) Index range: CHARACTER; components: numeric (INTEGER or FLOAT)

    (c) Index range: an enumeration type other than CHARACTER; components: numeric

    (d) Index range: an enumeration type other than CHARACTER; components: an enumeration type

13.1.2 Can the base type of an array's index range be FLOAT? Explain.

13.1.3 Create the text file described in Exercise 12.11.1 (unless you have already done so). Then write a program to read this file character by character, write it to the screen, and at the end tell how many times each letter of the alphabet occurred in the file.

13.2.1 Consider the array variable Hours_Worked of type WEEKLY_INFO, introduced in Section 13.1, where we declared

```
         type DAYS_OF_WEEK is (Sun, Mon, Tue, Wed, Thu, Fri, Sat);
         type WEEKLY_INFO is array (DAYS_OF_WEEK) of INTEGER;
```

If we wish to assign values to the components of Hours_Worked by an assignment statement in the form

```
         Hours_Worked := ( ... );
```

with an array aggregate on the right of the assignment operator, which of the following may be used for this purpose? Explain each answer.

(a) (0,6,6,6,6,6)

(b) (Sun..Wed => 8, Thu..Sat => 0)

(c) (Mon | Wed | Fri => 8, Tue | Thu | Sat => 3)

(d) (Mon..Fri => 8, Sat..Sun => 0)

(e) (Sun..Thu => 7, Wed | Fri => 8, Sat => 0)

(f) (Sun..Tue => 8, Thu..Sat => 5, Wed => 0)

(g) (0, Mon..Fri => 8, 0)

(h) (0, 0, Tue..Sat => 8)

(i) (0, 0, others => 8)

(j) (others => 4)

13.2.2 Referring to the type WEEKLY_INFO of Exercise 13.2.1 and the type INTEGER_ARRAY, which we have several times declared to be **array** (NATURAL **range** <>) **of** INTEGER, we declare

```
Hours_Worked: WEEKLY_INFO := (0, 8, 8, 8, 8, 8, 0);
Four_Ints: INTEGER_ARRAY(0..3)   := (5, 2, 5, 1);
Five_Ints: INTEGER_ARRAY(11..15) := (2, 5, 2, 5, 2);
```

Tell whether each of the following assignments is or is not valid. Justify each answer.

(a) Five_Ints := Four_Ints;

(b) Four_Ints := Five_Ints(12..15);

(c) Five_Ints(12..14) := Four_Ints(0..2);

(d) Five_Ints(11..14) := Five_Ints(12..15);

(e) Four_Ints(0..2) := Four_Ints(2..3);

(f) Hours_Worked(Sun..Tue) := Hours_Worked(Thu..Sat);

(g) Hours_Worked(Tue..Fri) := Hours_Worked(Sun..Tue);

(h) Hours_Worked(Mon..Fri) := Five_Ints;

13.2.3 Referring to the variables Hours_Worked, Four_Ints, and Five_Ints of Exercise 13.2.2, tell whether each of the following conditions is True, False, or invalid. Explain each answer.

(a) Five_Ints(11..12) < Four_Ints

(b) Five_INTS(12..14) >= Four_Ints(0..2)

(c) Five_Ints(11..12) < Four_Ints(0..2)

(d) Five_Ints(12..15) >= Four_Ints

(e) Four_Ints < Five_Ints

(f) Hours_Worked(Sun..Tue) >= Hours_Worked(Thu..Sat)

(g) Hours_Worked(Mon..Tue) < Hours_Worked(Thu..Sat)

(h) Hours_Worked(Mon..Tue) > Five_Ints

13.2.4 Consider the array variables Rain and Snow of Figure 13.2.3. Make a sketch (like that of **Rain and Snow** in that figure) for each of the arrays **Rain or Snow**, **Rain xor Snow**, **not Rain**, **not Snow**.

13.2.5 Referring again to the declarations of Exercise 13.2.2, show (in the form of array aggregates) the results of each of the following catenation operations:

(a) `Four_Ints & Five_Ints`
(b) `Five_Ints & Four_Ints`
(c) `Four_Ints(0..2) & 2`
(d) `2 & Four_Ints(0..2) & 2`
(e) `Four_Ints(0..2) & Five_Ints(13..15)`
(f) `Five_Ints(11..13) & Four_Ints(0..2)`

13.3.1 We have stressed that although an array *type* may be unconstrained (as is the type STRING), *objects* of this type (variables and constants) must be *constrained*. But observe that Ada allows a declaration such as the following:

```
President: STRING := "George Washington";
```

(a) Comment on this situation. Does this contradict the requirement that all array variables be constrained? What is the index range of the variable President? Could a different STRING literal be assigned to President in an assignment statement? If so, what restrictions (if any) would there be on such a literal? Test your answers with a short program.

(b) Recall the declaration

```
type INTEGER_ARRAY is array (NATURAL range <>) of INTEGER;
```

and suppose we declare

```
Three_Ints: INTEGER_ARRAY := (-1, 0, 1);
```

How does this situation relate to that of part *a*? If this declaration is acceptable, what would you expect the index range of the array variable Three_Ints to be? Write a test program to verify your answers.

(c) Now consider the declarations

```
type ARRAY_OF_INTS is array (INTEGER range <>)
   of INTEGER;
Three_Ints: ARRAY_OF_INTS := (-1, 0, 1);
```

Answer the same questions as in part *b*.

13.3.2 Declare

```
subtype STRING_30 is STRING(1..30);
```

and adapt the procedure Sort_Up (Section 10.6) to sort an array of names of subtype STRING_30. Then write a test program to read in an array of names from a data file, invoke Sort_Up, and display the names in alphabetical order.

13.3.3 Write a procedure to accept a character string (of any length) and reverse the order of the characters in it. Do this without declaring any local STRING variable within the procedure.

13.3.4 Write a BOOLEAN-valued function to accept a character string (of any length) and determine whether or not it is a palindrome. A *palindrome* is a word or phrase whose characters read the same in both directions (forward and backward). Examples are MADAMIMADAM (Madam, I'm Adam) and AMANAPLANACANALPANAMA (A man, a plan, a canal, Panama).

13.3.5 It was stated in Section 13.3 that Text_IO's procedure Get_Line obtains characters from the keyboard and places them in the STRING variable named as its first parameter (but not exceeding the length of that string) until End_of_Line was detected. If the first index of the string variable is 1, Get_Line then sets the second (NATURAL) parameter to the number of characters obtained, a number between 0 and the length of the string, inclusive. It was also asserted that if the number of characters was less than the length of the string, the remaining locations in the string variable were left indeterminate. To be more precise, the remaining loactions are simply *not* used, so whatever was in those locations prior to the call to Get_Line remains there. Verify this by executing the following small program, and tell why it establishes what we have just claimed. (You will have to abort the program's execution abruptly, unless you add some statement within the loop, such as

```
exit when Str(1) = '!'
```

for a controlled termination of the loop.)

```
with Text_IO;

procedure Get_String is

   Str:   STRING(1..30);
   Len:   NATURAL;

begin
   loop
      Text_IO.Put ("Enter a string: ");
      Text_IO.Get_Line (Str, Len);
      Text_IO.Put_Line (Str);
      Text_IO.Put_Line (Str(1..Len));
      Text_IO.New_Line;
   end loop;

end Get_String;
```

(a) Make your first input string relatively short (5 characters or so).

(b) The next input string should be almost long enough to fill the entire string (but no more than 30 characters).

(c) Now enter a few more strings of varying lengths (but less than 30). Is an *empty* string acceptable to the program? (An empty string is created when the ENTER key is pressed immediately at the prompt.)

(d) Enter several strings of length greater than 30. Explain in detail what you conclude from the resulting output. What happens when you enter a string *exactly* 30 characters long?

(e) The results of part *d* should suggest the use of Skip_Line at some appropriate place in the program. Where? What effect does the Skip_Line have? (This is a bit tricky, for if the length of the input string is less than 30, in effect Skip_Line has already been executed, and the resulting program may not behave as expected. You will have to experiment a bit with various values of the Len variable and make appropriate patches to the program.)

(f) What does the second Put_Line do, and why?

13.3.6 Write a program that opens a text file, reads it on a character-by- character basis, and writes each character to a second text file. (That is, write a file copy program.) The names of the input and output files should be obtained as strings from the keyboard by using the results derived from Exercise 13.3.5. In addition to an exception handler to intercept End_Error, you also have to be concerned with a potential Name_Error (see Section 7.16).

13.3.7 Modify the file copy program of Exercise 13.3.6 above to:

(a) Remove multiple spaces between words as characters are written to the output file (see the program of Figure 12.3.3).

(b) Remove multiple blank lines when the output file is written (thus three consecutive blank lines are to be reduced to a single blank line, but a single blank line is to be left as is).

(c) Remove multiple spaces between words *and* multiple blank lines.

13.4.1. Consider the declarations

```
type ROW  is array (1..3) of INTEGER;
type ROWS is array (1..2) of ROW;
New_Table:  ROWS;
```

The array variable New_Table is different from the variable Table (Figure 13.4.1). New_Table has exactly *two* components, each of which is a *three*-component array.

How might New_Table be pictured, so as to distinguish it from Table? (Suggestion: consider Figure 13.4.5.)

13.4.2 In Section 13.3 we saw the declarations

```
subtype NAME_STRING is STRING(1..30);
type NAME_ARRAY is array (NATURAL range <>)
    of NAME_STRING;
Name_List:  NAME_ARRAY(1..100);
```

and we compared the meanings of Name_List, Name_List(25), and Name_List(25)(1). Suppose we had declared

```
Name_List: array (1..100, 1..30) of CHARACTER;
```

How might we picture such an array? How, if at all, could we refer to the twenty-fifth name in the array? How, if at all, could we refer to the first character of the twenty-fifth name in the array? How might the twenty-fifth name be displayed?

13.4.3 Refer to the two-dimensional array type WEEKLY_INFO declared in Section 13.4 and to the description of the array variable

```
Sales:  WEEKLY_INFO;
```

What would be the interpretation (significant in a business context) of the column sums and column averages of this array?

13.5.1 Complete the package body INTEGER_TABLES (Figure 13.5.2).

13.6.1 Consider the array Employees declared in this section:

```
Employees: array (INTEGER range 1..Max_Num) of EMPLOYEE_INFO;
```

Tell how to reference each of the following:

(a) The entire array of employee information records
(b) The 20th employee's record in the array
(c) The 20th employee's name
(d) The 20th employee's birth date
(e) The 20th employee's birth month
(f) The 20th employee's city
(g) The first three digits of the 20th employee's zip code

13.6.2 Write a procedure Display_Card that accepts a single **in** parameter of (record) type CARDS and displays the value and suit of the parameter in the form

<value> of <suit>

For example, Display_Card ((Eight, Hearts)) would display

EIGHT of HEARTS

13.6.3 In the game of bridge all 52 cards are distributed to 4 players, so that each player has a hand of 13 cards. Consider the bridge hand determined by the following declarations:

```
type Bridge_Hand is array (INTEGER range 1..13) of CARDS;

Hand:  Bridge_Hand :=

         ((Two,Hearts),     (Jack,Clubs),    (Ace,Clubs),
          (Nine,Diamonds),  (Nine,Spades),   (Four,Hearts),
          (Queen,Clubs),    (Six,Hearts),    (Seven,Hearts),
          (Ace,Diamonds),   (Ten,Hearts),    (Nine,Clubs),
          (Three,Spades));
```

(a) Use the procedure Display_Card to display the entire hand, one card to a line.

(b) Write a modified version of the Sort_Up procedure of Figure 10.6.4, named Sort_Up_Value, and use it to sort the cards in the array Hand into increasing order by Value. Test your procedure by sorting the array and displaying it as in part *a* above.

(c) Write a modified version of the Sort_Up procedure of Figure 10.6.4, named Sort_Up_Suit, and use it to sort the cards in the array Hand into increasing order by Suit. Test your procedure by sorting the array and displaying it as in part *a*.

(d) Define a function "<" among pairs of objects of type CARDS which establishes an order relation on this type. (See Section 11.8.) Specifically, "<" (Left, Right) is True if Left is a "lower card" than Right, where Left is *lower* than Right provided Left's Suit is "smaller" than Right's Suit (in the enumeration type sense), or in the event they have the same Suit, Left has a smaller Value than Right; otherwise, the function is to return False. Then write a modified version of the Sort_Up procedure of Figure 10.6.4, named Sort_Up_Cards, and use it to sort the cards in the array Hand. Finally, display the resulting array as in part *a*. The cards should be sorted in increasing order within suits, the suits also in increasing order.

(e) The arrangement of cards in part *d* is frequently used by bridge players to sort their hands; that is, they rearrange the cards dealt to them so that the suits increase left to right and within each suit the cards increase left to right. On the other hand, some bridge players prefer to arrange their cards so that the suits increase left to right, but within each suit the cards *decrease* left to right. Determine what modifications to the program of part *d* would be required to achieve this type of sort, and implement this new sort.

(f) Is the result of the sort Sort_Up_Cards the same as applying Sort_Up_Value (part *b*) *followed by* Sort_Up_Suit (part *c*)? Should it be?

Chapter 14

Generic Units

This chapter deals further with some aspects of a topic we have discussed before, namely, the development of *reusable software*. By now we have seen many instances of reusable software: the function GCD and procedure Exchange (Section 9.8), the package Rationals (Section 11.8), and the packages Int_Pack (Section 3.5), Integer_Arrays (Section 11.7), and Integer_Tables (Section 13.5). These subprograms and packages embody Ada code that has been compiled and is ready for use with any Ada program, provided only that the compiled version of the respective subprogram or package is in the program's library and is included in the program's context by means of a **with** clause.

Our aim here is to broaden the applicability of some of the subprograms and packages we have already written. We pointed out in Section 11.7 that the procedure Sort_Up included in the package Integer_Arrays could be adapted, by a mere change of type declarations, to sort any array of STRING components indexed by a NATURAL range; the result of such an adaptation could be used to alphabetize—sort into ascending order—an array of *names*. It could also easily be adapted to sort any array of FLOAT components indexed by a NATURAL range. The important point here is that there is no difference whatever between the *logic* involved in sorting an array of integers and that involved in sorting an array of strings, floating point numbers, or, for that matter, *anything*, provided only that, in each case, there is an order relationship among the components of the array so that it makes sense to speak of arranging them "in order." It is tempting, then, to seek to develop a universally applicable Sort procedure. While we are about it, we might wish to depart from the restriction that the array in question be indexed by a NATURAL range; could we go so far as to allow an index range of *any* discrete type?

The answer to this question, and to all these considerations on extending the applicability of subprograms, lies in an Ada feature known as a **generic unit**. A generic unit is either a **generic subprogram** or a **generic package**. As we first saw in Section 3.2, a generic unit provides a pattern, or **template**, that can be used to create specific *instances* by a process called *instantiation*. We have encountered several examples of generic packages— Integer_IO, Float_IO, and Enumeration_IO—each of which is contained in the package Text_IO.

In the sections that follow, we develop generic subprograms and packages of our own and see how they may be applied in various contexts. We look at generic subprograms first, and we begin with a very simple and familiar example.

14.1 A generic Exchange subprogram

As we are aware, the process of exchanging (or interchanging or swapping) two variable values is often used in programming. Every programmer knows that it requires an extra variable besides the two given ones and that it takes three assignments. In fact, because of its brevity, it is unlikely that we would actually use a procedure to accomplish it. However, because an exchange procedure has the advantage of illustrating several important concepts of programming, without the distraction of complicated program logic, we did in fact write such a procedure (Figure 8.7.1) to interchange the values of two INTEGER variables. It is clear that by merely changing the types of its formal parameters, this procedure could be adapted to exchange two CHARACTER values or two FLOAT values. It is because the Exchange procedure is so simple, as well as so widely applicable, that we use it to construct an example which we trace through successive stages of generalization.

Consider the parameterless procedure Exchange shown in the program skeleton of Figure 14.1.1. This procedure has been written in such a way that its use is limited to interchanging *only* the values of the INTEGER variables A and B in the program Example. It is called twice in the program, and each time it interchanges the values of these particular variables; indeed, it is not capable of accomplishing anything else.

```
procedure Example is

    .
    .
    .
A, B:  INTEGER;

procedure Exchange is

    Temp:  INTEGER := A;

begin

    A := B;
    B := Temp;

end Exchange;

begin -- Example

    .
    .
    .
Exchange;
    .
    .
    .
Exchange;
```

```
        .
        .
        .

    end Example;
```

Figure 14.1.1

Now consider the form of Exchange that appears in the program skeleton of Figure
14.1.2.

```
    procedure Example is

        .
        .
        .
    A, B, C, D:  INTEGER;
    procedure Exchange (X, Y: in out INTEGER) is

        Temp:  INTEGER := X;

    begin

        X := Y;
        Y := Temp;

    end Exchange;
    begin -- Example

        .
        .
        .
    Exchange (A, B);
        .
        .
        .
    Exchange (C, D);
        .
        .
        .
    Exchange (A, C);
        .
        .
        .
    Exchange (B, D);
        .
        .
        .

    end Example;
```

Figure 14.1.2

By introducing *parameterization* into the procedure Exchange of Figure 14.1.2, we have made it possible to apply this procedure to *different* pairs of INTEGER variables, as has been done. (We discussed this concept earlier, in Section 11.9.) Notice that this procedure is available for application *only* within the program Example. We are well aware, however, that the interchanging of INTEGER values is of common occurrence throughout programming in general. Thus as a further step toward improved applicability, we write the procedure Exchange in a separate file, as shown in Figure 14.1.3, and compile it separately, as was done in Section 9.8. Just as is the case with procedures that are main programs, this compilation unit, and the library unit that results from compiling it, has the name Exchange.

```
procedure Exchange (X, Y: in out INTEGER) is

   Temp:  INTEGER := X;

begin

   X := Y;
   Y := Temp;

end Exchange;
```

Figure 14.1.3

Now we may separately write and compile the program Example, as shown in Figure 14.1.4.

```
with Exchange;

procedure Example is

   .
   .
   .
   A, B, C, D:  INTEGER;

begin -- Example

   .
   .
   .
   Exchange (A, B);
   .
   .
   .
   Exchange (C, D);
   .
   .
   .
   Exchange (A, C);
   .
   .
   .
   Exchange (B, D);
   .
   .
   .
end Example;
```

Figure 14.1.4

The program Example of Figure 14.1.4 behaves just as it does in Figure 14.1.2. The difference is that the source code for Exchange is *not* included in this program; moreover, as we saw in Section 9.8, it is now possible to include the clause **with Exchange** in *any* program requiring the interchange of the values of two INTEGER variables.

This Exchange procedure has one serious restriction. Although the inclusion of the parameters X and Y has made it possible to apply Exchange to various pairs of variables, it still remains true that these must be <u>INTEGER</u> variables. Yet we may very well need to interchange the values of two variables of a type other than INTEGER—two FLOAT variables, say, or two STRING variables. Perhaps we might change the name of this procedure to Exchange_Ints and then write and separately compile procedures Exchange_Flts and Exchange_Strs to handle FLOAT and STRING variables, respectively. This would be an advance. If our program needed to do interchanging of INTEGER, FLOAT, or STRING variables—or perhaps of several of these—we could employ a **with** clause to make the necessary procedures available to the program. As another possibility, we might name all three of these procedures Exchange and incorporate them all into a separately compiled *package* for use with any program needing some or all of them.

This solution is only a partial one; we might have to interchange the values of *other* types of variables—variables of other floating point types, of enumeration types, or of any of the enormous variety of array or record types. Can we write and compile a *single* procedure to handle this degree of generality?

The answer is a qualified yes, and the key to it lies in the idea of parameterization. The introduction of the formal parameters X and Y in Figures 14.1.2 and 14.1.3 allowed the procedure Exchange to be used with *any* pair of INTEGER variables; what is needed here is a *formal parameter* to be used in place of the specific type INTEGER. If we could use a *formal* **type** parameter, instead of INTEGER, as the type of the procedure's parameters X and Y, then when employing the Exchange procedure, we could supply a corresponding *actual* type parameter and proceed to apply the procedure to variables of this type. Is all this simply wishful thinking? No, this is just what Ada allows us to do in the construct known as a **generic subprogram**.

Unlike an "ordinary" (nongeneric) subprogram, a generic subprogram must have not only a subprogram body but also a separately declared subprogram *specification*. For now we assume that the subprogram specification and body are in the *same* compilation unit, in which case the specification must *precede* the body. The generic subprogram specification begins with the reserved word **generic**, followed by declarations of generic formal parameters, followed by the ordinary specification of the subprogram. While generic formal parameters may stand for a variety of entities, our interest at the moment is in introducing a generic *type* parameter. To do so and to sum up the remarks we have made, we declare the generic procedure specification as follows:

```
generic

   type ITEM_TYPE is <information to be supplied here>;

procedure Exchange (X, Y: in out ITEM_TYPE);
```

Here, in the **generic** part, we specify what is generic about the procedure—it is the formal type ITEM_TYPE, used as the type of the procedure's parameters X and Y. Eventually, when the procedure is to be used, ITEM_TYPE will have to be replaced by some *specific* type name (actual type parameter), just as the formal parameters of any subprogram are replaced by actual parameters when the subprogram is called. Supplying actual parameters to replace the formal generic parameters of a generic subprogram is known as **instantiating** the generic subprogram; it creates a *specific instance* of the template—or pattern—of declarations and actions relative to the specified type. We will see shortly how this is done, but let us first see how to complete the declaration of ITEM_TYPE.

Ada allows us several ways of specifying what kind of type is allowable as an actual parameter corresponding to ITEM_TYPE. If we write

```
type ITEM_TYPE is range <>;
```

then the actual type parameter supplied in the instantiation of Exchange must be an *integer* type; at the same time, all the operations pertinent to integer types may be applied within the subprogram body to any objects declared to be of type ITEM_TYPE. But if we write

```
type ITEM_TYPE is (<>);
```

then we may supply the name of any *discrete* type when we instantiate the subprogram, but only the operations common to all discrete types may be applied to objects of type ITEM_TYPE within the subprogram body. To go one step further, we could declare

```
type ITEM_TYPE is digits <>;
```

and then the actual type parameter supplied in the instantiation of the procedure would have to be of a *floating point* type; correspondingly, the operations of floating point types would be available for objects of type ITEM_TYPE within the subprogram body.

Are we obliged to make a choice from among these possibilities? If so, we may not be able to create a *totally* general Exchange procedure, applicable to variables of virtually all types. But Ada provides us with a further possibility for this formal type parameter. We may use the declaration

```
type ITEM_TYPE is private;
```

In this case *any* of the types we have seen can be supplied as an actual parameter corresponding to the formal type parameter ITEM_TYPE when we instantiate the generic Exchange procedure. (We must modify this assertion slightly: the declaration

```
Temp:   ITEM_TYPE;
```

in the body of the procedure prevents us from using an *unconstrained* array type as an actual type parameter, since the variable Temp, like any variable, cannot be declared to be unconstrained.) The price to be paid for declaring ITEM_TYPE in this way is that the only operations available for use with objects of this type within the subprogram are assignment and comparison by means of the relational operators = and /=. Of course, the only operation we need to use in an Exchange procedure is assignment, and thus this restriction offers us no problem. Accordingly, we present the final form of Exchange in Figure 14.1.5. Notice that the generic procedure specification *precedes* the procedure body in this unit; alternatively, we could put the specification and body in distinct files and compile them separately, as long as we compile the specification *before* compiling the body. (We should point out that the meaning of Ada's reserved word **private**, when used in declaring a formal type parameter of a generic unit, is different from the meaning it has in a context like that of Figure 11.8.1; the latter meaning is described in the discussion following that figure.)

```
-- The generic procedure specification:

generic

  type ITEM_TYPE is private;

procedure Exchange (X, Y: in out ITEM_TYPE);


-- The generic procedure body:

procedure Exchange (X, Y: in out ITEM_TYPE) is

  Temp:  ITEM_TYPE := X;

begin

  X := Y;
  Y := Temp;

end Exchange;
```

Figure 14.1.5

Instantiating a generic subprogram is a simple matter, and it bears a close resemblance to instantiating a generic *package*, a process we have carried out many times with Integer_IO and other generic I/O packages. To illustrate it, we present a demonstration program in Figure 14.1.6. Here we have instantiated the generic Exchange procedure four times, to produce the four procedures Exchange_Nats, Exchange_Strs3, Exchange_Strs4, and Exchange_Recs. Recall that we are not allowed to use the *unconstrained* array type STRING as an actual type parameter in an instantiation of Exchange; for this reason we introduce the STRING subtypes STRING3 and STRING4 to use as actual type parameters in the instantiation. The program includes calls to each of these procedures.

```
  with Exchange;

procedure Make_Exchanges is

  subtype STRING_30 is STRING(1..30);
  subtype STRING_3 is STRING(1..3);
  subtype STRING_4  is STRING(1..4);

  type OFFICE_INFO  is
    record
      Name:    STRING_30;     -- Employee's name
      Assts:   NATURAL;       -- Number of assistants
```

```
        Office: STRING_3;        -- Office number
        Phone:  STRING_4;        -- Office telephone extension
     end record;

  Employee_Count:  constant NATURAL := <some suitable value>;
  Directory:  array (INTEGER range 1..Employee_Count) of OFFICE_INFO;

  procedure Exchange_Nats  is new Exchange(NATURAL);
  procedure Exchange_Strs3 is new Exchange(STRING_3);
  procedure Exchange_Strs4 is new Exchange(STRING_4);
  procedure Exchange_Recs  is new Exchange(OFFICE_INFO);

begin

  -- We assume that values have been assigned to the
  -- components of Directory (for example, by reading them
  -- from a file).

  Exchange_Nats (Directory(24).Assts, Directory(37).Assts);
  Exchange_Strs3 (Directory(24).Office, Directory(37).Office);
  Exchange_Strs4 (Directory(24).Phone, Directory(37).Phone);
  Exchange_Recs (Directory(1), Directory(4));

end Make_Exchanges;
```

Figure 14.1.6

Notice that the instantiations of Exchange bear a resemblance to the instantiations of Integer_IO and other generic packages we have seen, except that the word **package** has been replaced by **procedure**. Similarly, we would use the word **function** to instantiate a generic function.

14.2 A generic Sort_Up procedure: Generalizing the index type

In this section we take a step toward generalizing the procedure Sort_Up that appears in Figure 10.9.4. Recall that we had declared

```
type INTEGER_ARRAY is array (NATURAL range <>) of INTEGER;
```

and that the procedure Sort_Up itself had the following specification:

```
procedure Sort_Up (Int_Data: in out INTEGER_ARRAY);
```

As it stands, Sort_Up will sort into ascending order the components of an array of type INTEGER_ARRAY. As we have already noted, this means not only that the array must have INTEGER components but also that it must be of an unconstrained array type whose index set is a range of the subtype NATURAL. To begin generalizing this procedure, we remove the latter restriction and allow the unconstrained array type to be indexed by a range from *any* discrete type. Since *every* array must be indexed by a discrete range—that is, a range of either an integer type or an enumeration type—our generic Sort_Up procedure has achieved full generality, at least in this respect. In the next section, we move toward generalizing the *component* type of the array to be sorted; for now, we continue to deal with arrays having INTEGER components.

The generic procedure we are seeking to develop has the specification shown in Figure 14.2.1.

```
generic

   type INDEX_TYPE is (<>);
      -- This declaration generalizes the index type.

   type INT_ARRAY is array (INDEX_TYPE range <>) of INTEGER;
      -- This declares a (new) unconstrained array type
      -- with INDEX_TYPE as the base type of its index range.

      -- Procedure Sort_Up takes as a parameter any array of
      -- type INT_ARRAY (an unconstrained array type, indexed
      -- by a range of type INDEX_TYPE, and with components of
      -- type INTEGER), and sorts it into ascending order.

procedure Sort_Up (Int_Data: in out INT_ARRAY);
```

Figure 14.2.1

To implement this procedure, we again use the selection sort method employed several times before, in Chapters 10 and 11. In fact, we may repeat almost verbatim the code that appears in Figure 10.9.4. We must be careful, however, that we do not attempt to perform on the array's indexes any operations that are peculiar to *integer* types (such as the subtype NATURAL that was originally used for the indexes), since now the indexes may be taken from an *enumeration* type as well. In Figure 10.9.4, this situation occurs in two places only: The integer operation + is performed with an array index twice, both times in the expression

```
Int_Data'First + 1
```

This does not pose a real problem for us, since we may use

```
INDEX_TYPE'Succ (Int_Data'First)
```

in its place. It is now a simple matter to write the body of our generic Sort_Up procedure. Making the adjustment mentioned, we repeat the code of Figure 10.9.4, but change a few type names as needed. The resulting procedure body appears in Figure 14.2.2.

```
procedure Sort_Up (Int_Data: in out INT_ARRAY) is

   Max_Loc:  INDEX_TYPE;    -- index of largest component
   Max_Val:  INTEGER;       -- value of largest component

begin

   for End_Index in reverse
     INDEX_TYPE'Succ (Int_Data'First)..Int_Data'Last loop
```

```
        -- Initialize Max_Loc and Max_Val to beginning of
        -- array

  Max_Loc := Int_Data'First;
  Max_Val := Int_Data(Max_Loc);

        -- Search through array, replacing Max_Loc and
        -- Max_Val whenever a larger component is found

  for Index in
    INDEX_TYPE'Succ (Int_Data'First)..End_Index loop
      if Max_Val < Int_Data(Index) then
        Max_Loc := Index;
        Max_Val := Int_Data(Max_Loc);
      end if;
  end loop;

        -- Exchange the largest and the last of the components
        -- indexed by the range Int_Data'First..End_Index

  Int_Data(Max_Loc)     := Int_Data(End_Index);
  Int_Data(End_Index)   := Max_Val;

    end loop;

  end Sort_Up;
```

Figure 14.2.2

It is difficult to think of a realistic situation in which we would want to sort an array of INTEGER components indexed by a range of an enumeration type. There is nothing unusual about employing arrays of this kind, as we have seen in the examples of Chapter 13. However, the ordinary reason for choosing an enumeration type to index an array is that we want to maintain an association between each enumeration type value (the index) and a corresponding integer value (the component). Thus, it is unlikely in this context that we would want to sort the array, which would destroy this association. (The same may be said of arrays indexed by a "special" integer index range, such as a particular span of years.) However, to illustrate the instantiation and use of the generic procedure Sort_Up, we offer the program skeleton shown in Figure 14.2.3. Notice that the array types used as actual type parameters are *unconstrained*, as is the formal type parameter INT_ARRAY of the generic Sort_Up procedure. In general, formal and actual *array* type parameters must match in this respect, as well as in the kind of component types and index types they have.

```
with Sort_Up;

procedure Test_Sort is

    type MONTHS is (Jan, Feb, Mar, Apr, May, Jun, Jul,
        Aug, Sep, Oct, Nov, Dec);
    type MONTH_DATA is array (MONTHS range <>) of INTEGER;

    type INTEGER_ARRAY is array (NATURAL range <>) of INTEGER;
```

```
Year_Sales:     MONTH_DATA(Jan..Dec);
Summer_Sales:   MONTH_DATA(Jun..Sep);
Population_20:   INTEGER_ARRAY(1901..2000);
Grade_List:     INTEGER_ARRAY(1..38);

procedure Sort_MDat is new Sort_Up (MONTHS, MONTH_DATA);
procedure Sort_Ints is new Sort_Up (NATURAL, INTEGER_ARRAY);

begin

  -- Assign values to the array variables

     .
     .
     .
  Sort_MDat (Year_Sales);
  Sort_MDat (Summer_Sales);
  Sort_Ints (Population_20);
  Sort_Ints (Grade_List);
     .
     .
     .

end Test_Sort;
```

Figure 14.2.3

14.3   A generic Sort_Up procedure: Toward generalizing the component type

Our goal in this section is to begin the process of generalizing the generic Sort_Up procedure we developed in the preceding section, so that it will sort arrays having *various* component types. As we might expect, we have to introduce another generic formal parameter into the generic procedure, this time one to stand for the component type of the array. The generic procedure specification has the form shown in Figure 14.3.1.

```
generic

  type INDEX_TYPE is (<>);
  type ITEM_TYPE is <information to be supplied here>;
  type ITEM_ARRAY is array (INDEX_TYPE range <>) of ITEM_TYPE;

    -- Procedure Sort_Up takes as a parameter any array of
    -- the unconstrained array type ITEM_ARRAY, indexed by
    -- a range of INDEX_TYPE, and with components of type
    -- ITEM_TYPE.  It sorts the array components into
    -- ascending order.

procedure Sort_Up (Item_Data: in out ITEM_ARRAY);
```

Figure 14.3.1

As we saw when we developed a generic procedure Exchange in Section 14.1, the applicability of this generic procedure Sort_Up depends on the declaration given for the formal type parameter ITEM_TYPE. We may use any of the generic type declarations

```
type ITEM_TYPE is range <>;
type ITEM_TYPE is (<>);
type ITEM_TYPE is digits <>;
```

Then, as we stated in Section 14.1, the actual type parameter corresponding to ITEM_TYPE (here, the component type of any array type for which this generic procedure is to be instantiated) must be of an integer type, a discrete type, or a floating point type, respectively. In each case, the operations of the respective class of types may then be applied in the procedure body to objects of the type ITEM_TYPE.

If we inspect the code of the procedure body Sort_Up as it appears in Figure 14.2.2, we find that apart from assignments, the only operation applied to objects of the component type is a comparison by means of the relational operator <:

```
if Max_Val < Int_Data(Index) then ...;
```

In the generic procedure we are developing, both Max_Val and Item_Data(Index)—which replaces Int_Data(Index)—are component values, and therefore both will be of type ITEM_TYPE. Consequently, if we declare ITEM_TYPE in any of the ways mentioned, the relational operator < used in this comparison will be the one applicable to integer types, discrete types, or floating point types, respectively.

If we were interested in constructing a generic sort procedure to deal only with arrays having components of one of these classes of types, we could do so immediately by merely completing the generic type declaration of Figure 14.3.1 and writing the procedure body—a simple matter, since all that need be done is to repeat the code of Figure 14.2.2, with INTEGER changed to ITEM_TYPE in the one place where it occurs (the declaration of the local variable Max_Val), with the type name changed to ITEM_ARRAY, and with Int_Data changed to Item_Data throughout.

But as in the case of the procedure Exchange, we would like to produce a generic procedure to handle *any* of these types and more besides—STRING types, certainly, and possibly others. As before, it would seem that we can accomplish this by using the declaration

```
type ITEM_TYPE is private;
```

However, there appears to be a problem. If we use this declaration, the only operations *immediately* available for use with objects of the component type ITEM_TYPE are assignment and comparison for equality and inequality but *not* comparison by means of the relational operator <. The way of getting around this difficulty—and it requires considerable explanation—is to pass the appropriate relational operator as an actual *function* (subprogram) parameter corresponding to a formal function (subprogram) parameter which we must include in our generic sort procedure specification. We need to do two things: (1) Discuss in further detail a topic introduced in Section 11.8, namely, the idea of an operator as a *function*, and (2) describe the use of *subprograms* as formal parameters in a generic unit.

To this end, we digress for the moment and devote the following section to an investigation of the first of these topics.

14.4 Operators as functions

In Section 11.8 we introduced the package Rationals in which we declared a type RATIONAL with its associated arithmetic and relational operator functions. The multiplication operator, for example, was declared by means of the function declaration

```
function "*" (Left, Right: RATIONAL) return RATIONAL;
```

We saw that in a program including the clause **with Rationals**, we may declare RATIONAL variables X and Y and write their product as **Rationals."*" (X, Y)**. If the program also has the clause **use Rationals**, the name of the package Rationals may be omitted and the product may be written simply as **"*" (X, Y)**, or, in the more familiar infix notation, **X * Y**.

Actually, the operators we have taken from the start to be predefined are declared as functions in the package Standard where, for example, the following specifications appear:

```
function "+" (Left, Right: INTEGER) return INTEGER;
function "+" (Left, Right: FLOAT)   return FLOAT;
```

These two "+" functions are distinct, as is clearly indicated by the fact that they have different parameter types and different value types. Therefore, the symbol "+" provides an example of **operator overloading**, a concept that we also discussed in Section 11.8.

A peculiarity of the package Standard is that we never include the context clause **with Standard** or **use Standard** in a program; these clauses are implicitly understood by Ada to be part of every program. Thus we may always use the "+" operator in infix form, without quotation marks, in such expressions as

```
X := A + B;
```

The other predefined operator functions from package Standard are also used in this same way.

Now consider the following, again from the package Standard:

```
function "<" (Left, Right: BOOLEAN) return BOOLEAN;
function "<" (Left, Right: INTEGER) return BOOLEAN;
function "<" (Left, Right: FLOAT)   return BOOLEAN;
function "<" (Left, Right: STRING)  return BOOLEAN;
```

These specifications make it clear that "<" stands for several different functions, all of them BOOLEAN-valued. Furthermore, it suggests that the *programmer* might declare one or more further functions designated by "<", each of them taking two parameters of the same given type and returning a BOOLEAN value and each of them with its own function body indicating how this function "works."

To construct an example—in fact, a practical one—we declare a record type and show two ways of defining a function "<" that can be used to compare records of this type in order to determine which one "is less than" (that is, precedes) the other in some meaningful sense.

```
subtype ID_RANGE is INTEGER range 1111..9999;

type PERSONAL_INFO is
  record
    Name:   STRING_30;
    ID_No:  ID_RANGE;    -- 4-digit ID number
    .
    .   -- declarations of other fields
    .
  end record;
```

Suppose that we had an array with components of this type. For example, suppose the records represented information about members of some organization and we declare

```
type MEMBER_INFO is array (NATURAL range <>) of PERSONAL_INFO;

Max_Membership:     constant NATURAL := <some suitable value>;

Members:            MEMBER_INFO(1..Max_Membership);
```

The variable Members would now be an array of records, each record containing the personal information of a particular member. Is there a natural *order* among these records? To put it differently, can we write a comparison such as

```
Members(23) < Members(17),
```

or, more generally,

```
Members(J) < Members(K)
```

and expect this comparison of records to be meaningful and, specifically, to yield a well-determined value of either True or False?

First of all, these comparisons do not automatically make sense; Ada provides no built-in order relationship among objects of this or any other record type. In dealing with a record type, we cannot immediately say that a given value of this type *precedes* another given value of the type. But we may *impose* an order on the type by defining a function "<" by which particular record values may be compared. The usual way to proceed is to select one of the fields of the record, called a **key** field, and consider the records to be ordered according to an order that may already exist among values of this field's type. Thus, if we choose to order the records according to their Name field (in which we assume a person's last name to be given first), the order imposed on the record type might naturally be that of *character strings* (an order already defined in Ada)—specifically, the records will be ordered according to the alphabetical order of the names appearing in their Name fields. Alternatively, we might choose to order the records according to their ID_No field, considering one record to precede another if the ID_No of the first precedes that of the second in integer order. We use these ideas to write two possible implementations of a function "<" applicable to parameters of the record type PERSONAL_INFO. In Figure 14.4.1, we regard the records as ordered in terms of their Name fields.

```
function "<" (Left, Right:  PERSONAL_INFO) return BOOLEAN is

begin

  return Left.Name < Right.Name;    -- uses "<" for type STRING

end "<";
```

Figure 14.4.1

If instead we choose to order the records according to their ID_No fields, we may write the function body as in Figure 14.4.2.

```
function "<" (Left, Right:  PERSONAL_INFO) return BOOLEAN is

begin

  return Left.ID_No < Right.ID_No;  -- uses "<" for type INTEGER

end "<";
```

Figure 14.4.2

We have shown here how the operator < can be further overloaded by writing (in either of two ways) a function "<" applicable to parameters of the type PERSONAL_INFO. However, it is *not* permissible to declare *both* "<" functions of Figures 14.4.1 and 14.4.2 in the same module, since *both* are BOOLEAN-valued functions with two parameters of type PERSONAL_INFO. We could do the same for the relational operators <=, >, and >= as well, and we could similarly devise operators applicable to other data types. In general, Ada allows us to overload in this way any of the operators shown in the operator precedence table of Figure 5.4.1. As a simple example to conclude this section, we offer a function "+" that returns the vector sum (that is, the component-by-component sum) of two vectors (arrays of FLOAT values, indexed by 1..N).

```
N:  constant POSITIVE := <some suitable value>;
subtype RANGE_N is POSITIVE range 1..N;

type VECTOR is array (RANGE_N) of FLOAT;

function "+" (Left, Right:  VECTOR) return VECTOR is

  Sum:  VECTOR;

begin

  for K in RANGE_N loop
    Sum(K) := Left(K) + Right(K);  -- uses "+" for type FLOAT
  end loop;
  return Sum;

end "+";
```

Figure 14.4.3

14.5 A generic Sort_Up procedure: final form

Now that we have seen the possibility of defining an order relationship on a given data type—or, equivalently, of defining an operator "<" on the given type if one has not already been predefined—we can conclude our development of a generic sort procedure for arrays with a broad span of component types. In our generic sort procedure declaration, we include, as before, the formal type parameters INDEX_TYPE, ITEM_TYPE, and ITEM_ARRAY, by using the declaration

```
type ITEM_TYPE is private;
```

This time we also include a formal *function* parameter "<", which is to be replaced by a corresponding actual function parameter (a relational operator function), appropriate for the given component type, when the generic procedure is instantiated. We assume that at the point where the generic procedure is instantiated, there is available a relational operator function applicable to values of the component type, whether this operator function is predefined (as for BOOLEAN, INTEGER, FLOAT, STRING) or programmer-defined (as shown, for instance, in the examples of Figure 14.4.1 or 14.4.2). The declaration of a formal function or procedure parameter in a generic unit takes a somewhat strange form, which is illustrated in the present case by

```
with function "<" (Left, Right: ITEM_TYPE) return BOOLEAN;
```

As is evident from the declaration, we must give the full specification of the function used as a formal parameter, so that when a corresponding actual parameter is supplied at the time of instantiation, the Ada compiler may check that the actual and formal function parameters match. Thus the relational operator function (actual parameter) used in the instantiation must be a BOOLEAN-valued function that compares values of the actual component type (the actual type parameter corresponding to ITEM_TYPE) specified in the instantiation.

Summing up what we have said, we may write the generic procedure declaration as it appears in Figure 14.5.1.

```
generic

    type INDEX_TYPE is (<>);
      -- any discrete index type

    type ITEM_TYPE is private;
      -- any component type

    type ITEM_ARRAY is array (INDEX_TYPE range <>) of ITEM_TYPE;
      -- an unconstrained array type with components of
      -- type ITEM_TYPE and indexes of type INDEX_TYPE

    with function "<" (Left, Right: ITEM_TYPE) return BOOLEAN;
      -- relational operator (function) for the component
      -- type ITEM_TYPE

      -- Procedure Sort_Up takes as a parameter any array of
      -- the unconstrained array type ITEM_ARRAY, indexed by a
      -- range of type INDEX_TYPE, and with components of type
```

```
-- ITEM_TYPE and a relational operator "<" on this type.
-- The procedure sorts the components of the array into
-- the ascending order specified by the formal function
-- parameter "<".

procedure Sort_Up (Item_Data:  in out ITEM_ARRAY);
```

Figure 14.5.1

The procedure body remains the same as in Figure 14.2.2, with INTEGER replaced by ITEM_TYPE in the declaration of the local variable Max_Val, with the array type changed to ITEM_ARRAY, and with Int_Data replaced by Item_Data throughout. This revised procedure body is shown in Figure 14.5.2.

```
procedure Sort_Up (Item_Data: in out ITEM_ARRAY) is

   Max_Loc:  INDEX_TYPE; -- index of largest component
   Max_Val:  ITEM_TYPE; -- value of largest component

begin

   for End_Index in reverse
     INDEX_TYPE'Succ (Item_Data'First)..Item_Data'Last loop

       -- Initialize Max_Loc and Max_Val to beginning of
       -- array

     Max_Loc := Item_Data'First;
     Max_Val := Item_Data(Max_Loc);

       -- Search through array, replacing Max_Loc and
       -- Max_Val whenever a larger component is found

     for Index in
       INDEX_TYPE'Succ (Item_Data'First)..End_Index loop
         if Max_Val < Item_Data(Index) then
           Max_Loc := Index;
           Max_Val := Item_Data(Max_Loc);
         end if;
     end loop;

       -- Exchange the largest and the last of the components
       -- indexed by the range Item_Data'First..End_Index

     Item_Data(Max_Loc)    := Item_Data(End_Index);
     Item_Data(End_Index)  := Max_Val;

   end loop;

end Sort_Up;
```

Figure 14.5.2

To show how this generic procedure would be instantiated and how instances of it might be used, we offer in Figure 14.5.3 a modification of the program of Figure 14.2.3. We

have changed the component type to FLOAT in the declaration of the array type
MONTH_DATA and have included some declarations from Section 14.4. The result is a
strange, and undoubtedly quite unrealistic, mix of types; nevertheless, it does serve to
illustrate the breadth of applicability of our generic Sort_Up procedure. (The reference
numbers in brackets at the right margin are, of course, not part of the program.)

```
with Sort_Up;

procedure Test_Sort is

    type MONTHS is (Jan, Feb, Mar, Apr, May, Jun, Jul,
      Aug, Sep, Oct, Nov, Dec);

    subtype STRING_30 is STRING(1..30);
    subtype ID_RANGE is INTEGER range 1111..9999;

    type PERSONAL_INFO is
      record
        Name:   STRING_30;
        ID_No:  ID_RANGE;    -- 4-digit ID number
          .
          .   -- declarations of other fields
          .
      end record;

    type MONTH_DATA is array (MONTHS range <>) of FLOAT;

    type INTEGER_ARRAY is array (NATURAL range <>) of INTEGER;

    type MEMBER_INFO is array (NATURAL range <>)
        of PERSONAL_INFO;

    Year_Sales:      MONTH_DATA(Jan..Dec);
    Summer_Sales:    MONTH_DATA(Jun..Sep);
    Population_20:   INTEGER_ARRAY(1901..2000);
    Grade_List:      INTEGER_ARRAY(1..38);
    Max_Membership:  constant INTEGER := 200;
    Members:         MEMBER_INFO(1..Max_Membership);

    function "<" (Left, Right: PERSONAL_INFO) return BOOLEAN;

    procedure Sort_MDat is new
      Sort_Up (MONTHS, FLOAT, MONTH_DATA, "<");              [1]
    procedure Sort_Ints is new
      Sort_Up (NATURAL, INTEGER, INTEGER_ARRAY, "<");        [2]
    procedure Sort_Recs is new
      Sort_Up (NATURAL, PERSONAL_INFO, MEMBER_INFO, "<");    [3]

    function "<" (Left, Right: PERSONAL_INFO) return BOOLEAN is

    begin
      return Left.Name < Right.Name;
    end "<";

begin  -- Test_Sort

    -- Assign values to the array variables
```

```
        .
        .
        .
    Sort_MDat (Year_Sales);
    Sort_MDat (Summer_Sales);
    Sort_Ints (Population_20);
    Sort_Ints (Grade_List);
    Sort_Recs (Members);
        .
        .
        .

end Test_Sort;
```

Figure 14.5.3

In this program three instantiations of Sort_Up are declared in the lines numbered [1], [2], [3]. In these instantiations, three different actual function parameters designated by "<" have been used:

[1]   a predefined function (operator) "<" for values of type FLOAT;

[2]   a predefined function "<" for values of type INTEGER;

[3]   a function "<" defined in the program for values of the record type PERSONAL_INFO. (Ada has no predefined function "<" to compare objects of this type.) Note that the function *specification* of the relational operator "<" for type PERSONAL_INFO must *precede* the use of this operator function as an actual parameter in the instantiation of Sort_Up for arrays with components of type PERSONAL_INFO; otherwise, the operator would not be visible at the point of instantiation. However, the body of this function must *follow* the instantiation, since an instantiation is a **basic declaration**, and basic declarations must precede subprogram bodies.

In each case the Ada compiler determines which operator function matches the formal parameter "<" once an actual type parameter has been supplied in the instantiation to match the formal type parameter ITEM_TYPE, thus determining the type of the values to be compared by means of "<".

One further point is that in the declaration of the formal function parameter "<" in Figure 14.5.1, we may supply a default for this parameter by placing the phrase "**is <>**" at the end of the declaration:

```
with function "<" (Left, Right: ITEM_TYPE) return BOOLEAN is <>;
```

The effect of "**is <>**" is to cause the formal parameter "<" to be replaced at the point of instantiation by whatever BOOLEAN-valued function designated by the *same* symbol "<", and with two parameters of the actual component type (corresponding to ITEM_TYPE), is *visible* at this point. Thus, if this form of declaration was used in the generic procedure specification, the instantiations appearing in lines 1, 2, and 3 of Figure 14.5.3 could have been written *without* an actual parameter corresponding to "<":

```
procedure Sort_MDat is new
   Sort_Up (MONTHS, FLOAT, MONTH_DATA);
procedure Sort_Ints is new
   Sort_Up (NATURAL, INTEGER, INTEGER_ARRAY);
procedure Sort_Recs is new
   Sort_Up (NATURAL, PERSONAL_INFO, MEMBER_INFO);
```

In each case the formal parameter "<" would be replaced by the same actual parameter as in lines 1, 2, and 3 of Figure 14.5.3:

1.   The function "<" predefined for values of type FLOAT;

2.   The function "<" predefined for values of type INTEGER;

3.   The function "<" defined in the current program for "values" of type PERSONAL_INFO. Note again that this function is specified *ahead* of the instantiation at line 3 and is therefore visible at this point.

Of course, just as is the case with default values of subprogram parameters, the default value of the generic function parameter "<" may be *overridden* at the point of instantiation simply by explicitly supplying a different actual parameter (a BOOLEAN-valued function with two parameters of the actual array's component type).

14.6 A generic Sort procedure

Over the course of the preceding four sections, we have introduced several new ideas in order to arrive at a Sort_Up procedure that is completely general. The procedure is "completely general" in the sense that it can sort into ascending order an array of any unconstrained array type, no matter what the (discrete) base type of its index range is and no matter what the type of its components is—provided that there is some kind of order relationship < between values of the component type. In order to achieve this level of generality for the component type of the array, we introduced the generic type parameter ITEM_TYPE and found that we had to use the formal type declaration

```
type ITEM_TYPE is private;
```

This in turn required the introduction of a formal function parameter "<" in the generic procedure, with the understanding that when the procedure is instantiated, this parameter is to be matched—possibly by default—by a corresponding *actual* function parameter (a comparison operator) applicable to the component type of the array.

But recall the relationship between formal and actual parameters. When a subprogram is called (and thereby executed), each of its formal parameters is in some fashion replaced by the corresponding actual parameter. In an analogous way, when a generic unit is instantiated (and thereby elaborated), each of its generic formal parameters is likewise "replaced" by the corresponding actual parameter. In particular, when the generic procedure Sort_Up is instantiated, the formal function parameter "<" is replaced by the actual function parameter (appropriate for the given component type), which we have also designated by "<".

Where does the operator "<" occur in the body of the procedure Sort_Up? As a matter of fact, it occurs only once (see Figure 14.5.2), in the conditional statement that is used (within a loop) to find the location of *largest* of the array components indexed by Item_Data'First..End_Index:

```
if Max_Val < Item_Data(Index) then
   Max_Loc := Index;
   Max_Val := Item_Data(Max_Loc);
end if;
```

As we noted when we first studied the selection sort in Section 10.6, replacing "<" by ">" at this point is all that is needed to change the procedure Sort_Up to a corresponding procedure Sort_Down that will arrange the array components into descending (decreasing) order.

It follows that there is no need to write a generic procedure Sort_Down; all that is necessary is to replace the formal parameter "<" of Sort_Up by the actual parameter ">" (applicable to the component type)—rather than by the actual parameter "<"—when instantiating Sort_Up. For this reason, it will suffice for us to have a generic procedure Sort with a formal function parameter "<"; the sort can be specified as ascending or descending by employing in its instantiation the *actual* function parameter that we ordinarily designate for the component type as "<" or ">", respectively. In Figures 14.6.1 and 14.6.2 we offer the specification and body of the generic procedure Sort; the code for this procedure is the same as that of Sort_Up (Figures 14.5.1 and 14.5.2) except that several identifiers and comments have been changed to fit the context.

```
generic

   type INDEX_TYPE is (<>);
      -- any discrete index type

   type ITEM_TYPE is private;
      -- any component type

   type ITEM_ARRAY is array (INDEX_TYPE range <>) of ITEM_TYPE;
      -- an unconstrained array type with components of
      -- type ITEM_TYPE and indexes of type INDEX_TYPE

   with function "<" (Left, Right: ITEM_TYPE) return BOOLEAN;
      -- relational operator (function) for the component
      -- type ITEM_TYPE

      -- Procedure Sort takes as a parameter any array of the
      -- unconstrained array type ITEM_ARRAY, indexed by a
      -- range of type INDEX_TYPE, and with components of type
      -- ITEM_TYPE for which an order (relational) operator is
      -- defined.  The procedure sorts the components of the
      -- array into the ascending order specified by the formal
      -- function parameter "<".  According to whether the
      -- corresponding actual parameter is the component type's
      -- "<" or ">" operator, the resulting instantiation sorts
      -- array components into ascending or descending order,
      -- respectively.

   procedure Sort (Item_Data:  in out ITEM_ARRAY);
```

Figure 14.6.1

```
procedure Sort (Item_Data: in out ITEM_ARRAY) is

   Extr_Loc:   INDEX_TYPE;       -- index of extreme component
                                 -- ("largest" component in the
                                 -- order specified by the formal
                                 -- parameter "<")
   Extr_Val:   ITEM_TYPE;        -- value of extreme component

begin

   for End_Index in reverse
     INDEX_TYPE'Succ (Item_Data'First)..Item_Data'Last loop

        -- Initialize Extr_Loc and Extr_Val to beginning of
        -- array

     Extr_Loc := Item_Data'First;
     Extr_Val := Item_Data(Extr_Loc);

        -- Search through array, replacing Extr_Loc and
        -- Extr_Val whenever a "larger" component is found

     for Index in
       INDEX_TYPE'Succ (Item_Data'First)..End_Index loop
         if Extr_Val < Item_Data(Index) then
           Extr_Loc := Index;
           Extr_Val := Item_Data(Extr_Loc);
         end if;
     end loop;

        -- Exchange the "largest" and the last of the
        -- components indexed by the range
        -- Item_Data'First..End_Index

     Item_Data(Extr_Loc)   := Item_Data(End_Index);
     Item_Data(End_Index)  := Extr_Val;

   end loop;

end Sort;
```

Figure 14.6.2

14.7 A generic package: Numeric_Arrays

The generic units we have developed in this chapter have all been subprograms (in fact, procedures), and we have stressed the fact that their specifications and bodies may be separately compiled, with the resulting object files saved for ready use in any program that may need them. In particular, our Sort procedure provides a realistic example of widely applicable off-the-shelf software. But recall that our first encounter with sorting occurred in Section 10.6, where we developed the selection sort for arrays that were of a *constrained* array type, with index range 1..N and with components of type INTEGER. Later, we extended this sort routine to a form in which it could be applied to arrays of the *unconstrained* type INTEGER_ARRAY, declared by

```
type INTEGER_ARRAY is array (NATURAL range <>) of INTEGER;
```

We incorporated the procedures Sort_Up and Sort_Down into the package Integer_Arrays (Section 11.7), which provided a collection of frequently used routines (Sum, Max, Index_of_Max, Min, Index_of_Min, and Location) that could be applied to arrays of type INTEGER_ARRAY. By now, as a result of our efforts in this chapter, we have a free-standing Sort routine whose applicability is by no means restricted to arrays of this type.

Could we generalize the other routines in the package Integer_Arrays so as to make them more widely applicable? The answer is that we can do so, and we carry out such a project in this section by developing a generic package to achieve this end. But first let us reflect on what degree of generalization we should seek to attain.

Recall that the function Location in the package Integer_Arrays takes two parameters —the name of an array to be searched and a value to be sought among the components of the array. If the given value is in the array, the function returns the index of a component having this value; if the value is *not* in the array, the function "signals" this absence in a way that can be checked by the program that calls the function. (In Integer_Arrays, the function does this by returning −1, a number that lies outside the range of the index type NATURAL, and that therefore cannot be an actual index.) It is easy to see that a routine such as Location would be of practical application in *any* array context, no matter what the index type and component type of the array.

On the other hand, in what circumstances might we wish to find the Max or Min component of an array (or the indexes at which they occur)? If the components of an array were of an enumeration type (including CHARACTER) or of a STRING type, say, we could meaningfully speak of finding the greatest or least component value in the array, but would it be useful in practice to do so? Probably not; the greatest and least elements of an array are of interest principally when they are *numeric*. This suggests that we might develop our package for use with arrays of numbers, whether integer or real.

Finally, if our generic package is to contain a Sum routine, it will only be applicable to arrays whose components can be *added*; thus, if we are to understand addition in any ordinary sense, we should plan to apply our package to arrays with integer or floating point components.

With these reflections in mind, we generalize the package Integer_Arrays to a generic package Numeric_Arrays that can be applied to arrays with components of any integer or floating point type. As for the index ranges of these arrays, one possibility would be to use the declaration "NATURAL range <>"—as was done in the package Integer_Arrays. Nevertheless, we will instead deal with an unconstrained array type with indexes from any discrete type, as we did in developing our generalized Sort procedure.

It is difficult to see how in our generalized context, a function Location could handle the situation in which the value sought is *not* in the array. The function must return a value of the index type, and there is no value of this type that might *not* be used as one of the actual indexes of the array we are searching. For this reason, we replace the function Location by a procedure Locate which has two **in** parameters (the name of the array to be searched and the value to be sought) and two **out** parameters (the index at which the search terminates and a BOOLEAN parameter to indicate whether or not the given value has been found at this location).

Since we want to be able to apply the package Numeric_Arrays to arrays with either integer or real components, we must declare the formal type parameter for the component type to be **private**; therefore, it is necessary to include the formal function parameters "+" and "<" to permit array components to be added and compared. These are the *only* operators (other than = and /=) that can be directly applied to array components in the package body; in particular, all comparison of component values must be done without using ">". This is no problem for us, since the effect of using a comparison of the form A > B can always be achieved by using B < A instead; similarly, A <= B can be replaced by A < B **or** A = B.

Figure 14.7.2 shows the specification of the generic package Numeric_Arrays. But first we offer a syntax diagram (Figure 14.7.1) for the specification of *any* generic unit (whether a subprogram or a package). It should be noted that both these kinds of generic units have the same form of *specification*, as will be clear from Figure 14.7.1. Furthermore, we offer no special syntax diagram for the *body* of a generic subprogram or package; the syntax diagrams for these subprogram bodies and package bodies are precisely the ones we have seen before in the context of *nongeneric* subprograms and packages: Figures 8.3.1*a*, 8.7.4*a*, and 11.3.1*c*. Finally, we observe that Figure 14.7.1 refers to several syntactic constructs whose syntax diagrams we have already seen: **subprogram specification**, which appears in Figures 8.3.1*b* to *d* and 8.7.4*b* to *d*; **package specification**, shown in Figure 11.3.1*b*; and **array type definition**, as in Figure 13.4.2.

a

generic specification

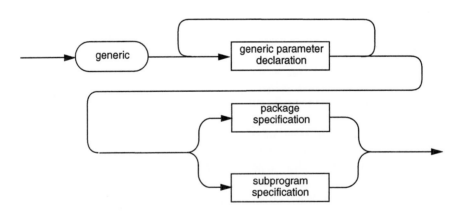

b

generic parameter declaration

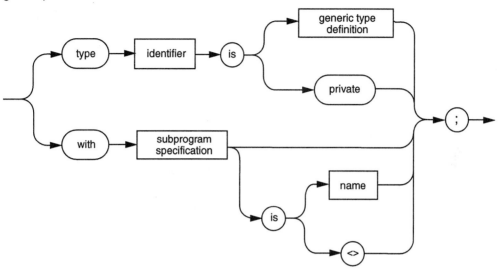

c

generic type definition

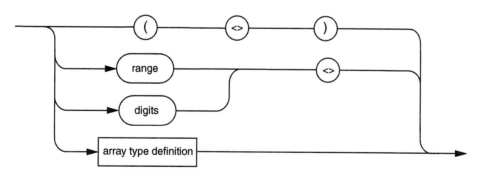

Figure 14.7.1

The specification of the generic package Numeric_Arrays appears in Figure 14.7.2.

```
generic

    type INDEX_TYPE is (<>);
        -- any discrete index type

    type ITEM_TYPE is private;
        -- any component type
```

```
    type ITEM_ARRAY is array (INDEX_TYPE range <>) of ITEM_TYPE;
        -- an unconstrained array type with components of
        -- type ITEM_TYPE and indexes of type INDEX_TYPE

    with function "+" (Left, Right: ITEM_TYPE) return ITEM_TYPE is <>;
        -- addition operator (with default) for component type

    with function "<" (Left, Right: ITEM_TYPE) return BOOLEAN is <>;
        -- relational operator (with default) for component type

package Numeric_Arrays is

    -- Function Sum returns the sum of the components of the
    -- array passed to it as a parameter.

    function Sum (Item_Data: ITEM_ARRAY) return ITEM_TYPE;


    -- Function Max returns the maximum of the components of
    -- the array passed to it as a parameter.

    function Max (Item_Data: ITEM_ARRAY) return ITEM_TYPE;


    -- Function Index_of_Max returns the index of the maximum
    -- of the components of the array passed to it as a parameter.
    -- If this maximum value occurs more than once in the array, it
    -- returns the first index at which it occurs.

    function Index_of_Max (Item_Data: ITEM_ARRAY) return INDEX_TYPE;


    -- Function Min returns the minimum of the components of
    -- the array passed to it as a parameter.

    function Min (Item_Data: ITEM_ARRAY) return ITEM_TYPE;


    -- Function Index_of_Min returns the index of the minimum
    -- of the components of the array passed to it as a parameter.
    -- If this minimum value occurs more than once in the array, it
    -- returns the first index at which it occurs.

    function Index_of_Min (Item_Data: ITEM_ARRAY) return INDEX_TYPE;


    -- Procedure Locate searches an array for a particular
    -- component value; it takes as its first two parameters the
    -- name of the array to be searched and the value to be sought;
    -- it returns in its second two parameters the index at which
    -- the search ended and a BOOLEAN value indicating whether the
    -- given value was found at this location.

    procedure Locate

        (Item_Data:  in  ITEM_ARRAY;
         Target:     in  ITEM_TYPE;
         Loc:        out INDEX_TYPE;
         Found:      out BOOLEAN);

end Numeric_Arrays;
```

Figure 14.7.2

We next display the body of this generic package. The function and procedure bodies are much as we have seen them in earlier versions, with the function Location replaced by the procedure Locate, except for the following: (1) the generalizations needed to accommodate an arbitrary discrete index type have been made (as in the generic procedure Sort); (2) no comparisons of array values have employed any operator other than = or /= or <; and (3) in the function Sum, the local variable Total has been initialized to the first component value of the array rather than 0, with the summation then starting from the second array value (why?).

```
package body Numeric_Arrays is

   function Sum (Item_Data: ITEM_ARRAY) return ITEM_TYPE is

      Total: ITEM_TYPE := Item_Data(Item_Data'First);

   begin

      for Index in INDEX_TYPE'Succ (Item_Data'First) .. Item_Data'Last loop
        Total := Total + Item_Data(Index);
      end loop;
      return Total;

   end Sum;


   function Max (Item_Data: ITEM_ARRAY) return ITEM_TYPE is

      Max_Val: ITEM_TYPE := Item_Data(Item_Data'First);

   begin

      for Index in INDEX_TYPE'Succ (Item_Data'First) .. Item_Data'Last loop
        if Max_Val < Item_Data(Index) then
          Max_Val := Item_Data(Index);
        end if;
      end loop;
      return Max_Val;

   end Max;


   function Index_of_Max (Item_Data: ITEM_ARRAY) return INDEX_TYPE is

      Max_Loc: INDEX_TYPE := Item_Data'First;
      Max_Val: ITEM_TYPE  := Item_Data(Max_Loc);

   begin

      for Index in INDEX_TYPE'Succ (Item_Data'First) .. Item_Data'Last loop
        if Max_Val < Item_Data(Index) then
          Max_Loc := Index;
          Max_Val := Item_Data(Max_Loc);
        end if;
      end loop;
      return Max_Loc;

   end Index_of_Max;
```

```
    function Min (Item_Data: ITEM_ARRAY) return ITEM_TYPE is

      Min_Val: ITEM_TYPE := Item_Data(Item_Data'First);

    begin

      for Index in INDEX_TYPE'Succ (Item_Data'First) .. Item_Data'Last loop
        if Item_Data(Index) < Min_Val then
          Min_Val := Item_Data(Index);
        end if;
      end loop;
      return Min_Val;

    end Min;


    function Index_of_Min (Item_Data: ITEM_ARRAY) return INDEX_TYPE is

      Min_Loc: INDEX_TYPE := Item_Data'First;
      Min_Val: ITEM_TYPE  := Item_Data(Min_Loc);

    begin

      for Index in INDEX_TYPE'Succ (Item_Data'First) .. Item_Data'Last loop
        if Item_Data(Index) < Min_Val then
          Min_Loc := Index;
          Min_Val := Item_Data(Min_Loc);
        end if;
      end loop;
      return Min_Loc;

    end Index_of_Min;

    procedure Locate (Item_Data: in  ITEM_ARRAY;
                      Target:    in  ITEM_TYPE;
                      Loc:       out INDEX_TYPE;
                      Found:     out BOOLEAN)      is

      Index: INDEX_TYPE := Item_Data'First;

    begin

      Found := False;
      while Index < Item_Data'Last and Item_Data(Index) /= Target loop
        Index := INDEX_TYPE'Succ (Index);
      end loop;
      Loc := Index;
      if Item_Data(Index) = Target then
        Found := True;
      end if;

    end Locate;

  end Numeric_Arrays;
```

Figure 14.7.3

Figure 14.7.4 shows a demonstration program to illustrate applications of the package Numeric_Arrays. The program is very simple, yet it does demonstrate the instantiation and use of this generic package and of all the routines it contains. The package is applied to an array of FLOAT components indexed by a range of an enumeration type MONTHS and to an array of INTEGER components indexed by a range of subtype NATURAL.

```
with Text_IO, Numeric_Arrays;

procedure Test_Arrays is

    type MONTHS is (Jan, Feb, Mar, Apr, May, Jun, Jul, Aug,
        Sep, Oct, Nov, Dec);
    type FLT_ARRAY is array (MONTHS range <>) of FLOAT;
    type INT_ARRAY is array (NATURAL range <>) of INTEGER;

    package Flt_Arrays is new Numeric_Arrays (MONTHS, FLOAT, FLT_ARRAY);
    package Int_Arrays is new Numeric_Arrays (NATURAL, INTEGER, INT_ARRAY);

    package Int_IO is new Text_IO.Integer_IO(INTEGER);
    package Flt_IO is new Text_IO.Float_IO(FLOAT);
    package Mon_IO is new Text_IO.Enumeration_IO(MONTHS);


    Flt_Data: FLT_ARRAY(MAR..SEP) := (2.3, 6.4, 1.5, 5.8, 7.2, 3.1, 4.0);
    Int_Data: INT_ARRAY(3..12)    := (4, 8, 2, 7, 6, 10, 1, 9, 3, 5);

    Found: Boolean;
    Mth_Loc: MONTHS;
    Nat_Loc: NATURAL;

begin
    for Index in Flt_Data'Range loop
      Mon_IO.Put (Index);
      Text_IO.Put ("         ");
      Flt_IO.Put (Flt_Data(Index), 0, 0, 0);
      Text_IO.New_Line;
    end loop;
    Text_IO.New_Line;
    Text_IO.Put ("The sum is ");
    Flt_IO.Put (Flt_Arrays.Sum (Flt_Data), 0, 0, 0);
    Text_IO.New_Line;
    Text_IO.Put ("The maximum is ");
    Flt_IO.Put (Flt_Arrays.Max (Flt_Data), 0, 0, 0);
    Text_IO.Put (" at index ");
    Mon_IO.Put (Flt_Arrays.Index_of_Max (Flt_Data));
    Text_IO.New_Line;
    Text_IO.Put ("The minimum is ");
    Flt_IO.Put (Flt_Arrays.Min (Flt_Data), 0, 0, 0);
    Text_IO.Put (" at index ");
    Mon_IO.Put (Flt_Arrays.Index_of_Min (Flt_Data));
    Text_IO.New_Line;
    Flt_Arrays.Locate (Flt_Data, 4.0, Mth_Loc, Found);
    if Found then
      Text_IO.Put ("The index of 4.0 is ");
      Mon_IO.Put (Mth_Loc);
```

```
      else
        Text_IO.Put ("4.0 not found");
      end if;
      Text_IO.New_Line;
      Flt_Arrays.Locate (Flt_Data, 25.8, Mth_Loc, Found);
      if Found then
        Text_IO.Put ("The index of 25.8 is ");
        Mon_IO.Put (Mth_Loc);
      else
        Text_IO.Put ("25.8 not found");
      end if;
      Text_IO.New_Line (2);
      for Index in Int_Data'Range loop
        Int_IO.Put (Index, 2);
        Text_IO.Put ("        ");
        Int_IO.Put (Int_Data(Index), 2);
        Text_IO.New_Line;
      end loop;
      Text_IO.New_Line;
      Text_IO.Put ("The sum is ");
      Int_IO.Put (Int_Arrays.Sum (Int_Data), 0);
      Text_IO.New_Line;
      Text_IO.Put ("The maximum is ");
      Int_IO.Put (Int_Arrays.Max (Int_Data), 0);
      Text_IO.Put (" at index ");
      Int_IO.Put (Int_Arrays.Index_of_Max (Int_Data), 0);
      Text_IO.New_Line;
      Text_IO.Put ("The minimum is ");
      Int_IO.Put (Int_Arrays.Min (Int_Data), 0);
      Text_IO.Put (" at index ");
      Int_IO.Put (Int_Arrays.Index_of_Min (Int_Data), 0);
      Text_IO.New_Line;
      Int_Arrays.Locate (Int_Data, 7, Nat_Loc, Found);
      if Found then
        Text_IO.Put ("The index of 7 is ");
        Int_IO.Put (Nat_Loc, 0);
      else
        Text_IO.Put ("7 not found");
      end if;
      Text_IO.New_Line;
      Int_Arrays.Locate (Int_Data, 25, Nat_Loc, Found);
      if Found then
        Text_IO.Put ("The index of 25 is ");
        Int_IO.Put (Nat_Loc, 0);
      else
        Text_IO.Put ("25 not found");
      end if;
      Text_IO.New_Line (2);

   end Test_Arrays;
```

Figure 14.7.4

In Figure 14.7.5 we show the output of this demonstration program. You should check this output, along with the source code in Figure 14.7.4, to verify that the program has made proper use of the generic package Numeric_Arrays and that the routines of this package have performed as described in their documentation.

```
MAR        2.3
APR        6.4
MAY        1.5
JUN        5.8
JUL        7.2
AUG        3.1
SEP        4.0

The sum is 30.3
The maximum is 7.2 at index JUL
The minimum is 1.5 at index MAY
The index of 4.0 is SEP
25.8 not found

  3         4
  4         8
  5         2
  6         7
  7         6
  8        10
  9         1
 10         9
 11         3
 12         5

The sum is 55
The maximum is 10 at index 8
The minimum is 1 at index 9
The index of 7 is 6
25 not found
```

Figure 14.7.5

14.8 Exercises

14.1.1 Write the specification and body of a generic function to accept as parameters two values of any discrete type and return the larger of them. Write a brief program to test this function.

14.1.2 Write the specification and body of a generic function to accept as parameters two values of any discrete type and return a natural number indicating how many values there are in the range that has the first of these parameters as its first value and the second of them as its last value. Write a brief program to test this function.

14.1.3 Write the body of the generic function having the following specification:

```
generic

    type DISCR_TYPE is (<>);

    -- Function Mid_Val returns the "middle" value of
    -- range the of DISCR_TYPE.

    function Mid_Val return DISCR_TYPE;
```

Write a brief program to test this function.

14.2.1 Explain what effects the sorts in the program of Figure 14.2.3 actually have. Are any of these useful?

14.4.1 Using the Name field of the record type PERSONAL_INFO as the key field, write function bodies for the operator functions "<=", ">", and ">=" applicable to parameters of type PERSONAL_INFO. Can you make use of the function "<" of Figure 14.4.1?

14.4.2 Recall the two-dimensional array type declared in Section 13.4 by

```
subtype ROW_RANGE is INTEGER range 1..2;
subtype COLUMN_RANGE is INTEGER range 1..3;

type INTS_2X3 is array (ROW_RANGE, COLUMN_RANGE) of INTEGER;
```

How might an operator function "<" be defined for "values" of this type?

14.4.3 Extend the example of Figure 14.4.3 by defining the *scalar product,* or *inner product,* of two vectors. Look up the definition of this product (the resulting value is of type FLOAT), and write the definition using the symbol "*". Then write a small test program to verify that your definition produces the expected results.

14.4.4 Extend the example of Figure 14.4.3 and Exercise 14.4.3 by defining the component-by-component product of two vectors (analogous to the component-by-component sum of Figure 14.4.3). Explain why the symbol "*" cannot be used for this product. Instead, we might try using some suggestive symbol such as the "cross," for which we can substitute the letter X. Explain why we cannot define the term-by-term product by the function "X," and then use X in an infix form: V1 X V2. Finally, implement this product using the symbol "**". (Why can this be used?) Once again, test your resulting function.

14.6.1 A possible objection to the body of the procedure Sort, Figure 14.6.2, is the line

```
if Extr_Val < Item_Data(Index) then
```

The problem lies in the fact that the symbol < suggests "less than," while after generic parameter replacement this symbol could as well become >; that is, there is a potential for misleading the reader, unless care is taken to read the accompanying documentation in detail (an activity that we would scarcely discourage in any event). Show that the potential for misinterpretation is significantly reduced if the < in this line is changed to **, inasmuch as ** could never be taken to be exponentiation in the present context. What other changes in the generic procedure are required, if any?

14.6.2 Explain the effect of changing the generic declaration

```
with function "<" (Left, Right: Item_Type) return Boolean;
```

in the specification of the procedure Sort, Figure 14.6.1, to

```
with function "<" (Left, Right: Item_Type) return Boolean is <>;
```

In this context, why would the suggestion of Exercise 14.6.1 above be inappropriate?

14.7.1 Rewrite the package Int_Pack of Chapter 3 as a generic package that extends it from a package of INTEGER routines to one that deals with as general a type as possible. Begin by examining the present package specification (Figure 3.5.1) and package body (Figure 3.6.1) to see what characteristics are required of the underlying type.

14.7.2 Take full advantage of the capabilities of the generic package Numeric_Arrays to redo, as simply as possible, Exercise 13.6.3.

Appendix A

ADA Reserved Words

The following 63 words are *reserved*; none of them may be used as a programmer-declared identifier.

abort	else	mod	renames
abs	elsif		return
accept	end	new	reverse
access	entry	not	
all	exception	null	select
and	exit		separate
array		of	subtype
at	for	or	
	function	others	task
begin		out	terminate
body	generic		then
	goto	package	type
case		pragma	
constant	if	private	use
	in	procedure	
declare	is		when
delay		raise	while
delta	limited	range	with
digits	loop	record	
do		rem	xor

Appendix B

Table of ASCII Codes

The ASCII codes for the standard 7-bit character set, shown in their decimal representation.

Character	Code	Character	Code	Character	Code	Character	Code
NUL	0	SP	32	@	64	`	96
SOH	1	!	33	A	65	a	97
STX	2	"	34	B	66	b	98
ETX	3	#	35	C	67	c	99
EOT	4	$	36	D	68	d	100
ENQ	5	%	37	E	69	e	101
ACK	6	&	38	F	70	f	102
BEL	7	'	39	G	71	g	103
BS	8	(	40	H	72	h	104
HT	9	)	41	I	73	i	105
LF	10	*	42	J	74	j	106
VT	11	+	43	K	75	k	107
FF	12	,	44	L	76	l	108
CR	13	−	45	M	77	m	109
SO	14	.	46	N	78	n	110
SI	15	/	47	O	79	o	111
DLE	16	0	48	P	80	p	112
DC1	17	1	49	Q	81	q	113
DC2	18	2	50	R	82	r	114
DC3	19	3	51	S	83	s	115
DC4	20	4	52	T	84	t	116
NAK	21	5	53	U	85	u	117
SYN	22	6	54	V	86	v	118
ETB	23	7	55	W	87	w	119
CAN	24	8	56	X	88	x	120
EM	25	9	57	Y	89	y	121
SUB	26	:	58	Z	90	z	122
ESC	27	;	59	[	91	{	123
FS	28	<	60	\	92	|	124
GS	29	=	61	]	93	}	125
RS	30	>	62	^	94	~	126
US	31	?	63	_	95	DEL	127

Appendix C

Syntax Diagrams

In the diagrams of this appendix, an object enclosed in a circle or oval represents a *terminal* of the language, namely, a **reserved word** (Appendix A) or **punctuation** or other symbol. An object in a rectangle represents a *nonterminal* whose syntax is defined by another diagram or diagrams. For example, in the diagram

exception handler

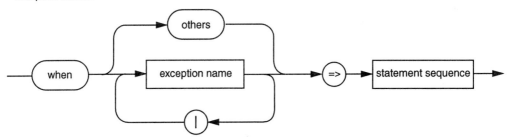

when, **others**, |, and => are terminals; **exception name** and **statement sequence** are nonterminals (with corresponding diagrams **name** and **statement**).

This appendix does *not* describe the complete syntax of the Ada language; only the constructs described in the book itself are given here. And some of the diagrams that are included here are incomplete, when the corresponding construct is more extensive or complex than what we feel to be appropriate to a beginning text.

actual parameter part

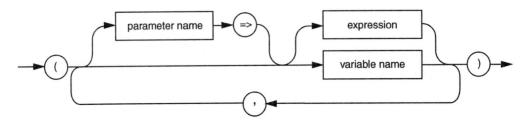

array type

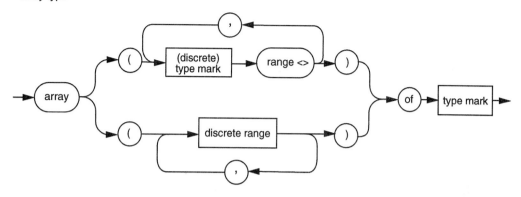

assignment statement

basic declaration

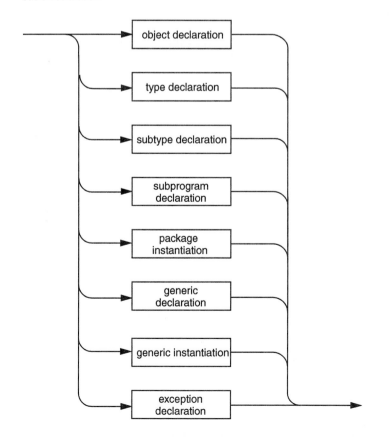

block statement

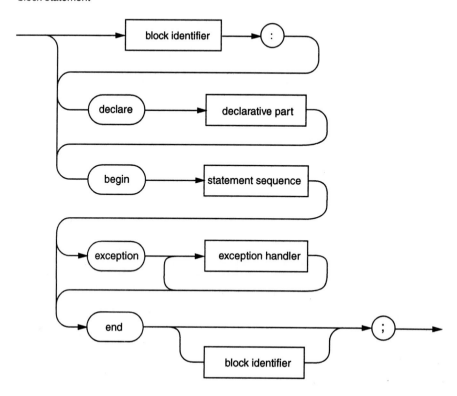

case statement

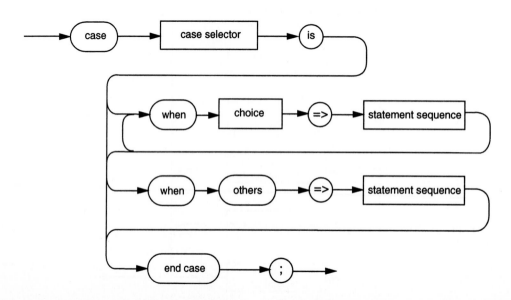

choice

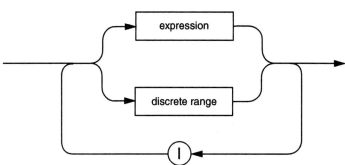

component declaration

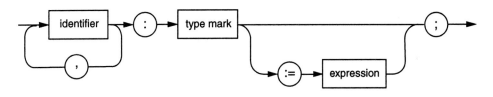

condition

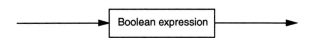

constant declaration

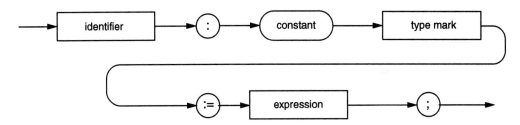

context clause

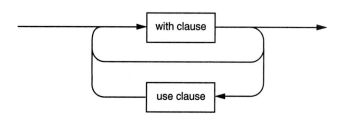

declarative part

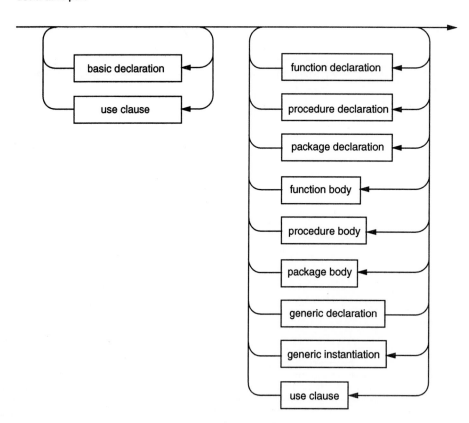

digit

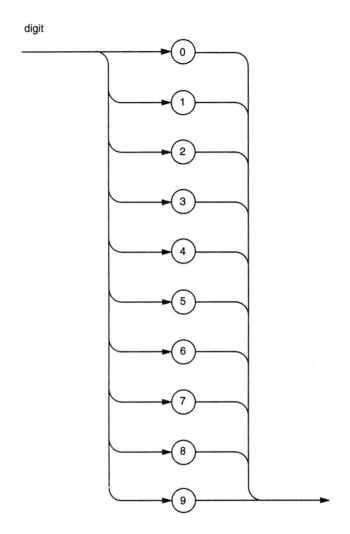

discrete range

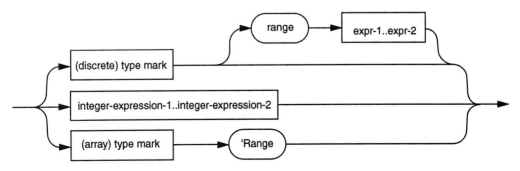

enumeration type definition

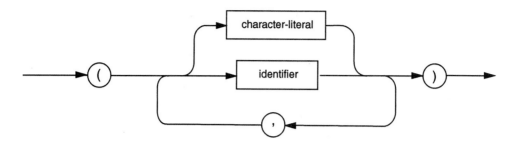

exception declaration

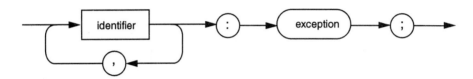

exception handler

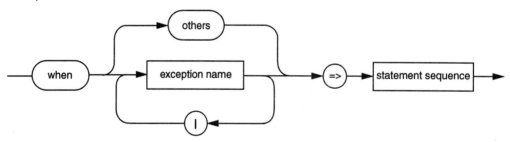

exit statement

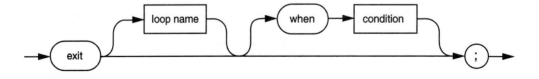

for loop statement

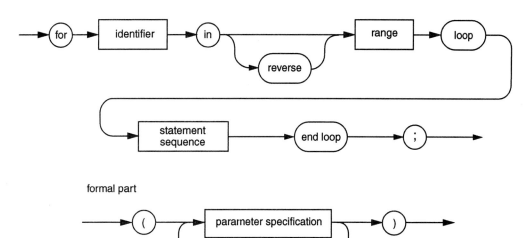

formal part

function body

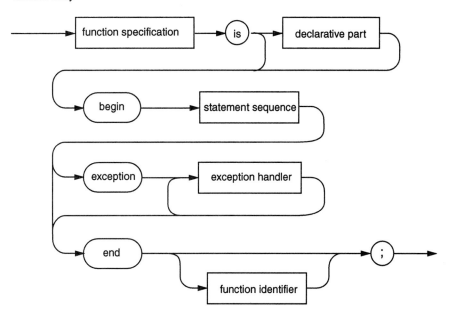

function call

function specification

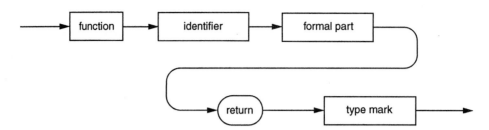

generic actual part

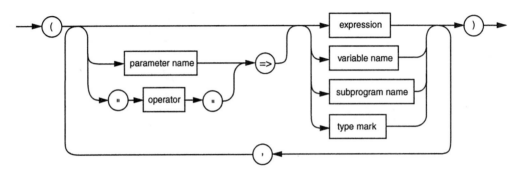

generic declaration

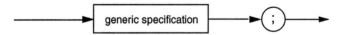

generic instantiation

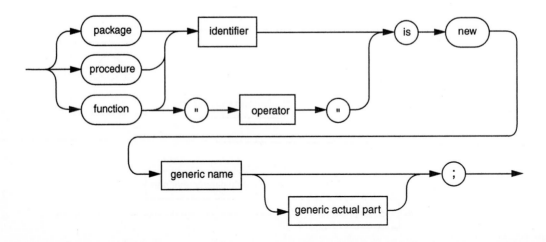

generic parameter declaration

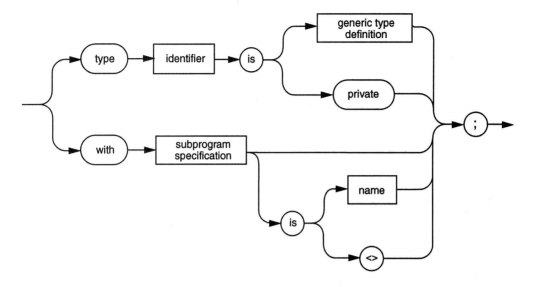

generic specification

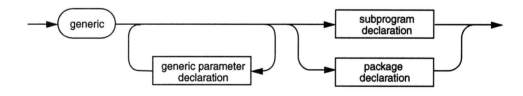

generic type definition

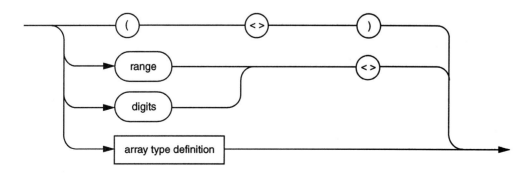

identifier

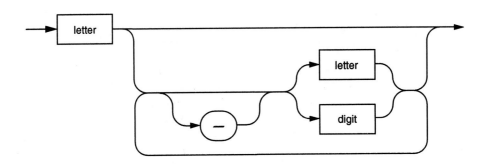

if statement

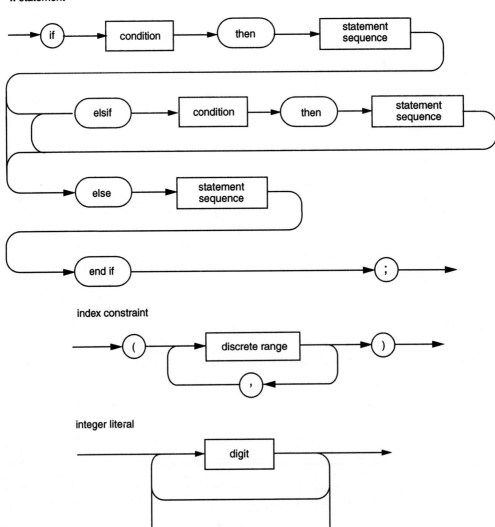

index constraint

integer literal

letter

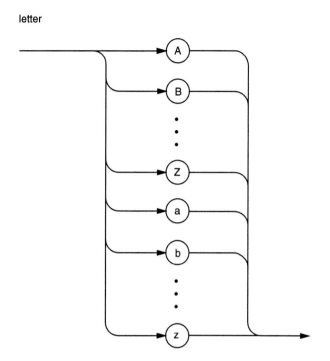

loop statement

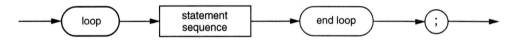

name

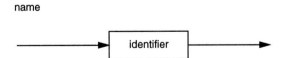

package body

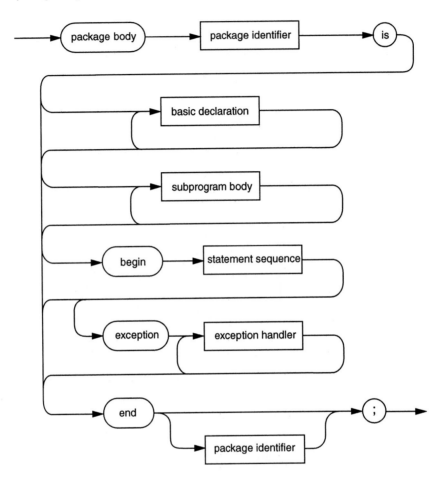

package specification

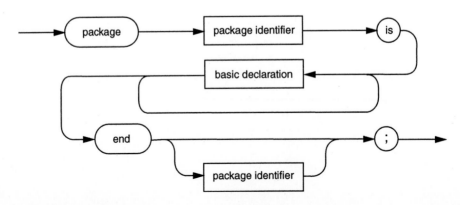

parameter specification

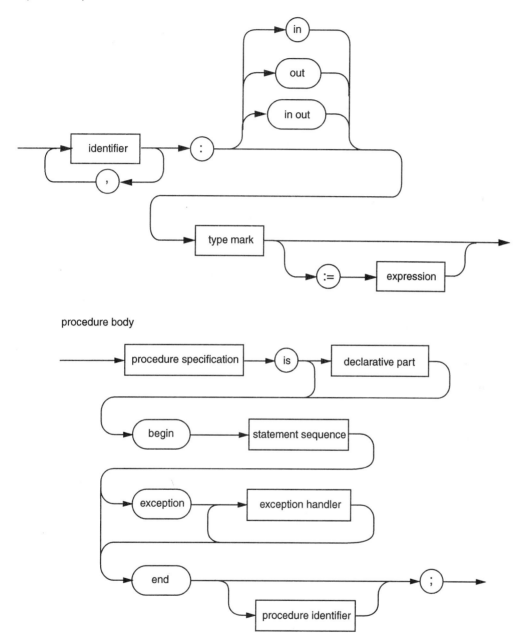

procedure body

procedure call

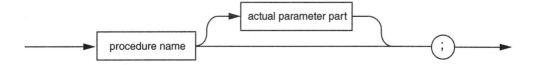

procedure specification

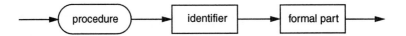

raise statement

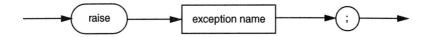

range constraint

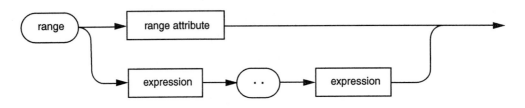

record type

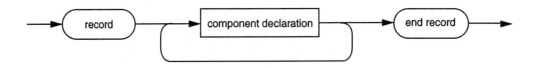

return statement

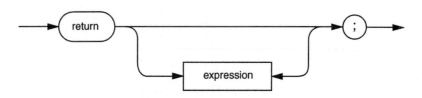

statement

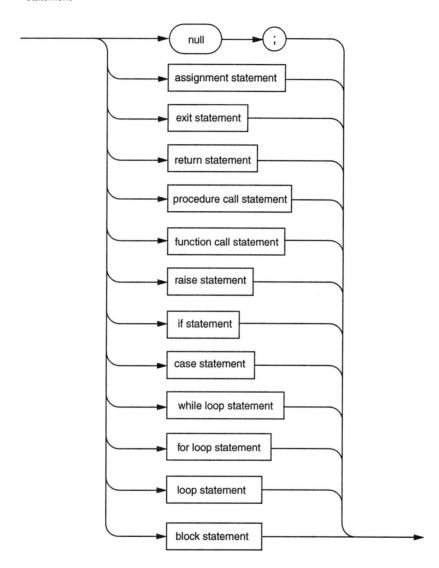

string literal

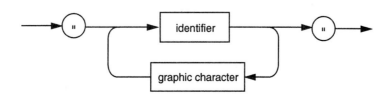

string literal

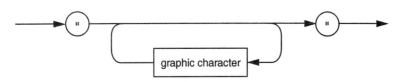

subtype declaration

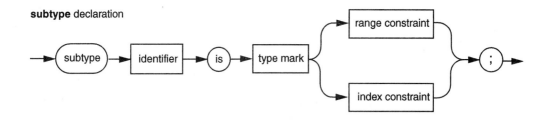

type conversion

type mark

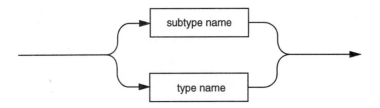

use clause

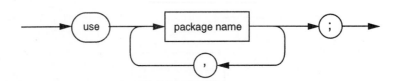

variable declaration

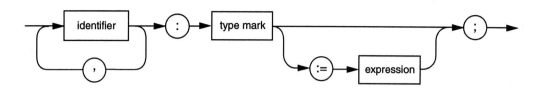

while loop statement

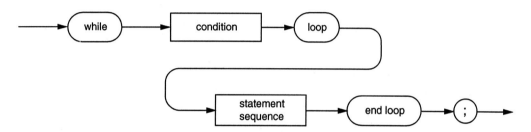

with clause

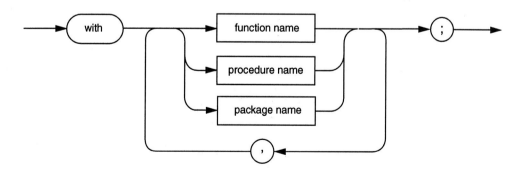

Appendix D

The Packages Text_IO and Standard

The packages in this appendix are taken from the *Ada Language Reference Manual (LRM)*, Section 14.3.10, and Appendix C.

D.1 The package specification Text_IO

```
    with IO_EXCEPTIONS;

package TEXT_IO is

  type FILE_TYPE is limited private;

  type FILE_MODE is (IN_FILE, OUT_FILE);

  type COUNT is range 0 .. implementation-defined;
  subtype POSITIVE_COUNT is COUNT range 1 .. COUNT'LAST;
  UNBOUNDED : constant COUNT := 0; -- line and page length

  subtype FIELD       is INTEGER range 0 .. implementation-defined;
  subtype NUMBER_BASE is INTEGER range 2 .. 16;

  type TYPE_SET is (LOWER_CASE, UPPER_CASE);

  -- File Management

  procedure CREATE(FILE : in out FILE_TYPE;
                   MODE : in FILE_MODE := OUT_FILE;
                   NAME : in STRING := "";
                   FORM : in STRING := "");

  procedure OPEN(FILE : in out FILE_TYPE;
                 MODE : in FILE_MODE;
                 NAME : in STRING;
                 FORM : in STRING := "");
```

```
procedure CLOSE(FILE :  in out FILE_TYPE);
procedure DELETE(FILE : in out FILE_TYPE);
procedure RESET(FILE : in out FILE_TYPE; MODE : in FILE_MODE);
procedure RESET(FILE : in out FILE_TYPE);

function MODE(FILE : in FILE_TYPE) return FILE_MODE;
function NAME(FILE : in FILE_TYPE) return STRING;
function FORM(FILE : in FILE_TYPE) return STRING;

function IS_OPEN(FILE : in FILE_TYPE) return BOOLEAN;
-- Control of default input and output files

procedure SET_INPUT(FILE : in FILE_TYPE);
procedure SET_OUTPUT(FILE : in FILE_TYPE);

function STANDARD_INPUT return FILE_TYPE;
function STANDARD_OUTPUT return FILE_TYPE;

function CURRENT_INPUT return FILE_TYPE;
function CURRENT_OUTPUT return FILE_TYPE;

-- Specification of line and page lengths

procedure SET_LINE_LENGTH(FILE : in FILE_TYPE; TO : in COUNT);
procedure SET_LINE_LENGTH(TO   : in COUNT);

procedure SET_PAGE_LENGTH(FILE : in FILE_TYPE; TO : in COUNT);
procedure SET_PAGE_LENGTH(TO   : in COUNT);

function LINE_LENGTH(FILE : in FILE_TYPE) return COUNT;
function LINE_LENGTH return COUNT;

function PAGE_LENGTH(FILE : in FILE_TYPE) return COUNT;
function PAGE_LENGTH return COUNT;

-- Column, Line, and Page Control

procedure NEW_LINE(FILE    : in FILE_TYPE;
                   SPACING : in POSITIVE_COUNT := 1);

procedure NEW_LINE(SPACING : in POSITIVE_COUNT := 1);


procedure SKIP_LINE(FILE    : in FILE_TYPE;
                    SPACING : in POSITIVE_COUNT := 1);

procedure SKIP_LINE(SPACING : in POSITIVE_COUNT := 1);


function END_OF_LINE(FILE : in FILE_TYPE) return BOOLEAN;
function END_OF_LINE return BOOLEAN;

procedure NEW_PAGE(FILE : in FILE_TYPE);
procedure NEW_PAGE;

procedure SKIP_PAGE(FILE: in FILE_TYPE);
procedure SKIP_PAGE;
```

```
function END_OF_PAGE(FILE : in FILE_TYPE) return BOOLEAN;
function END_OF_PAGE return BOOLEAN;
function END_OF_FILE(FILE : in FILE_TYPE) return BOOLEAN;
function END_OF_FILE return BOOLEAN;

procedure SET_COL(FILE : in FILE_TYPE; TO : in POSITIVE_COUNT);
procedure SET_COL(TO   : in POSITIVE_COUNT);

procedure SET_LINE(FILE : in FILE_TYPE; TO : in POSITIVE_COUNT);
procedure SET_LINE(TO   : in POSITIVE_COUNT);

function COL(FILE : in FILE_TYPE) return POSITIVE_COUNT;
function COL return POSITIVE_COUNT;

function LINE(FILE : in FILE_TYPE) return POSITIVE_COUNT;
function LINE return POSITIVE_COUNT;

function PAGE(FILE : in FILE_TYPE) return POSITIVE_COUNT;
function PAGE return POSITIVE_COUNT;

-- Character Input-Output

procedure GET(FILE : in FILE_TYPE; ITEM : out CHARACTER);
procedure GET(ITEM : out CHARACTER);

procedure PUT(FILE : in FILE_TYPE; ITEM : in CHARACTER);
procedure PUT(ITEM : in CHARACTER);

-- String Input-Output

procedure GET(FILE : in FILE_TYPE; ITEM : out STRING);
procedure GET(ITEM : out STRING);

procedure PUT(FILE : in FILE_TYPE; ITEM : in STRING);
procedure PUT(ITEM : in STRING);

procedure GET_LINE(FILE : in FILE_TYPE;
                   ITEM : out STRING;
                   LAST : out NATURAL);

procedure GET_LINE(ITEM : out STRING;   LAST : out NATURAL);


procedure PUT_LINE(FILE : in FILE_TYPE; ITEM : in STRING);
procedure PUT_LINE(ITEM : in STRING);

-- Generic package for Input-Output of Integer Types

generic
  type NUM is range <>;
package INTEGER_IO is

  DEFAULT_WIDTH : FIELD := NUM'WIDTH;
  DEFAULT_BASE  : NUMBER_BASE := 10;


  procedure GET(FILE  : in FILE_TYPE;
                ITEM  : out NUM;
                WIDTH : in FIELD := 0);
```

```
    procedure GET(ITEM : out NUM; WIDTH : in FIELD := 0);


    procedure PUT(FILE  : in FILE_TYPE;
                  ITEM  : in NUM;
                  WIDTH : in FIELD := DEFAULT_WIDTH;
                  BASE  : in NUMBER_BASE := DEFAULT_BASE);


    procedure PUT(ITEM  : in NUM;
                  WIDTH : in FIELD := DEFAULT_WIDTH;
                  BASE  : in NUMBER_BASE := DEFAULT_BASE);


    procedure GET(FROM : in STRING;
                  ITEM : out NUM;
                  LAST : out POSITIVE);


     procedure PUT(TO   : out STRING;
                   ITEM : in NUM;
                   BASE : in NUMBER_BASE := DEFAULT_BASE);

end INTEGER_IO;

-- Generic package for Input-Output of Real Types

generic
  type NUM is digits <>;
package FLOAT_IO is

  DEFAULT_FORE : FIELD := 2;
  DEFAULT_AFT  : FIELD := NUM'DIGITS-1;
  DEFAULT_EXP  : FIELD := 3;


  procedure GET(FILE  : in FILE_TYPE;
                ITEM  : out NUM;
                WIDTH : in FIELD := 0);

  procedure GET(ITEM : out NUM; WIDTH : in FIELD := 0);


  procedure PUT(FILE : in FILE_TYPE;
                ITEM : in NUM;
                FORE : in FIELD := DEFAULT_FORE;
                AFT  : in FIELD := DEFAULT_AFT;
                EXP  : in FIELD := DEFAULT_EXP);

  procedure PUT(ITEM : in NUM;
                FORE : in FIELD := DEFAULT_FORE;
                AFT  : in FIELD := DEFAULT_AFT;
                EXP  : in FIELD := DEFAULT_EXP);


  procedure GET(FROM : in STRING;
                ITEM : out NUM;
                LAST : out POSITIVE);
```

```ada
   procedure PUT(TO   : out STRING;
                 ITEM : in NUM;
                 AFT  : in FIELD := DEFAULT_AFT;
                 EXP  : in INTEGER := DEFAULT_EXP);

end FLOAT_IO;

generic
   type NUM is delta <>;
package FIXED_IO is

   DEFAULT_FORE : FIELD := NUM'FORE;
   DEFAULT_AFT  : FIELD := NUM'AFT;
   DEFAULT_EXP  : FIELD := 0;


   procedure GET(FILE  : in FILE_TYPE;
                 ITEM  : out NUM;
                 WIDTH : in FIELD := 0);
   procedure GET(ITEM : out NUM; WIDTH : in FIELD := 0);


   procedure PUT(FILE : in FILE_TYPE;
                 ITEM : in NUM;
                 FORE : in FIELD := DEFAULT_FORE;
                 AFT  : in FIELD := DEFAULT_AFT;
                 EXP  : in FIELD := DEFAULT_EXP);

   procedure PUT(ITEM : in NUM;
                 FORE : in FIELD := DEFAULT_FORE;
                 AFT  : in FIELD := DEFAULT_AFT;
                 EXP  : in FIELD := DEFAULT_EXP);


   procedure GET(FROM : in STRING;
                 ITEM : out NUM;
                 LAST : out POSITIVE);


   procedure PUT(TO   : out STRING;
                 ITEM : in NUM;
                 AFT  : in FIELD := DEFAULT_AFT;
                 EXP  : in INTEGER := DEFAULT_EXP);

end FIXED_IO;

-- Generic package for Input-Output of Enumeration types

generic
   type ENUM is (<>);
package ENUMERATION_IO is

   DEFAULT_WIDTH   : FIELD := 0;
   DEFAULT_SETTING : TYPE_SET := UPPER_CASE;

   procedure GET(FILE : in FILE_TYPE; ITEM : out ENUM);
   procedure GET(ITEM : out ENUM);
```

```
        procedure PUT(FILE  : in FILE_TYPE;
                      ITEM  : in ENUM;
                      WIDTH : in FIELD := DEFAULT_WIDTH;
                      SET   : in TYPE_SET := DEFAULT_SETTING);

        procedure PUT(ITEM  : in ENUM;
                      WIDTH : in FIELD := DEFAULT_WIDTH;
                      SET   : in TYPE_SET := DEFAULT_SETTING);
        procedure GET(FROM  : in STRING;
                      ITEM  : out ENUM;
                      LAST  : out POSITIVE);


        procedure PUT(TO    : out STRING;
                      ITEM  : in ENUM;
                      SET   : in TYPE_SET := DEFAULT_SETTING);

    end ENUMERATION_IO;

    -- Exceptions

    STATUS_ERROR   : exception renames IO_EXCEPTIONS.STATUS_ERROR;
    MODE_ERROR     : exception renames IO_EXCEPTIONS.MODE_ERROR;
    NAME_ERROR     : exception renames IO_EXCEPTIONS.NAME_ERROR;
    USE_ERROR      : exception renames IO_EXCEPTIONS.USE_ERROR;
    DEVICE_ERROR   : exception renames IO_EXCEPTIONS.DEVICE_ERROR;
    END_ERROR      : exception renames IO_EXCEPTIONS.END_ERROR;
    DATA_ERROR     : exception renames IO_EXCEPTIONS.DATA_ERROR;
    LAYOUT_ERROR   : exception renames IO_EXCEPTIONS.LAYOUT_ERROR;


    private

      -- Implementation-dependent

    end TEXT_IO;
```

D.2 The predefined package Standard

```
package STANDARD is

    type BOOLEAN is (FALSE, TRUE);

    -- The predefined relational operators for this type are as follows:

    -- function "="  (LEFT, RIGHT : BOOLEAN) return BOOLEAN;
    -- function "/=" (LEFT, RIGHT : BOOLEAN) return BOOLEAN;
    -- function "<"  (LEFT, RIGHT : BOOLEAN) return BOOLEAN;
    -- function "<=" (LEFT, RIGHT : BOOLEAN) return BOOLEAN;
    -- function ">"  (LEFT, RIGHT : BOOLEAN) return BOOLEAN;
    -- function ">=" (LEFT, RIGHT : BOOLEAN) return BOOLEAN;


    -- The predefined logical operators and the predefined logical
    -- negation operator are as follows:
```

```
-- function "and" (LEFT, RIGHT : BOOLEAN) return BOOLEAN;
-- function "or"  (LEFT, RIGHT : BOOLEAN) return BOOLEAN;
-- function "xor" (LEFT, RIGHT : BOOLEAN) return BOOLEAN;

-- function "not" (RIGHT : BOOLEAN) return BOOLEAN;


-- The universal type universal_integer is predefined.

type INTEGER is implementation_defined;
-- The predefined operators for this type are as follows:

-- function "="   (LEFT, RIGHT : INTEGER) return BOOLEAN;
-- function "/="  (LEFT, RIGHT : INTEGER) return BOOLEAN;
-- function "<"   (LEFT, RIGHT : INTEGER) return BOOLEAN;
-- function "<="  (LEFT, RIGHT : INTEGER) return BOOLEAN;
-- function ">"   (LEFT, RIGHT : INTEGER) return BOOLEAN;
-- function ">="  (LEFT, RIGHT : INTEGER) return BOOLEAN;
-- function "+"   (RIGHT : INTEGER) return INTEGER;
-- function "-"   (RIGHT : INTEGER) return INTEGER;
-- function "abs" (RIGHT : INTEGER) return INTEGER;

-- function "+"   (LEFT, RIGHT : INTEGER) return INTEGER;
-- function "-"   (LEFT, RIGHT : INTEGER) return INTEGER;
-- function "*"   (LEFT, RIGHT : INTEGER) return INTEGER;
-- function "/"   (LEFT, RIGHT : INTEGER) return INTEGER;
-- function "rem" (LEFT, RIGHT : INTEGER) return INTEGER;
-- function "mod" (LEFT, RIGHT : INTEGER) return INTEGER;

-- function "**"  (LEFT  : INTEGER;
--                 RIGHT : INTEGER) return INTEGER;

-- An implementation may provide additional predefined integer types.

-- It is recommended that the names of such additional types end with
-- INTEGER as in SHORT_INTEGER or LONG_INTEGER. The specification
-- of each operator for the type universal_integer, or for any
-- additional predefined integer type, is obtained by replacing
-- INTEGER by the name of the type in the specification of the
-- corresponding operator of the type INTEGER, except for the right
-- operand of the exponentiating operator.


-- The universal type universal_real is predefined.

type FLOAT is implementation-defined;

-- The predefined operators for this type are as follows:

-- function "="   (LEFT, RIGHT : FLOAT) return BOOLEAN;
-- function "/="  (LEFT, RIGHT : FLOAT) return BOOLEAN;
-- function "<"   (LEFT, RIGHT : FLOAT) return BOOLEAN;
-- function "<="  (LEFT, RIGHT : FLOAT) return BOOLEAN;
-- function ">"   (LEFT, RIGHT : FLOAT) return BOOLEAN;
-- function ">="  (LEFT, RIGHT : FLOAT) return BOOLEAN;

-- function "+"   (RIGHT : FLOAT) return FLOAT;
-- function "-"   (RIGHT : FLOAT) return FLOAT;
-- function "abs" (RIGHT : FLOAT) return FLOAT;
```

```
-- function "+"    (LEFT, RIGHT : FLOAT) return FLOAT;
-- function "-"    (LEFT, RIGHT : FLOAT) return FLOAT;
-- function "*"    (LEFT, RIGHT : FLOAT) return FLOAT;
-- function "/"    (LEFT, RIGHT : FLOAT) return FLOAT;

-- function "**"   (LEFT : FLOAT; RIGHT : INTEGER) return FLOAT;

-- An implementation may provide additional predefined floating point
-- types. It is recommended that the names of such additional types
-- end with FLOAT as in SHORT_FLOAT or LONG_FLOAT.  The specification
-- of each operator for the type universal_real, or for any
-- additional predefined  floating point type, is obtained by
-- replacing FLOAT by the name of the type in the specification of
-- the corresponding operator of the type FLOAT.

-- In addition, the following operators are predefined for universal
-- types:

-- function "*" (LEFT  : {universal_integer};
--                RIGHT : {universal_real})
--                          return {universal_real};
-- function "*" (LEFT  : {universal_real};
--                RIGHT : {universal_integer})
--                          return {universal_real};
-- function "/" (LEFT  : {universal_real};
--                RIGHT : {universal_integer})
--                          return {universal_real};


-- The type universal_fixed is predefined.  The only operators
-- declared for this type are

-- function "*" (LEFT  : {any_fixed_point_type};
--                RIGHT : {any_fixed_point_type})
--                          return {universal_fixed};
-- function "/" (LEFT  : {any_fixed_point_type};
--                RIGHT : {any_fixed_point_type})
--                          return {universal_fixed};


-- The following characters form the standard ASCII character set.
-- Character  literals corresponding to control characters are not
-- identifiers;  they are indicated in italics in this definition.

type CHARACTER is

   ('nul', 'soh', 'stx', 'etx', 'eot', 'enq', 'ack', 'bel',
    'bs',  'ht',  'lf',  'vt',  'ff',  'cr',  'so',  'si',
    'dle', 'dc1', 'dc2', 'dc3', 'dc4', 'nak', 'syn', 'etb',
    'can', 'em',  'sub', 'esc', 'fs',  'gs',  'rs',  'us',

    ' ',   '!',   '"',   '#',   '$',   '%',   '&',   ''',
    '(',   ')',   '*',   '+',   ',',   '-',   '.',   '/',
    '0',   '1',   '2',   '3',   '4',   '5',   '6',   '7',
    '8',   '9',   ':',   ';',   '<',   '=',   '>',   '?',

    '@',   'A',   'B',   'C',   'D',   'E',   'F',   'G',
    'H',   'I',   'J',   'K',   'L',   'M',   'N',   'O',
    'P',   'Q',   'R',   'S',   'T',   'U',   'V',   'W',
    'X',   'Y',   'Z',   '[',   '\',   ']',   '^',   '_',
```

```
    '`',   'a',   'b',   'c',      'd',   'e',   'f',   'g',
    'h',   'i',   'j',   'k',      'l',   'm',   'n',   'o',
    'p',   'q',   'r',   's',      't',   'u',   'v',   'w',
    'x',   'y',   'z',   '{',      '|',   '}',   '~',   'del');

    -- for CHARACTER use  --  128 ASCII character set without holes
    --      (0, 1, 2, 3, 4, 5, ..., 125, 126, 127);
    -- The predefined operators for the type CHARACTER are the same
    -- as for any enumeration type.



package ASCII is

   --   Control characters:

    NUL        : constant CHARACTER := 'nul';
    SOH        : constant CHARACTER := 'soh';
    STX        : constant CHARACTER := 'stx';
    ETX        : constant CHARACTER := 'etx';
    EOT        : constant CHARACTER := 'eot';
    ENQ        : constant CHARACTER := 'enq';
    ACK        : constant CHARACTER := 'ack';
    BEL        : constant CHARACTER := 'bel';
    BS         : constant CHARACTER := 'bs';
    HT         : constant CHARACTER := 'ht';
    LF         : constant CHARACTER := 'lf';
    VT         : constant CHARACTER := 'vt';
    FF         : constant CHARACTER := 'ff';
    CR         : constant CHARACTER := 'cr';
    SO         : constant CHARACTER := 'so';
    SI         : constant CHARACTER := 'si';
    DLE        : constant CHARACTER := 'dle';
    DC1        : constant CHARACTER := 'dc1';
    DC2        : constant CHARACTER := 'dc2';
    DC3        : constant CHARACTER := 'dc3';
    DC4        : constant CHARACTER := 'dc4';
    NAK        : constant CHARACTER := 'nak';
    SYN        : constant CHARACTER := 'syn';
    ETB        : constant CHARACTER := 'etb';
    CAN        : constant CHARACTER := 'can';
    EM         : constant CHARACTER := 'em';
    SUB        : constant CHARACTER := 'sub';
    ESC        : constant CHARACTER := 'esc';
    FS         : constant CHARACTER := 'fs';
    GS         : constant CHARACTER := 'gs';
    RS         : constant CHARACTER := 'rs';
    US         : constant CHARACTER := 'us';
    DEL        : constant CHARACTER := 'del';

-- Other characters:

    EXCLAM     : constant CHARACTER := '!';
    QUOTATION  : constant CHARACTER := '"';
    SHARP      : constant CHARACTER := '#';
    DOLLAR     : constant CHARACTER := '$';
    PERCENT    : constant CHARACTER := '%';
```

```
AMPERSAND   : constant CHARACTER := '&';
COLON       : constant CHARACTER := ':';
SEMICOLON   : constant CHARACTER := ';';
QUERY       : constant CHARACTER := '?';
AT_SIGN     : constant CHARACTER := '@';
L_BRACKET   : constant CHARACTER := '[';
BACK_SLASH  : constant CHARACTER := '\';
R_BRACKET   : constant CHARACTER := ']';
CIRCUMFLEX  : constant CHARACTER := '^';
UNDERLINE   : constant CHARACTER := '_';
GRAVE       : constant CHARACTER := '`';
L_BRACE     : constant CHARACTER := '{';
BAR         : constant CHARACTER := '|';
R_BRACE     : constant CHARACTER := '}';
TILDE       : constant CHARACTER := '~';

-- Lower case letters:

LC_A : constant CHARACTER := 'a';
LC_B : constant CHARACTER := 'b';
LC_C : constant CHARACTER := 'c';
LC_D : constant CHARACTER := 'd';
LC_E : constant CHARACTER := 'e';
LC_F : constant CHARACTER := 'f';
LC_G : constant CHARACTER := 'g';
LC_H : constant CHARACTER := 'h';
LC_I : constant CHARACTER := 'i';
LC_J : constant CHARACTER := 'j';
LC_K : constant CHARACTER := 'k';
LC_L : constant CHARACTER := 'l';
LC_M : constant CHARACTER := 'm';
LC_N : constant CHARACTER := 'n';
LC_O : constant CHARACTER := 'o';
LC_P : constant CHARACTER := 'p';
LC_Q : constant CHARACTER := 'q';
LC_R : constant CHARACTER := 'r';
LC_S : constant CHARACTER := 's';
LC_T : constant CHARACTER := 't';
LC_U : constant CHARACTER := 'u';
LC_V : constant CHARACTER := 'v';
LC_W : constant CHARACTER := 'w';
LC_X : constant CHARACTER := 'x';
LC_Y : constant CHARACTER := 'y';
LC_Z : constant CHARACTER := 'z';

end ASCII;


-- Predefined subtypes:

subtype NATURAL  is INTEGER range 0 .. INTEGER'LAST;
subtype POSITIVE is INTEGER range 1 .. INTEGER'LAST;


-- Predefined string type:

type STRING is array(POSITIVE range <>) of CHARACTER;

pragma PACK(STRING);
```

```
-- The predefined operators for this type are as follows:

-- function "="  (LEFT, RIGHT : STRING) return BOOLEAN;
-- function "/=" (LEFT, RIGHT : STRING) return BOOLEAN;
-- function "<"  (LEFT, RIGHT : STRING) return BOOLEAN;
-- function "<=" (LEFT, RIGHT : STRING) return BOOLEAN;
-- function ">"  (LEFT, RIGHT : STRING) return BOOLEAN;
-- function ">=" (LEFT, RIGHT : STRING) return BOOLEAN;

-- function "&" (LEFT  : STRING;
--               RIGHT : STRING)    return STRING;
-- function "&" (LEFT  : CHARACTER;
--               RIGHT : STRING)    return STRING;
-- function "&" (LEFT  : STRING;
--               RIGHT : CHARACTER) return STRING;
-- function "&" (LEFT  : CHARACTER;
--               RIGHT : CHARACTER) return STRING;

type DURATION is delta implementation-defined
                            range implementation-defined;


-- The predefined operators for the type DURATION are the same as for
-- any fixed point type.

-- The predefined exceptions:

  CONSTRAINT_ERROR : exception;
  NUMERIC_ERROR    : exception;
  PROGRAM_ERROR    : exception;
  STORAGE_ERROR    : exception;
  TASKING_ERROR    : exception;

end STANDARD;
```

Index

Ada operators are shown in italics.